THE GREAT
SYMPHONIES
THE GREAT ORCHESTRAS
THE GREAT CONDUCTORS

Edited by
Clive Unger-Hamilton and
Peter van der Spek

Contributors:
Janny de Jong
Clive Unger-Hamilton
Neil Fairbairn
Peter van der Spek
Jan Taat
Derek Walters

THE GREAT
SYMPHONIES

THE GREAT ORCHESTRAS
THE GREAT CONDUCTORS

SIDGWICK & JACKSON

LONDON

Contents

First published in Great Britain by Sidgwick & Jackson Limited Originally published by Uniepers bv/Marix Evans & Chilvers 1983

Copyright © 1988 by Uniepers bv, Amsterdam, The Netherlands The English Copyright © 1988 by Sidgwick & Jackson Ltd., London

ISBN 0-283-99694-3

Design and production: Uniepers bv, Amsterdam

Translation: Rollin Cochrane and Cynthia Wilson

Illustrations: Fabbri, Milan; Phonogram, Hilversum; Phonogram International; A3-Studio; Michael Evans, London; EMI-records Holland; Polydor, Hilversum; CBS, Haarlem; RCA Hilversum; 'Luister', Amersfoort; AVRO, Hilversum; Werner Neumeister; Bibliothèque Nationale, Paris; Oesterreichischer Nationalbibliothek; Nationalbibliothek, Berlin; Wiener Stadtbibliothek; 'Preludium', Concertgebouw Amsterdam.

Printed in the Netherlands by Ten Brink, Meppel for Sidgwick & Jackson Limited 1 Tavistock Chambers, Bloomsbury Way London WC1A 2SG

Foreword 11
by Leo Boudewijns,
Vice-Chairman International Federation of Phonogram and Videogram Producers

Introduction 13

The origins of the symphony 14
by Clive Unger-Hamilton

1 Haydn and Mozart 19
by Clive Unger-Hamilton

2 Beethoven 45
by Neil Fairbairn

3 Schubert 64
by Janny de Jong

4 Mendelssohn and Schumann 74
by Neil Fairbairn

5 Brahms and Bruckner 88
by Janny de Jong

6 Tchaikovsky, Dvořák and Sibelius 106
by Janny de Jong

7 Mahler 126
by Derek Walters

8 The twentieth century 134
by Jan Taat

9 A guide to the great conductors 153
by Peter van der Spek

10 A guide to the great orchestras 183
by Peter van der Spek

11 Discographies 196
by Peter van der Spek

Index 242

Composers

Hugo Alvén 196
William Alwyn 197
Thomas Arne 20, 197
Malcolm Arnold 197
Kurt Attenburg 197
C.Ph.E. Bach 197
J.Chr. Bach 21, 197
Mily Balakirev 110, 198
Samuel Barber 133, 198
Arnold Bax 198
Ludwig von Beethoven 45, 198
William Sterndale Bennett 202
Niels Bentzon 202
Luciano Berio 202
Hector Berlioz 104, 203
Leonard Bernstein 203
Franz Adolf Berwald 91, 203
Georges Bizet 93, 203
Arthur Bliss 150, 204
Ernest Bloch 136, 204
Karl-Birger Blomdahl 204
Luigi Boccherini 22, 204
Arrigo Boito 204
Alexander Borodin 116, 204
William Boyce 20, 204
Johannes Brahms 89, 204
Johannes Bernardus van Bree 81
Havergal Brian 206
Benjamin Britten 136, 206
Max Bruch 116, 207
Anton Bruckner 94, 207
Geoffry Bush 209
Elliot Carter 209
Ernest Chausson 96, 209
Carlos Chavez 209
Luigi Cherubini 50, 209
Muzio Clementi 55, 209
Arnold Cooke 209
Aaron Copland 145, 210
Cesar Cui 109
Anton Diabelli 61
Karl Ditters von Dittersdorf 23
Peter Maxwell Davies 148, 210
Paul Dukas 108, 210

Antonin Dvořák 114, 210
Edward Elgar 129, 211
Zdenek Fibich 109, 212
César Franck 102, 212
Niels Gade 83, 212
Vittorio Giannini 212
Alexander Glazunov 116, 212
Reinhold Glière 112, 213
Karl Goldmark 213
Eugene Goossens 213
François Joseph Gossec 23
Charles Gounod 111, 213
Edvard Grieg 115, 213
Johann Halvorsen 213
Howard Hanson 213
Roy Harris 213
Karl Hartmann 146, 213
Hamilton Harty 214
Franz Joseph Haydn 19, 214
Michael Haydn 215
Victor Hely-Hutchinson 215
Hans Werner Henze 148, 216
Alfred Hill 216
Paul Hindemith 144, 216
Alun Hoddinott 216
Vagn Holmboe 216
Gustav Holst 149, 216
Arthur Honegger 151, 216
Alan Hovhaness 217
Vincent d'Indy 128, 217
Charles Ives 141, 217
Leos Janáček 125, 217
Daniel Jones 217
Joseph Jongen 217
Wilfred Josephs 218
Wilhelm Kalliwoda 86
Olav Kielland 218
Otto Klemperer 218
Oliver Knussen 218
Jonas Kokkonen 218
Leopold Kozeluch 218
Franz Krommer 218
Edouard Lalo 218
Rued Langgaard 218
Adolf Lindblad 218
Franz Liszt 101, 218
George Lloyd 219
Witold Lutoslavski 151, 219

Johann Nepomuk Maelzel 52
Albéric Magnard 219
Gustav Mahler 126, 219
Frank Martin 131, 222
Bohislav Martinu 151, 222
Vincenc Masek 222
William Mathias 223
Felix Mendelssohn-Bartholdy 75, 223
Olivier Messiaen 147, 224
Nicolai Miaskovsky 224
Darius Milhaud 145, 224
Anthony Millner 224
Ernest Moeran 224
Leopold Mozart 32
Wolfgang Amadeus Mozart 29, 224
Modest Mussorgsky 125
Carl Nielsen 132, 228
Gösta Nystroem 228
Hubert Parry 228
Wilhelm Peterson-Berger 228
Willem Pijper 148
Walter Piston 228
Sergei Prokofiev 133, 228
Sergei Rachmaninov 121, 229
Joachim Raff 230
Ture Rangström 143, 230
Alan Rawsthorne 230
Ferdinand Ries 52
Nicolai Rimsky-Korsakov 124, 230
Cyril Rootham 230
Gioacchino Rossini 67, 230
Albert Roussel 130, 230
Edmund Rubbra 149, 231
Anton Rubinstein 108
Camille Saint-Saëns 96, 231
Antonio Salieri 24
Aulis Sallinen 231
Giovanni Battista Sammartini 22
Franz Schmidt 231
Arnold Schoenberg 131, 231
Franz Schubert 64, 232
Robert Schumann 84, 233

Alexander Scriabin 142, 234
Humphry Searle 234
Dmitri Shostakovich 146, 235
Jean Sibelius 123, 235
Bedrich Smetana 124, 237
Ludwig Spohr 76, 237
Johann Stamitz 25, 237
Charles Stanford 237
Wilhelm Stenhammer 132, 237
Robert Still 237
Richard Strauss 105, 237
Igor Stravinsky 134, 238
Karol Szymanovski 143, 238
Piotr Ilyich Tchaikovsky 107, 238
Michael Tippett 240
Eduard Tubin 240
Ralph Vaughan Williams 147, 240
Johannes Verhulst 87
Matthijs Vermeulen 143
Jan Vorisek 241
Georg Wagenseil 20
Richard Wagner 103, 241
William Walton 241
Carl Maria von Weber 53
Kurt Weill 241
Bernard Zweers 122

Conductors

Claudio Abbado 153
Ernest Ansermet 153
John Barbirolli 154
Daniel Barenboim 154
Thomas Beecham 155
Eduard van Beinum 155
Roberto Benzi 156
Leonard Bernstein 156
Karl Böhm 161
Pierre Boulez 161
Adrian Boult 161
Frans Brüggen 162
Ricardo Chailly 162
Andrew Davis 162
Colin Davis 162
Antal Dorati 163
Charles Dutoit 163
Wilhelm Furtwängler 163

Alexander Gibson 164
Carlo Maria Giulini 164
Eugene Goossens 164
Charles Groves 164
Bernard Haitink 165
Nicolaus Harnoncourt 165
Christopher Hogwood 166
Neeme Järvi 166
Eugen Jochum 166
Armin Jordan 166
Herbert von Karajan 166
Erich Kleiber 167
Otto Klemperer 167
Kyrill Kondrashin 168
Serge Koussevitsky 168
Josef Krips 169
Rafael Kubelik 169
Raymond Leppard 169
Lorin Maazel 170
Charles Mackerras 170
Nicolai Malko 170
Igor Markevitch 170
Neville Marriner 171
Jean Martinon 171
Kurt Masur 171
Zubin Mehta 172
Willem Mengelberg 172
Yevgeny Mravinsky 172
Charles Münch 173
Ricardo Muti 173
Václav Neumann 173
Roger Norrington 174
Eugene Ormandy 174
Seiji Ozawa 174
André Previn 175
John Pritchard 175
Mstislav Rostropovich 175
Gennadi Rozhdestvensky 176
Kurt Sanderling 176
Wolfgang Sawallisch 176
Giuseppe Sinopoli 177
Georg Solti 177
William Steinberg 178
Leopold Stokowsky 178
Evgeny Svetlanov 178
George Szell 178
Klaus Tennstedt 179
Michael Tilson-Thomas 179
Arturo Toscanini 179
Edo de Waart 180
Bruno Walter 181

Orchestras

Academy of St Martin - in - the - Fields 183
Academy of Ancient Music 183
Bamberger Symphoniker 183
Berliner Philharmoniker 183
BBC Symphony Orchestra 184
Boston Symphony Orchestra 184
Bournemouth Sinfonietta 184
Chicago Symphony Orchestra 185
Cleveland Orchestra 185
Collegium Aureum 185
Concertgebouw Orchestra 185
Czech Philharmonic Orchestra 193
Detroit Symphony Orchestra 186
Dresden Staatskapelle 186
XVIII Century Orchestra English Chamber Orchestra 186
English Concert 186
Ferenc Liszt Chamber Orchestra 186
Hallé Orchestra 186
Israel Philharmonic Orchestra 186
Leipzig Gewandhaus Orchestra 187
Leningrad Philharmonic Orchestra 187
London Philharmonic Orchestra 187
London Symphony Orchestra 188
Los Angeles Philharmonic Orchestra 188
Luzern Festival Orchestra 188
Montreal Symphony Orchestra (Orchestre Symphonique de Monréal) 188
NBC Symphony Orchestra 189

New York Philharmonic Orchestra 189
Orchestra of the XVIII th Century 189
Orchestre des Concerts Colonne 190
Orchestre des Concerts Lamoureux 190
Orchestre Philharmonique de Radio France (Orchestre de ORTF) 190
Orchestre National de France 190
Orchestre de Paris 190
Orchestre de la Suisse Romande 191
Philadelphia Orchestra 191
Philharmonia Hungarica 192
Philharmonia Orchestra 191
Philharmonic Orchestra of Budapest 192
Philharmonic Orchestra of Oslo 191
Pittsburgh Symphony Orchestra 191
Rotterdam Philharmonic Orchestra 192
Royal Philharmonic Orchestra 192
San Francisco Symphony Orchestra 192
Scottish Chamber Orchestra 192
Scottish National Orchestra 192
Sinfonie Orchester des Bayerischen Rundfunk 190
Stockholm Philharmonic Orchestra 192
Symphonie Orchester des Oesterreichischen Rundfunks 189
Toulouse Capitol Orchestre 193
USSR State Symphony Orchestra 193
Vienna Philharmonic 193
Vienna Symphony Orchestra 194
Washington National Symphony Orchestra 193

Foreword

The ability to reproduce music is barely one hundred years old. Thomas Edison succeeded in recording sound for the first time in 1877. It was as late as 1925 before the gramophone record was mature enough to be an accepted medium for the enjoyment of classical music. Records have played the most important part in the reproduction of serious music up until the last few years. Without all these wonderful performances, first on 78 record then on LP and now on CD, the general audience would know and love much less repertoire. The public is now well acquainted with all the classics, from Bach's six Brandenburg Concertos up to and including all fifteen of Shostakovich's symphonies and much more.

Of all the forms taken by classical music throughout its history, one emerges as foremost in the affections of the general public, The Symphony. Is this due to the genre itself with its ever-changing moods and tempi, or is it because so many masterpieces happen to have taken this form? That we do not know. The fact remains that the great symphonies of Mozart, Haydn, Beethoven, Schubert, Brahms, Mahler and Bruckner can never be played too often. The music loving public will always demand more.

Records are always accompanied by books. What is not expressed in the musical note is compensated for by the written word. The great composers and their works continue to be the subject of numerous publications. This particular book is different, better than many that have preceeded it.

The information contained within is extensive. The language used is clear and appealing. The authors are never pretentious nor boring. These authors dare to take opinions that many will not especially appreciate: record companies, performing artists, colleagues. The best aspect of this publication is, without doubt, the all-encompassing listings of LP's and CD's, compiled independently, thoroughly sorted and reviewed. It will prove useful to all music lovers searching through the ever growing and ever confusing supply of recordings available. Edison could never comprehend this book. It was his cherished and unfulfilled dream to record Beethoven's Ninth Symphony 'with an orchestra of seventy-five players' at least once in his lifetime. There are forty-four such recordings listed here!

Leo Boudewijns
Vice-Chairman, International Federation of Phonogram and Videogram Producers

Hector Berlioz conducting characteristically massive forces in the hall of the Cirque - Olympique, Paris.

Introduction

The Great Symphonies is meant for all those who through their work or leisure cultivate a love of classical music. This book, divided into four main chapters, covers the entire symphonic repertoire from the eighteenth century to the present day and analyses the masterpieces of this repertoire. Despite our intentions to be as thorough as possible, no previous knowledge of classical music's theories or history is assumed. Since the appearance of the first edition of *The Great Symphonies*, much has changed in the world of music. The compact disc has entered the scene and conquered an enormous part of the record market. The registration and reproduction of music has evolved greatly. New digital techniques are ever improving the quality of recordings. Older, historical performances are once again available thanks to the new remastering techniques.

In this second, completely revised edition of *The Great Symphonies*, the four chapters deal respectively with:

1. the birth and development of the symphonic form as well as the evolution of the arts of orchestration and direction;
2. the composers and their works (all the most renowned symphonies are considered and are placed in music history);
3. biographies of the conductors, a summary of their repertoire and a description of the orchestras heard today on record, radio or television or in the concert hall;
4. an extensive discography.

The discography covers more than 1500 recordings (LP, cassette and CD). This impressive survey includes the masterpieces as well as lesser known works of the symphonic form. A Beethoven symphony can have up to 200 performance listings, a Mahler symphony around 100. The accompanying commentaries are meant to emphasize the differences between the numerous recordings available. The discography can be helpful to the record collector, the radio listener, concert-goer or music student.

The form of this revised and extended version of *The Great Symphonies* is clear and straightforward. A complete index of names is included at the back of the book.

The Argyll Rooms in London; watercolour by W. Westall (1825). In this concert hall the London Philharmonic Society played the British premières of Beethoven's Fifth, Seventh and Ninth Symphony. (London, reproduced by Courtesy of the Trustees of the British Museum.)

The origins of the symphony

An orchestral concert *c* 1830.

The classical symphony was a product of the mid-eighteenth century, the age of elegance, but its origins extend much further back in time. Two hundred years before then, before the introduction of major and minor keys, a perpetual problem for composers of instrumental music was how to 'go on', how to write an extended work that would not become boring to listen to.

Most of the orchestral music heard today comes from the repertoire of the eighteenth and nineteenth centuries, when a satisfactory system of keys and key relationships was well established – and ever enlarging. Before this structure had evolved, music was generally restricted to staying in one key throughout, with the result that any piece much longer than five minutes' duration could become extremely monotonous to the ear, particularly in instrumental music, which lacks words to help sustain the interest and divert attention from the paucity of modulation (key-changing) available. This is why Elizabethan music, for example, relies heavily on such forms as short pairs of dances, or sets of variations on popular songs such as William Byrd's *The Carman's Whistle* for example.

The paired dances, one slow (Pavane) in duple or quadruple time and one much livelier (Galliard) in triple time, evolved in the seventeenth century into the suite, itself an ancestor of the sonata and the symphony. The suite form is basically two sets of paired dances linked together by a common key: Allemande (moderately slow), Courante (fast), Sarabande (slow) and Gigue (fast). If a suite needed to be longer, extra dance movements such as a Minuet, Gavotte or Bourrée could be interpolated, or there might be a free, rhapsodic Prelude at the beginning. From the suite – generally a keyboard medium – and alongside it, grew orchestral overtures, concertos and sinfonias.

These again would have separate contrasting sections, three or four in number, and more extended as composers discovered how to modulate through other keys and return to close in the original one. In the first half of the eighteenth century, both Bach and Handel (particularly the latter) wrote fairly extended orchestral works this way. Bach's Brandenburg Concertos are probably the best-known examples, though not completely typical since they feature solo instruments in opposition to the body of the orchestra. Orchestral forces in this period, the late Baroque, were fairly small, with rarely more than a dozen string players and such woodwind – a pair of oboes, for example – as was available or necessary. (Woodwind, incidentally, was always popular for performance outdoors, since its sound carried much better than that of the strings.) The ensemble would be supported by a harpsichord, whose function was to keep the players together, cue in the players' entrances and fill out the supporting performances. These 'continuo' harpsichordists fulfilled the role of conductor, and frequently the composer himself would direct performances of his music from the keyboard. But then, as now, the four-part string section (first and second violins, violas and cellos, equivalent to the four parts of a choir: treble, alto, tenor and bass) formed the main body of the orchestra; other, more exotic sounds such as trumpets, trombones or percussion were used for special effects and found their way into the symphony orchestra from their use in the opera house.

As Bach's sons (three of them composers) discovered, little more could be done with the complex intricacies of counterpoint than their father – the supreme master of the art – had achieved. Accordingly they set out to evolve a simpler and more natural approach to composition that relied less on such learned devices as fugue and canon, and used a more straightforward, direct and less elaborate approach.

They and their contemporaries used instead themes that were readily identifiable and short, contrasted with others and pursuing a relatively constant and predictable series of key progressions that came to be known as 'sonata form' and enabled their music to 'go on', as we said earlier, without tiring the ear.

At this point matters become more complicated, for the term 'sonata form' has two separate meanings: as well as referring to the structure of a movement (particularly the first and most important movement, hence the occasional use of 'first movement form' for this meaning), 'sonata form' also embraces the structure and arrangement of the movements within the entire work. It must also be stressed that, in the Classical era at least, the structure of a symphony, string quartet or sonata is fundamentally the same: a symphony is a sonata for orchestra, and a string quartet is in symphonic form but written for four solo instruments alone.

The first movement is generally the most extended, sometimes with a slow introduction, and most commonly with two contrasted themes or 'subjects'. The second movement is usually the slow one (though it may change places with the third), and is followed by a dance movement. This, in triple time, is a Minuet – later evolved by Beethoven into the scherzo. Designed to let a little air into a listening experience that could become a little overpowering, the Minuet (or scherzo) is in form a dance-within-a-dance. The first dance, in two halves – each repeated – is followed by a Trio. This trio, again in two repeated halves and sometimes given to wind instruments alone, is succeeded by a reprise of the original minuet but this time without the repeats. To listen to, this form (known sometimes as A-B-A) is much less complicated than a description seems on paper. Haydn in particular has a lot of fun in the minuets of his symphonies, trying to throw the listener off balance, as it were, and make him lose count of the familiar one-two-three one-two-three rhythm of the dance.

The last movement is usually the lightest of all. It may be in 'first-movement form', it may be a set of variations (the finale of Beethoven's Eroica symphony, for example), or it may be a rondo. Rondo form, explained in textbooks as A-B-A-C-A-D-A etc, is at its simplest a tune whose repetitions are separated by contrasted episodes in contrasting keys. The last movement of Mozart's Eine Kleine Nachtmusik is a well-known rondo. Other, more elaborate, rondos use two themes with contrasting episodes in between; and since such a shape resembles first-movement form, they are sometimes called 'sonata-rondos'.

The contents and relationships of these four movements are the very essence of musical thought during the period known as the Classical era, and a familiarity with this generalized outline of the structure will give the listener a rough idea of what he may reasonably expect to happen when listening to a symphony, sonata or string quartet by, say, Mozart or Haydn. Next we must look at the sonata form more closely, to see how a typical first movement is made up.

As stated earlier, the form is not one imposed upon the music by composers, but evolved as a convention to enable a piece to be of some substance and length without becoming tiring to the ear. Its origins are to be found in the more truncated binary music of the baroque period, exemplified by the short, one-movement, keyboard 'sonatas' of Domenico Scarlatti (1685–1757) and by the dance movements in the suites and preludes of J.S. Bach (1685–1750). Each of these pieces, though only an average of three minutes' duration, clearly divides into two halves, each repeated, with the first half

The famous Neapolitan opera composer Alessandro Scarlatti (1660-1725) wrote a set of 12 *Sinfonie* as early as 1715.

coming to a close in a different key from its opening and with the second half leading the music back to end in the original key. Sometimes the resemblances to classical first-movement form are even closer, displaying in microcosm the identifiable landmarks of symphonic first-movement shape, which depends on a final, more or less full restatement of all the opening material contained in the first half after a free discussion of some of those themes has taken place at the beginning of part two. This of course unbalances part two, which now has to contain all the weight of the development as well as a restatement of what happened in part one. But discussion of themes can be fairly rudimentary, and doesn't have to make the music much longer: a familiar piece in typical first-movement form is the overture to Mozart's *The Marriage of Figaro,* a mature work from the middle of the Classical period, which lasts in its entirety – as an observer once remarked – for the exact time required to boil an egg.

After an optional slow introduction, which composers sometimes feel necessary to call the listeners' attention to what is about to take place, just as a drum roll at the circus announces that the tamer's head is about to enter the lion's mouth, the movement begins with a theme (its 'first theme', often coldly referred to as 'first subject' in books on musical theory) which will be in the home key (called the 'tonic') of the piece, to fix the music with a tonality and give it somewhere to come back to. The first theme will also be plainly identifiable to the ear, for if it is to be discussed later during the development section, it is essential that we shall be able to recall the speaker's original argument. For this reason too, the theme is often repeated more than once (perhaps, for variety, on different instruments) and is frequently too short to be called a 'tune'.

When statements of the first theme are complete the music moves away to another, closely related, key for its second theme. This, to provide contrast to the usually terse opening material, tends to be of a more lyrical and extended nature and may consist of not just one, but two or even three, linked tunes of generally more whistleable character; and the first half closes in the new key with a series of cadence-figures (the coda) at what musicians know as a 'double bar', which is a sign that they must go back to the beginning and repeat the entire section over again (though omitting the slow introduction, if there has been one).

The 'exposition' having been played twice, to fix its material in the listener's mind, the music is now set to embark on its second (development) section. Here there are no rules: the composer most frequently makes use of his first theme to a substantial degree, perhaps even starting a fugue with it. He may ignore his second theme altogether and introduce fresh material entirely at his fancy. New and distant keys are explored. All we can be sure of is that when the development comes to an end the music will have been led back to the home key, ready for another restatement of the opening section – part three: the 'recapitulation'.

Though there may be a number of differences between this restatement and the original exposition, one is of especial importance. This lies in the preparation of the music now for its second theme(s), so that it takes place not this time in any new key but in the tonic, so that the movement can close in the key that it began. The final coda, too, may be more extended as further proof of the music's imminent end (Beethoven's coda for the first movement of the *Eroica symphony* is 140 bars long). These few facts are quite sufficient for any listener to follow, and identify the landmarks in, a straightforward first movement in sonata form. Though it has been outlined in little more than five hundred words, it will always stubbornly remain more confusing to read about than to hear. One's ear will quite readily pick out certain points of reference along the way.

The double bar at the end of the exposition is usually the easiest to spot – particularly the second time it comes round. Great masters of the form such as Haydn, Mozart and Beethoven found it a marvellously malleable mould for their ideas: about three-quarters of the latter's entire output depends upon just this structural medium for its shape. This is not to say that Beethoven composed mostly first movements and left everything unfinished, for slow movements and finales can just as easily utilize this compact and satisfying ternary shape.

In fact, by the time Beethoven had finished with the form, after nine symphonies, sixteen string quartets and thirty-two piano sonatas, it is hardly surprising that composers after him felt more than a little daunted by his achievements within it. Conformity with a pattern failed to meet the needs of the Romantic age that followed Beethoven, and the formal approach that had governed the construction of symphonic movements became less easy to identify, if indeed it was present at all. But the four-movement structure endured much longer in the works of some musicians, as we shall see.

The Count Unico Willem van Wassenaer *left* may have been another composer of the earliest symphonies, for long wrongly attributed to the young Giovanni Battista Pergolesi (1710-36).

A caricature by Grandville of Berlioz entitled, aptly enough, 'Concert with Cannon'.

Joseph Hayd'n

1

Haydn and Mozart

Joseph Haydn

'The Father of the Symphony'. This well-known axiom needs careful qualification, for Haydn was by no means the first composer to write a symphony. That honour belongs to any one of a number of much less well-known composers; either in Italy, such as Galuppi or Sammartini, or else at the court of Mannheim in southern Germany such as Monn, Wagenseil or Stamitz, and the truth is by no means established. But Haydn was the first composer of great symphonies, and he fathered more than one hundred of them. (In addition, incidentally, he wrote eighty-three string quartets, over fifty piano sonatas, more than twenty operas and at least 125 full-length works for baryton, a now obsolete cello-like instrument favoured by his employer, Prince Nicolaus Esterházy. Small wonder that most of his output remains unknown today.) Haydn was beginning to write symphonies when Mozart was born and he was still writing them after Mozart was dead. The magnificence of his works in this genre established the symphony as the leading orchestral form of his day and, indirectly, of all succeeding generations. He was first to see the apparently limitless variety of which the symphony was capable, and he brought to it an entire world of human emotions: from rough, knockabout comedy and the more elegant wit of the drawing-room, through intense passion to profound sorrow. In this sense is Haydn the father of the symphony. He forged its template.

He also brought to it an extra movement, the minuet, not the mincing progressions of an effete nobility across the ballroom floor but a virile country dance that reveals his own peasant origins. He delights in imitating the squawling bagpipes and clodhopping rhythms of the village green, and loves to play tricks upon the listener's ear, throwing the music off beat as if the revellers had lost their way in the steps of the dance. By the time he was in his early twenties, with a few minor successes to his credit, Haydn was beginning to compose chamber music, mostly for string quartet with the occasional addition of horns or oboes, and by applying the styles he had learned from his studies of the younger Bach's keyboard music, evolved his own form of symphonic music – and also the classical string quartet. To begin with, there was little difference between the two, and it is often hard to say whether an early symphony with merely a few instruments is really a divertimento or serenade, or whether a string quartet with a couple of extra wind parts forms a rudimentary symphony. Ultimately, it does not matter. At Esterháza, however, the differences became much more clear cut when Haydn found himself with substantial orchestral forces at his command. Of his string quartet writing, incidentally, the great German poet Goethe remarked that 'One listens to four intelligent people conversing with each other; one expects to gain from their discourse and to learn to know the peculiarities of the instruments'.

Joseph Haydn

Joseph Haydn (1732-1809) stands alone among the great composers in being virtually self-taught. His father was an impoverished country wheelwright with twelve children to feed: of his family, incidentally, Joseph's younger brother Michael also became a composer. As a small boy, Joseph's sweet voice and ready ear brought him to the attention of a music loving relative, and at the age of eight he was placed in the choirschool of St Stephen's cathedral in Vienna.

Here, though he learned to play the violin and keyboard and to sing, there was no formal instruction in harmony, counterpoint or composition. Being forced to leave when his voice broke and having no funds to persue his studies, with borrowed money he bought an old clavichord and rented an attic room where he continued to practise the violin and, more importantly, studied the keyboard sonatas of C.P.E. Bach.

Taking the latter's revolutionary, non-contrapuntal style as his model, Haydn set to work to make himself master of the new 'galant' music. He also met the composer Porpora, whose servant he became in exchange for some grudging instruction in composition.

His first appointment, as musician in the house of a wealthy countess, came as the result of an early keyboard sonata he had written, and was soon followed by another job as music director to Count Morzin. This nobleman maintained his own band, which gave Haydn invaluable experience in composing for wind instruments - the opportunity for him in being able to write something for small orchestra and then to have it played through whenever he needed, cannot be over-estimated - and it was soon apparent that he was gaining a unique mastery of the new art of orchestration.

Two years later, in 1761, Haydn was taken up by the reigning prince of a great Austrian house, who had been impressed by the quality of the music when on a visit to Count Morzin. The Esterházys were a fabulously wealthy family, and the prince installed the young musician at his immense palace in the remote countryside of north-eastern Austria (now part of Hungary) where he maintained a substantial orchestra, a private theatre, and chorus and soloists to go with it. The next thirty years of the composer's life were spent here, in a happy fever of creativity. The one blot on the horizon was Haydn's wife: in 1760 he had married the elder sister of a girl who had taken holy orders - and with whom he had been deeply in love. His wife seems to have set out to make the composer's life a misery. They had no children, and after some years lived the rest of their lives apart. It was at Esterháza that nearly all his symphonies were composed and first performed, and as his fame spread through the visits to his employer of royalty and nobility, he became the most prized member of the Prince's household. And there he might have remained, but when in 1790 Prince Nicolaus died, his successor disbanded most of the musical establishment, and Haydn was pensioned off - not without a suitably princely annuity.

Now he was in a position to take up a handsome offer that had been made to him by a London concert promotor called Salomon: namely, to visit England and there conduct six new symphonies he should write for the occasion.

The visit, in 1791-92, was so successful that it was repeated two years later with six more symphonies, making up the twelve that are known today as the 'London' set. So magnificent was Haydn's welcome in England that it is conceivable he might have stayed, but the new Prince Esterházy summoned him back with more work to do. He returned to settle at Esterháza for the summer seasons and for the rest lived in Vienna, by now financially independent for the rest of his life.

After this there were no more symphonies. In his final active years Haydn wrote chamber music, his two oratorios *The Creation* and *The Seasons*, a wonderful succession of Masses for his patron - and his country's national anthem, the sublime *Austrian Hymn*, inspired by the impression made upon him by *God Save the King* on his visits to England. A few days before his death, on 31 May 1809, while the French were bombarding the gates of Vienna, he asked his servants to carry him to the piano where they heard him play this beloved and solemn melody.

Georg Wagenseil

The early Austrian symphonist Georg Wagenseil (1715-77) worked for nearly all his life as a musician at the imperial Austrian court. He made early successes as a composer of operas in the Italian style, and many of his (about thirty) symphonies were made up of material drawn from the overtures to these works. Though this music shows a ready command of the new musical form, and has often a sophisticated rhythmic propulsion, the melodies tend towards the commonplace and are not helped by rather unimaginative orchestration. But his fame was widespread: it is reported that the six-year-old Mozart, on tour at the Viennese court, asked to see Wagenseil. When the composer was brought before him, the little boy announced 'I am going to play a concerto of yours, you must turn the pages for me'.

Thomas Arne and William Boyce

In the rarefied native musical climate of the English eighteenth century, there were but two composers of any lasting distinction: Thomas Arne and William Boyce (1710-79). Arne worked primarily in the theatre while Boyce's career was much more synoptic, embracing church and instrumental music, masques and stage pieces (from one of which comes his famous song *Heart of Oak*), and eight symphonies. These were published in London around 1750 and have a refreshing and vigorous brilliance that has won them a lot of favour with present-day audiences. Perhaps Boyce's most significant work, however, was a large collection he assembled and edited of English cathedral music from the sixteenth and seventeenth centuries.

The nickname of 'Papa' that was often applied to Haydn was not given to him for his parentage of the symphony: it was a mark of the respect and genuine love that he inspired in those who were privileged to know him. The young Mozart, twenty-four years Haydn's junior, was an especially dear friend although the latter's demanding employer prevented any frequent personal intimacy between the two. Of his confinement in a remote corner of the Austrian Empire, Haydn observed in later years in reply to being asked how he had acquired his unique genius: 'I lived cut off from the world ... and I was forced to become original'. For all his fame and fortune he never lost the qualities of honesty, modesty and devotion that endeared him to so many of his peers. It was after a private performance of one of Mozart's string quartets (in which Haydn, Mozart and Mozart's father had taken part) that he made his celebrated remark to Leopold Mozart which seems to sum up his marvellous personality: 'Before God, and as an honest man, I tell you that your son is the greatest composer I have ever heard, or ever heard of'. Even the young Beethoven, to whom Haydn gave some rather unsuccessful lessons between his two visits to London, regarded his master with veneration – though at the time the truculent young genius, nicknamed by Haydn 'The Grand Mogul', had little patience with his teacher's careful methods. Haydn never forgot the good fortune that his genius and his environment had brought him: his manuscripts often ended with the words 'Laus Deo' as if in thanks for his happy and creative life.

He was successful with the opposite sex, as well. Separated from his termagant wife, Haydn captured many hearts, not least in England though already in his sixtieth year on his first visit there. This cannot be due to his appearance, which seems to have been singularly unprepossessing: though formal in manner and fastidious in dress, his plain, good-humoured face was permanently scarred in later life with the legacy of smallpox and by an unsightly growth on his nose, and he habitually referred to himself as an ugly man.

Though his symphonies were taken most enthusiastically to heart by audiences all over Europe and have remained his best-loved works for succeeding generations, Haydn seems to have favoured his operas and other vocal works beyond these, often seeing his purely orchestral compositions as occasional music of greater or less distinction Posterity seems right: each one of his 104 listed symphonies is of a gemlike brilliance, possessed of its own marvels. There will be no room here to analyse every one, and such a lengthy sermon would anyway bring the starry delights of this music down to earth with a bump. Besides, by no means all of them are familiar pieces in recording catalogues today. Posterity has chosen to favour about two dozen of them for regular performance: some half-dozen from the composer's apprentice and middle years, and from his maturity the symphonies he wrote for the 'Concerts spirituels' in Paris and the final twelve composed for Salomon in London.

Accordingly it is these, with one or two additions and subtractions, that are best examined separately, with one written between the Paris and London sets – no. 88 in G major – that it will be illuminating to put under a close lens, see the works behind the face, and watch how he put a symphony together.

Haydn: The Early Symphonies

Haydn wrote his first symphonies for Count Morzin, in the period before he moved to the much larger musical establishment at Esterháza. But, as the lively and invigorating symphony no. 1 shows, from the beginning these were no works of a musical apprentice: Haydn was already an experienced and mature artist.

Though it is now uncertain what the precise specifications of Count Morzin's band were, the forces of Prince Esterházy's orchestra when Haydn moved there in 1761 were much larger. At his command were:

A performance of Haydn's oratorio *The Creation* in Vienna in 1808. Beethoven was present at this performance.

two each of flutes, oboes, bassoons and horns backed up by about fourteen strings, while trumpets and timpani (kettledrums) could also be made available from the Prince's military band. The best known of the early works are nos 6, 7 and 8, which bear the titles of *Le Matin, Le Midi* and *Le Soir*. Though not among Haydn's most daring experiments in symphonic form (in fact they have a decidedly archaic ring in places, reminding one of the old concerto grosso form), these little works have probably retained their popularity thanks to their charming nicknames. It is often hard to know whether Haydn's symphonies become favourites because of their nicknames, or whether it is only the favourite ones that are given them. The next well-known work in the canon is no. 22 in E flat, known as *The Philosopher*, though no-one now knows why. This symphony has an exceptionally beautiful and grave opening movement, and makes use of an unusual instrument, the cor anglais (a sort of tenor oboe). A less often played work is no. 28 in A, dating from 1765, the year after *The Philosopher*. Its buoyant opening movement has a teasing, rhythmically ambiguous main theme with which Haydn has a lot of fun. Also worthy of extra attention in this work is the whirling gypsy dance that forms its minuet. From the same year too is no. 31, whose brassy summons at the beginning (and which also reappears at the symphony's end) has earned it the nickname of the *Hornsignal*.

Sturm und Drang

Much of the music of Haydn's middle years is of a less extrovert cheerfulness than audiences expect of their genial 'Papa', and charged with a high, nervous tension. This has led it to be known as his 'Sturm und Drang' period, after the German literary movement (*Eng*: Storm and Stress) that deals with mighty conflicts between the forces of good and evil. Two works from this period are symphonies nos. 44 in E minor and 45 in F sharp minor, the first of these, subtitled *Trauersymphonie* has hectic, frenzied outer movements that are balanced around a slow movement of the uttermost serenity and loveliness. (At the end of his life, Haydn is said to have asked for this movement to be played at his funeral.) No. 45 is also a marvellously constructed 'Sturm & Drang' work

Johann Christian Bach

Johann Christian Bach (1735-82) was the youngest son of Sebastian's second marriage, to Anna Magdalena. He studied music first with his elder brother, Carl Philipp Emanuel, and later with Martini in Italy. At the age of 27 he moved to England as music master to the wife of King George III, hence his nickname of the 'London' Bach. He remained there for the rest of his life, writing opera's, keyboard concertos, chamber music and about fifty symphonies. He is remembered today, however, as a friend of - and a profound influence upon - the boy Mozart during his stay in London, who modelled many of his earliest works upon those of the older master and began himself to write symphonies after he became acquainted with those of Johann Christian.

Giovanni Sammartini

Giovanni Battista Sammartini (c 1700-75) was the younger of two musician-brothers from Milan (where Giovanni remained for virtually all his working life). Though he was employed primarily as an organist, he is remembered now for his early works in symphonic form, which antedate those of Haydn by as much as twenty years. These brought him a lot of attention, though the music today seems rather nugatory and insubstantial; and its relevance rests mainly in the obvious link it provides between the Italian Overture style of Vivaldi and his contemporaries, and the early symphonic style of the young Mozart. Sammartini was an extraordinarily prolific, incidentally, with about 2000 compositions to his credit.

LUIGI BOCCHERINI.
Geb. in Lucca den 19 Jan. 1743
Gest. in Madrid 1805

Luigi Boccherini

The paradox of the Italian composer Luigi Boccherini (1743-1805), is that though he must be one of the most prolific composers of all time, with 155 quintets, 102 string quartets, 25 symphonies, 60 trios and a great deal more besides, his fame rests almost exclusively on one trifling minuet from one of the string quintets. Like Domenico Scarlatti before him, Boccherini spent much of his mature life in Spain, and his music is often redolent with the haunting and passionate discords of the Iberian folk heritage. Harmonically his music is extremely advanced for its time: the composer was a widely travelled man with a powerful intellect ever alert to new influences. His lyrical themes, subtle orchestration and pointed wit are the hallmarks of a unique musical mind that is too often neglected today in favour of more traditional, mainstream fare.

in a minor key, whose fierce emotions have unfortunately been overshadowed by the story that gave it the name of the *Farewell symphony*. It was time, thought the musicians, that Prince Esterházy should leave his palace for a while and give them a break, so Haydn designed the finale of this work to give his royal highness a hint. One after another the instruments ceased playing, and the performers each blew out the candles that illuminated their music, and left their seats. At the work's close there are just two violins carolling softly (in the extraordinary key of F sharp major): all the rest are gone. It is reported that Prince Nicolaus took the hint.

Perhaps the most tragic symphony Haydn wrote also comes from these years: no. 49 in F minor, *La Passione*. Each of the work's movements is in the minor key, and the first movement is an adagio of surpassing sadness. But it was not in Haydn's nature to remain serious for too long, and he returned to music that was happier, though no less sublime. Symphony no. 60, *Il Distratto*, is a glorious work in C major that features trumpets in addition to the usual line-up, and has six movements. The title comes from a play given at Esterháza for which Haydn wrote the incidental music. It is one of his merriest inspirations, and draws heavily on the folk music that was so dear to the composer. Symphony no. 73 in D has an especially gleeful finale, that has given it its nickname *La Chasse*. This movement was originally the overture to a jolly (but overlong) pastoral that Haydn had written for the opera house the year before in 1780. Unfortunately the other movements seem rather lacklustre beside this gay and spirited ending.

The Paris Symphonies

In 1784 Haydn was commissioned by a music society in Paris to write six symphonies. He was to receive twenty-five 'louis d'or' for each of them, and a further five upon publication of each. This was a lot of money, and the composer must have set about his work with an extra alacrity. What we now know as nos 82–87 were first performed in Paris in the season of 1787, with a much larger orchestra than Haydn had at home. His music, particularly his symphonies, was famous in France, and these concerts were patronized by the royal family.

They are all masterpieces, especially with regard to the beauty and style of their woodwind parts. Haydn is quoted as having said in his old age: 'I have only just learned . . . how to use woodwind instruments, and now I do understand them I must leave the world.' From this set of works it would seem the composer was seriously underestimating the craftsmanship of his late middle years. No. 82, *The Bear*, in C major, probably derives its nickname from the rustic, lumbering finale – just the sort of music to accompany a dancing bear on the village green. This work also has a lovely, simple-sounding set of variations as its slow movement, that hovers between F major and F minor. No. 83 in G minor, *The Hen*, must have been given its subtitle by Parisian audiences when they heard the chuckling second theme of the first movement (played on the violins). The slow movement is a glorious extended melody for strings that is an exquisite miniature of sonata form, complete with repeat of the first half and a development section. No. 85 in B flat was voted her favourite by Queen Marie Antoinette, hence it quickly became dubbed *La Reine*. The high point of its first movement comes at the very end of the development, when the key change that brings the music back to the B flat tonic makes the moment one of Haydn's great surprises.

The well-known set of variations that is the slow movement has as its theme an old French song, *La gentille et jeune Lisette*. Great effect is had here with one of Haydn's favourite devices in his slow movements: the sudden fortissimo outburst by the whole orchestra, as though it were picking up the tune and shaking it – like Alice with her naughty kitten. It is followed by one of the composer's most delightful and undanceable minuets that sandwiches a heartfelt little trio for oboes and horns, and rounded off with a rondo that makes the listener want to dance for joy.

Between writing these brilliant works for Paris and his first visit to London, Haydn composed five more symphonies, two for a rather unscrupulous violinist in the Esterházy orchestra, Johann Tost, to sell in Paris (nos 88 & 89); and three for a German princeling (nos 90–92), which were also sent to the same nobleman in Paris who had commissioned the 'Paris' set on behalf of the concert society.

Symphony no. 88 in G major
This merry and marvellous work was written in 1787, between the six *Paris* symphonies and the composer's first visit to London. It has been suggested that the only reason for this symphony's being less well-known than most of the 'London' set is due to its lack of a catch-penny nickname: it is without doubt one of the golden fruits of Haydn's sunny maturity.
Adagio-Allegro. The work opens, typically, with a slow introduction that serves as a call-to-arms for what is to follow. It is made up of a mere sixteen bars, in 3/4 time, with the jerky rhythm that characterizes the earlier overtures of Handel and his contemporaries. Audiences, as Haydn well knew, were notoriously bad at settling down and lending their noble ears to what was, after all, the paid performance of a band of lackeys. So if (as is the case with this symphony) the work proper was to open with a quietly-stated theme – which here dominates the entire movement – their attention must be grabbed from the very outset, and

Karl Ditters von Dittersdorf

Karl Ditters von Dittersdorf (1739-99) wrote more symphonies than Joseph Haydn - about 150 in all. He became famous as a violinist in his early twenties, and toured Italy in the company of his friend Gluck. He was befriended by the noble but disgraced bishop of Breslau, and entered into the latter's employment.
Much of his music was written for his patron's entertainment; including many operas and singspiele; these made him famous in Vienna, and were also responsible for his employer's elevating him to the nobility.
Apart from their quantity, Dittersdorf's symphonies are unusual in their often descriptive qualities: there is a set of twelve composed 'after the Metamorphoses of Ovid', another one 'in the style of five nations', and a symphony that describes the six humours, for example. Another attractive feature in his use, like Haydn, of folk tunes in his symphonies, though whether these are really traditional melodies or invented by Dittersdorf it is often impossible to say. He was also second violin in an occasional quartet in Vienna that met to play new works by its leader (Haydn) and viola player (Mozart).

François Joseph Gossec

In the mid-eighteenth century, Paris was an important centre of symphonic composition, and in the forefront of the new form's apologists was François Joseph Gossec (1734-1829). Born the son of a peasant in what is now Belgium, his musical gifts materialized early, and he was sent to Paris with a letter of introduction to the great Rameau. With such an invaluable master and helper, and with his own outstanding gifts, Gossec's career flourished in a most gratifying way. He succeeded Rameau as leader and conductor of an important Paris orchestra, and established a reputation as an outstanding musical innovator. His thirty symphonies have passages of tenderness and passion that recall the music of Haydn's 'Sturm und Drang' period to mind, particularly in the slow movements. Of all the lesser-known eighteenth-century symphonists, it is perhaps Gossec whose music is most unjustly neglected today.

The Empress Maria Theresa (in German, Theresia), after whom Haydn's symphony no. 48 was named when it was written for her visit to Prince Esterhàzy in 1773.

Antonio Salieri

Antonio Salieri (1750-1825) was a more successful composer in Classical Vienna than his rival, Mozart. He studied music in the Venetian Republic, and followed his teacher to Vienna. There he met the emperor, and probably as the result of a successful comic opera Le Donne Letterate was made court composer - and later Kapellmeister. Most of his compositions (which include two symphonies) are all but forgotten today.

Salieri is remembered instead as a famous teacher - of Schubert and Beethoven, most notably - and also Cherubini and Liszt. The rumour that he poisoned Mozart out of jealousy at the younger man's superior powers is almost certainly untrue, though he seems to have suffered much calumny in his time, being suspected as well of poisoning the composer Cimarosa - and of doing away with Gluck too, by pushing him out of a carriage.

The elegant lines of the palace of Schönbrunn, on the outskirts of Vienna, reflect the Classical forms of the music that was written for performance there.

this baroque convention fulfilled the composer's needs admirably. Little need be said about the melodic content of the opening adagio: it hovers around the scale of G major and moves purposefully to settle on the chord of D major (known to theorists as the 'dominant', or most nearly related, key to the tonic).

For the allegro of the movement, the tempo changes to a fast two beats in a bar. The jaunty opening theme (and who could not call it a tune?) once over, is immediately repeated forte by the full orchestra, this time with a spirited little ten-note figure accompanying it in the bass that is to become as important in the movement as the theme itself, as the ensuing bars that lead to the second theme well show.

As if to stand convention on its head, it is Haydn's second theme for this movement that is, if anything, terse. Clearly derived from the symphony's first tune, it seems to function only as an establishing of the new, dominant, key of D, in which the music bustles to a noisy close, with the little accompanying figure from the beginning (reminiscent of the opening of Mozart's *Figaro* overture, composed the year before) elbowing its little way into the foreground.

After the repeat of the exposition, it is this same little motif that leads tentative statements of the main tune through a surprising number of remote keys abetted by an irrepressible figure of three repeated notes that are exposed in Haydn's development section for being the husk of the main tune – and of its little accompaniment too. When the first

theme returns for the final, recapitulation, section it is now accompanied in the high treble by some insolent whistling from the flute, and from then on the music chases its own tail through to a rousing finish.
Largo. The only solemn minutes of this symphony are contained in its short and sublime largo. The ardent, hymn-like theme is repeated seven times throughout the movement, with different counterpoints and varied orchestrations. Haydn knew better than anyone that there was no need at all to meddle with such a glorious melody. It is simply a calm, reflective 'time without war' from the hurrying world around it.
Menuetto & Trio: Allegretto. It would be hard to imagine anything further from the concept of a courtly minuet than this lurching waltz that reels through a tipsy fourteen bars before its first repeat. The second part, of thirty bars' duration, incorporates a restatement of the opening after getting lost in some very unlikely keys. The trio has a typical bagpipe-style drone bass supporting an insistent little melodic line that keeps trying to throw itself off the beat, as it were. After the trio, the minuet is played once again da capo – but without the repeats.
Finale: Allegro con spirito. The theme of this blithe and merry rondo is strongly reminiscent of the theme that dominates the symphony's first movement, with its pairs of repeated notes. The theme itself is quite long (with some alarming modulations inside it) and only makes three hilarious appearances in the movement's short duration. After the third time, a general pause in the music is the signal for a headlong, rushing coda that brings the symphony to an end.

No. 92 in G major, the *Oxford*, is likewise one of the composer's finest works. Its nickname derives from the fact that Haydn conducted a performance of it at the Sheldonian Theatre in Oxford when he was awarded an honorary doctorate of Music by the university. It has a wonderfully evocative slow introduction, followed by one of the most unorthodox sonata movements, whose cheeky second theme only comes to the fore at the very end of the piece. The slow movement, in D major, is an adagio set of variations with the familiar fortissimo outburst in the middle and a remarkable passage in the minor. The symphony's wild and unbuttoned minuet is countered by a soothing trio featuring the horns; and the rondo finale presents a glittering series of episodes between a light-hearted but curiously perverse theme. The entire work is Haydn at his most habit-forming.

The London Symphonies
The twelve symphonies that many find to be Haydn's crowning achievement were composed in two sets of six: the first (nos 93–98) for his first visit to London in 1791–92, and nos 99–104 for his second trip there in 1794–95. They were performed at the Hanover Square Rooms, with Haydn himself directing the orchestra from the pianoforte.
No. 93 in D major is a typically delightful work. The second theme of the first movement is the one that predominates in the music's development while the slow movement, a theme and variations, is full of surprises, by turns martial and affectionate. The trio of the minuet has endearing little phrases for woodwind that seem built on to the dance as an afterthought, and the symphony's finale is yet another irrepressible and magical rondo. The last movements of classical symphonies, so often their weakest link, are always with Haydn the moments to cherish and relish.
The *Surprise* symphony (no. 94 in G major) must be one of the most famous in the entire symphonic repertoire. Its nickname derives from the loud explosion in the middle of the slow movement's theme, which is said to have been specifically written in by the composer to wake up audiences who always tended to nod off during slow movements. The work begins with a haunting slow introduction that moves eerily through distant keys. The ensuing allegro, in a cheerful, rocking rhythm, can hardly be said to boast a second theme for it is the opening motif that appears to take over most of the movement's fun and games. The

Johann Stamitz

Johann Stamitz (1717-1757) was one of 11 children. He received his first music lessons from his father, an organist and music teacher and one of the well-to-do men of his native city, Nemecky Brod (Deutschbrod). Johann was sent to a Jesuit school. Musical education was excellent in 18th century Bohemia, in compositon and performance, and the Jesuits had the best teachers in their schools. Johann Stamitz was most active in playing the violin. In 1741, while he played at royal functions in Prague, Stamitz was offered a court position by the Prince who admired his talents. The following year, he was introduced as the 'violin virtuoso' before playing a concert in Frankfurt. At the court in Mannheim, his reputation grew quickly; after only four years, Stamitz was concert master and director of court music. In 1744, Stamitz married and the couple had two sons, Karl (1745-1801) and Anton (1754-?) both of whom became composers.
Stamitz visited Paris in 1747. It was to be an important visit. His fame had preceeded him. His symphonies were already known in the French capitol, and his public performances as well as his salon engagements were greatly successful.
Little is known about Stamitz's last years. He died when only forty. He left 175 compositions behind, including concerti, sonatas and chamber music, 74 symphonies (19 of which date before 1745).
Stamitz has an important place in music history for two reasons. The first is that he developed both the sonata and the symphonic movement forms into what they were to be for classical composers. The second reason is his new orchestral style: he specified the general music trends of the time for use in large, orchestral works. His early works follow the usual three part Italian sonata form of allegro - slow movement - menuet with trio or variations. But Stamitz introduced sharper contrasts between themes in his later pieces, and paid more attention to the development of the themes he used. Considering the amount of work he produced, and the effect it must have had on a public used to Bach, Handel and Telemann, it is not surprising to know that Stamitz was warmly received by the music critics of his time. Equalling unsurprising is the fate history awarded Stamitz, a renewing force that is instantly forgotten as greater talents appear. Stamitz was branded 'a figure of historical importance only' mainly because his direct successors (including his sons Karl and Anton) could not match his talent, and used his new ideas in such a trivial way. The great classical masters owe not only new ideas to Stamitz, but a much improved orchestral tradition, built during his Mannheim years, which made it possible to perform the new, demanding, classical symphonies. Stamitz influenced many generations with his orchestral efforts.
If Stamitz, as we are led to believe, only cleared the field for Haydn and Beethoven, his fresh and lively melodies, driving rhythms and dynamic excitement, remain attractive still today.

A portrait of Haydn
(engraving ca. 1791)

andante and variations are too well-known to need much description. Suffice it to say that the composition of such a simple and artless tune is in itself a 'tour de force', a hallmark of genius that only Mozart and Schubert can seem to share with Haydn. Marvellous too is the symphony's finale, a sophisticated rondo whose fearsomely difficult violin writing must have needed lots of rehearsing to point up the music's muscle and wit.

Perhaps the loveliest feature of the next symphony, no. 95 in C minor, is the theme and variations it has for a slow movement, first stated by a solo cello. There is no slow introduction to the first movement, which is also distinguished by dramatic silences that punctuate the music's flow. The blithe, contrapuntal finale is in C major.

No. 96 in D major, is wrongly entitled the *Miracle*. Its name relates to an incident during a performance, when a chandelier fell in the auditorium during the slow movement and, miraculously, no-one was injured. But it seems that this happened during a later symphony, no. 102, on the composer's second London visit. The allegro first movement (hauntingly introduced by a descending little run on the oboe) is typically unorthodox, original, unique and entirely startling. The slow movement (in G major with a minor central section) has a cadenza just before the finish, as if it belonged to a concerto rather than a symphony.

No. 97 in C major is perhaps the least familiar of the twelve London symphonies, though it is difficult to see why. Its first movement is forthright, brilliant and powerful. A rhapsodic adagio contains unusual string sounds, where the performers are instructed to play with their bows much nearer the bridge (sul ponticello) than is customary, producing a thin and distinctive sonority. The trio of the minuet is one of the loveliest moments in the work, and the difficulties of the headlong finale must have given even the virtuoso London orchestra a very hard time.

Symphony no. 98 in B flat has, like the *Miracle* symphony, a cadenza, this time in the finale, and for piano – the autograph of the score is marked 'Haydn solo'. Another endearing feature in the work is the solo bassoon that takes over the trio of the minuet.

In the following work (chronologically the first of Haydn's second visit to England) clarinets make their debut in his orchestral line-up, and remain there for all the remaining symphonies save no. 102. No. 99 in E flat major's most wonderful feature is the central adagio, long and suffused with a sadness that we have not seen perhaps since *La Passione*. The minuet is dominated by the novelty of the clarinets that were, after all, relatively new arrivals on the musical scene, and the work concludes with another sublime and happy rondo.

The *Military symphony* (no. 100 in G major) shows every sign of having been written with English audiences in mind – and they loved it. Its name has come from the clashing percussion of the slow movement that is supposed to have been inspired by a military parade. After a poignant adagio introduction, Haydn opens the symphony proper with what sounds like a toy band: the first theme is played by solo flute and oboes alone. Neither is there any second subject, instead a repetition of the first theme in D (the dominant key). A second theme proper only appears well after the music has found its new key, and even for Haydn this proves to be one of the merriest little tunes ever written. Another theme and variations makes up the allegretto slow movement, full of surprises and at times hilarious when it tries to take itself too seriously. In contrast, the third movement is a fairly orthodox minuet, of an irresistibly dancelike character. The finale is in first-movement form, though the tune that starts it leads us to expect a rondo. The latter work vies for pride of place in popularity with no. 101 in D major, known as the *Clock* from the tick-tock accompaniment to the tune of the slow movement. The work was premiered at London's Haymarket Theatre, and lost no time in becoming one of the audience's favourites. An unusual feature of the first movement is the way the theme of the movement proper derives from material first presented in the slow introduction. Surprisingly, however, the jaunty first theme plays no part in the movement's development, which is taken over by the more pliable material of the second subject. As we have seen, what you can do with a tune is sometimes more relevant than what it merely sounds like. The well-loved andante of the slow movement is again in first-movement form, and succeeded by a bouncing minuet that contains a trio of matchless serenity. The last movement, marked vivace, is a perfect example of that art which conceals art, for within this rollicking, good-natured paperchase is contained the most complex fugal writing that supports the structure, without the listener ever becoming aware of it.

It is quite a claim to make that the symphony no. 102 (in B flat major) has the best slow movement of all, but it certainly seems like it. Haydn also thought very highly of it, for it was also used as the slow movement of a piano trio. The entire work is relatively short, though in no way deprived of material, and is profoundly dramatic, making a great feature of the timpani. From the hushed largo introduction through to the brilliant finale, the crackling pace and dazzling invention never flag for a moment.

The dramatic opening of no. 103 in E flat major has given it its subtitle of *Drum-roll.* The most surprising feature of the first movement is the recurrence of the slow introduction (complete with drum-roll) as part of the movement's development, a masterstroke that even Haydn had never thought of before. Two contrasting folk tunes, one in the minor, form the basis for a prolonged set of variations in which a solo violin features prominently. After a minuet of pronounced Slavonic flavour, the finale, again long but this time in the highest of spirits, is built entirely from the simplest of themes that is constantly subjected to such a variety of treatment which no-one but Haydn could ever have imagined. The tune itself is fairly simple, but the possibilities within it, never apparent before you hear them, are nothing short of marvellous.

The last symphony, no. 104 in D major, has for some reason won the distinction of being called the *London* symphony. Haydn never again wrote a symphonic work, and the first movement of this one has a gem-hard structure as if he wanted to finish with a firm, enduring masterpiece. The first theme after the introduction is tuneful, fast, but somehow grave, a bit like a speeded-up hymn melody. The development of this movement is constructed with the utmost ingenuity from part of this little theme. The andante slow movement is a heartwarming melody subjected to the customary explosions, and the minuet fairly straightforward – though its trio shifts to the remote key of B flat major. The finale is perhaps the best of all, a sort of rondo with only one theme accompanied by an insistent drone. Notice too the ease and obvious delight with which Haydn handles the woodwind in this last movement.

Muzio Clementi was dismissed as a musical hack by Mozart, who was probably jealous of his rival's international reputation.

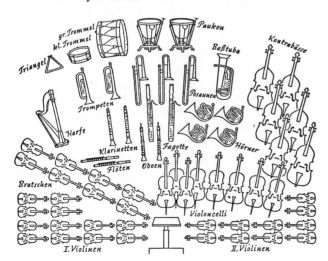

A typical disposition for an orchestra of the late eighteenth century.

Wolfgang Amadeus Mozart

The forty-odd symphonies of Mozart were written over a twenty-five year period of his life, starting in London when he was eight years old and ending in the musically glorious summer of 1788, when he completed his last three works in the form (nos 39–41) in one extraordinary six-week period of white-hot inspiration.

Give or take a few years, then, and we see that this is almost exactly the same period over which Haydn was composing *his* symphonies, though the few years' start that he had over the child Mozart was of crucial importance. When Mozart began, as we said above, he was in London, under the influence of Johann Christian Bach and his partner Carl Friedrich Abel (1723–87) who together ran an on the whole successful series of subscription concerts there. An early symphony that was for a long time accepted as being by Mozart (K.18) we now know to be a copy he made of a work by Abel. As is only to be expected of a young craftsman learning his trade, Mozart's early symphonies are generally derivative, modelled first upon the two worthies just mentioned, then upon such Continental masters as Wagenseil and Monn, and ultimately – and most important – on Joseph Haydn.

Mozart's first symphony (K.16) is a typical such work, in three simple movements, that resembles an opera buffa overture, and bearing all the marks of a youthful experiment. But one year later (1765), the young composer is handling the form with much more familiarity and freedom, as the charming symphony no. 5 (K.22) bears out. Over the next few years of his travels, Mozart continued to develop his control – and therefore by extension his originality – in orchestral writing and the symphonic shape at an alarming rate. By the time he was seventeen, he had absorbed it completely into his own language, as the first example we shall survey shows.

The conductor Nicolaus
Harnoncourt in Salzburg.

Symphony no. 25 in G minor (K.183)

Aside from the well-known *Great* G minor, this is Mozart's only symphony in the minor mode. It was apparently composed in 1773, when Mozart was seventeen, and we can think of it as his first mature work in the form.

From the very outset (as is frequently the case, he finds no need for the characteristic slow introduction) it is quite clear that this is no apprentice piece. The opening allegro has an urgency and rhythmic drive that gives the work a quite extraordinary power for the music of such a young mind. The texture of the scoring in the piece is richer too, for in addition to the customary pairs of oboes and bassoons, Mozart employs four horns instead of the usual two.

The slow movement is built upon a simple and lovely andante melody in the major, punctuated twice by a little second motif (it is too short to be called a theme) that recalls its composer's preoccupation with operatic melody. The minuet returns to G minor, and to the spirit of urgency that infected the opening; there is nothing gay or dance-like about this minuet. But it is interrupted by a trio in the major, for winds alone, of a touching and heartfelt serenity which points up all the more the starkness of the minuet on its return. The rapid finale resembles the first movement more than a little, with its jerky, dotted rhythms adding an undertone almost of suppressed hysteria to round off this small but perfectly formed masterpiece.

Symphony no. 29 in A major (K.201)

A few months after completing the above work, Mozart wrote this most melodic of his early symphonies. Though orchestrally on a smaller scale than no. 25 (in addition to the strings, it uses only a pair each of oboes and horns), it is the one other heavyweight symphony from this period in the composer's life.

The opening theme of the first movement (marked allegro moderato) climbs gently up the first four notes of the scale, a seemingly ingenuous little melody. We have to wait until the coda to find out how skilfully it can be combined against itself in three-part counterpoint. The slow movement, in sonata form, features a calm, broad melody with muted

Mozart

Wolfgang Amadeus Mozart was born in Salzburg, Austria, on 27 January 1756. His father, Leopold, must have been a consummate teacher, for the boy was fluent upon the harpsichord before he was five years old. Ever the opportunist, Leopold took the little prodigy (and his elder sister 'Nannerl') on a moneyspinning European tour through Brussels, Paris, London, Amsterdam and Zürich that lasted for over two years, and can scarcely have fortified Wolfgang's frail constitution.

When he was thirteen, his father took him twice to Italy where Mozart was quick to absorb the native operatic styles that were to have such a profound effect upon his musical language. He returned from there a fully-fledged professional composer, and picked up several important commissions.

Employed, along with his father, by the highhanded and capricious Archbishop of Salzburg, Mozart found the life of a musical lackey intolerable and obtained grudging leave to visit Paris. But the trip was something of a disaster: the opera commissions he was seeking were not forthcoming, and society was much less ready to be won over by a twenty-one year old genius than it had been by a pretty infant prodigy. Mozart's mother, who had accompanied him on this trip, died in Paris and Mozart returned home (via Mannheim) in January 1779. He soon set to work on an important commission for an opera (his twelfth) at Munich, *Idomeneo*, and moved to settle in Vienna when the Archbishop had him - literally - booted out of his job.

Over the next couple of years Mozart continued composing, playing and teaching; he also befriended Haydn, from whom he learned so much about symphonic and quartet writing, and married (much against his father's judgment) Constanze Weber, one of a family of singers he had met in Mannheim. Money was always short, even though the emperor himself was a fan of Mozart's music, and to cope with this difficulty Wolfgang wrote most of his sublime series of piano concertos for benefit concerts, featuring himself as soloist.

In 1784 he became a freemason, and soon after, his operas brought him to the attention of Lorenzo da Ponte, a librettist of genius who obtained the emperor's permission to set (with Mozart's music) Beaumarchais' subversive comedy *Le Mariage de Figaro*. The work was a great success, though it furthered his career in Vienna not at all. But in Prague the autorities set out straight away to commission another work from the pair, and *Don Giovanni* was produced there to great applause the following year (1787). On his return to Vienna he continued to compose prolifically, often for little or no money, and his financial situation became desperate. His last three symphonies were written over a six-week period in the summer of 1788.

Another opera *Così fan tutte* had its success checked by the emperor's death early in 1790, and for the remainder of that year Mozart was too exhausted and worried to write much more. In 1791 he completed his last two operas, *La Clemenza di Tito*, and *Die Zauberflöte* - the work he prized above all his other compositions. A Requiem he began as the result of a commission was destined to remain unfinished: it was as if, he said, he was writing the Requiem for himself. He died in the night of 4-5 December 1791, ill, neglected and impoverished, at the age of thirty-five.

A composite silhouette, dated 1785, of Haydn, Gluck, Mozart and Salieri.

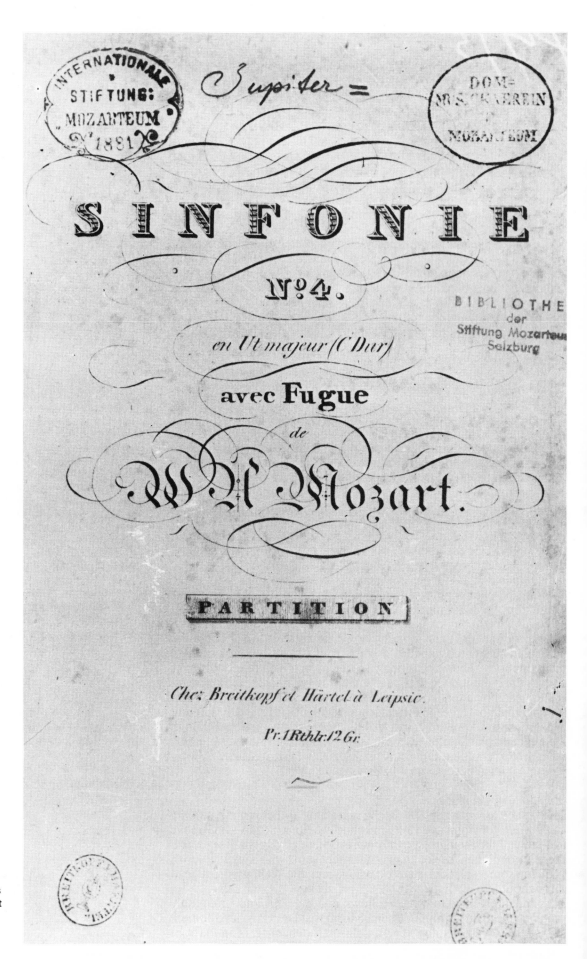

The title-page of Mozart's last symphony shows that the nickname of *Jupiter* was, at any rate, not the choice of its composer.

Mozart's birthplace in Salzburg.

Mozart's wife, Constanze, bore the composer two sons that survived their father.

strings and is succeeded by a delightful minuet in dotted rhythm, with 'echo' effects for the oboes and horns alone. The last movement, allegro con spirito, seems to return to the child within the composer in the innocent fun to be had with such lovely snatches of melody.

Symphony no. 31 in D major (K.297) – Paris Symphony
'You have no idea how they twice scraped and scrambled through it. I was really in a terrible way and would gladly have rehearsed it again, but there was no time left. So I had to go to bed with an aching heart and in a discontented and angry frame of mind.' Thus wrote the twenty-two year old composer to his father, in a typically chatty and interesting letter. What he left unsaid is more interesting: as he sat down dutifully to write home from Paris, his mother lay dead in the next room, a subject that Mozart seems to have found himself incapable of mentioning.
The performance of the symphony, however, went well, and Mozart was particularly delighted with the clarinets – the first time he had used them in a symphony. The work is richly scored in fact, with flutes, trumpets and drums in addition to the usual line-up. The brilliant first movement is succeeded by a tender andantino in a rocking 6/8 rhythm. But this lovely movement failed to impress the director of the Paris concerts, and Mozart substituted a 3/4 Andante in the same key (G major). Again in deference to Parisian taste, there is no minuet, so the music passes straight to its ebullient and frothy finale that contains a particularly witty passage of fugal development in its second subject.

Symphony no. 34 in C major (K.338)
This work was written in 1780, at the same time as the sublime *Sinfonia Concertante* for violin and viola, and shortly before Mozart's final move to Vienna. Like the *Paris* symphony it is on a relatively small scale, and there is no minuet. The opening movement starts with a joyful flourish as if for some splendid state occasion, and the feeling is sustained throughout.
The andante di molto which follows is a graceful and profoundly touching piece, in a simplified sonata form that lacks any development section. It is for strings alone, and has almost the character of an aria from

Leopold Mozart

Leopold Mozart (1719-87), the father of Wolfgang, was a gifted musician who put a promising career behind him to devote himself to the training of his two children. At the age of twenty he entered the employment of the Canon of Salzburg, but soon moved to the court of the Archbishop, where he was made court composer and, eventually, vice Kapellmeister. (His employer was the same narrow-minded and truculent despot who had the young Wolfgang kicked down the steps of his residence for insubordination.) In the same year that Wolfgang was born (1756), Leopold published his most famous work, a treatise on the art of violin-playing that earned him a wide reputation. He has often received a bad press for the demands he made upon his little son in touring him round Europe like a performing monkey, but just as it was important to make money, it was these travels that exposed Mozart to the influence of the latest and greatest music from all over Europe - giving him a more thorough and eclectic grounding in his art than would otherwise have been possible.

A charming silhouette of the Mozart family pursuing their customary occupations.

an unwritten opera. The finale is an infectious country dance, with an odd feature near the end when the music comes to a stop as if in anticipation of a cadenza, like a concerto.

Symphony no. 35 in D major (K.385) – Haffner Symphony

While at work on teething troubles of his opera *Die Entführung aus dem Serail,* Mozart received a request from his father that he supply a symphony to celebrate the ennoblement of a prominent Salzburg citizen, Sigmund Haffner. Six years before, he had written the *Haffner Serenade* for a wedding in the same musically discerning family. Mozart complied with his father's wish and sent this symphony, though originally in a slightly different form from the one we now know. It had two extra movements, both of which the composer removed when the work was later given its Viennese première.

The strongly defined first subject of the opening movement, with its two-octave leaps, makes an arresting and festive beginning; and this theme soon reappears as the counterpoint to a busy little second subject in the dominant key. The entire movement needs repeated listening and close attention to uncover all the little miracles Mozart works with this seemingly innocuous opening idea. It is a delight from start to finish, complete with a short visit in the development to the weird and distant key of F sharp major. The andante that follows is a passionate movement with a deceptively calm surface. In the codas to this piece, Mozart delays, as it were, the proper resolution of the chord progressions in a way that makes you feel as though you never want the music to stop. The minuet is bright and pompous, with a happy 'wrong-note' feature in the accompaniment, and a more restful trio which again seems to be extracted from some imaginary opera.

The finale is certainly extracted from an opera, but not imaginary this time. As we said above, Mozart had only just completed *Die Entführung* when he set to work on this symphony, and the theme of this light and fizzy ending is drawn from an aria in that work sung by Osmin, the fat and crafty guardian of the Sultan's harem.

Symphony no. 36 in C major (K.425) – Linz Symphony

In October 1783, on the way back from a visit to Salzburg, Mozart and his wife broke their journey at Linz. He wrote to his father, 'I am giving a concert in the theatre here and, as I haven't a single symphony with me, I am writing a new one at break-neck speed, which must be finished in time.' This marvellous and brilliant work, apparently composed in a matter of days, is unusual in that it opens with a slow introduction that reminds the listener of Haydn – as do other moments in this sunny, extrovert symphony.

The first movement teems with melodic invention. The second subject takes off, unusually, in a minor key before settling down in more orthodox fashion, and the development, though intense, is quite short and to the point. The poco adagio which follows is in a lyrical and gently swinging 6/8, and succeeded by a glittering and martial minuet, whose trio is a gentle rustic dance of the sweetest beauty. The symphony ends with a bustling presto, a seemingly artless movement that is constructed with the greatest craftsmanship and whose pungent wit is timed to perfection.

Symphony no. 38 in D major (K.504) – Prague Symphony

As will be apparent from the gaps between the 'Köchel' (K.) numbers, Mozart's symphonic writing thinned out a lot in his maturity, though the quality continued to climb to the dizziest heights of genius. The *Symphony without a Minuet,* as this work was once rather foolishly known, was written after *The Marriage of Figaro* and before *Don Giovanni.* Mozart had been invited to Prague with a commission to write the latter opera, and took this new work with him, where it was first performed on 19 January 1787.

A portrait of Johann
Christian Bach by
Thomas Gainsborough,
painted during the
composer's residence
in London. Johann
Christian, one of the
three great sons of J.S.
Bach, was nicknamed
the 'London' Bach
from his long stay in
the capital, which
lasted from 1762 until
his death twenty years
later. His music was an
important influence on
the young Mozart.

Carl Philippe Emanuel
Bach (1714-1788), third
son of Johann
Sebastian Bach and
his first wife Maria
Barbara, wrote 18
symphonies.

Antonio Stradivari
above in his workshop
at Cremona, famous by
the end of the
seventeenth century
for the skill of its
stringed instrument
makers. There are
many Stradivari
instruments still in
circulation in the great
orchestras of the
world; some estimates
claim he may have
made as many as 3000
during his long life
(1644-1737), all prized
for their masterly
craftsmanship and
inimitable tone.

Haydn's handwriting, in a letter written from Eisenstadt in his old age.

A concert in the Schönbrunn Palace near Vienna for the Austrian Imperial family (seated in the front row).

An eighteenth-century view of Salzburg, where Mozart was born in 1756.

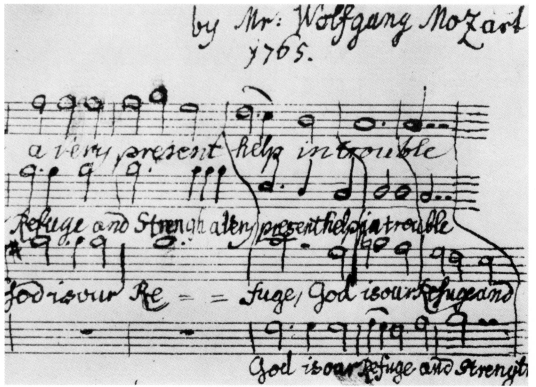

Mozart's autograph of a motet he wrote when he was nine years old during his stay in London, in 1765. The previous year, the young Mozart wrote his first symphony (in E flat) in London.

Haydn's studio in
Vienna.

Frontispice of the first
edition of one of
Mozart's compositions
in 1787.

The Graben, the
principal street of
Vienna, in the
eighteenth century.
Vienna, as the capital
(die Kaiserstadt) of a
multi-national empire,
attracted musicians
from all over the world,
including Italy, France,
England and Ireland, as
well as from its own
vast dominions.

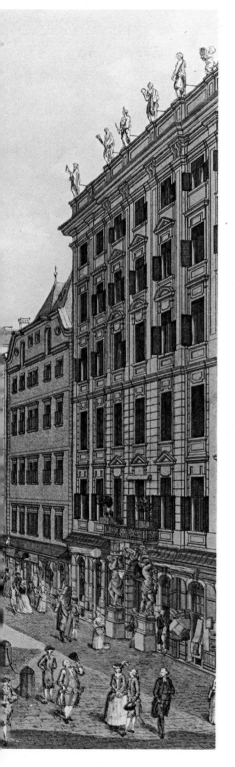

The young Mozart with his father, Leopold, and sister Nannerl. A watercolour painted in 1763 by Carmontelle.

Joseph Haydn. He was well aware of his good fortune in having the patronage of the princely Esterházy family, which gave him musical resources in the shape of an orchestra, singers and an opera house – and freedom from financial worry.

Leopold Mozart.

Again there is a slow introduction, infused with a drama that reminds us, and it can be no coincidence, of the music of the Commendatore's ghost in the latter opera. The allegro into which it leads is one of Mozart's greatest musical feats, where seemingly inexhaustible ideas are combined, explored and manipulated to an effect that is simply glorious. There is no space here to examine in any detail the wizardry of this movement's marvellous structure: it seems, however, to be a piece of which the ear can never tire. Melody abounds again in the exquisite andante, whose tunes are sweet but speak of a pathetic sadness. The last movement, a rushing presto, alternates a breathless anxiety tempered with flashes of Mozartean humour and comic relief, in particular from the horns and that traditional clown of the orchestra, the bassoon.

Symphony no. 39 in E flat major (K.543)
Mozart's last three symphonies, written between June and August of 1788, seem to have been composed with reference to a planned (but probably unrealized) series of concerts in Vienna. The scoring for no. 39 is unusual: one flute, two each of clarinets, bassoons, horns, trumpets – drums and strings. After a slow, richly scored introduction, a bright allegro theme in triple time propels this sunlit movement on its way. The musical ideas contained within it are legion, and contrasting phrases succeed each other all the time – though, such is Mozart's mastery of balance, never crowding each other out or jostling for attention.
The ingenuous, dotted theme of the andante which follows, has at first a Haydnesque simplicity about it, though a little later in the movement a repeated-note figure in the minor leads the composer off on some daring harmonic key changes and miraculous contrapuntal flights of fancy. The well-known minuet that succeeds it is, by contrast, simple and straightforward, and Mozart enjoys some delicious play with the clarinets on its trio section. The allegro finale recalls Haydn again, where one little melodic flake of nine notes is made strong enough to carry the weight of almost an entire movement. The piece never for a moment relaxes from being vibrant, joyful, and humming with life.

Symphony no. 40 in G minor (K.550)
Written as they were in an amazingly condensed space of time, Mozart's last three symphonies show an astonishing disparity of moods, and that of no. 40 is the hardest to pinpoint. It has been called 'tragic'; but a molto allegro opening, particularly with such a skipping rhythm (that it shares, by the way, with Cherubino's aria *Non so più* from *Figaro*) must give the lie to those kind of adjectives. Yet on the other hand it is assuredly not gay or frisky, and to call it neurotic or hysterical would be seriously to undervalue its powerful logic and structure. But there is a pathos in the affecting (major) second subject that temporarily checks the restless quaver flow of the movement.
It is followed by a lovely andante in E flat major. The calm of this movement, however, is never allowed to settle into complacency, being repeatedly disturbed by chromatic 'wrong' notes that show off what has been called Mozart's ability to 'poison' a musical phrase. And there is no emotional let-up in the minuet either: its grim, stern dissonances are only relieved by a wistful and soothing trio in G major. The finale, allegro assai, returns once more to the urgency of the opening movement. It also is in sonata form, and has a marvellous, classically pathetic second subject that lends a dignity and poise to the movement's demonic energy.

Symphony no. 41 in C major (K.551) – Jupiter
It was Haydn's impresario, Salomon, who gave this mighty work its nickname. More perhaps than any of the other symphonies discussed here, its strength lies in its development. In the first movement, allegro vivace, the opening flourish is rounded off by a tiny, climbing cadence and both are soon combined with a third

The Austrian scholar Ludwig Köchel (1800-77) lived in Salzburg for thirteen years, and while there compiled his catalogue of Mozart's works.

A portrait of the boy
Mozart hangs above the
composer's piano in his
birthplace at Salzburg.

figure whose most prominent feature is a staccato descending scale. All
this is quite easy to pick out, and occurs within the first minute of the
music. It soon gives way to a second – and third – subject, and the
development after the beautiful little coda makes a virtuoso display of
combining these several motives in magical and psychically satisfying
fashion, before the final recapitulation.

The strings are muted in the tranquil andante cantabile, which
resembles a soft, operatic aria whose peace is only ruffled by some
momentary syncopations that throw the music off its delicate but
insistent triple tread. The orchestration that underlies the melodic line in
this movement is particulary rich and fulfilling.

For a work in the often brilliant key of C major, the minuet is restrained,
though the downward chromatic slips in the little piece lend the music a
gorgeous feeling of quiet ecstasy.

All too often in the classical symphony, it is the finale which is its weakest
point, but in the *Jupiter* it is perhaps the concluding allegro molto that is
its crowning glory. Five themes are stated more or less consecutively and
then combined in the most dazzling fugal work-out.

One motif is made up simply of four long semibreves, as if from some
ancient chorale; another, complete with trill, seems like a snatch of
birdsong; and a very insistent little figure is scarcely more than a bustling,
self-important downward scale. These, and the other motifs, are all
readily and separately identifiable to the ear, but it takes close
concentration to follow and pick out all the interweaving, canonic
imitation, inverting and combining that Mozart can do with these simple
tools. It is as if we are being shown a complete catalogue of all that can
happen to these tiny elements. But this is no text-book display: all the
composer's ineffable artistry is directed towards achieving a consistent
and unified whole that sounds in our ears and our hearts with a sublime
and incomparable happiness.

The last portrait of Mozart
drawn from life:
A silverpoint made by
Doris Stock in 1789.

2

Beethoven

At half past six on 2 April 1800, the citizens of Vienna were invited to a concert at the Royal Imperial Court Theatre. The long programme concluded with 'a new grand symphony composed by Herr Ludwig van Beethoven'. No one in the audience could have foreseen that this engaging but modest work was the prelude to a towering achievement of European culture.

Beethoven wrote nine symphonies, not a great number for a composer of his generation, but these cover an emotional and stylistic range that few artists have ever equalled. He approached the symphonic form with a concentration that was unusual even by his own formidable standards. Piano variations or chamber music he might dash off and later live to regret (he despised his own tuneful and popular septet), but a symphony was a work to be taken seriously. He was twenty-nine when the first symphony, a work he had long intended to write, was performed, and his musical sketchbooks indicate fruitful gestation periods for several of the others. It was in his mind to write music for Schiller's *Ode to Joy* as early as 1793, for example. This idea only materialized in 1824 as the choral finale of the ninth symphony.

As a symphonist Beethoven was aided by a general improvement in the standard of orchestral playing (especially among the winds) and by the sheer number of professional musicians at hand. From the time of his first symphony, orchestras with sufficient strings and two each of flutes, oboes, clarinets, bassoons, horns, trumpets and timpani were available to him. He added another horn for the third symphony (the *Eroica*); the fifth included piccolo, contra-bassoon and three trombones. He dropped contra-bassoon and one of the trombones for the sixth and was content to revert to the smaller requirements of the first two (the so-called 'Beethoven orchestra') for the seventh and eighth, but for the ninth he assembled all his forces, doubling the horn section and adding triangle, cymbal and bass drum to the percussion.

Beethoven used the wind section as an equal partner of the strings. 'The only flaw was that the wind instruments were used too much,' wrote a critic at the première of the first symphony. A plaintive oboe cadenza in the first movement of the fifth symphony and stirring use of trombones in the last: the bizarre rattle of contra-bassoon in the finale of the ninth; and a daring confidence in the abilities of his French horns in the trio of the *Eroica* all mark Beethoven as an innovator in orchestration. He was also largely responsible for taming the kettledrums and for liberating the cellos and double-basses, drudges of an eighteenth-century orchestra, from their rôle as mere time-keepers. It has often been pointed out that Beethoven's symphonies fall into two broad categories: the cheerful and emotionally restrained even-numbered works contrast with the bold and passionate odd-numbered ones (excluding the first, which is taken as the exception that proves the

Ludwig van Beethoven

As Beethoven lay dying, a fierce hailstorm broke over Vienna and a great clap of thunder roused the composer for the last time. He opened his eyes and shook his clenched fist. Then, in the midst of the tumult, he died. This romantic account of Beethoven's death is generally unchallenged by even the most meticulous of scholars. It seems only appropriate that the greatest musical genius of his age should have died as passionately as he lived. Beethoven was born in Bonn in December 1770. His grandfather, Ludwig, was Kapellmeister (musical director) at the court of the Elector, and his father, Johann, was a tenor in the same service. Johann was a severe, intemperate man, who saw the spark of genius in his son and compelled him to practise long hours at the pianoforte and organ. The boy gave his first public recital when he was eight (though the programme boasted that he was only six). At fourteen, his formal education behind him, Beethoven became assistant organist at the court chapel. 'A second Wolfgang Amadeus Mozart,' predicted his master, the principal organist C.G. Neefe. Mozart, it is believed, was of the same opinion after hearing the youth play for him in Vienna in 1787. His mother's death and his father's increasing incompetence and alcoholism forced Beethoven to take responsibility for his two younger brothers while still in his teens. For some years he supported the family by teaching and by playing viola in the court orchestra, but the desire to seek recognition as a composer and virtuoso pianist was too great to be ignored. In 1792 Beethoven moved to Vienna, where he remained for the rest of his life.

He arrived in Vienna with glowing recommendations and soon found devoted and influential friends. Haydn, who briefly taught him composition, thought him prodigiously talented, if personally rather difficult; Salieri the popular rival of Mozart, taught him free of charge. As a performer he had no peers. His piano improvisations at private gatherings frequently moved the audience to tears. His compositions, dedicated to those willing to pay for the privilege, were equally well received. These early works, products of what is often called his 'first period', included piano sonatas, chamber music and two concertos for piano and orchestra. The success of his compositions, supplemented by the generosity of wealthy admirers, provided Beethoven with an adequate, if never abundant, income.

In 1800, at his first benefit concert, Beethoven conducted the C major symphony. Three years later a second symphony had its première. This ebullient and popular work is a mystery to those who attempt to match a man's life with his music, for at the time of its composition Beethoven was in a state of profound depression, struggling to admit to himself that the deafness which had irritated him sporadically for some years was progressive and incurable. 'I must live like an outcast,' he wrote in a moment of anguish. 'O Providence - do but grant me one day of pure joy.' The deterioration of his hearing gradually forced Beethoven to abandon the concert platform and to work single-mindedly as a composer. The music of his so-called middle period (1803-12) reflects an increased dedication to composition.

Milestones of this fertile decade include the third, fourth and fifth piano concertos, the *Appassionata* Sonata, the Violin Concerto, the opera *Fidelio* and the symphonies nos. three to eight. Throughout these years Beethoven was passionately moved by the philosophical issues of his day. Political liberty and human dignity inspired him to write some of his greatest works, including *Fidelio* and the *Ode to Joy* finale of the ninth symphony. (A belated discovery that Napoleon was not a champion of egalitarianism led him to destroy the original dedication of the third symphony.) The powerful emotions apparent in these works heralded the beginning of a Romantic movement in

The title-page of Beethoven's manuscript of the *Eroica* symphony, clearly showing where the composer obliterated the dedication to Napoleon on hearing that the latter had declared himself Emperor.

rule). There is some truth in this generalization. Robert Schumann called the fourth symphony 'a slender Grecian maiden between two giants'. The cheerful sixth (the *Pastoral*) is a conspicuous oasis of joy between the turbulent emotions of the fifth and seventh. The eighth, a favourite of Beethoven, is a concise and meticulous masterpiece, an unlikely forerunner to the sprawling ninth symphony that appeared ten years later.

These swings in symphonic mood are largely a manifestation of Beethoven's genius; they are also a product of the age in which he lived. Rebellion and the rights of man were the political keynotes of Beethoven's generation. Schooled in the formal traditions of the eighteenth century, he could, and frequently did, write as correct a counterpoint or as rigid a sonata as the most conservative of his elders. He was also a child of his times, full of hope, anger and frustration, emotions that found their way into his compositions.

Beethoven's symphonies, even his most ambitious ones, were generally well received. The *Eroica*, it is true, provoked growls of 'lawless' and 'wild' from the critics and, from an unidentified man in the audience at the first performance, the despairing remark, 'I'll give another Kreutzer if the thing will but stop.' At the tumultuous première of the seventh, however, the public demanded to hear the second movement repeated. A similarly joyful exhibition interrupted the first performance of the ninth. By then Beethoven was totally deaf and could hear neither the music nor the ovation.

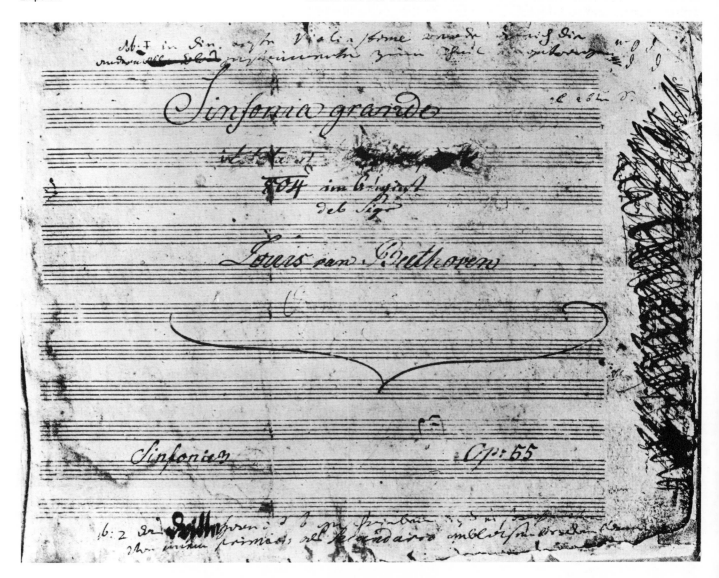

In the silence and sickness of his last years Beethoven continued to plan future compositions. On 18 March 1827 he wrote with characteristic confidence of a tenth symphony 'which lies already sketched in my desk'. Eight days later he was dead.

Symphony no. 1 in C major, opus 21

The orchestra at the première of Beethoven's first symphony (Vienna, 1800) was sloppy and spiritless, but behind this lacklustre performance one critic discovered 'considerable art, novelty and a wealth of ideas'. Since then the piece has continued to charm audiences, though it irritates those critics who think of Beethoven as a thunderous prophet and wince to see him on the dance floor in such an amiable mood.

Adagio molto – allegro con brio. Sustained chords in the woodwinds and ambiguous wanderings by the strings clear like morning mist as the adagio introduction resolves into C major and a sunny allegro. The bright, ascending first subject is played by the violins. Oboe and flute emerge as soloists in the graceful second subject, which concludes with a plaintive duet between cellos and woodwinds.

The development section seizes upon the rising dotted rhythm of the first subject, drawing it through a number of keys before descending to the recapitulation. Twenty-one bars of rousing C major dispel any final doubts about the home key.

Andante cantabile con moto. The second violins introduce this elegant movement with a tune which Haydn would have been proud to have written. Stately and sure-footed, it moves with the confidence of a courtly dance. Beethoven's voice is clearly audible across the ballroom, however, bringing the timpani quietly into play during a troubled middle section. Order is discreetly restored, and the initial tune, with delightful counterpoint, brings the movement to a close.

Menuetto – allegro molto e vivace. Here is a 'minuet' that is totally undanceable, the first of these movements that Beethoven was later to label scherzo. The violins rush in with an urgent ascending scale, creating an air of suppressed tension that finally breaks loose in the second section. Calm is suddenly imposed by the woodwinds in a magical trio. The violins hover impatiently while the imperturbable winds repeat their pulsing chords. In true 'minuet' style, the movement ends as it began, with excitement and speed.

Adagio – allegro molto e vivace. 'This is not Beethoven,' complained Hector Berlioz of the cheerful finale. It is not Beethoven of the *Eroica*, he should have said, but it is Beethoven the student of Haydn. The movement begins with a joke and continues in unflagging good humour. A C major scale hesitantly ascends during the introductory adagio section and after several false starts finally gathers courage and races into the allegro. A dance-like second subject enriches the musical material. It is tempting (though rather more picturesque than true) to interpret such wit and high spirits as Beethoven's symphonic farewell to the eighteenth century.

Symphony no. 2 in D major, opus 36

Having fulfilled his audience's expectations with the first symphony, Beethoven went on to surprise them with the second. A critic at the première (Vienna, 1803) was disappointed by what he called this 'striving for the new', and it is said that the violinist Rodolphe Kreutzer ran out of one performance with his hands to his ears. The good humour of this symphony soon proved irresistible, however, especially when compared to the monumental innovations of its successors.

Adagio molto – allegro con brio. An adagio introduction, with suggestions of melancholy and high drama, does not prepare the listener for the bustling first subject of the allegro. An equally cheerful second subject, like the chorus of a drinking song, is taken by the woodwinds. But Beethoven knew that there was more to a tune than meets the ear. With the four semiquavers of the first subject as his principal motif, he

music. Form was giving away to feeling. The elegant citadel of classical music, so carefully erected in the eighteenth century, began to crumble under the thunderous blows of Beethoven. For all his democratic ideals, Beethoven delighted in mixing with the privileged and powerful. When he first arrived in Vienna, his intense eyes, broad pockmarked face and mane of black hair, made him a striking, but never handsome man. In his later years, physical decay and personal neglect reduced him to a wildly eccentric figure. (On one of his country rambles he was detained by the police as a suspected tramp.) Yet he exerted a magnetism that absolved him from the petty obligations of Viennese society. He might dress like a peasant, roar with insulting laughter in a roomfull of high-born ladies, throw eggs at his cook, come to blows with his brothers in the street, accuse his most loyal friends of treachery - but be forgiven and remain beloved. His intense relationships with a succession of women, many of whom were married or his social superiors, give some suggestion of his compelling attractions.

Beethoven's birthplace in Bonn is a popular place of pilgrimage for music-lovers from all over the world.

A twentieth-century
sketch of Beethoven, by
Leonid Pasternak.

Despite a longing to share his domestic life, Beethoven never married. This unfulfilled desire for a family led to the disastrous years of legal battle over the guardianship op his nephew Karl. Beethoven finally won his case, but the emotional toll was immense, and Karl's abortive suicide attempt in 1826 may have hastened his uncle to the grave.

For a few years after the completion of his eighth symphony (1812), Beethoven's output dwindled, but his energy and inspiration returned during the last decade. The *Missa Solemnis* (1822), the *Diabelli Variations* for piano (1823), the ninth symphony (1824) and five profound string quartets (which include the last music he ever wrote) are the works not just of prodigious genius but of a priest-like devotion to Art.

Though never a concious religious man, Beethoven gratefully received the last sacraments of the Catholic Church on his deathbed, and surrendered himself to the God he had so often addressed in his diaries and in his music. Some 10,000 people jammed the streets of Vienna at his funeral (1827).

'Thus he was,' wrote the poet Franz Grillparzer, author of Beethoven's funeral oration, 'thus he died, thus he will live to the end of time.'

leads this rather banal material up to an unexpectedly emotional peak. Larghetto. As if to prove that he could write as good a tune as anyone, Beethoven begins this movement with a melting 'Schubertian' melody (Schubert was, at the time, five years old). While any other composer might have been content to write variations on this beautiful theme, and so end the movement, Beethoven adds a second and then a third subject, bringing the whole to a powerful climax before returning to the original theme. The romantic Hector Berlioz, entranced by this long movement, described it as 'the delineation of innocent happiness hardly clouded by a few accents of melancholy'.

Scherzo – allegro. The word scherzo means joke, and here Beethoven took the title literally, passing his boisterous three-note motif from strings to horns to oboes. The woodwinds attempt to introduce a note of quiet seriousness in the trio section, but the strings will have none of this and interrupt noisily to take the movement back to the beginning.

Allegro molto. The comedy of the scherzo continues in this light-hearted and eccentric finale. The principal theme is an explosive two-bar passage, a sort of musical sneeze that seems to catch Beethoven unaware whenever he threatens to become too earnest. A languorous second subject gives the woodwinds, especially the bassoon, a brief chance to float above the scurrying strings. And a mysterious pizzicato passage in the coda offers the glimpse of another world, before the jeering first subject brings the symphony to a happy close.

Symphony no. 3 in E flat major, opus 55 – Eroica
Beethoven's third symphony did not break completely with the past: within the first movement are the bones of a sonata form, and the scherzo could be described as a frenetic eighteenth-century minuet. But in size and emotional breadth the *Eroica* is revolutionary and truly heroic. Beethoven once remarked that if he understood the art of war as well as he knew the art of music he could conquer Napoleon. With this great symphony (first performed 1805) alone he could have gone confidently to battle.

Allegro con brio. Two massive E flat major chords assert this symphony's heroic intentions. The cellos then enter with the legato first subject, but they have already lost their grasp of it in the seventh bar, when an intrusive C sharp gives an early indication of ensuing conflict. It would be vain to attempt a coherent description of this huge movement in such a brief space, but the following are significant points of reference: a serene and organ-like second subject (though an abundance of themes and rhythmic motifs make conventional analysis difficult); massive syncopated chords at the end of the exposition and again (sounding as much like Stravinsky as Beethoven) in the development; a distant and dissonant solo horn introducing the recapitulation; bold, verging on the brutal, modulation at the beginning of the coda; and a cheerful contrapuntal passage, the horn again playing the simple first subject and leading the movement to an optimistic conclusion.

Marcia funebre – adagio assai. Simulated 'drum rolls' by the double basses accompany the slow tread of a solemn march. But this is no mere funeral procession. Hector Berlioz described it as 'a drama in itself', referring to the glowing C major interlude and a tempestuous fugue in F minor. Perhaps these are no more than fleeting impressions in the minds of the mourners, for in the end, the sombre theme returns, now with long cruel silences, as if drawing near the grave.

Scherzo – allegro vivace. Excited scurrying among the strings is aggravated by their apparent difficulty in finding the key of E flat. Their joyous arrival at the tonic is short-lived, however, as three French horns now begin the trio section with a triumphant fanfare. This exultant tune becomes a pensive hymn before the scherzo returns. Beethoven temporarily shatters the rhythm with four bars in duple time, but three-in-a-bar order is quickly restored. Horns and strings unite to conclude the movement on a resolute fortissimo.

Finale: allegro molto – poco andante – presto. As if trying to capture all the moods of the preceding three movements, Beethoven chose to write variations for this unconventional finale. At first he reveals only the bass line, introduced by pizzicato strings in a manner both mysterious and strangely comical. The theme itself is a light-hearted melody that lends itself to joyous, even playful, variations and fugues. Then suddenly it becomes the solemn vehicle for a beautiful andante chorale, one of the most moving passages Beethoven ever wrote. A concluding presto passage, the horns in full cry, recalls the heroic confidence of the very first two bars of the symphony.

Symphony no. 4 in B flat major, opus 60
In the summer of 1806 Beethoven stopped work on his C minor symphony (later to be known as the fifth) in order to compose this comparatively neglected masterpiece. It is an astonishing aspect of his genius that he could turn his attention with such apparent ease from an intense and stormy composition to one that so overflows with wit and good cheer.

Adagio – allegro vivace. The violins tiptoe mysteriously through a number of unexpected keys before coming triumphantly to rest on F major at the end of the adagio introduction. This chord is then, as it were, wound up until it springs into B flat major and one of the happiest first movements Beethoven ever wrote. The woodwinds contribute a robust and bucolic second subject, and such is the abundance of melodic

Luigi Cherubini

Despite his Italian nationality, Cherubini (1760-1842) is considered a French composer. According to the forward of the catalogue of his works, written by the composer himself and containing 305 works, Cherubini received his first music lessons from his father at the age of nine. Before turning sixteen, he had already composed three *Masses*, a *Magnificat*, a *Miserere* and a *Te Deum*, as well as an oratorium and three cantatas. In 1777, Cherubini received a scholarship to study with Sartie in Venice from the then Grand Duke of Tuscany, who was later to become Leopold II. There, the composer studied counterpoint and polyphony. Cherubini's first opera, *Quinto Fabio*, was performed in 1780 in Alessandria. The following eight years, he dedicated himself to composing only operas and music for the theatre.

Cherubini moved to London in 1784, where he composed four operas for The King's Theatre, without success. For one year, he was also 'Composer to the King'. In 1786, he left for Paris, where, in 1788, his opera *Démophon*, with a libretto by Marmontel, was performed. In this opera, Cherubini broke with the Neopolitian School, and laid the foundation for his development as a composer in the French style. He was put in charge of the Italian Opera in Paris, and in 1790, produced his opera *Lodoiska* with them. It was composed in a very new style, using courageous harmonic combinations and yet unknown instrumental effects. Its success with the public was great, but Cherubini's financial situation unfortunately did not improve as a result.

The Conservatoire de Musique was founded in 1795, and Cherubini was appointed into the degrading position of 'Inspecteur des Etudes'. Napoleon considered the composer rather second rate, and the sensitive Cherubini became depressed by the antipathy his music and person were subjected to. He clearly lost most of his interest in music as a result.

In 1795, Cherubini married Mlle Cécile Tourette which elevated his financial situation at least. The Imperial Theatre in Vienna commissioned an opera from him which led to Cherubini's introduction to Beethoven in 1805. Beethoven was in awe of the Italian, praising him as the leading composer of his generation, and obviously influenced by him. Cherubini was present at the première of *Fidelio*. Both *Wassertrager* (*Les Jeux journées*) and *Faniska* by Cherubini were performed in Vienna, but it was a bad time for expensive opera there as war had broken out. When Vienna was occupied in 1806, Cherubini was ordered to organize

material that the development section begins to digress with a theme of its own. Then, while the timpani roll apprehensively, the violins are allowed a rare moment to catch their breath before rushing back to the country dance with a joyful and boisterous recapitulation.

Adagio. Critics who seek biographical information from a composer's music see this voluptuous adagio as clear evidence that Beethoven was blissfully in love, with a dotted accompanying rhythm, for all the world like a lover's heart-beat. The movement is dominated by two beautiful melodies, the first introduced by the violins, the second by the clarinet – each characterized by sighing, descending slurs. These are repeated, the first with shimmering ornamentation, before a final 'heart-beat' from the timpani brings this lovely adagio to a close.

Allegro vivace; trio – un poco meno allegro. Between the raptures of an adagio and the excitement of a finale Beethoven was determined to prevent his audience from falling asleep. Here he mocks the complacent three-four rhythm of the minuet in a short movement of unsettling syncopation and unconventional harmony. The woodwinds establish a rustic interlude in the trio section, but the tipsy opening, with its sliding unisons returns to restore disorder.

Allegro ma non troppo. This bubbling finale gives the strings little respite. The ebullient semi-quavers of the opening bar continue relentlessly with only a brief pause when the winds play their relaxed second subject. Eleven bars from the end the tempo suddenly unwinds and the whole symphony grinds to a halt, only to pluck up courage again in a mad dash for the final double bar.

Symphony no. 5 in C minor, opus 67
Historical musical events are not always impressive at the time. Beethoven's fifth and sixth symphonies received first performances on the same evening (1808), but the only accounts of that remarkable concert tell how the *Choral Fantasy* (also receiving its première) came to an embarrassing halt. As if to make up for the ignominy of its birth, the fifth has become the most popular of all Beethoven's symphonies.

Allegro con brio. The four most famous notes in symphonic music – the familiar dot-dot-dot-dash 'victory' motif – establish a rhythmic pattern that persists throughout the movement. The fortissimo courage of these opening bars, however, does not continue. After this initial burst of confidence, the strings introduce a melancholy first subject, charged with a nervous energy that infuses the whole movement. Likewise, the horns boldly introduce a graceful second subject, which is quickly absorbed into the compelling rhythm of the opening. This tension between despair and courage is most evident at the end of the development section, where strings and winds exchange a series of panting, repetitive chords, to be fiercely revived by the opening theme, now played by the full orchestra. In a defiant coda Beethoven reasserts the determination of his first five bars.

Andante con moto. Resignation and triumph alternate in this stately slow movement. The opening theme in A flat major (a dotted rhythm that one critic has described as 'sadly suave') is introduced by the cellos and violas. It solemnly proceeds with a number of variations, but its progress is impeded by a triumphal procession in C major, with a band that includes trumpets, horns, oboes and timpani. A royal funeral and coronation have taken place on the same day.

Allegro. Cellos and basses slide almost imperceptibly into the first few bars of this extraordinary movement. Their mysterious reverie is shattered by the horns playing a fortissimo four-note motif – a distorted version of the opening bars of the symphony. The 'trio' section involves lower strings again, this time in an aggressive and grotesque fugue ('the gambols of a delighted elephant,' said Berlioz, possibly mistaking the technical struggles of the bass section for deliberate comedy). The timpani, echoing the horns' four-note rhythm, finally summon the entire orchestra without a pause to the finale.

Allegro – Presto. An ascending C major triad dispels all the doubt and darkness of the previous three movements. Reinforced by the piccolo, contra-bassoon and three trombones, the orchestra marches confidently through an exposition and development section, only to be recalled abruptly by a ghostly reminiscence of the four-note phrase that haunted the third movement. This disturbing presence is purged by the full orchestra in a triumphant recapitulation. Untroubled by any subsequent musical memories, the symphony comes to an emphatic and noisy close.

Symphony no. 6 in F major, opus 68 – Pastoral

Beethoven delighted in the country, drawing inspiration from the peace and beauty of his surroundings. 'My unhappy ears do not torment me here,' he wrote. 'It seems as if in the country every tree said to me Holy! Holy!' Although it could be argued that many of Beethoven's great compositions have their origins in the Austrian countryside, it was only in the sixth symphony (the Pastoral) that he chose to be explicit.

Allegro ma non troppo. 'The cheerful feelings excited by arriving in the country' was Beethoven's own subtitle for this movement. He achieves a sense of untroubled well-being by repeating the tumbling second bar of his first subject until it becomes a pulse for the whole movement. This repetitive two-beat unit (a quaver, two semi-quavers and two more quavers) provides no precise image. The listener must 'see' for himself the wind in the leaves or water falling over smooth stones. Because of its descriptive nature, it is easy to forget that this movement is written in strict sonata form: exposition, development and recapitulation are all in their 'correct' places.

Andante molto mosso. 'By the stream'. This is a broad and peaceful stream, its gentle murmur coming from the lower strings which 'flow' steadily throughout most of the movement. Above them a number of liquid melodies float among the violins and the winds, obscuring the fact that this movement, like the first, is written in traditional sonata form. A nightingale (flute), a quail (oboe) and a cuckoo (clarinet) emerge at nightfall in a delightful coda.

Allegro. 'A happy gathering of the peasants'. The peasants do not have long to celebrate, but they fit in a noisy and drunken dance before the impending storm scatters them. Their little wind band includes an oboist who plays consistently off the beat, a flamboyant clarinettist and a sleepy bassoonist who can manage only three notes. This scherzo modulates suddenly to the sombre key of F minor, and proceeds without pause to the next movement.

Allegro. 'Storm'. 'Listen to those rain-charged squalls of wind,' exhorted Hector Berlioz, referring to the turbulent opening of this movement. The staccato violins are quickly joined by an ominous growling from basses and cellos. The woodwinds shriek, the timpani rumble, and eventually trombones enter on a fortissimo that had the impressionable Berlioz trembling with fear and admiration. 'It is no longer merely rain and wind, but an awful cataclysm,' he wrote. The storm passes, and amid distant thunder the oboe and flute herald a serene sunrise.

Allegretto. 'Shepherds' song. Joy and thanksgiving after the storm'. Again there is no break between movements, as calls by solo clarinet and horn arise from distant mountainsides. The violins then enter with a gracious melody, the shepherds' hymn of thanksgiving. This is taken up by the full orchestra and remains, with exquisite variations, the central theme of the final movement. A muted horn, repeating the call of the first bars, brings the symphony to a tranquil close.

Symphony no. 7 in A major, opus 92

The première of the seventh symphony in 1813 marked a high point in Beethoven's popularity. Sad to say, the merits of this great work were partially eclipsed by another of that evening's first performances: Wellington's Victory (also known as the Battle Symphony), a noisy money-

A caricature of Beethoven walking in the streets of Vienna.

and conduct Napoleon's evening amusements at Schönbrunn. The composer returned to France a bitter and physically broken man. He retreated to the castle of his friend, the Prince of Chimay. Friends tried to interest him in church music. After a long while, Cherubini produced the Mass in F for three vocal parts and orchestra in 1809 which was to prove the beginning of a new period in his composing career.

During Napoleon's 100 days, Cherubini was named Chevalier de la Légion d'Honneur. In 1816, Louis XVIII appointed him to the Royal Chapel with the similarly royal salary of 3000 francs. All at once, Cherubini had received the honour, status and financial rewards he had previously lacked. He became director of the Conservatoire in 1822 where he was to be an important influence on French compositional talent for quite some time to come. Cherubini is also responsible for the book: 'Solfèges pour l'examen de l'école'.

In 1815, the newly founded Philharmonic Society paid Cherubini £200 to write a symphony, an overture and a vocal work, which the composer finished, travelling to London for the performance on May first of that same year. Later, in 1829, he transcribed the symphony for string quartet.

Cherubini's compositional idealism is evident throughout his works. His musical expression is always disciplined and never coarse. Recognition by the public was, therefore, always a problem. Even his newer, more dramatic, more French style, influenced tastes in France for only a short while. As soon as Boieldieu and Auber entered the French musical world, Cherubini's renown rapidly diminished. His most important work is undoubtedly the Requiem in C major. The Credo for 8 a capelle voices is an extraordinary example of pure and disciplined counterpoint. His influence is evident by Beethoven, especially in Fidelio, but his influence in France was, as has been mentioned, more coincidental than not. Cherubini's music has had more lasting favour in Germany, thanks to the efforts of Mendelssohn, and has always been regularly performed there.

The interior of
Beethoven's birthplace in
Bonn, with one of the
composer's pianofortes.

The title-page of
Beethoven's eighth
symphony.

Ferdinand Ries

Ferdinand Ries (1784-1838) was born into a family of court
musicians in Bonn. Although precociously talented on both the
violin and piano, his own musical future appeared in doubt after
the French invasion of Germany. His fortunes changed in 1801
when he arrived in Vienna and knocked on the door of Ludwig van
Beethoven. Delighted to be of assistance to the son of his old
teacher and benefactor Franz Anton Ries, Beethoven took the
young man on as his first official piano pupil, showering him with
musical encouragement and financial aid. Later in life, Ries
repaid Beethoven's generosity by acting as his agent in London.
To the world of Beethoven scholarship he is remembered for his
valuable and affectionate portrait (written with F.G. Wegeler),
Biografische Notizen über Ludwig van Beethoven.
Ries became an eminent solo pianist and composer, distinguished (according to the London *Harmonicon*) for the 'Romantic wildness' of his playing. His compositions owed everything to
Beethoven - except their inspiration. Eight symphonies, twenty-
six string quartets, twenty-eight violin sonatas and a myriad of
pieces for solo piano are among his many works.

Johann Nepomuk Maelzel

Although a talented pianist, Maelzel's (1772-1838) true genius
lay in inventing 'musical instruments', mechanical novelties that
intrigued the audiences of Europe and America. Even Beethoven
was beguiled by the Panharmonicon, a huge music box which,
with the aid of weights, cylinders and massive bellows, imitated
all the instruments of the orchestra. For this monstrous toy, at
Maelzel's instigation, Beethoven wrote his monstrous Battle
Symphony, also known as *Wellington's Victory*. Their relationship soured when the two fell out over the rights to an orchestral
version of this enormously successful gewgaw. Maelzel was,
according to the irate Beethoven, a 'rude fellow wholly without
education or breeding'. A simpler but more significant invention
was the metronome. Maelzel, in fact, borrowed the idea for this
classic machine, but with his flair for showmanship and sharp
practice was soon regarded as its solo creator. 'Every village
schoolmaster ought to use the metronome', wrote Beethoven in
1818, when the two had patched up their quarrel. Perhaps this
fulsome endorsement owed something to the efforts Maelzel
had expended in developing an ear trumpet for the deaf composer.
Maelzel died on board an American ship, while seeking new
markets for his eccentric genius.

spinner that Beethoven had turned out with Maelzel, inventor of the metronome and manufacturer of the composer's ear-trumpets.

Poco sostenuto – vivace. Here Beethoven returns to a practice he had seemingly abandoned: a slow introduction to the first movement of a symphony. This long and dignified passage, almost as much an overture as an introduction, leads to the key of E major (the dominant of A), where it begins a bouncing 6/8 rhythm that is to continue throughout the movement. A flute quietly introduces the first subject of the vivace, taking up the light-hearted rhythm. This bouncing single beat (dotted quaver, semi quaver, quaver) is clothed, but never fully disguised, in a splendid variety of dynamics and keys. As if trying to break its relentless grasp, Beethoven brings the music to a complete halt. After a stunned silence the orchestra recovers its balance and proceeds irrepressibly to the end.

Allegretto. Allegretto is a disconcerting direction for this most beautiful and mournful of movements. Beethoven presumably feared that a more conventional andante would encourage it to plod. The key is A minor; the rhythm a resigned and constant two-bar unit (crotchet, quaver, quaver; crotchet, crotchet). The lower strings lead this sombre, simple march. A plangent obbligato joins the procession, and twice the steady footfalls pause in deference to a melting tune in A major. The movement ends as it began, on a weary and unresolved A minor chord.

Presto – assai meno presto. Beethoven's mastery of the scherzo form was by now awesome. In the first few bars of this presto he skips playfully up an F major arpeggio; twenty bars later he lightly descends in the key of A major. The wonders of such harmonic sleights-of-hand are matched by the remarkable 'trio' section. The key abruptly changes to D major and the mood from impish gaiety to a serene pilgrims' hymn, one long suspended A suggesting that the pilgrims' organ is not entirely air-tight.

Allegro con brio. Two jarring and fortissimo E major chords introduce this exuberant finale. The whirling rhythm of the first subject (in A major), with its huge hammer blows on the second beat, dominate the movement. A dance-like second subject finds little time to expand before its massive companion comes thundering back. This great tune lurches forward with convulsive upward slurs and stumbling breaks in rhythm. The effect is both grotesque and unforeseeably sublime.

Carl Maria von Weber

Writing about his youth in 1811, Carl Maria von Weber (1786-1826) painted a characteristically Romantic picture. 'I have no happy childish days to look back upon,' he complained, 'no free open boyhood.' He was thinking of the restless years when his musical education was governed by the wanderings of his father's theatrical company. His greatest promise as a pianist and composer became evident in these early days, but his gifts did not fully mature until much later. Indeed, the young man's future did not look promising in 1810 when, employed by the dissolute Duke Ludwig at Stuttgart, he was accused of corruption and thrown into prison.

After this unfortunate episode he 'settled matters' with himself (as he put it) and rededicated his life to the performance and composition of music.

In 1813 he was appointed director of the Prague Opera, where he proved himself a first-rate conductor and astonished his colleagues with theatrical expertise in all fields, from prompting to scene painting. Among his hand-picked cast in Prague he found his future wife, Caroline Brandt.

Weber spent the last nine years of his life as director of the Dresden Court Opera. By this time he had already composed some of his greatest instrumental works, among them concertos for the piano, clarinet, horn and bassoon. These revealed his gift for ravishing melody and mastery of orchestration. At Dresden he composed the one work that established the direction German opera would take for the remainder of the century. From its first performance in1821, *Der Freischütz* was an astonishing success. Weber's music perfectly captured the menace and magic of the opera's Romantic plot. 'I tremble to think of the future, for it is scarcely possible to rise higher than this,' Weber wrote after conducting a performance in 1822. These words were prophetic. Neither *Euryanthe* (1823) nor *Oberon* (1826) surpassed *Der Freischütz* as works of art.

Weber died of consumption in London after the successful première of *Oberon*. Eighteen years later his remains were returned to Germany, where his funeral oration was read by his great successor, Richard Wagner.

Beethoven's ninth symphony was first performed in 1824 at the Kärntnertor Theatre in Vienna.

An engraving of
Beethoven in 1814

Symphony no. 8 in F major, opus 93

Beethoven was fond of his eighth symphony. He called it the 'little one', and when it was pointed out to him that this new work had not received the same applause as the seventh he replied sharply, 'Because it is much better'.

Notwithstanding the composer's approval, the eighth has remained a puzzle and, for some, a disappointment. To begin with, it is very short; only the first symphony takes less time to perform. Those who value a work by its sheer length will be bound to see this symphony – dwarfed by the sixth, seventh and ninth – as an inferior creation.

And then there is the problem of style. How can the man who wrestled with angels in the third and fifth symphonies suddenly turn his attention to clockwork soldiers? The eighth seems to be a conventional symphony in form, and yet it is full of wrong turns, surprises and deliberate jolts to the audience. What is it all about? The answer is partly in the question. Those who can only think of Beethoven as a marble bust, a noble figure staring at some distant mountain range, will for ever be disappointed with the earthy, witty and sometimes petulant craftsman of the eighth symphony. Yet here is Beethoven, a man of the world (or at least of Vienna), at the height of his powers. The jokes and anger of the first movement, the affectionate games of the second, the grace of the minuet and the fierce wit of the finale are as much a portrait of the composer as anything that remains on canvas or stone.

Allegro vivace e con brio. Without a note of introduction, the full orchestra bursts in with a cheerful first subject. This is a twelve-bar passage – four bars of determined forte and then, as if to compensate for such bravado, a dolce piano answer by the winds before the orchestra recovers its energy and completes the tune. An exuberant tutti seems to be leading to the second subject when the music suddenly develops a limp, coming down heavily and unexpectedly on the third (last) beat of

Muzio Clementi

The symphonic works of Muzio Clementi (1752-1832) are perhaps the least important part of this extraordinary man's output, which was mainly of piano music, but his works are important in the way they developed sonata form from the early Rococo period, right through the Classical era into the Romantic age. Imported to England while still a boy by a wealthy patron (a cousin of the eccentric pederast William Beckford), Clementi made his home and his fortune in that country. As well as composing about 100 piano sonatas and the famous *Gradus ad Parnassum* studies, he was also music publisher and founder of a piano factory (where he employed the young John Field as demonstrator of the instruments) in Soho, London. Almost the only symphonic work to be heard today of his, for he failed to publish most of his orchestral music, is the extraordinary *Great National Symphony*, which boasts an elaborate contrapuntal treatment of *God Save the King*.

Facing page
Beethoven. A portrait
by his friend Joseph
Mähler. The composer
was very pleased with
this likeness, and
wrote an affectionate
letter to the artist to
tell him so.

the bar. It finally hobbles to a halt. There is a bar of complete silence before the strings and solo bassoon, now soft and staccato, persuade the second subject to begin. This turns out to be a beautiful legato melody but in the 'wrong' key – not the anticipated C major (the dominant of F) but the harmonically distant D. The winds salvage the situation by repeating the passage in C, but even they are unable to bring it to a satisfactory cadence. It remains a tune without a proper ending.

In the development section Beethoven takes the opening (a crotchet and four quavers) and plays with it furiously, as a tiger would a mouse. He drags it through key after key – C, B flat, A, D minor. And in the climactic recapitulation only the bassoons, cellos and basses are allowed to continue with this ill-fated first subject. The rest of the orchestra rages at triple forte, a dynamic Beethoven used very rarely. Good humour returns for the second subject, but the excitement erupts again (and again in triple forte) during the long coda. As if deliberately calming himself, Beethoven stops the music for a complete bar and then, very softly, brings the movement to a delicate close.

Allegretto scherzando. This is the shortest symphonic movement that Beethoven wrote, lasting only about three minutes. It is said to have been inspired one boisterous evening in 1812 by the chronometer, an early form of metronome. Imitating its monotonous ta-ta-ta-ta, Beethoven wrote a simple canon in honour of the inventor, his friend Maelzel. This tune introduces the surprising allegretto scherzando. The chronometer, represented by woodwinds and horns playing pianissimo and staccato, accompanies a delicate first subject picked out by the violins. Characteristically, Beethoven does not let his audience drowse off to this hypnotic ticking. After only four bars of the second subject he shatters his fragile structure with a savage fortissimo from the strings and, two bars later, by another. The orchestra quietly picks itself up and finds its way back to the initial theme, whereupon the whole opening section is repeated with only minor variations.

As if impatient with his clockwork conceit, Beethoven ends the movement with a noisy and deliberately trite coda, mocking at once both his music and the expectations of his audience.

Tempo di menuetto. One of Beethoven's great achievements as a symphonist was to transform the traditional minuet and trio (the third movement) into an exuberant and passionate scherzo. Here, however,

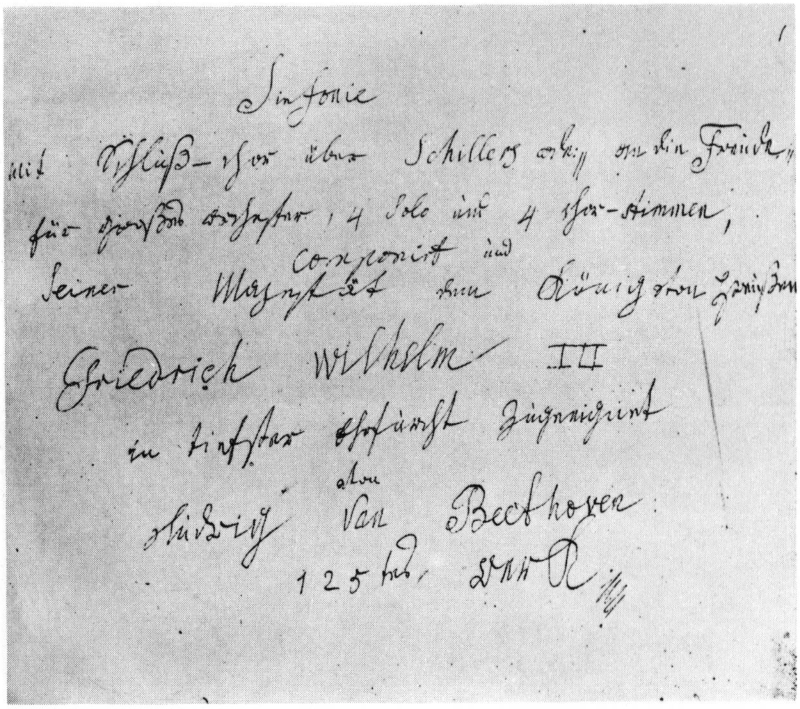

As the autograph shows,
Beethoven dedicated his
ninth symphony to
Friedrich Wilhelm III.

A mill at Grinzing, outside Vienna. Beethoven lived for a time nearby, and was influenced by the peaceful countryside to compose the Pastoral symphony.

The wedding of Napoleon and Marie Louise of Austria. Napoleon was at first hailed as a liberator by many countries seeking freedom from feudal traditions, and Beethoven too was fired by this enthusiasm. But Napoleon's dictatership and dynastic ideas soon turned the tide of liberal thought against him.

A catalogue in the *Allgemeine Musikaliche Zeitung*, advertising the latest publications for sale, including Beethoven's cello sonata, opus 69, and an arrangement of his fifth symphony for piano duet.

At Beethoven's funeral on 29 March 1827, 20,000 people filled the square in front of the Schwarzspanierhaus. Schubert (who was to follow him to the grave one year later) was one of the torchbearers, and the poet Grillparzer composed the funeral oration.

INTELLIGENZ-BLATT
zur Allgemeinen Musikalischen Zeitung.

October.   No. I.   1809.

Anzeige.

Schillers Lied von der Glocke, durch Andreas Romberg in Musik gesetzt, schon öfters in Hamburger Concerten mit dem grösten Beyfall aufgeführt, ist bey N. Simrok in Bonn verlegt und in allen guten Musikhandlungen zu haben. Die Partitur zu 16 Franken, der Klavierauszug zu 6 Fr. und die Orchesterstimmen zu 9 Franken. Der Klavierauszug kann auch bey der Aufführung als ausgeschriebene Singstimme benutzt werden, und so kann dies schöne Meisterwerk sogleich aufgeführt werden. Zur Verständlichkeit der Zuhörer ist der Text, nach der Behandlung in der Musik, besonders abgedruckt, und wird für 2 Gr. verkauft.

Dies Werk ist bey Breitkopf und Härtel zu haben

in Partitur für   4 Thlr. Sächs. Courant.
in Stimmen für   2 Thlr. 6 Gr. —
im Klavierauszug   1 Thlr. 12 Gr. —

Neue Musikalien, welche im Verlag der Breitkopf- und Härtelschen Musikhandlung in Leipzig erschienen sind.

Beethoven, L. v. Sinfonie à grand Orchestre. No 5. (C moll)   4 Thlr. 12 Gr.
— Sinfonie pastorale à gr. Orchestre. No 6. (F dur)   4 Thlr. 12 Gr.
Pär, F. Ouverture de l'Opéra: les Mines de Pologne, à gr. Orch.   1 Thlr.
— Ouverture de l'Opéra: Numa Pompilius, à gr. Orchestre   1 Thlr.

Für das Pianoforte.

Beethoven, L. v. grande Sonate av. Violoncelle. Op. 69.   1 Thlr. 12 Gr.
— 2 Trios p. Pianoforte, Violon et Violoncelle.   Op. 70. No 1. 1 Thlr. 12 Gr.
— do   do   — 2.   2 Thlr.
— 5me Sinfonie, arrangée à 4 mains 2 Thlr. 12 Gr.
Beethoven, L. v. 8 Variations sur le Trio: (Tändeln und Scherzen) del' Op: Soliman, No. 10.   16 Gr.
Dussek, J. L. 3 Sonates progressives à 4 mains Op. 67.   1 Thlr. 8 Gr.
— Notturno p. Pianoforte et Violon, avec un Cor ad libitum. Op. 68.   1 Thlr.
Fischer, M. G. Sonate à 4 mains. Op. 12. 1 Thlr. 12 Gr.
Gyrowez, A. Ouverture de l'Op. Agnes Sorel. 8 Gr.
Nözel, C. F. Sammlung v. Schottischen Anglaisen, Walzern u. Anglaisen f. d. Klavier. 14 Gr.
— Sammlung von 6 Montferino's, Quadrillen, Ecossaisen, Walzern und Massurischen Tänzen f. d. Pforte mit Begleit. einer Flöte und Violine.   16 Gr.
Righini, V. Ouverture de Tigranes.   8 Gr.
Steibelt, D. 6 Sonates doigtées d'une difficulté graduée.   Liv. 1.   1 Thlr.
— do   do   — 2. 1 Thlr. 12 Gr.
— grande Sonate p. le Pianoforte av. accomp. de Violon obligé.   Op. 79.   12 Gr.
— grande Sonate av. Violon obligé. Op. 80. 16 Gr.
— grande Sonate av. Violon obligé. Op. 81. 1 Thlr.
— Fantaisie av. 9 Variations sur une Walse Russe.   16 Gr.
— Methode de Piano, ou l'art d'enseigner cet Instrument. (Französisch und Deutsch).   2 Thlr. 12 Gr.

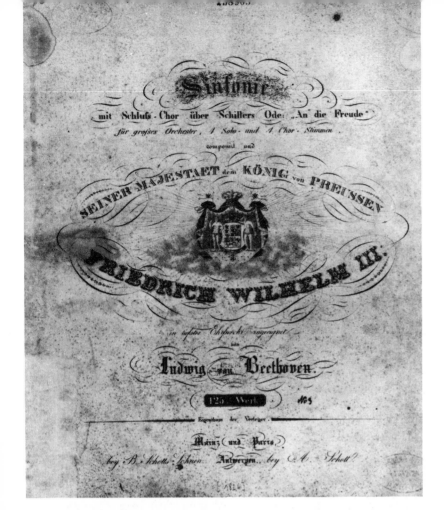

9th Symphony
The title-page of
Beethoven's symphony
no. 9, the *Choral*.

he deliberately returns to the elegance of pre-revolutionary Europe, as if to apologize for his previous irreverence. The one-two-three rhythm is boldly established for two bars by strings and bassoons before the violins enter with a smooth descending line that is both graceful and, for once, danceable. Beethoven cannot resist the temptation to throw the dancers off their beat in the second strain of the minuet, but the bassoonist quickly finds his place and restores order.

Two French horns and solo clarinet, accompanied by an athletic cello, introduce a ravishing trio section, 'this most charming of all idylls', as Richard Wagner called it. The violins, who next take up the tune, fail to improve upon this opening, and the music passes back to winds and lower strings before returning to the stately minuet.

Allegro vivace. With the first few lively bars of this finale Beethoven seems determined to remain in the eighteenth century, among the untroubled tunes of Haydn. Only when his skittish opening is rocked by a discordant C♯, does it become clear that Beethoven the practical joker is waiting in ambush. Time and again throughout the movement he surprises his audience wiith sudden changes in dynamics, startling silences, abrupt key changes and bizarre orchestral effects. Again, as in the first movement, a lyrical second subject enters in the 'wrong' key, and again the conscientious woodwinds put it right. A short development section attempts to introduce a note of seriousness which ends in burlesque when bassoon and timpani go bouncing off on their own for an extended solo. Beethoven was never more full of fun or of invention. In the lengthy coda he begins a stately march, forces it to quicken its pace and finally to jog into the distance, once again with the bassoon and kettledrums. Then, just as the cheerful first subject reappears, it is compelled to enter the jarring key of F♯ minor. Having hijacked his own tune (his weapon being the sudden C♯ heard earlier in the movement), Beethoven finally brings the symphony to a jolting and noisy close. His own laughter is almost audible above the crashing F major chords.

Anton Diabelli

Today Anton Diabelli (1781-1858) is not generally remembered for his accomplished songs, Masses and piano music, nor for the successful Viennese music publishing company that bore his name. He is known instead for the simple waltz tune upon which Beethoven based his thirty-three *Diabelli Variations*, one of the great monuments of the solo piano repertory Diabelli had not expected to unlash a masterpiece of these dimensions. His original plan had been to commission fifty variations, each by a different composer (including Schubert and the young Franz Liszt). Beethoven, it seems, got carried away with enthusiasm for the project.

Diabelli made a more deliberate contribution to the history of music in recognizing the genius of Franz Schubert and, with the song *Erlkönig* (opus 1), becoming his first publisher.

Symphony no. 9 in D minor, opus 125

None of Beethoven's symphonies have caused so much controversy as his ninth. This is the result of its great length ('at least twice as long as it should be', complained the *Harmonica* after the English première in 1825), its enormous difficulty to perform and the unprecedented choral finale, a setting of Friedrich Schiller's 'An die Freude' (Ode to Joy). For some these difficulties remain, but most now share the farsighted opinion of Robert Schumann: 'In this work the great man has given us of his greatest'.

Allegro, ma non troppo, un poco maestoso. The symphony opens with ten bars of shimmering suspense, while the violins hesitantly pick out sparse descending notes. Then, as if a dam has broken, the full orchestra bursts out with the fierce theme that dominates this movement. The woodwinds exercise a calming influence in their legato second subject, but this is only a false peace, soon disturbed by the unsettling beat of the kettledrums. Likewise, a fugue in the development section, suggesting stern resignation, is shattered by the angry return of the opening theme. In the long coda the winds finally accept the prevailing passion and, to a growling repetitive bass, begin a funeral march that leads to the defiant conclusion.

Molto vivace - presto. This ebullient 'scherzo' is a perfect antidote to the emotional rigours of the preceding movement. Strings, timpani and then full orchestra pounce on the audience in eight introductory bars. Then begins a buoyant fugue that gradually builds in intensity until it has become a wild dance, its joy bordering on frenzy. As if alarmed at losing his good humour, Beethoven now takes the music into a major key and a pastoral mood for the trio section (marked presto). The movement concludes as it began, both playful and violent, like a kitten with its claws extended.

Adagio molto e cantabile – andante moderato. In profound stillness the strings introduce the beautiful adagio. Each phrase is echoed by a choir of winds, their organ-like tones enhancing the religious tranquillity. The tempo now changes to andante and the key from B flat to D major, with violins and violas playing a yearning, restless melody. This wistful andante emerges once more, but the remainder of the movement consists of exquisite variations on the adagio theme. The serenity is briefly challenged by the brass, but peace descends once more and the movement ends as calmly as it began.

Presto – allegro ma non troppo – allegro assai – presto – allegro assai vivace – alla marcia – andante maestoso – adagio ma non troppo, ma divoto – allegro energico, sempre ben marcato – allegro ma non tanto – prestissimo – maestoso – prestissimo. A violent chord from the full orchestra introduces a long declamatory recitative by cellos and basses. As if uncertain where to proceed, the orchestra next plays snatches from each of the three preceding movements before discovering the beautiful anthem that is the subject of this finale. The bass soloist now enters, resuming the recitative heard earlier and then putting words (from Schiller's Ode to Joy) to the majestic tune. He is followed by full chorus and then solo quartet. The rest of the movement consists of five sections, each of which is an extended variation on the Ode to Joy theme. Briefly these are a spirited 'Turkish' march with tenor and men's chorus; a devout choral episode; a boisterous and brassy exhibition piece for chorus; a variation for combined forces, concluding with a solemn adagio; and a tearaway prestissimo which is reigned back for a prayerful section before the tumultuous final bars.

The young Beethoven, at
the height of his powers
as a lion of the keyboard.

Beethoven's tomb in
Vienna.

Below: Napoleon's forces
marching into Vienna.
When the French were
bombarding the city,
Beethoven was forced to
seek refuge in a cellar.

3

Schubert

Franz Schubert

Schubert (1797-1828) was born in Liechtental, on 31 January. His father was the parish schoolmaster, and the family lived in genteel poverty. The household was a musical one: Franz learned the violin and piano at home, before being sent away to the imperial 'Convict' seminary in Vienna where he had won a choral scholarship. His most important teacher there was Salieri, but such was the boy's precocious talent that even the grand old pedagogue (who had given Beethoven lessons) found he could teach Schubert very little. He was obliged to leave there when his voice broke, attended teacher training college, and in 1814 became an assistant teacher in his father's school - a job he detested. That same year, at the age of just seventeen, he wrote his great song (to words from Goethe's *Faust*), *Gretchen at the Spinning-wheel*.

Four years later he decided to give up teaching and support himself through his compositions, an especially difficult situation since Schubert was no virtuoso pianist or conductor and could not earn his living through performances. But he continued to compose at an astonishing rate, despite poverty, and serious illness. He remained almost always cheerful and optimistic, and knew at least the comfort of a devoted circle of friends who believed in his music and loved him as a brother. Only at the end of his short life there were signs that he was going to become successful.

Till then, his fortunes had been at a perpetually low ebb, allowing himself to be bilked by unscrupulous publishers. Paradoxically the year of his greatest creative output was 1828, the year of his death. It was as if he was hurrying to complete his life's work. That year produced a succession of masterpieces: the *Great C major* symphony, the wonderful C major quintet, the three last piano sonatas, twenty songs, church music and the miraculous *F minor Fantasy* for piano duet. Weakened by syphilis, he contracted typhoid fever in October and died in the arms of his brother Ferdinand the following month.

It took the musical world many years before they knew what a mighty genius they had lost. Only those close to the composer realized the true scale of the tragedy.

'Schubert is dead,' wrote his friend Moritz von Schwind, 'and with him all that we had of the brightest and fairest.' At his own wish, he was interred next to the grave of his hero, Beethoven.

On the strength of a single work, the symphony no. 8 in B minor (known as the 'Unfinished'), Schubert has become one of the most popular and best loved orchestral composers in the world. But anything even approaching such acclaim was totally unknown to the composer during his lifetime: his genius was recognized and appreciated by only a small circle of friends, who occasionally met at 'Schubertiads' to perform his songs, piano pieces and chamber music in a genial atmosphere of conviviality. But such a lack of recognition was no great cause of distress to Schubert: he died at the age of only thirty-one, young enough to be still buoyed up with optimism, and on the edge of yet greater discoveries. The tragedy is ours, not his.

But it remains a remarkable fact that such a relatively large part of his (admittedly copious) output remains little-known and unperformed – much more than is the case with Mozart, say, or Beethoven – and this curious state of affairs is well exemplified in his symphonies. In some respects, the neglect is understandable. In an output of more than 600 *Lieder,* even if we ignore the difficult and subjective problem of variation in quality, there would still remain the practical impossibility of more than a fraction of these pieces achieving any broad popularity; and on the whole posterity has opted to favour the most tuneful among them, such as 'The Trout', *An die Musik* (which has even been successfully transformed into an instrumental rock number), and perhaps a couple of dozen more. Schubert's fifteen operas too are almost entirely neglected, for while they contain much music of outstanding beauty, their plots unfortunately are so trumpery and two-dimensional as to render them virtually unperformable to all but the composer's most ardent apologists.

The symphonies fall into two groups: nos 1–6, which are predominantly works of the composer's youth, and nos 8 & 9 (the *Unfinished* and the *Great* C major), both masterpieces of Schubert's maturity. There is no seventh symphony: this was originally the number given to the ninth, mentioned above, and (to add to the confusion) sometimes to an incomplete and unpublished work in E minor. In addition to these, there is strong evidence for a lost symphony written in 1825, known as the *Gmunden-Gastein* symphony after the places where it was composed. (The musicologist Otto Erich Deutsch, compiler of the chronological catalogue of all Schubert's works, has even given it a 'Deutsch' number: D 849.) Some Schubert scholars also believe that the marvellous Grand Duo for piano duet is an arrangement for four hands of a symphony, and there are piano sketches too for a projected symphony in D (D 615).

As mentioned above, not all of these works are familiar to audiences. Several of the works from the composer's apprentice years have much in them that is juvenile and obviously derivative (particularly of Haydn). But they have nevertheless a noticeable personality of their own, and anyone concerned to understand the development of Schubert's ineffable genius will find much food for thought in the early symphonies, as well as rich delights. Even in the first symphony, written while the composer was still at school, there are moments we can already hear to be 'typically Schubertian', such as the sudden switches from major to minor, the long-spanned and seemingly spontaneous melodies, and the fondness for rocking triplet rhythms.

The orchestration is, on the whole, unadventurous. The forces used are typical of the period, and display a frequent preference for the woodwind section. The scoring in all of the symphonies is not yet what we think of as 'Romantic': Schubert had studied the art at first hand, playing symphonies of the earlier classical period in the school orchestra, and this background is obviously reflected in the early works. It must be remembered as well that the young man hoped and intended that these works would be performed. Their only opportunity, of course, would be amateur performance, so conformity in instrumentation was additionally important.

Symphony no. 1 in D major, D 82

Franz Schubert put his first symphony on paper while still a schoolboy, at the age of sixteen. No sketches of it remain, nor of the following two. We know only when and how it happened from recollections by fellow-students and letters Schubert himself wrote to his parents. The first performance took place within the closed circle of the school orchestra

Caricature of Schubert (right) and his friend, the singer Heinrich Vogel.

A Romantic and imaginary conception of Schubert at work.

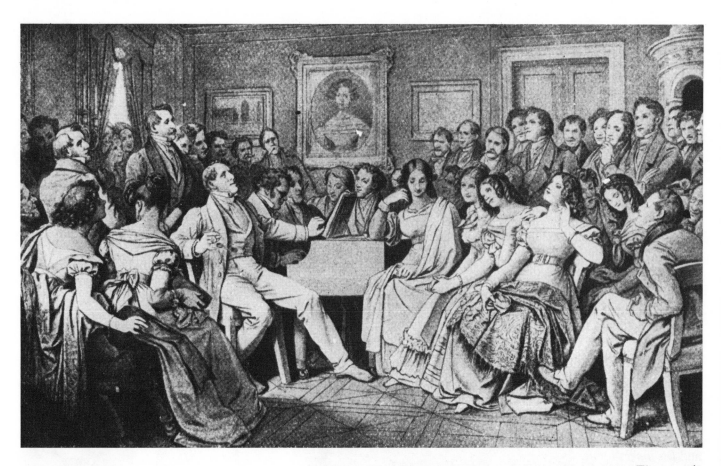

An impression of a *Schubertiad*, with the composer at the piano accompanying the great singer Joseph Vogl at his side.

in which Schubert played, but little more than this is known. The genesis of the first three symphonies remains largely undocumented. They may also have been put before the amateur orchestra of which Schubert's father was a member. Schubert completed the work on 28 October 1813. For a sixteen-year-old he shows an exceptional grasp of form. He was well-acquainted with Haydn and Mozart, and no doubt Beethoven as well. But aside from these he can have had few other examples to follow, as his familiarity with the repertoire was slight.

The first symphony begins with a slow introduction, leading to the first allegro vivace. In this movement Schubert is not yet recognizable as the lyrical master he was to become. The first and principal theme is nothing more than a scale; but the second theme is more melodic, introduced by the violins with subsequent support by the woodwinds.

The second movement, an andante, is extremely simple and lyrical. It could just as well have been written for string quartet, for all the important melodic and harmonic elements are given to the strings.

After the andante comes a minuet which makes a resolute and purposeful impression. The rhythm is sturdy and pointed, the trio, a dance-like melody for violins and bassoons.

The finale, allegro vivo, is an almost naive, ingenuous movement. Here again the strings take precedence, with a rhythmic melody in the first violins, a staccato accompaniment in the second violins and melodic ornamentation in the winds.

The first symphony suffers from a typical 'Schubertian' defect: excessive prolongation of material containing only a few ideas. But Schubert is not the only one who sometimes seems unable to cut his music short. It was Schumann who referred to its 'heavenly length'.

Symphony no. 2 in B flat major, D 125
Between 1813 – the year of the first symphony – and 1815, Schubert devoted himself intensively to the creation of compositions other than symphonies. A number of string quartets, an unsuccessful opera and his

first religious work, the Mass in F major, were written during these two years. But above all, this period saw a milestone in the history of the *Lied, Grettchen am Spinnrade*. Schubert managed instinctively to set the essentials of Goethe's poem in *Faust* to music, with a rhythmic piano accompaniment imitating the whirr of the spinning-wheel and above this, a simple but eloquently expressive melody for the voice. The genius of this song and the seeming ripeness of the Mass in F major find a surprising counterweight in the youthful immaturity of the second symphony.

Schubert follows the customary path: a slow largo introduction to the first movement's allegro vivace. The main theme is a spiritedly accented melody built of scale figures. The second theme is of a more lyrical character, though the concluding triplet provides a suggestion of restlessness. The second movement, andante, presents a theme, both lovely and simple, in the violins. Schubert's preoccupation with smaller forms is clearly evident; the melody could easily have served as a theme for one of his *Moments musicaux* for piano. Five variations follow the theme, the only instance of Schubert's use of the variation form in orchestral music. The third movement a minuet has more the character of a scherzo. A forceful melody, played loudly in 3/4 time, forms the movement's principal material, interrupted by a trio section consisting of an airy oboe melody. The finale, presto vivace, offers a combination of witty and lively themes cast in a somewhat unusual form midway between a rondo and a sonata.

Symphony no. 3 in D major, D 200
The third symphony was composed in the summer of 1815, and though a lovely piece and full of invention, must pale beside important progressions that Schubert made that year in his songwriting: *Der Erlkönig* and *Die junge Nonne*.

Notable is the first movement's introductory clarinet theme, given to this instrument rather than to the strings which Schubert normally favoured. We know from letters that he made a first attempt at writing a theme for horns and oboes, then another for strings, finally opting for a simple clarinet melody. This adagio maestoso introduction is short and its melodic material is of no further importance in the rest of the movement. The second movement is not the traditional slow movement, but an allegretto in the middle of which the clarinet again assumes prominence. The third movement is a scherzo-like minuet with a trio reminiscent of a Viennese waltz. Here Schubert's partiality for the woodwinds can be clearly heard. The last movement, presto vivace, has its principal theme a rhythmic melody in 6/8 time. The movement in its entirety strongly recalls that well-known Italian dance, the tarantella.

Symphony no. 4 in C minor, D 417 – Tragic
The name *Tragic* was given to the symphony by Schubert himself, though just why is not clear. Possibly by using this suggestive nickname he wished to awaken the interest of the public, for in the years of early Romanticism symphonies were not widely popular. Opera was held in high regard, but since Beethoven the symphonic repertory had fallen into a certain neglect. C minor is the key of Beethoven's fifth symphony, though this is the only occasion on which Schubert used it in his orchestral works. Another explanation for the nickname *Tragic* is that Schubert simply wrote it above the score as a joke, perhaps thinking of the continual monetary difficulties which obliged him to earn a living in what was for him a highly unsympathetic way: teaching.

It is true that in the period previous to this fourth symphony Schubert was occupied setting to music texts of a more or less tragic nature, having to do with melancholy, death, nostalgia, love and longing. Typical Romantic concerns in a nutshell: *Der König in Thule, Lodas Gespenst, Das Grab, Des Mädchens Klage, Lied der Mignon* ('Nur wer die Sehnsucht kennt'). But the origin of this utterly inappropriate sub-title

Gioacchino Rossini

Gioacchino Rossini (1792-1868) was born in the Italian town of Pesaro and received musical instruction in Bologna, but soon left all academic learning behind. He wanted simply to write music and to avoid being crushed under a burden of theoretical ideas. His first one-act opera, *La cambiale di matrimonio*, presented in 1810, was a great success with both public and press alike. As of the second performance of *Il barbiere di Siviglia* (the première itself was not successful), Rossini's name was definitively established. He wrote one opera after another, usually on commission, and always in a remarkably short time.

At the age of thirty-seven he turned his back on opera composition to produce only salon pieces and two larger works. He wrote in a romantic *bel canto* style. Extremely melodic arias with lively orchestral accompaniments, 'catchy tunes' which nearly always proved instantly memorable, were the chief ingredients of his success.

Rossini travelled widely throughout Europe, eventually taking up permanent residence, along with his second wife, in Paris in 1855. He was by now extremely wealthy, and lived and entertained on a lavish scale. There he was visited by many musicians, among them Arthur Sullivan and Richard Wagner, and at his death left a fortune worth more than one million pounds.

Schubert (right) with
his friends Jenger and
Hüttenberger. Portrait
by Josef Telscher
(1827).

remains a mystery. In the entire work there is not one trace of sadness or melancholy, of 'dark thoughts' or drama. On the contrary, the music manifests only a natural, lively and melodic beauty. Without preliminary sketches or other preparatory work, Schubert wrote the symphony directly in score.

Again the first movement, allegro vivace, begins with a slow introduction, adagio molto. A robust opening chord is followed by a lyrical melody of almost solemn magnificence, played by the violins with a lovely recapitulation by the cellos. If this introduction gives a somewhat sombre impression, this is immediately dissipated by the beginning of the allegro whose first theme sparkles as if glittering in sunlight. The second theme is lyrical, but as both themes are developed Schubert concentrates mainly on the first lively material with its many small rhythmic ideas.

The second movement, andante, displays a similarity with the famous *Impromptu no. 6, D 935* for piano. The theme is in the same key and distils the same atmosphere. The graceful theme is unfolded by the strings as if by a string quartet. The second theme is distinguished by the continual repetition of the same note in the accompaniment. The first theme eventually returns, as befits the rondo form, and both combine to bring the andante to its conclusion.

The following minuet has nothing in common with the traditional minuet, but is actually a lively scherzo in which the theme is immediately proclaimed by fortissimo winds and strings. The trio is short, dance-like and airy. If there were a 'tragic' element in the symphony, it certainly would not be found here.

The finale, allegro, consists of short motivic themes which seem to some extent to get in one another's way and as a result are not truly developed, but rather undergo a long series of repetitions. In this movement a number of unusual harmonic progressions can be heard. The movement leads to a festive conclusion in C major.

Symphony no. 5 in B flat major, D 485
This symphony is one of easily accessible charm and melodic richness. To express what he here has to say, Schubert needs only a small orchestra: strings, one flute, two oboes, two horns and two bassoons. As

The great German writer
Wolfgang van Goethe was
a friend of Beethoven,
though he had no time for
Schubert's miraculous
settings of his poetry.

a consequence the symphony has come to be known as 'the symphony without trumpets and timpani', but just as remarkable for Schubert is the absence of clarinets. The work dates from the last half of 1816 when Schubert was nineteen years old.

Though the music still bears traces of Haydn's influence, and is suffused with a Mozartean delicacy, it is at the same time replete with so many of those unmistakeable Schubertian fingerprints that the listener loves to identify. There is no need here for any portentous slow introduction: the bright, gauzy allegro springs to life with the help of a vivacious little violin figure, from which the more reflective second theme also seems to derive. The entire, life-enhancing movement is all too soon at an end, and the ensuing andante con moto takes itself much more seriously. This is just such a movement as Haydn might have written, with a lovely melody 'so simple that one feels one has always known it' accompanied and embellished with the utmost tenderness, and a beautiful excursion into the minor.

The third movement, Menuetto: allegro molto is in the minor, balanced by a warm and bucolic country-dance as its trio section (in G major). This movement is altogether more of a traditional minuet than the racy third movements in the previous symphonies, perhaps in order to give the ear enough time to hear the chromatic notes in the theme; and its setting in another key than the home B flat of the symphony is a typically wayward trick of the composer's musical thought.

In the last movement, marked allegro vivace, there are again many Haydnesque touches. The irrepressible gaiety of the (often repeated) first theme buoys the entire movement along, and is counterbalanced by another melody which, this time, could belong to no-one else than Schubert. To convey the impression of apparent spontaneity within the carefully-wrought framework of an orchestral score as Schubert does here, not withstanding the wit and good humour of the movement, is a masterstroke of craftsmanship.

Symphony no. 6 in C major, D 589
With the first of Schubert's C major symphonies, we come to the end of his first period of symphonic composition. It was completed in February

Romanticism

The word 'Romantic' signifies something different for everyone, its intensity varying from individual to individual. The most common definition implies a highly personal and emotional manner of expression. Another refers to a more or less defined period in the nineteenth century.

The word itself is of French origin - literature written no longer in Latin but in Old French was given the name of 'lingua romana'. From this derived the word 'romance', a short poem of epic-lyric character. This lyricism in turn gave rise to the use of the word 'Romantic' to indicate anything which is considered free, individual, spontaneous, imaginative, emotional, heroic or fantastic. The word became fixed in common usage when in 1813 E.T.A. Hoffmann employed it in an article concerning individual expression in Beethoven's instrumental music.

The specific period of Romanticism spans nearly 100 years, from about 1800 until the century's end. The beginning of this era must be seen as a reaction against the previous period of rationalism, in which the emphasis was upon man as a rational, intellectual being fully capable of expressing his thoughts and feelings in clear language and of solving problems in a sane and intelligent way. Romanticism rebelled against this cerebral approach to existence. 'Feeling' assumed a place of central importance. A need for greater space was felt in order to allow external influences to penetrate to the fullest. A love of nature and the beauties of the countryside gained ascendancy. An early outstanding example is Beethoven's sixth symphony, the *Pastoral*.

Another hallmark of the Romantic period is the consciousness of national or individual identity. Subjective sentiments sought liberation from dominating rules and laws, leading to revolutions in Europe in the wake of the French revolution and the subsequent Napoleonic empire.

This observation by Jean-Jacques Rousseau is characteristic of the period: 'I am distinct from all others. I may be no better, but at least I am different.'

These new ideas and ideals inspired a search for innovation and

SLAVSIA Chœur Triomphal de la VIE pour le TSAR

Paris, AU MÉNESTREL, 2bis Rue Vivienne. HEUGEL & FILS, Editeurs

renewal in the arts. The dramatic musical form *par excellence*, opera, developed rapidly, encompassing all the elements of Romanticism, from the supernatural, as in Weber's *Der Freischütz*, through nationalism, as in Glinka's *A Life for the Tsar*, to the summit of operatic history, Wagner's mythology-based 'Total art work', *The Ring*.

Purely instrumental music also underwent changes. The symphony as an abstract musical phenomenon became less popular. Composers endeavoured to link their works to nature, literature, painting. 'Programme music' came into being: Liszt with his *Faust* and *Dante* symphonies, Mendelssohn with his *Hebrides* Overture, Smetana with his symphonic cycle *My Fatherland*, Richard Strauss with his *Tod und Verklärung* and *Also sprach Zarathustra*, to mention only a few. These last are examples of the symphonic poem, usually a one-movement work based on extra-musical particulars.

Two paths presented themselves: one, the inclusion of innovative Romantic ideas in a renewed symphonic form, the other, avoidance of new currents in favour of continued development of the traditional symphony, as was the case with Brahms and Bruckner. A clear somewhere in the middle were the composers who were subjected to influences from both sides, such as Tchaikovsky, who eschewed programme music but could not entirely avoid it, and Dvořák, who avidly embraced whatever was new and used what appealed to him. Romanticism also seemed particularly appropriate to the development of smaller musical forms.

The *Lied* underwent a rapid evolution, from Schubert to Hugo Wolf and Richard Strauss. Short pieces, mostly for piano, became widely current and were given titles such as 'Impromptus', 'Nocturnes', 'Fantasiestücke', 'Mazurkas', 'Preludes', 'Waltzes', etc.

Hundreds of examples can be found in the piano music of Chopin, Schubert, Schumann and Brahms.

Compositional techniques were also considerably revolutionized. The old rules of harmony, based on the hierarchy of the notes of the scale, were overthrown and, in principle at least, any succession of keys became possible. The search for additional means of musical expression resulted in the expansion of the size of the orchestra and the use of more and varied instruments. The music of Wagner, Mahler and Berlioz (particularly in his *Messe des Morts*) offer obvious examples.

1818, and shows many echoes of Rossini, whose operas were coming very much into vogue in Vienna at that time. Coincidental with its composition was Schubert's decision to abandon school-teaching as a means of earning his living and make his compositions support him: this may be why he adopted such a frankly popular approach to symphonic writing in this work.

After an introductory adagio, the cheerful first movement weaves a merry and predictable way through some delightful modulations.

The central andante is a Romantic 'song without words', enhanced by a strongly rhythmic central section and some delightful, quasi-operatic part-writing for the woodwind.

The third movement, for the first time, is a scherzo and not a minuet. There are possible comparisons with Beethoven's seventh symphony to be drawn here, not least in the relationship of the trio's key to that of the scherzo proper (E major to C; and in Beethoven, A major to F).

The finale is again operatic in much of what it has to say. Melodic ideas abound – indeed Schubert, of all composers, was never short of them – but there is little attempt at reasoned development. Nevertheless, the movement provides a bright and happy *envoi* to this lesser-known group of early works.

Symphony no. 8 in B minor, D 759 – Unfinished

Why Schubert never finished this symphony will always remain a mystery, unless, as some suggest, the manuscript was subsequently lost by his friend Hüttenbrenner. Only the first two movements exist in their entirety, plus a few bars of the third.   The finale is missing altogether.

Overleaf: A contemporary silhouette of Schubert at the piano.

The score, complete or just these two movements, was passed to Hüttenbrenner and thence to Johann Herbeck, conductor of the orchestra of the *Gesellschaft der Musikfreunde* in Vienna. In any event, the two existing movements awaken a desire for more. The first movement, allegro moderato, begins with a dark, eight-bar motif in the basses succeeded by the first theme proper on oboe and clarinet, an anguished expression of great longing. But the best-known theme is the second subject, an extended melody for cellos. The development, however, depends on the material used at the very opening of the work rather than on either of the subjects as such.

The second movement, andante con moto, is unhappily all-too-often played so slowly that it drags. Its subject-matter is poetical in the extreme: if ever any orchestral work can be considered the harbinger of Romanticism, this must be it. Repeated listening to the heavenly and serene themes of the movement, and their reappearances within it makes one aware of the marvellously constructed balance of the piece, which is perhaps its most perfect and satisfying element. It is pitched in the unlikely key of E major, which again seems to set an ethereal mood, enhanced by some of Schubert's most magical key changes.

The title page of Schubert's *Heidenröslein*, to a romantic verse by Goethe.

Frédéric Chopin, one of
the leading figures of the
Romantic movement.

Symphony no. 9 in C major, D 944 – Great

This and the *Unfinished* are Schubert's most important symphonies.
The work dates from February or March, 1828. In November of the same
year Schubert died. His request to the *Gesellschaft der Musikfreunde* in
Vienna to perform the symphony was denied by reason of the work's
great length and difficulty, thus Schubert himself never heard it
performed. After Schubert's death, his brother Ferdinand took an
interest in the composer's unpublished works and thanks to a visit paid
him by Robert Schumann, the symphony was finally performed in 1839
by the Gewandhaus orchestra of Leipzig under the direction of
Mendelssohn, albeit in a shortened version.

The opening andante can not be considered a mere introduction to the
allegro ma non troppo. It is a slow lengthy section on its own terms, cast
in a rondo form. The opening melody for the horns is extremely
beautiful. The *allegro*'s principal theme is strongly rhythmic. The
second theme is short with a characteristic triplet motif. In developing
these two short themes Schubert was unfortunately unable to avoid
rather too many repetitions of the themes themselves or of elements
drawn from them.

The second movement, andante con moto, contains a very lovely
principal theme, played by the oboe and recurring many times. Before
one of the repetitions there occurs a passage which is often referred to as
the most beautiful in all Schubert's symphonic œuvre. Robert
Schumann described it in these terms: 'There is a passage … in which the
horn sounds from afar, as if coming from another world'. A small
rhythmic motif taken from the principal theme turns up again and again
throughout the entire movement.

The scherzo which follows manifests a scintillating vitality, its main
subject a waltz-like theme. The trio, ushered in by the horns, unfolds a
broad flowing melody. The finale is built upon three themes, but suffers
from the 'Schubertian defect' mentioned earlier: the too frequent
repetition of material of relatively minimal interest.

4

Mendelssohn and Schumann

The symphony is a slow, conservative beast. When the first fireworks of Romanticism exploded behind its back, it did not leap up and charge into the new century. Instead it merely ambled forward, forcing composers to drag their heels alongside or to run ahead after the more excitable songs, operas and caprices.

Beethoven and his great predecessors Haydn and Mozart were largely responsible for creating this monster. These three geniuses devoted much of their lives to writing symphonic masterpieces. By the time Beethoven had finished his monumental ninth symphony, there appeared to be little more that could be said. Yet the challenge was still there, and few Romantic composers could resist the temptation of trying to urge that mammoth creature to move at their own bidding.

Two men who succeeded in impressing the symphony with their own particular stamp of genius were Felix Mendelssohn and Robert Schumann. In education and temperament these two were quite dissimilar. Mendelssohn was a wealthy, highly trained and intensely self-disciplined musician – a well-established composer by his twenty-first birthday. Schumann was emotionally volatile (in later life mentally ill) and largely self-taught; he had composed next to nothing when he was twenty-one. Despite their differences, both Mendelssohn and Schumann approached the symphony in the same manner, revealing caution and respect that is not popularly associated with the Romantic movement. Neither man fundamentally challenged the division of the symphony into four movements, or even the form these movements took; there was still the opening allegro in traditional sonata form, still the light-hearted scherzo or minuet, still the eloquent adagio and the rousing finale. What then distinguishes these 'Romantic' symphonies from their classical ancestors? To begin with, there is a modest but insistent attempt at description. Pure form was not always enough; music could be improved upon with an idea or an image behind it. Mendelssohn may not have had a precise picture in mind when he wrote the first movement of his *Scottish* symphony, but he was clearly trying to describe in music the grey and rugged 'feel' of Scotland. There is also a Romantic reverence for the distant past, beautifully captured by Schumann, for example, in the fourth movement of his *Rhenish* symphony, a musical tribute to the Gothic splendour of Cologne Cathedral. An interest in folk music, which was later to become a school of composition in itself, is evident in Mendelssohn's ebullient *saltarello* (symphony no. 4) or Schumann's ländler (the second movement of symphony no. 3). Perhaps the most significant innovation was the effort by both men to unify their symphonies internally with common musical themes and thus to invest a traditional, formal structure with a modern life of its own.

Other men did their best to lead the classical symphony into the Romantic age. The Frenchman Hector Berlioz hauled it off the beaten track on an extraordinary diversion that few could follow. Niels Gade in Denmark, Johannes Verhulst in Holland and the durable old campaigner Ludwig Spohr each made worthy, but generally forgettable, contributions. It remained to Mendelssohn and Schumann, with their old-fashioned minds and modern sensibilities, to forge a permanent link between the nineteenth century's two greatest symphonists, Beethoven and Brahms.

The symphonies of Mendelssohn

For young Felix Mendelssohn there was no escaping the symphony. He was more than just a teenage prodigy, an able pianist and a precocious composer. He clearly possessed genius as well, and was thus the unfortunate heir-apparent to Beethoven, whose symphonies cast an

Felix Mendelssohn

Mendelssohn (1809-47) was born in Hamburg but grew up in Berlin, where his family moved when he was three. His father Abraham was a wealthy banker, who oversaw the education of his children with a severe affection. Young Felix and his older sister Fanny began their day at 5 a.m., a discipline that encouraged their precociousness in music. At the age of nine, Felix made his first public appearance as a pianist. By then he had already begun to study composition, and at sixteen he confirmed his genius with the Octet for strings, one of the century's great chamber works. 'Ce garçon est riche,' pronounced the crusty old composer Cherubini (without the hint of a 'double entendre').

Mendelssohn's adult life is a bewildering series of travels and musical triumphs. Leipzig, where he conducted the Gewandhaus orchestra and founded the Conservatory in 1842, became his spiritual home, but London had an almost equally strong claim. His first trip to Britain, when he was twenty, inspired two of his finest works, the *Scottish* symphony (No. 3) and the *Hebrides* overture. By his tenth visit, in the year of his death, he was a friend of Queen Victoria and Prince Albert, and the undisputed idol of English musical society. This public figure was in sharp contrast to Mendelssohn the family man, a devoted husband and the father of five children.

Mendelssohn's influence extended far beyond his own compositions. When only twenty he conducted Bach's *St Matthew Passion* in Berlin, the first performance of that work since the composer's death. Throughout his life he tirelessly championed the music of Bach. He also conducted the first performance of Schubert's C major symphony, which his friend Robert Schumann had discovered in manuscript on a visit to Vienna.

Mendelssohn composed with obsessive energy throughout his life. Some of his more superficial works are justly neglected but much remains to be rediscovered and reappraised. His status declined in the late nineteenth and early twentieth centuries, when the charm and skill of his music was mistaken for mere facility, his conservatism for timidity. But certain masterpieces have survived the sternest critical scrutiny: the *Italian* symphony (No. 4), the violin concerto, the overture and incidental music to *A Midsummer Night's Dream* (written when he was seventeen and thirty-four respectively) and several of the *Songs Without Words* for solo piano.

Weakened by years of overwork Mendelssohn was unable to recover from his shock at the death of his beloved sister Fanny. He died at thirty-eight, the most celebrated symphonic composer of his day.

Facing page: By the age of twelve, Mendelssohn was already an accomplished composer. *Left:* A sketch by the composer of the garden-house at the family home in Berlin.

Mendelssohn's beloved
sister Fanny, little more
than three years older
than her brother, wrote
several songs and some
chamber music. Her
death in May 1847
shocked Felix terribly and
hastened his own end,
less than six months later.

Ludwig Spohr

In his own day, Ludwig (or Louis) Spohr (1784-1859) was
ranked alongside Beethoven and Mendelssohn as a composer of
genius. He was born and educated in Brunswick, and first
achieved fame as a virtuoso violinist. His many compositions
include four oratorios, eleven operas, thirty-three string quartets
and nine symphonies. Among the latter works, written between
1811 (when Mendelssohn was two years old) and 1849 (when
Mendelssohn was two years dead) are several interesting experiments. In the sixth symphony each movement imitates a different style, from the Baroque to the 'modern'; the seventh is written
for two orchestras; the ninth depicts the seasons.

intimidating shadow across the path of his successors. Mendelssohn
began confidently enough. No one denies that his first symphony was a
remarkably mature work for a fifteen year-old composer. But his later
efforts did not fare so well. Poor Mendelssohn has been at times judged
trite, cautious, academic, over-sentimental and passionless. Above all,
he has been rebuked for what he lacked. He was not, like Beethoven,
engrossed in the struggles between suffering and joy; he was not, like his
contemporary Berlioz, an outrageous bohemian, intent upon sensation.
Mendelssohn was not, in fact, a natural symphonist. His talent was for
the miniature, whereas the age clamoured for another Beethoven. Yet in
spite of this hostile environment, which has existed to some extent since
his death, the third and fourth symphonies are recognized as masterpieces because of what Mendelssohn possessed. Meticulous craftsmanship, boundless energy and an abundance of enchanting tunes create
more than mere charm. They invest these works with enduring genius.

Mendelssohn: the early string symphonies
Sunday morning was a time for informal music-making in the
Mendelssohn household. This was the ideal opportunity for young Felix
to hear the compositions he had been working on during the week. Piano
sonatas, chamber music, even chamber operas had their premières at
these get-togethers. Among the more ambitious works were twelve
symphonies for strings, written between 1821 and 1823, before the boy's
fifteenth birthday. These are no masterpieces, but they do reveal
Mendelssohn's uncanny ability to imitate his great predecessors. Here is
a fugue by Bach, an overture by Handel, an allegro by Haydn or a rondo
by the young Mozart. Mendelssohn goes through his paces, generally
content to remain in the shadow of his masters, but every so often a spark
of irresistible originality brightens these student compositions. It is as if
the schoolboy, having correctly recited Latin verses all day, now bursts
out of doors and turns cartwheels in the playground.

Symphony no. 1 in C minor, opus 11
Mendelssohn wrote his first symphony for full orchestra (first
performed in 1827) when he was fifteen years old. It is a work of
originality and technical maturity, far greater than the apprentice piece of
a precocious adolescent.
'A searing fire pours out of this first allegro,' wrote his friend Adolf Marx
at the first private performance. The second movement, andante, makes
up in warmth what it lacks in fire, and reveals the teenage composer's
astonishing mastery of orchestration. In the third movement, a robust
menuetto (allegro molto) contrasts movingly with an ethereal trio
section. The symphony ends with an allegro con fuoco. This finale is
more vigorous than truly passionate, but an interlude for solo clarinet
and pizzicato strings adds a charming and novel touch.

Symphony no. 2 in B flat major, opus 52 – Hymn of Praise
Mendelssohn's second symphony (first performed 1840) is neither his
second, nor a symphony in the conventional sense. It consists of three
movements for orchestra, followed by an oratorio for two soprano
soloists, tenor, chorus and orchestra. Mendelssohn was very fond of the
work; so, at first, was the public. But the novelty of its structure has not
been able to sustain a general lack of musical fibre. The first movement
(maestoso con moto – allegro) begins with a gusty solo for trombones, a
tune that unfortunately reappears sporadically throughout the work.
The second movement (allegretto un poco agitato) is a charming
Italianate melody with some striking touches of writing for the
woodwinds. The symphonic section ends with an adagio religioso, after
which the orchestra subsides into accompaniment. The remainder of
the work, nearly two-thirds of its length, is for chorus and soloists.

Schubert's birthplace at Liechtental, a working-class suburb of Vienna.

Overleaf:
Above In 1818 Schubert lived at the Schloss Zseliz as music master tot the Esterházy family. His own room is at the left of the illustration. It was at Zseliz that he wrote his sixth symphony.

Overleaf: Below Dancing in the garden at Atzenbrugg, by Schubert's friend, the Romantic painter Moritz van Schwind. It was a favourite place for merrymaking of Schubert and his friends; he once wrote a set of Atzenbrugger dances.

Overleaf: Facing page The Romantic movement in Russian music arrived with Glinka's opera *A life for the Tsar*, containing this lively chorus.

 SCHLOSS ZELIZ

In 1835 Mendelssohn became the director of the Leipzig Gewandhaus orchestra, and eight years later founded the famous Conservatory there. His sister Fanny painted this watercolour of his living-room in Leipzig.

The title-page of the first edition of Mendelssohn's symphony no. 1.

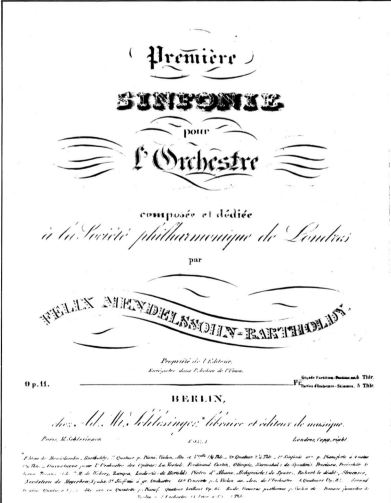

The young Mendelssohn, drawing by W. Hensel, ca. 1820.

Felix Mendelssohn in
1844.

The pianist Clara Wieck
(1819-96), painted in
1840, the year of her
marriage to Robert
Schumann.

1844

AU THEATRE MICHEL.

Vendredi, 17. Mars,

MADAME CLARA SCHUMANN,
NÉE WIECK,

première pianiste de S. M. l'Empereur d'Autriche,

aura l'honneur de donner un

DERNIER
CONCERT,

AVANT SON DEPART,

dans lequel elle jouera plusieurs fois avec ac
compagnement d'orchestre.

Première partie.

1. Ouverture.
2. Concerto, en Sol mineur pour le piano avec accompag-
   nement d'orchestre . . . . F. MENDELSSOHN-
   BARTHOLDY.
   exécuté par Mme Clara Schumann.
3. Air, chanté par Mr Versing. . . MOZART.
4. a) Scherzo . . . . . CLARA SCHUMANN.
   b) «Gretchen am Spinnrad» Lied de
   Schubert, transcrit pour piano par F. LISZT.
   c) Etude en La mineur . . . F. CHOPIN,
   exécutées par Mme Clara Schumann.
   Seconde partie.
5. Ouverture.
6. a) «Lied ohne Worte» . . . MENDELSSOHN-
   BARTHOLDY,
   b) Etude «wenn ich ein Väglein wär» A. HENSELT.
   c) Prélude et Fugue . . S. BACH (demandée),
   exécutées par Mme Clara Schumann.
7. Lieder, chantées par Mr Versing.
8. Concertstück pour piano, avec accom-
   pagnement d'orchestre . . . C. M. v. WEBER,
   exécuté par Mme Clara Schumann.

ON COMMENCERA A 8 HEURES DU SOIR.

Symphony no. 3 in A minor, opus 56 – Scottish

Inspired by the ruined chapel at Holyrood Palace in Edinburgh, the twenty year-old Mendelssohn conceived an idea for his *Scottish* symphony. Thirteen years later this composition was finally completed and performed in 1842. It is an exciting and picturesque work in which the occasional glimpse of Scotland is dwarfed by a magnificent panorama of Romantic Germany.

A melancholy introduction (andante con moto) establishes the Scotland of Mendelssohn's Romantic imagination, a world of twilit ruins and brooding skies. This opening passage also provides the first theme of the allegro un poco agitato. Scotland now becomes stormy and dangerous. The unquiet rhythm and restless swells in volume are, in fact, more reminiscent of the ocean than of the mountainous Highlands. Marine images become inescapable in the long coda, when several massive chromatic waves come rolling out of the string section. The last bars return to the theme of the opening andante as if Mendelssohn (who was very prone to sea-sickness) had gratefully stepped ashore.

For all his love of Scotland, Mendelssohn could not bring himself to write an orchestral imitation of the bagpipe. He came closest to meeting this challenge in the vivace non troppo (a 'scherzo', though it is written in strict sonata form). Here the clarinet introduces a spirited 'Scottish' dance. But this is a pipe without a bag, for Mendelssohn wisely omitted reproducing the overpowering drone.

Any visions of Scotland vanish into the mist during the beautiful third movement, an extended adagio. It is as if the composer here stands up to reassure his audience that he is still the sentimental German traveller they all love.

Mendelssohn originally called his finale allegro guerriero (warlike), which says more about the fierce enthusiasm of its opening theme than the conventional allegro vivacissimo that remains. The second subject extracts from the storm-tossed first movement a prayer for victory. This, it seems, is granted, for in the coda (allegro maestoso assai) all the sullen thoughts and clouds of Mendelssohn's Scotland are transformed into a major key and a triumphant hymn of praise.

Symphony no. 4 in A major, opus 90 – Italian

'I can continue to enjoy nature and the blue sky without thinking of anything else,' wrote Mendelssohn from southern Italy in 1831. This was not entirely true, for he had already begun to work on a symphony, now known as the *Italian* (first performed in 1833). Surprisingly, Mendelssohn went through agonies composing this most sunny work. In the end he was dissatisfied with the results, and the symphony remained unpublished during his lifetime.

From the first bar of the allegro vivace the winds establish an air of quivering excitement with rapidly repeated chords. Out of this shimmering accompaniment the violins spring with joyful energy. The upward leaps of this delightful opening melody and of the second subject that bounds along after it are irresistibly optimistic. It is difficult to bear in mind that Mendelssohn struggled in writing this spirited movement. The first movement shows us little of Italy except sunshine. The second, andante con moto, is said to portray a religious procession that Mendelssohn encountered in Naples. Cellos and basses describe the devout tread of the marchers with a steady pizzicato. Above this, violas, oboe and bassoon (an unusual and particularly effective combination) play the hymn-like tune, a perfect blend of piety and suppressed joy. Curiously, any sadness here comes not from the D minor melody itself but from a sighing tune in A major, introduced by the clarinet midway through the movement.

The third movement, con moto moderato, is a gracious and flowing

Johannes Bernardus van Bree

The music of Beethoven, Schumann and Mendelssohn found a versatile Dutch champion in Van Bree (1801-57). He began his career as a solo violinist but by the 1830s had turned his attentions to conducting. His Caecilia Orchestra tirelessly played music of contemporary German masters to sceptical Amsterdam audiences. From 1849, as leader of his own string quartet, he continued to preach the same gospel in the field of chamber music. In 1853 he became director of the new Amsterdam school of the Society for the Promotion of Music.

Van Bree was also the leading Dutch composer of his generation. His music includes two symphonies, five violin concertos, several Masses, operas and choral works.

Facing page: Clara Schumann, at this period in her life much more famous than her husband, used to promote her husband's works by performing them in public on tour. On this occasion in St Petersburg, however, she included one of her own works instead.

Mendelssohn by Aubrey
Beardsley, a more
restrained and respectful
caricature than many of
the artists' other
impressions.

FELIX
MENDELSSOHN
BARTHOLDY.

dance, troubled only by a mysterious summons from the French horns
in the trio section.

Dancing continues in the finale, called saltarello after the vigorous
Italian dance of that name. This movement remains in A minor
throughout, a highly unusual way to end a symphony that started so
brightly in a major key. The opening is both airy and earthbound, as if
danced by rustic gnomes rather than ethereal sprites. This gives way to a
second dance, a quietly intense tarantella, whose reckless triplets have
proved too much for many an unwary string section. The movement
ends with a wistful farewell to the opening theme of the symphony, now
strangely transformed by the minor key.

Symphony no. 5 in D minor, opus 107 – Reformation
Mendelssohn loathed his *Reformation* symphony. Of all his compositions, he claimed, this was the one he would choose to burn. So it
comes as a pleasant surprise to find that it is a work of power and often
great beauty. The number five is misleading. Mendelssohn completed
this symphony when he was twenty-one, but it was published and
numbered posthumously. It was written on commission to celebrate the
300th anniversary (1832) of Lutheranism.

A religious atmosphere is established in the opening andante, which ends with a devout cadence known as the 'Dresden Amen'. The muscular allegro con fuoco that follows is more the Church Militant than the Church Penitent, but this bold posturing is unexpectedly interrupted by the Dresden Amen, and when the allegro resumes it is soft and subdued, as if chastened by a divine rebuke.

The second movement, allegro vivace, is a delightful scherzo that seems to have escaped from Mendelssohn's music to *A Midsummer Night's Dream*. The trio section is a lilting serenade, more the stuff of Italian piazzas than Lutheran cathedrals. There follows the beautiful andante, a brief interlude of sheer peace and reflection before the struggles of the finale (andante con moto – allegro maestoso). This is introduced by solo flute playing Martin Luther's famous chorale, *Ein feste Burg ist unser Gott*. Mendelssohn's own contributions are frail compared to Luther's majestic anthem, and in the last thunderous bars the full orchestra returns to this chorale before a final mighty amen.

The symphonies of Robert Schumann

'Sometimes I would like to smash my piano,' wrote Schumann in 1839, 'it has become too narrow for my thoughts.' The orchestra, he confessed, was the medium for which he longed to write. Two years later his wish came true. In 1841 he completed his first two symphonies and a three movement work, a near-symphony called Overture, scherzo and finale. Schumann was thrilled with this new venture. 'I wish you knew my symphony,' he wrote of the first to a friend, 'How I enjoyed hearing it performed.' But critics have not always shared his enthusiasm. They point out, and Schumann would have agreed, that his knowledge of orchestral writing was slight. As a result, his beautiful melodies sometimes lack clarity, thickened by too many instruments playing the same line. Rejection of Schumann's orchestration reached such a point that at the end of the century Gustav Mahler rescored all four symphonies in order to reveal what he called the 'latent treasures ... which the composer's imagination but dimly perceived'.

Today Schumann is treated with greater respect. Although no one claims that he used the orchestra as inventively as Berlioz or Mahler, his symphonies abound in passion, energy and ravishing melodies. The flaws in works of such genius are best left untouched.

Symphony no. 1 in B flat major, opus 38 – Spring

Schumann began writing his *Spring* symphony in mid-winter, 1841. By the end of February it was complete, and on the 31 March, on the brink of the season it celebrates, Felix Mendelssohn conducted the première in Leipzig. The symphony was inspired by a poem, and at one point Schumann considered giving each of the movements titles: *Spring's Awakening, Evening, Merry Playmates* and *Spring's Farewell*. These name-tags he wisely discarded – only the first may help describe a story behind the music. A work as confident as this needs no supporting text to evoke the vigour and freshness of spring.

'I should like the trumpets to sound as if from on high, like a call to awaken,' Schumann wrote of the andante un poco maestoso, the introduction to the first movement. The grip of winter is not immediately broken, but the liquid strains of a flute gradually soften the frozen earth, and with the allegro molto vivace Spring arrives bubbling and tumbling like a mountain torrent. This boisterous weather subsides in the coda when a beautiful hymn-like melody briefly suggests the warmth of June. Gusty, exuberant April then blows back to bring the movement to a close.

The second movement, larghetto, is a tender, wordless love song played first by violins, then cellos, and finally by oboe and horn. A chill creeps into this idyllic scene in the last few bars when trombones quietly draw the key from E flat major to G minor and prepare us for the unsettled emotions of the scherzo.

Niels Gade

Niels Gade (1817-90) won fame as a violin virtuose in his native Copenhagen but achieved wider recognition when he became Mendelssohn's assistant conductor in Leipzig. In 1848, shortly after Mendelssohn's death, he returned to Copenhagen, where he spent the rest of his life. His compositions, which include eight symphonies, bear witness to the overpowering influence of his early friendship with Mendelssohn and Schumann.

In addition to being a composer of great genius, Schumann was also a music critic of rare wit, sympathy and perception.

Robert Schumann

Robert Schumann (1810-56) spent his early years in Zwickau, Saxony, where his father, August, was a prosperous bookseller and publisher. The boy began piano lessons when he was seven and soon revealed a precocious ability at improvisation. All encouragement he received from his family in this field, however, died with his father in 1826. Robert, then sixteen years old, reluctantly took the advice of his mother and guardian to pursue a respectable career in law. Shortly after his twentieth birthday he had persuaded the law faculty at both Leipzig and Heidelberg Universities (and, finally, his mother) that his was not a legal genius. The rest of his life he devoted single-mindedly to music. Schumann's early compositions were for the piano, works of great imagination and descriptive power, including the exuberant *Carnaval*, three sonatas, *Kinderscenen* and the *Etudes Symphoniques.* A permanent injury to his right hand in 1832 forced him to give up any ambition of becoming a virtuoso pianist, but he found a more valuable outlet for his abilities in critism. As founder, chief contributor and, until 1844, editor of the *Neue Zeitschrift für Musik*, he became a perceptive champion of what was worthwhile in modern music, being the first to publicly acknowledge the brilliance of his contemporary Chopin and, years later, of the much younger Brahms.

In 1840 Schumann married Clara Wieck, who at twenty years old was already a distinguished concert pianist. For years this match had been bitterly opposed by Clara's father, Schumann's former piano teacher Friedrich Wieck. In the exultation of his love, Schumann sought words for his music and composed in that one year nearly 150 songs, including the great cycles *Liederkreis* and *Dichterliebe.* 'I should like to sing myself to death, like a nightingale,' he wrote to Clara. In the year following their marriage he turned with equal passion to the orchestra, completing the first two of his four symphonies (now, confusingly, numbers one and four). In 1842 he wrote almost exclusively for chamber ensembles. Three string quartets and the famous quintet for piano and strings date from this year.

Schumann's health, undermined by syphilis, now began to fail. He and his family moved to Dresden, seeking a peaceful life, but he was not a moderate man and continued to overwork. The great A minor piano concerto and two more symphonies are among the best works from his last decade. In 1850, his creative powers dwindling, he began an unfortunate period as director of music at Düsseldorf. Madness finally descended in 1854. After attempting to drown himself in the Rhine, he was taken to a private asylum near Bonn, where he remained until his death two years later. `

Marked molto vivace, the third movement is a tug-of-war between its sombre first theme and the gayer tunes that attempt to displace it. If spring is still in the air, then this is a squally day of black clouds and grey sky, which ends, as a spring day will, with an unexpectedly tranquil sunset.

The spirit of the first movement returns with the playful and robust finale – allegro animato e grazioso. A soulful horn call, followed by the trilling cadenza of a lonely flute, suggests that there is still sadness in this bright world. But the rest of the orchestra has no time for clouds or contemplation, and dances on to the sunny conclusion.

Symphony no. 2 in C major, opus 61

Schumann suffered a mental and physical breakdown in 1844 and was still feeling its effects when he composed this symphony two years later. He described it as a struggle between the spirit and the body, and admitted that only in the finale did he begin to feel himself again. Although traditionally his 'second' symphony, this was the third such work he had completed. A dark and passionate masterpiece, it is the least played of Schumann's four symphonies.

In a slow introduction, sostenuto assai, trumpets, horn and trombone promise to break through the dark murmurings of the strings. But instead of the glorious sunrise we had anticipated, this day dawns in wind and rain. The turbulent allegro ma non troppo establishes a feverish mood, its double-dotted rhythms lashing out restlessly. At the end of this long storm the brasses attempt, again fruitlessly, to shine through the ragged clouds.

This nervous energy persists in the second movement: scherzo – allegro vivace. Violins scurry desperately with incessant semiquavers before subsiding, as if into an uneasy sleep, during the first trio. A second trio establishes some welcome calm, if not contentment. But the unhappy semiquavers wake up and bring us back to the restless opening.

Like a pool that interrupts the tumult of a noisy stream, the adagio espressivo affords a moment of peace. This is peace of the body and not of the mind, for a minor key and great sighing leaps in the melody allow the spirit little rest. Here Schumann confounds those critics who find fault with his orchestration. Woodwind solos are beautifully handled and give the movement a simplicity and purity that his music sometimes lacks.

Felix Mendelssohn, who conducted the first performance of this symphony, must have been surprised to discover a similarity between the opening bars of the allegro molto vivace and the first movement of his own *Italian Symphony*. The resolute good cheer of this finale, however, does not survive, and Schumann's unquiet spirit returns in the development section. Then, as if determined to recover his tranquillity, he brings the music to a complete halt and introduces a new tune, a quiet, flowing melody that carries him to the end of the movement. Drums and brass contribute noisily to the final bars, as if Schumann needed all their support to sustain his newfound confidence.

Symphony no. 3 in E flat major – Rhenish
Robert and Clara Schumann moved to Düsseldorf in 1850, where he became conductor of the city's flourishing orchestra and chorus. This was a disastrous step. Schumann had never studied conducting and in the previous few years had become increasingly subject to fits of physical and mental depression. (So withdrawn and emotionally unsuited for this work was he that on one awful occasion, the entire chorus stopped in confusion without Schumann noticing anything wrong.) Yet his genius, though fitful, had not deserted him. In the first three months of his residence at Düsseldorf he completed this confident and melodious work. He called it his *Rhenish* symphony, in celebration of the River Rhine and the country surrounding his new home. It is his last symphony (the fourth was actually written in 1841, nearly ten years earlier) and one of his last indisputably great compositions before madness ended his creative life.

Lebhaft (lively). The symphony opens with a joyous and powerful theme, as if Schumann had succeeded in shaking off the demon of depression that had clung to him for so long. The time signature is 3/4, a metre commonly used for dance music, but here Schumann employs syncopation to give his tune a march-like quality, as if to portray the confident strides of a hero. Suddenly the mood changes and the 3/4 rhythm asserts itself in a quiet and yearning dance (the second subject) introduced by the oboes. This is at first no more than a wistful interlude, but it re-emerges throughout the movement like a sad memory. At one point it would seem that Schumann is succumbing to its melancholy, but he calls upon his brass section to drive away these unwelcome thoughts. The French horns now take up the noble opening theme and urge the full orchestra back to its original optimism. Trumpets and drums finally gallop upon the scene, like an army of reinforcements arriving in the nick of time, to bring the first movement of a triumphant conclusion.

Scherzo – sehr massig (moderate). Schumann called this movement a scherzo, but it lacks the fierce wit of a scherzo by Beethoven. Instead it sounds like an old-fashioned minuet in peasant garb. The rhythm is a slow but good-humoured one-two-three, and the tune is sedately introduced by lower strings and bassoon. This gives way to the livelier rhythm of a new dance that begins competing with the first. The horns enter with a solemn chorale and the dancing ceases, as if a black cloud threatened to send the revellers inside. This interlude is short-lived. The original theme returns, now strengthened by full orchestra. Two mighty horn calls finally signal that the dancing is at an end, and the music winds down to perfect stillness.

Nicht schnell (not fast). The dancers have departed and night has fallen. The human bustle and simple good spirits of the scherzo give way to this lyrical slow movement and its world of melancholy reminiscence. Clarinets and bassoons introduce the first theme, a melody heavy with the perfumed night air, and followed by a mournful second theme for bassoon and strings. Lest too much slowness and sweetness should begin to resemble syrup, Schumann recalls his original theme and concludes this brief and nostalgic excursion into the realm of sentiment.

Feierlich (solemn). Shortly after settling in Düsseldorf, Robert and Clara Schumann made a brief excursion up the Rhine to Cologne. There, in the magnificent Gothic cathedral, they attended the ceremony that inspired this solemn movement. In his slow and measured music, Schumann evokes not only the formal occasion but the antiquity and

Robert Schumann's wife, Clara Wieck, was the daughter of his piano teacher Friedrich Wieck.

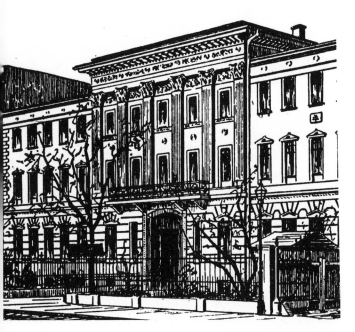

The house in Inselstrasse, Leipzig, where Robert and Clara Schumann lived from 1840 to 1845.

strength of the building itself. The trombones (heard here for the first time) introduce a stately procession that remains the principal theme throughout the movement. In its deliberate pace, resonant orchestration and austere counterpoint the music recreates the atmosphere of an earlier age. The excitement mounts as restless semiquavers on the strings suggest a great crowd of people pressing into the cathedral. There is a moment of holy silence, and then the brass section plays two magnificent fanfares which seem to reverberate in the great dome high above the heads of the congregation. The strings and woodwinds respond in awe, and the movement ends with hushed and reverent chords.

Lebhaft (lively). Scarcely have the last organ chords died away than the finale begins a joyful dance. With gusts of contagious glee, it blows away the last remnants of solemn devotion. A slower second subject is compelled to hobble along after the dancers, wheezing with laughter. The grave processional of the preceding movement now reappears transformed, as if the Cardinal himself had buckled on his dancing shoes and joined the celebration. Only near the end of the movement do the revellers pause, silenced by a moving cry of thanksgiving from the brass section. The dance then bounds onwards to the final tumultuous bars. So near his own unhappy end, Schumann had created one of the happiest endings in symphonic literature.

Symphony no. 4 in D minor, opus 120

In 1841, with characteristic enthusiasm and speed, Schumann wrote his first two symphonies. The *Spring* symphony was an immediate success; the second, in D minor, was less popular and remained neglected for ten years. Schumann finally returned to it in 1851, when a revised version was published, misleadingly described as symphony no. 4. This work is a rich source of pleasure for musicologists, who find in its opening bars ideas that link all four movements. Ignorance of such complexity detracts in no way from our joy in this symphony's energy and beauty.

A sombre introduction, marked ziemlich langsam (rather slow), leads directly into the main section of the first movement, the dramatic lebhaft (lively). Violins introduce the principal subject, a fiery wave of semi-

Johann Wenzel Kalliwoda

One of the most admired and industrious contemporaries of Schumann and Mendelssohn was the Bohemian composer and violinist Johann Wenzel Kalliwoda (1801-66). He was born and educated in Prague but spent most of his life in Germany as conductor of the court orchestra at Donaueschingen. There he attracted some of the greatest soloists of the day: Liszt, Clara Schumann and Sigismond Thalberg.

His compositions were treated respectfully by contemporary critics. Robert Schumann admired the fifth symphony (there were seven in all). About Kalliwoda's eighteen concert overtures, however, he was less enthusiastic. They were pleasant enough, he complained, but all sounded the same. The subsequent neglect of Kalliwoda's music has confirmed Schumann's judgement.

quavers, that at first threatens to overwhelm all other musical ideas. This aggressive theme eventually encounters stiff competition from a resolute three-chord motif. Then, as if from nowhere, emerges the majestic melody that carries the movement to its end.

A slow and plaintive melody, played by oboe and cellos, introduces the romance. Although Schumann wrote few more lovely tunes than this, he drops it immediately for the unsettled quavers that introduced the first movement. A solo violin, playing delicate triplets above the rest of the orchestra, suddenly emerges from the gloom and spans the movement like a rainbow. At its end there is a pot of gold – a final glimpse of the tune that began this enchanting romance.

The third movement – another lebhaft – starts life as a footstamping country dance. This is transformed by the airy trio section, in which the same rainbow as in the preceding movement appears in the sky. The music continues without a pause into the solemn introduction to the finale, marked langsam (slow). Violins quietly recall their semiquaver passage in the first movement and crescendo to the main section, the mirthful lebhaft. This is based on the three dramatic chords originally encountered in the first movement. A light-hearted second subject appears to complete the musical material. But upon reaching his logical conclusion, Schumann strikes a rich new seam of ideas with which, like a conjuror, he dazzles us in the exciting coda.

A cartoon of the Leipzig Gewandhaus Orchestra, drawn in 1850 by the cellist Carl Reiners. Conducting the band is Julius Rietz.

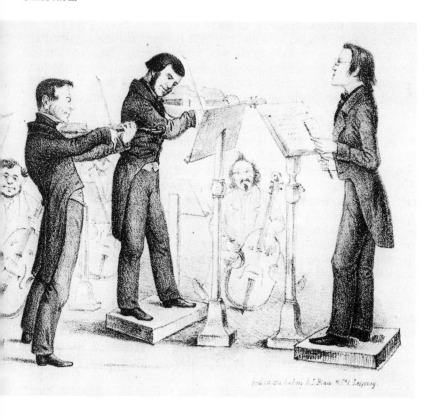

Johannes Verhulst

Johannes Verhulst (1816-91) was born in The Hague where, at seventeen, he became a violinist in the court chapel. His real musical education began in 1838, however, when he settled in Leipzig as conductor of the Euterpe orchestra. There he became a friend and admirer of both Mendelssohn and Schumann. As a member of the Davidsbund, a society dedicated to overthrowing musical philistinism, he fell particularly under the influence of Schumann, to whom he submitted many of his compositions. Schumann was an indulgent critic, comparing the nationalism of Verhulst (in one flattering critical essay) to that of Chopin. He later stood as godfather to Robert, Verhulst's first son.

In 1842 Verhulst returned to Holland, where he embarked upon a long and influential conducting career in Rotterdam, The Hague and Amsterdam. As a composer he was an ardent disciple of German Romanticism, and his varied output reflects Schumann's encouragement to him: 'You are quite right to cultivate every style'. Among his compositions are choral works, songs, overtures, two string quartets and a much-admired symphony in E minor.

5

Brahms and Bruckner

The young Brahms (seated), with his friend the violinist Joachim.

Classical Romanticism

The second half of the nineteenth century marked turbulent years in the history of the symphony. The great genius of symphonic form, Beethoven, had brought the classical symphony to a point of perfection which could scarcely be surpassed. High Romanticism, giving more importance to individual and personal expression, made its appearance. The form best suited for such expression gave rise to a clear-cut divergence of opinion. Liszt, Wagner and Richard Strauss elected to abandon traditional form and seek new pathways for saying what they had to say musically. 'Programme music' came into being, music with a story, based on literary particulars or personal experiences. Wagner turned his back on the orchestral form as a self-sufficient means of expression and created the *Gesamtkunstwerk*, the total blending of all the arts. The 'invention' of the symphonic poem is credited to Franz Liszt. Brahms and Bruckner clothed their Romantic ideals in classical dress, employing traditional compositional techniques in matters of form, melody and harmony, although Bruckner made frequent harmonic detours under the influence of Wagner.

In France during this period relatively little importance was assigned to the symphony as a compositional form. Hector Berlioz wrote symphonic poems, including the *Symphonie fantastique*, despite his calling it himself a symphony. Charles Gounod wrote three authentic symphonies, Georges Bizet wrote one at the age of seventeen, Saint-Saëns, three, among them the celebrated 'Organ' Symphony, and César Franck composed one. Wagner's influence had indeed seeped into France, but the French symphonies were nonetheless cast in orthodox moulds. Of these, only the works of Berlioz, Saint-Saëns's third symphony and that of Franck have remained in the standard repertory. Both Bruckner and Brahms sought a synthesis of the classical and Romantic traditions. Brahms's approach was to fit Romantic ideas into concise, intellectual forms, based on those of his predecessors. Bruckner sought to link himself to the innovators, Wagner in particular. He developed one specific style and in the main held to it without deviating. This accounts for the well-known aphorism that Bruckner did not compose nine symphonies, but one symphony nine times. He was, and still is, criticized for saying the same thing in each of his symphonies, whereas Brahms, in each of his, expresses himself in a totally different manner. For Bruckner, the Church and a deep 'God-consciousness' were of extreme significance; for Brahms, not at all. Lines can be traced from both these composers back to Johann Sebastian Bach, the similarities being for Brahms an intensive use of counterpoint, for Bruckner, his frequent use of sequences, repetitions. As mentioned, Bruckner admired Wagner greatly, while Brahms rejected him.

Johannes Brahms

Throughout his entire life Brahms clung doggedly to traditional compositional forms and maintained for himself, personally and as a composer, an exacting sense of discipline. The musicologist Alfred Einstein described him as a 'musical thoroughbred' who never met with disappointments such as those experienced by the idealistic, innovative, decadent Richard Wagner. His disillusionments were of a different nature, namely those of a classical composer born too late. Brahms was extremely unsympathetic towards the new pathways taken by Liszt in his symphonic poems. Liszt's creations were one-movement orchestral pieces in which themes borrowed from literature were varied in a great number of ways. The renunciation of strict tonality, of which both Liszt and Wagner became passionate champions, was, to Brahms's way of thinking, outlandish. He had been thoroughly trained by his teacher Eduard Marxsen in the old-fashioned ways, deeply rooted in musical history from Palestrina to Beethoven. He had learned to use conventional sonata form and fugue, and studied Bach and Handel as did no other composer of his time.

Brahms was forty-three years old when he unveiled his first symphony before the public. For fourteen years he had carried it around in his head, though some of it had been written down. Brahms was careful, refusing to begin something whose consequences he could not foresee. And he realized that by publishing a symphony he might well 'burn his fingers'. In the first place, he sought to develop a personal orchestral sound in the instrumentation. His orchestration tends towards dark colourings. In the second place, Beethoven bothered him, in a positive sense. In the eyes of his contemporaries, Beethoven, with his ninth symphony, had achieved the acme of symphonic form; and Brahms, with his traditional orientation, was hesitant to stand in the former's shadow. He did compose for chorus and orchestra, notably in the *German Requiem*, but not for orchestra alone. Before publishing his first symphony, he tried out his purely orchestral skills by composing the *Variations on a theme of Haydn*.

Brahms made use of the usual complement of the symphony orchestra of his time: double woodwinds, an occasional third flute, four horns, two trumpets, three trombones, timpani and strings. His preference was always for the middle and lower registers of the instruments, particularly the resonant bass instruments. He used trombones not only for dynamic amplification, but also for soft chorale-like themes. Occasionally he made use of the tuba and double-bassoon to reinforce the bass line. The harp was absent from his scores, and string parts were often divided. Although at present modern instruments are naturally used to perform Brahms's symphonies, he himself wanted nothing to do with modern instruments. He held fast to the old natural horn and trumpet. His themes are always lyrical, sometimes reminiscent of folk music, sometimes motivic. The slow movements often have long-spanned themes. Brahms's style is distinguished by a frequent use of parallel thirds and sixths, and skilful use of counterpoint. Some maintain that in his contrapuntal working-out of themes he surpassed even Beethoven. Rhythmically, simultaneous use is frequently made of uneven rhythms such as two against three.

The success of the *Variations on a theme of Haydn* probably gave Brahms the courage to bring out his first symphony, to which he put the finishing touches in 1876.

Symphony no. 1 in C minor, opus 68

Brahms struggled with his first symphony for a long time. From a letter dated July, 1862, we know that he was then working on the first movement. In this letter, Clara Schumann quotes the first measures of the allegro. Six years later Brahms sent the theme of the last movement to his friend Clara Schumann with the greeting *Hoch auf'm Berg, tief im tal, grüss ich dich, viel Tausendmal*, a text which fits the theme. Fourteen

Johannes Brahms

Johannes Brahms (1833-97) was born in Hamburg on 7 May. His father played the double-bass, and according to report, none too well. But he did give his son music lessons at a very early age. From his seventh year Brahms received piano lessons from an official teacher and gave signs of possessing an extraordinary talent for the instrument. Three years later he went to the celebrated teacher Eduard Marxsen, who also instructed him in theory and composition. At this time Brahms earned money by playing the piano in bars in the red-light harbour district of Hamburg, and learned early on to accept life as it is, lost all belief in God and armed himself against his own sensitivity behind a mask of indifference.

On 21 September 1848 in Hamburg, he gave his first public piano recital. By 1853 the way to fame lay open. Robert Schumann helped greatly in this regard by writing enthusiastically about Brahms in his *Neue Zeitschrift für Musik*. Brahms became friends with Schumann and his wife Clara, an acclaimed concert pianist. In 1857 he received a permanent appointment to the court of Lippe-Detmold, giving music lessons to Princess Friederike and working as choral director. With only a few short interruptions, he remained there until 1860. During one of these, he founded the Hamburg Women's Chorus, composing for them and giving many concerts. In 1863 he accepted an invitation from the *Singakademie* in Vienna to join them as their permanent director. This position was of short duration, but he was to remain in Vienna. By this time he had become a celebrated pianist in his own right and a respected composer, both of which activities allowed him to lead a life of relative ease.

As a pianist he made tours of Germany, Austria, Switzerland, Denmark and Holland. He refused an invitation to pay a visit to Cambridge University in England in order to receive an honorary doctorate, not daring to cross the sea. In 1896, at the age of 63, he was sent to Karlsbad for a healthcure during which it was discovered he was suffering from cancer of the liver. He returned to Vienna, where he died on 3 April 1897.

His output includes many works for solo piano, including a large number of arrangements, compositions for piano duet and two works for two piano duet and two works for two pianos. A small number of organ works, many songs (including folk-song arrangements) and marvellous chamber music also came from his pen. In addition to the four symphonies, his orchestral works include the *Tragic Overture*, the *Academic Festival Overture*, the two piano concertos, the Concerto for violin, cello and orchestra, and Serenades and the *Variations on a theme of Haydn*. Brahms also composed large-scale works for chorus and orchestra, with or without soloists, of which the *German Requiem* is the best-known.

years separate the beginning of the symphony and its first rehearsal, which took place in Karlsruhe on 4 November 1876. Even during this rehearsal he was hesitant about the work, making cuts on the spot and contemplating changes in the finale. The symphony was well-received by the public, and Brahms himself conducted performances in Mannheim, Munich and Vienna.

What Brahms had often feared came true: his approach *à la* Beethoven in the first and last movements caused him to be elected to the position of the 'third great B', the last in the well-known line of Bach, Beethoven and Brahms. Debates about the symphony flared up. He was accused of having 'lifted' the theme in C of the last movement from the finale of Beethoven's ninth symphony, the *Ode to Joy*. The conductor Hans von

Brahms at home.

Bülow defended Brahms, asserting that he had carried on the great tradition of Beethoven and proclaiming the symphony 'Beethoven's Tenth'.

Yet it is not amiss to speak of the work as a typical Brahmsian symphony. The first and last movements begin with a slow introduction which contains the thematic material. The rhetorical power of these introductions does in fact recall Beethoven. But the middle movements have nothing to do with the earlier master. In the place of a slow movement and scherzo, Brahms composed two movements with an intermezzo character. Notable is the violin solo in the second movement, a reminder of Schumann's fourth symphony with its violin solo in the romanze. The orchestration of the symphony is sometimes rather thick, less well-balanced than in the later symphonies.

Symphony no. 2 in D major, opus 73

The second symphony was given the nickname of *Pastorale*, though this is now rarely used. Many authors point to the 'country' quality of the work. The author Edwin Evans, who, for the benefit of musicians, provided a measure-by-measure rhythmic table for all of Brahms's orchestral *œuvres*, could not escape this same characterization, speaking of the second symphony as reflecting a mood which 'like it or not, carries us away to green meadows'. Another current of opinion considered the name *Viennese* to be more appropriate. Viennese, because the public of this musical city valued the symphony highly from the outset and because Brahms, in the first movement, seems to be giving an ironic wink to the Viennese waltz and Johann Strauss, whose music he held in high esteem.

No programmatic idea lies behind the symphony, in any event not one originating with Brahms himself. Brahms worked on the second symphony in the summer of 1877 in Pörtschach on the Wörthersee in Carinthia, and in the autumn of that same year in Lichtental near Baden-Baden. During his summer holidays in Pörtschach in the years 1877–79, Brahms clearly felt himself inspired. One work after another flowed from his pen. The Violin Concerto was composed in this period, as well as the Sonata for violin and piano, no. 1, opus 78. The period of creation necessary for his first symphony was as long as that required by his second symphony was short.

Initially Brahms caused some confusion regarding his second symphony. He proclaimed it to be a very sorrowful, melancholy work and advised his publisher Simrock to print a black mourning-band around the score. It proved however to be a buoyant and animated piece, full of melodic incursions, for which no mourning-band could be considered appropriate.

In the first movement, allegro non troppo, a lyrical theme unfolds containing all the elements on which the first movement is thematically based. The second theme is also lyrical, written in the characteristic parallel thirds, and supported by a pizzicato bass. The flowing horn solo in a bedding of strings just before the end, followed by the wink given to the Viennese waltz (played by woodwinds and strings), are also characteristic. In this symphony, Brahms added a tuba to the trombones. The second movement, adagio, was written in sonata form and immediately introduces two themes. One is played by the bassoons, and the other by the cellos. Both themes remain in contact, but are developed and varied in different ways, ending in an unexpected fugato.

The third movement, allegretto grazioso, was also a reason for the nickname of *Viennese* symphony. The ländler theme, introduced by the oboe, recalls Schubert, as do the alternations between major and minor. The movement unrolls in the manner of a serenade with two fast intermezzi, characterized by a shifting rhythm.

The finale, marked allegro con spirito, begins with a theme in which motifs from the first movement theme recur; these motifs disappear into the background as the second theme is introduced. In the coda Brahms

Franz Adolf Berwald

It was not until after his death that Franz Adolf Berwald (1796-1868) was recognized as an important composer. He began his musical career as a very young boy, playing violin concerts at the age of nine. Having grown up in Uppsala, Berwald moved to Stockholm to join the Royal Orchestra there. The conductor at that time, Du Puy, became Berwald's counterpoint and composition teacher. Together with his brother, the violinist Christian August, Berwald even toured Finland (1819), Russia (1819) and Norway (1827). Despite his early successes, he decided to end his career as a solo violinist. He dedicated himself, in spite of his limited education up to that point, to broadening his general musical knowledge.

Berwald made his début as a composer in 1818 with *Fantasy For Orchestra*. The Royal Orchestra performed most of his premières, including his *First Symphony*, now, unfortunately lost to us. Seeking international recognition, Berwald moved to Berlin in 1829 where he composed 2 operas that were never performed. He had no success in either composing or performing and was forced to find some other means of support. In 1835, Berwald opened an orthopaedic institute having been earlier a successful inventor of orthopaedic gymnastics. The institution made it financially possible for him to leave Berlin in 1841, and move to Vienna where he continued his musical work. It was there that Berwald composed *Symphonie Singulière*. Recognition for his work was practically non-existent, and in 1842, Berwald was forced to return to Sweden to again find new means to support his family.

A few of Berwald's symphonies enjoyed faint recognition, but never broad public appeal. He travelled to Paris, Vienna and Bavaria trying to promote his work, sometimes successfully, most often not. The Mozarteum in Salzburg did name him an honorary member, but a new disappointment awaited him in Sweden where he was denied the leadership of the Royal Orchestra. The University of Uppsala also refused him a teaching position.

Finances again necessitated Berwald to find employment outside the world of music. He accepted the directorship of a glass factory in Angermanland from 1850 until 1858. He composed in his leisure time, and wrote many articles for papers and magazines. His opera *Estrella de Soria* was performed in 1862 at the Royal Theatre in Stockholm, but with little success.

Berwald was finally named to the Music Academy in 1864 and was also finally appointed to teach at the Conservatory in 1867. Despite all the disappointments of his musical career, Berwald is now recognized as the first true symphonicus in Sweden and the greatest of his country's 19th century composers. The musical recognition denied him during his lifetime had a great deal to do with Berwald's originality. The composer himself was convinced that the music was too personal, and yet foreign influences are obviously present in his work. The harmonic structure reveals a clear relationship with Germanic romantic music. His unexpected modulations are reminiscent of Schubert. The formal structure of some compositions is so unexpected as to be considered avant-garde. For example, a scherzo is placed in the middle of a slow movement, or a piece is written in one, unbroken movement in which many tempo and key changes take place. It was most likely these originalities that made it so difficult for Berwald's contemporaries to appreciate his work.

Long after Berwald's death, the Swedish public began to take notice of him. In 1946, for the celebration of the 150th anniversary of his birth, *Estrella de Soria* was again performed. There was also a festive series of concerts given featuring his most representative compositions.

made generous use of the brass. The three trombones bring the work to its conclusion with a sustained enunciation of the keynote. It is a robust movement whose rhythm and tempo scarcely flag as it rushes to its dramatic close.

Symphony no. 3 in F major, opus 90

Brahms completed the third symphony in Wiesbaden in the summer of 1883. The work presents certain enigmas. One of the theories of the poet Max Kalback, author of a substantial biography of Brahms, was that the two middle movements were originally intended as incidental music to Goethe's *Faust*. It is true that the composer was occupied with Goethe while working on his third symphony. His friend, the violinist Joachim, felt the finale to have a mythological origin. In a letter to Brahms, dated 27 January 1884, he wrote: 'I do not like to look for poetic backgrounds in music, but with this piece I cannot get the image of Hero and Leander out my mind. The image of the gallant swimmer passes again and again unbidden before my eyes.' Here Joachim was referring to the story from Greek mythology about Hero, priestess of Aphrodite, in Sestos on the Hellespont. Her lover, Leander, who lived on the other side of the Hellespont, swam across nightly to reach her. During a storm Leander was drowned and at the sight of his body cast ashore, Hero threw herself into the sea and was also drowned. Brahms did not react to Joachim's remarks, but clearly there was something in them. The deep friendship between Joachim and Brahms was troubled at this time, but in the third symphony Brahms's musical motto keeps returning. This is the notes F-A-F, the first letters of the phrase *Frei aber Froh*. And this phrase was a variant of Joachim's motto, F-A-E, meaning *Freu aber Einsam.*.

The first movement, allegro con brio, opens with the F-A-F motto in a dissident way, for the A is lowered to A flat, an immediate conflict between major and minor which continues throughout the movement. The second movement is an andante and begins with a simple melody played by the clarinets and bassoons. The trombones have their say, but trumpets and timpani are absent.

In the third movement, poco allegro, the cellos play a prominent role in the introduction of the theme, which is later repeated in various ways by horn, oboe and violins. In the finale, allegro, Brahms uses short motifs instead of melodic themes; these are developed rhythmically in various ways. The symphony comes full circle at the end as the F-A-F motif returns in the original key.

The world première was given by the Vienna Philharmonic Orchestra under the direction of Hans Richter, who with the same orchestra had also given the first performance of the second symphony.

Symphony no. 4 in E minor, opus 98

Brahms had begun his purely orchestral work with a set of variations, the *Variations on a theme of Haydn* (1873) and he concluded it with another brilliant variation-piece, the fourth symphony. For with the exception of the Double Concerto for violin, cello and orchestra, Brahms was to write no great orchestral work after his fourth symphony.

The fourth symphony, which came into being in Murzuschlag in Stiermarken in the summers of 1884 and 1885, was first performed in Hamburg by the symphony orchestra of Meiningen under the direction of Brahms himself. The work still requires attentive listening. Prominent contemporaries of Brahms had trouble with it and during a performance in Leipzig, the audience left the hall before the finale. Brahms cast the finale in one of the most complex forms of composition, one which since Bach and Handel had scarcely been used: the passacaglia. The passacaglia was originally an old Spanish or Italian dance. Opinions vary as to the origin of the word. Some see in it the Spanish words *pasar* (walk) and *calle* (street). Others point to a similarity with the Italian *gallo* (rooster). The latter might refer to the three-part rhythm of the dance, the rhythm of 'the rooster's halting gait'. In any

Facing page : An anonymous drawing of Brahms, now in the municipal museum in The Hague.

Georges Bizet

Georges Bizet (1838-75) was born in Paris and died just outside the city three weeks after the première of his *magnum opus*, the opera *Carmen*. He grew up in a middle-class and musical environment, and entered the Conservatoire before the age of ten, where Gounod was one of his teachers. While there he wrote his only symphony, in C major, at the age of seventeen, though it was not performed until sixty years after his death.

As well as *Carmen*, whose failure was the most bitter blow of its composer's life, Bizet's orchestral music has kept his name prominent in the repertory: *L'Arlésienne Suite* (from incidental music he wrote for Daudet's play), and *Jeux d' enfants* (originally a piano duet) are favourites everywhere. Most of the rest of his two dozen operas however, apart from *The Pearl Fishers* and a once-popular Serenade from *The Fair Maid of Perth*, have so far been condemned to oblivion by posterity.

Anton Bruckner

Anton Bruckner (1824-96) was born in the Austrian town of Ansfelden. His grandfather and father were both schoolmasters and Bruckner was destined to follow in their footsteps. A pupil in his own father's class, Bruckner showed himself to be an extremely gifted student and as he also proved to be musical, he was committed to the care of the music teacher Johann Weiss. An attempt was made to educate him in the most all-round way possible, so as to allow him to teach virtually any subject, including music. Under Weiss he learned the art of organ improvisation and studied the compositions of Mozart, Haydn, Bach and Handel. When his father fell seriously ill, Bruckner was called upon to return to his family in order to replace him as schoolmaster and music teacher, no mean task for a youngster of twelve.

Upon his father's death, Bruckner left for the Volksschule in St Florian, where he followed a regular course of instruction supplemented by lessons in piano, organ, violin and music theory. In 1840 he moved to Linz in order to receive teacher training and worked as a student-teacher in various places. Meanwhile, time permitting, he devoted himself to music-making and composition. In 1848 he became organist at the Stiftkirche in St Florian. Following a successful performance of his *Mass in B flat*, Bruckner decided to leave teaching and dedicate himself fulltime to composition and performance. In 1856 he became organist at the cathedral in Linz, a distinguished position which carried a stipend commensurate with the dignity of the post. But as a composer he remained very unsure of himself and so decided to study 'modern' compositional techniques and counterpoint. For the latter, Bruckner went to Otto Kitzler, conductor of te theatre orchestra in Linz, whose performances of Wagner's *Flying Dutchman* and *Tannhäuser* had made a confirmed Wagnerian of the aspiring composer. He remained in Linz until 1868, the year in which his first symphony was given its première. He then moved to Vienna where he taught music theory and organ at the conservatory and paid regular visits to the Wagner-paradise of Bayreuth. As a composer he was frequently exposed to heavy criticism, but as an organist his career was extremely successful. He was a much praised organ improviser and made a number of tours, including visits to France and Germany. Criticism of, and even outright hostility towards, his compositions owed much to his great admiration for Wagner and his borrowing of Wagner's ideas, while failing to develop his own individual style.

event it is a slow dance with a continuous bass-line, over which various instruments improvise. The form was adopted and assigned strict rules by seventeenth- and eighteenth-century composers. One of the most famous is by J.S. Bach (for organ in C minor, BWV 582). Unlike a typical theme with following variations, in a passacaglia the theme is heard uninterruptedly, with variation supplied by secondary figures worked in above, below or within it. Symphonically it was a very unusual form and it almost seems as if in this movement Brahms wished one more time to display his classical training. The idea runs throughout the entire symphony, although it is only in the finale that this uncommon form is actually employed.

Brahms borrowed the theme from his great predecessor Bach, from the latter's cantata BWV 150 *Nach dir, Herr, verlanget mich*, from the section *Meine Tage in den Leiden, endet Gott dennoch zu Freude*. In the very first measures of Brahms's symphony elements of it are recognizable in the melody and the bass. Another recognizable figure is the descending succession of thirds. In the first three movements this manner of treating the melody returns repeatedly. In the first movement, allegro non troppo, all these elements are exposed and give to the entire symphony an elaborately cohesive character. The second movement, andante moderato, with a horn theme, is highly concentrated and economically written. Using various procedures, Brahms makes the most of every small melodic, harmonic and rhythmic figure. The third movement, allegro giocoso, is a sturdy rhythmic scherzo, neither charming nor lightweight, but storming onward to the big finale, in which the theme is introduced by the brass at full strength.

As the first performance showed, the fourth symphony was not an immediate popular success. The conductor Hans von Bülow championed the work, and took it on tour. When the Vienna Philharmonic played the symphony on 7 March 1897, Brahms, extremely ill, was in attendance. At the close of the first movement an ovation went up from the audience, and this was repeated after each of the successive movements. So four weeks before his death, Brahms received enthusiastic acclaim for this work.

Anton Bruckner

The nine – or rather, eleven – symphonies by Bruckner had little popular appeal in the composer's time, and caused a certain amount of misunderstanding. On the one hand Bruckner was an advocate of the innovators Wagner and Liszt. On the other, he reached backward to baroque methods of composition, particularly in his use of sequences, repetitions, to move from one theme or key to another. Bruckner paid little heed to the length of a symphony as established by Beethoven. He was a proponent of the large form, thus continuing the line of Schubert and following in the footsteps of Wagner. But his 'baroque' methods and refined contrapuntal treatment of themes stood in direct opposition to these expansive formal tendencies. Among Bruckner's teachers was Otto Kitzler, conductor of the theatre orchestra in Linz, whose performances of Wagner's *Flying Dutchman* and *Tannhäuser* made a deep impression on Bruckner and transformed him into a confirmed Wagnerian. He drew the antagonism of the Viennese critic Eduard Hanslick, who was devoted to Brahms and wanted nothing to do with Wagner. And Hanslick, a leading critic who set the tone, tore Bruckner's work to pieces, abetted, though somewhat in the background, by Brahms. Neither composer cared for the other's work. Bruckner did find an admirer and follower in Gustav Mahler, who made a piano arrangement of the third symphony and conducted the première of the sixth in 1899.

In addition to their exceptional length, Bruckner's symphonies are remarkable for the use of the long organ-like 'pedal-points' and long silences between various sections within movements. Bruckner himself jokingly called his second symphony the 'Symphony of Silences'. On a number of occasions he used three themes in the outer movements and sometimes in the slow movements as well. Such a third theme usually makes its appearance in unison passages, which has led some authors to see a connection with Gregorian chant, not so much in the melody as in its essential atmosphere. Another of Bruckner's frequently encountered hallmarks is the so-called *Gesangsperiode*: two melodies appearing simultaneously, the lower one treated contrapuntally in relation to the upper. This is especially true for the second themes of sonata-type movements. Bruckner was originally an organist, familiar with the works of Bach and, as a result, with counterpoint.

A typical Bruckner symphony begins with a quiet tremolo in the strings. From this a theme blossoms forth while the accompanying tremolo rises

Facing page: Brahms in his study, at the end of his life.

Above: The Belvedere, where in 1891 Bruckner was invited to live by the Emperor Franz Josef.

Wagner's death in 1883 inspired Bruckner to compose the adagio of his seventh symphony. In 1891 Bruckner accepted a pension from the conservatory. Able to walk only with difficulty and subject to respiratory problems, he received an offer from the Emperor Franz Josef to come and live in the Belvedere Palace. He gave up all regular work and devoted himself entirely to the completion of the ninth symphony, a goal he did not achieve, despite the efforts he made up to and including the very day of his death, in Vienna on 11 October 1896. During the memorial service held in the Karlskirche, the adagio from his seventh symphony was played under the baton of Hans Richter in an arrangement for brass made by Bruckner's pupil Ferndinand Löwe. Johannes Brahms observed the coffin being carried into the church and left muttering: 'Soon it will be my turn.' Scarcely half a year later he too was dead.

Bruckner's body was interred in the Stiftskirche in St Florian. In addition to his nine symphonies, Bruckner composed a number of motets, organ works, a Te Deum, several Masses, a Requiem and several chamber works.

Ernest Chausson

Ernest Chausson (1855-1899) studied law at first, and only entered the Paris conservatory at the age of 25, staying only a year with Jules Massenet before leaving to study privately with Cesar Franck until 1883. A well-to-do man, Chausson wrote very little considering the fact that he could devote all his time to composition. Only sixteen years remained for him to work before he was killed in an accident near Nantes while riding his bicycle when only 44. Chausson worked very slowly and carefully which may explain the limited size of his oeuvre.

Chausson became famous to a certain extent in his role as secretary of the Société Nationale de Musique. His opera, *Le Roi Arthur,* for which he was also responsible for the libretto, had its première four years after Chausson's death, in 1903, and not in France, but in Belgium. His *Symphony in B Flat* (1890) was performed for the first time in Paris in 1897. Chausson's music is definitely a product of the Franck school, but there are traces of Wagnerian influences as well, especially in his symphony. The composer was not a confident man, rarely daring to promote his own works for performance. His *Poème for violin and orchestra* is still well known. He also wrote some especially beautiful lieder, reminiscent of Duparc.

Camille Saint-Saëns

Camille Saint-Saëns (1835-1921) was writing music by the time he was six years old. Born in Paris, he was an exceptionally gifted pianist, and was admitted to the Conservatoire for study in piano and organ when he was thirteen. His piano and organ career - he was organist at the church of the Madeleine in Paris - progessed splendidly, but as a composer he was not immediately appreciated. He was reproached for being too 'heavy', and was so easily and uncritically influenced as to be unable to develop any individual voice until later in his life. Of his three symphonies, the third, known as the *Organ Symphony*, has become far and away the most popular. He also wrote concertos for violin (3), cello (2), and piano (5), symphonic poems, including *Danse macabre*, and a great deal of chamber music. Of his thirteen operas, *Samson et Dalila* is the only one still to enjoy a measure of popularity. But most famous of all is *Le Carnaval des animaux*, a work which its composer was terrified would earn him a reputation for frivolity.

to a crescendo. In his finales Bruckner tends to follow the same procedure. Other characteristics are: an increasingly shorter and more highly-accented rhythm, a rhythmic use of the triplet, the frequent repetition of main themes for full orchestra with long rests between phrases, chorale melodies as third themes and the conclusion of a symphony with a long coda restating all the themes expansively.

Bruckner seems to have derived his orchestral colours from the organ. Sound-groups are blended to function almost like organ registers. In principle he thought in terms of a typical nineteenth-century orchestra. For the last two symphonies he used a double complement of woodwinds, four horns, two trumpets, three trombones, timpani and strings. And the larger forms he indulged in added forces, including piccolo, triple woodwinds, triple brass, bass tuba, timpani, harp and strings. (The eighth symphony includes a part for three harps.)

Although one generally speaks of Bruckner's nine symphonies, he in fact composed eleven. The *Exercise* symphony in F minor and the 'Symphony No. 0' in D minor were not considered seriously enough by him to be included in the numbering. Bruckner was working on the last movement of his ninth symphony on the day he died. He was unable to complete it.

Bruckner was a sensitive person and touchy in matters of criticism. The barrage of criticism he received drove him to rework his symphonies. Sometimes he did this himself, sometimes he delegated the work to his students. Revisions had mainly to do with the instrumentation and abridgement of, in particular, the sequential passages. Confusion about the various versions, or *Fassungen*, of Bruckner's symphonies is still great. His revisions may be summarized as follows:

The first symphony was written between 1865 and 1866 and received the nickname *Linzer*. The work was revised in 1868, 1877 and 1884. In 1890 Bruckner reworked the symphony for the fourth time, creating the so-called *Viennese* version. The first performance took place in 1868 in Linz under the direction of the composer.

The second symphony was written between 1871 and 1872. He reworked it in 1873 and conducted the first performance in that same year. Further revisions took place in 1875–76, 1877, 1878 and 1891.

The third symphony has three important versions. The first version was made between 1872 and 1873, and reworked in 1874. The second version was written between 1876 and 1877 and Bruckner conducted its first performance in the latter year. The third version was written in the years 1888–89.

The fourth symphony has two versions, the first dating from 1874, the second from 1878 and completed in 1880, the composer adding a new scherzo. The first performance took place under the direction of Hans Richter in 1881. Bruckner reworked the finale five times.

The fifth symphony was begun in 1875 and completed in 1876. The first two movements were revised by the composer in 1877–78. The first performance took place in Graz in 1894 under the direction of Franz Schalk, but the composer was too ill to attend the première.

The sixth symphony was written between 1879 and 1881. Several movements were played in Vienna in 1883 under the direction of Wilhelm Jahn.

The seventh symphony which Bruckner began in 1881, underwent several modifications after its completion in 1883. The first performance took place in Leipzig in 1884 under the direction of Arthur Nikisch. This is the only symphony which has remained virtually unchanged.

The eighth symphony exists in two versions. The first was written between 1884 and 1887, the second, between 1889 and 1890. In the same period Bruckner also returned to the first symphony, creating the so-called *Viennese* version.

The ninth symphony remained incomplete and unmodified. Bruckner began work on it in 1887. The last movement, adagio, dates from 1894.

Wagner's Festival
theatre at Bayreuth in
1876, the year of its
completion.

Anton Bruckner in
1893, by Anton Miksch.

Facing page, above: The beautiful monastery of St Florian, on the Danube, where Bruckner was first a student, and later organist and choirmaster.

Facing page, below: Liszt with his daughter Cosima, who was later to marry the gentleman on her left, Richard Wagner. At the right of the picture (painted by Cosima's mother, the Countess Marie d'Agoult) is the German writer on music, Hans von Wolzogen.

Above: Bergen, Norway, the birthplace of Grieg in 1843.

Johannes Brahms. He was forty-three years old when he unveiled his first symphony before the public.

Wagner's birthplace in
Leipzig.

Wagner's caricature,
drawn by André Gill in
1861.

The versions listed above are those made by the composer. Confusion is increased by revisions made by his students Franz Schalk and Ferdinand Löwe. They prepared the symphonies for publication and shortened them substantially. Halfway through the 1930s a heated discussion arose when, on the initiative of Max Auer, Robert Haas and Alfred Orel, among others, the original versions of the fifth and ninth symphonies were performed. Schalk and Löwe had little defence against the charge that they had mutilated Bruckner's symphonies. The original manuscripts of the fifth and ninth symphonies were lost at the publisher's. Knowing that his works had not achieved publication undamaged, Bruckner had fortunately bequeathed authentic manuscripts to the library in Vienna. On the basis of these, more or less original versions of his symphonies could be published and played. It would be too complex to treat all Bruckner's versions and the editorial modifications in this chapter; those interested are referred to the *Essence of Bruckner* by Robert Simpson.

In 1980, in Bruckner's home town of Linz, a symposium was held concerning these matters and published in 1981 under the title *Die Fassungen*. Here, insofar as possible, the original versions are taken as the most authentic.

In addition to the problem of the *Fassungen*, Bruckner's music gives rise to another difference of opinion. Some see in him a worthy musician who, in his symphonies, did not express himself to the best of his ability. True enough, they do not differ widely from one another.

Others see a religious character in Bruckner's orchestral work. The author Frank Wohlfart divided them into three categories. Symphonies nos. 3, 5 and 9 are the most sacramental. The relation to God and worship speaks most strongly from them because of their chorale-like themes. Symphonies nos. 4, 6 and 7 have a less exalted atmosphere and awaken an idea of sensitivity to nature. The first, second and eighth symphonies all share the same key of C minor, the 'fate key' of Beethoven's fifth symphony.

Symphony no. 1 in C minor – Linzer

Like Brahms, Bruckner was no longer young when he wrote his first symphony. He was forty-one when he completed it, and revised the work in 1890. The allegro begins in march time, leading to the introduction by the violins of a gentler melody. A quick, very loud climax follows. The woodwinds put forward a lyrical second theme, one of the so-called

Franz Liszt

Franz Liszt (1811-86) was born in Hungary. He was a prominent and revolutionary figure in many areas of life: as a pianist he introduced innovative virtuoso piano techniques, as a composer he created the 'symphonic poem', as a writer he left to posterity an intelligent analysis of the music of his time. His pianistic gifts were unequalled, and he first made his reputation travelling Europe as the greatest virtuoso in the world.

After many travels and wanderings as a concert musician, he retired from the concert platform and took up residence in Weimar, where he became director of the *Musikhochschule*. This was in 1848 and the previously tranquil town of Weimar was transformed into a centre of great prestige within the musical world. His unparalleled success earned him a great deal of money, allowing him to lead an untroubled and aristocratic existence. With his fortune he made generous contributions to various musical institutions and gave aid and support to a number of less fortunate fellow-musicians.

Between 1835 and 1839 he carried on a notorious relationship with the Countess Marie d'Agoult. The liaison produced three children, one of them being Cosima, who was later to marry Richard Wagner after a failed marriage to Liszt's pupil, the conductor Hans von Bülow.

In addition to an enormous output of piano music, Liszt wrote the *Faust* and *Dante Symphonies*, symphonic poems such as *Les Préludes*, and *Mazeppa*, church music, songs and two piano concertos. He also made a large number of piano arrangements of such works as Beethoven's symphonies, Schubert's songs and selections from Wagner's operas.

Liszt playing the piano for some friends, including (standing behind the piano) Berlioz and Carl Czerny.

Wagner in Bayreuth,
accepting the
congratulations of his
admirer, Anton Bruckner.

César Franck

César Franck (1822-90) was taken to Paris from his native Liège by his father, when the boy's gifts as a pianist had made themselves apparent at a very early age. At the Conservatoire, he astonished his teachers with his virtuosity, which was only hampered by a shy and retiring temperament. Perhaps for this reason Franck became progressively more involved with the organ, where the performer is safely shielded from the public gaze. After graduation, he earned his living as an organist in Paris, though his majestic compositions for the instrument failed to achieve much popularity.

Later he became professor of organ at his old *alma mater*, the Paris Conservatoire, and aroused the hostility of his colleagues Saint-Saëns and Gounod, for devoting much of his lesson time to the teaching of composition. (His pupils included d'Indy, Duparc and Chausson.) As a composer himself, Franck matured late, and his greatest music - including his D minor symphony - was written after the age of sixty. He died as the result of an accident with an omnibus, just as his compositions were beginning to win him the fame he so richly deserved.

Gesangsperioden. After a long sequential passage, a third theme is proposed by the trombones. The movement concludes with the same accentuated rhythm that began the work in the violins.

The second movement, adagio, begins with a low horn introduction over a dark rhythm played by the strings. After a theme from the cellos, the dynamics are quickly raised in a crescendo. The flutes, followed by the clarinets, introduce the next melody. At this point the violas repeat the accompaniment to the first theme, played earlier by the violins. The woodwinds remain important throughout the entire adagio.

The following scherzo, the third movement, makes a fresh, dance-like impression. A certain influence of the Austrian peasant dance can be felt. The simple theme is repeated many times and by means of ample repetitions leads to a contrasting trio with a lovely horn motif.

The finale is built around two energetic themes. The first has a 'Wagnerian' brass colour; the second is given to the more peaceful violins. The sound-level of this movement causes one to suspect the use of an extremely large orchestra, though this is not the case. The work ends in a happy, assertive C major.

Symphony no. 2 in C minor

Bruckner began this work in London in 1871. In this composition he makes an impression of someone with too many symphonic ideas at once, unable to develop all of them. The symphony was at first poorly received by both the public and the critics, and Bruckner struggled for a long time to adapt himself to the standards of others.

The Vienna Philharmonic Orchestra played the symphony twice, and then consigned the score and orchestral parts to the archives, judging it to be a work of little interest.

The moderato first movement opens with a characteristic *tremolo* from the violins, after which the cellos introduce a theme. The second theme is again a *Gesangsperiode*. The third theme is played by the woodwinds over a relentlessly rhythmic bass. In the development the three themes are handled contrapuntally.

The andante is written in a simple form, with two themes alternating. The first theme is initially played by the violins, and the second by the horn. At the end of this second movement there is a quotation from Bruckner's own Mass in F minor, taken from the *Benedictus*.

The scherzo is monothematic. The single theme is developed harmonically in a variety of ways.

The first theme of the following finale recalls the opening theme of the first movement. The two themes of this finale are handled by Bruckner in a broad and expansive manner. Again there is a quotation from the Mass in F minor, this time from the Kyrie.

Symphony no. 3 in D minor
The third symphony is one of the most Wagnerian, and was in fact dedicated to that composer. The first version of the work contains quotations from Wagner's operas, namely, *Die Walküre, Tristan und Isolde* and *Die Meistersinger*. Later Bruckner removed these quotations, but dedicated the work to Wagner and in doing so, pronounced the death sentence for the symphony, which was thoroughly damned by the fashion-setting, anti-Wagnerian critic Eduard Hanslick. Although not a direct quotation, the opening theme of the symphony strongly recalls the beginning of *Der fliegende Holländer*.
The first movement is not one of Bruckner's strongest compositions. He seems unable to develop the lovely opening theme. The second theme is a *Gesangsperiode*. Triplets predominate rhythmically in this movement, but the impression given remains static.
The succeeding adagio makes a classical-Romantic impression, with lovely string melodies. The tension built up from juxtaposition of musical ideas in this movement is finally resolved in a rapturous and tender conclusion.
The third movement is a boisterous dance, such as can also be heard in the first symphony, although this movement leaves behind a less passionate impression.
The first theme of the finale has its origin in the first theme of the opening movement. The second theme is played by the violins, supported by a chorale-like accompaniment in the brass. A third theme, played by the wind instruments, bears out the work's liturgical character with a deceptively innocent chorale melody.

Symphony no. 4 in E flat major – Romantic
The fourth symphony has become the most popular of Bruckner's symphonies. The work underwent its last revision in 1874. In 1954 Hans Redlich made a new reworking of it, prompted by the belief that so many years after the composer's death, it would be good to assemble all the successful parts in a new version.
The first movement, *Ruhig bewegt*, begins with the customary string tremolo, above which is sounded a motif played by the horn. Bruckner continues with this idea until the introduction of the second theme, consisting of an up-and-down melody of two 'long' notes, followed by a triplet, a rhythmic figure so typical of the composer, and pastoral in character. In the development Bruckner exploits these elements, in contrary motion, repetitions and miraculous harmonic transformations. The movement concludes with an extensive repetition of the first horn theme.
The andante which now follows is written in sonata form. After a short introduction the cellos begin the mournful first theme. The second theme is also unfolded by the cellos, and a chorale melody can be heard at the end of the exposition. Following the development and repetition of all the themes, the movement ends with a coda in which only the first theme is used, with solemn, quiet sounds upon the kettledrums.
The third movement, bewegt, scherzo , leaves behind the impression of a typical Austrian hunting party. The contribution of the horn recalls this strongly and the entire movement is dominated by the brass. The melody of the trio has its origins in the folk tradition and is reminiscent of the ländler.
The fourth movement, bewegt, doch nicht zu schnell, opens like the first movement, softly with dissonant harmonies. The introduction grows in tension and culminates in a dynamic forte with the customary triplets and emphatic use of the brass. The horn theme from the first movement

Richard Wagner

Even today Richard Wagner (1813-83) remains probably the most controversial of all composers. Points of dissent are his so-called revolutionary spirit, his individual vision of Christianity and his anti-Semitism.

His anti-Semitic writings have frequently, though somewhat exaggeratedly, been taken as the basis of Hitler's ideas on such matters. His life-style has also drawn criticism: he led a life of great luxury, a speculating 'swindler' who spent money like water, constantly borrowing and seldom repaying his debts.

Wagner is of no significance whatsoever as a purely orchestral composer. His great strength lay in his operas, from such early attempts as *Die Feen* and *Das Liebesverbot* to his sublime masterpiece *Der Ring des Nibelungen*, and his creation *Gesamt-kunstwerk*, a synthesis of music, literature, painting and theatre, all of it conceived, written and directed by one man: Richard Wagner.

Wagner's influence on musical life was enormous, and he took no account of established values in regard to music. He put down on paper what he heard in his thoughts; nothing like this had ever happened before. The compulsive power of his approach found many followers - as well as opponents - among composers in Western Europe.

Hector Berlioz

Hector Berlioz (1803-69) was the son of a doctor, and born near Grenoble in the French Alps. As a child he showed no special musical ability, and never achieved mastery of any instrument. It was not until he went to Paris to study medicine that he became infatuated with music and attended the Conservatoire.

Unfortunately he also became infatuated with a neurotic English actress, Harriet Smithson, who was playing a season of Shakespeare in the city. The relationship gave him a love of Shakespeare's plays, which stayed with him for the rest of his life. (They married, and were divorced in 1840; Harriet was by then a truculent alcoholic.) But their stormy courtship also inspired his magnificent *Symphonie fantastique*, which he subtitled 'Episodes in the life of an artist'.

But is is not for any great symphonic output that Berlioz is remembered. He was concerned with many forms of music, and possessed a unique talent for imaginative orchestration. Works such as his great Requiem, the operas *Benvenuto Cellini* and *The Trojans*, and the extraordinary concerto/symphony for viola and orchestra *Harold in Italy* (which he wrote for Paganini) are some of the inspired products of his marvellous imagination.

But as well as listening to his music, another delight for music-lovers is a shrewd and witty volume of memoirs he wrote, documenting his extraordinary life.

is heard again. After a pause, the strings introduce the second theme. In this movement Bruckner again struggles with the development of a surplus of thematic material. He creates themes open to too many possibilities and seems unable to make decisions. He obliges himself to keep to the classic sonata form, but it is clear that his ideas lie outside the boundaries of this form. Harmonically, marvellous things happen in this movement, recalling Wagner; and Bruckner concludes the symphony with the horn-call from the first movement.

Symphony no. 5 in B flat major

In the first movement Bruckner gradually builds up tension in the home key of B flat. The piece begins adagio with pizzicato cellos and double-basses and a melody in the bassoon and violas. The composer then drifts off into more remote keys. Not until the allegro does the main key sound in the minor mode. It is a dynamic movement, in which strings are often doubled in octaves, and have some enchanting melodies to play.

The adagio is more quietly balanced harmonically. The first theme begins in the minor, played by the oboe. The second theme consists of intervals of a seventh. Again there are wonderful melodic passages for the strings.

After a typical and frisky scherzo, there follows a finale with an unusual form. Like the first movement, the finale begins adagio. The allegro is a fugue. After the complete fugue, the brass bursts forth in a festive and thrilling chorale.

Symphony no. 6 in A major
This symphony has frequently been judged a masterpiece, though it is perhaps less often performed than it deserves. The first movement, maestoso, opens very rhythmically, and the main theme dominates the entire movement. The adagio is made up of three contrasting elements: a wistful oboe melody, restrained but rhapsodic string passages, and a grim, purposeful march. The scherzo makes a poetic impression, but does have a ländler trio. The finale contrasts a busy march rhythm with less energetic tunes that Bruckner seems to have drawn from the countryside he loved so much.

Symphony no. 7 in E major
In the first movement the cellos, together with horn, violas and clarinet, play an exceptionally long and rapturous theme over an underlying tremolo. This dominates the entire movement: what follow are motifs rather than themes in the ordinary sense. The long, lyrical theme undergoes a number of harmonic transformations in this glorious hymn to nature.
The adagio contains many themes. While Bruckner was at work on his seventh symphony he was also occupied with the masses in F and D minor. Its tragic flavour was imparted by the news he received, while at work on this movement, of the death of his idol, Richard Wagner. For the first time he uses Wagnerian tubas, which play the movement's main theme as a quartet.
The scherzo is traditional, with a rhythmic but poetic trio for strings alone. The finale is characterized by a chorale melody as second theme, while the first theme bears a relation to the long melody from the first movement.

Symphony no. 8 in C minor
The eighth symphony is the last Bruckner completed. It was first performed in 1887, but again was not well-received. It is known that in this period Bruckner was no longer capable of coping with the rejections of conductors and critics, in addition to those of his own students. In the beginning of 1890 he revised the symphony and completed the revision on 10 March of that year. The winds play a very important role in the work, which is dominated by an inexorable 'fate' motif. A lyrical second theme tries to induce a gentler mood, but the remorseless rhythm of destiny returns to remove all optimism from this music.
The second movement is an invigorating scherzo, thus deviating from the expected succession of movements. The movement has an energetic theme, with a quiet trio. For the first time Bruckner uses a battery of harps.
The succeeding adagio is one of Bruckner's most interesting scores in terms of orchestration. The six-part division of the strings is particularly uncharacteristic of him. A dark main theme is alleviated by a chorale melody which constitutes the second theme, played by five tubas, and together these elements build the movement to a shattering climax. The finale is likewise on an enormous scale, and contrasts a number of different themes which are brought together in the movement's glorious coda as if to show that man, ultimately, is the master of his own destiny.

Symphony no. 9 in D minor
The last movement of this symphony is missing, and so the symphony ends with an adagio. It is on a large scale, nevertheless. Bruckner marked the first movement misterioso. The themes are all developed at mighty length, with a grave and powerful coda. The scherzo, in which the timpani play a prominent part, offers a series of variants and repetitions of a grim-sounding theme. The final adagio opens with chromatic harmonies. Wagner again springs to mind because of the abandonment of strict tonality, but there is no weakness in this heavenly music, that was to be the last Bruckner ever wrote. He did not live to see the symphony performed.

Richard Strauss

Richard Strauss (1864-1949) has no connection with the waltz king of Vienna. He was born in Munich, where his father was a horn player in the opera orchestra. During his student years, he received much help and encouragement from Hans von Bülow, who in 1885 procured for him the prestigious job of assistant director of the celebrated Meiningen orchestra. The next year he became third conductor at the Munich Opera and worked hard to perfect his conducting skills, while at the same time writing some attractive, if not outstandingly original, music. It was not until 1889 that he produced his first major work, the 'tone poem' *Don Juan*.

In this and other orchestral works, *Till Eulenspiegel, Also sprach Zarathustra, Don Quixote* and *Ein Heldenleben* for example, Strauss used orchestras of enormous size, and had detailed 'programmes' in mind for each of them. His fame grew all the time: in 1898 he became conductor of the Royal Opera in Berlin, and co-director of the Vienna Opera at the end of the First World War.

After his orchestral successes (and failures), Strauss turned to the composition of operas; between 1900 and 1940 he produced more than a dozen masterpieces for the stage, such as *Der Rosenkavalier, Elektra, Salome* (to a translation of Oscar Wilde's play) and *Arabella*. Many of these were written in inspired collaboration with the poet, Hugo von Hofmannsthal.

Salome, incidentally, shocked audiences with its frank portrayal of the heroine's lasciviousness, and Kaiser Wilhelm II declared that it would do the composer much damage - damage which, Strauss remarked, paid for his villa at Garmisch.

Above: Richard Strauss (seated), with his friend, the conductor Mengelberg.
Facing page: A letter from Bruckner to his friend Rudolf Weinwurm.

6
Tchaikovsky, Dvořák and Sibelius

The nationalists

1848, a year of rebellion, with the February uprising in Paris and the subsequent revolts in Germany and Austria, was not without repercussions in the world of music. Nationalistic sentiments, unleashed by the struggles for liberty, readily lent themselves to expression in musical terms. Chopin, in the first half of the century, was one of the earliest to give utterance to such feelings, followed, in some cases considerably later, by Smetana and Dvořák in Czechoslovakia, Bernard Zweers in Holland, Jean Sibelius in Finland and Mikhail Glinka in Russia.

Nationalism developed variously with each composer, never manifesting itself twice in exactly the same way. In Tsarist Russia, a group of five composers, comprising Alexander Borodin, Mily Balakirev, César Cui, Modest Mussorgsky and Nicolai Rimsky-Korsakov (in addition to their hero Glinka), laid great emphasis on the national character in their music, finding their inspiration in the national folk idiom, in Russian history or in the beauties of the Russian countryside.

Tchaikovsky's was a case of another sort. Like his teacher Anton Rubinstein, composer of six no longer performed symphonies, he opposed the blatant expression of nationalistic feeling, considering this to be superficial and searching for a more direct connection with the Western musical tradition. His symphonies excel, not in matters of form, but in their strikingly melodic nature. That these melodies often derived from folk music Tchaikovsky freely admitted, arguing for their appropriateness not as evocations of nationalistic sentiment but as simple mementos of his early youth in the country. Tchaikovsky thus takes his place in history as a 'Western' Russian nationalist, exhibiting a Western European approach to composition, yet nationalistic in spite of himself, due to this persistent use of Russian musical elements.

Anton Dvořák's development took place along different lines. At that time Czechoslovakia was part of Austria, but the year 1848 saw the emergence of strong patriotic feelings in Bohemia and Slovakia, sentiments which received great encouragement from Northern Italy's successful secession from the mighty Austrian empire in 1859.

The cry was increasingly heard for a national theatre in which dramatic and operatic productions would be performed in the Czech language. In November 1862 this dream became a reality. Bedřich Smetana, at the forefront of Czech composers, energetically devoted himself to the organization of a national musical life and the composition of typically Czechoslovakian works, operas in the native language and symphonic poems with nationalistic ties, of which *The Moldau* from his *My Fatherland* is the most celebrated example. Within the national patriotic struggle an internal feud was also smouldering between Slovakia and Bohemia. Although Dvořák in his first three symphonies did not concern himself overtly with nationalism, once he had come under Smetana's influence by studying the older composer's works in detail,

Tchaikovsky at about the time of his disastrous marriage.

the expression of Bohemian ideals and atmosphere began to be heard in his compositions. In his fifth symphony of 1875, despite its conspicuous debt to Beethoven, this tendency is unmistakable. Dvořák's so-called 'Slavic period' is generally conceived of as ending with the sixth symphony of 1880, but the Bohemian element is by no means absent from the subsequent symphonies. Even the ninth, the famous *From the New World*, written in 1893 shortly after the composer's arrival in the United States, represents a mixture of the new American and the old Bohemian worlds.

Of the three composers under discussion, Jean Sibelius is probably the only one who, for a considerable period at least, can be regarded as a conscious exponent of nationalism. Freedom to make use of the national language was a continual point of contention in the wars of independence waged in the second half of the nineteenth century. Already as a schoolboy Sibelius became fascinated with the great Finnish national epic, the *Kalevala*. This, together with Nordic mythology and nature poetry, in which he professed an extreme interest, formed an inexhaustible source of musical inspiration. In 1892 Sibelius married Aino Jarnefelt, daughter of an influential military officer and leading advocate of the use of the Finnish tongue. This milieu and the struggle for independence from Russia served to intensify Sibelius's national consciousness. Only in 1904 did he distance himself from expressly nationalistic Romanticism. The label of 'nationalist' is due not only to Sibelius's use of folk material, but more importantly, to the atmosphere, so difficult of description, which his music distils.

The symphonies of Tchaikovsky and Sibelius may be seen as high points in their respective national symphonic traditions, those of Dvořák, as the basis for a new national symphonic order. Tchaikovsky and Dvořák are alike in their utilization of conventional forms, in contrast to Sibelius who pursues an entirely individual course in each of his symphonies. Of the three, Tchaikovsky is prominent as an orchestrator, Sibelius as an innovator and Dvořák for his eclecticism.

Tchaikovsky

Tchaikovsky himself was well aware that whatever distinction his symphonies possessed, they were not shining examples as regards form. His strength lay, not in the development of long movements with well-knit structures, but in the realization of shorter, simpler forms, the scherzo, the waltz or the march. This 'deficiency', as he called it, undoubtedly arose from his strong affinity for melodic invention. Not only his symphonies *per se*, but all his large-scale instrumental compositions are based chiefly upon lyricism and melody, enriched by appropriate harmonies and orchestral colouring. To his patroness Nadezhda von Meck he expressed regret that so much of the melodic material he devised had to be discarded or completely reworked in obedience to the practical dictates of form. Hardly surprising then, as he continued throughout his lifetime to struggle with the classical ideals of orderliness and structural organization, that his admiration for Mozart knew no bounds.

Always averse to the mere stringing-together of 'empty' phrases and harmonies, he developed an antipathy towards programme music, music based upon an underlying story. Music, for Tchaikovsky, must itself have something to say, without external allusions.

Tchaikovsky did not take an active part in the contest then current in Western Europe between the adherents of Brahms, with his respect for classical design, and those of Wagner, with his rejection of this tradition in favour of freer, more organic structures. But he did nonetheless take sides by choosing the conventional symphonic form as the vehicle most suitable for the expression of his Romantic musical ideas.

Mozart remained for Tchaikovsky a kind of master teacher on paper, but his true source of inspiration was the lyric stream of Russian folk music and Italian opera. He professed a great liking for the operas of Verdi and

Piotr Ilyich Tchaikovsky

Piotr Ilyich Tchaikovsky was born in 1840 in Wotkinsk, a remote area of Russia, and died in St Petersburg in 1893. His father was director of the state mines in Wotkinsk. The Tchaikovsky family showed little interest in culture and was not musically inclined. In the charge of his governess the ten-year-old future composer left for St Petersburg where he began studies in law. Interested in music as he was, he took piano, voice and music theory lessons. At nineteen he left law school and took a job as a functionary in the Ministry of Justice. Three years later he resigned and registered as a student at the newly-founded conservatory in St Petersburg, whose director was Anton Rubinstein. A few years later he left St Petersburg to accept a position as teacher of music theory at the equally new conservatory in Moscow. This appointment was due to the intervention of Anton Rubinstein who recommended to his brother Nicolas, the conservatory's new director, to engage Tchaikovksy's services, taking him into the family. This occurred literally, as Tchaikovsky lived for a considerable time in Nicolas's home. In 1877 Tchaikovsky was given the opportunity to stop teaching in order to concentrate entirely on composition. This he could permit himself because his new rich admirer-friend, the widow Nadezhda von Meck, supplied him with a yearly income. In addition to composing, he worked as a music journalist for a Russian paper.

Shortly before he met Nadezhda von Meck (in writing alone, they never met in person), he was married for a very short while to Antonina Milyukova. The alliance lasted ten weeks. The relationship with von Meck lasted until 1890. She broke off all ties with him on the pretext of no longer having sufficient financial means. Tchaikovsky travelled frequently and far. He visited Italy, England, France, Switzerland, the United States, and heard Wagner in Bayreuth.

Much speculation surrounds his death. The official version is that he died from cholera after drinking a glass of contaminated water. Unofficial sources speak of suicide, and the most recent information points to his being sentenced to take poison by a secret tribunal as a result of a homosexual relationship with a nephew of the Tsar. One piece of evidence against the cholera theory is the fact that Tchaikovsky's body lay in state, whereas this was strictly forbidden for those dead of cholera, due to the danger of contagion. He was buried in the artists' cemetery on the Alexander Nevsky Prospect in St Petersburg. In addition to symphonies he wrote a large number of chamber works, ballets, concertos and operas, the latter including *Eugen Onegin*, *Mazeppa* and *The Queen of Spades*.

Paul Dukas

Paul Dukas (1865-1935) entered the Paris Conservatory in 1882 where he studied with Mathias, Dubois and Guiraud. His cantata, *Velléda*, won a second Grand Prix in Rome. Dukas also wrote two unpublished overtures as well as unpublished lieder, symphonic sketches and choral works.

In 1892, an overture that Dukas composed for *Polyeucte* by Corneille, was performed. In spite of the obvious Wagnerian influence, Dukas was instantly recognized as a French compositional talent with a great future in store for him. His *Symphony in C major* followed in 1896, premièring under Paul Vidal to whom the work is dedicated. The Andante of this piece made an extraordinary impression at the time. A year later, Dukas himself conducted the première of *L'Apprenti sorcier* at the Société Nationale de Musique; this work especially secured fame for the composer and instantly became standard repertoire for all major orchestras. It is a symphonic scherzo on a ballad by Goethe. With its logical development, ironical rhythms, furious movements and brilliant scoring, this piece became a model for new compositions in a far from simple genre. This classic was followed in 1901 by *Sonata in E flat minor*, reminiscent of Beethoven, and *Variations, interlude and finale* on a theme by Rameau. Dukas honoured his friendship with Debussy in 1921 with *La Plainte, au loin, du faune*. In spite of all these successful works, Dukas truly came into his own as a composer in the world of opera. His comic opera in three acts, *Ariane et Barbe-Bleue* (with a text by Maurice Maeterlinck), was performed in 1907 at the Opera Comique in Paris. This was the first of many operatic successes.

Between 1910 and 1913, Paul Dukas was professor of orchestral direction at the Conservatoire, and from 1913 until his death, he taught composition at the conservatory as well as at the Ecole Normale de Musique. Dukas was an extraordinary teacher, inspiring his students to understand musical techniques as the mere tools of expression in the service of more important creative, musical ideas. Dukas was also greatly admired as a music critic. He contributed to many journals and papers. Dukas was an officer in the Légion d'Honneur and inspector for the Beaux Arts. He succeeded Vincent d'Indy as chosen president of the Union Syndicales des Compositeurs. In 1934, under great pressure from its members, Dukas also took on the presidency of the Academie des Beaux Arts. His energy was in high demand; he dedicated himself entirely to the tasks at hand. In his later years, his health suffered as a result, but Dukas remained faithful to his responsibilities.

Dukas's limited amount of compositions is the result of his unscrupulous self-criticism and perfectionism. However limited in number, all his works are monuments to his poetic and sensitive nature.

Rossini, frequently performed in St Petersburg at that time; and with Bizet's *Carmen*, which he came to know during a short stay in Paris, he maintained an almost love-sick infatuation throughout his life. This opera's permeating atmosphere of inevitable fate transmuted into musical terms of frequently sparkling tunefulness, vitality and even gaiety, a contradictory atmosphere so similar to the character of Tchaikovsky's own music, could hardly fail to captivate him.

Tchaikovsky's masterly technique as an orchestrator is of the first importance. The author Preston Stedman gives seven typical characteristics which combine to produce Tchaikovsky's highly individual and expert orchestral sound-colouring:

1. Rhythmic motifs are generally given to the brass and woodwinds.
2. Expressive melodies are played in octaves, usually by strings or woodwinds.
3. Orchestral families are kept strictly apart and only instrumental groups which accord well are used simultaneously.
4. Scale passages frequently serve to decorate important melodies or harmonic figures, most notably when leading to a climax.
5. Strings are often required to play pizzicato.
6. Melodies for woodwinds are preferably given to the instruments' lower register.
7. All instruments are assigned equal importance.

Tchaikovsky wrote all his symphonies for the typical symphony orchestra of his time, without recourse to the larger forces called for by such composers as Wagner or Mahler.

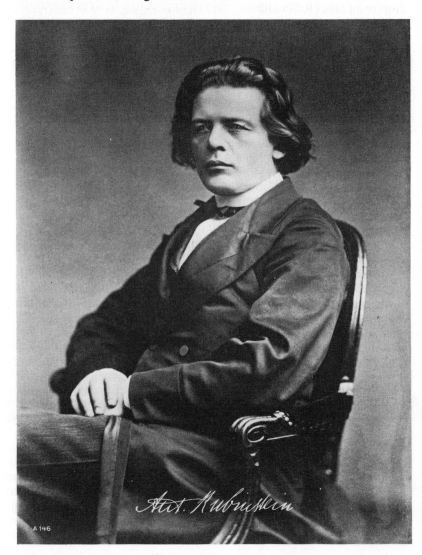

Anton Rubinstein, hailed in his lifetime as a great symphonist, is remembered today as the teacher of Tchaikovsky, a much greater one.

Symphony no. 1 in G minor, opus 13 – Winter Dreams

Tchaikovsky's work on his first symphony resulted in a case of almost total nervous exhaustion as he laboured ceaselessly far into the night in order to produce his first symphonic creation. Despite his dislike of programme music, he did give a loose programme to the work by himself calling it *Winter Dreams* and assigning a title to each of the first two movements, 'Winter Daydreams' and 'Forlorn country, misty country'. The country was most certainly Russia, the use of a country or place as a musical 'hero' having been foreshadowed by Mendelssohn with his *Scottish* and *Italian* symphonies and his *Hebrides* overture.

In February 1866 Tchaikovsky began work on the symphony, which was always to retain a special place in his heart. Having orchestrated the entire work between June and November of that year, he showed it to his teacher Anton Rubinstein, with whom he entertained extremely cordial relations and who had recently procured for him a teaching position at the Moscow Conservatory. Rubinstein condemned the work out of hand. Tchaikovsky approached the director of the Conservatory, Nicolas, Anton's brother, requesting a public performance of one movement of the symphony, the scherzo. The request was granted, but the performance was not a success. Tchaikovsky took the advice of Anton Rubinstein to heart and rewrote the symphony in accordance with his recommendations. The final version was completed in 1883 and first performed in Moscow on 1 December of that year, under the direction of Nicolas Rubinstein. Neither in the West nor in Russia has the first symphony achieved firm status in the repertory, although, despite its many formal imperfections, it remains a fresh and charming work. The third movement, scherzo, marks the beginning of a new tradition in symphonic history, a true dance movement, its trio Tchaikovsky's first symphonic waltz. The last movement, which makes use of the folk song *The garden is in bloom*, can be considered one of the first examples of the so-called 'festive Russian finale'. In his subsequent symphonies, the sixth excepted, Tchaikovsky also favoured such exuberant finales. Tchaikovsky himself regarded *Winter Dreams* as a valuable souvenir of his cherished youth.

Symphony no. 2 in C minor, opus 17 – Little Russian

Tchaikovsky began work on his second symphony in 1872 while staying with his sister Alexandra and brother-in-law Lev Davidov on their estate in Kamenka in the Ukraine. Not surprisingly, a few Ukranian folk tunes are present in the work, accounting for its nickname of *Little Russian*, i.e. Ukranian, given to the symphony by the critic Nicolai Kashkin. The score was met with great enthusiasm by fellow composers who were adherents of nationalistic expression in music. Yet it had not been Tchaikovsky's intention to express himself in a nationalistic manner. He regarded the folk-songs only as promising melodic material for symphonic treatment and in the entire work only three actual folk tunes can be isolated.

The first movement begins with a lengthy introduction, andante sostenuto. A solo trumpet, followed by a bassoon, against pizzicato accompaniment form cellos and basses, play a Ukranian variant of the folk melody *On the banks of Mother Volga*. At the conclusion of the movement, this melody is again quoted in its entirety. The rest of the melodic material is original. Two of the most striking original themes make their appearance in the brilliant allegro vivo and are developed along traditional lines.

Prompted by the success of his first opera, Tchaikovsky began a second in 1869. But this second attempt, *Undine*, was a failure and retaining only a few successful sections, he destroyed the score. One of these commendable fragments was the wedding march intended for the opera's third act. Tchaikovsky used this march as the second movement of his symphony. In place of the expected slow movement we encounter an andantino marziale. The first theme, introduced by the clarinets and

Anton Rubinstein

Anton Rubinstein (1829-94) was a pianist and composer who had received his training in Berlin. As a pianist he was a strong competitor of Franz Liszt, and was instrumental in setting up the conservatories in St Petersburg and Moscow. His brother Nicolas was a first rate pianist and conductor.

Anton Rubinstein is of minor importance as a composer. His *Melody in F* is practically his only composition which is still known, although he did write six symphonies and some symphonic poems, including *Russia*.

Zdenek Fibich

Unlike the great Czech masters, Smetana and Dvorak, Zdenek Fibich (1850-1900) was the son of rather well-to-do parents; his musical education was therefore more orthodox than that of his famous colleagues. From 1865 until 1867, Fibich studied at the Conservatory in Leipzig, harmony with Richter and piano with Moscheles. In 1868, he studied for a year at the Conservatoire in Paris, finishing up his studies with Vincenz Lachner in Mannheim.

Fibich returned to Prague in 1870, where he married Ruzena Hanusiva. He took on a teaching position in Vilna, but resigned in 1874 due to the ill health of his wife. Ruzena Fibich died shortly thereafter, and Fibich married his sister-in-law, Betty Hanusova, a well-known singer at the National Theatre in Prague. Fibich was appointed second conductor at this same theatre, staying on there until 1878. He then went on to conduct at the Russian Church until 1881, when he resigned to spend more of his time composing.

Zdenek Fibich's life ran smoothly, as lives of composers go, until he met Anezka Schulzova in 1893. Fibich became so involved with this woman, that he abandoned his family for her. For the rest, we know very little of his life, even how the composer died remains for the most part a mystery.

Fibich demanded the very best from himself as a composer. His music is very personal, and can in that way be compared to Delius. Influences of Liszt and Wagner can be heard especially in his later pieces, but the reserve which dominates most of Fibich's works, is evidence of a strong empathy with French music. Harmonically, Fibich was very progressive for his time. But he was at his most original in terms of dynamic. Most of his best passages are marked pp or ppp. He was the first to play with the notion that important musical ideas could be very effective when whispered, not screamed. Fibich's originality in the use of soft dynamics is what often gives his compositions their unusual strength.

Fibich's works for orchestra all date from the years 1873 to 1893. There are 7 *Symphonic Poems*, 3 *Ouvertures* and 2 *Symphonies*. His *Third Symphony* he finished in 1898. All his symphonic works are very well structured. *The Second Symphony*, for example, is completely built up out of the two themes from the first movement, but in such a subtle way, that only through studying the score, does this structure become apparent. This ability to conceive such refinement of structure, makes Fibich the undisputed master of Czech symphonic music.

César Cui

César Cui lived from 1835 to 1918. He was the son of a French army officer who had remained in Russia and a Lithuanian mother. He received his musical education from Moniuszko. Cui was a qualified engineer and worked in this capacity. In addition he was not only a composer but also a music journalist for Russian, French and Belgian publications.

An early ninetheenth-century view of St Petersburg, then one of the most beautiful cities in the world.

Mily Balakirev

Mily Balakirev, born in 1837, began his studies as a mathematician and applied himself to musical studies and composition on the side. He worked as a pianist and music teacher in St Petersburg. In 1857 Mussorgsky and César Cui became his students. Four years later Rimsky-Korsakov joined the group and again a year later, Alexander Borodin. In 1868 he became director of the music academy in Leningrad and conductor of the city's orchestra. For several years he withdrew completely from musical life and took a job with the railway. In his last years of composing he wrote a great deal of piano music. His most important works include the oriental fantasy *Islamey* for piano, various overtures on Russian national themes and several symphonies which are no longer performed.

bassoons, is a dark–hued military melody. The second theme provides a rhythmic response to the first, and the third theme is again a folk song, *Spin, fair spinner*, a melody Tchaikovsky had treated in his earlier collection for piano duet, *Fifty Russian Folk Melodies*, published in 1868–69.

The third movement of the second symphony is a spirited scherzo whose fluctuating rhythm (3/8, 2/8) recalls folk music, though the material is original. The main theme of the fourth movement is another Ukranian folk song, the then very popular *The Crane*, followed by a series of variations. A strongly rhythmic second subject forms an appropriate counterbalance to the popular melody.

The first performance of the second symphony took place on 7 February 1873 in Moscow. Tchaikovsky reworked the entire first movement in 1879. The final version, as we now know it, was first heard in St Petersburg on 12 February 1881.

Symphony no. 3 in D major, opus 29 – The Polish
The third symphony hardly represents a high point in Tchaikovsky's symphonic output. Rather than an example of deeply-felt creative genesis, the work was for the composer a form of creative therapy necessary after another of Anton Rubinstein's harsh judgments, stated in no uncertain terms, this time of the composer's first piano concerto. It is the only symphony in a major key and the only one having five movements. In this work, Tchaikovsky gave himself almost entirely over to strict formal considerations and was later to look back on it as a decisive step forward in his struggle with form. The fifth movement, in the style of a polonaise with the marking tempo alla polacca, gave the symphony its nickname, *The Polish*, despite the total absence of any other Polish elements, or even of Russian folk melodies.

The symphony begins with a funeral march leading into an allegro brillante. The second movement resembles an Austrian ländler and bears the marking alla Tedesca. Notable here is the generous use of pizzicato in the strings accompanying the melody. The following movement is an andante elegiaco, its themes typically Tchaikovskian in their melodiousness. The fourth movement is a short, brilliantly orchestrated scherzo which recalls Mendelssohn, and the fifth movement is the above-mentioned virtuoso polonaise. The first performance took place in Moscow on 19 November 1875, under the direction of Nicolas Rubinstein.

Symphony no. 4 in F minor, opus 36

The story of the birth of the fourth symphony marks in two respects a significant point in Tchaikovsky's life. It was at this time that he began his long correspondence with Nadezhda von Meck. In 1876 he received from her an insignificant musical commission, but the contact thus established was to grow into an extensive and intimate exchange of over a thousand letters. Under the one stipulation that they were never to meet, the extremely wealthy Madame von Meck undertook to furnish Tchaikovsky with an income sufficient to provide for his material needs, permitting him to set aside his teaching and to devote himself entirely to composition. As an expression of this strange intimacy, Tchaikovsky dedicated his fourth symphony to Nadezhda von Meck, inscribing 'Dedicated to my best friend' on the title page of the score, in accordance with her wishes to remain anonymous. In his letters the composer refers again and again to 'our symphony'.

It was also at this same time that Tchaikovsky, in order to put a stop to (partially imagined?) rumours regarding his homosexuality, took the decision to marry. Perhaps he even hoped, by means of this marriage, to find a solution to his struggle with homosexuality itself. In any event, on the spur of the moment he married a young student who adored him, Antonina Milyukova. Within a few weeks the marriage proved disastrous and Tchaikovsky was nearly driven to suicide, a prompt divorce his only salvation.

Again in spite of his rejection of programme music, Tchaikovsky provided this symphony with a programme, explaining the argument himself in letters to Nadezhda von Meck. The first movement, andante sostenuto; moderato con anima, begins with a sweeping fanfare indicative of irrevocable fate 'which hangs like a sword of Damocles above our heads'. This same fanfare brings the movement to its conclusion. The oboe, which plays the melancholy theme of the second movement, andantino in modo di canzona, represents the composer's own disposition, the sorrowfulness and pain of the past. The third movement, scherzo, pizzicato ostinato, portrays dreaming, fantasies providing an escape from reality. The pizzicato sections are inspired by the sound of the balalaika. This movement's trio, with its drunken oboe melody, is 'the memory of inebriated farmers', as Tchaikovsky wrote to Madame von Meck. The fourth movement, allegro con fuoco, is an uncommon explosion of passion and fire. Critics have frequently objected to this finale, reproaching Tchaikovsky for having created nothing more than a piece of noisy vulgarity, but if we are aware that the composer had in mind a faithful rendering of a typical Russian revel, we must admit that the musical portrayal conforms admirably to reality. The main theme of the finale is again a folk song, *A birch stood in the meadow*. The fate motif of the first movement suddenly re-emerges, but does not succeed in extinguishing the celebratory fervour.

The world première took place in Moscow on 22 February 1878 under the direction of Nicolas Rubinstein.

Symphony no. 5 in E minor, opus 64

For the first time, it was Tchaikovsky himself who, on 17 November 1888, conducted the first performance of one of his own compositions. Ten years elapsed between the premières of the fourth and the fifth

Charles Gounod

Charles Gounod (1818-1893) was born of an artistic family. His father was a painter (Grand Prix de Rome in 1783) and his mother was a gifted pianist who gave him his first music lessons. In 1836, Gounod entered the Conservatoire in Paris. He won the Second Prix de Rome in 1837 and the Grand Prix in 1839. The influence that Gounod's travels to Italy had on his work are very clear. There, he studied the great Italian masters, especially Palestrina. Gounod's music was heard for the first time in Vienna in 1842, where his *Mass* for three a capella voices was performed. Travelling through Austria, he came in contact with Schubert's work. In Berlin, he met Mendelssohn.

Back in Paris, Gounod studied theology as an external student at a seminary, and made music only in his role as church organist. It seemed that he would enter the priesthood, but Gounod realized in time that he was not really suited for such a life. During these years of retreat, the composer did study works by Schumann and Berlioz. He re-entered the musical world in London, surprisingly enough, where his *Messe Solenelle* for soloists, choir and organ in G major was performed in 1851 to great critical acclaim.

Gounod was, despite his varied interests, destined to spend most of his composing talents in service of the theatre world. 1851 saw the première of his first opera, *Sapho*. His opera *Faust* premièred in 1859 in the Theatre Lyrique, instantly propelling him to the top among living composers. His operas, successful as they were, were very different from Mozart's, and this is surprising as Gounod was a known devotée of Mozart's work. Gounod wrote of his admiration in his book 'Le Don Juan de Mozart', published in 1890.

Gounod was truly a great musician and orchestral master. His ambition was to try all musical forms, and he wrote several symphonies, two of which have survived. These symphonies have been successfully performed by the Association des Jeunes Artistes. These works are, however, second in importance to the rest of Gounod's pieces.

Tchaikovsky photographed with his bride in 1877.

The title-page of
Tchaikovsky's *Manfred*
Symphony, dedicated to
Balakirev.

Reinhold Glière

Despite his Belgian ancestry, Reinhold Glière (1874-1956) is
considered a Russian composer, conductor and teacher. His
father was a wind instrument builder. As a young boy and violin
student, Glière was already busy composing pieces that were
then played by the many musicians that visited his home. In
1884, Glière went to study violin and composition at the music
school in Kiev. He entered the Conservatory in Moscow in 1894
to study violin, harmony, counterpoint, composition and instrumentation. Glière earned his diploma by writing an oratorium on
a text by Byron: *Heaven and Earth*. After graduation, he found
work teaching, but also devoted time to composing; lieder, 2
soloconcertos, piano pieces and his *Second Symphony* (dedicated to Koussevitsky) were soon realized.
From 1905 until 1907, Glière studied direction with Oscar Fried
in Berlin, and returned to début as a conductor in Russia in 1908.
His symphonic poem, *The Sirens* was a great success for him
also in 1908. He finished his *Third Symphony 'Ilia Muromets'* in
1910.
Glière was appointed to the Conservatory in Kiev in 1913; the
following year, he became director of the same institute. Glière
returned to live in Moscow in 1920, working as a music pedagogue there, but also busying himself with social work. He
toured many times, taking advantage of his travels to study the

Below: Tchaikovsky, by
this time the grand old
man of Russian music.

symphonies. In the intervening period Tchaikovsky had devoted
himself chiefly to opera, both as composer and conductor, acquiring a
certain international renown and making, as guest-conductor, a tour
throughout Europe. His diary speaks of meetings with Brahms, Dvořák,
Gounod, Grieg and Massenet. At the conclusion of this journey, he took
up residence in a house in the country near the village of Klin, a tranquil
setting which afforded him great pleasure and allowed him to find the
necessary discipline for intensive composition. In a few summer months
the fifth symphony had been written, and although Tchaikovsky did not
rate it as highly as the fourth, it has become one of his most popular
works. Again Tchaikovsky seems unable to completely avoid a
programmatic idea behind the music, several notations making the programme, at least for the first movement, quite clear: 'Complete
abandonment to fate, or rather the inscrutable ways of Providence.
Allegro: murmurs, doubts, complaints, reproaches to XXX! Must I
throw myself into the arms of faith?'
Whether or not Tchaikovsky with XXX had in mind a specific person is
unclear. More unlikely he was referring to his greatest problem, his
homosexuality. If we consider the first movement in the light of the
aforementioned notations, the beginning of the movement, andante,

can be called the 'Destiny theme', introduced by the clarinets. The following allegro con anima, also put forward by the clarinets, expresses the 'murmurs and doubts'. For the rest Tchaikovsky leaves us in uncertainty, although the 'Destiny theme' repeatedly recurs throughout the work. It is said of the second movement, andante cantabile, con alcuna licenza, that it is expressive of love which cannot be attained. Tchaikovsky however gives no indication to this effect. The movement begins with an imperishable horn melody, followed by a counter-melody introduced by the oboes. It is a highly emotional section, full of drama and tenderness, dynamic outbursts and unremitting changes of tempo. Midway through, the 'Destiny theme' reappears. The theme of the third movement, valse, allegro moderato, derives from a song which the composer had heard in the streets of Florence. The waltz's trio begins with spiccato violins which later return to embellish the re-capitulation of the principal waltz theme. Here again we find, very near the end, a reminder of the 'Destiny theme', softly played on low clarinets. The finale begins with the 'Destiny theme' in E major rather than minor, the first step toward the victoriousness which characterizes the entire movement. After the introductory andante maestoso, a rhythmic allegro vivace flares into life, building to a bombastic but triumphant conclusion.

Symphony no. 6 in B minor, opus 74 – Pathétique
Tchaikovsky's final and most important symphonic work is the sixth symphony. The name *Pathétique*, suggested by his brother Modest, came to replace the original name given to the work by the composer himself, that of *Programme symphony*. A symphony with a story, but not one to be told in words. Tchaikovsky confided to his cousin Vladimir Davidov that the programme arose from deep personal feelings and that during the symphony's composition he often found himself in tears. The day before the première Modest paid a visit to his brother at home and discovered him worrying anxiously about the problem of a suitable name, as the score was to be sent off that same day to the publisher. 'Tragic,' suggested Modest at first, then, 'Pathétique'.
The idea for the symphony was born during a concert tour. At the beginning of 1893 Tchaikovsky conducted in Brussels, then went on to Cambridge where he joined the illustrious company of Grieg, Bruch and Saint-Saëns as the recipient of an honorary doctorate. In Cambridge he conducted *Francesca da Rimini*; in London, his fourth symphony. Back in Russia, he directly set to work on the elaboration of his ideas and in a matter of weeks the symphonic score was ready for performance.

national folk culture of his country, and the music of this culture. Many of his compositions were thus affected by the national music of Russia, the Ukraine, Azerbeidsjan, Uzbekistan and other Soviet republics. In the first few years following the revolution, Glière was put in charge of the office of Music and Education in Moscow, where his reputation as a composer was equalled by his fame as an organizer of concerts and pro-grammes for the working class.
In 1923, Glière went to study the culture of Azerbeidsjan. He based his newest opera, *Sah Senen* on what he found there. In the same manner, Glière based his opera *Hulsara* on the sounds he heard in Uzbek. These were followed by Ukrainian songs.
Glière became president of the Union of Composers in Moscow in 1937. He has been honoured with both the Order of the Red Banner and the Order of Achievements, as well as an honorary doctorate for his studies of musical folklore.
The two most important phases of Glière's career as a composer were quite different. His early period was clearly aimed at the west: he was then strongly influenced by the conservative trend at the time, namely, western classicism and romanticism. Later on, Glière turned to face the East, becoming, through his travels and studies, an important promoter and transcriber of the indiginate music of the Soviet republics.

A group of Tchaikovsky's friends bidding farewell to the composer as he leaves Tiflis for a trip to France (1886).

Antonin Dvořák

Antonin Dvořák was born in 1841, the son of a café owner and village butcher. The only trace of musical schooling in his early life was his active participation in the village orchestra. Only when he was fourteen years old did he begin to receive regular musical instruction.

Talented as he showed himself to be, he went on to a music academy in Prague, the Organ School. His studies were paid for by an uncle who was a man of means, after which he played the viola and worked for eleven years in the orchestra of the Czech opera. In 1873 he married Anna Cermákrová, a contralto in the opera's chorus. They had six children, several of them dying young. From the moment he left the Organ School he devoted himself to composing. A nationalistic work for chorus and orchestra, entitled *The Lands of the White Mountain*, was a success and procured him enough money to take the risk of leaving his job with the orchestra in order to apply himself chiefly to composition. His career progessed smoothly. In Vienna he made the acquaintance of Brahms and of Hans von Bülow, who was to champion his work.

Dvořák travelled and was repeatedly acclaimed. In Cambridge he became an honorary doctor of the university and he was awarded this same tribute by the university of Prague in 1890. From 1892 to 1895 he was director of the conservatory in New York and after he returned to Prague, he became artistic director of the conservatory there.

Dvořák wrote symphonic poems, chamber music, concertos, works for chorus and orchestra, for a cappella choir, short works for orchestra (including the celebrated *Slavonic Dances*), operas such as *Rusalka* and *Armida*, many songs and works for piano solos.

Tchaikovsky conducted the première in St. Petersburg on 28 October 1893. The title page of the manuscript bears a dedication in Tchaikovsky's own handwriting to his beloved cousin Vladimir 'Bob' Davidov.

Although we officially know very little about the programme behind the sixth symphony other than that it moved the composer profoundly, it is allowable to speculate on the probabilities governing these emotions. Three years earlier Nadezhda von Meck had written to Tchaikovsky, breaking off their relations. A year later his sister died and at the same time he was confronted with the deaths of three good friends. It is perhaps likely, though we have no way of knowing for certain, that his own death greatly occupied his thoughts.

In any event the sixth symphony is a symphony in which death plays an undeniable rôle. Notes found among Tchaikovsky's papers after his death indicate that the symphony was an expression of 'life, love, disappointment and death'.

The first movement, allegro non troppo, begins with a low bassoon melody, supported by threatening harmonies from the strings and giving rise to the first theme. The well-known second theme, often referred to as the 'love theme', is introduced by the strings, undergoes a development involving many changes of tempo and subsides into a slow pianissimo played by a bass clarinet. A startling outcry from the full orchestra ushers in an allegro vivo which, after substantial development leading to a climax, is followed by the melody of a burial hymn deriving from the Russian Orthodox liturgy. The first movement is brought to a close by brass and woodwinds accompanied by pizzicato strings.

The second movement, allegro con grazia, is an orchestral waltz, distilling an airy charm, but at the same time by no means alien to Tchaikovsky's despondent temperament. The 5/4 time signature gives the waltz a halting character which continues throughout, even in the trio, as if the music were locked within an impenetrable and relentless circle.

The third movement, a march, allegro molto vivace, has been considered by some critics to be a funeral march and is certainly one of the most marvellous that Tchaikovsky conceived. The movement builds with intensely dramatic tension, variations on short motifs rising through descending scales for full orchestra to a tremendous climax.

The fourth movement, adagio lamentoso, is an unusually lengthy section for the conclusion of a symphony. The strings begin with a downward leaping theme and the entire movement is characterized by descending melodies and changes of tempo. The symphony ends with a hushed pianissimo bassoon melody over darkly coloured ostinato strings.

In addition to the six symphonies, Tchaikovsky composed a truly programmatic symphony, the *Manfred Symphony*, inspired by Balakirev, who himself devised the programme, based upon Lord Byron's dramatic poem. It is an elusive programme, full of earth, air and water, Alpine sprites and magical enchantments. The symphony is not a particularly inspired composition and Tchaikovsky himself remained ambivalent towards it. This elusive quality, together with the work's great length and difficulty, has caused *Manfred* to be seldom performed.

At the beginning of the 1960s sketches were found for an eighth symphony in E flat major, dating from 1892. The work was reconstructed by Bogatreiv and given in performance, but has not gained acceptance as a true symphonic creation of Tchaikovsky.

Antonin Dvořák

Dvořák's style is characterized by a continual alternation between the 'Germanic' style and nationalistic sentiments manifested in the use of folk material. Modality and rhythms rooted in the folk tradition are a constant feature of his nine symphonies.

Dvořák was influenced by many other composers, but chiefly by

Brahms, whom he much admired. Yet Beethoven's influence can also be clearly heard in short pithy motivic statements or the long-spanned themes of the slow movements. Schubert provided a rich lyrical stimulus and is recalled in certain modulations and the manner in which themes are repeated. Some harmonic progressions bring Wagner to mind.

Dvořák made no clear decision to compose in a nationalistic way. Nor did he choose sides in the then prevailing contest between followers of Brahms and followers of Wagner and Liszt. He constructed his symphonies along traditional lines, while indulging in freer compositional techniques by writing a fairly large number of symphonic poems. The influence of Smetana on Dvořák's nationalistic manner of composing has already been mentioned.

Orchestral composition absorbed Dvořák throughout his lifetime, the orchestra apparently being the best 'instrument' with which he could express his creativity. His chamber and vocal music was written either in periods of repose or concurrently with orchestral works and operas.

Dvořák is a less interesting orchestrator than Tchaikovsky, clear and transparent but more conventional. His fundamental guideline was that everything must sound natural. A theme written for a particular instrument must conform to the individuality of that instrument. A violist himself, Dvořák wrote beautifully for strings, and his experience as a member of the village orchestra in Zlonice gave him a great affinity for wind instruments. He showed a predilection for the infrequently heard alto oboe and bass clarinet, and used horns, trumpets and trombones not only to supply harmonic weight, but for the introduction of themes. Harmonically, Dvořák may be thought of as a traditionalist.

The ninth symphony, *From the New World*, has become the most popular of Dvořák's symphonies – to the detriment of the other eight. And unjustly so, for the eighth symphony especially is most certainly its equal, and in fact each of them has its individual charm.

Dvořák is the typical nineteenth-century symphonist, avidly taking in all outside influences, yet developing his own personal, spontaneous, even occasionally naive style. Confusion due to various instances of deferred publication still exists as to how the symphonies should be numbered, and the numbering given is that of their order of composition.

Eduard Grieg

Gesine Judith Grieg, the composer's mother, was an accomplished pianist in Bergen, Norway. Married to the businessman Alexander Grieg in 1836, the couple had five children, Eduard (1843-1907) was the fourth. The further story of Grieg's youth and student years can be read in his autobiography, My First Success (1908). His first music lessons were given by his mother. The family home was, of course, full of music and Eduard was especially attracted to works by Mozart, Weber and Chopin. In 1838, one Ole Bull heard Eduard play at home, was so impressed, and convinced his parents to send him to the Conservatory in Leipzig for a proper education. Thus poor Eduard ended up at the famous institution as a lonely young boy of fifteen, an experience he would recall with disgust in his later years. Eduard's first piano teacher there was rather pedantic. He was only allowed to study Czerny, Kuhlau and Clementi, sterile music according to the unfortunate Grieg. His next teacher was more successful with the young Norwegian. A personal friend of Schumann's, this teacher interested Grieg in Schumann's music; his enthusiasm would last for the rest of his life. Later, Grieg studied piano with the famous Moscheles, and harmony and counterpoint with E.R. Richter.

While in Leipzig, Grieg was fortunate to be able to attend Gewandhaus Concerts. There he heard Clara Schumann play her husband's music, as well as performances of Wagner. Having returned to his birth place, Grieg gave a performance of his own *Piano pieces, opus one*, his first public recital. In that same year, he played Beethoven's C minor concerto as well.

The Norwegian government denied Grieg a scholarship in 1863, and angry Grieg left for Copenhagen, then the cultural centre of both Denmark and Norway. There he met Niels Gade, a well-reputed composer considered to be the leader of the Scandinavian romantic school and a personal friend of both Schumann and Mendelssohn. Gade was helpful to Grieg and encouraged him to be more productive. Gade sent Grieg away with the task of writing a symphony, something Grieg felt incapable of at the time. All over the eventual manuscript, the unsure composer had scribbled: Not Ready For Performance. Grieg's first symphony was never published as a whole, but the two middle movements are mentioned in his catalogue of works as *Two Symphonic Pieces for piano duo*.

Grieg has become very well-known for certain of his works: his *Piano Concerto* (1868), his *Holberg Suite* (1885), both *Peer Gynt Suites* (1876), piano works and lieder.

Dvořák's autograph of the first page of his 6th symphony, in D major.

Alexander Borodin

Alexander Borodinwas nine years old when he composed the piano polka *Hélène*. He was born in 1833, the son of a member of the nobility named Gedeanov. His exceedingly youthful interest in music was ignored and he was obliged to study medicine. He finished his studies in 1858 and became an army doctor. As a composer he was largely self taught. In 1864 he became professor at the academy of medicine in Leningrad. His best-known composition is the opera *Prince Igor*, whose ballet music the *Polovtsian Dances*, has become world-famous. *In the Steppes of Central Asia* is also regularly performed. He wrote two symphonies, and a third was completed by his fellow composer Glazunov. Borodin died in Leningrad in 1877.

Alexander Glazunov

Alexander Glazunov was a composer who became known as such at a very early age. In Weimar Franz Liszt performed one of his symphonies, which Glazunov had written at the age of sixteen. Glazunov left the Soviet Union in 1928 because of problems with the authorities, and established himself in Paris. He was born in 1865 and died in 1936. He was a composer of much chamber music, ballets, choral works and eight symphonies.

Max Bruch

Max Bruch (1838-1920), born in Cologne, was the son of a civil servant and an accomplished singer. His mother's family was also very musical. Young Max's musical development was watched carefully; he received his first lessons in Bonn from Breidenstein. It was soon obvious that Bruch had an exceptional talent. In 1852, Bruch received a four year scholarship to study in Frankfurt at the Mozart Gesellschaft. Later, he studied with Heller, Reinecke and Breuning in Cologne, already a little famous as a composer himself. Long visits to Leipzig and Munich were also important for his musical development. Between 1858 and 1861, Max Bruch taught in his native city where his operette *Scherz, List und Rache* (text by Goethe) was also performed. It was works for choir that brought Bruch fame in his own country (for example, *Frithjof-Scenen* for solo, men's choir and orchestra, opus 23).

In 1865, Bruch was appointed director of the Konzert Institute in Koblenz and in 1867, he became Kapellmeister to the Prince van Scharzburg-Sondershausen. Bruch quit these posts in 1870 to concentrate fully on his composition, first in Berlin and later in Bonn. His opera *Hermione* (based on Shakespeare's The Winter's Tale) was performed in Berlin in 1872 but was not very successful. Bruch conducted the Stern Gesellschaft in Berlin for

Symphony no. 1 in C minor, opus 3

The score of Dvořák's first symphony, written in Prague between 14 February and 24 March, 1865, was entered in a competition in Germany and mislaid. It was not until twenty years after the death of the composer that the work was rediscovered, and received its first performance in Brno on 4 October 1936. Dvořák remained unperturbed by the loss of the symphony, remarking, 'I'll simply write another one'. The symphony bears the name of *The Bells of Zlonice*, although there is no indication of this on the manuscript. The composer is reported to have mentioned this name to his students in Prague and it is by no means unthinkable that he may have associated the work with his youth in Zlonice. The symphony, with its extremely long finale, shows definite influences of Beethoven and Schubert.

Symphony no. 2 in B flat major, opus 4

The second symphony, inhabiting the world of Wagner and Liszt, is formally speaking Dvořák's weakest. The outer movements contain such a wealth of thematic material as to give an overall impression of excessive density and inadequate development. The score, completed on 9 October 1865, was fully rewritten in 1888 and received its first performance in Prague on 11 March of that year.

Symphony no. 3 in E flat major, opus 10

During the ten years which separate the second and third symphonies Dvořák concentrated on composition in other musical forms, writing much chamber music and two operas. The three-movement symphony was given its name of *Eroica* because of its ultra-Germanic character, and the shadows of Schubert, Beethoven and Wagner are indeed never far away. The symphony was completed on 4 July 1873 and received its first performance soon afterwards in Prague under the direction of Smetana.

Symphony no. 4 in D minor, opus 13

In this symphony, despite certain echoes of Wagner, Dvořák began to find his personal voice, with the emergence of nationalistic sentiments expressed in both melody and rhythm and orchestration of exemplary clarity and transparency. The slow second movement is significant in Dvořák's work as an example of the free-variation form. The third movement was played in public in 1864, and although the work was completed in its entirety in that same year, it did not receive its world première until 6 March 1892 under the direction of the composer.

Symphony no. 5 in F major, opus 76

This symphony was dedicated to the conductor Hans von Bülow, who described Dvořák as 'together with Brahms the most inspired composer of his time'. It is the most Czechoslovakian, or rather, the most Bohemian, of Dvořák's symphonies, unmistakably rooted in folk lore, the Furiant rhythm of the first movement's second theme being an obvious example. A work of youthful élan, it exhibits scarcely a trace of imitative neo-Romanticism. The orchestration was completed on 23 July 1875 in Prague, where the first performance was given on 25 March 1876.

Symphony no. 6 in D major, opus 60

A performance on 16 November 1879 of the *Slavonic Rhapsody No. 3*, given by the Vienna Philharmonic under the baton of Hans Richter, prompted the conductor to request that Dvořák write a new symphony for the orchestra. Thus the first signs of international recognition were on their way. The work has its origins in folk music. The traditional scherzo is replaced by a Furiant, a typical Czech dance, partially based on an actual folk melody. Despite echoes of Brahms – the same key signature as the latter's second symphony and a similar spirit in the final movement – the symphony fully inhabits Dvořák's own world.

Acrobats in Admiralty
Square, St Petersburg.

Riots in Prague in 1848.
That fateful year saw
revolutions all over
Europe, often
culiminating in fierce
fighting against the
powers of the great
Empires. Prague was
no exception, and was
the scene of a famous
bombardment before
being brought back to
order.

The Winter Palace at St
Petersburg in about
1836, the year that
Glinka's opera *A life for
the Tsar* – a milestone
in Russian music – had
its first performance.

Right: Rimsky-
Korsakov, and the
sumptuous cover of his
Sadko, opus 5.

A religious procession in Kursk, by Ilya Repin. The rich Russian folklore and the intense Orthodox religion were important sources of inspiration to the Russian nationalist composers.

Bedřich Smetana (1824-84) as a young man. His opera *The Bartered Bride* (1863) is the comic masterpiece of Czech music.

Slavonic dancing in Moravia. Dvořák was very sensible to Slav aspirations, and much of his music, such as the Moravian Duets, celebrated his native folklore.

Dedicated to Hans Richter, who considered this a great honour, the work was first performed in Prague on 25 March 1881.

Symphony no. 7 in D minor, opus 70
Dvořák's reputation continued to grow internationally and in 1884 he was given honorary membership of the London Philharmonic Society, which at the same time commissioned from him a new symphony. This was completed on 17 March 1885 and taken into the repertory of three conductors, Hans Richter, Hans von Bülow and Arthur Nikisch. Each of them gave successful performances, notably three in Boston under Nikisch, but it was Dvořák himself who first introduced the work to the public in London on 22 March 1885.
International recognition, the stimulus of the commission and the requirement Dvořák imposed upon himself to achieve a level of craftsmanship equal to that of Brahms in his third symphony combined to produce in the composer exceptional enthusiasm and single-mindedness as he completed work on the symphony. Moreover, he had set himself the challenge of adding a great work to Czech musical culture, and the entire composition radiates the exhilarating freshness of the Bohemian countryside.

Symphony no. 8 in G major, opus 88
Two features of the eighth symphony are immediately prominent, the variety of sentiments expressed, the wholesome, robust virility of the outer movements contrasting with the poetic, meditative mood of the middle two, and the conspicuous Slavic character, stronger than ever before, which infuses not only the melodies, but rhythms and harmonies as well. Dvořák wrote the symphony following a period of intensely emotional exertion while seeking rest and a renewal of energies in his house in Vyoská in Bohemia with its much-loved garden and surrounding woodlands and meadows. His intention was to produce a symphony unlike any that had gone before, to prove himself capable of developing thematic material in a totally original way. In this he

two years (beginning in 1878); he then became conductor of the Liverpool Philharmonic for three years. 1881 saw his marriage to Clara Tuczek, and in 1883, he led the Orchestra of Breslau, where he was to stay for seven years. The Hochschüle für Musik in Berlin named him professor of composition in 1892. Bruch has received honorary degrees from Cambridge (1893), Breslau (1896), and Berlin (1918) and he is a member of the Académie des Beaux Arts in France. In 1908, he received the Order of Accomplishments from the Prussians. Bruch retreated to Friedenau, near Berlin in 1910 for his last years.
At present, Bruch is known almost exclusively for his two violin concertos, the *Kol Nidrei Variations for Cello and Orchestra* and his *Ave Maria for Soprano* (from the cantata, *Das Feuerkreuz*).

Sergei Rachmaninov

Sergei Rachmaninov (1873-1943) is extremely well-known as the composer of solo piano works and piano concertos. But his compositional activities went further than piano playing and composing for that instrument. He wrote chamber music, choral works, a symphonic poem, songs and three symphonies.

Above: The composer and pianist Rachmaninov (right) with Eugene Ormandy, conductor of the Philadelphia Orchestra 1938-80. *Left:* A letter to Dvořák from Hans von Bülow. 'Next to Brahms you are the most excellent of composers', he affirms.

Bernard Zweers

Bernard Zweers (1854-1924) is referred to as the father of Dutch composition. He was an avowed nationalist. His vocal works have only Dutch texts. His third symphony, *To My Fatherland*, is still known. One of his choral works is still a favourite of male choirs, *The Big Dog and the Little Cat*.

PHILHARMONIC SOCIETY OF NEW YORK

FIFTY-SECOND SEASON, 1893-1894.

Synopsis of Compositions

TO BE PERFORMED AT THE

Second Public Rehearsal and Concert

ON DECEMBER 15th and 16th, 1893, AT

✷ MUSIC HALL ✷

ANTONIN DVORAK :
Symphony No. 5, E minor, op. 95 (Manuscript.)
"FROM THE NEW WORLD."

Above: An advertisement announcing the première of Dvořák's Symphony 'From the New World'. *Right:* Folk dances were the inspiration of many Slav composers in the nineteenth century.

succeeded admirably, for although he retained the traditional symphonic form, he contrived to charge the customary structures with enormous ripeness, naturalness and novelty of expression.

The first movement, allegro con brio, opens with a stately and ceremonious chorale, giving way to a second theme for cellos and winds, which returns as a motto figure throughout the movement, although never serving as developed thematic material. Marked use is made of the Mixolydian mode, suggestive of neither major nor minor, endowing the work with an unmistakable folk character.

In the second movement, an adagio in C minor, a dark mood predominates. Several critics have pointed to the similarity between this atmosphere and that of another of Dvořák's compositions, *In the Old Castle*. The stormy, agitated middle section of the adagio is followed by the return of the poetic theme in the violins.

The allegretto grazioso third movement is much lighter in character, free of emotional outbursts. An elegant and charming theme is introduced by the violins and undergoes a number of chromatic transformations.

The finale, allegro ma non troppo, is eminently robust and again strongly recalls the folk tradition. After a cheerful opening fanfare by the trumpets, the rigorously rhythmic main theme is announced by the cellos, followed by a series of masterly variations. A fast coda brings the work to a spontaneous close.

The symphony was written between 6 and 23 September 1884 in Vyoská, the orchestration completed on 8 November in Prague. The première was given in that city of 2 February 1890, followed by performances in London and Frankfurt, all under the direction of the composer.

Symphony no. 9 in E minor, opus 95 – From the New World
This, the most popular of all his symphonies, was completed on 24 May 1893, shortly after Dvořák's arrival as director of the conservatory in New York, a position he held from the latter part of 1892 until the spring of 1895. In the *New York Herald* of 12 December 1893 Dvořák refutes the opinion, then generally current, that he had made widespread use of negro themes. 'I borrowed not a single one of these melodies. I wrote my own themes, applying characteristics of Indian music and developing them by the use of modern rhythms, harmonies, counterpoint and orchestral colour.'

The 'American' element is most noticeable in the overall atmosphere: the Bohemian in busy Manhattan; an avidity for all things new.

The first performance took place in Carnegie Hall on 16 December 1893 and was immediately an overwhelming success.

Jean Sibelius

As stated earlier, of the three composers treated Sibelius was the one most conscious of his national background, evidenced by his symphonic poems *Finlandia, En Saga* and *Four Legends from the Kalevala*. In his symphonies, however, he turned away from nationalistic programme music to follow a highly individual path. His orchestral *œuvre* shows Sibelius to be a master of the orchestra with a deep instinctive understanding of form and a highly original approach to it.

None of Sibelius's symphonies serves as a prototype from which a general principle can be taken which would characterize them all. He never addressed himself twice in the same way to the problem of symphonic composition, arriving at a unique, though not always equally approachable style. Certain distinguishing features of his manner of composition can however be noted: a definite preference for minor key signatures, short motivic themes, frequent use of a descending fifth in the melodic line, usually falling on an unaccented beat, and the continual recurrence of darkly hued, sustained, static chords in the brass. As to the magnitude of the orchestra, Sibelius's music calls for little out of the ordinary. Woodwinds are doubled with added bass clarinet in the sixth symphony, together with four horns, three trumpets, three

Jean Sibelius

Johan Julius Christian Sibelius, better known as Jean Sibelius, was born in Tavastehus, Finland in 1865 and died in the same country in Järvenpää in 1957. He came from an academic milieu, his father was a doctor, and during his school years he developed a great interest in the *Kalevala*, the Finnish national epic. Another great source of inspiration for him was nature, and he loved the nature poetry of the Swedish poet Runeberg.

Later he studied composition with Martin Wegelius, a confirmed adherent of Wagner with little respect for Tchaikovsky, who had strongly impressed Sibelius in his younger years. In 1889 he went to Berlin for further study. Armed with a letter of introduction from the composer and pianist Busoni, he then went to Vienna in order to meet Brahms, but Brahms refused, and Sibelius returned to Finland less than two years later. In 1892 he married Arno Järnefelt, daughter of a leading propagandist for the Finnish language. His first sizeable work, the choral symphony *Kullervo*, was a great success. International recognition followed at the turn of the century. His work was played at the World's Fair in Paris and at the Proms under Sir Henry Wood. After 1925 he wrote no more works of significance. Only several light works came from his pen, written for money in order to pay for the large debts which resulted from his luxurious and selfindulgent life style. In addition to *Kullervo* and the seven symphonies, Sibelius wrote symphonic poems, including *Finlandia*, overtures, suites, chamber music, and a few works for other combinations of voices and instruments.

Bedrich Smetana

Bedrich Smetana (1824-84) was a composer, pianist and founder of the music school in Prague, a school which flourished thanks to financial assistance from Franz Liszt.

He spent a number of seasons in Gothenburg in Sweden, conducting the orchestra there, but he always remained a steadfastly nationalistic Czech. His best-known works are his string quartet *From My Life*, the opera *The Bartered Bride* and his cycle of symphonic poems *My Fatherland* which includes the world-renowned *Moldau*.

Nicolai Rimsky-Korsakov

Nicolai Rimsky-Korsakov, born in 1844, was a naval officer as well as a brilliant composer. During a sea voyage he wrote a symphony which proved to be a great success when performed. He became a pupil of Balakirev and threw himself wholeheartedly into composing. He was a very important teacher and conductor, whose most famous pupil was Igor Stravinsky. He was also the author of a book on the art of instrumentation which is still highly regarded. He wrote three symphonies, chamber music, choral works, operas, concertos and symphonic poems, including *Scherezade*. He died in 1908.

A set design for a 1930 Paris production of *Boris Godunov*. Thanks largely to Diaghilev and the Ballets Russes, Russian music of all kinds was especially popular in France.

trombones, timpani and strings. The first symphony calls for slightly larger forces, adding tuba, triangle, bass drum, cymbals and extra timpani.

The first two symphonies were written in what is referred to as Sibelius's Finnish period, the first, performed in Helsinki in 1894 and 1897, composed in the shadow of Tchaikovsky's *Pathétique*. The third is a product of composer's classical period. The fourth, dating from 1911, took shape at a time of unrest, and of personal malaise due to illness and the threat of the First World War. The fifth symphony, completed 8 December 1915 on the occasion of the celebration of the composer's fiftieth birthday, has been seen as an even more telling example of ominousness expressed in musical terms. The sixth and seventh symphonies date from the years after the war, years of full maturity.

After 1925 Sibelius composed no works of significance. In the early 1920s he may have began work on an eighth symphony, but even if it were completed, no trace of it has ever been found. His first large-scale piece for orchestra, the symphonic poem *Kullervo*, was suppressed by Sibelius during his lifetime and only rediscovered in the 1960s.

The first, second and fifth symphonies, as well as the one-movement seventh, are regularly performed. Less well-known is the fourth, a starkly powerful work, nonetheless, filled with intensely personal ideas and an unmitigated sense of brooding.

Symphony no. 4 in A minor

Reaction to the fourth symphony, first performed early in 1911, was more one of bewilderment than of approval. This was the first large-scale work Sibelius wrote following his serious illness. Suffering from cancer of the throat, he underwent an operation in 1908 which could scarcely fail to confront him, a dedicated *bon vivant*, with the sober questions of life and death.

The symphony's four movements are held together by a dominating motif which returns in each, the triplet. Sibelius seems to be foreshadowing his seventh symphony, which consists of a single continuous movement. Various symphonic elements recur in the fourth symphony, recalling the Wagnerian use of leitmotif.

In the first movement, tempo molto moderato, quasi adagio, seven basic motifs can be isolated, two of them being especially significant. The first is the triplet, used melodically as well as harmonically, the second is a

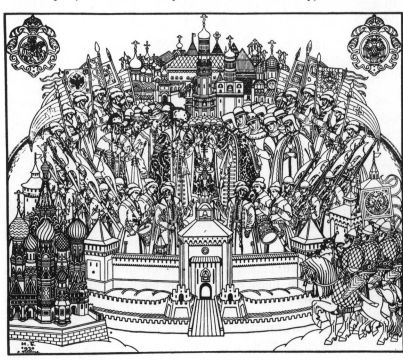

A caricature of the Czech composer Martinů by Ondrej Sekora.

short rising melody in major and minor thirds. After a brief development of these two ideas, the remaining figures are introduced. The almost primitive orchestration gives no evidence of a search for colouristic effects, the various motifs and fragments following one another without benefit of colourful linking material.

The second movement, allegro molto vivace, has the character of a scherzo, though Sibelius himself did not qualify it as such. The movement contains a large number of short themes, succeeding one another in various dance rhythms and in the majority of which the triplet again plays an important rôle. Despite the cadences of the dance, the movement displays no buoyancy or light-heartedness.

The third movement, il tempo largo, is one of the loveliest, as well as one of the most complex slow movements in all of Sibelius's symphonies. After some preliminary material based on short motifs, in which the triplet is again prominent, the main theme is stated by unison strings, an expansive melody constructed of smaller fragments.

The fourth movement, allegro, is also complex in structure. The main motif can be traced to the beginning of the symphony, with short melodies and triplets constructed largely of major and minor thirds. After an intricate development, the work dies away with soft indeterminate chords in the strings.

In Finland there was no great symphonic tradition before Sibelius. Neither have any significant works been written since his death. Sibelius seems to have been a unique high point.

In Russia however the symphonic tradition continued. Tchaikovsky's younger contemporary Glazunov composed eight highly Romantic, fairly unoriginal symphonies. Rachmaninov wrote three symphonies which are weaker than his piano concertos and Scriabin wrote his in a mystical-impressionistic style. In the Soviet Union Tchaikovsky is still regarded as a shining example for many composers, although no one has attained his greatness, unless an exception is made for Shostakovich, who, with difficulty and under political pressure, succeeded in developing a personal symphonic style.

In Czechoslovakia, Bohuslav Martinu was at first strongly under the influence of Smetana and Dvořák. He wrote his symphonies in America, but they are clearly Czech in character. In the compositional world of Czechoslovakia in the 1980s nationalism, often fostered by political circumstances, quietly persists. Martinu's six symphonies have a deeply-thought and intense musical feeling, and are loved by all who know them. Of no. 1, the American critic Virgil Thomson wrote: 'The shining sounds of it sing as well as shine . . . personal indeed is the delicate but vigorous rhythmic animation . . . the singing syncopation that permeates the whole work.'

Modest Mussorgsky

Modest Mussorgsky, world-famous for his *Pictures at an Exhibition*, was born in 1839 and was an officer of the regimental guard in St Petersburg. He appears to have been an excellent pianist, and listening to the original piano version of *Pictures at an Exhibition*, this is easy to believe. As a composer he was almost entirely selftaught. In 1859 he left the army to establish himself as an independent composer, but failed. His lack of compositional facility made the progress of his work too slow and too uncertain for building a career. He accepted a government job to earn a living, but took to heavy drinking and died from alcohol abuse in 1881. As a composer he is important for his operas, of which *Boris Godunov* is the best known.

Leos Janácek

Leos Janácek (1854-1928) received his musical education at the conservatories in Prague, Vienna and Leipzig, but quickly returned to settle in his fatherland where he remained for the rest of his life. In 1881, he founded an organ school in Brno where he was also conductor of the Philharmonic Society. Janácek was appointed composition professor at the new Conservatory in Brno in 1919.

Janácek was not noticed for a long time. However, in 1924, he was given an honorary doctorate at the University of Prague for his efforts on behalf of Czech music. Janácek, the third together with Smetana and Dvorak of the three Czech masters, relied on folk music for his inspiration, perhaps even more so than his two colleagues. He published Moravian folk songs together with Bartok and he wrote an article on their musical structure. On the other hand, Janacek's music is quite modern and independent. His efforts to combine the traditional elements of the folk culture of his country with contemporary musical ideas, caused his work to be dismissed by the general public for quite some time. It took a long time for audiences to appreciate the importance of Janácek and his work.

Janácek was also 40 before he began work on his first important piece, his opera *Jenufa*. It finally arrived in Vienna in 1918. Janácek was 60 before fame reached him. An unusual work, with an unusual orchestration (including 11 trumpets!), is Janácek's *Sinfonietta*. His *Slavic Festival Mass* appeared in 1928, combining religious and national elements in an inspiring manner. Janácek also left us with a theoretical work: 'Concerning Chords and their Progression', published at first in the Czech language.

7

Mahler

Gustav Mahler

Although the life of Mahler (1860-19110) has been the vehicle for a somewhat subjective film, it is not the stuff of which romances are usually made. Rather it is the story of a brilliant executive, an administrator who by the age of 37 had been appointed to one of the most prestigious posts in the musical world. Much of his music was composed between appointments at various opera houses throughout German speaking Europe, or else, during his incumbency at the Vienna Opera House, at his lakeside holiday home at Maiernigg, near Klagenfurt.

He was born in Kaliste, then part of the Austro-Hungarian Empire, and went to school in Iglau, now Jihlava in Czechoslovakia. He was the second child of twelve children, of Jewish parents. Five of his siblings died in infancy, a sixth child died at thirteen, a seventh of a brain tumour, an eighth committed suicide, and the surviving brother emigrated to America to escape importunate creditors. That let Gustav Mahler himself, and two sisters, who were his family security after his parents died. This depressing necrologue, though unremarkable a century ago, may have contributed significantly to the dark side of Mahler's creative development, or neurosis, as the practitioners of the new science of psychiatry were to term it.

As a child, Mahler showed promise as a pianist of talent, and his father supported his entry into the Vienna Conservatory, where he displayed a marked gift for composition. He left the Conservatory in 1878 to pursue a University course in musical philosophy, but this was discontinued. In 1880 he took up his first musical post as Musical Director for a summer season appointment in Hall, near Innsbruck. From that small-time job (during which, incidentally, he completed his first major work, *Das klagende Lied*, a cantata for voices and orchestra, originally intended as an opera) Mahler climbed steadily up the ladder of success. Those who engaged him were impressed by his drive and confidence; those subordinate to him were to find him intolerant and ambitious.

The following year he was at Laibach (Ljubljana, now in Yugoslavia) followed by an appointment at Olomutz, after which he returned temporarily, in 1883, to Vienna.

This was a significant time for Mahler; he visited Bayreuth and was profoundly affected by Wagner's *Parsifal*, and it was also the year when he finished the song-cycle *Lieder eines fahrenden Gesellen* (Songs of a travelling Journeyman), the result of a blighted love affair. An appointment at Kassel in Germany, which gave him the opportunity to conduct opera of a wide variety of styles, revealed his dissatisfaction with the inadequate, and two years later he took an appointment in Prague with a more competent company. But shortly afterwards the director went on tour leaving Mahler in charge, and Mahler began to shape the resources at his command. Although lack of time prevented his composing, the germs of the first two of his symphonies were

The music

Most listeners have been beckoned to Mahler's music through one of two doors: the shadowy adagietto of the fifth symphony (the *Death in Venice* music) or the giant architecture of the eighth – the *Symphony of a Thousand*. The universal acclaim now quite properly accorded to Mahler is actually a very recent phenomenon, due in no small measure to the success of that haunting film, the beauty of Venice being sensitively matched with music which was, at that time, relatively little known. A generation or two ago, Mahler's lack of popularity was due, on the one hand, to the conservatively-minded distrusting anything modern, while the modernists disparaged anything that savoured of a bygone era. Now, having stood the test of time, Mahler's music receives the veneration paid to old and respected masterpieces.

With the music of the masters such as Bach, Mozart, or even Beethoven, the craftsmanship, construction, and cleanliness of melodic line can be seen on mere perusal of the written music; but with Mahler, the heart-beats and the agony are not to be found on the page, but only by listening to, and experiencing, the sound of the music. One obstacle to the enjoyment of Mahler is the sheer length of the works; they are mountainous, to be sure, but the best view from a mountain is from the summit, not the foot.

At first, Mahler wrote lengthy descriptive explanations embodying non-musical imagery as programme notes for his symphonies – but these effusive 'programmes' were later discarded, even scoffed at, by the composer, who said that the music should be able to stand up without the crutch of a narrative. Even regarding the one movement of all his symphonies which was actually written to a programme – the 'Huntsman's Funeral' in the first symphony – Mahler declared 'it is quite irrelevant to know what is being portrayed; it is only important to grasp the mood of what is being expressed.'

And yet . . . Mahler was to find that music was not enough to express his moods. In the second, third, and fourth symphonies, and later in the trilogy which included the eighth, ninth, and *Das Lied von der Erde* (Song of the Earth) he calls upon voices to express the emotions he portrayed in words. And when he could not find, in existing literature, the texts to express his thoughts, he wrote the words himself.

In 1897 he wrote: 'Whenever a plan for a great musical structure occurs to me, I always arrive at a point where I have to call in words to convey my musical ideas. It must have been the same with Beethoven in his ninth' (wherein Beethoven adds his own words as an introduction to Schiller's poem). He may at the time have been planning his fourth symphony. But then, following the fourth, he embarked on the purely instrumental group of symphonies – the fifth to seventh – perhaps as if to prove to himself that he could write without the necessity for verbal expression. More remarkable is the fact that a composer who spent his life working with opera should never, despite several false starts, have written one himself.

The symphonies

One of the ways in which Mahler expresses the agonies of his mind is through the appoggiatura - a clear fingerprint of the composer. This musical device is the placing of a note of melody slightly higher than the accompanying chord, with which it clashes harmonically, before the melody settles on to its rightful resolution. It is like a billiard ball tantalizingly perched on the edge of a pocket before at last sinking into place - or else, as might happen in the music of later Mahler - rolling away instead, thus creating new possibilities of musical tension.

Mahler is justly renowned for his use of the orchestral palette; the huge orchestra he uses is not novel - Richard Strauss had employed similar forces before him - nor are the forces used merely for the effect of their sheer volume. Rather, it was to provide a greater degree of shading in the tone-colours. Flutes are used for their ethereal, rather than pastoral quality; over a choir of trombones in sombre harmony a single trombone utters a plaintive cry; bassoons, in their higher registers become plangent rather than comic. In forte passages, clarity of line is preserved by handing the melody to a single, strident, trumpet. He often intentionally used the banal to effect musical irony. Again, the obvious example is the third movement of the first symphony, but the numerous trumpet calls that resound through his music are echoes, perhaps, of the bugles at the Iglau barracks. Mahler revealed that a formulative incident in his creative development occurred when he was a child; his parents caught in a violent quarrel, the distressed young Mahler fled from the house into the strains of an organ grinder's *O du lieber Augustin*. That is why, on

being nurtured. Ideas for his *Resurrection* symphony (no. 2, not completed until 1894) were being incubated as early as 1883. From Prague he moved to Leipzig, as assistant to Artur Nikisch, eventually leaving this post to work on his symphony no. 1. His first real directorship came in 1888, when te took over the Opera House at Budapest, whose music at that time was in a somewhat parlous state. He agreed to stay for ten years, and although his productions there increased his reputation, winning the admiration of no less a personage than Brahms, he stayed only two years. For the next six years, in the closing decade of the nineteenth century, he spent a happy time at Hamburg in a less demanding job which gave him the opportunity to produce the long-gestating *Resurrection* symphony, and the third symphony in D minor. A visit to London with a troupe from Hamburg to play selections from German operas at Drury Lane and a guest appearance at Covent Garden took place in 1892, but much more significant a happening during that period was his conversion to Catholicism, which played such an eventful part in his development as a creative artist.

Then in 1897 Mahler went to Vienna. The appointment, opened to him on his formal conversion to the Catholic faith, was to have a tremendous impact on both Mahler and his public. His ten years there, firstly as Kapellmeister at the Court Opera, and then as its Artistic Director, were to be be known as the opera house's 'golden age' while to the world at large he became regarded as a Viennese composer.

Burning with tremendous zeal, living only for music, he hired and fired as the necessity took him, oblivious to the personal feelings of those who were there to make the notes sound. It was a time of his greatest creative output, the masterful canvases produced including the fourth to the eighth symphonies. Another significant personal event was his marriage to Alma Maria Schindler, who gave him the support he needed during this period of intense - perhaps too intense - activity.

Never having been really comfortably off, his eventual decision to leave Vienna was tied up with the need to make provision for his retirement, and he thought that he could do this by going to America. He made several visits to the USA between 1907 and 1910, taking up the post of the conductorship of the New York Philharmonic Society in 1908. He introduced Smetana's *Bartered Bride*, and Tchaikovsky's *Queen of Spades*, but by 1910 the position was deteriorating. Unfortunately, his natural acerbity did not endear him to society, and perhaps the vital flame was guttering. Offhanded with people first, and next with the music under his direction, he became too ready with tactless excuses. Madame Mahler complained to the press that in Vienna not even the Emperor dared dictate to him, but in New York he was at the beck and call of ten ladies (the Board of the Philharmonic Society) who ordered him round like a puppet.

Then Mahler's health declined rapidly, and after a collapse, he returned to Vienna with only a few months to live.

Although his symphonies are built round transcendental questions, the queries, it has been said, savour more of the neurotic than the deeply philosophical. 'Will the meaning of Life be revealed by Death?' he asked his friend, Bruno Walter.

He had a superstitious dread of finishing a ninth symphony, for neither Beethoven, Schubert nor Bruckner completed a tenth. For this reason alone, he entitled his ninth *Das Lied von der Erde* no doubt thinking by such means to avoid the taboo. That done, he went on to write his ninth-numbered symphony, which was to be his last, the so-called tenth remaining incomplete at his death, at the age of 50, in May 1911.

Vincent d'Indy

Descended from a noble family in Vivarais (the Ardeche), Vincent d'Indy (1851-1931) was brought up in Paris by his grandmother Madame Théodore d'Indy. Madame d'Indy insisted on a musical education, and later put her grandson in the charge of the well-known pianist and teacher Marmontel.

The young Vincent was recognized early as a wonder child. He studied harmony with Albert Lavignac (the musical master of Debussy at a later date) as a boy of only 14. At 16, Vincent read Berlioz's 'Traité d'instrumentation' and became completely obsessed with Berlioz and his music.

After the Franco-Prussian War of 1870, d'Indy plunged into the Parisian musical life. He ignored his aristocratic childhood friends, preferring the company of composers, critics and musicians. He came into contact with the conductor Jules Pasdeloup who performed d'Indy's *Symphony Italienne*. This piece was admired by Bizet and Saint-Saëns among others, and d'Indy's star began to rise. D'Indy was introduced to César Franck and studied counterpoint and composition with him as well as organ at the Conservatoire. The young d'Indy took on all musical tasks offered to him in his unlimited enthusiasm. He performed as a pianist, as an organist, played the horn and percussion until he was appointed permanently as a percussionist with the Concerts Colonnes in 1873. That same summer, d'Indy travelled throughout the German speaking countries, hearing and admiring the German masters: Bach, Beethoven, Weber and Wagner. He spent time with Liszt and his students. He learned a great deal about teaching music history, something he would use in practice later as director of the Schola Cantorum. In Dresden, Munich and Vienna, he flew from musical discovery to musical discovery. He attended concerts and rehearsals and even heard Russian music (including Rimsky-Korsakov), all of which gave him a definite advantage over his French colleagues. His official début as composer came in 1874 when Pasdeloup performed one of his three ouvertures from *Les Piccolomini: Max et Thécla*. The piece was very successful. People found it Wagnerian, when it was actually closer to Weber or Schumann. The following year, the Société Natonale performed d'Indy's symphony, written in the memory of Janos Hundayi. This symphony was never again performed and never published.

In 1876, d'Indy attended Bayreuth for a performance of Wagner's *Ring*. It made an immense impression on him. He was an instant and enthusiastic Wagnerian. His dream was to introduce a new, Wagnerian, musical-dramatic art form in France. Traces of this dream can be found in all the works that followed. D'Indy did not, however, completely ignored the French tradition hereafter. He attended the performance of Berlioz's *La Damnation de Faust* in 1877 and remained a great admirer of his fellow Frenchman. D'Indy also remained involved in the ongoing discussion concerning the revision of French opera. Together with his master César Franck, it was often difficult for him to reconcile his French loyalties with his Germanic tendencies.

In 1878, Pasdeloup conducted d'Indy's symphonic ballet, *La Foret enchantée*. Including the obvious Weber and Wagner influences clearly heard in this piece, it is characteristic of d'Indy's qualities as a composer. It is clear, brilliant and light, pure and true of colour and very reminiscent of Berlioz. *Le Chant de la Cloche* for soloists, double choir and orchestra (on a poem by Schiller), premièred in 1883. The critical acclaim for d'Indy's work was now extensive; it would never be popular with the public though. D'Indy's work was too complicated to ever appeal to a wide audience. The composer's best work is undoubtedly *Symphonie crévenole*, 1885, based on the folksongs d'Indy discovered and studied in the Ardeche.

His *Symphonie sur un chant montagnard français* did cause a sensation at its première in 1887 when it was performed by the Concerts Lamoreaux.

hearing those trumpet calls, one must be prepared to ponder, are these the trumpet calls of fate, or ironic echoes of the banal trivia of everyday life? At least, that is what Mahler asks us to do. While the giant tapestries of his symphonies were being woven in his brain, the composer, as administrator of an opera house, would be constantly caught up in the humdrum world of bills and box-office, and the endless disputes between artist and artisan.

The symphonies fall neatly into three periods – the classification is Mahler's own, but apparent enough on the most cursory inspection. The three groups are symphonies 1 to 4, 5 to 7, and the final group, including *Das Lied von der Erde*. In fact, a neater classification is made by putting the first symphony in a category of its own – a kind of introduction to the others which then fall into three trilogies, the central one being the purely instrumental symphonies.

The first symphony, the *Titan*, in D major, is closely linked with the song-cycle *Lied eines fahrenden Gesellen* for which Mahler wrote not only the music, but the words as well (he had not yet encountered the collection known as *Des Knaben Wunderhorn*.) The conformist nature of this first work can be seen in the conventional four movement construction, and the fact that the first three movements never stray far from the tonic or related keys. Even the last movement, with its incursion into the remote key of D flat pays lip-service to Beethoven's ninth by the reiteration of themes from other movements.

Apart from linking themes, there is a predominant motif, a falling fourth, which runs throughout the work. In the first movement, played by the woodwind against held strings, it suggests the 'Titanic' Austrian scenery; played rapidly it becomes a cuckoo call; played boldly by the brass, a military theme. In the popular third movement based on *Frère Jacques* in a minor key, the fourth is a persistent bass.

Autograph of Mahler's Tenth Symphony, with the words 'Erbarmen!' and 'O Gott! O Gott! Warum hast du mich verlassen?'

The first trilogy, symphonies 2 to 4, not only have a common emotional link – the search for spiritual assurance – they are unusual in that they each have movements including voices, using texts drawn from *Des Knaben Wunderhorn* (an anthology set by many other composers, including Brahms). According to Mahler's friend and biographer Bruno Walter, in the second symphony he asks the reason for the tragedy of human existence, in the third, he is assured of the almighty love that forms all things, while the fourth is a declaration of the certainty of the heavenly life. The strivings for spiritual recognition found their resolution when Mahler became a Catholic; after his conversion, he wrote the fourth symphony which reveals the Paradise offered to the soul after death.

The second symphony, *The Resurrection* calls upon gigantic forces: an enormous string section, with several harps, is needed to support quadruple woodwind, a vast brass section (with an additional brass band) an array of percussion, organ, female soloists and full chorus. He was not to employ such vast resources again until his eighth symphony. The full contingent is however reserved for the climactic fifth and last movement – *a dies irae* and jubilant hymn in juxtaposition. Neville Cardus regarded the third symphony as a true test of the Mahler enthusiast. There are six movements, and the first lasts for nearly three-quarters of an hour. Such a complex structure defies conventional analysis, but the multitude of short themes has been likened to the structure of early Mozart movements where contrasted groups of motif-like phrases take the place of well-contrasted themes. This expansive first movement (called in the original programme note 'Summer Marches In') is followed by a contrasting pastoral minuet, a bucolic scherzo, and a sombre aria. The fifth movement begins with an unusual choral effect, a women's chorus singing against boys' voices imitating the tolling of bells. This tolling persists for most of the movement, in which the violins are silent throughout. As the bells fade away, the well-

Vincent d'Indy's most important work was one of organization and not of composition. As director of the Société Nationale de Musique, he was an inspiration in the efforts to develop French music. Under the influence of the great Germans, and with Franck, a Belgian with German ancestry, in the forefront, d'Indy had a lasting impact on French musical life. His power was even greater when he became director of the Scola Cantorum as well. This alternative to the Conservatorium became an important meeting place for Franck's followers, the revisionists who would give French music more impact worldwide. D'Indy's efforts were carried on by Albert Roussel and later by Milhaud and Honegger. D'Indy was a great and well-loved man. His 'Cours de composition musicale' (in four parts, 1903-1950) has yet to lose its significance in the teaching of composition. Unfortunately, d'Indy's music is seldom performed outside of France today.

Edward Elgar

Though Elgar (1857-1934) is Britain's only symphonist of the classical and Romantic periods, and a late starter at that, the two symphonies are not the best known of his works. The huge popularity of the *Pomp and Circumstance* marches at one extreme, the almost reverential awe accorded to *The Dream of Gerontius* at the other, with such masterpieces as the *Enigma Variations* and the Cello Concerto in between, have elbowed the academically respectable symphonies to one side. Too derivative, the modernists declared. Only three years, but a noticeable growth in creative development, separates the two symphonies. The first, in A flat, was given its first performance in 1908 at the Free Trade Hall in Manchester under Hans Richter, to whom the work is dedicated. It was written while Elgar was fulfilling the only academic post in his life, the Chair of Music at Birmingham University. Its interest lies in the thematic material for the whole symphony being built from the simple melody which opens the first movement. The second symphony is regarded as a much maturer work, though it was received less enthusiastically, perhaps because the emotional content, whilst suited to the symphony's stated purpose (a memorial to King Edward VII) was, in a way, anticlimatic: it begins gloriously, and ends with quiet restraint.

Elgar was virtually self-taught as a composer. His early skills he had from his father, a musical general factotum. After a short spell in a legal office, Elgar concentrated on making music his career, performing in a provincial orchestra, teaching the violin, and doing musical hackwork. Serious acclaim did not reach Elgar until he was forty; much of the main driving force in bringing Elgar's music to public notice was due to his wife, eight years his senior. When she died, Elgar seemed to lose his creative spirit and he began to lead the life of a country gentleman. When, however, he mentioned off-the-cuff that he had written a third symphony but that nobody wanted it, there was a public outcry. Money was advanced for its performance, and Elgar found himself having to write the symphony which he had only sketched out. At his death two years later, only fragments of each movement had actually been written.

The Vienna Opera House,
an engraving from 1838.

Albert Roussel

Born in Tourcoing, Northern France, Albert Roussel (1869-1937) was orphaned at seven, and brought up by his uncle and grandfather. He entered the Navy where in his spare time he made his first attempts at composition. A musical fellow officer suggested that he ought to pursue his studies more seriously, whereupon Roussel resigned his commission and entered the Schola Cantorum under the composer d'Indy. His time in the Navy had given him the opportunity to visit Indo-China, which made a deep impact on his musical development.

Following a further private visit to Cochin, China and India in 1909 he embarked on his opera-ballet *Padmavati*. During the First World War he enlisted, serving with the Red Cross and Motor Transport, then after the conclusion of the war, once again began to compose. His idiom is marked by the interweaving of melodic lines, rather than an overall harmonic structure. His greatest works date from his later life, from his fifties onwards, and include the second symphony in B flat, commenced after the end of the war, the virile third symphony in G minor, which appeared in 1922; and what is sometimes regarded as finest if not his most popular work, the fourth symphony in A major, commissioned by the Boston Symphony Orchestra.

tailored finale begins with a soft string passage. Mahler planned a seventh movement for the symphony, which would have been an anti-climax to this great work, but rejected it, using the material instead for the fourth, the final symphony in the trilogy, described in more detail later.

The fifth symphony begins the purely orchestral second trilogy. Although in five movements, it is divided into three 'parts', the third part – the fourth and fifth movements – beginning with the popular adagietto for harp and strings.

The sixth symphony uses an unusual device – a major chord followed by a minor one, portraying the fall from optimism to despair, to make the connecting link between the subject matter of the symphony. The finale is another movement of extreme length, often a barrier to the understanding of this complex work whose thematic development captures the growth of Mahler's own musical development.

The seventh symphony is again in five movements, and displays many traits of Mahler's later style: shifts of tonality bringing the work to a close in a key unrelated to the one in which it commenced, thus achieving a directional impulse. Here too, are uncompromising contrapuntal lines which led, not just to an awareness of the tonal possibilities, but in the hands of Schoenberg, into a whole new school of musical construction. Now, seemingly having proved that he could express his feelings in music without the aid of words or voices, he embarked on his massive eighth symphony, and although two more symphonies were to follow it, by any standard it must be counted his greatest achievement. It consists virtually of two huge choral cantatas, the first a setting of the hymn *Veni*

The artist Otto Böhler's
impression of Gustav
Mahler on the podium.

Frank Martin

Joseph Lauber was Frank Martin's (1890-1974) teacher in
Geneva. Martin's first compostions: *Violin Sonata* (1913),
Symphonie pour orchestre burlesque (1915), his choral work
Les Dithyrambes (1918), and his *Piano Quintet* (1921) all reveal
a strong influence from Franck, Fauré and Ravel in the young
composer. After coming into contact with Jacques-Dalcrose,
however, Martin began to give the rhythmic elements in his
pieces a much more important place.
A serious study of Schoenberg's twelve tone system led Martin
to use his own version in works composed after 1930. His
Symphonie of 1937 is the first of a series of works written in a
completely new style, the culmination of which is the dramatic
oratorium *Le Vin Herbé*.
Martin's use of the twelve tone system is unorthodox. It is not
placed in the forefront; it does make it possible to create new and
beautiful melodies and harmonies that are emotionally and
rhetorically very strong. His mastery of orchestration is evident
in, for example, the *Petite symphonie concertante* for harpsichord, harp, piano and double string orchestra (1945). It is an
important work in Martin's oeuvre: not only for the superlative
sound colouring but also for the rich harmony and first rate
thematic material.

Arnold Schoenberg

Arnold Schoenberg (1874-1951), the founder of the Second
Viennese School and inventor of the 'twelve-note' method of
composition was vitually self-taught. As a child he had violin
lessons, and when a young man, lessons in counterpoint from
a friend. His earliest attempts at compositions were, he admitted
later, pastiches - mere copies of pieces he admired. But after the
death of his father he was very much influenced by the opinions
of friends in his circle, and gained the conviction to resist
convention in his music. A performance of a string quartet gave
him the confidence to proceed with the early masterpiece, the
sextet *Verklärte Nacht* written in the amazingly short time of six
weeks. When it was first performed it was regarded as controversial and uncompromising, though today its highly chromatic,
even luscious, writing is unexceptional. But this was an early
work, and there was a long way to go. It was the period of
Mahler's later symphonies, which pointed away from tonality,
and this was the direction which Schoenberg took.
Early pieces were beginning to arouse hostility, yet it was not
until 1908 that the first works which totally broke with tonality,
Six little Piano Pieces, appeared. In 1913 he conducted a concert
which included his own early Chamber Symphony and works by
two of his pupils - Anton Webern and Alban Berg. The riot which
ensued broke up the concert, before the final item, Mahler's
Kindertotenlieder could be performed.
Since the classical structure of a symphony was based on sonata
form, and this, virtually by definition, relies on well-defined tonal
centres, it follows that in the 'new music' the concept of a
symphony was going to need redefinition.
Thus Schoenberg's Chamber Symphonies are quite different
from those of the classical and Romantic schools. The same
quandaries faced his pupils; Berg wrote nothing with the title
'symphony' and Webern only one, minimal, piece. In addition to
his treatises on twelve-note music, Schoenberg also wrote
several text-books on conventional harmony. A curious anec-
dote concerns Schoenberg's superstitious fear of the number
13. During his last illness, he believed that if he could survive July
13th, he would recover. He died 13 minutes before the day
expired.

Wilhelm Stenhammer

Wilhelm Stenhammer (1871-1927), born in Stockholm, began studying the piano with Richard Andersson, and went on to study with Barth in Berlin from 1892 until 1893. He studied theory and composition at the Conservatory in Stockholm, graduating in 1890 with a degree for organ as well. His début as conductor was in 1897. Stenhammer also performed with the Tor Aulin String Quartet as pianist. In 1898, he received a commission to write an opera for the new Opera Theatre there, his opera *Tirfing*. Stenhammer was an important musician in his role as conductor of the Royal Symphony Orchestra in Stockholm. He also conducted in Göteborg which made him all the more popular with his countrymen. Stenhammer's *First Symphony* appeared in 1903, his *Second Symphony* in 1915. He wrote *Symphonic Cantata* for the 150th anniversary of the founding of the Swedish Music Academy in 1915.

Carl Nielsen

Carl Nielsen's (1865-1931) compositions were in great vogue during the middle of this century, but knowledge of his music outside his native Denmark was virtually restricted to his symphonic music. In fact this represents just a fraction of his output, which includes chamber music, choral works, solo instrumental music (including a symphonic suite for piano) and two fullscale operas.

Nielsen came from a large, and consequently poor, family, and in his early working life he was a shepherd boy. But his musical talents showed in his playing the violin for street dancing, and his joining the town band in nearby Odense when he was fourteen. His popularity prompted friends to help him take up fulltime musical studies, and he entered the Royal Conservatory, Copenhagen, under Nils Gade in 1884. After two years he left to join a theatre orchestra, but was later awarded a travelling scholarship to visit Germany, Italy and France. It was in Paris that he met his future wife, the Danish sculptress Anne Marie Brodersen.

He had by now sketched the first movement of an unfinished symphony which was to become his *Symphonic Rhapsody*. Much of his completed music of this time was instrumental or chamber music, but he embarked on his first symphony proper (in G minor) in 1892, completing it in 1894. The second symphony, the *Four Temperaments* in which each of the movements is allied to one of the four 'humours' - the slow movement *Melancholy* for example - dates from the next decade, and already shows one of the hallmarks of his style - the simultaneous playing of passages in different keys. In 1908 he became conductor of the Royal Opera, which no doubt influenced his decision to use wordless voices in his third symphony. He left the Royal Opera in 1914 to concentrate on conducting and composition. His fourth symphony, *The Inextinguishable*, written between 1914 and 1916, during the First World War, is probably his best known. It is worth noting that the 'nicknames' of his compositions, such as *Sinfonia espansiva* for the third, were apparently coined by Nielsen *after* writing the works in order to make them more widely understood; the parallel is Mahler's writing 'programmes' for his symphonies. Symphony no. 5, which has a cadenza for the side-drum, is only in two movements, but generally regarded as his finest work. The title *Simple Symphony* for his sixth, and last, is regarded as a somewhat ironic title. Though his music shows polytonality, it never strays far from a defined key scheme.

Creator Spiritus, and the second the closing scene of Part II of Goethe's *Faust*. Eight solo voices, double chorus and organ, with appropriately enormous orchestral forces have earned this symphony the nickname *Symphony of a Thousand*. It was the first of Mahler's works to achieve unanimous acclaim.

Eight months after its first performance, Mahler was dead. He never heard his next works. The first of these, *Das Lied von der Erde*, to translations of Li Po and other Chinese poets, is altogether different in both structure and concept from anything he had previously written. Dark and delicately orchestrated, the use of the pentatonic scale gives a faint suggestion of the exotic. Here too, is the extension of tonality which was to be its dissolution.

His last complete symphony, the ninth, is again in the conventional four movements, but the whole structure is innovative. It begins, not brashly, but with a lyrical easy-moving andante comodo, and ends, not with a grand finale, but with a sustained adagio movement finishing on hushed strings.

There were sketches of a tenth symphony which Mahler's wife Alma could not bear to destroy (as Mahler willed). Instead, sufficient material

Carl Nielsen

remained to enable movements from the work to be performed. It is intensely personal, and the manuscript ends with anguished words of farewell from the composer to his wife.

The fourth symphony

Although Mahler is usually associated with massive works, the smaller scale of the fourth symphony enables us to look at this work in some detail. It is Mahler's happiest symphony, and after the enormous resources of the second, and the intellectual demands of the third, the fourth symphony comes almost as a respite. It is not only that the orchestra is reduced in numbers, but its forces are used sparsely and delicately, the overall texture founded, as in the classical symphony, on the strings instead of the wind. Furthermore, the naive lines and the skilful counterpoint show the symphony to be an extension of Haydn, rather than Beethoven. Two melodies are quoted, *Es sangen Drei Engel* associated also with the third symphony, and one from the *Wunderhorn*, on which the quiet last movement is built, *Wir geniessen die himmlichen Freuden*. The first movement is constructed from a number of folk-like themes, unequivocally major, uncluttered by chromatic notes or accidentals, which never stray far from the tonic or related keys. The effect is of childlike simplicity. Sometimes themes run together hand-in-hand so that it is difficult to say what the predominant theme is at certain points; rather, it is the pairs of themes which are the signposts, their inextricable links being part of the thematic texture. Three themes, however, act as a guide through the movement, although there are in fact at least five forming the opening section. The opening clucking melody soon turns into a rapid musical figure which is a thread through most of the movement. Another important distinctive theme (marked *Ton!*) for the cellos tells us that we are nearing the end of the exposition. The development section introduces a happy flute theme – the symbol of childhood. The second movement is a light ländler-type movement, in which Mahler compensates for the reduced size of the orchestra by using several curious devices and effects, including a solo violin tuned a tone higher to give an antique 'fiedel' sound. There is a suggestion that this movement owes something to Saint-Saëns's *Danse Macabre*, but the 'Freund Hein' who leads the children through Limbo into the world beyond is not the Devil, but a kind of spiritual Pied Piper.

The symphony's slow movement is its third; but it is marked only poco adagio, for a movement too grave would be out of place for a child's entry into Paradise. It is one of the loveliest movements in all Mahler's music. It begins with the lower strings alone; the violins enter, their melody being taken up by the oboe as a counterpoint to the opening theme. From then on the texture thickens and the movement takes the form of variations of increasing complexity which reveals the adult Mahler, yearning perhaps for his lost childhood. The movement leads triumphantly to the gates of Paradise, marked by sustained brass chords against which the horns call, with the timpani beating confidently. The strings descend, harp arpeggios leading to an unusual cadence (the chords of E, C, and D) leaving only the faintest whisper of woodwind and strings to close the movement. The final movement begins with a clarinet introduction, after which the soprano soloist sings of the heavenly paradise. The clucking figure of the first movement returns; the end is a quiet lullaby. It marks not just the close of the movement, and the symphony itself, but the end of the trilogy – even the passing of childhood. The work is now even more impressive, for we, with hindsight, know what music still lay ahead. Not even Mahler knew that.

Serge Prokofiev

Serge Prokofiev (1879-1953) was born in the Ukraine. He began composing at the age of seven and studied privately with Reinhold Glière before, at the age of thirteen, he was admitted to the conservatory in St Petersburg. There he studied with Liadov, Rimsky-Korsakov and Tcherepnin. At this time he created a sensation as a pianist. His performance of his Piano Concerto no. 1 won him the Anton Rubinstein prize. In 1918 Prokofiev left his own country. He remained in the West until 1927, travelling through Germany, Italy, Spain, Belgium and America, performing chiefly his own compositions arranged for piano. Important compositions from this period are *The Love of Three Oranges*, the Symphony no. 2, the Quintet in G minor and the Overture in B flat.

Between 1927 and 1936 he spent periods of varying length in Russia and the West. Only in 1936 did he decide to again definitely take up residence in the land of his birth. This marked a period of great creativity: *Romeo and Juliet*, *Peter and the Wolf*, the second violin concerto, and piano sonatas nos. 6,7 and 8. Prokofiev died on 5 March 1953, the same day as Stalin. His music was banned by musical officialdom in his own country and not reinstated until 1959.

Samuel Barber

Samuel Barber (1910-1981) is one of the most important 20th century, American composers. His musicality was evident early on. Barber was admitted to the Curtis Institute of Music in Philadelphia when only thirteen. He graduated in 1932 with degrees in piano, voice and composition. Barber was honoured in 1935 with the American Prize in Rome and, both in 1935 and 1936, with the Pulitzer Prize for Music in the United States. In 1945, he was also awarded a Guggenheim Fellowship.

In 1936, Samuel Barber's *First Symphony* premièred in Rome. This performance was conducted by none other than the renowned Molinari. The following year, *First Symphony* was performed at the Salzburg Festival; both events truly honoured the 27 year old American composer. The honours increased when Bruno Walter decided to record this same symphony.

Barber invests a great deal of thought in his melodies, making them quite exceptional. His compositions are more lyrical and romantic than classical in form. Barber's compositional talent has proved capable of even the most brilliant escapades. Yet only in his later years did he find his own idiom. Early Barber is reminiscent of Stravinsky. His later works are more original, more personal. His *Adagio for Strings*, *Snag for Orchestra*, nos. 1 and 2, and *Music for a Scene from Shelley* are well known both in the United States and Europe. *Apalachian Spring* and *Billy the Kid* have become true American classics. Barber's *Second Symphony* premièred under Koussevitsky in 1944 with the Boston Symphony. Eugene Ormandy performed the première of his ballet suite: *Medea*, in 1947 in Philadelphia. Samuel Barber was awarded the 1946 Critics Award for his cello concerto, reconfirming his importance among 20th century American composers.

8

The twentieth century

Igor Stravinsky

Igor Stravinsky (1882-1971) was born in Oranienbaum, near St. Petersburg. In spite of the fact that his father was a popular opera singer, and despite the early piano lessons, Igor Stravinsky's parents did not envisage a musical career for their son. Igor was

'It seems to me that since Beethoven ample proof has been given of the uselessness of the symphony.' These words are those of none other than the French composer Debussy, who continues: 'Even with Schumann and Mendelssohn it is merely a respectful repetition of the same forms but lacking the same power. Yet the ninth was a brilliant guidepost, a magnificent attempt to expand and liberate habitual forms by giving

'It is not music's job to express anything', said Igor Stravinsky; 'Composers combine notes. That is all.'

them the harmonious dimensions of a fresco ... Beethoven's true lesson was not to conserve old forms, nor to follow slavishly in his footsteps. But to look through open windows towards the freedom of the sky ... '

These observations, the remark regarding Mendelssohn's and Schumann's symphonic art aside, are not only typical of Debussy; they suggest the place of the symphony itself in music in the twentieth century, particularly in Western Europe. The most important principles of symphonic form and structure have always had their basis in the reliable mainstay of tonality. The tones making up a symphonic composition are distributed according to a set system around a ground-tonality or tonal centre, and are of varying degrees of importance. The entire compositional coherence of a symphony rests upon there being in each movement a continuous ebb and flow around this tonal centre, as the music moves either to escape it temporarily or to be drawn back. Traditionally, a set relationship also exists between each of the various movements.

From the beginning of the twentieth century, however, the sovereignty of tonality has been on the decline. Composers have been searching for other methods of achieving cohesiveness in their compositions. Some have gone very far indeed and abandoned all the traditionally observed relationships among the notes, with atonality as a result. The most important representatives of this trend are the composers of the second Viennese School, Schoenberg, Berg and Webern. Others, less radical, have made use of freer forms of tonality, or sought ways to employ two or more tonal centres simultaneously in the same composition (Darius Milhaud). The consequences are these: where tonality has suffered its greatest crisis, the symphony has suffered its greatest crisis as well; where tonality has remained unchallenged (largely Eastern Europe), the symphonic form is still an important means of musical expression.

To return to Claude Debussy – he wrote no symphonies. Yet he gave admirable support to the opinions quoted above by creating *La Mer*, which he sub-titled 'Symphonic Sketches', pointing on the one hand to the painterly effect (wind, sea, light, colour, atmosphere), and on the other to the symphonic latitude and liberation he so fervently advocated. Although he stayed well away from the academic rules of symphonic composition, his development of the musical material can be called symphonic in that there is a clearly contrasted thematic structure, a recognizable symphonic design with an introduction, scherzo and rondo-finale. *La Mer* has no traditional tonal centre, but seems to be seeking one throughout.

Arnold Schoenberg, in his chamber symphony no. 1 opus 9 (1906), found a highly personal solution to the problem of form. To begin with, this work brings into question the suitability of a large orchestra as the primary medium for the presentation of symphonic form. Written for fifteen solo instruments (ten winds and five strings), it represents a reaction against the supremacy assigned to the strings by the nineteenth century. Schoenberg does not only strike at the 'big sound', but also at full-scale structural expansiveness. He compresses the structure of this five-movement work into what may be loosely considered an example of the classical sonata form. The first of the five continuous movements is an allegro exposing the main themes, the following scherzo introduces new themes, the third movement can be seen as a development of the material from both these sections, and it is in turn followed by an adagio which presents further new figures. The fifth movement acts as a reprise of the themes from the first and fourth movements. Although Schoenberg does challenge nineteenth-century practices, he nevertheless concurs with the need for thematic coherence among the various movements. In this respect he belongs to the Romantic school. The symphony as a formal problem was only of moderate interest to Schoenberg. In addition to this opus 9, he completed in 1939 a second chamber symphony, opus 38, on which he had worked extensively while

sent to study law at the university and stayed there until he was 23. One of his fellows students was Vladimir Rimsky-Korsakov, son of the famous composer, who introduced Stravinsky to his father. From that moment on to his death in 1908, Rimsky-Korsakov played an important part in Stravinsky's musical education. Stravinsky acknowledged his debt to Rimsky-Korsakov in his later years.

In 1905, Stravinsky finished his degree at the university and in 1906, married his cousin, Nadeja Soelima. He finished his *First Symphony*, some shorter works and a symphonic poem, *Feu d'Artifice* for the wedding of Rimsky-Korsakov's daughter. These were all performed in the years 1907 until 1909 in St. Petersburg. Diaghilev heard Stravinsky at this time, and asked him to write music for his new ballet, *L'Oiseau de Feu*. *Firebird* was performed in Paris in 1910 and caused a great sensation. It was brilliant and the orchestration was extraordinary.

After revising the score, Stravinsky's *First Symphony* was performed at the festival in Montreux with Ansermet conducting. Stravinsky was in demand, especially with Diaghilev who commissioned more ballet music beginning with *Petrouchka*. Stravinsky had an obvious flair for exciting rhythms and daring harmonies and together with Diaghilev, conquered first Paris and then the rest of the musical world.

Stravinsky was at this point extremely celebrated. He turned to new ideas instead of resting on his laurels. A symphony with a theme of primitive, seasonal rites occupied his creative energies. Diaghilev talked Stravinsky into yet another ballet instead of his planned symphony and in 1913, *Le Sacre du Printemps* was performed. It caused an incredible sensation. Gone were the folksey, tempered sounds of *Petrouchka* and the colourful naiivieté of *Firebird*. Here were brash dissonances and barbaric, offensive rhythms.

During the First World War, Stravinsky lived in Switzerland. He composed a theatrical piece on a small scale: *L'Histoire du Soldat*. Its première was in 1918 in Lausanne and this piece heralded a new type of composition for the young master. Ths style was more compact; he traded in a full orchestra for 2 voices, violin, double-bass, clarinet, bassoon, cornet, trombone and percussion. Stravinsky was at the time, also busy making a name for himself as performer of his own works, as pianist and as conductor. With a forthcoming tour to the United States in mind, he composed *Concerto for Piano and Wind Instruments* in 1925. Stravinsky settled in Paris in 1934 and became a naturalized Frenchman. He toured regularly. At the outbreak of the Second World War, he settled in America and became a citizen there in 1945.

With his ballet, *Pulchinella* (1920), Stravinsky began a new, neo-classical period in his composing career. In 1923, his opera-bouffe, *Mavra*, followed. This was based upon a story by Poesjkin, written to illustrate his theory of the superiority of the traditional operatic model, what Poesjkin called 'The Russian-Italian model'. *Mavra* was attacked by the critics who considered it a step backwards for Stravinsky. They disdained the traditionally formed arias with accompaniment and called it a 'village humpa-pa'. More appropriate would be to consider the piece in its own right as an experiment with its own intrinsic value. After Poesjkin, Stravinsky turned to Sophocles with a text in Latin supplied by Jean Cocteau, he wrote an opera-oratorium, *Oedipus Rex*. This work, that premièred in 1927 in Paris, is considered one of the composer's most important. It successfully summons up the monumental, classical atmosphere using very contemporary means.

Stravinsky not only made a name for himself with music for the theatre, but also left us with a no less important oeuvre in the 'pure' classical genres. In 1920, he wrote *Symphony of Wind Instruments* (for 23 instruments) that was dedicated to the memory of Claude Debussy and was performed for the first time under Koussevitsky in London in 1921. *Symphony of Psalms* is undoubtedly one of his most beautiful works. It was commissioned by Koussevitsky for the 50th birthday of the Boston Symphony Orchestra in 1930. Stravinsky used Biblical texts in the Vulgate version, and inscribed his manuscipt with the dedication 'to the honour of God'. According to many, the *Symphony of Psalms* surpasses the rest of Stravinsky's work in its ability to involve its listeners emotionally. He finished his *Symphony in C* in 1940 and his *Symphony in Three Movements* in 1945.

Benjamin Britten

Benjamin Britten (1913-76) was a pupil of Frank Bridge. Later he studied composition with John Ireland and Arthur Benjamin. From 1935 to 1939 he worked in close cooperation with W.H. Auden, who supplied him with librettos for films, theatre and radio. Britten was a pacifist, during the war he lived and worked in the United States. He was one of the co-founders in 1947 of the English Opera Company, and in 1948 the Aldeburgh Festival was inaugurated at his instigation. Britten conducted many of his own works and was the regular accompanist for the tenor Peter Pears, with whom he began an especially fruitful collaboration upon his return from America.

Britten died in 1976. In addition to chamber music, songs, choral works and orchestral pieces, Britten left behind a large number of important operas, of which *Peter Grimes*, set on his beloved Suffolk coast, is probably the bestknown.

Benjamin Britten
accompanying the tenor
Peter Pears.

Ernst Bloch

Ernst Bloch (1880-1959), born in Geneva, received his first music lessons from Jean Dalcroze. At only fifteen, Bloch composed his first string quartet and an *Oriental Symphony*. In 1897, this young talent was sent to Brussels to study with Isaije and Rasse. There he composed as well, but these pieces have never been published. Bloch went to Frankfurt to further his composition studies with Iwan Knorr in 1900. A year in Munich followed (with Ludwig Tuille), before Bloch went to Paris. In Paris, in 1903, Bloch's *Historiettes au crépuscule* for voice and piano was published. While in Paris, he composed *Macbeth*, based on Shakespeare, with a libretto by Edmond Fleg, which he finished in 1909 and which was premièred in 1910 at the Opéra Comique. Bloch also travelled to Switzerland at this time, conducting there, and in 1915, for his appointment to the Conservatory in Geneva to teach composition. After only a year of teaching, Bloch left to tour America with Maud Allen.

composing the first. The other two important representatives of the second Viennese School also devoted little attention to the symphony *per se*. According to the musicologist Hans Redlich, Alban Berg's Three Pieces for Orchestra, opus 63 should be considered as 'Berg's active discussion of Gustav Mahler's conception of the symphony'. Anton Webern, in his symphony, opus 21, has only two movements. The first is a combination of sonata form and double canon, so subtly put together as to be scarcely discernible to the ear.

Apart from his symphony no. 1, opus 1, a youthful work written between 1905 and 1907 and thoroughly bound by academic restrictions, Igor Stravinsky made four essays into symphonic form; this statement, however, needs qualification. The symphonies for wind instruments (1920) do not constitute a symphony in the classical-Romantic sense. Stravinsky harks back to an earlier meaning given to the word, signifying 'to sound or play at the same time'. The work, dedicated to the memory of Debussy, exhibits no conformity with any of the symphonic conventions. Its single movement is constructed from six elements made to cohere by motivic inter-relationships.

Neither is the *Symphony of Psalms* (1930) to be considered as a true symphony. Rather it should be regarded as a musical document portraying the drawing-together of the symphony and the oratorio in the twentieth century. Together with the two orchestral symphonies, the symphony in C and symphony in three movements, it marks Stravinsky's neo-classical period. The term 'neo-classical', must here be taken to refer to an orientation towards models considered 'classical', without in any strict manner conforming to the style of that period. The *Symphony of Psalms*, for example, might more accurately be labelled 'neo-baroque'. Of the three movements, prelude, double fugue and sinfonia-allegro, the first two may be seen as a reflection of the baroque principle of form: an introduction wedded to the subsequent primary section. This main section looks back to Bach in its large-scale vocal and instrumental design. Symphonic cohesion is achieved in two ways, firstly by the appearance in all three movements of a particular motif, an intervallic figure of two interlocking minor thirds, and secondly by reminiscences of the introduction in the finale.

Stravinsky composed the symphony in C in the years 1938–40 while delivering a series of lectures at Harvard University on, among other things, form and structural principles. It was his intention to demonstrate in the work his belief that certain principles of form remain valid regardless of composition. He took as his point of departure the smaller orchestra of the Viennese classicists, finding his chief model in Haydn, though certain features of the first movement (in sonata form) point to Beethoven. The symphony in C has four movements: the outer movements are interrelated, the second movement, larghetto concertante, is an arioso for solo woodwinds, and the third, allegretto, is a dance movement, with the succession minuet-passepied-minuet, exhibiting a definite scherzo character. As in the *Symphony of Psalms*, the cohesive element for the entire work is an intervallic figure, this time consisting of a rising second and a descending fourth. The first movement's main theme arises from this motif and returns in the coda as a chorale-like conclusion. A significant characteristic of the symphony in C is its concertante quality, exemplifying the way in which twentieth-century composers detached themselves from the pathos of the nineteenth.

The Symphony in three movements, from the years 1942–45, is also a concertante work. As in the *Symphony of Psalms* and the symphony in C, Stravinsky here again attempts to explore the formal principles of classical scores without adopting the musical vocabulary of their time. Structurally, old models are brought together to form a novel unity. In the first movement it is chiefly sonata form which is used to distinguish the symphonic and concertante elements in two separate expositions. Both elements are jointly recapitulated. The middle movement, a

Right: Arnold Schoenberg, a self-portrait painted in 1910. As well as being one of the most revolutionary of composers, Schoenberg was a remarkable painter, a member of the 'Blaue Reiter' school. His music was championed in America by Leopold Stokowski (*left*), conductor of the Philadelphia Orchestra.

Stravinsky studied law
in his birthplace, St
Petersburg, and had
lessons at the same
period with Rimsky-
Korsakov; the
impresario Diaghilev
heard some of his early
works and
comissioned a ballet.
With *The Firebird* (1910),
the 28-year-old
composer leaped into
world-wide
prominence.

The avant-garde composer Karlheinz Stockhausen is mystified by the strong animosity his work arouses in many listeners. 'My music makes sense to me', he says.

Luciano Berio. In his *Sinfonia*, the experimental Italian composer combined elements of Bach, Wagner, Martin Luther King and the Swingle Singers.

Jean Sibelius. Like Rossini before him, Sibelius retired from composition in middle life and wrote little more.

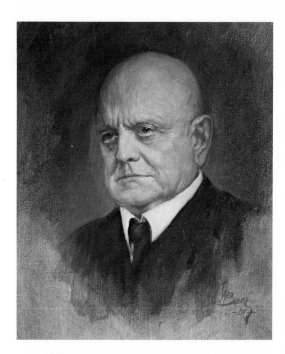

The Moldau, Prague, by Kokoschka.

homage to Rossini, forms the core of the composition. It was originally written to accompany film footage taken of occupied China during the Second World War. It is a sensitive andante in three-part form (ABA), in which the melodic part for harp and the equally solo-like flute part are given free room for expansion. Noteworthy in the instrumentation is also the repeated use of timpani and piano, which lends particular strength to the keen syncopated rhythms of the outer movements. These rhythms inevitably recall *Le Sacre du Printemps*, written thirty years earlier. But the finale also foreshadows to a certain extent the strict serial style which Stravinsky would later adopt.

In contrast to Stravinsky, who occupied himself with the phenomenon of the symphony only during his neo-classical period, his countrymen Prokofiev and Shostakovich espoused the form throughout their compositional careers. This surely has something to do with the fact that Stravinsky settled outside Russia after the revolution, whereas Prokofiev, after a fourteen-year stay in the West, returned; and Shostakovich spent his entire life in the country of his birth. In eastern Europe, particularly in Russia, tonality has remained the basis of all music-making, and this holds true today. Therefore the symphony has continued to occupy a position of importance in Russian musical life. Of Prokofiev's seven symphonies, only the first, the so-called *Classical*, has proved to be an unqualified success. Written in the troubled period before the outbreak of the Russian Revolution of 1917, it offers, in its purity and simplicity, a reaction against the excesses of late Romanticism. As Stravinsky was later to do in composing his symphony in C, Prokofiev took a Haydn symphony as his point of departure. Prokofiev however went much further, composing his symphony as if it were in fact by Haydn, without actually plagiarizing him. The outer movements are constructed according to the classical sonata form and provide a frame for a larghetto in three-part song-form and a gavotte, which replaces the classical minuet, giving an overall form perfectly within the classical tradition. Prokofiev's desire in composing his second symphony (opus 40, 1924) was to write a work of 'iron and steel' and no greater contrast to the first symphony is imaginable. The composition is modelled on Beethoven's last piano sonata, opus 111. The tormented mechanical restlessness of the work makes it almost inaccessible. With the third and fourth symphonies, Prokofiev attempted to transfer music previously written for his opera *The Flaming Angel* and for several ballets, to the symphonic form. The third symphony is predominantly sombre in colour, but of exceptional formal clarity. The fourth, on the other hand, is the most cheerful of them all. For the first time, in this symphony's finale Prokofiev offers a response to the positivism required by the Soviet authorities. Music must not exist for its own ends, but must function as an audible stimulus for the people. The finale is understated, but at the same time concludes ostentatiously: a cynical response.

The positivistic concept also colours the last movements of Prokofiev's fourth, sixth and seventh symphonies. In the seventh and last, dedicated to the youth of the Soviet Union, this ultimately leads to a level approaching that of mediocre light music. But it is Prokofiev's fifth symphony which is indisputably his masterpiece. A classical equilibrium reigns throughout. It is a score patterned on the classical-Romantic model and exhibiting great expressive power and melodic richness. The stately sobriety of the first movement is followed by a nervously fluttering scherzo. The third movement, adagio, begins gravely, but an abrupt shift into the major mode gives it a more benevolent character. Thematic elements from the first section of the adagio are reproduced in the finale.

The fifteen symphonies of Dmitri Shostakovich give every indication of being direct descendants of the nineteenth century. His first symphony can only be described as the ingenious undertaking of a nineteen-year-old. Here Shostakovich seems clearly to have had his origins in the world of Tchaikovsky and Bruckner, although Prokofiev's symphonic ideas

In America, Bloch was invited by Karl Muck to conduct his own *Trois Poèmes juifs* with the Boston Symphony Orchestra. In 1916, Bloch settled in New York and was given a teaching position at the Mannes School of Music. During this time, he conducted many renowned orchestras in the United States in performances of his own works. Bloch wrote his first violin sonata in 1920, the same year in which he was appointed director of the Conservatory in San Francisco. After ten years there, he returned to Europe, retreating to the Swiss Ticino and later, living in Chatel in the Haute Savoie. Bloch settled nowhere for very long, but he did honour all his various homes with compositions. Switzerland was honoured with a 'symphonic fresco', *Helvetia*. The United States were the subject of an 'epic rhapsody', *America*. (The première was performed by the New York Philharmonic in 1928). Bloch was again on the move after his newest stay in his native land. He travelled to France where several of his works were heard in Paris, including *Sacred Service*, written for liturgical, Hebrew texts. But it was in Italy that Bloch settled for a while at least, enjoying reasonable success there as well. In 1938, Bloch's opera *Macbeth* was performed in Naples to enthusiastic audiences (the piece having been neglected for thirty years). He was given an honorary membership in the Accademia di Santa Cecilia in Rome in 1929. These successes could not, however, negate the strong anti-semitism of Italy in the thirties, so Bloch again travelled to America.

The other land where Bloch's compositions were well-received was England. The Ernst Bloch Society was founded in 1937. The City of Birmingham Orchestra has performed many of his works including *Evocations for Orchestra*. Bloch's cello *Rhapsodie Schelomo*, and his *Piano Quintet* (1923) are both quite well known, and his *Concerto Grosso* for strings and piano (1925) is popular indeed. Even so, some of Bloch's pieces have never been performed.

Charles Ives

Charles Ives (1874-1954) was born in Danbury, Connecticut. His early musical education was from his father, an amateur musician who had been a military bandleader during the Civil War. Musically Ives's father was something of an eccentric, making his son sing 'Swanee River' in E flat while accompanying him in C - 'to stretch his ears'. Young Charles took to his father's love of dissonance and polytonality like a duck to water. At Yale, his music teacher (the composer Horatio Parker) was shocked and nonplussed at the musical ideas and irreverence of this brilliant young man who found Chopin 'soft' and Mozart 'effeminate'.

Ives graduated from Yale in 1908, the same year that he married Harmony Twitchell, and embarked on a prosperous career in insurance that enabled him to retire at the age of fifty-five. As a musical initiator, he was generations ahead of his time, using toneclusters, polyrhythms, microtones (intervals smaller than two adjacent notes on the piano), jazz and random elements in his music years before any of the 'serious' European masters. Socially he kept very quiet about his activities as a composer, and refused all royalties on his music - which he published at his own expense. In later years, however, when fame (much to his displeasure) had reached him, Ives tried to explain his outrageous harmonies and anarchic approach: 'I found I could not go on using the familiar chords early. I heard something else', he commented.

Alexander Scriabin

The Conservatory in Moscow was where Alexander Scriabin (1872-1945) was trained both as pianist and composer. He was received as a brilliant pianist early on in his career, making extensive tours and often playing his own works. From 1903 onwards, a piano student of Scriabin's supported him and beginning in 1908, Koussevitsky paid him a yearly salary in his role as publisher of Russian music at his company in Berlin. Scriabin was also featured as a soloist with Koussevitsky's orchestra on several of their tours.

In Scrabin's early works, up until about opus 25, the strong influence of Chopin is clearly heard. Thereafter, Scriabin developed his own very specific musical language. Hexachords, freed tonality, sharp motives and free forms are characteristics found in his later works. Scriabin had a deep mystical side to his character which inspired him to approach all art forms in a personal way. His ultimate aim was to unite all artistic disciplines in service of his mystical beliefs. His premature death from blood poisoning at the age of 45 defeated his ambitions.

Scriabin's *First Symphony in E major*, opus 26, is a hymn to art as a kind of religion. The *Third Symphony,* opus 43 from 1903, furthers this idea in its title: *Divine Poem.* Opus 54, *Poem of Ecstasy,* expresses the spiritual satisfaction inherent in creative work.

Following the First World War, Scriabin's work was very much the fashion, but was soon almost completely forgotten by the fickle music public. This was partly due to his theosophical ideas. The relationship between his philosophy and his work were not appropriate to the tastes of the thirties. Thanks to virtuoso pianists of today, Scriabin's works have a more constant following.

The conductor Eugene Ormandy (in a dark shirt) with, on his left, the cellist Mstislav Rostropovich and Dmitri Shostakovich.

have not left him untouched. (Shostakovich wrote his first symphony only six years after Prokofiev wrote his.) The work provides ample evidence of Shostakovich's early mastery of form and instrumentation. This is particularly true of the first three movements, in which there is not only a continual shifting of tempi but also an ever-increasing extravagance of musical thought. The finale, in which unremitting variety is raised to the level of a formal principle, does not wholly succeed in fulfilling the promise of the earlier movements. The second and third symphonies, entitled *To October* and *The First of May* respectively, are both in a single movement with a choral conclusion. Both are a result of questing and experimentation, neither particularly successful in matters of form. Yet the musical expression is spacious and daring. Passages such as those at the beginning and end of the second symphony, containing no trace of a tonal basis, remain unique in Shostakovich's output.

The fourth symphony, opus 43, was not heard until 1961, a quarter of a century after its composition, as Shostakovich withdrew it following the first orchestral rehearsals. Again the composer embraced the classical-Romantic principle of form, and the musical language of Tchaikovsky, Bruckner and Mahler. The first movement is written in true sonata form with an emormous development section, complete with the quasi-baroque concertante interpolations so widely favoured at the time. Characteristic of the symphony as a whole is the way in which Shostakovich spotlights individual instrumental groups, a procedure similar to that employed by Mahler and Ives. The conclusion of the second movement is a masterpiece of instrumentation, its graceful string figures artfully combined with explosive percussion. The finale shows the composer juxtaposing passages of extreme contrast in a short space. A vehement beginning is followed by a waltz and pastoral sections, in which the cuckoo's cry is to be heard, and the work ends with a long melancholy coda. The fifth symphony, bearing the programmatic title *The Stabilization of Personality,* is essentially a late-Romantic work incorporating Wagnerian harmony. As in the sixth symphony, the motto of optimism, *From darkness into light,* dictated by the Soviet authorities, tends towards triviality. The seventh and eighth symphonies reflect various war-time events in a patriotic way. Fascinating in the first movement of the seventh symphony is a protracted ostinato which takes

the place of the development. As in Ravel's *Bolero*, this *ostinato* works toward an enormous climax, but the character is much more sinister. Symphonies eleven to fourteen, like much music written in the years between 1950 and 1970, were conceived as programme music. No. 11, opus 103 (1957) commemorates the year 1905, the year of revolution, in which Rimsky-Korsakov made his liberalism explicit. The twelfth symphony, *The Year 1917* (opus 112, 1961), was dedicated to Lenin. Symphony no. 13 (1962) is not only of a programmatic nature but vocal as well. A chorus declaims poems by Yevgeny Yevtushenko, including his famous *Babi Yar*, with its denunciation of anti-semitism. When Premier Krushchev withdrew his support of Yevtushenko, Shostakovich's thirteenth symphony also disappeared. The fourteenth symphony, for soprano, bass and chamber orchestra, is a song-cycle in which the increasing asperity of the musical idiom is closely bound up with the textual content. In the fifteenth symphony (1971), Shostakovich does not strive for profundity. A gentle sound predominates. This and the many instances of persiflage, such as the quotation of Rossini's William Tell theme, exclude the work from the influence of true symphonic art. The only symphony completely within this tradition is the ninth, which can be regarded as a pendant to Prokofiev's *Classical Symphony*.

Just as the symphony in Russia could flourish thanks to the dominance of tonality, so in the rest of Europe the symphony could only blossom where confinement to a tonal centre was still held in esteem. Such a group of composers centred itself around Paul Hindemith. Hindemith used the denomination 'symphony' for the first time in 1937, employing it more and more frequently as he became increasingly conscious of his place in musical history. In total he uses the classifications of 'symphony' or 'symphonic' eight times.

Best-known is the symphony *Mathis der Maler* (1934). From his opera of the same name about the sixteenth-century painter Mathis Grünewald, who was ever in conflict with the authorities, Hindemith extracted three symphonic episodes. These were inspired by pieces of Grünewald's Isenheimer altar in Colmar: Angelic Concert, Burial, and the Temptation of St Anthony. Hindemith tastefully works two chorale melodies into the symphony: in the first movement, *Es sangen drei Engel ein süssen Gesang* and in the third, *Lauda Sion Salvatorem*.

The process for *Die Harmonie der Welt* was the reverse: Hindemith later used this symphony, which treats the life and work of the scholar Johannes Kepler, as a basis for an opera. The symphony provides a clear link with the sound and expressive world of Bruckner. This is also true for the *Symphonische Tänze*, which may well have been intended as dances, but provide an example of a true symphony in their interrelation. The symphonic procedure is also visible in *Symphonische Metamorfosen Carl Maria von Weberscher Themen*, in which four pieces for piano duet are so reorganized, transformed and enriched in a variety of ways, as to allow one to speak of a proper symphony. Less successful is Hindemith's attempt to transfer his ideal of *Spielmusik* to the symphonic form, as in the symphony in B flat for concert band, the *Sinfonia Serena* and the symphony in E flat. These all have a concertante character coupled with the application of polyphony. Admittedly this combination leads to a number of surprising and original solutions to problems of form, such as the partial layering of originally separate structural elements and the use of fugal components.

In the footsteps of Hindemith and his concertante polyphony followed Karl Amadeus Hartmann, Johann Nepumuk David and, to a certain extent, the Swiss composer Arthur Honegger. Hartmann joins Hindemith's techniques of construction with the late-Romantic tradition of Bruckner and Mahler. His eight symphonies are without exception charged with tragic expression and extremely elaborate as regards constitution. Polyphonic structure for Hartmann is a very sophisticated affair, which derives from three basic rules. According to

Ture Rangström

Ture Rangström (1884-1947) was famous in Sweden as a composer, conductor and music critic. He studied in Stockholm and in Munich (with Pfitzner) as well as voice in Berlin. As a music critic, Rangström wrote for various magazines and journals from 1909 until 1921. He conducted the Symphony Orchestra of Göteborg from 1922 until 1925.

Rangström's early works are clearly influenced by impressionism, but later on, he developed a more personal and definitely more Swedish style. Between 1910 and 1912 a number of his symphonic poems were popularly received. After these came his symphonies: *August Strindberg in Memoriam*, 1915; *My Country*, 1919; *Song Under the Skies*; *Fourth Symphony, 'Invocatio'*, 1936.

Ture Rangström wrote a great deal of important, varied music. He left us many suites for orchestra, lots of chamber music and especially lieder. It is for these lieder in particular, that Rangström is so loved in his native Sweden.

Karol Szymanowski

Polish musical life in the first part of this century, and the part Karol Szymanowski (1882-1937) played therein, both fall outside the interests of the western classical music lover. Szymanowski's music is not part of any movement in the 20th century. Between the masters Stravinsky on the one hand, and Schoenberg on the other, were composers who followed their own, different paths. They were not part of any given trend, were not the focal point of any known clique, in short, they were not fashionable. Their music was, compared to the great masters mentioned, for the most part, ignored. Karol Szymanowski was such a composer.

Szymanowski was born in Timoshovka on his father's estate near Kiev, one of many such estates under the Polish crown in the Ukraine. Timoshovka was a Polish enclave in the middle of the Ukrainian people and was the centre of culture with a lively musical life. Father Szymanoski upheld the musical standard, and Mozart and Beethoven were the first masters the children came into contact with.

Szymanowski received his first music lessons also from his father. Later, he was a student at the Gustav Neuhaus school. During a trip to Vienna, where he heard Wagner's *Lohengrin*, Szymanowski decided to make music his life. He returned home with piano transcriptions of all of Wagner's operas which he studied intensely.

In 1901, Szymanowski went to Warsaw to study with Zawinski and Naskowski. He had already a few compositions to his credit, several of which were already published. (The *Third* of *Four Suites* became world famous because Paderewski included it in his repertoire) In Warsaw, Szymanowski befriended the conductor Gregor Fitelberg who later performed many of his works, as well as the pianist Arthur Rubinstein. Szymanowski did find the music life in the Polish capital very conservative. The rest of the world was listening to Wagner and Richard Strauss, but Warsaw was still busy with Mendelssohn. In 1905, Szymanowski founded a group with other young Polish composers known under the name Young Polen in Music. Berlin, ironically enough, eventually became their headquarters.

Paul Hindemith

The story goes that Hindemith (1895-1963) ran away from home at the age of eleven when his parents refused to allow him to become a musician. The young Hindemith supported himself by playing in cafés and dance orchestras. In 1909, he began his studies at the Dr. Hoch Konservatorium in Frankfurt, following courses in violin, counterpoint and composition. He was already busy composing his opus 1 through 8.

In 1915, Hindemith was given the post of concertmaster in the orchestra of the Opera. That same year, he toured Holland, Germany and Spain as a member of the Rebner Quartet. Right after the First World War, Hindemith was busy with his first operas: *Mörder, Hoffnung der Frauen* and *Das Nusch-Nuschi*. His relationship with the Donaueschinger Musiktage, the most important music festival of its time, began in 1921. In 1922, Hindemith resigned from the Rebner Quartet and helped found the Amar Quartet with which he toured Europe. Hindemith accepted a post teaching composition at the Hochschule für Musik in Berlin in 1927.

Paul Hindemith had an intense interest in all aspects of music. He wrote works for mechanical piano, mechanical organ, for the Trautonium * and for the gramophone as an autonomous instrument. Hindemith was a great promoter of 'Zeitoper': the new genre combining the newest texts and music.

Hindemith's enthusiasm and energy, his weakness for new things, made him an extremely popular figure, especially with the German youth. There were others, though, that campaigned against Hindemith's person and everything he stood for. Those in the German Socialist movement worked against the composer inside and outside of Germany, making it extremely difficult for him to work, and finally declaring Hindemith 'politisch untragbar' in 1934. The Nazis removed him from his post at the Musik Hochschule and forbade performance of his music. Personally, all these awful experiences had no negative effective on Hindemith. His enthusiasm and energy for his work was rather intensified by the trauma and persecution he was forced to undergo.

Hindemith remained in Berlin until 1938, doing his best to ignore the boycott. He went to serve the Turkish government in their attempts to revive the musical life of their country from 1934 until 1937. Hindemith also toured the United States every year, finally moving there permanently in 1940.

The first mature masterpiece that Hindemith wrote was his *Opera Mathias der Mahler* which he wrote in 1934 in Lenzkirch in the Black Forest. Parts of this piece were and are performed as a symphony under the same title. In Germany, *Mathias* was considered a none too subtle attack on the political powers of the time, misusing their muscle to persecute artists. The hero of the opera is the painter Mathias Grünewald and the plot concerns an altar piece that hangs in Colmar. It is evident that Hindemith, despite his posture of calm, was deeply troubled and hurt by the events around and concerning him.

Hindemith wrote two more symphonies during his American period. After 1946, he slowly renewed his European contacts, performing and lecturing there once again. Beginning in 1951, he taught at Yale University and in Zurich and he conducted more and more on both continents. Hindemith returned to settle in Switzerland in 1953 where he composed, among other things, *Symphonie Harmonie der Welt*.

A synopsis of Hindemith's work is not easy to give. His oeuvre is, in the first place, very extensive. His interests covered practically every possible aspect of music as well.

* Trautonium: from the German, Trautwein (1924), one of the oldest electronic musical instruments. It is very difficult to play. It belongs to the same group as the 'Ondes Martenot', an instrument that Messiaen wrote for.

these, melodies lend themselves primarily to: 1. variation 2. fugue and 3. all possible forms of imitation (for instance, from back to front, or in contrary motion from high to low using the same pattern of intervals). By these and other means he often achieves shattering climaxes in an expanded tonal idiom with extremely well-thought-out constructions. For example, under the title of *Toccata variata*, in the second movement of his sixth symphony, Hartmann presents three fugues, bound together by means of variation-techniques, and by accelerating the metric impulse and thickening the polyphonic structure, he achieves enormous intensity using melodies which are in themselves quite simple.

The symphonies of the Austrian composer Johann Nepomuk David are all monothematic, built out of a single motif. In order to avoid the risk of monotony this might produce, David exploits constructional procedures similar to those used by Hartmann, and with a Bach-like polyphony.

The symphonic art of Arthur Honegger is on the one hand firmly rooted in the nineteenth century, yet his harmonic idiom, joining an expanded tonal sense to an archaic-sounding diatonic system, allows him to achieve an authentic style. His connections with the past emerge above all in the breadth of his melodic invention, his retention of the three-part symphonic form (with the exception of the *Monopartita* of 1951) and his inclination towards the programmatic. Not only did Honegger come to the symphony via the symphonic poem, the last three of his five symphonies were assigned programmes: *Symphonie Liturgique* (1946), *Deliciae basiliensis* (1946) and *Di Tre Re* (1947). The first movements of his symphonies always demonstrate a very personal approach to sonata form. In the first symphony, the three themes of the exposition are sounded simultaneously in the recapitulation. The first movement of the second symphony has two development sections. The first movement of the fifth symphony has no development, but two groups of themes and a recapitulation. The second symphony, which Honegger wrote while deeply concerned with the events of the Second World War, exhibits his strong urge towards 'autobiographical' music. It is written for string orchestra with a solo trumpet in the finale.

Like Honegger, Albert Roussel stands at the frontier between two epochs. In his four symphonies Roussel proceeds along the path from programme music to an absolute symphonic form. The first symphony, from 1908, bears the title *Poème de la forêt*. High points are the third symphony of 1930 and the fourth (in A major) of 1935, both of which have maintained a place in the repertory. Echoes of Mahler can be heard in the Romantic understructure of these symphonies, but the rugged motive power, the daring melodies and a preference for great masses of sound recall Prokofiev and Stravinsky.

The symphonic work of Honegger's contemporary Darius Milhaud falls into two distinct groups. Between 1917 and 1923 he wrote six symphonies for reduced forces (the sixth, for example, is for vocal quartet, oboe and cello). Each of them is a short ironic piece of raillery, poking fun at established symphonic forms and procedures. Only in 1939 did he address himself to large-scale symphonic form. He wrote thirteen symphonies, some calling for a chorus (no. 3, *Te Deum*, 1946; no. 13, *Pacem in Terris*, 1966, from the encyclical of Pope John XXIII) and some with titles (no. 8, *Rhôdanienne*, 1957; no. 12, *Rurale*, 1961). In these works Milhaud shows himself to be an impressive and imaginative orchestrator.

Among twentieth-century French symphonists, mention must also be made of Henri Dutilleux and Henri Barraud. In his first symphony (1951), second symphony *Le Double* (1959) and *Métaboles pour orchestre* (1964), by making use of expanded tonality Dutilleux achieves works which are virtuoso and strictly organized, as well as clear and transparent. The second symphony owes its name to the fact that the principle of concerto grosso is applied within the symphonic form: a

Darius Milhaud (1892-1974), whose witty essays in polytonality gave his music a considerable vogue.

small ensemble, a concertino of twelve instruments, confronts the full orchestra.

Dutilleux and Barraud have in common their attempt to bridge the gap between the various twentieth-century currents, from impressionism up to and including serialism, even endeavouring to bring these different worlds into contact with each other. Barraud however bases his style more explicitly on the strict contrapuntal methods of Hindemith, which gives his works a darker quality than those of his colleague.

An isolated case is the ten-part symphony *Turangalîla* by Olivier Messiaen. Although the work does not fit into any traditional symphonic conception, because of its thematic relationships, scope and power, it has its place in the world of the symphony.

The American composer Charles Ives wrote four symphonies, the first two in the period before 1900 and the last two well after the turn of the century. The fourth symphony, which Ives wrote in the years 1911–16, is indisputably the most important. It is a four-part composition for large orchestra with two pianos and a mixed chorus in the first and final movements. The work bears little relationship to traditional symphonic form. With the exception of the third movement, a conventional fugue, the symphony seems consciously to be pointing towards the future. After a majestic and monumental opening (based on the poem *Watchman, Tell us of the Night* by Lowell Mason), there follows a lengthy allegretto of an extremely sombre and oppressive nature. After the fugue, this atmosphere is again evoked in the fourth movement. Noteworthy in Ives's method of composition is the division of the orchestra into independent, sometimes even spatially separated, sound-groups. The consistent use of these independent groups leads to a frequent piling-up of various rhythms one above another simultaneously and the occurrence of elaborate polytonal and polyphonic situations. A great deal of the melodic material is borrowed from, or even quotes directly, American tunes, whether instrumental or vocal. These include, for example, *Yankee Doodle; Hail Columbia, the Gem of the Ocean; Joy to the World* and *In the Sweet By and By*. In addition Ives also re-uses material from his own earlier compositions.

The collage-technique which Ives employs is also used by the American Elliott Carter in his *Symphony of Three Orchestras*, written in 1976.

Samuel Barber composed his first single-movement symphony in 1935–36. The work breathes a Romantic atmosphere with certain influences

Darius Milhaud

Darius Milhaud (1892-1974) comes from a Jewish merchants family that long ago settled in Aix-en-Provence. In 1909, Milhaud entered the Conservatoire in Paris where his teachers included Dukas, Leroux, Widor and d'Indy. He planned on becoming a violinist, but was more and more attracted to composition as his studies progressed. Milhaud greatly admired Debussy, and had a distinct dislike of Wagner and Ravel.

Milhaud's first worthy composition is his *Sonata for violin and piano* from 1911. While still a student, he came into contact with Honegger and Auric, as well as Durey, Poulenc and Germaine Tailleferre, with whom he organized first the 'Société des nouveaux jeunes', and later the famous 'Groupe des Six'.

From 1917 until 1919, Milhaud worked as the secretary for the French ambassador in Brazil, Paul Claudel. South American sounds can be found in pieces like *Saudadas do Brazil* and *Scaramouche*. Black jazz fascinated Milhaud as well: its rhythm, harmony and specific instrumentation can also be found in his work. Satie, Stravinsky, Meyerbeer and Berlioz also inspired Milhaud throughout his life.

After his return to Paris in 1919, Milhaud undertook many concert tours throughout Europe and America, mostly conducting his own work. He spent the Second World War in California, teaching composition at Mill's College. In 1945, Milhaud was appointed as composition professor at the Conservatoire in Paris.

The oeuvre Milhaud produced is extensive and varied, and sometimes lacks the necessary self-criticism that should have limited it to some degree. The opus number is far beyond 300, an amount rarely equalled even by composers who were free to work constantly. All possible genres are represented as well as important, revolutionary pieces like *La Création du Monde*. However, there are in this number, pieces whose spirit or technique is so conventional as to be disappointing in performance.

During the twenties, Milhaud was definitely the most creative and versatile of his composing contemporaries. Having written the music for Cocteau's ballet *Le Boeuf sur le Toit* however, in which Milhaud had arranged many Brazilian elements, he realized the dangers involved, the possibility of being dismissed as only fashionable. He thereupon decided to dedicate himself more seriously to his work, not to fall prey to the dangers of commercial success.

There are nine known symphonies from Milhaud's hand: *Le Printemps*, 1917; *Symphony nr. 1*, 1939; *Pastorale*, 1918; *Symphony nr.2*, 1944; *Sérénade*, 1921; *Hymnus ambrosianus* (with choir), 1946; *Ouverture, Choral and Etude for Strings*, 1922; *Symphony nr.5 for wind instruments*, 1922; *Symphony 1848*, 1947.

Aaron Copland

Aaron Copland (b. 1900) is one of the foremost composers to come out of the United States. After receiving his earliest music lessons from his sister and studying piano with V. Wittgenstein and Clarence Adler, he received instruction in composition from Rubin Goldmark, nephew of the well known Karl Goldmark and, in Paris, from Nadia Boulanger. In 1924 he returned to America where he took an active role in contemporary musical life. Copland assimilated jazz elements into his music, and later added both North and South American folk elements. After 1950 his work also shows signs of twelve-tone techniques. In addition to his compositions, Copland wrote a great deal about music: *What to Listen for in Music* (1938), *Our New Music* (1941), *Music and Imagination* (1952) and *Copland on Music* (1960).

Dmitri Shostakovich

Between 1919 and 1925, Shostakovich (1906-1975) studied at the Conservatory in Leningrad, piano with Nikolajev and Steinberg and composition with Glazunov. In 1925, Shostakovich had finished his *First Symphony*, opus 10, a beautiful, mature work which was performed for the first time a year after its completion in his place of birth. He was immediately recognized as a very important compositional talent and his name became quickly famous throughout Russia and beyond. The *First Symphony* was performed in Berlin under Bruno Walter in 1933.

The following two symphonies: *October Assignment*, 1927, (the month of the Russian Revolution) and *May First Symphony*, 1928, were both less spectacular than the *First Symphony*. Works that then followed were more disappointing. Nevertheless, Shostakovich's career continued to be very successful. He was recognized more and more as composer and as pianist. In 1934, his second opera, *A Lady Macbeth from Mitsensk*, was, upon its première in Leningrad, instantly recognized as a first class masterpiece. It became a sensation in America, whereas the reception in London was less enthusiastic. In 1936, the Soviet authorities dismissed the work as bourgeois, unhealthy and unsuited for the people. Shostakovich was truly shocked by all the different reactions. Despite the 'official' reaction in his country, Shostakovich's career continued to blossom. He was considered the foremost composer of his generation. His dedication to his country was emphasized by Shostakovich's behaviour during World War Two, when the composer refused to leave the threatened Leningrad. His *Seventh Symphony, the Leningrad Symphony*, appeared in 1941 and was a great triumph.

Shostakovich's music is very nationalistic despite the traceable influence of both Berlioz and Mahler in his work. Characteristic are the pathos, the daring rhythms and orchestrations and often, the satire. In spite of the often trivial thematic material, often written under pressure from Soviet authority, Shostakovich survives as an independent and masterful composer in most of his work.

In 1943, Shostakovich was named professor at the Conservatory in Moscow. Five years later, he was again accused by the Soviet authorities, this time for supposedly writing music in opposition to communist ideals. He survived yet again this official attack, and was named 'Artist of the People of the USSR' in 1954.

Official opinion changed to a degree in 1958, and the ban on *A Lady Macbeth from Mitsensk* was lifted. The composer revised the work which was thereafter known under the title: *Katerina Izmalova*.

Shostakovich wrote an enormous amount of piano works in all forms: solo concertos, with choir, lieder, for films and ballets. His greatest achievement, however, is undoubtedly the group of 15 symphonies written between 1926 and 1971, as well as his 15 string quartets. These pieces belong among the greatest of monuments of classical music history.

Karl Hartmann

Karl Hartmann (1905-1963) studied at the Music Academy in Munich. After having worked for three years as a freelance composer upon graduation, he was appointed director of Musica Viva, an organization sponsored by the State Opera in Munich and dedicated to the promotion of contemporary music. Hartmann was a devotee of Alban Berg's. He used the Zwölf Ton Technik without adhering to the system's rules too strictly. Hartmann was considered a foremost representative of the new German school already during his own lifetime. Hartmann included six symphonies in his work.

from the young Prokoviev. In this symphony Barber made a startling formal discovery. Although written in one continuous movement, the composition contains a scherzo and adagio which are worked into the development of the large sonata form of the whole, after which the exposition themes again make their appearance.

The second symphony (1944–47) also adheres to the Romantic tradition. The first movement (allegro ma non tanto) is in true sonata form with three clearly defined themes, a development and a recapitulation. This is followed by a pastoral andante un poco mosso and the work concludes with a passionate allegro risoluto, The symphony was, however, withdrawn by the composer.

Less important as a symphonist than either of these Americans is Aaron Copland. Yet his *Dance Symphony* of 1925 must be mentioned, a work in which, like Hindemith, he succeeded in adapting dances to the symphonic form while maintaining their dance-like character.

Leonard Bernstein, who has won greater fame as a conductor than as a composer, has three symphonies to his credit. The first and third are bound up with elements of the Jewish liturgy. The first *Jeremiah*, dates from 1942 and is based on Hebrew melodies. The first movement, which uses the Jewish vocal patterns of the *Amidah* and *K'rovoh*, symbolizes Jeremiah's prophecy of the destruction of Jerusalem. The second movement portrays the mocking reaction of the corrupt priests, symbolized by jazz rhythms, while the main theme of the first movement is proclaimed distortedly braying horns. The third movement harks back to the first, but what then was presented as prophecy now is sounded as a lamentation, with passages from Jeremiah's eponymous book sung by a mezzo-soprano.

The second symphony, *The Age of Anxiety*, is based on a poem by W. H. Auden. Bernstein divides the poem into two three-part sections: a prologue with two series of variations, followed by an elegy, 'The Dirge', a scherzo 'The Masque', and an epilogue. The work has a programme: four people philosophise about their own future and the future of the world. The third symphony, the *Kaddish* (1963), exhales an atmosphere similar to the first. Notable in the build-up of melodies and structures is a compositional technique, which approaches that of Johann Nepomuk David or Willem Pijper: small units are used as building-blocks to create larger lines which constantly renew themselves, piece by piece, without breaking the over-all musical coherence.

For a long time it seemed as if Dutch symphonic music, heavily influenced by late German Romanticism, might suffocate under the burden of its own rigidity. Fortunately a few composers, though still dependent upon the Romantic idiom, experienced an impulse towards innovation. Hendrik Andriessen wrote five symphonies and one symphonic étude, characterized by classical construction and a French sound-palette with room for Romanticism à la César Franck and impressionism in the manner of Debussy.

Also the composer of five symphonies, Jan van Gilse perpetuated the German Romantic idiom of Richard Strauss.

Henk Badings, who composed no less than fifteen symphonies between 1930 and 1970, also has based his work on the German tradition. In matters of form and instrumentation he demonstrates strong ties with the past as well as a certain individuality.

Whereas the sound-worlds of Andriessen and Badings appear uninfluenced by the developments advanced by the Viennese School, Stravinsky and Bartók, the innovations coming out of Vienna and Paris proved to be of great significance for Willem Pijper and Matthijs Vermeulen. Although both of them held the opinion that the direction taken by the Viennese School, with its emphasis on atonality and the twelve-tone system, would provide consequences ultimately unacceptable for such aspects of composition as form, rhythm and melody, leading finally to a disintegration of sound as we know it, they were sufficiently stimulated to develop their own structural principles. Pijper and Vermeulen also have in common a great admiration for Stravinsky, even though this finds expression in their symphonic work in widely divergent ways.

Vermeulen's seven symphonies, written between 1914 and 1965, are characterized by a continual use of 'polymelodies', various melodies appearing simultaneously in the different instrumental groups, each retaining its own independence. Vermeulen combines this with a forceful motoric drive, from which ear-catching rhythmic or metrical accentuation is absent, but thick orchestration obscures the compact structures and undifferentiated lines.

Willem Pijper's works demonstrate a greater refinement. His use of a great variety of unexpected rhythmic and metrical shifts results in a continual revivification of structure. While with Vermeulen harmony as an important musical ingredient is sacrificed to the 'polymelodic', Pijper achieves a true polytonal harmony in which different keys appear at the same time. A very personal aspect of Pijper's compositional methods is the 'germ-cell system', which he himself developed: a minute motif, itself extremely unobtrusive, permeates and influences large sections, or even the entire composition, as all musical components (melody, rhythm, harmony, etc.) are grafted onto it. Pijper's best-known symphony is his third and last. It bears the motto: 'if I can not reach heaven, then I will raise hell.' With satanic rage, hell is indeed raised by the full orchestra in the finale; from the outset a climax begins to build, becoming almost unbearable near the end, followed by no sense of resolution, and leaving behind a feeling of despair. In the 1950s Dutch composition was heavily influenced by Pijper's music.

During the same period, through the work of Kees van Baaren and his students, the twelve-tone system and serialism also became influential, with their emphasis on the confinement of all musical parameters into ordered series. Since the beginning of the 1970s, a reaction against this has produced a return to tonality, though it is a tonality charged with a different and more personal character.

Peter Schat, who in his earlier compositions turned his back purpose-

Ralph Vaughan Williams

Ralph Vaughan Williams (1872-1958) received his instruction in composition from Max Bruch and, much later, from Maurice Ravel. Originally an organist, he found himself increasingly attracted to composition. In 1918 he became a professor of composition at the Royal College of Music. Like Bartók, Vaughan Williams made an extensive study of folk music. He studied, collected and arranged a large number of English folk songs: they had a profound effect upon his own compositions too, particularly in the field of orchestral music.

In his own country, Vaughan Williams belongs to the most influential composers of his generation. His reputation became definitively established with the *Sea Symphony* (1910), and his great hymn, *For All the Saints*, remains one of the most popular in the English canon.

Olivier Messiaen

Olivier Messiaen (1908-?) is of half Flemish, half Provençale ancestry. His father was a literature professor, and a well known translator of Shakespeare. Messiaen spent his youth in Grenoble where, as a boy of eight, he taught himself to play the piano. When only 11, he entered the Conservatoire in Paris where his most important teachers were Marcel Dupré (organ) and Paul Dukas (composition). Messiaen was honoured with many prizes while still a student. He has also made a life study of Hindu and Greek music, as well as birdsong. In 1931, Messiaen was appointed organist at the church La Trinité and in 1939 added the posts of professor at both the Ecole Normale de Musique and the Schola Cantorum in Paris. He was a co-founder of the avant-garde composer's group 'Jeunes France' in 1939 along with André Jolivet, Daniel Lesur and Yves Baudrier.

The inspiration for and the philosophy behind Messiaen's work is his deep mystical, religious belief. Symbolically, his beliefs can be traced in all of his compositions. Many of his titles are Biblical or liturgical. Messiaen calls himself 'compositeur de musique et rythmicien', calling to attention himself the importance rhythm plays in his works. His rhythms are intensely varied and are drawn from such different sources as the Hindu tala rhythms and medieval models.

Messiaen is a master of orchestration, using extremely varied percussion instruments as well as vibraphone, celesta and Ondes Martinot. The spectrum of rhythmical effects in his compositions is almost unlimited. Messiaen is also the author of 'Technique de mon Language Musical' which he wrote in 1944 explaining his compositional methods.

Since the end of the Second World War, Messiaen has been recognized as a foremost French composer. He is still so recognized to this day. He is perhaps most appreciated in the world of church and especially organ music, a field where he especially unites his musical talents and religious beliefs.

Aaron Copland

Peter Maxwell Davies

Peter Maxwell Davies (1934-) studied at the Manchester College of Music. There, he was one of the founders of the Manchester New Music Group for which he wrote several compositions including *Five Pieces For Piano* in 1956. In Rome, Davies studied with Petrassi. In his early years, he was clearly under the influence of serialism and total serialism and the rhythmic experiments of Olivier Messiaen. His first important work, *Prolation* of 1958, is clearly an example of these influences.

Davies worked in the United States from 1962 until 1964 at Princeton University. Medieval manners of composition crept into his work at this time (*Alma Redemptoris Mater*, 1957 and *Ricercar*, 1959). Returning from America, Davies settled in Dorset. Theatre music now became an important element in Davies's work (*Eight Songs for A Mad King*, 1969, for example). He wrote an important opera, *Taverner*, about the 16th century composer Taverner who ended up in jail as a protestant heretic. This opera had its première at the Royal Opera House Covent Garden.

Hans Werner Henze

Hans Werner Henze (1926-) was first a student of Wolfgang Fortner's at the Heidelberg School for Church Music, and then of René Leibowitz's in Paris. Henze was successful even as a very young man. His opera *Das Wundertheater* was published in 1949 when Henze was only 17!

Henze belongs to the most avant-garde of the German composers of his time. Despite the fact that he is not a strict adherent, his music is often based on or influenced by Schoenberg's Zwölf Ton Technik. Throughout his life, Henze was recognized as an important contemporary composer.

In 1951, Henze was awarded the Robert Schumann prize in Düsseldorf for his Chamber music for piano, flute and strings (1946). He was appointed music director of the ballet at the opera in Wiesbaden from 1950 until 1952, and did a great deal to promote dance in Germany in those years.

Henze's early works are clearly influenced by his teacher Fortner, and the music of Stravinsky. Later, he developed a more personal style, using his own version of the twelve tone system already mentioned. His works are known for their amazing structures, sharp rhythms and effective orchestration. One of his most successful pieces is Henze's *Third Symphony* from 1951. It begins with an unusual declamation by the god Apollo and culminates in a magical dance.

Hindemith's descriptive symphony *Mathis der Maler* is among the most enduringly popular of all his works.

Overleaf: Elgar never completed his third symphony. In this sketch for the Adagio, the opening bars are surmounted by the beginning of his Piano Quintet, opus 84.

fully on all traditional forms, composed a symphony in 1978 in which he attempted to reach a synthesis between classical form and non-traditional elements: twelve-tone techniques, uncommon instruments within the orchestra and unusual metres. Younger composers such as Tristan Keuris, whose *Sinfonia* (1972) was an overnight success, and Jan Wagemans (symphony, opus 3, 1972), have kept the symphonic form alive in Holland.

In Great Britain, after Edward Elgar, the most important exponent of English late Romanticism, Ralph Vaughan Williams, attracted attention as a symphonist. Nationalistic tendencies, deriving from an early interest in folk song, are present in most of his symphonies. Actual folk material is seldom quoted; rather the music breathes a melodic atmosphere

evocative of the folk spirit. His links with the traditions of the sixteenth and seventeenth century polyphonists are apparent in his harmonies, often based upon the old modes, and in his clearly constructed counterpoint. His first three symphonies – *Sea Symphony* (1905-10), *London Symphony* (1914) and *Pastoral Symphony* (1922) – are written in an easily assimilable style. In the fourth symphony (1935), Vaughan Williams makes a sudden departure from this folk-influenced style. The work is violent and dramatic, full of dissonance and dark sounds. With his fifth symphony (1943) he returns to his familiar musical language with its folk character. The sixth, seventh and eighth symphonies share, in addition to unconventional formal structures, an increasing use of dissonance and harmonic tension. In his ninth symphony (1956-57) Vaughan Williams succeeds in exploring new sound possibilities: there are important passages for saxophone trio and for flugelhorn.

Eleven years his junior, Arnold Bax, with seven three-movement symphonies to his credit, characterized his music in the following words: 'My music is the expression of emotional states.' Bax is a perfect example

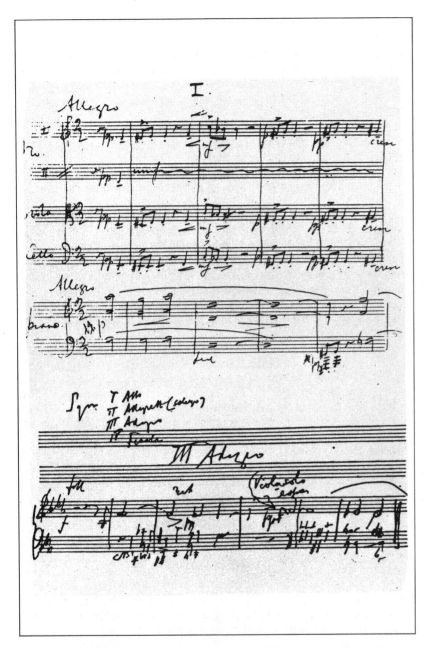

Gustav Holst

Gustav Holst (1874-1934) was the village organist as a very young man, responsible for the choral activities, and with a small orchestra also in his charge. These youthful experiences would prove important for his later career. In 1893, Holst entered the Royal College of Music in London (to become a fellow of that same institution 27 years later). He tried 8 times to receive a scholarship, all of them unsuccessful. After having studied theory, he finally received a scholarship for composition and went to study with Stanford. Holst also studied piano and organ, but because of a nerve infection in his hand, was forced to trade in the two keyboard instruments for the trombone. As a trombonist, Holst played in many orchestras, including the Scottish Orchestra, experiencing first hand the problems of interpretation which was very profitable for him in his composing career. While still a student, Holst became friends with Vaughan Williams, someone who was to have a great deal of influence on Holst throughout his life.

Important for Holst's music were his travels to Algeria (the *Beni Mora Suite*, 1910), to Saloniki in 1918 and to Constantinople and the Far East in 1919. 1925 saw Holst's most public success. His opera *Boar's Head* was performed in Manchester and his *First Choral Symphony* (for soprano, choir and orchestra with texts by John Keats) was premièred at the Leeds Festival.

Holst's *Cotswolds Symphony* was premièred in Bournemouth in 1902. After this piece, Holst concentrated on only choral composition and the study of folksongs. He finished a *Somerset Rhapsody* in 1907. This was in what was referred to as his 'Sanskrit period', a time in which the composer was strongly attracted to Hindu epics and the hymns of Rig-Veda. The result was Holst's chamber opera, *Savitri*. This piece as well as the *Beni Mora* caused the public to associate Holst very often with the east. Holst has remained known, especially outside of England, for his suite, *The Planets*. When his short orchestral work *Egdon Heath* appeared in 1927, the public was intensely disappointed. The piece was only tolerated 'because it was at least from Holst'. The composer himself, however, considered *Egdon Heath*, together with his *First Choral Symphony*, his best work.

Edmund Rubbra

Despite his working class origins and unlike the rest of his family, young Edmund Rubbra (1901-), born in Northampton, was deeply attracted to music. At an early age, he had already worn out a string of piano teachers, all of these local unknowns. He was forced to earn his living working, for while in a shoe factory and at another time, for a train company. Even during his school years, Rubbra shyly and self-consciously attempted to compose. Rubbra studied music with Cyril Scott, a revolutionary composer he admired greatly (he idolized Debussy). Later, he also studied with Gustav Holst and Ralph Vaughan Williams.

Rubbra's musical personality is most successfully expressed in his symphonic as well as his vocal works. What impresses one the most are the melodies in both types of compositions, but it is the five symphonies that are the nucleus of Rubbra's oeuvre. The five are progressively more successful. In the first two, Rubbra is so busy following the rules of traditional symphonic development, that the listener is sorely tried. The tension never lets up for even the shortest while. The *Third* and *Fourth Symphonies* are more relaxed whereas the *Fifth* is a highpoint in Rubbra's creative evolution.

Apart from composition, Rubbra built up quite a reputation in the thirties as a music critic. He was also an exceptional pianist. Ironically enough, as a composer, he never wrote for his own instrument.

of a 'threshold composer', someone standing midway between the old and the new. He shares with Vaughan Williams his affection for old traditions, but impressionism by no means left him untouched. His work is therefore somewhat ambiguous, colour and form hover between the Romantic and the modern. A more interesting symphonist of the same generation is Havergal Brian, composer of thirty-two symphonies, twenty-one of which he completed after the age of 80 (he died at the age of 86). Brian's musical language is compact and functional. His early symphonies lack the compactness of his later work and are remarkably ambitious. His music is classically tonal, sober and meticulously crafted. Michael Tippett too, in his four symphonies, seems preoccupied with the possibilities of the classical form. The fourth symphony in particular is intense, melancholy, and deeply felt. It is a profoundly moving work, and most rewarding to come to know.

The most prominent British composer during the years after the Second World War is undoubtedly Benjamin Britten. His talent revealed itself very early: the delightful *Simple Symphony* for strings, published in 1934, is based upon material from compositions he wrote between the ages of nine and twelve. His two greatest contributions to the symphonic

Sir Arthur Bliss

Arthur Bliss (1891-1975) studied in Rugby and went to university at Cambridge. He attended the Royal College of Music in London for one year, and furthered his studies with Stanford, Vaughan-Williams and Gustav Holst. Bliss studied orchestral direction along side of his more important composition courses, but his talents and direction were obvious.

During the First World War, Bliss served in France. While Bliss was at the front, two string quartets of his were performed and published. For one of these, he received a prize. Returning from the war, however, Bliss had the engraving plates destroyed as well as all the unsold copies.

In 1919, theatre music that Bliss had arranged from Elizabethan pieces was performed at the Shakespeare Festival at Stratford-on-Avon. He also composed chamber music that was performed at the Aeolian Hall in London in 1920. The composer himself considered *Madam Noy*, a piece for soprano and 5 instruments, as his first mature composition. *Rhapsodie for soprano, tenor and 6 instruments* (1917) was performed at Salzburg at the ISCM (International Society for Contemporary Music) Festival, as was *Rout*, for soprano and 10 instruments (1922). Towards the end of the twenties, Sir Arthur Bliss had, with these three pieces, built up quite a reputation as a very original compositional talent. Always attracted to experimentation, Bliss worked with sonority and colouring, busy trying all sorts of new ideas. These early compositions were inspired in part by Ravel, Stravinsky, and, perhaps more subtly, by the works of 'les Six'.

In 1923, Sir Arthur Bliss left England and settled in Santa Barbera, California. While there, he composed a string quartet, the lieder cycle *The Women of Yueh* (with chamber orchestra accompaniment) and some piano pieces. Bliss returned to London three years later.

The Concertgebouw Orchestra under Pierre Monteux performed the première of Bliss's *Hymn To Apollo* in 1924. Another important composition is *Introduction And Allegro* for orchestra, premièred in London during the Promenade Concerts, and in America, by the Philadelphia Orchestra under Stokowsky (1927). These works bear witness to Bliss's classical spirit; they are his version of 'absolute' music. The *Oboe Quintet*, the *Clarinet Quintet*, the *Violin Sonata* and *Music For Strings* are reiterations of this classical, absolute approach. Another *Oboe Quintet* followed, written on commission in 1927, and performed in Venice by Leon Goossens and the Venetian Quartet. Other than the works already mentioned, the most successful pieces composed by Bliss are his *Pastoral* for choir, mezzo soprano, flute, percussion and strings (dedicated to Elgar); *Seranade* in four movements, two for orchestra and two for baritone solo (performed at the Courtauld-Sargent Concert in London in 1930); *Symphony Morning Heroes* for choir, narrator and orchestra (also a 1930 première) and Music For Strings (performed at the Salzburg Festival of 1935). Bliss also wrote music for film, for example, 'The Things To Come' for H.G. Wells. During the World's Fair in New York in 1939, Solomon performed the Piano Concerto written by Bliss; Adrian Boult was conducting.

There was a third period of composition for Bliss, after his first, experimental, and second, classical periods: he turned his attentions to the theatre. The ballet *Checkmate* is still very successful. *Miracle in the Gospels* has also become quite renowned. It was Bliss's intention with *Miracles*, to compose an opera that was immediately comprehensible for the public, a rarity indeed.

In 1953, Sir Arthur Bliss succeeded Arnold Bax as Master of the Queen's Music. In all of his numerous and varied oeuvre, Bliss wrote but one symphony.

repertory are the *Sinfonia da Requiem* (1940) and the *Cello Symphony* (1963).

William Walton wrote two magnificient symphonies, the first including a splendid scherzo marked con malizia. Among the younger generation of British composers, Malcolm Williamson, born in Australia, stands out in the symphonic field, with his remarkable second symphony (1969), in which he manages to unite traditional symphonic form with highly modern techniques, serialism among them.

In his six symphonies, which he himself calls 'orchestral pieces given the name of symphonies', the German Hans Werner Henze devotes himself to the same problem, that of resolving the conflict between sonata form and the twelve-tone system. He often finds his solutions in variation techniques. In his second and third symphonies he uses the form of the chaconne. His fourth symphony, originally created as the finale of the opera *König Hirsch* (King Stag), is a one-movement work with a cyclical form. The finale of the fifth symphony consists of a series of variations on music from the second part of the work. When Henze uses sonata form, as in the first, fourth and fifth symphonies, his approach is free in the extreme, allowing him to develop well-ordered, logical structures which escape the repressive bonds of traditional rules of structure and development. Henze's attitude towards the twelve-tone system is also characterized by a very free approach, enabling him to achieve a colourful palette of widely expressive means, musical transparency and flowing, almost lyrical lines, fused with dense, compact contrapuntal and motivic structures. His sixth symphony is constructed in a particularly interesting way. There are no actual themes as such, but rather a number of associated musical elements which emerge again and again in the various movements, rhythmic, intervallic and harmonic structures which, in their endless variation, acquire ever-new dimensions.

The Polish composer Witold Lutoslawski has found a highly individual way of disengaging himself from the dictates of form. After his neo-classical first symphony, written in 1946, he turned to the twelve-tone system. His second symphony, dating from the years 1966–67, is based on this system, with the addition of 'aleatoric counterpoint' *i.e.* that the plurality of voices is only partially set down, with the result that a certain element of chance is built in to the music played by the ensemble, initiated either by the conductor or individual members of the orchestra. Naturally there can no longer by any talk of themes, exposition, development, etc. But coherence and compactness still give the work a symphonic allure, to which in any event the oldest definition of 'symphony' is applicable: 'sounding together'.

Witold Lutoslawski

Witold Lutoslawski (1913-) is one of a group of avant-garde composers who came into prominence after the Second World War. In his music, Lutoslawski combines folk melodies with serial and later 'aleatorical' techniques. (The term 'aleatory' entered musical language in the fifties. It is used to designate performances where the element of chance plays an important role. Therefore, no two performances are alike.) Lutoslawski's *Funeral Music For Strings*, 1958, made an enormous impression. The structure of the piece, based on a canon with variations, is very well built up, and the emotional content is considerable. His *Concerto for Orchestra*, 1954, is quite popular.

Bohuslav Martinu

Martinu (1889-1959) was born in Policka (Bohemia). At only eight, Bohuslav Martinu had already written his first string quartet, and in 1906, he entered the Conservatory in Prague. Distracted by his love for literature and theatre, Martinu was suspended from the Conservatorium twice for failing to live up to expectations. He finally left the Conservatory and went to enter the Organ School instead.

In 1913, Martinu became a violinist in the Czech Philharmonic Orchestra. He remained there for 10 years. During the First World War, Martinu refused military service and returned to his native village to become a music teacher.

The National Theatre in Prague performed Martinu's ballet *Istar* in 1922. In that same year, the renowned violinist Joseph Suk persuaded Martinu to return to the Conservatory, something the composer was less than happy about. In 1923, he left for Paris where he stayed until 1940. Martinu became a student of Roussel's, a composer he greatly admired. While in Paris, he was also successful in promoting his own work with several conductors. Talich performed some of Martinu's work in his homeland, Sacher and Ansermet in Switzerland, Henry Wood in England and Koussevitsky in America. Publishers also began to notice Martinu. In 1928, the ISCM choose his *Second String Quartet* for their Festival in Siena. In 1932, he won a prize for his *String Sextet*. Financial troubles, however, continued to plague the newly married composer. More success came when, in 1941, Koussevitsky premièred Martinu's *Concerto Grosso* in Boston, one of the most successful and popular of Martinu's works. Sacher performed the première of another important piece: the *Concerto for Two String Orchestras, Piano and Tympani*. Martinu's *First Symphony* appeared in 1942 (commissioned by Koussevitsky), and his *Second Symphony* in 1943 (première in Cleveland). 1944 produced both a *Third Symphony* and a *Violin Concerto*, and the *Fourth Symphony* followed in 1945.

As many critics praise Martinu as dismiss him. Perhaps due to his unorthodox and incomplete training, the quality of his compositions is far from consistent. Some works are masterly while others are highly disappointing. Nevertheless, Martinu's importance as a composer is unquestioned. His music is always lively and very often, extremely original.

Arthur Honegger

Born and raised in France, Honegger (1892-1955) held the Swiss nationality until his death. He studied at the Conservatoire in Paris with, among others, Caplet (harmony), Widor (composition) and d'Indy (orchestral direction). While a student, Honegger became friends with Darius Milhaud together with whom he founded 'Les Nouveaux Jeunes' in 1918, later known as 'Groupe des Six'. The other members were Aurc, Durey, Poulenc and Germaine Tailleferre. Les Six were, at their outset, strongly influenced by the poet Jean Cocteau and the composer Eric Satie. Honegger attained world fame as young as 28 when his oratorium, *Le Roi David*, a dramatic psalm (1921) for brass, woodwinds, double-bass, piano and harmonium, premièred at the Theatre du Jorat in Mézières. Honegger used this unusual instrumentation to achieve his extraordinary goals.

Honegger was married to the pianist Andrée Vaurabourg for whom he wrote his piano concertino. This is one of the few pieces wherein Honegger used 'sounds of the times', namely jazz elements. Aside from composing, Honegger was also for many years a composition teacher at the Ecole Normale de Musique during the period when Alfred Cortot was director. Honegger toured both North and South America, the Soviet Union and Europe, often conducting his own works. He also travelled extensively in his role of president of the Société des Auteurs et Compositeurs de Musique after his election in 1892. Pieces from his extraordinarily varied oeuvre that should be mentioned include his *Movement symphonique no.1 'Pacific 231'*, 1923, for orchestra, that imitates a locomotive in motion; *Movement symphonique no.2 'Rugby'*, 1928; *Symphonie no.1*, 1930; *Movement symphonique no.3*, 1933; *Symphonie no.2 for strings and trumpet*, 1941; *Symphonie liturgique*, 1946; *Symphony no.4 'Deliciae brasiliensis'*, 1946 and *Symphonie no.5 'Di tre re'*, 1951. Honegger wrote the score for Paul Claudel's oratorium (or concert opera) *Jeanne d'Arc au bûcher* (1935). In his later works, Honegger used a more sombre tone. There is a tragic lyricism not found earlier. His *Cantate de Noël*, 1953, which would be his swan song, had this lyricism and is considered a high point in Honegger's composing career.

Stockhausen's *Refrain*, an elegant example of today's graphic notation.

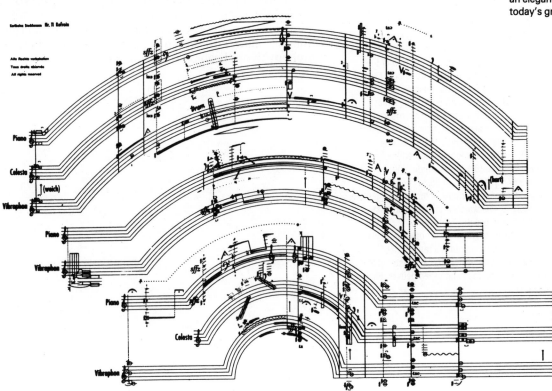

9

A guide to the great conductors

Claudio Abbado
born in Milan, June 26, 1933

Claudio Abbado already knew at the age of eight what he wanted to become. 'Someday I want to conduct Debussy' he wrote in his diary. He completed his studies at the Conservatory in Milan at the age of nineteen with a degree in piano, and two years later, with one in conducting and composition. He furthered his conducting studies with Hans Svarovsky, 1957), head of the 'Kapellmeister' class at the Music Academy in Vienna. Abbado sang in the Academy choir in performances of the *St Matthew Passion*, and the Brahms *Requiem*. He considered this experience as an extremely important one for his later conducting.
In 1958, Abbado won the Koussevitsky Prize at Tanglewood, in the United States. He was appointed to the Conservatory in Parma to teach chamber music. Abbado made his début at the Scala in 1960, during the Scarlatti tricentenary. In 1963, he won first prize at the Mitropoulos Competition. Abbado turned down a position with an American orchestra to be able to accept Karajan's offer to conduct at Salzburg. There he conducted Mahler's *Second Symphony*. This was his first encounter with the Wiener Philharmoniker where Abbado became principal guest conductor in 1971. After Salzburg, he conducted *Mort Atomique* by Manzoni (1965) at the Scala. He opened the new season there two years later with Bellini's *Capuletti ed I Montecchi*. Back in Salzburg in 1968, he conducted the *Il Barbiere di Siviglia*. He is a frequent guest at Salzburg and at the Viennese Festwochen. In 1968, Abbado was appointed principal conductor, and three years later, artistic director of the Scala in Milan.
Abbado founded the Philharmonic Orchestra of the Scala in 1982, to concentrate solely on concert (as opposed to operatic) repertoire. In 1977, he added the Youth Orchestra of the Common Market to his many activities.
Abbado is well loved in the city of his birth, Milan, due to his natural and contemporary allure. He is close to Paolo Grassi, Luigi Nono, Maurizio Pollini and Giorgio Strehler, living together in a city with a lively musical climate. His rehearsals are open to the public; he gives concerts in factories and schools and he has founded a musical workshop there.
In 1975, Abbado worked with Pollini on Nono's opera, *Au Grand Soleil d'Amour Chargé,* with Lioubimov as stage director. Not only does Abbado enlarge the accepted reper-

toire, but he appeals to a very wide audience.
In 1971, he was awarded a medal by the Mozart Society of Vienna. In that same year, he began to tour the world conducting Verdi, Rossini, Brahms, Mahler, as well as Berg (*Wozzeck*), Mussorgsky (*Boris Godounov*), Schoenberg, Boulez, Stockhausen and Penderecki.

Ernest Ansermet
born in Vevey in 1883, died in Geneva in 1969

Both of Ernest Ansermet's parents were amateur musicians. Their son was drawn to music early in life and played the clarinet, the violin and all the brass instruments in the band. This early experience enabled Ansermet to compose marches for the Swiss army, later in life, pieces he himself considered worthless. His dedication to music was only equalled by his dedication to mathematics, and in 1903, he received his degrees in mathematics and physics from the University of Lausanne. He taught at the College in Lausanne until 1906, when he returned to his studies, this time at the Sorbonne, taking classes at the same time at the Conservatory in Paris. Ansermet returned to Lausanne as a mathematics professor, but decided to dedicate himself to music after only one year. He was appointed conductor of the Kursaal Orchestra in Montreux after winning a competition there. He befriended Ramuz, and was introduced to Stravinsky, then living at Clarens. Ansermet assisted Stravinsky while he wrote *Le Sacre du Printemps, Petrouschka, l'Histoire du Soldat, Les Noces* and *Renard*. Very important for his conducting career was meeting Diaghilev in Geneva. The Orchestre des Concerts in Geneva wanted him as conductor just as Diaghilev invited him to conduct the Ballets Russes. His first performance with them was a gala at the Grand Théatre in Geneva, on the 20th of December, 1915, performing Massine's *Soleil de Nuit* with music by Rimsky-Korsakov. That same evening, Stravinsky introduced his *Firebird*. Ansermet and the Ballets Russes toured the United States in 1916, the beginning for him of a long double career, conducting in Geneva and touring the world. Through the continued success of these tours, Ansermet established his international reputation. He conducted the première performances of Stravinsky's *l'Histoire du Soldat* in 1918, *Le Chant du Rossignol* and *Pulcinella* in 1920, *Renard* in 1922 and *Les Noces* in 1923. The friendship and co-operation between these two men lasted so long that

Left: Claudio Abbado

their names became inseparable. Ansermet did more, however, than conduct Stravinsky. He was also responsible for the première of Satie's *Parade* in 1917 and of de Falla's *El Sombrero de tres Picos*.

Having settled in Geneva in 1915, Ansermet divided his talents and attention between three orchestras. Outside of his work for the Ballets Russes, he was the force behind the entire musical life of French speaking Switzerland. He also founded a national Argentinian orchestra in Buenos Aires. For ten years, he spent his winters in Geneva and his summers in Argentina. Ansermet was considered the very best when it came to the French and Russian repertoire (serving even as a model for the great Karl Böhm!). In spite of the many offers made, especially by American orchestras, Ansermet chose to dedicate himself to the musical tradition in his native land at the expense of his international career. He founded the first Orchestra Romand in 1918 in Geneva with 63 musicians. He obtained a contract with Radio Geneva in 1932, guaranteeing the broadcasting of all concerts given by the OR. Nevertheless, his own orchestra was taken from him after only three years. The Swiss Radio Society moved it to Lausanne. With a great deal of effort, Ansermet founded an orchestra in Geneva yet again. He negotiated again with the Radio Society to support his 84 musicians with broadcasts from Geneva, Lausanne, in the Grand Theatre and in the studio. This Orchestra de la Suisse Romande finally débuted in 1940, and Ansermet conducted it until his death in 1969. They performed both in Switzerland and on tour (in the United States, Poland, Greece and Japan) with amazing success. In addition, he gave 450 concerts in the radio studios of Geneva which now bear his name.

As a composer, Ansermet is remembered in connection with Debussy, whose piano works he orchestrated, for example, *Les Epigraphes Antiques*. He enthusiastically promoted Swiss composers. Arthur Honegger's works, *Horace Victorieux* (1921), *Chant de Joie* (1923), and *Rugby* (1928) all premièred under him. Frank Martin dedicated many works to Ansermet, including the following whose première Ansermet also conducted: *Symphonie* (1938), *In Terra Pax* (1945), *La Tempête* (1956), *Le Mystère de la Nativitè* (1959), *Monsieur de Pourceaugnac* (1963) and *Les Quatres Elements* (1964).

After the Second World War, Ansermet and his orchestra recorded numerously for Decca, then the most outstanding of all record companies. (They had a special procedure: full frequency range recording). The value of these recordings is clearly more than just historical.

Ernest Ansermet was never impressed by fame and remained critical of conductors whose showmanship was a performance in itself. 'Conducting is not a profession', he once said, in justification of his views and his self acquired skills.

Daniel Barenboim

Sir John Barbirolli

born in London in 1899, died in London in 1970

Sir John Barbirolli, born in London of Italian lineage, began his career as a cellist with the Queen's Hall Orchestra. He performed as a solo cellist under the name of Giovanni Barbirolli. He was educated at the Royal Academy of Music

(1912-17). In 1925, Barbirolli was contracted to conduct for the first time a number of concerts in Chelsea with the Guild of Singers and Players there. He conducted the Scottish Opera from 1933 until 1937. When Toscanini's contract with the New York Philharmonic ended in 1936, Barbirolli was named his successor. He lived in New York until 1943, and while there, conducted the première of Benjamin Britten's *Violin Concerto* and the *Sinfonia da Requiem*.

In 1943, Barbirolli was chosen principal conductor of the Hallé Orchestra in Manchester. The orchestra had had no permanent leader since the departure of Hamilton Harty in 1933. Barbirolli reorganized the group, and under his direction, the playing and interpretation were restored to their old glory. In the fifties, it was considered one of the best orchestras in Europe. After the Second World War, Barbirolli took this orchestra on many tours. He conducted the newly discovered Mozart oboe concerto, with Evelyn Rothwell as soloist, in the first Salzburg Festival after the war. Beginning in 1947, the Hallé Orchestra was featured in the Cheltenham Festival of Contemporary English Music, playing the premières there of, for example, Rawsthorne's violin concerto, and symphonies by Arthur Benjamin and Racine Fricker. He also conducted them at the Edinburgh Festival of 1948, 1950 and 1951, where both orchestra and conductor easily stood up to foreign 'competition'.

Barbirolli chose his programs from a wide spectrum of works of varying styles, using the late Classics as a foundation. Exceptional was the painstaking preparation that preceeded every concert. This precision was matched by a wonderful liveliness in performance. Early on, the attention to detail was accompanied by tension and uneasiness, however his later interpretations had a very grand air about them, especially when he performed the large symphonic classics. Barbirolli always approached a movement as a separate entity, not some piece of a whole.

In 1949, Barbirolli was knighted (King's Birthday List) and in 1950, he received the Gold Medal of the Royal Philharmonic Society.

Daniel Barenboim

born in Israel in 1942

Born in 1942, the Israeli Barenboim was a child prodigy as a pianist. He began conducting in 1964, and has pursued this career side by side with that of a pianist ever since. Performances of Mozart operas have won him great acclaim; and as a symphonic conductor since becoming artistic director of l'Orchestre de Paris (1975) he has explored and made recordings of the nineteenth-century French repertoire, notably Berlioz and Saint-Saëns. Barenboim has a great ability to control and bring out the form in such large-scale orchestral works, which he performs with a rare and passionate sensibility

At the age of seven Daniel Barenboim gave his first public recital in his native Buenos Aires. He concluded the programme with seven encores, stopping only when he had exhausted his repertoire. The child is father of the man. Today, both as pianist and conductor, Barenboim is one of the most exuberant and tireless of modern musicians.

His parents, who were of Russian-Jewish origin, moved to Israel in 1952, but Barenboim's precocious talent was fostered in Europe. He studied conducting with Igor Markevich and piano with Edwin Fischer in Salzburg; composition with Nadia Boulanger in Paris, while in Rome he graduated from the Accademia di Santa Cecilia. The great Wilhelm Furtwängler called him a phenomenon. And all before his fifteenth birthday.

In 1955 Barenboim played a Mozart concerto in the Royal Festival Hall, and two years later he made his American début with the *Symphony of the Air* under Leopold Stokowski. His career as a concert pianist was well under way, but as a conductor he had to wait until 1964, when he began a long and fruitful relationship with the English Chamber Orchestra. Conducting from the piano, Barenboim performed and recorded the twenty-seven Mozart concertos with the ECO. 1967 was an astonishing year. He played all thirty-two of the Beethoven sonatas at the Queen Elizabeth Hall in London, celebrated a popular (and highly publicized) marriage with the English cellist Jacqueline du Pré, toured the United States with the Israel Philharmonic and, with the New Philharmonia, appeared for the first time in Europe as a conductor of a symphony orchestra. The following year, when Istvan Kertesz fell ill, he made his New York conducting début with the London Symphony Orchestra. 'Mr Barenboim is a born conductor', wrote Harold C. Schonberg in the New York Times. Since then his right to a musical existence apart from the piano has remained unquestioned.

As any lingering resentment of the teenage wonderchild subsides, his musical opinions are treated with increasing respect.

In 1975, after years of guest appearances, Barenboim became permanent conductor of l'Orchestre de Paris, expanding his largely Germanic repertoire to include the works of Berlioz, Saint-Saëns and Debussy. His many recordings with the orchestra, added to an already vast discography, have made him the most inescapable of modern musicians and, in early age, one of the 'grand old men' of music.

Sir Thomas Beecham

born in Saint Helens (Lancashire) in 1879, died in London in 1961

One of the most important British conductors. Though much of his best-remembered work was done in the opera house, his symphonic career was also distinguished. He founded the London Philharmonic Orchestra (1932) and the Royal Philharmonic Orchestra (1946).

Beecham had little formal training and was at times a laughably poor technician. He was immensely rich and felt no shame in hiring his own orchestras when no one else would employ him. He was often careless and inconsistent during performance. He treated many great masterpieces with contempt and appeared to revere what was second rate. He was vain, insufferably rude and unbelievably extravagant. Yet, unlike most 'amateur' conductors, he could make even a poor orchestra play, for one evening at least, like the best in the world; with the best orchestras he created some of the century's most memorable performances.

He was born in Lancashire, heir to the fortune amassed by his father in the manufacture of 'Beecham's Pills'. His musical training was private, but at the age of twenty he felt confident enough to stand in as conductor at a local concert in place of the venerable Hans Richter. Confidence was a quality Beecham never lacked. While still in his twenties he went to London, where his father sponsored his expensive education in conducting.

In 1910 opera became his passion and Covent Garden his plaything. He was eventually responsible for over 120 productions, including works by Strauss, Delius, Debussy and Ethel Smyth. Financial problems forced him to retire completely for three years in 1920, but by then his apprenticeship was over, and on his return he was recognized as England's foremost conductor. He formed the London Philharmonic Orchestra in 1932 and with this group established his reputation on the Continent.

During the war he travelled throughout Australia and the United States, often urging mediocre orchestras into performances well above their normal capacities. In England again in 1946 he established the Royal Philharmonic Orchestra. By now his musical Midas-touch was infallible, and the new orchestra quickly matured to become one of the best in Europe. Beecham the savage wit has been a subject of legends since long before his death. (In a relatively genial moment he could accuse his Tristan of making love to Isolde like 'that estimable quadruped, the hedgehog'.)

Beecham the musician is more of a mystery. His memory was extraordinary and his repertoire vast. In Haydn and Mozart he inevitably discovered a freshness and grace that came as a revelation to audiences. Bach he disregarded entirely; Beethoven he found awkward; Mahler he treated like an unpleasant odour. Of all modern composers, he reserved his greatest affection for Frederick Delius. Claiming that his 'barbarous age' could never properly appreciate music with such 'a sense of regret and craving for beauty', Beecham betrayed a tenderness that his acerbic intellect too often concealed.

Eduard van Beinum

born in Arnhem in 1900, died in Amsterdam in 1959

The story goes that the fourteen year old Eduard van Beinum, while listening to the annual Cecelia concert given by the Concertgebouw Orchestra in his home town of Arnhem, said to his mother: 'You'll see, some day I'll be standing in front of that orchestra!'. These words uttered in youthful enthusiasm were to prove true. In 1931, van Beinum was named second conductor and in 1938, he took his place beside Bruno Walter and Willem Mengelberg as first conductor. He was to retain this position until his death in 1959. Nevertheless, it did not at the outset seem that van Beinum would indeed fulfill his boyhood dream.

Eduard was not the only musical member of his family. His father played the bass in the Arnhem Orchestral Society. His older brother Co played the violin well and was happy to teach his little brother music. Eduard thus learned to play the violin early on. Eduard studied the piano with Frans Hillen and proved to be especially good at sight-reading. Even as a school boy, he enjoyed a good reputation as an accompanist in the circle of musicians that surrounded him in

Eduard van Beinum
photo: G. de Groot

Sir Thomas Beecham

his youth. He was offered a place as a violinist with the Arnhem Orchestra when only 16. Everything was going so smoothly that there was little musical direction to be found in his young career. It was decided that Eduard should follow a strict course to remedy the situation. Enrolled in the Amsterdam Conservatory, van Beinum studied musical theory with Bernard Zweers and Sem Dresden. His greatest musical mentor was the renowned pianist, J.B. de Pauw. Van Beinum's final examination at the piano was brilliant, and he soon became known at the Dutch orchestras as a talented piano soloist.

Van Beinum made his début at the Concertgebouw playing César Franck's *Variations Symphoniques.* He gave many chamber music concerts with his brother and with his wife, who played the first desk of the Second violins of the Concertgebouw Orchestra. They often played together in the chamber music room of the great hall in Amsterdam. Van Beinum was much in demand with singers, known for his reliable, poetic and inspiring piano accompaniment. He was really on his way to become a famous pianist, when fate intervened.

The young pianist worked in the city of Zutphen with an amateur orchestra, something he really enjoyed doing. After a walk along the beach with his future wife, he saw an advertisement for a conductor. He applied at once and on the 10th of October, 1927, began to work as the conductor of the Orchestral Society of Haarlem. He was 27 at the time. A great risk had been taken to employ him, considering van Beinum's very limited conducting experience. The risk paid off though, and van Beinum stayed in Haarlem for four years, reorganizing and reforming the orchestra and elevating the provincial city's musical life in general.

In 1929, van Beinum was invited to conduct in the summer series at the Concertgebouw. He made a surprising début, performing the *Oxford Symphony* by Haydn and Saint-Saëns's *Third Symphony.* More guest appearances followed and in 1931, he was rewarded with a regular season concert. When Cornelis Dopper resigned as second conductor in September of that same year, van Beinum was approached to succeed him without a second thought. He débuted in his new position with the *Eighth* of Beethoven and the *Eighth* of Bruckner. The Bruckner performance was repeated 25 years later while celebrating his jubilee with the Orchestra. People started to notice van Beinum internationally as well. He was invited to conduct in Aachen, Geneva and Paris, for summer concerts with the Philharmonic in Leningrad (in Bahu on the Caspian Sea), and as a guest with the London Philharmonic a few months of every year from 1949 until 1952. It was in London that van Beinum conducted the first complete performance of the *St Matthew Passion.* Also in London, he introduced Benjamin Britten's *Spring Symphony,* having conducted the world première of this piece in 1949 during the Holland Festival. Van Beinum crossed the Atlantic Ocean in 1953 to conduct the Orchestra Sinfonia Brasiliera in Rio de Janeiro, Buenos Aires and Sao Paulo. He also performed with the Philadelphia Orchestra in both New York and Philadelphia, and starting in 1956, was a guest at the Los Angeles Philharmonic for two months of every season.

Leonard Bernstein

Roberto Benzi
born in Marseille in 1937

Early on, Roberto Benzi received piano lessons from his father, a music teacher. At the age of 11, he conducted his first concerts in 1948 in Bayonne and in Paris with the Orchestra of Colonne. Two years later this wonderchild appeared in two movies: *Prélude à la Gloire* and *L'Appèl du Destin.* Benzi studied conducting music while busy performing it, until 1958. Cluytens was his mentor from 1947 until 1950. In 1954, having immersed himself in opera, he performed an extremely successfull *Carmen* in the Garnier Palace in Paris. Benzi took this *Carmen* on tour throughout Japan. Tours have also taken him throughout Europe and North Africa. He débuted in 1975 at the Metropolitan in New York with *Faust.* The next year, Benzi was appointed conductor and artistic director of the Orchestre of Bordeaux-Aquitaine.

Leonard Bernstein
born in Lawrence (Massachusetts) in 1918

The concert in which Leonard Bernstein replaced Bruno Walter in 1943 was broadcast by radio throughout the United States. After the initial disappointment of having an almost completely unknown young man substitute for the famous Walter, the audience grew extremely enthusiastic, overwhelmed by the mastery with which Bernstein controlled the orchestra. This won him instant fame. From 1945-1948 he was musical director of the New York City Orchestra. He also conducted the Philharmonic Orchestra of Israel, staying on there as musical adviser until 1949. Bernstein toured with Koussevitsky and was a guest conductor with the great orchestras of Vienna, Milan, Paris and London. From 1951-55 he conducted classes in composition at the Berkshire Music Centre; in this same period he taught at Brandeis University. In 1957 he conducted the New York Philharmonic together with Mitropoulos. After becoming chief conductor of the New York Philharmonic in 1958, he was, in 1969, given the title of honorary conductor for life, in appreciation of his many merits. He was the first American exclusively trained in his own country, to be offered such an important position. Bernstein was the first American to be invited to conduct the Scala in Milan (*La Bohème* and *La Somnambula*). In 1964 Bernstein débuted at the Metropolitan, in 1966 at the Vienna State Opera. Since 1969 he has been welcomed as a great conductor around the world.

Bernstein's repertoire is remarkable in its extreme eclecticism. He is famous for his Mahler, Gershwin and Stravinsky. He introduced the *Second Symphony* of Charles Ives, the *Turangalîla Symphony* of Messiaen (1949) and the *Fifth Symphony* of Henze (1963). His vitality and enthusiasm have made him popular with a wide audience, and his television concerts are famous indeed. Professionals consider him a natural at conducting. Bernstein's approach to music-making before an audience has often been criticized for its showmanship. But for anyone having an ear for the musical flow of his interpretations as well as an eye for his athletic movements, there can be no doubt as to the seriousness of his approach and the depth of his dedication. For

Bernstein music is an art which cannot be exercised in isolation, in a studio for example. He makes music for listeners whose presence he must sense. He is convinced that only then can great interpretations be achieved, that musicians must be able to see those for whom they are performing. This explains why he currently makes his recordings almost exclusively before a live audience.

Karl Böhm
born in Graz in 1894, died in Salzburg in 1981

Böhm was descended from a family of physicians and lawyers. While studying law, he visited the Conservatories of Graz and Vienna, staying to study in Vienna with Eusébius Mandyczevski, a friend of Brahms. He began his musical career in 1917 as a coach at the opera in his birthplace. In 1921 he was appointed 'Kapellmeister' of the State Opera in Munich and in 1927 he became the 'Generalmusikdirektor' in Darmstadt. Next he went to the Hamburg Opera after which he succeeded Fritz Busch (forced to resign for political reasons) at Dresden in 1943. Through the intervention of Richard Strauss, Böhm was engaged by the Vienna Opera that same year. Böhm conducted *Ariadne auf Naxos* for the 80th birthday of Richard Strauss, many of whose operas he had already 'baptised'. After the war, like his colleagues Furtwängler and Karajan, he was forbidden to conduct. In 1947 he was given the direction of the Konzerthausgesellschaft and the Gesellschaft der Musikfreunde in Vienna. From 1950 to 1953 Böhm was active in the German opera season in Buenos Aires. In 1954 he returned to the Vienna State Opera and in 1962 he made his first appearance in Bayreuth with a performance of *Tristan and Isolde*. In 1968 Böhm published an autobiography entitled *Ich erinnere mich genau*.

Böhm's conducting style is distinguished by great spiritualism, youthful élan, great sensitivity and unquestioned authority. His own personality he gladly offers up to the service of the score. Böhm's conducting is so natural that it is difficult to consider it an interpretation. Not yearning to 'Hineininterpretation', he has built his reputation as an honest and simple musician, capable of objective and loyal performance.

Böhm was a great conductor of Mozart. Towards the end of his career, he recorded all the Mozart symphonies. He is also responsible for restoring *Cosi fan tutte* to the accepted repertoire, it having been neglected for more than a century.

Pierre Boulez
born in Montbrison (France) in 1925

Pierre Boulez received piano lessons with his sister beginning in his seventh year. School was spent at a Catholic Secondary. While there, he was in contact with amateur musicians, played chamber music and sang in the college choir. His father, an important figure in the steel business, envisaged a career in research for his son. Pierre studied mathematics and technical sciences in Lyon, but was so attracted to music that he broke off his studies. Boulez travelled to Paris and enrolled at the Conservatory (1944) to study harmony with Messiaen. There he discovered Stravinsky,

Bartók and the Viennese School.

In 1946 Boulez left Messiaen, as he would also leave René Leibowitz, having discovered atonal and serial music. That same year, he became director of an experimental theatre group, La Compagnie Renaud-Barrault. He began to conduct, to write, to attack Berg's new romanticism, to compose and to immerse himself in art and poetry.

Beginning around 1955, he enjoyed a certain renown as a composer (*Le manteau sans maître*). He settled in Baden-Baden in 1959, having been invited by the Südwestrundfunk (radio) and taught analysis and orchestral direction in Darmstadt and Basel. He taught at Harvard as well around this time (1962-63), concentrating more and more on conducting. That same year Boulez appeared with the Viennese Philharmonic at the Salzburg Festival and in 1963, he conducted a brilliant *Sacre du Printemps* with the Orchestre de Paris that was also released on record. He conducted the first French performance of Alban Berg's *Wozzeck* at the Opera. In 1966 he conducted *Parsifal* at Bayreuth. Boulez' conducting is distinguished by a new approach, striving, with absolute precision, towards objective perfection.

A man of many inner contradictions, Boulez lives musical history backwards. He dismisses Stravinsky at first, only to later become one of his greatest interpreters. Bartók, Wagner, Liszt, all are dismissed only to be conducted at a later date, unveiling numerous new aspects of the pieces in performance. Boulez and Marcel Landowski have a lively, continuous debate concerning their differences in musical politics. Boulez left France in 1967, deciding never again to conduct there, and started to build an international career. Boulez became principal guest conductor of the Cleveland Symphony Orchestra in 1969, and following that, artistic director of the BBC Symphony Orchestra (1971-75) and the New York Philharmonic (1971-77). He conducted *Der Ring des Nibelungen* in New York in 1976-80. Also in New York, Boulez organized the 'Rugs', popular concerts inspired by the English Proms, meant to appeal to a wider audience. Returning to France in 1976, he became the director of IRACM (Institut de Recherche et de Coordination Acoustique-Musique) and the Ensemble Intercontemporain. More recently, Boulez has spent less of his time conducting, and more composing and doing musicological research.

Sir Adrian Boult
born in Chester in 1899, died in Farnham in 1983

Adrian Boult attended Westminster School and Christ Church, Oxford. He completed his musical studies at the Leipzig Conservatory with Max Reger (1912-13) and came in contact with the great Nikisch there. He returned to England and conducted at Covent Garden. At the request of the composer, Boult conducted movements of *The Planets* by Gustav Holst in 1919. He taught at the Royal College of Music in London from 1919 until 1930. As a conductor, he worked with many orchestras in England and abroad. He was principal conductor of the City of Birmingham Symphony Orchestra from 1924-1930 and added the assistant musical direction of Covent Garden to his duties in 1926. Boult conducted the Bach Choir from 1928 until 1931, and

Left: Leonard Bernstein, honorary conductor for life of the New York Philharmonic Orchestra since 1969.

Karl Böhm
photo: S. Lauterwasser

Pierre Boulez

was the principal conductor of the BBC Symphony Orchestra from 1930-1950, a position that brought him much renown and invitations to guest conduct: in Vienna (1933), Boston and Salzburg (1935) and New York (1938-39). He conducted the Proms from 1942 until 1950 and directed the music at the coronation of King George VI in 1936.

Beginning in 1950, Boult was principal conductor of the London Philharmonic Orchestra, excusing himself in 1957 and accepting only invitations as a guest. He has made a great deal of recordings, most of them dedicated to performing English music. Boult conducted *Dream of Gerontius* by Elgar for television at Canterbury Cathedral in 1968. He returned to the City of Birmingham Symphony Orchestra from 1959-60 and to the Royal College of Music in 1962. He retired from the concert stage in 1979.

Sir Adrian Boult was a remarkable but modest musical personality who contributed a great deal to the fame enjoyed by English repertoire at home and abroad. Vaughan-Williams dedicated *Job, a Masque of Dancing* to him and *Novelle*, his *Concerto for Strings*. Boult conducted the premières of Arthur Bliss' *Music for Strings* (1935) and *Pianoconcerto* (1939) as well as Vaughan-Williams' *A Pastoral Symphony* and *Symphonies no. 4* and *6*. Adrian Boult wrote *The Point of the Stick* (1920, revised in 1968) from which a film was made.

Frans Brüggen
born in 1934 in Amsterdam

Recorder player and conductor Frans Brüggen is internationally recognized as one of the foremost specialists in the performance practices of baroque music. When only 21, Brüggen was given a position at the Conservatories in both Amsterdam and The Hague to teach the recorder and Early Music in general. He is also well respected as an editor of early music. His more than 100 concerts annually are well received throughout the world. Luciano Berio once wrote of him: ' Brüggen is a musican who is not an archeologist but a great artist'. The New York Times agreed: 'his playing transcends academic correctness, for it is animated by an uncommon rhythmic verve, polished by a sovereign technique, and musically distinguished by a rare sensibility'. Brüggen taught at Harvard University for a year as an Erasmus Professor in 1972 and at Berkeley University as a Regents Professor in 1973-74. He has often worked with the two other leaders in his field, Gustav Leonhardt and Nicolaus Harnoncourt.

A second career as conductor began when Philips engaged Brüggen to direct various ensembles ad hoc. He went on to lead the Mozart Ensemble Amsterdam. Brüggen now conducts The Orchestra of The Eighteenth Century, a group he founded in 1981. He has also conducted 18th century programs as a guest with the Minnesota Orchestra, the Concertgebouw Orchestra, the San Francisco Symphony Chamber Orchestra and the Northwest Chamber Orchestra of Seattle.

Sir Adrian Boult

Frans Brüggen

Ricardo Chailly

Ricardo Chailly
born in Milan in 1953

Ricardo Chailly began his musical education with his father, the composer Luciano Chailly. Later, he studied at the Conservatory in Milan with Franco Caracciolo. He also followed courses with Piero Guarino in Perugia and Franco Ferrara in Sienna until 1972. Chailly made his début in 1970 in Milan, and two years later, conducted *Werther* in the Teatro Nuovo. Claudio Abbado choose him as his assistant at the Scala, while Chailly himself endeavoured to build up a career as a guest conductor, specializing in opera. The Opera of Chicago has been inviting him to conduct regularly since 1974 (*Madame Butterfly, Rigoletto, Cavaleria Rusticana*) and in 1977, he was invited to San Francisco by the opera there. His official début at the Scala was in 1978 with Verdi's *I Masnadieri*. A year later, Sir Colin Davis invited him to conduct Donizetti's *Don Pasquale* at Covent Garden. In 1982 Chailly became principal conductor of the RIAS (Radio Symphony Orchestra of Berlin). In 1988 he became the principal conductor of the Concertgebouw Orchestra.

Chailly has conducted the premières of *Requiem pour les Enfants* (1979) and *E flat Concerto* (1984), both composed by his father, as well as *La Foresta Incantate* by Tutino (1983).

Andrew Davis
born in Ashridge (Kent) in 1944

Andrew Davis studied the organ with Peter Hurford and Piet Kee before attending King's College, Cambridge (1963-67). He then studied orchestral direction with Franco Ferrara at the Accademia di Santa Cecilia in Rome. In 1969 he attended a seminar for young English conductors in Liverpool, after which he was appointed second conductor of the BBC Scottish Orchestra (1970-72). Davis was appointed second conductor of the New Philharmonia Orchestra in 1973, and in 1975, musical director of the Toronto Symphony Orchestra. He has also conducted quite regularly at the Glyndebourne Festival. His repertoire is strongly French (Franck, Fauré, Duruflé) and he has made numerous recordings of these works.

Sir Colin Davis
born in Weybridge in 1927

The first time that Davis experienced a concert performance of *L'Enfance du Christ* of Berlioz, he was so impressed that he decided then and there to become a conductor. He had already completed his studies as a clarinettist at the Royal College of Music in London, but he got the chance to conduct the Chamber Orchestra in Kalmar, Sweden, and later, the Chelsea Opera Group, where he was praised for his Mozart in the early fifties. In 1952 Davis became the principal conductor of the Ballet of the Royal Festival Hall, and from 1957-59, second conductor of the BBC Scottish Orchestra. In the following years he drew attention through a number of spectacular substitutions for leading conductors, such as Klemperer in 1959 for *Don*

Giovanni and Beecham in 1960 for *Die Zauberflöte*. In 1961 he was appointed musical director of the Sadler's Wells Opera, where he later became artistic director (1961-65). Davis has frequently been asked to conduct the London Symphony Orchestra and has toured and also made recordings with this orchestra. He was principal conductor of the BBC Symphony Orchestra from 1967 until 1971 and, after that, artistic director of Covent Garden from 1971-1986. In 1972 he became permanent guest conductor of the Boston Symphony Orchestra, occupying for several years a similar position with the Concertgebouw Orchestra in Amsterdam. Since 1983, Davis has been principal conductor of the Orchestra of the Bayerische Rundfunk in Munich. He is first guest conductor of the London Symphony Orchestra and honorary guest conductor of the Boston Symphony Orchestra. He has made recordings as guest conductor of the Staatskapelle of Dresden.

Colin Davis has a passion for Mozart, Handel and Berlioz. Numerous recordings bear witness to his great clarity and vitality.

Antal Dorati
born in Budapest in 1906, American citizen since 1947

Antal Dorati's father was a violinist and his mother taught him the violin and piano. From his fourteenth until his eighteenth year he studied at the Franz Liszt Academy in his birthplace. Simultaneously, he followed courses at the University of Vienna. Dorati studied with Béla Bartók and Zoltán Kodály; for Kodály, he was destined to work vigorously collecting information about musical folklore in Hungary. At the close of this period, having received honours in composition, piano and conducting, he began his career as a conductor. Dorati was the youngest assistant conductor to have ever performed with the Royal Opera in Budapest (1924-28). He conducted the Hungarian première of Stravinsky's *Le Chant du Rossignol* and *Oedipus Rex* in 1928. Thereafter, he became Fritz Busch's assistant in Dresden and was named principal conductor in Münster in 1929 (until 1932). For eight years, Dorati worked with the Ballets Russes in Monte Carlo: as second conductor from 1933 until 1938 and as artistic director from 1938 until 1941. He toured the world with this company, finally settling in New York in 1941 and becoming the musical director of the American Ballet Theatre. This directorship lasted until 1945 when he started to build up a new career as a guest conductor. He was first a guest with the New York Opera Company from 1941-1942. The Dallas Symphony Orchestra followed; he led that organization from 1945-49, concentrating from then on on orchestral direction only. Dorati then conducted all of the following orchestras: the Minneapolis Symphony Orchestra (1949-1960), the BBC Symphony Orchestra from 1962-66, the Stockholm Philharmonic Orchestra from 1966 to 1975, as well as the National Symphony Orchestra of Washington D.C. from 1970 onwards, and in 1974, the Royal Philharmonic Orchestra in London. In 1977 Dorati was named musical director of the Detroit Symphony Orchestra.

With the Philharmonia Hungarica, founded in Vienna in 1957, he recorded for Decca, beginning in 1969, all the symphonies of Joseph Haydn. Gifted with a phenomenal memory, Dorati always refers to himself as 'the doctor of the orchestra'. His repertoire is immense: he is a contemporary representative of Bartók and Kodály, there is Stravinsky, Messiaen and Dallapicola which he has performed and promoted throughout the world, as well as the complete Haydn already mentioned. He has made over 500 recordings. There have also been important premières: *Sinfonia serena*, Hindemith 1947, *Concerto for Orchestra*, Gerhard 1965 and *Concerto for Viola*, Bartók, 1949.

Antal Dorati is also a composer. In 1975 he wrote a concerto for his wife, the pianist Ilse von Alpenheim.

Charles Dutoit
born in Lausanne in 1936

Charles Dutoit was educated at the Conservatory in Lausanne (violin, piano and orchestral direction) and also at the Conservatory of Geneva (viola and orchestral direction). He graduated in 1958 and travelled to Sienna to study further with Alceo Galliera. His travels took him to Tanglewood in 1959. In this same period (1957-59), he performed as a violist with a number of orchestras in Europe and South America. Back in Switzerland, he worked with choirs and student orchestras. Dutoit began conducting the Orchestre de la Suisse Radio and l'Orchestre de Chambre de Lausanne in 1959. In 1964, he was appointed conductor of the Orchestre of Radio Zurich where he stayed for two years. At the Vienna State Opera (1965-67), Dutoit worked with Massine on *El Sombrero de tres Picos* and with Noureyev on *Le Lac de Cygnes*. He succeeded Paul Klecki as conductor of the Symphony Orchestra of Berne (1966-78). He has conducted at the Scala and at the Philharmonie in Berlin. Dutoit has worked with the National Symphony Orchestra of Mexico (1973-750, the Symphony Orchestra of Göteborg (1975-78) and as principal conductor of the Symphony Orchestra of Montreal (1977). Dutoit's repertoire spans from Monteverdi to Messiaen, his preference is for Stravinsky. His recordings have enjoyed rave reviews by the international music press.

Wilhelm Furtwängler
born in Berlin in 1886, died in Baden-Baden 1954

From 1922 until his death in Baden-Baden on November 30, 1954, Wilhelm Furtwängler, born in Berlin on January 25,1866, was inseparably bound up with German and Austrian musical life. After study in composition and orchestral conducting with Joseph Rheinberger and Max von Schillings, he began his career as director of the Theatre in Strasbourg. Later he was conductor for the Berlin State Opera, then succeeded Artur Nikisch as conductor of the Gewandhaus Orchestra in Leipzig. After a time with the Vienna Philharmonic Orchestra he was given, in 1952, lifetime conductorship of the Berlin Philharmonic Orchestra with which he had been regularly associated since 1922. Furtwängler first drew particular notice as a conductor when he was given the opportunity to conduct one of his own works. Having to present a full evening's programme, he selected Brucker's *Ninth Symphony* to supplement the performance of his own composition. Later he declared that

Sir Colin Davis

Antal Dorati

only during the extensive preparations for this concert culminating in his appearance on the podium did he himself become aware of his conducting talent. From that moment on he gave up his aspirations as a composer and set to work developing his conducting techniques. His path was a long and difficult one. Assistant conductorships in Breslau, Zurich and Munich led to an appointment as Kapellmeister in Strasbourg and, in 1911, in Lübeck. In 1915 he became director of the Opera in Mannheim, in 1921, concert director of the Tonkünstlerorchester in Vienna, and a year later, director of the Musikfreunde. There then followed his important appointments in Vienna, Leipzig and Berlin. Upon the death of Nikisch in 1922, a successor was sought both in Leipzig and Berlin. The young Furtwängler's capacities were so valued he was given both positions, quickly rising to the top of German musical life.

Furtwängler developed a personal conducting technique based on observation of the styles of Nikisch and Weingartner, whose movements were rounded and supple rather than angular. Furtwängler did not so much mark time, but seemed, as it were, to sketch the music in the air.

Sir Alexander Gibson
born in Motherwell in 1926

Sir Alex Gibson, having completed his studies at the University of Glasgow, enrolled at the Royal College of Music in London. He then continued his studies with Igor Markevich at the Mozarteum in Salzburg, and with Van Kempen at the Accademia Chigiana in Sienna. He was a prize winner at the International Competition of Besançon, and shortly thereafter became first rehearser and then first assistant conductor at Sadler's Wells Theatre. He left to become first assistant of the BBC Scottish Orchestra (1952-54) but returned to Sadler's Wells as principal director (1954-57) and subsequently musical director (1957-59). The Scottish National Orchestra named him principal conductor in 1959 (until 1984). In 1962 Gibson helped found and artistically direct the Scottish Opera where he performed the first complete *Les Troyens* (1969) and *Der Ring des Nibelungen* (1971). Since 1981 Gibson is principal guest conductor of the Houston Symphony Orchestra.

Wilhelm Furtwängler

Carlo Maria Giulini
born in Barletta (Italy) in 1914

Studying at the Accademia di Santa Cecilia, where he took first prizes in viola (1936), composition (1939), and conducting (1941), Carlo Maria Giulini played under Otto Klemperer and Bruno Walter. Having chosen conducting as his craft, he studied further with Molinari. In 1944 Giulini was assistant conductor to Fernando Previtali of the orchestra of the Italian Radio in Rome. From 1950 until 1953 he conducted the symphony orchestra of Radio Milan. Giulini made his début at the Opera in 1948 with *La Traviata*. During this time he made friends with Arturo Toscanini with whom he studied from 1951 to 1975. From 1952 to 1956 Giulini was associated as conductor with La Scala in Milan (making his début there with De Falla's *La Vida Breve*), at first as assistant to Victor de Sabata, later as ar-

Carlo Maria Giulini

tistic director (1953-55). Giulini worked with Visconti on *Don Carlos* (Covent Garden, London) and with Zefferelli on *Falstaff*. 1960 brought his first tours to the United States and Japan. In 1963 he was back at the Scala to conduct *Don Giovanni* and in 1969, he was guest conductor of the Chicago Symphony Orchestra. He became principal conductor of the Wiener Symphoniker in 1973, but stayed only three years, preferring his artistic freedom. Guilini succeeded Zubin Mehta in 1978 as conductor of the Los Angeles Symphony Orchestra with which he has toured Europe. Specializing in opera (he has conducted all but *Aïda* of Verdi's operas), he was a great admirer of Maria Callas.

Even though Giulini loves to travel, he remains loyal to his own Italy, staying there half of every year 'to work and to ponder'. His repertoire, not only limited to opera, includes Mozart, 19th century choral works, the German symphonies, Beethoven, Mahler, Moussorgsky, Dvorák, Prokofiev and Britten.

Giulini prefers to conduct from memory, considering this a necessary condition for greater freedom during a performance, there then being no danger of distraction from looking at the score. His gestures, consonant with his early training as a string-player, are extremely ardent. He is an autocrat, allowing no misunderstandings of his intentions and rejecting discussion of his insights by members of his orchestra.

Sir Eugene Goossens
born in London in 1893, died in Hillingdon in 1962 as an American citizen

Eugene Goossens, brother of the oboist Leon Goossens, studied at the Conservatory of Brugge, the College of Music in Liverpool (until 1907) and the Royal College of Music in London (1907-10). He was a violinist (1911-1919) in the Queen's Hall Orchestra and made his début there, conducting one of his own pieces during the Proms of 1912. He played in the Langley-Mukle Quartet and later founded the Philharmonic String Quartet. Goossens was Thomas Beecham's assistant from 1916 until 1920. Between 1921 and 1923, he conducted the Carl Rosa Opera Company en the Ballets Russes. In 1921 he performed the first concert version of *Le Sacre du Printemps* and in that same year he was appointed musical director of the Handel Society. After this, most of Goossens' career was spent in America, although he faithfully returned to England every summer to conduct. He began at the Rochester Philharmonic (1923-31) and from there went to the Cincinnati Symphony Orchestra (1931-46). In 1947, Goossens moved to Australia to conduct the Sydney Symphony Orchestra (1947-56) and to be director of that city's Conservatory. His career ended prematurely when Goossens was accused of customs fraud.

Sir Charles Groves
born in London in 1915.

Groves began his musical life as a choirboy in St Paul's Cathedral and studied organ and piano at an early age. He was fortunate enough to rehearse the choir for *Ein Deut-*

sches Requiem of Brahms that Toscannini was to conduct. Groves made his début as a choir director with the BBC in 1938, and was appointed second conductor for the BBC Theatre Orchestra in 1942. He led the BBC Northern Orchestra from 1944 until 1951 when he was given charge over the Bournemouth Symphony Orchestra. In 1963 Groves left Bournemouth to conduct the Royal Liverpool Philharmonic Orchestra, a position that he combined for many years with the Royal Philharmonic Orchestra. As successor to Sir Charles Mackerras, he then became director of Sadler's Wells Theatre.

Bernard Haitink
born in Amsterdam in 1929

As a boy of eleven, Haitink already felt drawn to music. He studied violin at the Amsterdam Conservatory and studied orchestral conducting with Felix Hupka. Upon graduation he became a violinist with the Radio Philharmonic Orchestra. Haitink continued his conducting studies under Ferdinand Leitner who appointed him (1955) as second conductor of the Dutch Radio Union. In 1956 he made his début with the Concertgebouw Orchestra. He became principal conductor of the Radio Philharmonic in 1957. After the sudden death of Eduard van Beinum in 1961, Haitink was named conductor of the Concertgebouw Orchestra, together with Eugen Jochum. He was thirty-five at that time. The appointment as principal conductor followed in 1964. His star was rising rapidly, in spite of the fact that Haitink considered himself a 'late bloomer'. Invitations to guest conduct arrived from around the world. His love affair with England began in 1967; Haitink accepted the post of principal conductor and (two years later) of artistic director of the London Philharmonic Orchestra. A true anglophile in the making, he shuttled back and forth from Amsterdam to London, popular in both cities. In 1977 Haitink left the London Philharmonic to succeed John Pritchard as artistic director of the Glyndebourne Festival.
Bernard Haitink is considered one of the great Mahler interpreters: he has recorded all the symphonies with the Concertgebouw Orchestra, some even twice. In a series spanning years, he has performed Mahler for the Eurovision Christmas concert broadcasts. His Bruckner is also renowned, and he has a weakness for Beethoven, performing him more and more as his career progresses. Haitink's recordings of Debussy and Ravel are well-loved, and more recently, he has concerned himself with Dmitri Shostakovich, recording his works as well.
Bernard Haitink left the Concertgebouw Orchestra in 1988 to become musical director of the Royal Opera House Covent Garden. As a conductor Haitink stands for a profound vision, deep analysis, sobriety and craftmanship, all in the service of the score being performed. His style is known for its intense concentration and great reliability.
Jo Hekster, a violinist in the Concertgebouw Orchestra under Mengelberg, van Beinum and Haitink, says: 'In comparing the three, I would always choose Haitink as the greatest. Expansive, with a dose of energy which is simply fantastic. The modern conductor, a man of our times ... Haitink is in full control of his material. You can feel it from the very opening bars of a Mahler symphony. He has an

overview of the totality of even the longest work. He doesn't slacken for one second. And when it's all over and he seems completely "emptied", you haven't got over your surprise at how well he managed his reserves. Orchestral musicians like a conductor who fascinates. Somebody who "gets to you". A real personality. Haitink is that kind of man.'

Nicolaus Harnoncourt
born in Berlin in 1929

Nicolaus Harnoncourt comes from a musical family. He began his musical career as a cellist, studying with Paul Grümmer in Graz and from 1948 onwards with Emanuel Brabec in Vienna. Having graduated with honours he joined the cello section of the Vienna Philharmonic (1952-69).
His years with the orchestra didn't satisfy him musically, and so, with a group of colleagues he founded (1952) Concentus Musicus. Their aim was to have a more personal contact with the repertoire of the Middle Ages, Renaissance and Baroque through an intense study of early music and old instruments. To achieve this, the ensemble decided to play authentic instruments or copies of them and worked with these instruments for four long years before making their début in 1957. Tours began in 1960.
Their first international success came with their recording of the *Brandenburg Concertos* in 1962. Other musicians interested in early music, for example Gustav Leonhardt, made acquaintance with Harnoncourt and immediately decided to work co-operatively. Since then, the names of Leonhardt and Harnoncourt are inseparable, for example, in the great project they have together to record the complete *Cantatas* of J.S. Bach.
Harnoncourt opts for the performance of Renaissance and Baroque music according to old principles on period instruments or copies 'not for historical reasons, but artistic ones. For music of any period can be presented in the liveliest and most convincing way only in the sound-terms of its own time.' In a long career as player and conductor, Harnoncourt has continued his study of old styles and performance practices. His specific opinions have been the source of several important publications. As his studies continued, Harnoncourt has changed his opinion over details often as he learns more and more deeply about his specific repertoire.
Three large projects have contributed the most to Harnoncourt's international fame: the Bach project already mentioned (which includes the *St Matthew Passion*), his complete and authentic recording of *L'Incoronazione di Poppea* of Claudio Monteverdi, and his Mozart project with the Concertgebouw Orchestra (some symphonies and a piano concerto) for Telefunken (1981). There are some who say that, especially in the Mozart, Harnoncourt makes too many concessions in respect to his artistic credo, working with the Concertgebouw Orchestra, an orchestra untrained in authentic practices. Nevertheless, Harnoncourt as always tries with the means at hand, to come as close as possible to 18th century sound ideals.
There is no doubt indeed that Harnoncourt's influence (far from complete as yet) will be monumentally important in

Nicolaus Harnoncourt

Bernard Haitink

terms of 20th century musical interpretation.

Anyone watching Harnoncourt, winner of the Ernst von Siemens music prize in 1974 and of the Dutch Erasmus Prize in 1980, will know immediately that he is completely untrained in matters of conducting technique. As one colleague rather baldly put it: 'It looks as though he is constantly hanging out the washing.' But with his unsophisticated gestures he succeeds in drawing from his players persuasive interpretations. His rhythmic and dynamic delivery combine to form an interpretative style which has had immense influence on traditional performance practices.

Christopher Hogwood
born in Nottingham in 1941

Christopher Hogwood studied music while following traditional undergraduate courses at Pembroke College Cambridge, receiving his Bachelor's Degree in 1964. Influenced by Raymond Leppard and Thurston Dart, he furthered his studies with Rafael Puyana and Gustav Leonhardt. Hogwood received a scholarship from the British Council that enabled him to study in Prague at the University and Music Academy. Back in Cambridge, he came in contact with David Munrow and took part in Munrow's Early Music Consort of London as a harpsichordist. In 1973 he founded his own orchestra, the Academy of Ancient Music, dedicated to the performance of the Baroque and Classic styles on early instruments using authentic performance practices.

Hogwood is considered one of the best interpreters of William Byrd and Elizabethan music in general. Nevertheless, he has also recorded other styles, including even the symphonies of Mozart and Beethoven.

Neeme Järvi
born in Tallinn (Estonia) in 1937.

Järvi's first music teacher was his brother Vallo. He studied choir direction and percussion in his native city before going to Leningrad to study orchestral direction with Nicolai Rabinovich and Evgeni Mravinsky. Järvi began as a percussionist with the Radio Symphony Orchestra of Estonia, but eventually became conductor there in 1963. That same year, he was appointed principal conductor at the Opera in Tallinn. Järvi won first prize in 1971 at the International Competition in Rome. 1980 saw him turn his attention to the USA where he was invited to guest conduct some major orchestras including the Metropolitan. Järvi became conductor of the Symphony Orchestra of Göteborg in 1982 and of the Scottish National Orchestra in 1984. He has recorded the complete symphonies of Glazounov and the orchestral works of Sibelius.

Eugen Jochum
photo: S. Bayat

Eugen Jochum
born in Babenhausen in 1902, died in 1986.

Eugen Jochum studied piano and organ in Augsburg from 1914 until 1922, following that with studies in orchestral direction with Walterhausen at the Music Academy in Munich. He became rehearser at the Opera in Munich in 1924, then in Kiel (1926) where he was appointed conductor in 1927. In this same period, he conducted symphony concerts in Lübeck. Jochum's career developed from Mannheim (1929) to Duisberg (1930-'32), combining that post with Radio Berlin and the Berlin Opera, then on to Hamburg (1934-1949) where he succeeded Karl Böhm as 'Generalmusikdirektor'. In 1949, Jochum founded the Symphony Orchestra of the Bavarian Radio where he was to remain until 1960. He shared the post of principal conductor of the Concertgebouw Orchestra with Bernard Haitink from 1961 until 1964, where he often returned as a guest conductor in later years. The last concert at the Concertgebouw was in 1986, when Jochum conducted a wonderful Bruckner's *Fifth Symphony*. He headed the Bamberger Symphony Orchestra from 1969 until 1971, and was named 'Conductor Laureate' of the London Symphony Orchestra from 1975 until '78.

Jochum has combined these functions with performances as guest conductor throughout the important musical centres of the world, including appearances in Bayreuth (1953, '64 and '71) and Salzburg. He was considered one of the great German conductors of his time, an artist who bridged the old and new generations with smoothness. Jochum has also done his part to keep the tradition of the late Romantics intact.

Armin Jordan
born in Luzern in 1932.

Jordan's father was a German Swiss, his mother a French Swiss. Armin Jordan began his musical studies at the piano at the age of twelve. He furthered his studies at the University and Conservatory of Fribourg, taking courses in literature, law theory and music. He studied conducting in Lausanne and later in Geneva with Marussia Lemarc-Hadour.

In 1949 Jordan founded his own orchestra in Fribourg. He worked for six years as rehearser in Bienne-Soleure before being appointed to the Zurich Opera. After five years, he moved on to Sankt Gallen and in 1973, he became principal conductor and director of the Opera in Basel. In that same year, Jordan took on the Chamber Orchestra of Lausanne, which, under his direction would become one of the most requested orchestras in Switzerland. They made many recordings for Erato together, including *Pelléas et Mélisande* in Monte Carlo and *Ariane et Barbe-Bleue* by Paul Dukas. In 1981 Jordan conducted the music for Hans-Jürgen Syberberg's filming of *Parsifal*, playing the part of Amfortas as well.

Jordan became principal conductor of the Orchestre de la Suisse Romande in 1985.

Herbert von Karajan
(Heribert Ritter von Karajan)
born in Salzburg in 1908

Herbert von Karajan studied at the piano as a boy of four, and followed lessons at the Mozarteum in his birthplace while still a schoolboy. Following the advice of Bernard

Paumgartner, Karajan went to study at the Music Academy in Vienna with Frans Schalk and Alexander Wunderer. In 1927 he returned to Salzburg to make his début with *Fidelio*, at the age of 19. His début at the Mozarteum was in 1929. He was conductor of Ulm from 1928 until 1934. From 1934 until 1941 Karajan was conductor, principal conductor, and artistic director in Aachen, making him the youngest 'Generalmusikdirektor' in Germany. His début at the Vienna State Opera was in 1937, and the next year at the German State Opera in Berlin, where he was principal conductor from 1939 until 1945.

At the end of the thirties, Karajan made his first recordings. During the war, he regularly conducted at the Opera in Paris. In 1946 he made his début with the Wiener Philharmoniker which was the beginning of many years of performing together. He was, however, forbidden to conduct that very same year, due to his sympathies for the German National Socialist Party during the war.

The Salzburg Festival saw him début in 1948 with *Le Nozze di Figaro*. The Scala received him for the first time the very next year, in a season of German music. He often returned to the Scala in the fifties. The Festival of Luzern made him their director in 1950, and the Wiener Singverein declared him their conductor for life. Walter Legge convinced Karajan to go to London to conduct his newly founded London Philharmonic. Karajan was also busy in this period, making many recordings, using the newest techniques of the time. Bayreuth was reopened in 1951, and Karajan was naturally invited. With Furtwängler's death in 1955, Karajan was appointed principal conductor and artistic director of the Berlin Philharmonic. The direction of the Salzburg Festival was added the next year, as well as succeeding Karl Böhm at the Vienna State Opera (1957). In 1965 Karajan left Vienna in a huff. His demands exceeded the acceptable, and many were tired of his dictatorial attitude. In that same year he conducted the music of *La Bohème* for Franco Zefferelli's film of the opera, founding for this occasion his own film company, Cosmotel.

In 1967, Karajan started a series at the Easter Festival in Salzburg, conducting and directing an opera every year, beginning *Der Ring des Nibelungen*. The Herbert von Karajan Foundation was founded in 1968 to organize two competitions, one for conductors and one for amateur orchestras. The Orchestre de Paris named him as their musical adviser from 1969 until 1971, only to see him leave as he left Vienna: no one was prepared to meet his exorbitant demands. He did eventually make peace with Vienna in 1977. Karajan became fascinated with the possibilities presented by video, worked with a foundation in Munich, Unitel, only to found his own company, Télémondial, in 1982.

Serious back problems and partial paralysis forced him to take it easy for six long years. After surgery in 1983 he could move normally again and stand straight up. The traditional New Years concert in Vienna was broadcast on television with Karajan conducting. The merciless cameras showed a very aged man. Nevertheless, the orchestra's performance was amazing.

No doubt exists as to the effectiveness of his gestures which are extremely controlled, but differences of opinion exist as to the poetry and evocative power of his music-making. Opinion spans from 'too cerebral, cold, eccentric, stub-

born' all the way to 'the miracle Karajan'. In the last few years certain mannerisms have crept into Karajan's conducting: artificially switched-on tempos, unusual accents and dynamic extremes.

Erich Kleiber

born in Vienna in 1890, died in Zurich in 1956.

Characteristics which earned admiration for Austrian conductor Erich Kleiber were his decisiveness and feeling for proper proportions and justice. These characteristics induced Kleiber to take up residence in South America in 1935. He had been forbidden to perform Alban Berg's opera *Luka* in 1934. Kleiber had always been opposed to the meddling of the Nazi regime in artistic affairs and could not accept being forbidden to perform new 'difficult' music (Stravinsky, Hindemith, Mahler and many others).

Kleiber was often a guest in Amsterdam (Concertgebouw, 1933-1938), in Milan (the Scala, 1935) and in Moscow where he conducted the State Symphony Orchestra in 1936. Having moved to South America, he performed German opera at the Colón Theatre in Buenos Aires. Kleiber also conducted the Philharmonic in Havana for three years. He functioned as a musical missionary, performing German repertoire throughout Latin America, even with orchestras of questionable quality.

Erich Kleiber studied in Prague: at the Conservatory (violin and composition) and at the University (philosophy and history). He made his début as a choir director in 1911 at the National Theatre in Prague. That was the begin of a busy career. He filled positions in Darmstadt (1912-18), in Wuppertal (1919-21), Mannheim (1922) and Düsseldorf (1923).

His first big opportunity as a conductor came in 1923 when he was appointed to lead the Berlin State Opera and given unlimited powers. These he put to advantage, holding for example 150 rehearsals for the première of Alban Berg's *Wozzeck*, a sign of his seriousness and dedication as well as of his affection for contemporary music. Other important premières were Darius Milhaud's *Christoph Colomb* in 1930 and in 1928 Schreker's *Der Singende Teufel*.

Kleiber returned to Europe after the hostilities were over, and was received as a guest at the Royal Opera House Covent Garden regularly (1950-53). He returned to the German State Opera in Berlin as principal conductor , but left after only one year, in protest to the political meddling in his artistic policies by the East Germans.

Kleiber is renowned for his interest in and knowledge of 20th century music, but he is equally at home with the great classic masters: Haydn, Mozart and Beethoven. His recordings of the Beethoven Symphonies, made with the Concertgebouw Orchestra, are still well loved by connoisseurs.

Otto Klemperer

born in Breslau in 1885, died in Zurich in 1973.

Klemperer began his musical studies at the Hochschule in Frankfurt in 1901. There he studied piano with James Kwast and music theory with Ivan Knorr. Kwast he met again at the Klindworth-Scharwenka Conservatory in

Herbert von Karajan

Otto Klemperer

Berlin where he studied orchestral direction and composition with Pfitzner as well. Klemperer débuted in 1906 with Offenbach's *Orphée aux Enfers*. Having had an important introduction to Mahler a year earlier, he was appointed rehearser to the German State Opera in Prague in 1907 on Mahler's recommendation. He was quickly appointed principal conductor there, and making his début with Weber's *Der Freischütz*.

Again on Mahler's recommendation, Klemperer became principal conductor at the Hamburg Opera in 1910. The Opera of Strasbourg followed from 1914 until 1917. He then became 'Generalmusikdirektor' in Cologne from 1923-1924. While there, Klemperer brought *Die tote Stadt* by Korngold in première. From Cologne he moved to Wiesbaden (1924-1927) and to the Kroll Opera in Berlin. This company was one of the most respected in Europe; it had a new production style and a profusion of premières, drawing attention to its director, Klemperer. Some of the important premières performed there were: *Oedipus Rex* (Stravinsky, 1928), *Neues vom Tage* (Hindemith, 1929), *Erwartung* (Schoenberg) *Cardillac* (Hindemith) and *Z mrtvého domo* (*From the Ossuary*) of Janácek.

The Kroll Opera closed in 1931. Klemperer stayed on at the State Opera for two years before emigrating to the United States. He became principal conductor of the Los Angeles Philharmonic (1933-1939) and conducted the Pittsburgh Symphony Orchestra in those same years. On top of that, he studied composition with Schoenberg.

In 1939 Klemperer underwent surgery for a brain tumour, an operation that was not completely successful and left him partly paralysed. He nevertheless resumed his work, conducting as a guest until being named principal at the Opera in Budapest in 1947. His condition worsened greatly after a nasty fall at the Montreal airport, forcing him to conduct sitting down from then on. Passed sixty-five, partially invalid, Klemperer continued to travel, but it always accompanied by his doctor. The Philharmonia Orchestra in London named him conductor-for-life in 1955. He returned to his first love, the opera, conducting and directing at Covent Garden every year. Some of his famous productions were: *Fidelio* (1961), *Die Zauberflöte* (1962) and *Lohengrin* (1963).

Heir to the great German conducting tradition of the 19th century, Klemperer was equally influenced by Mahler in his work. He was differently affected by the composer than, say, Bruno Walter, following Mahler's dynamic temperament in a continuous stream of revision and creation. The years saw him become a conductor of great stature, a true traditionalist. His tempi became extremely slow, much slower than his early recordings. His interpretations were witness to his dramatic power, sometimes equalling the great Furtwängler. Klemperer also worked throughout the world to promote the works of his mentor, Mahler.

Klemperer is known as a composer to a limited circle of admirers. He wrote one opera, *Das Ziel*, 6 symphonies, 9 string quartets, one *Missa Sacra* and some Lieder.

Kirill Kondrashin
born in Moscow in 1914, died in Amsterdam in 1981

Kirill Kondrashin was born of a musical family. He studied

piano and music theory with Nicolai Zhulyayev. After making his début in 1931 in the Stanislavski Theatre in Moscow, Kondrashin was determined to make conducting his career. He studied with the Russian greats of his time: Alexander Gaouk and Boris Khaikin at the Moscow Conservatory (1932-36). He was appointed assistant chief (1934-37) at the Nemirovich-Danchenko Music Theatre. Kondrashin received his diploma with honours at the first Russian conducting competition in 1938, and was immediately appointed principal conductor of the Maly Theatre in Leningrad (1938-43). He worked for thirteen years (beginning in '43) at the Bolshoi Theatre where he strove to widen the repertoire and better the quality of performance.

In 1956 he left the world of opera being greatly attracted to symphonic music. Kondrashin became conductor of the Moscow Philharmonic and was guest at other Russian orchestras. He introduced many Western pieces to the symphonic repertoire as artistic director of the Moscow Philharmonic (1960-1976), intensifying his relationship with Western Europe. Change came in 1979: then a professor at the Conservatory in Moscow, Kondrashin was invited to conduct the Concertgebouw Orchestra in Holland where he defected. He was welcomed as principal guest conductor there, beside Bernard Haitink.

Kondrashin was an artist of great humility who effaced himself in favour of the music he performed. This did not, however, mean that he was not at the same time a demanding perfectionist, desirous of performing every score with the utmost faithfulness. The demands he made often resulted in an approach of enormous intensity.

Most of his recordings have been made for the label Melodia. Kondrashin was an important performer of his friend Shostakovich's music, recording the complete symphonies and conducting the premières of the 4th ('61), 12th ('61) and 13th (1962). In his years in Western Europe he recorded a number of other works, including radio recordings, and these are being made available again, certain proof of his artistry.

Sergei Alexandrovich Koussevitsky
born in Vichny-Volochok in 1874, died in Boston in 1951
became an American citizen in 1941

In 1905 Koussevitsky married Nathalie Ushkov, the daughter of a very wealthy man with a lot of real estate and a tea business. His new father-in-law instantly became his enthusiastic personal patron.

Koussevitsky used his new found fortune to move to Berlin where he made his début with the Philharmonic in 1908. Back in Moscow in 1909 he founded a music publishing house which was to become the most important weapon in the promotion of young, Russian composers. He published Scriabin, Rachmaninov, Prokofiev, Stravinsky and Glazunov. In 1915, he incorporated the Gutheil Fund and opened an office in Berlin. One in Paris followed shortly thereafter. Thanks to his familial patron, he even founded his own orchestra. They toured together, performing mostly Russian repertoire. They even made three tours along the Volga river (1910, '12, '14) on a specially built barge. After the Revolution, Koussevitsky was ordered to take over the State Orchestra of Petrograd (the old court orchestra, later

Kirill Kondrashin

to become the Leningrad Philharmonic). He stayed for three years before leaving his fatherland.

After staying for a short while in Berlin and Rome he settled in Paris in 1920. There he conducted Russian operas, and founded the 'Concerts symphoniques Koussevitsky' at the Opera House, an élite group of musicians dedicated to performing Russian and young French repertoire (1921-1928). Koussevitsky became music director of the Berlin Symphony Orchestra in 1924, a position he would hold until 1949. Under his direction, it would become one of the best orchestras in the world. Not only did the orchestra perform many new works, Koussevitsky commissioned many new pieces for the group. In 1931, for example, on the occasion of the Boston Symphony's fiftieth anniversary, he commissioned Stravinsky's *Symphony of Psalms*, Prokofiev's Fourth Symphony, Honegger's Third Symphony, Hindemith's *Concert Music for Strings and Brass* and Respighi's *Metamorphoses*. The Nathalie Koussevitsky Foundation, founded in 1942, also commissioned such important compositions as Stravinsky's *Ode*, Bartók's *Concerto for Orchestra* and Schoenberg's *A Survivor from Warsaw*.

It can be concluded, without exaggeration, that Koussevitsky played a vital role in the evolution of musical life in the twentieth century.

Josef Krips
born in Vienna in 1902, died in Geneva in 1974

Joseph Krips was a student with Mandyczevsky and Weingartner. After the Second World War, he became a leading international conductor. His career lasted for more than 50 years taking him all over the world to conduct the most important orchestras.

After studying in Vienna and Dortmund, Krips became the youngest Generalmusikdirektor in Germany, posted in Karlsruhe. From 1933-1938 he was conductor of the Vienna State Opera as well as a professor at the Academy of Music there. From there, Krips went to Belgrado to the State Opera until 1939 when the Hitler regime forbade him to continue conducting. After the war he returned to Vienna working to restore musical life there (at the Opera and the Hofmusikkapelle) until 1950. He was also busy building up the Salzburg Festival (beginning in 1946).

Touring with the Vienna Opera and Wiener Philharmonic resulted in invitations as a guest conductor at the London Symphony Orchestra (1954-1963), San Francisco Symphony Orchestra (1963-1970) and other renowned groups in the United States, Europe, the Soviet Union, Mexico, Canada, Australia, New Zealand and Israel. Krips conducted the opera in Berlin and at Covent Garden. The many honours bestowed upon him during his career included honorary conductor (and citizen) of San Francisco, the honorary Ring of the UNO, the Bruckner medal in both Europe and the United States, the Ring of Honour of Vienna and the Mozart ring of Austria.

Rafael Kubelik
born in Bychory (Prague) in 1914, a Swiss national since 1967

As the son of the famous violinist, Jan Kubelik, it was natural for Rafael to attend the Conservatory in Prague where he studied piano, composition, violin and orchestral direction.

He marked the taking of his final diplomas at that institution with the composition of a *Fantasy for violin and orchestra*, the playing of a Paganini violin concerto and the conducting of Dvorak's overture *Othello*.

The time Kubelik spent at the Conservatory was of great importance for his formation as a conductor. Throughout those five years he was part of the Conservatory's orchestra in various capacities: member of the First violin section, First-chair violist and finally, leader of the entire orchestra. Here Kubelik learned the value of good teamwork between orchestra and conductor. He thus became a conductor who attempted to work with his orchestra in a spirit of friendly and harmonious co-operation rather than one of coercion and forceful dominance, an attitude he has maintained from his first appearance as conductor with the National Theatre of Brno (1936-'41).

Kubelik headed the Czech Philharmonic Orchestra from 1941 until 1948. He left his fatherland in 1948 and spent a few years in the United States. He was music director of the Chicago Symphony Orchestra from 1950 until 1953, whereupon he became director at Covent Garden for three years, following that with the Orchestra of the Bavarian Radio from 1961 until 1979. Kubelik was awarded the Gustav Mahler Medal for his continual promotion and performance of Mahler's symphonies, having been the first to record them completely. The New York Metropolitan Opera was also in his charge for three years in this period.

Kubelik's repertoire is extremely varied, including nearly everything from Mozart to Schoenberg, with a special affection for the works of Dvorák, Janácek and Mahler. His interpretations are charged with an impulsive spontaneity and a fiery temperament.

Rafael Kubelik has composed three *Requiems*, a number of operas, symphonic works and chamber music.

Raymond Leppard
born in London in 1927

Raymond Leppard is a British conductor, harpsichordist and musicologist. He studied at Cambridge University from 1948 to 1952, eventually joining the faculty of Trinity College as Fellow and University Lecturer in Music (1957-67).

Leppard made his conducting début in 1952 in London's Wigmore Hall. In 1959 he conducted for the first time at Covent Garden and three years later at Glyndebourne. From 1973 to 1980 Leppard was principal conductor of the BBC Northern Symphony. His most significant symphonic activities, however, have been with the English Chamber Orchestra since 1963. With this ensemble he has been able to explore to his heart's content his areas of special interest: early Baroque music and contemporary compositions. Leppard has earned respect for his critical editions of the

Josef Krips

Raymond Leppard

operas of Monteverdi, Cesti and Cavalli, and for numerous recordings, including Handel's *Concerti a due cori*, as well as for conducting the world première of Nicholas Maw's *The Ring of the Moon* in 1970.

Lorin Maazel
born in Neuilly-sur-Seine in 1930

Lorin Maazel started piano and violin lessons at the age of five, and was, as such a small child, already interested in conducting. He studied with Vladimir Bakalenikow in Pittsburgh, and at the young age of nine, made his début conducting a student orchestra at the World's Fair in New York. Soon after, he conducted the Los Angeles Philharmonic in the same concert as Stokowski. In 1941 Toscanini invited him to conduct the NBC Philharmonic Orchestra, and this led to his being invited to conduct the New York Philharmonic in one of their summer concerts, in Lewisohn Stadium, of all places, and for an audience of 8,500 people. Maazel is soon considered a true wonderchild and is asked to conduct all the major orchestras in the United States: Cleveland (1943), Philadelphia, Chicago, Los Angeles, San Francisco ...

To avoid being forever branded as a prodigy, from 1946 to 1950 Lorin Maazel attended the University of Pittsburgh studying mathematics, languages and philosophy. During this period he remained busily involved with music: he was leader and assistant conductor of the Pittsburgh Symphony Orchestra and founded the Fine Arts Quartet in which he played First violin.

Koussevitsky invited him to Tanglewood in 1951 to conduct Stravinsky's *Symphonie des Psaumes*. A Fulbright scholarship in 1952 enabled Maazel to study Baroque music in Italy. In that same year, he conducted in Europe for the first time, replacing Pierre Dervaux in Catania. This was to be the first of many performances in Europe: in 1955 in Vienna, in '56 in Berlin, and in 1960 as the youngest and first American to conduct in Bayreuth.

Maazel toured Australia in 1961 and the USA (with the orchestra of the O.R.T.F.) in 1962. In that same year he conducted *Don Giovanni* at the Metropolitan in New York. *Le Nozze de Figaro* brought him both to Salzburg and Japan in 1963. He succeeded Ferenc Fricsay as conductor of the Symphony Orchestra of Radio Berlin in 1965, staying there until 1975. In the meantime (1971), he added the Opera of West Berlin to his list of accomplishments.

Maazel was second conductor to Otto Klemperer at the Philharmonia Orchestra from 1970 until 1972, when he succeeded George Szell as conductor in Cleveland. He stayed in Cleveland until 1982, performing many works by young Americans.

Maazel worked on the sound of two opera films done by Joseph Losey: in 1979, with the orchestra and choir of the Opera of Paris, for *Don Giovanni*, and in 1983 for *Carmen*. In this same period (beginning 1977), he was principal guest conductor of the National Orchestra in France.

Maazel was appointed director of the Vienna State Opera in 1982 but left after only two years due to irreconcilable differences. He returned to the United States to become musical director of the Pittsburgh Symphony Orchestra until 1986.

Sir Charles Mackerras
born in Schenectady (USA) in 1925

After having completed his studies at the Conservatory in Sydney, Charles Mackerras became an oboist in the orchestra of that city (1943-1946). He then travelled to England for a year and went on to study in Prague with Talich at the Music Academy. He made his début at Sadler's Wells Theatre, where he remained as principal conductor until 1953. He followed that by becoming principal of the BBC Concert Orchestra for two years. Invitations to guest conduct followed from numerous opera houses until Mackerras was appointed to the Hamburg Opera (1966-1970). He then became director at Sadler's for seven years and principal guest at the BBC for two years (1977-79). Mackerras also performs regularly at the Paris Opera and Covent Garden.

Charles Mackerras is a great interpreter of Janácek, having performed two opera premières in England. Lesser known is the fact that Mackerras is an accomplished musicologist, editing works by Handel and Janácek.

Nicolai Malko
born in Brailov (USSR) in 1883, died in Roseville (Sydney) in 1961

Nicolai Malko studied philosophy at the University of St Petersburg, and composition with Rimsky-Korsakov, Liadov and Glazunov, and orchestral direction with Tcherepnine at the Conservatory. He continued his conducting studies with Mottle in Munich. Upon returning to St Petersburg, he was appointed to conduct opera and ballets at the Opera House (1908-1918). He then moved to Moscow to teach at the Conservatory there (1922-25) before again returning to Leningrad to conduct the Philharmonie (1926-29). Malko emigrated to Denmark in 1929 where he became principal conductor of the Symphony Orchestra of the Danish Radio (1929-32). Malko was also a teacher in Denmark and the Danish King was one of his conducting students.

Nicolai Malko made his American début in Chicago in 1938. He returned to Denmark for two years (1938-40), taught at the Mozarteum in Salzburg, before settling permanently in Chicago where he became a professor at De Paul University. He is a frequent guest with the Boston Symphony Orchestra (1941-42) and conducted for a year in Mexico (1943). Malko was conductor of the Grand Park Orchestra in Chicago from 1945 until 1954, then worked with the Yorkshire Symphony Orchestra in Leeds for two years (1954-56) before finally settling in Australia. He was principal conductor of the Sydney Symphony Orchestra from 1956 until 1961.

Igor Markevich
born in Kiev in 1912, died in Antibes in 1983

The Markevich family left Russia in 1912 and settled in Switzerland. Young Igor was trained as a pianist there and played Chopin for the first time in public when only eight. The renowned pianist, Cortot, heard Igor when he was

sixteen and convinced his family to move to Paris where Igor studied with Cortot at l'Ecole Normale de Musique. Cortot took him under his wing, arranged composition lessons for Igor with Nadia Boulanger, orchestration with Rieti and directing lessons with Herman Serchen.
Diaghilev approached Markevich in 1929 to commission music for Diaghlev's ballet *l'Habit du Roi*. He made his conducting début the next year with the Concertgebouw Orchestra. Markevich married Nijinski's daughter, Kyra, and dedicated himself to composing until the war. The war broke out while he was still in Italy. After the liberation, Markevich was put in charge of the May Festival in Florence. His career as a conductor took off immediately after that: from 1949 until 1956 he gave yearly conducting courses during the Salzburger Festspiele, he became principal conductor of the Stockholm Symphony Orchestra (1952-55), and of l'Orchestre des Concert Lamoureux (1957-61). He conducted the Havana Symphony Orchestra (1957-58), gave conducting courses in Mexico and in St Jacques de Compostella, conducted the Montreal Symphony Orchestra (1958-61), was principal conductor of the Symphony Orchestra of the Spanish Broadcast (1965-72), became in 1968 director of l'Orchestre National de l'Opéra de Monte Carlo, and left this post in 1973 to become principal conductor of the Orchestra of the Accademia di Santa Cecilia in Rome (until 1975).
His conducting career came to an end when he started showing signs of acoustic aphasia, but he continued working as an important musical pedagogue.
His most important compositions are: the *Piano concerto*, 1929, a *Partita for piano and orchestra*, 1936, a *Cantata* upon a text by Jean Cocteau, 1930, and the oratorium *Paradis Perdu*, 1935.

Neville Marriner
born in Lincoln, England in 1924.

Neville Marriner was obliged to interrupt his studies at the Royal College of Music during the Second World War. Having fulfilled his military duties he again took up his music studies at the Paris Conservatoire with René Benedetti. After teaching music for a year at Eton College (1947-48), Marriner devoted himself to musical performance as second violinist with the Martin String Quartet and as co-founder of the Jacobean Ensemble, specializing in the interpretation of seventeenth- and eighteenth-century music. He taught violin at the Royal College of Music from 1949 until 1959, at the same time taking lessons in conducting from Pierre Monteux during the latter's summer courses in Maine (USA). From 1952 onwards he was violinist with the Philharmonia Orchestra and from 1956-68, leader of the Second violins of the London Symphony Orchestra. In the years Marriner spent with the London Symphony Orchestra, he formed first the Virtuoso String Trio and, in 1959, the Academy of St Martin-in-the-Fields. This ensemble has made him world-famous (and very well-to-do). He is still the artistic director of this ensemble.
Putting to use his experience as an ensemble violinist, Marriner has moulded an orchestra of extreme refinement and polish.
In 1969 he was appointed conductor of the Los Angeles

Chamber Orchestra. From 1971-73 he directed the Northern Sinfonia in Newcastle, and from 1975 to 1979 he assumed André Previn's responsibilities for the concert series in the Elizabeth Hall of the Greater London Council for the South Bank Summer Music. In 1978 Marriner was appointed director and conductor of the Minnesota Orchestra.
In that same year, he conducted *Le Nozze di Figaro* at the Festival in Aix-en-Provence. He is also often invited by the National Symphony Orchestra of France. In 1983, Marriner was appointed principal conductor of the Symphony Orchestra of the Süddeutschen Rundfunk in Stuttgart.

Jean Martinon
born in Lyon in 1910, died in Paris in 1976

Jean Martinon began studying at the Conservatory in Lyon, but graduated with a first prize in violin from the Conservatory in Paris. He furthered his studies with Roussel, D'Indy, Désormière and Munch. Just before the war he made his début as a conductor, but his career really started after the Second World War: he then became second conductor next to Charles Munch in Bordeaux with the Société des Concerts (1946-48). From 1951-58 he was principal conductor of the Dublin Radio Symphony Orchestra and of the Orchestre des Concert Lamoureux, in 1958-60 principal conductor of the Israel Philharmonic Orchestra, from 1960-66 Generalmusikdirektor in Düsseldorf, and from 1963-68 artistic director of the Chicago Symphony Orchestra. From 1968-74 he conducted the Orchestre National de France and in 1974-76 the Residential Orchestra of The Hague.
Jean Martinon has travelled the world as an ambassador of French music. He has recorded this repertoire almost exclusively (including complete works by Ravel, Debussy and Saint-Saëns, most of the works of Roussel, as well as the complete symphonies of Prokofiev). He was awarded the Gustav Mahler Medal in 1968.
Martinon composed one opera, two violin concerti, four symphonies, a cello concerto and two string quartets.

Jean Martinon
photo: G. Neuvecell

Neville Marriner

Kurt Masur
born in Brieg (Silesia) in 1928

When he became fifteen, Masur went to study the piano and violin in Breslau, proceeding to the Conservatory in Leipzig in 1946-48 where he studied orchestral direction. He was appointed principal conductor in Erfurt (1951-53), Leipzig (1953-55) and Dresden (1955-58). Masur became Generalmusikdirektor in Schwerin from 1958 until 1960 when he was given a post at the Comic Opera of Berlin (East Germany). He remained there until 1964.
Masur was awarded the job of principal conductor at the Gewandhaus Orchestra in Leipzig in 1970, and became principal guest of the Dallas Symphony Orchestra in 1976.
Kurt Masur is a conductor from the Eastern bloc who, exceptionally, is better known outside of his own country. He has performed throughout the world with the finest orchestras, and has made a great deal of reputable recordings. One of his projects has been to record the complete symphonies of Mendelssohn.

Kurt Masur

Zubin Mehta
born in Bombay in 1936

Zubin Mehta who studied at the Music Academy in Vienna, is of Indian origin. As a musician, however, he feels himself to be thoroughly Viennese. The son of a violinist and founder of the Symhony Orchestra of Bombay, Mehta was familiar with music-making by the age of seven. He played both the violin and the piano. After pursuing a course of medical studies, he decided in 1954 to devote himself full-time to music. In that year he began his studies in Vienna, in particular receiving instruction in conducting from Hans Svarovsky. Later he attended the summer courses given in Sienna by Carlo Zecchi and Alco Galliera and also studied at the Berkshire Music Centre in Tanglewood, USA, with Eleazar de Carvalho. In 1958, after winning first prize in the Liverpool International Conducting Competition, Mehta was appointed assistant conductor of the Royal Liverpool Philharmonic. The following year his replacement of the ailing Eugene Ormandy with the Vienna Philharmonic was an outstanding success. In 1960 a similar opportunity came his way when he was called upon to substitute for Igor Markevich with the Montreal Symphony Orchestra. Mehta was associated with this orchestra until 1967. In 1962 he received the additional appointment of permanent conductor of the Los Angeles Philharmonic. Under his direction both orchestras developed remarkably. In 1969 Mehta was named chief conductor and musical adviser of the Israel Philharmonic Orchestra. Since 1978 he combines these functions with the music directorship of the New York Philharmonic Orchestra. In his performances Mehta, in his own words, seeks to find 'a mid-point between the clarification of structure and the expression of content, without being a purely emotional musician.' Harold Schonberg of the New York Times gave the following description: 'Mehta is a Romantic through and through, and he draws from his orchestra an especially rich sound. His beat is a pleasure for an orchestral player... There is something Toscanini-like about it.'
Metha's dynamic interpretations are known for their rhythmically power and robust sound.

Willem Mengelberg
born in Utrecht in 1871, died in Zuort (Switzerland) in 1951

Willem Mengelberg began his musical studies in the city of his birth with Richard Hol, M.W. Petri and Anton Averkamp. He continued his studies in Cologne where he graduated with a first prize for piano, composition and orchestral direction. He débuted as a pianist as a very young man. In 1891, Mengelberg was appointed the city music director in Luzern where he was responsible for the Conservatory and the city's orchestra. Only four years later, he became the principal conductor of the Concertgebouw Orchestra, a post he was to maintain for half a century.
Mengelberg added the direction of the Toonkunst Choir, an internationally renowned group, in 1897. It became a famous traditon that this Choir annually sang the *St Matthew Passion* at the Concertgebouw.
Mengelberg met Gustav Mahler for the first time in 1902. They were to remain friends for life. Mengelberg also

Willem Mengelberg

became a major promoter of Mahler's music. From 1907 until 1920, Mengelberg organized the Museum Concerts in Frankfurt, and from 1921 until 1929, he conducted the National Symphony in New York. While in New York, many guest conductors took over his duties at the Concertgebouw, for example Bruno Walter, Karl Muck and Pierre Monteux. After a hefty argument with Toscanini in the 1928-29 season, Mengelberg left New York to return to Amsterdam.
The University of Utrecht funded a chair in musicology in 1933 especially for Mengelberg.
His response to the German occupiers was too sympathetic during the war, and this resulted in Mengelberg's being banned from conducting in 1945. He left the Netherlands to settle in Switzerland, lonely and inert for the last few years of his life.
Mengelberg was an enthusiastic conductor, accurate and passionate, and he was one of the best interpreters of Mahler. In 1920, in celebration of his silver jubilee with the orchestra, he conducted all the Mahler symphonies in a series of nine concerts. It was a Mahler festival unrivalled in music history.
Contemporary music also played an important role in Mengelberg's repertoire, especially the French. He organized a festival for these pieces in 1922. Richard Strauss dedicated *Ein Heldenleben* to Mengelberg and he was honoured by Rachmaninov with his symphonic poem, *The Bells*. Mengelberg conducted the premières of Kodaly's *Hary János Suite* (1927), Bartók's Second Violin Concerto (1939) and Milhaud's *Carnival d'Aix* (1928).

Yevgeny Mravinsky
born in 1903, died in 1988

When Yevgeny Mravinsky died at the age of 84 in January,1988, he was considered the greatest Russian conductor both in and outside of the Soviet Union and one of the most amazing talents this century has known.
Born in St Petersburg, Mravinsky worked as a rehearser at the Imperial School of Ballet while studying biology at the University of Leningrad. He enrolled at the Conservatory to study composition with Alexander Gauk and Nicolai.
In 1930, Mravinsky was appointed principal conductor of the Leningrad Opera also making his début with the Symphony Orchestra there. The Symphony appointed them their principal in 1938, a post he held for fifty years. His name is closely associated with Shostakovich; Mravinsky performed the première of many of Shostakovich's symphonies: (the *Fifth* in 1937, the Sixth in 1943, the Eighth, dedicated to Mravinsky, in 1943, the *Ninth* in 1945, the *Tenth* in 1953). He also premiered the violin and cello concerti (1955 and 1959 respectively).
Mravinksy toured Europe with his orchestra three times, in 1960, 1972 and 1978. The first tour was especially impressive. DG recorded the last three Tchaikovsky symphonies in London during this tour (now available on CD). During the Wiener Festwoche in 1978, performances of Weber, Brahms, Tchaikovsky and Shostakovich were made for EMI and later transferred to CD by JVC.
Debussy, Prokofiev, Kabalevsky and Hindemith were also Mravinsky favourites. Despite his failing health, the con-

ductor continued to work becoming something of a recluse only in his final years, unapproachable for all but a select few and certainly no Westerners. Those fortunate to have seen him at work speak of a strong personality and absolute perfectionist. He fascinates his musicians with his concentration and feeling for detail. The rehearsal schedule is rigorous and unquestioned. When, shortly before his death, Mravinsky heard rumors concerning possible sucessors, he declared angrily that he would conduct 'his' orchestra even if they had to carry him in on a stretcher!

Charles Münch
born in Strasbourg in 1891, died in Richmond (Virginia) in 1968

Son of an organist, violinist, choir director and teacher at the local Conservatory, Charles Münch may have seemed destined to enter musical life. At the age of twenty-one he left his birthplace of Strasbourg for medical studies in Paris. But the violin lessons he received there gradually gained the upper hand.
He continued his studies in Berlin with Carl Flesch. Münch was drafted into the army as an Elzasser during the First World War and did not make his début until after the hostilities were over. In 1919 he was appointed to teach at the Conservatory in Strasbourg and also became concertmaster of the municipal orchestra there (until 1926).
Münch continued to teach at the Conservatory in Leipzig (1926-1932) and played for seven years as concertmaster in the Gewandhaus Orchestra under Furtwängler and Bruno Walter. He even conducted series of concerts in the Thomas Church from the concertmaster's place. His real début as a conductor however was in Paris in 1932. There he studied with Alfred Szendrei and quickly developed into one of the most promising young conductors of his day. He founded the Orchestre Philharmonique in Paris and was its first conductor. Münch was then appointed principal conductor of the Societé des Concerts de Conservatoire (1938-1946). In 1939 he added a position teaching orchestral direction at the Conservatory to his list of accomplishments.
It was after the Second World War that Münch's career became international. He was a regular guest with the National Orchestra and toured the USA with them in 1948. He succeeded Koussevitsky at the Boston Symphony Orchestra the following year and also directed the Berkshire Music Festival at that time. In 1967 Münch founded the Orchestra of Paris and became its first artistic director. Charles Münch was an unusual figure in the French musical world. He was almost completely self-taught as a conductor. Intuition played an important part in his accomplishments, which could vary from day to day as a result. He was warm and charismatic, had a good relationship with the players under him as he held the orchestra as a whole family in his grasp. In spite of his many students, he did not particularly establish his own school. His work was too personal to imitate. During a period in which conducting in France was rather sterile and chauvinistic, Münch was able to gather attention for various styles and schools, especially the great German tradition. He was, nevertheless, a great champion of French music, had a passion for Berlioz, and gave wonderful performances of Ravel, Fauré and Roussel.

Münch performed many works in première by Honegger, Jolivet, Schmitt, Dutilleux, Martinu, Poulenc, Von Einem, Copland, Barber, De Villa Lobos and Tansman.
His autobiography, *Je suis chef d'orchestre*, was published in 1954.

Ricardo Muti
born in Naples in 1941

Being the son of a physician, it was not difficult for Ricardo Muti to finance his studies. At an early age, he chose music and started with piano lessons. He was admitted to the Conservatory in Naples where he studied with Vincenzo Vitale, himself a student of Alfred Cortot's. Muti filled in for a colleague unexpectedly one day and conducted a student orchestra. He was so enthralled that he went immediately to study in Milan with Antonio Votto.
In 1967 he won first prize in the international Guido Cantelli Conducting Competition and this immediately resulted in a number of important offers. Muti conducted his first concert the following year with Svatoslav Richter as soloist, during the May Festival in Florence. Muti was appointed principal conductor for the festival from 1969 until 1973. He débuted at the Salzburg Festival in 1971. Two years later, he succeeded Otto Klemperer as principal conductor of the Philharmonia Orchestra (1973-'82). The Philadelphia Orchestra asked him as principal guest in 1977, and as musical director in 1980.
Muti conducted the first complete performance of *Wilhelm Tell* in Florence in 1972, working on the renaissance of opera in that city that had previously had such a strong operatic tradition. His first recordings were of Verdi, *Aida* and *Un Ballo in Maschera*. Muti is a wonder at Verdi. His performances are warm and lively and possess great lyrical passion. Muti succeeded Claudio Abbado as principal conductor at the Scala in Milan in 1986.

Vaclav Neumann
born in Prague on September 29, 1920

While still a student at the Conservatory, Vaclav Neumann founded the Smetana String Quartet in which he himself played the viola (1941-1947). His début as a conductor was in 1948, with the Czech Philharmonica. Neumann then became assistant to Rafael Kubelik who was then principal of that orchestra. Between 1951 and 1964, Neumann was conductor with various orchestras including the Symphony Orchestra of Karlovy Vary, The Brno Symphony, The Prague Symphony and the Czech Philharmonic. During these same years, he conducted frequently at the Comic Opera in Berlin. In 1964, Neumann was honoured with the principal's post of the Gewandhaus Orchestra in Leipzig as well as the Opera there. He returned to Prague in 1968 to succeed Karel Ancerl as principal again at the Czech Philharmonic. He was also (between 1970 and 1972) Generalmusikdirektor of the Opera in Stuttgart.
Vaclav Neumann is a prominent promoter of Czech composers. He has also recorded important series of the complete symphonies of Mahler and Martinu.

Ricardo Muti

Roger Norrington
born in 1934 in Oxford

Roger Norrington débuted as a conductor as early as 1962 and held important positions in England (musical director of the Opera in Kent, conductor of the Schutz Choir in London, conductor of the London Strings Players and the London Baroque Ensemble). International acclaim, however, was late and very sudden with the release of his *Second* and *Eighth* Symphonies by Beethoven, performed with the London Classical Players in 1987. The recordings were completely surprising and caused a great sensation. One critic wrote: ' An orchestra without limitations, playing at Beethoven's own controversial tempi, strongly accented, with fortissimi that challenge the galant style and do Beethoven perfect justice.'

Eugene Ormandy
born in Budapest on November 18, 1899, died in Philadelphia on March 12, 1985, an American citizen since 1927

Eugene Ormandy was sent by his father to the Music Academy in Budapest as a little boy of only five. Two years later he gave his first concert. He was accepted to study with the great violinist Jenö Hubay and also studied composition and counterpoint with Zoltán Kodály and Leo Weiner. Ormandy graduated with soloist's diplomas at the age of eighteen. He received honours for piano, counterpoint and composition, and was immediately offered a position to teach at the Royal Academy in Budapest.

Friends encouraged Ormandy to tour the United States because of his exceptional talents as a violinist. He made the journey in 1921. Abandoned by his manager and with only a few more dollars in his pocket, Ormandy tried everything to keep his head above water. He auditioned for Mengelberg in New York who was duly impressed with the young Hungarian violinist. Mengelberg thought he would make a fine concertmaster for the Concertgebouw Orchestra ... if a vacancy as such ever presented itself. Desperate Ormandy had to reconcile himself with playing in a cinema orchestra, at the Capitol Theatre in New York, for the present at least. Ironically, it was that ensemble that was the start of his career as a conductor when Ormandy was given the job of running the orchestra in 1924. He worked so hard on his direction techniques, that he quickly became a conductor worthy of notice. Ormandy was the conductor of the CBS Radio Orchestra from 1928 until 1931. In 1931, Toscanini had to cancel an appearance with the Philadelphia Orchestra at the last minute. Eugene Ormandy stepped in to replace the famous Italian and in this risky situation, won instant renown. In that same year, Ormandy was called in to replace the sick conductor of the Minneapolis Symphony; he was offered a five year contract after only the second rehearsal. More invitations as a guest conductor followed. Some of these were again in Philadelphia, where Ormandy was quickly named second conductor to Stokowsky. In 1938, when only 36, Eugene Ormandy was named principal conductor in Philadelphia, a position he was to hold for more than forty years (until 1979).

Ormandy's achievements as a conductor inspired invitations to conduct around the world. In 1953, he was the guest of the Concertgebouw Orchestra, where he conducted Hindemith's *Mathis der Maler* and Prokofiev's *Sixth Symphony*. In 1955, Ormandy returned to conduct again in Amsterdam. He toured Europe very successfully with the Philadelphians in that same year.

Eugene Ormandy is still considered a very great conductor, a craftsman of considerable technique and an exceptional musical talent. Some critics dislike his taste in sound, complaining that it relies too heavily on brilliant, superficial effects. Others admire him for exactly that, his sound: produced by warm and polished string playing. 'My conducting is the way it is because I am a violinist. Toscanini always directed, inspired by his cello. Conductors that are pianists have a sharper, tighter sound in their orchestras.' An orchestra led for so long under such a great talent inevitably gets branded by its conductor. The Philadelphia Orchestra under Ormandy was famously branded in this way. The recordings that Ormandy made with his orchestra include practically the entire symphonic repertoire, from early classical to the most contemporary.

Seiji Ozawa
born in Hoten, Japan on September 1, 1935

Forced to abandon his piano studies due to a hand injury sustained during a rugby match, Seiji Ozawa devoted himself to composition and conducting. He received his training at the Toho Music School in Tokyo, continuing his studies in Europe beginning in 1959. Ozawa won first prize in the international conducting competition in Besançon and in 1960, the Koussevitsky Prize. He has been assistant to Herbert von Karajan and Leonard Bernstein, who asked Ozawa to accompany him with the New York Philharmonic on their tour to Japan in 1961. After several years of guest conducting, Ozawa was appointed director of the Ravinia Festival of the Chicago Symphony from 1964 until 1968. He then became principal conductor of the Toronto Symphony from 1965 until 1969, followed by the San Francisco Symphony from 1970 until 1976. Ozawa has been associated with the Boston Orchestra since 1970.

Ozawa, who usually avoids interviews, did tell the British press some years ago in Tokyo: 'It was incredible that the Boston Symphony Orchestra should ask me to become its musical director. It is a very traditional orchestra and I am not a traditional musician. Coming from Japan, which has no history or tradition of performing western music, I am at a distinct disadvantage. I still must learn so much music. But this disadvantage also has its benefits. As my great teacher Saito said to me, I have no bad habits and can choose from the emotional world of Latin, German, French or Russian music.' This lack of tradition has become the subject of various opinions. Richard Dyer wrote in the Boston Globe in 1978, 'Ozawa knows how to forge a direct link between orchestra, music and audience. His body is a brilliant medium of communication... He possesses a vital feeling for instrumental colour, he knows how to concentrate an orchestra and keep it alert... But his work also displays moments of surprising tastelessness. More serious, for such breaches of taste are relatively rare, is Ozawa's continual inability to penetrate beyond the direct link between orchestra, music and audience... Too much is

Roger Norrington

Seiji Ozawa

superficial.' Seiji Ozawa has proved himself to be a great conductor in spite of and perhaps as a result of his unique position. He still retains strong ties with his native Japan, his young family lives there, refusing to ignore his musical and personal heritage simply to fit a mould supplied by western traditionalist.

André Previn
born in Berlin on April 6, 1929

André Previn, American conductor and composer is, no doubt due to his Christian name, frequently thought to be of French origin. Actually he was born in Berlin as Andreas Ludwig Priwin, son of German parents of Russian-Jewish descent. In any event, Previn, who as a child studied piano at the Berlin Hochschule für Musik and at the Paris Conservatoire, is a true American. Escaping the Nazi regime, the Previn family emigrated to the United States in 1939, where André's uncle was a music director at Hollywood's Universal Studios.

Newly settled in Los Angeles, Previn studied with Castelnuovo-Tedesco, the classical composer who himself had fled Naziism. Previn then launched a career as a jazz pianist and film orchestrator. In 1951, while in the Armed Forces, he studied conducting with Pierre Monteux and after several years, began a new career as concert pianist and conductor. Previn made his conducting début in 1963 with the St Louis Symphony Orchestra. Four years later he became principal conductor of the Houston Symphony (1967-1970). He made recordings with the London Symphony in 1965 whose principal Previn would later become from 1969 until 1979. The London Symphony also honoured him with the status of 'Conductor Emeritus'. In 1975, André Previn was appointed chief conductor of the Pittsburgh Symphony Orchestra.

Alongside his many activities in the field of classical music, Previn has not shrunk from serving the popular muse as pianist, arranger, conductor and composer. He has made recordings of his own jazz music, among them *A Different Kind of Blues* together with the violinist Itzhak Perlman. As a conductor, Previn has a strict preference for music with an apparent nationalistic motive or strongly coloured features.

The abstract symphonic repertoire is not his most successful field. In this respect, it is not surprising that his recordings with the London Symphony Orchestra of Vaughn William's symphonies and works by William Walton and Rachmaninov, are especially highly regarded.

Sir John Pritchard,
born in London on February 5, 1921

The name John Pritchard is strongly associated with the entire symphonic repertoire even if his early career tended towards more vocal direction. As the son of a violinist, Pritchard received his first music lessons from his father. He travelled to Italy to study piano, viola and orchestral direction. Once he served as the conductor of the little known Derby String Orchestra from 1943 until 1945. Pritchard worked mainly in the world of opera from 1947 onwards. He was rehearser at the Glyndebourne Festival where he replaced Fritz Busch at the last minute to conduct Don Giovanni. This same festival asked him to return as a musical advisor in 1963. In that year, Pritchard was appointed conductor of the Huddersfield Choral Society and in 1978, he became musical director of the Opera in Cologne. In 1981, the Théâtre Royal de la Monnaie in Brussels named him their musical director. Pritchard has performed many premières of important contemporary operas including works by Britten and Tippett. Despite this concentration of work in the vocal world, Sir John Pritchard has made his mark in the symphonic world as well. Between 1957 and 1963, Pritchard was conductor of the Royal Philharmonic in Liverpool. He became principal guest at the BBC Symphony Orchestra in 1979, and principal conductor there in 1982.

Mstislav Rostropovich
born in Baku in 1927

Mstislav Rostropovich received his first music lessons from his parents. His mother was a concert pianist, his father, a cellist of note, pupil of Casals and teacher at the Gnesin Institute in Moscow where he studied with

André Previn

Rostropovich conducting the Berlin Philharmonic Orchestra.

Shostakovich, among others. Having completed his studies with the highest honours, in the late 1940s he took prizes in cello competitions in Moscow, Prague and Budapest. In 1956 he became a professor at the Moscow Conservatory and in 1975 received an honorary doctorate in music from Cambridge University.

Rostropovich made his conducting début in 1968 with Tchaikovsky's *Eugene Onegin* at the Bolshoi Theatre in Moscow. His wife, Galina Vishnevskaya, whom he also regularly accompanies at the piano, sang the role of Tatjana. He made his conducting début in Western Europe with the same work, also with the Bolshoi Theatre, in Paris from December 1969 to January 1970. A recording of the opera was also made at this time. Following his appointment as musical director of the National Symphony Orchestra of Washington DC in 1977, he became permanent guest conductor of the London Symphony Orchestra, with which he has made a number of recordings, notably of the Tchaikovsky symphonies.

Rostropovich has an instinctive feeling for the intentions of the composer. This is to be heard in performances of contemporary music as well as of the traditional repertoire.

Gennadi Rozhdestvensky
born in Moscow in 1931

Gennadi Rozhdestvensky received his first instruction in music at the Moscow State Conservatory from his father Nikolai Anosov (conducting) and from Lev Oborin (piano). While still at the Conservatory he made his conducting début, having taken part in 1951 in a conducting competition at Moscow's Bolshoi Theatre and was immediately thereafter appointed student conductor there.

Studying during the day at the Conservatory and working in the theatre in the evening, he became acquainted not only with the ballet and theatre world in its smallest details but also with the conditions necessary for becoming a first-rate conductor. When Rozhdestvensky completed his studies at the Conservatory, he was already a highly regarded conductor both inside and outside Russia. He was conductor and chief conductor of the Bolshoi Theatre in the periods 1951-61 and 1964-70. In 1961 he was named artistic director and principal conductor for life of the Symphony Orchestra of the Russian Radio. In Western Europe he made a name not only as guest conductor with most of the front-ranking orchestras but also as director of the Stockholm Philharmonic Orchestra (appointed in 1974) and as chief director of the BBC Symphony Orchestra (appointed in 1978). Equipped with a brilliant and supple technique, Rozhdestvensky offers a clear portrayal of the structure of a composition as well as of its emotional content. His performances, a combination of analysis, intuition and apparent spontaneity, frequently bring undiscovered aspects of a composition to the fore. Alongside an interest in the younger generations of Russian composers, Rozhdestvensky also shows an affinity for the classics. The recent revival of interest in the symphonies of Prokofiev is largely due to his efforts.

Wolfgang
Sawallisch

Kurt Sanderling
born in Arys in East Prussia on September 19, 1912

The German conductor Kurt Sanderling became, in 1931, a coach at the State Opera in Berlin, staying there until 1936, when he was obliged to flee Germany for political reasons. This obligatory emigration launched him upon his eminent career. Shortly thereafter, Sanderling took up residence in Moscow and in 1936 he was appointed conductor of the Moscow Radio Symphony Orchestra. He became principal conductor of the Philharmonia in Karkov in 1939 and this post was followed by the principal's position with the Philharmonia in Leningrad in 1942, together with Mravinski.

Sanderling returned to Germany in 1960 where he was appointed conductor of the Symphony Orchestra of East Berlin. From 1964 until 1967 he was also conductor of the Dresden Staatskapelle. Sanderling is a much sought after guest conductor, with successful appearances at festivals in Prague, Vienna, Salzburg and Warsaw to his credit.

Kurt Sanderling's large repertoire consistently shows an instinctive feeling for form and a great attention to detail. He has a particular affection for the music of Mahler, Prokofiev, Shostakovich, Sibelius and Tchaikovsky.

Wolfgang Sawallisch
born in Munich on August 26, 1923

When as a child, Wolfgang Sawallisch first heard Humperdinck's opera *Hansel und Gretel*, he knew he was destined to become a conductor. Chance dictated that the first opera he was to conduct, in Augsburg in 1947, was in fact, *Hansel und Gretel*.

After graduation from the Conservatory in Munich, Sawallisch won the Sonata Prize, together with the violinist Gerhard Seitz, at the International Competition of Geneva in 1949. Two years later, he studied orchestral direction with Igor Markevitch and assisted him at the Salzburg Festivals of 1952 and 1953. Sawallisch's début as a symphonic conductor was in 1952 with the Berlin Philharmonic. He was appointed Generalmusikdirektor in Aachen (1953-1958) and went on in the same function to Wiesbaden in 1958. Sawallisch became the first director of the Vienna Symphony Orchestra in 1960, as well as director of the Opera in Cologne. He also taught orchestral direction at the Conservatory in Cologne.

At the Bayreuth Festival in 1957, Sawallisch conducted *Tristan and Isolde*, the youngest artist to have been invited to the festival up to that time. Hamburg appointed him their Generalmusikdirektor in 1961. Through numerous guest appearances, Sawallisch has built up an extensive international reputation.

In 1971, Sawallisch was named musical director of the Bavarian State Opera in Munich and became the intendant there in 1982. Between 1970 and 1980, he was the musical director of l'Orchestre Suisse Romande as well.

Sawallisch also regularly appears as a pianist, usually in the role of accompanist, as, for example, in the integral recording of Schubert's secular music for more than one voice, but also as a concerto soloist, often conducting from the keyboard.

Wolfgang Sawallisch invests an enormous amount of energy in his work. His musical ideas and interpretations are founded upon deep study and musical analysis. He is known for his ability to absorb the details of any score, giving his interpretations their freshness and naturalness. While working on a recording of Schubert's symphonies, Sawallisch did such far-reaching musicological research, that a completely new edition of the symphonies was warranted. His discography is extensive and is dominated by complete series of the symphonies of Schubert, Schumann and Mendelssohn.

Giuseppe Sinopoli
born in Venice on November 2, 1946

Giuseppe Sinopoli has many talents. He studied both music at the Conservatory of Venice (from 1965 until 1967) and medicine at the University of Padua. His doctoral thesis concerned criminal anthropology. Disappointed in the music lessons in Venice, Sinopoli travelled to Darmstadt in 1968, where he worked with Bruno Maderna and Karl Stockhausen. Between 1969 and 1973, he studied with Donatoni, becoming his assistant as well at the summer courses in Sienna. In 1972, Sinopoli began direction lessons with Hans Swarowski in Venice, deciding to settle permanently there. He did however continue to teach at the B. Marcello Conservatory in Venice, giving classes in orchestral direction and contemporary music. Sinopoli founded the Bruno Maderna Ensemble in 1975. He is also considered an expert on the works of Boulez. Since 1983, he is the permanent conductor of the orchestra of the Academia Santa Cecilia in Rome, and since 1984, he holds the same position with the Philharmonia Orchestra. Sinopoli made his début at the Metropolitan Opera conducting Tosca in

1985. In the course of his career so far, he has also made many symphonic recordings, including the Mahler symphonies.

Georg Solti
born in Budapest in 1912

Several colourful incidents mark the career of Sir Georg Solti. On the evening of his début with the Budapest Opera, 12 March 1938, news came that Hitler's troops had invaded Vienna and spread quickly through the theatre where the performance was taking place. By the time the opera, *Figaro*, was over, hardly any of the audience was left. Nazi injunctions made it impossible for Solti to continue working in Hungary and he went to Switzerland where, forbidden to seek employment, he made an intensive study of the piano. At the end of the war when Germany was occupied by the Allied Forces, Solti was invited by the American authorities to assume direction of the Bavarian State Opera in Munich at the age of thirty-four and with scarcely any conducting experience behind him.

As musical director at the Frankfurt Opera from 1952-61, Solti won international fame as one of the greatest interpreters of Wagner, and he went next to London's Royal Opera House (1961-71), where his efforts transformed Covent Garden into a world-class company and earned him a knighthood in 1971. He has been musical director of the Chicago Symphony Orchestra since 1969, a close and cherished association.

Solti remains young and vigorous at seventy, bringing a unique freshness, insight and excitement to all his performances. He is well aware of the dangers of performing familiar works from the standard repertory too often. For example, when he recorded his widely-acclaimed perform-

Giuseppe Sinopoli

Sir Georg Solti conducting the Vienna Philharmonic Orchestra.

ance of Mahler's *Second Symphony* for Decca, he had not looked at the score for eight years, feeling that only in this way could an interpreter approach such well-known music with fresh perception.

William (Hans Wilhelm) Steinberg
born in Cologne in 1899, died in New York in 1978

William Steinberg was a naturalized American conductor, born and educated in Europe. He studied the violin and piano, finishing up under Hermann Abendroth and Otto Klemperer. While still a teenager (15-18), he was an orchestral instrumentalist, playing both violin and viola. Klemperer discovered the youth's more extensive talents, and remained a great supporter throughout Steinberg's career. In 1921, Steinberg's first directorial position came at the Opera in Cologne. A year later, he was appointed to the German Opera in Prague. Between 1929 and 1936, Steinberg worked in Frankfurt, first as Generalmusikdirektor at the Opera there, and later as conductor of the Museum Concerts. He conducted the première of Schoenberg's *Von Heute auf Morgen* in 1930. Steinberg was also a frequent guest at the State Opera in Berlin.

The Nazi régime made it impossible for Steinberg to function. He did give a few concerts for the Jewish people in association with the Israeli Cultural Liason. In 1936, Steinberg left Germany. Together with Bronislav Hubermann, he founded the Palestine Symphony Orchestra, which was later to become the Israel Philharmonic, conducting himself for the first two seasons. An invitation from Toscanini to conduct the NBC Symphony drew Steinberg to the United States, where he became associate conductor at NBC.

Seven seasons long, Steinberg was very successful with the Opera of San Francisco. He was also regularly invited to work in South America. He was a guest director of all the prominent American orchestras: New York, Philadelphia, Chicago, San Francisco, Detroit, Los Angeles, Cleveland and Minneapolis, Buffalo and Pittsburgh. He conducted the London Philharmonic from 1958 until 1960. Steinberg became senior guest at the New York Philharmonic and principal conductor in Boston from 1969 until 1972. Especially in Pittsburgh, where Steinberg first worked in 1952, his influence was felt in all aspects of that city's musical life. In 1953, Steinberg returned to Europe for the first time since the war. He performed in Italy (Scala in Milan, Rome, Turin and Naples) and even conducted in his native Cologne. Steinberg conducted a Beethoven cycle in Amsterdam with the Concertgebouw Orchestra in 1955. In his later years, Steinberg returned to America where he was permanent guest conductor of both the New York Philharmonic and the Metropolitan Opera.

George Szell

Leopold Stokowski
born in London in 1882, died in Nether Wallrop (Hampshire) in 1977

Leopold Stokowski a London-born American of Polish-Irish origin, studied at The Queen's College, Oxford, and at the Royal College in London. After a period as organist at St James in Piccadilly, he pursued further studies in Paris, Munich and New York. He received his first important appointment as conductor of the Cincinnati Symphony Orchestra. In 1912 he was also given the direction of the Philadelphia Orchestra. In this thirty years with the latter, he transformed it into a world-famous ensemble.

Stokowski was a controversial musical phenomenon. On the one hand, he added to his prestige by continually championing new works, which he often himself premièred. Schoenberg and Varèse, for example, owe him a great deal. On the other hand, he considered it perfectly normal to perform compositions from the eighteenth or nineteenth centuries in arrangements which often differed enormously from the originals. In addition Stokowski did not hesitate to publicly reprimand an ill-behaved audience, and he changed the disposition of the orchestra on the platform. He was also known to give instructions to the strings by imitating their movements, and it is clear that Stokowski produced considerable perplexity in the average concert-goer. Stokowski also worked in films, most notably in his collaboration with Walt Disney in *Fantasia*. At the advanced age of ninety-five, Stokowski was still energetically at work, giving concerts and making recordings.

Yevgeny Svetlanov
born in Moscow in 1928

The Russian conductor, composer and pianist Yevgeny Svetlanov, came from a family of theatre people. His mother was a member of a pantomime group soloist with the Bolshoi Theatre. This proved decisive for his future career. At the age of seven he played a small part in an opera and made occasional appearances with the pantomime theatre. He breathed deeply and gladly of this theatrical atmosphere, which later worked greatly to his advantage as an opera conductor.

Svetlanov began his conducting career in 1953 while still a student at the Moscow Conservatory, taking the direction of the Radio Orchestra in the same city. In 1955 he was appointed assistant director of the Bolshoi Theatre, becoming its principal conductor in 1962. Although Svetlanov concentrated mainly on opera during this period, he did not neglect the concert repertory. His reputation as a conductor of symphonic works was, however, not established until 1965 when he was made chief director of the USSR State Symphony Orchestra. His repertory contains both classics and moderns, with particular emphasis on symphonists from his own country, Miaskovsky, Shostakovich, Prokofiev and Khachaturian. International acclaim was accorded to him for his recordings of Tchaikovsky's symphonies.

George Szell
born in Budapest on 7 June 1897, died in Cleveland, Ohio in 1970

Hungarian conductors who have pursued a career in the West have, without exception, earned great admiration and respect: Solti, Richter, Nikich and Dorati, for example. This list must also include George Szell, an American conductor of Hungarian origin. He grew up in Vienna, studying composition with Foerster and Reger, and piano with Richard Robert. At the age of eleven he made his piano début, playing his own compositions. Five years later he conducted the Vienna Symphony Orchestra. Shortly there-after he made his début in Berlin, in the role of pianist, composer and conductor. In 1915 Richard Strauss engaged him for the Berlin State Opera. For twelve years he was di-rector of the German Opera and of the Prague Philharmo-nia. He then left the continent, going first to Britain, where he conducted the Scottish Orchestra from 1937 tot 1939. Finally settling in America, he conducted various orches-tras, though his name will for ever be associated with the Cleveland Orchestra.

When in 1946 Szell was invited to assume the direction of the Cleveland Orchestra, he declared himself willing only on the condition that he be given carte blanche on every level. And during his years with the orchestra, until his death in 1970, Szell was indeed given free rein. This allowed him to mould the Cleveland Orchestra into one of the finest orchestral ensembles in the world.

Szell, whose interpretations have been characterized by some as both self-indulgent and unimaginative, has won particular respect for his extraordinary professionalism. He conducted everything from memory, even accompani-ments in concertos. More than any other conductor, he knew the peculiarities of each instrument and could give not only bowing suggestions but advice to wind instrumen-talists on the proper use of keys, valves and reeds.

Klaus Tennstedt
born in Mersebourg (Germany) on June 6, 1926

Klaus Tennstedt studied violin and piano at the Conserva-tory in Leipzig. He was appointed concertmaster of the orchestra of the Municipal Theaterhalle in 1948 where he also became first conductor in 1952. Dresden named him director of the National Opera in 1958, where Tennstedt would remain until 1962. That same year, he moved to take over the State Orchestra in Schwerin. Tennstedt stayed in Schwerin for nine years. He then defected to the west, leaving behind a great deal of his family and all of his friends. Since then, Tennstedt has refused to speak of his past behind the Iron Curtain.

Tennstedt found work in Sweden, at the Stora Theater in Göteborg and with the Swedish Radio Orchestra. Shortly afterwards, he accepted the Generalmusikdirektor's post in Kiel. The manager of the Toronto Symphony heard Tenn-stedt perform and immediately arranged a guest appearance in Canada. Boston also invited him to guest conduct and he was successful with the Americans as well. It didn't take long for all the prominent American orchestras to take notice, and invitations began to pour in. Europe followed after Tennstedt's new European début in London in 1976. He became an international conductor. Tennstedt settled in West Germany in 1979, taking on a permanent position with the North German Radio Orchestra in Hamburg. The London Philharmonic appointed him their principal in 1983.

Tennstedt considers it a priceless advantage to have worked for years as an orchestral string player. 'This makes it possible for me to draw out a string sound which many conductors, those coming to the profession via the piano for example, would find difficult. String players trust me and follow my directions much more easily.'

Tennstedt approaches recordings with respect. He consid-ers records a new medium, 'an ideal possibility to come into contact with various musical genres.' He is himself an excellent studio conductor, aware of the infinite possibili-ties of making even the tiniest details audible. Tennstedt enjoys a large reputation as a Bruckner and Mahler inter-preter.

Michael Tilson-Thomas
born in Hollywood on December 21, 1944

Michael Tilson-Thomas studied at the University of South-ern California, composition with John Crown, piano with Ingolf Dahl and harpsichord with Alice Ehlers. He studied orchestral direction in Bayreuth (1966) and at the Berkshire Music Centre in Tanglewood, where he won the Kousse-vitsky Prize in 1968. The Boston Symphony appointed him assistant conductor for the 1969 and 1970 seasons. The next year they promoted him to second conductor, and in 1972 principal guest. In the meantime, Tilson-Thomas was made musical director of the Buffalo Philharmonic Orchestra where he remained until 1980. Tilson-Thomas, still young and still considered a rising American star, has a very wide musical interest that stretches from Gregorian chant up through to jazz and which included everything in between, both popular and classical. He is dedicated to playing American compositions in all his programmes. Tilson-Thomas is also a gifted pianist. For the 1969 and 1970 seasons, he performed as a member of the Boston Sym-phony Chamber Players.

Arturo Toscanini
born in 1867, died in 1957

The Toscanini name is legend for many. Toscanini, the ideal performer of the 20th century. The numerous colour-ful anecdotes concerning him, stuff enough for several thick biographies, help in preserving the legend that is Toscanini.

Arturo was born on March 25, 1867 in Busseto (near Par-ma), the son of a tailor. He was a student at the Conserva-tory in Parma when only nine years old. A few years later he was admitted to Professor Carini's cello class. Toscanini graduated with honors (Con lode distinta) for cello, piano and compostion when he was 18.

He took a job as cellist in a traveling ensemble where he amazed his colleagues with his phenomenal memory. During a performance of Verdi's *Aïda* in Rio de Janeiro, the conductor suddenly refused to continue because of some difference of opinion, and when the second conductor also refused, Toscanini was encouraged to take the podium by his fellow musicians. The 20 year old stood up, closed the score, and proceeded to conduct the entire *Aïda* from mem-ory. It would be the first of many magical performances Toscanini would lead. The legend goes that the ovation in the hall was deafening.

Word spread and Toscanini was contracted in Italy and

Klaus Tennstedt

beyond: in 1898, principal conductor of the Teatro alla Scala in Milan and in 1907, the Metropolitan Opera in New York. Especially in New York, Toscanini was to prove to be the greatest Italian conductor of his time, perhaps of all time.

Milan and New York were the two most important centres where the conductor worked for the rest of his life. The Italian's heard their opera classics performed with an unknown intensity and intellectual depth, but not only their own repetoire. Toscanini performed Wagner, Debussy, Richard Strauss and introduced early Stravinsky. He was equally dedicated to Brahms. One of his first successes in America was with Beethoven's *Ninth*, intense yet miraculously subtle of mood and tone.

Toscanini took the New York Philharmonic on a European tour in 1930. He made his début in London on the same trip. Five years later he returned (with Brahm's *Fourth*, Beethoven's *Seventh* and Debussy's *La Mer*). Both times, the English public and press were amazed at the perfection of every single interpretation.

Toscanini conducted the Residence Orchestra in The Hague in 1937. In Amerca and abroad, many leading orchestras tried to pin Toscanini down as their principal conductor. He did have longer contracts with New York but never anything permanent. It did finally happen though. The Americans succeeded in granting all Toscanini's wishes, keeping

New York Philharmonic Orchestra.

him with one orchestra, the famous studio ensemble, the NBC Symphony Orchestra, for 17 years. The maestro refused to record at first. There are, however, recordings he eventually made with 'his' orchestra still available. A number of these have been transferred to CD. Most inspiring are his *Eroica*, Brahm's *First Symphony* and Mozart's *Haffner Symphony*.

Edo De Waart
born in Amsterdam on June 1, 1941

Edo De Waart began piano lessons when he was eight years old, and began the oboe when he became sixteen. He studied with Cees van der Kraan and Haakon Stotijn. De Waart graduated from the Conservatory in Amsterdam in 1961 with honours. He became an oboist in various Dutch orchestras, including the Concertgebouw (1963-1964), gaining the necessary experience for his later conducting career. De Waart's first direction teacher was Jaap Spaanderman.

In 1964, Edo de Waart won first prize at the International Competition for Conductors in New York. The prize included both money, and more importantly, a one year's assistantship at a renowned American orchestra. Leonard Bernstein choose De Waart as one of his three assistants for

the season 1965/1966. 1965 also took him to Spoleto, where he conducted Stravinsky's *L' histoire du Soldat* at the Festival of Two Worlds. The Concertgebouw Orchestra appointed him assistant conductor in 1966, a post he left to become conductor of the Rotterdam Philharmonic, at first, together with Jean Fournet, later, independently as musical director from 1973 until 1979. After a total of twelve years in Rotterdam, De Waart left for the United States in 1975, to accept various invitations as a guest conductor. He was musical director of the San Francisco Symphony from 1977 until 1985.

Edo De Waart has not restricted himself to symphonic direction but has built up a substantial reputation in the opera world as well. He made his operatic début during the Holland Festival of 1970. In 1979, he conducted Lohengrin at Bayreuth, and in 1986, *Die Meistersinger*, again in the Holland Festival. Edo De Waart was appointed musical director of the Dutch Opera in 1986, but he held that position for only a short time, deciding to take his leave in the wake of continuous management problems at the newly opened Muziektheater in Amsterdam. After spending a year in America, De Waart returned to his native Holland where he conducted as a guest with all the important orchestras. He has been appointed chief conductor of the Dutch radio orchestras as of September, 1988.

Bruno Walter
born in Berlin in 1876, died in Beverly Hills (USA) in 1962

Bruno Walter's assertion, 'I hate reticence in art, but in life I love it', might have been the motto of this German conductor, who was born in Berlin on 15 September 1876 and died in Beverly Hills on 17 February 1962. For over half a century he belonged in the front-rank of conductors, while continually demonstrating a great reserve, even shyness in his private life.

At Gustav Mahler's suggestion, Bruno Walter dropped his surname of Schlesinger upon taking Austrian citizenship in 1911. At that time he had been conducting alongside Mahler for ten years at the Hofoper in Vienna. From 1914 to 1922 he was Generalmusikdirektor in Munich, followed by two years devoted entirely to guest conducting, after which, between 1924 and 1931, he directed the German opera performances at Covent Garden in London. During these years he appeared in various capacities in Germany, but in 1933 the political climate impelled him to again return to Austria. Subsequently he took up residence in Paris, changing his nationality to French. In 1939 he re-settled in the United States where he made numerous guest appearances with leading orchestras, the Los Angeles Symphony Orchestra, the NBC Symphony Orchestra, the New York Philharmonic - where he was musical advisor from 1947 to 1949 - and the Philadelphia Orchestra.

From 1948 onwards Walter also appeared regularly with all major European orchestras. He made a name as an exceptional interpreter of Mozart and Mahler, and in his autobiography 'Theme with Variations' gives a direct insight into his conducting methods. He had learned from Mahler that small movements are sufficient to produce enormous results and that the degree of expressiveness achieved had nothing whatsoever to do with the breadth of vehemence of gesture. This accorded perfectly with Walter's reserved nature, as did his manner of conducting rehearsals. He did not coerce his players, but brought them gently over to his point of view. In this way he achieved an astonishing orchestral unity, with a warm sound and noble Romantic expression.

Edo De Waart

Rotterdam Philhar-
monic Orchestra.

10
A guide to the great orchestras

Academy of St Martin-in-the-Fields
founded in 1956

Conductors: Sir Neville Marriner, when complete, from 1956 until 1975 (still returns to conduct recordings), Iona Brown and Kenneth Sillito, concertmasters (leaders), when only strings, from, respectively, 1974 and 1980.

The extraordinary success of the Academy of St Martin-in-the-Fields is a triumph both for the group's unquestioned excellence, and for the vigour of the recording industry. In 1958, the twelve founding members (eleven string players and a harpsichordist) made their début in the London church from which they took their name. Their aim was to promote music of the late Baroque period, performed without a conductor, in the true spirit of chamber music. Neville Marriner, a violist with the London Symphony Orchestra, was chosen as leader. His job was to direct with 'nods and smiles' (as one member put it), while playing first violin. Early concerts attracted virtually no attention, but a trial tape interested one record company enough to take a risk with this unusual (for the time) ensemble. In 1961, 'A Recital By The Academy of St Martin-in-the-Fields' was released. The Academy played on this record 'with more sense of style than all the other chamber orchestras in Europe put together'. When complete (with woodwinds, brass and percussion), the orchestra numbers between 40 and 50 musicians. Very often it performs with only its core of 16 strings. Since 1975, the Academy has worked with a choir conducted by Laszlo Heltay.
During its brief, intense existence, the Academy's idealistic commitment to clarify authenticity and ensemble playing has been surprisingly little affected by the glamour of its reputation.
The Academy's repertoire stretches from the early Baroque (Albioni and Corelli) via Bach, Handel and Mozart (the three most respon-sible for their commercial success) to Schoen-berg and Britten. Alfred Brendel has recorded the complete Mozart piano concerti with the Academy. Sir Neville Marriner conducted the Academy for the sound track of the extraordi-narily successful film 'Amadeus'. The orches-tra has also performed the following pre-mières: *Sonata for Strings* (Walton, 1972), *Métamorphoses* (Bennet, 1980) and *Sinfonia Concertante* (Maxwell-Davies, 1983).

Academy of Ancient Music (Cambridge)
founded in 1973 by Chistopher Hogwood

The Academy of Ancient Music takes its name from a nineteenth century group dedicated to the performance of old music. This new group is also dedicated to 'authentic' performance of the Baroque and Classical repertoires. Its members are specialists in 17th and 18th cen-tury music and play original instruments or copies thereof. The effectiveness of this ap-proach is completely dependent on the appro-priateness of the repertoire. As tradition dic-tates, Christopher Hogwood conducts the or-chestra from the harpsichord.
The Academy plays in 18th century section-ing: the first violins left, the second violins to the right and the low strings in the middle. These instruments are strung with gut. The woodwinds are of a much simpler design than their modern counterparts. Vibrato is used as an ornament, not continually as became the habit later.
The first fifteen years of the Academy's exis-tence were a time of great evolution. That was true of their repertoire but also true of their public. What was first sarcastically referred to as 'a bunch of health food fanatics in sandals' grew to include enough of the regular concert-going audience to interest the record compa-nies in the Academy's work. The greatest change came when such a company financed the enormous, 7 volume Mozart project. In the Eighties, the Academy of Ancient Music sold more records than Luciano Pavarotti! The Academy evolves still. With the appearance of their 1988 Beethoven project (all the piano concerti), this group widened the scope of the authentic repertoire even more.

Bamberger Symphoniker
founded in 1946

Conductors: Joseph Keilbert (1940-45), Her-bert Albert (1947-48), Georg-Ludwig Jochum (1948-50), again Joseph Keilberth (1950-68), Eugen Jochum (1969-71), James Loughran (1978-83), Witold Rowicki (1983-85), Horst Stein (since 1985).

Joseph Keilberth (1908, Karlsruhe-1968, Munich) founded the Bamberger Symphoni-ker with musicians from the old German Opera of Prague.

Berliner Philharmoniker
founded in 1882

Conductors: Franz Wüllner (1883-84), Karl Klindworth, Hans von Bülow (1887-93), Richard Strauss (1893-95), Arthur Nikish (1895-1922), Wilhelm Furtwängler (1922-45 and 1948-54), Leo Borchard (1945), Sergiù Celibidache (1945-48), Herbert von Karajan (since 1955).

The Berliner Philharmonic was formed when more than fifty musicians broke away from the orchestra of Benjamin Bilse to form their own self-governing body. They found a concert hall in a former roller skating rink (renamed the Philharmonie) and teetered on the verge of financial collapse for several years, despite the immediate support of Brahms and the violist Joseph Joachim. Artistic security at least was secured when Hans von Bülow became the first permanent conductor in 1887. A mercurial and deeply serious musician (who once performed Beethoven's *Ninth Symphony* twice in an evening), von Bülow had no patience with the ephemeral. 'I will no longer promote bad music,' he announced during his first season at Berlin, and proceeded to concentrate on the symphonies of Beethoven and Brahms. He stayed with the orchestra only five years but established a precedent of virtuoso performance that has remained a hallmark of the Berlin Philharmonic.

Arthur Nikisch, von Bülow's successor, became permanent conductor in 1895. He was a man of enormous charm, who directed the orchestra with apparent ease. Tchaikovsky, whose music Nikisch frequently programmed, once said of him: 'He doesn't conduct, rather it seems as if he indulges in a mysterious magic'. Nikisch favoured romantic composers. Beethoven, Liszt and Brahms received regular performances as did contemporaries Richard Strauss and Anton Bruckner. Throughout these years, Strauss was a frequent guest conductor.

There was no possibility of finding a suitable replacement for Arthur Nikisch when he died suddenly in 1922, but in Wilhelm Furtwängler, the orchestra chose an inspiring successor. Furtwängler was a man for whom interpreting great music was a sacred experience. His devotion to the works of Beethoven, Brahms and Bruckner, could turn the old skating rink where the orchestra still played, into a cathedral of music. His intensely personal interpretations were occasionaly critizised by foreigners, but rarely by Berliners themselves. Perhaps it was Furtwängler's other wordly reverence for music that enabled him to remain in Germany during the Second World War, when the only Jewish face in the Philharmonic was the plaster bust of Mendelssohn, mysteriously neglected by the Nazis.

The Philharmonic in ruins, and Furtwängler in temporary disgrace, the orchestra struggled on with only a six-week interruption at the fall of Berlin in 1945. Furtwängler returned in 1947 and remained until his death in 1945. The orchestra, a democratic organization with an obvious fascination with musical dictators, then selected the 46 year old Herbert von Karajan as its next permanent conductor. A man of enormous personal power, Von Karajan has made the orchestra so much his own that he has referred to it as an extension of his arm.

Worshipped by many, disdained by some, Von Karajan has definitely become the most controversial conductor of the orchestra, the instrumentalists and their talents, and through his momentous expectations and fanaticism, Von Karajan has taken the Berlin Philharmonic to a technical level yet unreached by any other orchestra. The conductor's personal development has been extremely interesting. To discover the extent of it, one need only listen to and compare the different Beethoven and Brahms cycles that he has recorded for Deutsches Grammaphone throughout his career.

Since 1963, the Berlin Philharmonic has played in the round at a new Philharmonie, a building known to some as the 'Circus Karajani'.

BBC Symphony Orchestra
founded in 1930

Conductors: Sir Adrian Boult (1930-50), Sir Malcolm Sargent (1950-57), Rudolf Schwarz (1957-63), Antal Dorati (1963-67), Sir Colin Davis (1967-71), Pierre Boulez (1971-75), Rudolf Kempe (1975-76), Guennadi Rozhdestvenski (1978-81), John Pritchard (since 1982).

The BBC Symphony was founded by Adrian Boult; its original purpose was not solely to act as an radio orchestra, but it sprang into being as a result of the possibility of the Queen's Hall promenade concerts being dissolved. Since then, the BBC has taken over sponsorship of the world-renowned 'Proms', now held at the Royal Albert Hall, although they still bear the name given by their orginator, Sir Henry Wood. Since being televised, it would not be exaggerating to say that the last night of the Proms season is one of the world's most extraordinary musical events.

Boston Symphony Orchestra
founded in 1881 by Henry Lee Higginson

Conductors and musical directors: Georg Henschel (1881-84), Wilhelm Gericke (1884-89), Arthur Nikisch (1898-93), Emil Pauer (1893-98), Wilhelm Gericke again (1898-1906), Karl Muck (1906-08), Max Fiedler (1908-12), Karl Muck again (1912-18), Henri Rabaud (1918-19), Pierre Monteux (1919-24), Serge Koussevitzky (1924-49), Charles Munch (1949-62), Eric Leinsdorf (1962-69), William Steinberg (169-72), Seiji Ozawa (since 1973).

In the spring of 1881, Major Henry Lee Higginson, a wealthy businessman and music lover, announced the formation of a 'full and permanent orchestra, offering the best music at low prices'. That October, under direction of Georg Henschel, the Boston Symphony Orchestra made its début. Sixty local musicians were employed to play twenty concerts, the programmes included works by contemporary composers such as Dvorák, Wagner and Brahms.

It was the first American orchestra to employ a full time manager, the first to make a recording (1917), and the first to consult an accoustical engineer in the design of what was to become the magnificient Symphony Hall, which opened in 1900.

The orchestra became truly famous under Koussevitsky. This rich Russian immigrant ran the Boston Symphony Orchestra like a true despot; their achievements together were exceptional indeed. Four of the unprecedented nine commissons given by the orchestra for its 50th anniversary celebration were: the *Concert for orchestra* (Bartók), *Symphonie des Psaumes* (Stravinsky), the *Fourth Symphony* (Prokofiev) and the *First Symphony* (Honegger). At the 75th and 100th anniversary celebrations, more important commissions were given, including: the *Sixth Symphony* (Martinu), the *Sixth Symphony* (Walter Piston), the *Eleventh Symphony* (Villa Lobos), and the *Second Symphony* (Maxwell-Davies).

During the summer, the orchestra performs at the Festival of Tanglewood in the Berkshire mountains, in an outdoor, accoustical shell. Many of the better known instrumentalists then taught at the Berkshire Music Centre. Between the regular season and Tanglewood, as well as at Christmas, many of the orchestra's members let down their hair for a series of light concerts performed by the Boston Pops Orchestra. Founded and made very popular by Arthur Fiedler (their conductor from 1929 until 1979), these concerts are still virtually always sold out month in advance. Highlights are the traditional outdoors Carols Singing at Christmas, and the rendering (complete with cannon fire) of the *1812 Overture*, also outdoors, on the Fourth of July. Since Arthur Fiedler's death, the Pops have been led by various conductors, including the composer, John Williams.

Bournemouth Sinfonietta
founded in 1968

Conductors: George Hurt (1968-71), Maurice Gendron (1971-73), Kenneth Montgomery (1973-76), Volker Wangenheim (1977-80), Ronald Thomas (1980-83), Norman del Mar (since 1983).

The orchestra is made up of 35 musicians. These are other players than those of the Symphony Orchestra of Bournemouth. Since 1974, the Bournemouth Sinfonietta performs during the autumn tour of the Glyndebourne Festival.

Chicago Symphony Orchestra
founded in 1891 by Ferdinand W. Peck

Conductors and music directors: Theodore Thomas (1891-1905), Frederick Stock (1905-42), Désiré Defauw (1943-47), Artur Rodzinsky (1947-48), Rafael Kubelik (1950-53), Fritz Reiner (1953-63), Jean Martinon (1963-68), Sir Georg Solti (since 1963). Carlo Maria Giulini has been a frequent guest conductor for many years.

Briefly it was to be the Theodore Thomas Orchestra, but in 1912 assumed its present name. Its second conductor, Frederick Stock, may not be remembered as a great interpreter, but he prepared the ground in which a great orchestra could flourish. He established a civic orchestra in which young musicians could be trained, and introduced a summer season at the Ravinia Festival north of Chicago. He also encouraged the performance of new music, including premières of works by Stravinsky, Kodály, Milhaud, Prokofiev and Walton. Under Fritz Reiner, the orchestra became recognized as one of the finest in America. A series of brilliant recordings (many still available) persuaded even sceptical Europeans of this fact. Under the long tenure of Sir Georg Solti, the orchestra has combined flawless technique with a magnificent sound. Carlo Maria Giulini has called his long relationship with Chicago, 'a twenty-four year love affair'.

Cleveland Orchestra
founded in 1918

Conductors: Nikolai Sokoloff (1918-33), Artur Rodzinsky (1933-43), Eric Leinsdorf (1943-46), George Szell (1946-70), Lorin Maazel (1972-82), Christoph von Dohnáyi (since 1984).

In December 1918, fifty-seven local musicians played a concert to raise funds for St Ann's Church in Cleveland. To everyone's surprise, this pick-up group was encouraged to give a further 27 concerts that season. It has continued to this day as the Cleveland Orchestra. Nicolai Solokoff, a Russian born violist, was the first conductor. He was the discovery of Mrs. Adella Prentice Hughes, the orchestra's first manager and principal benefactor, known locally as the 'Mother of the Cleveland Orchestra'. Sokoloff remained for fifteen years, during which time the orchestra moved into Severance Hall, its permanent home since 1931.
Two distiguished Europeans, Rodzinsky and Leinsdorf, succeeded Solokoff, but the emergence of Cleveland as an internationally fa-

mous orchestra was the sole work of George Szell. Under Szell's precise and stern direction, the orchestra achieved an astonishing clarity and uniformity of sound, ideally suited to the classic repertoire. The American conductor, James Levine, for six years Szell's assistant, thought the orchestra at times 'too dry, almost without breath', but Szell, not known for his humour, once wittily defended his balanced and controlled interpretations: 'I cannot pour chocolate sauce over asparagus'. In 1972, Lorin Maazel, who had first conducted the orchestra as a thirteen year old prodigy, returned as Szell's successor. Like many American orchestras, Cleveland plays throughout the year. During the summers since 1868, it has moved to the wide open spaces of the nearby Blossom Music Centre, where it can entertain audiences of over 18,000.

Collegium Aureum
founded in 1964 by Harmonia Mundi and Franzjosef Maier

Collegium Aureum specializes in the performance of Baroque and Classic music on authentic instruments. This ensemble is considered very important: pioneers in the field of authentic performance practice. Very often they work with the Dellar Consort. Since 1976, they have enlarged their repertoire to include 19th century music. For these works, they play on modern instruments, but continue to perform in authentic style.

Concertgebouw Orchestra
founded in 1888

The Concertgebouw performed in public for the first time on November 3,1888 led by the conductor Willem Kes. Kes is remembered in the Concertgebouw's history as the director most responsible for educating both the orchestra and its public. His reforms meant the end of such laughable habits as the public's talking and eating during a performance and the orchestra's tendency to play out of tune. Aside from that, Kes organized the group well. He also greatly widened the accepted repertoire of his day. When Kes left Amsterdam in 1895 to conduct the Scottish Orchestra, he left behind a first rate orchestra. He was succeeded by the 24 year old unknown, Willem Mengelberg. Mengelberg spread the Concertgebouw's fame far around the world. In hindsight, Mengelberg was able to accomplish so much with his orchestra thanks to the enormous efforts of his predecessor.
During Mengelberg's reign the orchestra

developed close contacts with important composers (Gustav Mahler and Richard Strauss) as well as famous conductors (Hans Richter, Karl Muck, Bruno Walter, 1934-1939, Pierre Monteux, 1925-1934, and others). Many composers directed their own work in Amsterdam in this period: Debussy, Ravel, Stravinsky, Schoenberg, Pierné, Casella, Hindemith, Milhaud... an impressive list of music's most influential stars in the first half of the 20th century.
In 1945, Mengelberg was forbidden to conduct and the second conductor, Eduard van Beinum, succeeded him as principal. Van Beinum was extremely popular in the postwar years with both his musicians and his public. Bruckner and the French repertoire were his favourites and became the public's favourites as well. During the Van Beinum period the orchestra was also led by Kubelik and Szell. In April,1959, Van Beinum died suddenly during a rehearsal.
Eugen Jochum and Bernard Haitink shared the saddle for a few years before Haitink became sole principal conductor in 1963. This was to be the beginning of a new, glorious era for the orchestra. Haitink not only continued the strong Bruckner and Mahler traditions of his predecessor, he was also successful in putting his personal mark on the Concertgebouw. He has recorded the complete symphonies of both Bruckner and Mahler several times as well as performing Strauss, Debussy, Ravel, Brahms, Tchaikovsky and Shostakovich. In the season of 1987-88, Haitink was named artistic director of the Royal Opera House Covent Garden in London. In April, 1988, he took his leave from the orchestra he had led so magnificently for 27 years.
Kirill Kondrashin shared the post of principal conductor with Haitink between 1979 and 1981. Kondrashin was formerly the musical director of the Bolshoi Theatre and the Philharmonic Orchestra of Moscow. This great orchestral teacher brought the musicians together in unique moments of musical oneness, an artistry mourned with his sudden death in 1981.
In the 1988-89 season the orchestra is being led by Ricardo Chailly, a young Italian whose première with the Concertgebouw in 1985 was acclaimed by orchestra, public and press. The Concertgebouw has miraculous acoustics. The Large Hall is famous for its velvety sound. It is considered one of the three best halls in the world (the other two being the Musikverein in Vienna and Boston's Symphony Hall). Since 1967, Philips master technician Volker Strauss has made around one hundred recordings there.
The Concertgebouw first toured America in 1954 with Eduard van Beinum and Rafael

Kubelik. A second tour followed in 1971 and a third in 1978. In 1970, the orchestra performed four times in the Henry Wood Promenade Concerts in London as well as at the Edinburgh Festival and the Beethoven Festival in Bonn. Japan was toured in both 1974 and 1986. The first Russian tour was in 1974. Vienna and Switzerland followed the next year. Extensive European tours (including East Germany, Yugoslavia and Spain) were made in 1976 and 1988.

More important for the international fame of the Concertgebouw than these tours are certainly the Eurovision Christmas Concerts they give for a viewing and listening audience of between 80 and 100 million. Haitink conducted his twelfth and last Christmas Concert in 1987, performing Mahler's *Ninth Symphony*.

To celebrate the 100th birthday of the Concertgebouw, a unique series of compact discs have been released including both old and new performances, for example: the *Eroica* under Monteux, 1962, Beethoven's *Fifth* and *Sixth Symphonies* under Eric Kleiber made in the fifties, Mahler's *Fourth* directed by Van Beinum in 1956 and by Solti in 1961, Tchaikovsky's *Fifth* directed by Paul van Kempen and seven Haydn symphonies led by Sir Colin Davis.

Detroit Symphony Orchestra
founded in 1914

Conductors: Weston Gales (1914-17), Ossip Gabrilowitsch (1918-36), Franco Ghione (1936-40), Victor Kolar (1940-42), Karl Krueger (1943-49), Paul Paray (1951-63), Sixteen Ehrling (1963-73), Aldo Ceccato (1973-77), Antal Dorati (1977-81), Gary Bertini (1981), Günther Herbig (since 1984).

The Detroit Symphony Orchestra was run until 1942 by the Detroit Symphony Society. The forties were difficult years for the group until 1951, the industrialist John B. Ford, Jr. reorganized the orchestra and alleviated the situation.

Premières that Detroit have performed include: *Ora* (Berio, 1971), *Horizon circled* (Krenek, 1967), and *Three New England Sketches* (Walter Piston, 1959).

Dresden Staatskapelle
founded as court orchestra in 1548

Conductors and artistic directors: Julius Rietz (1874-77), Franz Wüllner (1877-84), Ernest von Schuch (1884-1914), Fritz Reiner (1914-21), Fritz Busch (1922-33), Karl Böhm (1934-42), Rudolf Kempe (1950-53), Franz Konwitschny (1953-55), Lovro von Matácic (1956-58), Otmar Suitner (1960-64), Kurt Sanderling (1964-67), Martin Turnovsky (1967-68), Herbert Blomstedt (1975-85), Hans Vonk (since 1985).

The history of this orchestra is a long one, since its founding in the sixteenth century at the Dresden court. First there was only a choir, but towards the end of the century, instruments were added for court church services. Famous composers have held the position of court cantor including Michael Praetorius (1613-17), Heinrich Schütz (1617-55), and later Johann Hasse (1731-61). In the nineteenth century, one of the conductors was Carl Maria von Weber.

The Dresden Staatskapelle has performed premières of *Danses de Marosszék* (Kodály, 1930), *Sonata for thirteen wind instruments* (Richard Strauss, 1944), and *Concert avec plusieurs instruments* no. 3 (Dittrich, 1979). The Dresden Staatskapelle now gives symphonic concerts and accompanies performances at the Dresden Opera. The Dresden Chamber Soloists (founded in 1965) are seven instrumentalists from the orchestra, led by the flautist, Johannes Walter.

English Chamber Orchestra
founded in 1948

The English Chamber Orchestra was founded by Arnold Goldsbrough, Lawrence Leonard and Quintin Ballardie and assumed its present name in 1960. It is the only permanent chamber orchestra in London. Since 1960, the orchestra performs without a permanent conductor, but from time to time 'preferred guest conductors' have led the group, including: Britten, Barenboim, Perahaia, Leppard and Ashkenazy.

Since 1961, the ECO has performed regularly at the Aldeburgh Festival. There have been only three concert masters (leaders) since the orchestra's founding: Emmanuel Hurwitz, Kenneth Silito and José Luis Garcia. Premières that the ECO have performed include many works by Benjamin Britten, for example, *A Midsummer Night's Dream* (1960), *Owen Wingrave*, *Paraboles* and *Symphonie Concertante*. Other premières have been Bennett's *Concert for Double Bass*, 1978, Holst's *Capricio*, 1968, Goehr's *Sinfonia*, 1980, and works by Arnold, Blake and Henze.

English Concert
founded in 1973

The harpsichordist Trevor Pinnock founded this orchestra and is its conductor. Originally it was made up of only seven musicians (five strings, flute and harpsichord) but has gradually grown to normal chamber orchestra size. Their repertoire is exclusively 17th and 18th century. Pinnock conduct from the harpsichord, and the musicians play authentic instruments in appropriate style.

Ferenc Liszt Chamber Orchestra
founded in 1963 in Budapest

Conductors: Frigyes Sándor (1963-79), János Rolla (since 1979).

Sixteen strings and a harpsichord make up this orchestra. All the musicians were at one time students at the Franz Liszt Academy in Budapest. The group became independent of the institution at a later date. At present, the orchestra performs without a conductor, led by the concertmaster, János Rolla.

Hallé Orchestra, Manchester
founded in 1858

Conductors: Sir Charles Hallé (1858-95), Sir Frederic Cowen (1896-99), Hans Richter (1899-1911), Michael Balling (1912-14), Sir Thomas Beecham (1914-20), Sir Hamilton Harty (1921-33), Sir Thomas Beecham and Sir John Barbirolli (1943-70), James Loughran (1970-83), Stanislaw Skrowaczewski (since 1984).

Israel Philharmonic Orchestra
founded in 1936

Few cities have had such an eager audience for symphonic music as Tel Aviv in the 1930's. On the eve of its first concert in December, 1936, tickets for the Palestine Symphony Orchestra (as the Israel Philharmonic was known until 1948) were selling on the black market for the unprecedented price of one pound each, and the applause at the end lasted for more than half an hour. Aturo Toscanini, who had amazingly controlled his temper throughout the rehearsals, announced that Palestine had one of the best orchestras in the world. His claim was more prophetic than strictly accurate. This 'orchestra of concertmasters' assembled by the violist Bronislaw Huberman, having come from many different musical cultures, took several years to achieve a homogeneous sound of its own. The first decade of the orchestra's existence posed difficulties quite apart from the musical ones. On tour in remote parts of the new country, orchestra members were obliged to erect their own makeshift stages. During the war, the half deleted orchestra, often without a conductor, played before half empty concert halls and allied army bases. The worst of these struggles ended in 1945 when the Italian conductor, Bernardo Molinari bullied the orchestra into a higher standard than it had previously known. Since then, the Israel Philharmonic had gradually assumed a place as one of the best and busiest of the world's orchestras. The international popularity of Zubin Metha, musical advisor since his appointment in 1969, has ensured many recordings and international tours.

For the beleaguered state of Israel, the Philharmonic has assumed an extra-musical importance as an ambassador of goodwill. 'No diplomatic mission sent abroad', said Prime Minister Golda Meir, 'could have accomplished what the orchestra's tours produce for our country'.

Leipzig Gewandhaus Orchestra
founded in 1781

Conductors since the Second World War: Herman Albert (1946-48), Franz Konwitschky (1949-52), Václav Neumann (1964-68), and Kurt Masur (since 1970).

The Leipzig Gewandhaus Orchestra derives its name from the Hall of the Guild of Cloth Merchants, where some of its earliest concerts were given, in the period between 1778 and 1884, the same period in which J.S. Bach was cantor of the St Thomas Church in Leipzig. The orchestra's original name was: 'das Grosse Concert'. The first performance took place in a private home in 1743. Its first conductor, Johann Friedrich Doles, was a pupil of Bach's, and Bach himself played at the earliest concerts. The group had sixteen members at that time. No concerts were held during the Seven Year War, but they were resumed in 1763, conducted by J.A. Hiller. Hiller took responsibility for all the concerts, calling them 'Concerts for devotees'. The group was enlarged to thirty members and so performed until 1778. After an interlude of three years, concerts were again held, as mentioned earlier, in the Gewandhaus, in a hall also used for dancing. The move to the Gewandhaus was encouraged by the mayor of Leipzig, Karl Wilhelm Müller, making him, in a way, the true founder of the Gewandhaus Orchestra as we know it. Together with eleven friends, Müller formed a committee that appointed Hiller conductor,

and invited the public to subscribe to a series of 24 concerts, the first of which was held in September, 1781.

The Gewandhaus proved impractical and too small and so in 1784, a new building was arranged for the orchestra. This contains both a large and small concert hall for all types of symphonic and chamber concerts.

Musicians that have regularly conducted the Gewandhaus include: Felix Mendelssohn (beginning in 1835), Julius Rietz (beginning in 1848), Niels Gade and Ferdinand David (beginning in 1852), Carl Reinecke (beginning in 1860), Arthur Nikisch (beginning in 1895), Wilhelm Furtwängler (beginning in 1922), Bruno Walter (beginning in 1929), and Herman Abendroth (beginning in 1934).

The most brilliant periods of this orchestra's history were working with Mendelssohn, Nikisch, Furtwängler and Abendroth.

Leningrad Philharmonic Orchestra
founded in 1921

St Petersburg was the centre of musical life in nineteenth century Russia. Even the turmoil of a revolution and a world war could not break the traditions of music-making in the old Imperial city. The court orchestra established in 1882, weathered these social storms, and survied three name changes to emerge in 1921 as the Leningrad Philharmonic. On the eve of this final metamorphosis, still the Petrograd orchestra, it was conducted by Serge Koussevitsky (1917-20). He was succeeded by Emil Cooper (1921-23), Nikolai Malko (1926-29), Alexander Gauk (1930-33) and Fritz Stierdry (1934-37). In 1938, Yevgeni Mravinsky won a national competition and became principal conductor. Kurt Sanderling has conducted the orchestra between 1948 and 1960. Since 1953, the orchestra has performed in various strengths: the Philharmonic, under Mravinsky, the Symphony under Arvid Jansons, Youri Temirkanov (1968-76), and Alexandre Dmitriev, and the Chamber Orchestra of Leningrad, conducted by Alexandre Serov.

Under Mravinsky's baton, the Leningrad Philharmonic became well known in the west. Immediately following his examinations at the Conservatory, this 35 year old was saddled with leading the oldest orchestra in the Soviet Union. Mravinsky toured with the orchestra to England, Finland, Switzerland and Austria and triumphed at every stop. Panofsky, the famous critic in Munich, wrote that Mravinsky was 'one of the greatest conductors of our time'. His fame was the result of brilliant performances of the large symphonic works. Mravinsky's knowledge of this repertoire is

unrivalled, and complimented by an extraordinary musicality. Together with his orchestra, he also successfully persuaded western audiences that Soviet music was worth airing. A long and fruitful relationship with Dmitri Shostakovich resulted in the premières of his fifth, sixth, eighth, ninth and tenth symphonies.

St. Petersburg has always been a progressive center of the recording industry, nevertheless Russian recordings sounded primitive and were accordingly ignored when they were first introduced to the Western audience. In a 1952 catalogue, of the 52 versions of Tchaikovsky's Pathétique presented, only one was made by Russians: an old 78 record performed by the USSR National Symphony Orchestra under Mravinsky. In those years, Moscow ensembles were almost the only ones recorded. Change came in 1956 when the Leningrad Philharmonic toured Europe. DG recorded the last three Tchaikovsky symphonies in the studio during that tour. Westerners were exhilarated by these performances. The virtuosity and discipline of the Leningrad players was sublime. Those fortunate to hear this group's European concerts in the Sixties will never forget them. Whole new aspects of the Russian repertoire came to light with these exceptional instrumentalists. Leningrad has always been important in keeping the Tchaikovsky tradition alive, doing so with authentic, Russian brilliance.

As might be expected, the Leningrad Philharmonic excels in the music of Tchaikovsky. 'They play with a conviction born of absolute belief in the work', wrote a critic in the Sunday Times after hearing Mravinsky conduct Tchaikovsky's Fifth Symphony. Despite a new name and a Soviet repertoire, the Leningrad Philharmonic can still live up to its majestic origins in the Tsarist court of St Petersburg.

London Philharmonic Orchestra
founded in 1904

Conductors: Thomas Beecham (1932-39), Eduard Van Beinum (1948-50), Adrian Boult (1951-57), William Steinberg (1958-60), John Pritchard (1962-66), Bernard Haitink (1967-79), Georg Solti (1979-83), Klaus Tennstedt (since 1983).

In 1931, Sir Thomas Beecham discussed with Sir Robert Mayer the possibility of forming a new orchestra, and was assured of engagements with many of the country's leading musical societies, including the Royal Choral Society and the Royal Philharmonic Society. The germ of an idea became reality when the wealthy industrialist Samuel Courtauld advanced £30,000 to fund the new venture. Assembled in 1932, some 106 of the country's finest musicians were guaranteed more than 70 concerts annually, and a season at Covent Garden. The orchestra's début was on the 7th of October, 1932, at Queen's Hall (destroyed by bombing during the war). Critics hailed the performance as a triumph, and under the baton of Sir Thomas Beecham the orchestra dominated the London musical scene. The war brought an end to the relationship between Beecham and the Philharmonic. The group was formally terminated, but that was to stick for only two weeks. It was again founded, and reformed as a self governing group. The new Philharmonic toured England during the war, threatened the whole way by German bombing raids. Beecham was invited to lead the orchestra once more at the war's end, but he declined, deciding to commit his energies once again to the formation of a new orchestra which was to become the Royal Philharmonic. Fate dealt yet another blow to the orchestra when Walter Legge, an important man at Columbia Records, established the Philharmonic Orchestra, taking the best musicians with him. A period full of tensions and problems followed. There was a lack of discipline, bad conductors and second rate performances. Change finally came in the decision to look for a top rate conductor willing to stay an entire season. The orchestra regained its old excellence through conductors like Furtwängler, and new talents like Solti, and Bernstein. Bernard Haitink conducted the London Philharmonic between 1967 and 1979, doing his share of restoration work with the group. Since 1964, the orchestra has been featured at the Glyndebourne Festival.

Premières played by the London Philharmonic have included: *Symphonie Pastorale* (1922) and *Symphony no. 5* by Vaughan Williams, *Our Hunting Fathers* (1936) by Britten, *A Child of Our Time* (1944) by Tippett, and *Paroles Tissées* (1965) by Lutoslawski.

London Symphony Orchestra
founded in 1904

According to its own contemporary programme notes, the London Symphony Orchestra was 'second to none in Europe' at its first concert in June, 1904. There may have been some truth to an extravagant claim, for the new group consisted of some of London's best musicians, who had broken away from Henry Wood's Queen's Hall Orchestra over a dispute about the use of deputies in concerts. Emulating the orchestras of Berlin and Vienna, the LSO established itself as a musical

republic, a limited company with directors chosen solely from within the orchestra and every member a shareholder, to be paid by the concert rather than by the season.

This unusual venture was an immediate success. The orchestra chose as its first principal conductor the eminent Wagnerian Hans Richter. His successors included Arthur Nikisch, Albert Coates, Sir Hamilton Harty and Josef Krips. The orchestra has a tradition of adaptability of both style and repertoire, having been exposed to most of this century's great conductors, (many of whom were also important composers), such as Savanav, Arbos, Mlynarski, Koussevitsky, Elgar, Steinbach, Mengelberg, Beecham, Furtwängler, Sokolov, Goossens, Boult, Barbirolli, Malko, Weingartner, Kubelik, and Van Beinum.

The niveau of performance has had its fluctuations, running parallel to the crises in its organization. At the end of the twenties, for example, the self satisfaction of its members in their own self government, led to a drastic change in quality. The tough competition of other renowned London orchestras did however make the LSO change its ways. In 1945, W.H. Reed became director of the group, and forced it to reorganize. Reed made it a non-profit distributing company, chose Sir William Walton as president of this new company, and generally gave the instrumentalists less say in the management. The orchestra also became associated with the Arts Council. A conductor was contracted as principal, the first being Eduard van Beinum, in order to ensure a better consistency of performance.

In 1961, eighty-six year old Pierre Monteux optimistically signed a twenty-five year renewable contract with the orchestra. His benign but undisciplined rule ended with his death in 1964, whereupon the directors chose the Hungarian Istvan Kertesz. Here was a man of sterner stuff, who alienated the administration with unacceptable demands for greater control. Meanwhile the orchestra had lost both its secretary and its chairman (the principal horn, Barry Tuckwell) in an unsettling spell of boardroom infighting. Kertesz left in 1968 to be succeeded by the young American, André Previn. The decade ended with a particularly fruitful series of concerts conducted by Pierre Boulez.

The seventies were relatively sunny, with Previn proving such a successful choice that he remained for an unprecedented eleven years. This was truly a prosperous period, rich in broadcasting and recording sessions, which are the life-line of modern orchestras. In 1982, the LSO, now under the direction of Claudio Abbado, moved into its first permanent home, the modern Barbican Centre in the City of London.

Los Angeles Philharmonic Orchestra
founded in 1919

Conductors: Walter Rothwell (1919-27), Georg Schneevoigt (1927-1929), Artur Rodzinski (1929-1933), Otto Klemperer (1933-1939). There were only guest conductors until 1943, when Alfred Wallenstein became principal (1943-1956), followed by Eduard van Beinum (1956-1959), Zubin Mehta (1962-1977), Carlo-Maria Giulini (1978-1984) and André Previn (since 1986).

The Los Angeles Philharmonic was the brainchild of Williams Andrew Clark, a music loving millionaire. In 1919, with an initial grant of one million dollars, Clark transformed the Old Symphony Orchestra into the Philharmonic, greatly expanding its concert schedule and increasing its membership to 94. Walter Rothwell, formerly an assistant to Gustav Mahler, was the first conductor, remaining with the orchestra until 1927.

Even under these eminent Europeans the Philharmonic failed to achieve the reputation of its patrician rivals in the east: Boston, Cleveland, New York and Philadelphia. But when Zubin Mehta, then only twenty-five, became principal conductor in 1962, the Philharmonic's fortunes began to turn. Mehta remained for sixteen years, leaving his successor with an orchestra regarded as one of the best in the world. Yearly national and international tours continue to confirm this reputation. The Philharmonic is known as a relaxed and friendly group, unlikely to call a new conductor 'maestro' for more than a few rehearsals. Since 1964, it has played for its winter season in the Music Center of the Dorothy Chandler Pavilion. In the summer it moves outside to the vast Hollywood Bowl.

Luzern Festival Orchestra

This orchestra is brought together for the duration of the Festival of Lucern. It is made up of instrumentalists from the foremost Swiss orchestras. Originally, Ansermet founded the group in 1943, to provide employment for his musicians in addition to the usual winter season. His instrumentalists were very grateful for the extra income.

Orchestre Symphonique de Monréal
founded in 1842

Founded under the name 'Société des Concerts Symphonique de Monréal', the orchestra received its present name in 1953. The Montreal Symphony has sponsered a competition since 1937. Principal conductors have been: Wilfrid Pelletier (1935-40), Désiré Delfauw (1940-48), Igor Markevitch (1958-61), Zubin Metha (1961-67), Franz-Paul Dekker (1967-75), Rafaël Frübeck de Burgos (1975-77), Charles Dutoit (since 1977).

New York Philharmonic Orchestra
founded in 1842

Conductors and music directors: Anton Seidl (1892-98), Emil Pauer (1898-1902), Walter Damrosche (1902-3). The next three years, there were four guests: Henry Wood, Felix Weingartner, Richard Strauss and Fritz Steinbach. Then followed: Vasily Safonov (1906-9), Gustav Mahler (1909-11), Josef Stransky (1911-23), Willem Mengelberg (1923-29), Arturo Toscanini (1928-36), Sir John Barbirolli (1936-42), Arthur Rodzinski (1943-47), Bruno Walter (1947-49), Leopold Stokowski and Dimitri Mitropoulos (1949-57), Leonard Bernstein (1958-69), Georg Szell (advisor, 1969-70), Pierre Boulez (1971-77), and Zubin Mehta (since 1978).

The oldest orchestra in the United States had an unpromising youth. In December 1842, the newly-formed New York Philharmonic Society gave its first concert: *Beethoven's Fifth* followed by an uneven medley of shorter compositions by Hummel, Weber, Rossini, and Mozart - with three conductors sharing the evening's responsibilities! For many years, the orchestra plodded on in this benign manner, giving no more than six annual concerts, finding conductors from among the musicians themselves and sharing the profits at the end of the season. By the time Theodore Thomas took charge in 1877, one musical journal had already dismissed the Philharmonic as 'antiquated and old foggish'. Thomas and his successor Anton Seidl (1891-98) had great personal followings, and transformed an evening with the Philharmonic (in Carnegie Hall since 1892) into a glamorous social occasion. This metamorphosis was not a moment too soon. New Yorkers had already begun to look elsewhere for their orchestral music, especially to the New York Symphony, founded in 1878. In the early years of the century, the success of the Philharmonic again began to wane. Gustav Mahler's two stormy seasons as conductor (1909 and 1911) did nothing for either the orchestra's music or its morale. Then a bequest of nearly a million dollars in 1911 from Joseph Pulitzer (on the condition that the organization be restructured) gave the Phil-

harmonic new life. Josef Stransky was the conductor from 1911 trough 1923, during which period the Philharmonic and the Symphony merged. During the thirties, several distinguished Europeans, including Willem Mengelberg (1921-30) and Wilhelm Furtwängler (1925-27) shared the conducting; but the glory of the decade was stolen by Arturo Toscanini (1927-33). He terrified his musicians as he entranced his New York audiences. Sir John Barbirolli (1937-40) understandably failed to recreate the fierce exuberance of Toscanini's rule. Subsequent conductors, however, have maintained the Philharmonic's position as one of America's great orchestras. Arthur Rodzinski (1942-1947) and Dimitri Mitropoulos (1949-58) were followed by Leonard Bernstein (1959-69). His sound musicianship, combined for a sure instinct for 'showbiz', inspired an enthusiastic following in the concert as well as on national television. In 1962, Bernstein and the orchestra moved into the new (acoustically not particularly successful) Lincoln Center. For this occasion, the following compositions were commissioned: *Connotations*, Aaron Copland; *Symphony no. Eight*, W. Schuman; *Andromache's Farewell*, Samuel Barber; *Ouverture Philharmonique*, Milhaud. Bernstein's successor, the composer Pierre Boulez (1971-1977), startled audiences with an uncompromisingly contemporary repertoire, but the popular Zubin Mehta (since 1978) has reintroduced a more familiar and therefore successful path.

Sinfonie Orchester des Österreichischen Rundfunks (ORF) (Austrian Radio Symphony Orchestra)
founded in 1969 in Vienna

Conductors: Max Schönherr (1945-69), Milan Horvat (1969-75), Leif Segerstam (1975-81), Lothar Zagrosek (since 1982).

This orchestra grew out of the Radio Symphony Orchestra that was formed in 1945 in Vienna.
Premières performed: *Concerto pour ondes Martenot*, Jolivet, 1948; *Ballade pour alto et orchestre*, Frank Martin, 1973; *Magnificat*, Penderecki, 1974; *Clocks and Clouds*, Ligeti; *Il Vitalino Raddoppiato*, Henze, 1978.

NBC Symphony Orchestra
founded in 1937 in New York

The National Broadcasting Symphony Orchestra was founded by Toscanini when he

returned to New York after having retreated to Italy for a year. The group was trained by Rodzinski, gave its first radio concerts under Montreux, and performed under Toscanini himself for the first time at Christmas. The great maestro stayed until his death, leaving only between 1941 and 1942, when Stokowski took over the concerts. The NBC Orchestra gave 24 concerts each winter season, 16 of them conducted by Toscanini. It died as an orchestra with Toscanini in 1954, but remained together as a group as the Symphony of the Air, until 1964.
For many seasons, the orchestra would perform an entire opera on the radio, dividing it into two programs. Many great conductors have been a guest with the NBC, including: Boult, Sargent, Stokowsky, Molinari, Mitropoulos, Reinder, Szell, Ansermet and Cantelli.

The Orchestra of the XVIIIth Century
founded by Frans Brüggen in 1981

'At one point', Frans Brüggen tells us, 'I approached about 25 people that I had regularly worked with. We came together and rehearsed for awhile without much thinking about it. That went so well that we decided to continue'. With the end of the Eigthies in sight, no other ensemble has so quickly and non-chalantly established its name as this Orchestra of the XVIIIth Century.
The orchestra is made up of about 45 members from all over the world, representing 14 nationalities. All of the musicians are well-known specialists in 18th century music and they play authentic instruments or copies of such. Their purpose is clear: to perform the classic masterpieces of Mozart, Haydn and the young Beethoven, as well as the repertoire of the earlier 18th century, Bach and Rameau, according to the practices of the day. Brüggen's group has the luxurious scope of a 'classic' ensemble as was often heard in Mannheim, Paris or Vienna.
The sound produced is the result of a few specific factors: they play at a lower pitch (a sounds a half step lower, like a modern g sharp), the strings are gut and the bows of a different design than their modern counterparts, the vibrato is handled completely differently as are other ornaments and questions of phrasing.
In the beginning, The Orchestra was supported by friends around the world before finally being recognized and supported by the Prince Bernard Fund and the Dutch National Government. From 1983 until 1988, they were sponsored by I.B.M. Europe S.A. The Euro-

pean Cultural Fund also contributed in 1986. The Orchestra assembles only twice a year for international tours (in the Netherlands, Belgium, the United States and Italy). They have performed five times for the Holland Festival. Since 1985 the group has been busy with recordings but has never made more than two records in any given year. These are always live recordings of public performances. A rehearsal is taped and kept for possible editing. Both the conductor, Frans Brüggen, and his players prefer this manner of recording, eager to capture the excitement of live performance. In the words of the concertmaster of The Orchestra, Lucy van Dael:'sparks can also fly from a record (or CD)!'

Orchestre Des Concerts Colonne
(Orchestre Colonne-Paris)

Georgy Hartmann founded this orchestra in 1873 under the name Concert National. The name was changed within a year, however, by Edouard Colonne to l'Association Artistique des Concerts Colonne and was changed again in 1910 to l'Orchestre des Concerts Colonne. Since 1917 it bears the simple name of l'Orchestre Colonne. Conductors: Eduoard Colonne (1873-1910), Gabriel Pierné (1910-1934), Paul Paray (1944-1956), Charles Munch (1956-1958), Pierre Dervaux (1958). The orchestra is self-governing and has been active in the important theatre productions of the Théâtre Musical de Paris since 1980.
Early on, the competition from Pasdeloup's Concerts populaires inspired Colonne to perform the young French repetoire. This was a brilliant move, including Massenet, Lalo, Dukas and Franck in his concerts.The real breakthrough came when Colonne performed all of Berlioz's works with choir. Colonne had artistic flair but was less than brilliant technically. His opposite in that respect was his contemporary, Lamoureux.

Sinfonie Orchester des Bayerischen Rundfunks (Bavarian Radio Orchestra)
founded in 1949

Conductors: Eugen Jochum (1949-1960), Rafael Kubelik (1961-1979), Sir Colin Davis (since Spring, 1983). Two ensembles have been formed from members of the orchestra: the Quatuor Koeckert and Munich Nonetto. Premières: Hartmann's *Symphonie no. 3* (1948), no. 4 (1953) and *Symphonic Hymns* (1975); Von Einem's *Tanz-Rondo* op. 27; Von Bose's *Symphonie no. 1* (1978), Xenakis's *Aïs* (1981) and Schuller's *Piano concerto* (1981).

Orchestre des Concerts Lamoureux
founded in 1881

Charles Lamoureux (1834-1899) graduated from the Conservatory in Paris as a violinist, and was admitted as a member to the Société des Concerts du Conservatoire. Lamoureux, however, dreamed of a greater role for himself in French musical life. In 1860, he founded a group with Colonne to promote chamber music. He was the first, for example, to perform the Brahms sextets in France. After visits to Germany and England, having heard performances of Handel, Bach and Mendelssohn, Lamoureux was determined to duplicate such performances in France. In 1873, he organized a festival in the Cirque des Champs-Élysées where he performed a laudable *Messiah*. The *St Matthew Passion* followed the next year. Both were extremely successful, proving Lamoureux to be a great conductor, unsurpassed in precision and with a strong feeling for musical expression.
Lamoureux was appointed conductor at the Opera in 1877. The following year, he was decorated with the Légion d'Honneur. After a difference of opinon over tempi in *Don Giovanni*, he decided to leave the Opera, choosing for complete independence from then on. With a great deal of work and care, Lamoureux founded his own orchestra in 1881, called 'Nouveaux Concerts' before it came to bear the name of its founder. The new orchestra was greatly successful. Lamoureux developed into a conductor of precision and strength, careful down to the smallest details, ever warm and passionate. He promoted contemporary French music (Saint-Saëns, Lalo, d'Indy, Chabrier, Franck, Dukas etc.) and used his orchestra to lead the Wagner movement in France, performing many national premières of Wagner's works. Lamoureux took his orchestra to England three times, where they played at Queen's Hall, London.

Orchestre Philharmonique de Radio France
founded in 1937

Conductors: Eugène Bigot (1945-65), Charles Bruck (1965-70).

The orchestra has had several names in its history: Orchestre Radio Symphonique (1937-55), Orchestre Symphonique de Radio Paris (1955-59), Orchestre Philharmonique de la RTF (1960-63), then the Orchestre Philharmonique de l'ORTF (1964-75). Since 1976, several orchestras have merged to form the new Orchestre Philharmonique de Radio France.

The orchestra's objective is to perform contemporary music, and it has been very successful in doing so. Some of the important composers whose works have been either premiered or performed are: Clostre, Martinet, Milhaud, Migot, Tansman, Landowski, Malec, Chaynes, Saguer, Inghelbrecht, Tisné, Nigg, Barraud, Guézec, Ballif, Rivier, Cage, Tabachnik and Xenakis.

Orchestre National de France
founded in 1934

The Orchestre National De France was an initiative of the French government. It performed for the first time in the Ancien Conservatoire in 1934. Toscanini conducted the ONF at the opera a few times beginning in 1936. During the Second World War, the orchestra was evacuated first to Rennes, then to Marseille. Returning to Paris in 1943, the orchestra played once a week at the Theatre des Champs-Élysées under many great conductors including Charles Münch (who became honorary chairman) and André Cluytens. The orchestra has had a double function since its founding: it is a radio orchestra and, a promoter/performer of French repertoire abroad.

Orchestre de Paris
founded in 1967

The Orchestre de Paris was founded to replace the orchestre des Concerts du Conservatoire. The financing was arranged by the city of Paris and the French national government, keeping the orchestra available throughout the whole year, not just the winter season. This made it possible to compete with the well-known orchestras of London, Berlin and Philadelphia. And as was hoped, the OdP greatly improved the French orchestral tradition that had suffered so greatly since the Second World War.
It was also hoped that this orchestra would improve the taste and musical exposure of ordinary Frenchmen by giving concerts in the provinces and the outskirts of Paris.
'They shall play Mozart, Dutilleux, Brahms and Schoenberg alongside one another', said the Minister for Music at a press conference prior to the orchestra's début. Charles Münch, then seventy-six, was the natural choice as Principal Conductor, a position he shared with Serge Baudo, another Frenchman. Münch auditioned all 400 candidates and formed an orchestra with a brightness of sound and suppleness of technique that critics frequently describe as 'characteristically French'. 'When it comes to French music,... it has to be played

by the French', said Münch. Münch died while on tour with the orchestra less than a year after his inaugural concert, since when the baton has fallen into foreign hands: Herbert von Karajan, Sir Georg Solti and, in 1975, Daniel Barenboim.

In its short life, L'Orchestre de Paris has made many recordings and tours, featuring an eclectic repertoire with a strong French accent. Barenboim, a conductor with little previous affinity for French music, has become something of a specialist in the works of Berlioz. True to Munch's dictum, the orchestra receives its highest praise for its national repertoire. When it strays far beyond this musical boundary, it is occasionally accused of sounding insecure, as if, like wine, it were still in need of maturing.

Orchestre de la Suisse Romande
founded in Geneva in 1918

Conductors: Ernest Ansermet (1918-67), Paul Kletzki (1967-70), Wolfgang Sawallisch (1970-80), Horst Stein (1980-85), Armin Jordan (since 1985).

The Orchestre de la Suisse Romande is made up of 115 musicians. They give a series of concerts in Geneva and Lausanne and a few other cities in French speaking Switzerland. The orchestra also plays large symphonic works for the Radio-Television Suisse Romande, and serves as a accompanist at the Grand Theatre in Geneva.

The ORS achieved great fame while conducted by Ansermet at the beginning of its history. A recording contract with Decca also helped spread their renown. Ansermet's name is especially thought of in connection with famous recordings of Debussy, Ravel and Stravinsky.

Philharmonic Orchestra of Oslo
founded in 1919

Conductors: George Schneevoigt (1919-21), Johan Halvorsen (1919-20), Ignaz Neumark (1919-21), Jose Eibenschütz (1921-27), Issay Dobrouwen (1927-31), Odd Grüner-Hegge (1931-33), Olav Kielland (1933-45), again odd Grüner-Hegge (1945-62), Oivin Fjeldstad (1962-69), Herbert Blomstedt (1962-68), Militiades Caradis (1969-76), Okko Kamu (1976-79) and Mariss Jansons (since 1979).

Philadelphia Orchestra
founded in 1900

Stunned by the prestige of orchestras in Boston and New York, music-loving Philadelphians asked the visiting German conductor Fritz Scheel to create an orchestra for them in 1900. The success of this new venture may have surprised a few of even its most enthusiastic founders. In 1902, The New York Times spoke of the Philadelphia Orchestra's 'uncommon excellence', and two years later, Richard Strauss declared it 'wunderschön'. The popular Scheel suffered a mental breakdown and died in 1907. His place was taken by Karl Pohlig, a fellow German with what was called 'a difficult disposition', who remained in an atmosphere of gathering animosity for five years. Leopold Stokowski, conductor of the Cincinnati Symphony Orchestra, became Pohlig's successor. His début in 1912 gave no indication of the career to follow. A critic at his first concert was impressed by this 'boyish' and 'thoroughly business-like young man', but Stokowski was also opinionated, temperamental and extremely eccentric. Over the next 23 years, he became the most controversial personality in Philadelphia and his orchestra one of the best in the world. He continually experimented in attempts to create better balance and greater sonority. He moved the second violins from the right of the stage to the position they generally occupy today - just beside the firsts on the left. He also abolished uniform bowing to establish the silky legato for which the orchestra grew famous. Claiming that Philadelphia 'must not be provincial but become universal', he assaulted his audiences with world and American premières: Schoenberg, de Falla, Shostakovisch, Stravinsky, Webern and then sold out performances of Mahler's *Symphony of a Thousand*. When his audiences coughed obtrusively, he lectured them from the podium for their 'disagreeable and disgusting noises'. Under Stokowski the orchestra became familiar to non-concert goers from its radio broadcasts and the sound tracks of three Hollywood films, including Walt Disney's classic, 'Fantasia'.

Eugene Ormandy, the young Hungarian who shared conducting duties for five years before taking over entirely in 1941, had the great advantage of being unlike Stokowski in every way except in his ability to make the orchestra play beautifully. He was reserved but gracious towards the public; polite and firm with his musicians. His choice of music was what one grateful reviewer called 'progressive rather than radical'. Far from declining, the standard of the orchestra soared. Virgil Thomson, praising its 'flexibility' and 'sensitivity' in 1952, declared that the Philadelphia Orchestra

under Ormandy was 'better... than any other orchestra has ever been'. Ormandy, a man not given to extravagant claims, became so identified with his orchestra that he could say in all modesty: 'The Philadelphia sound, its me'. It remained so until Ormandy's retirement in 1980, when the awesome responsibility of succeeding Stokowski and Ormandy fell to Ricardo Muti.

The Philadelphia Orchestra has played its winter season, since its founding, at the Academy of Music. In August, it moves to the countryside, to Saratoga Springs, New York, to play at the Performing Arts Center.

Premières performed by Philadelphia include: Varèse (*Amériques*, 1926; *Arcana*, 1927), Rachmaninov (*Symphonie no. 3*, 1936; *Danses Symphoniques*, 1941), Schoenberg (*Violin Concerto*, 1940), Martinu (*Concerto for two pianos,* 1943), Barber (*Symphony no. 1*, 1944), Bloch (*Suite Symphonique*, 1945), Bartok (*Piano concerto no. 3*, 1946), and Menotti (*Symphony no. 1*, 1977).

Philharmonia Orchestra
founded in 1945

Principal conductors: Herbert von Karajan (until 1959), Otto Klemperer (1955-73), Ricardo Muti (1973-82), Giuseppe Sinopoli (since 1984).

Between 1971 and 1973, Lorin Maazel was second principal conductor.

The Philharmonia Orchestra was founded after the Second World War by Walter Legge, primarily for producing recordings of the highest quality. Many of the orchestra's members were soloists in their own right. The orchestra has performed with a series of great conductors: Toscanini, Furtwängler, Giulini, Cantelli...

In 1964, the orchestra choose a new name, The New Philharmonia, playing for the public in concert halls for the first time. It changed back to its old name, however, in 1977.

Pittsburgh Symphony Orchestra
founded in 1895

In 1895 the Art Society of Pittsburgh established a symphony orchestra that rapidly became recognized as one of the finest in America. Although it attracted Victor Herbert and Emil Pauer as conductors, with Richard Strauss and Edward Elgar among its distinguished guests, the project foundered in 1910. It was not until 1926 that the present Pittsburgh Symphony Orchestra emerged to take its rightful place. The new organization, consisting mainly of local musicians, was slow to regain the reputation of its predecessor. But in 1937, Otto Klemperer and Eugene Goossens, Georges Enesco and Fritz Reiner, among others, shared a season's conducting, giving the orchestra a shakedown that marked the beginning of Pittsburgh's musical renaissance. Reiner became permanent conductor the next year, remaining until 1948. The young Lorin Maazel, though not yet twenty, moved from the violin section to the podium as apprentice conductor on Reiner's departure, but it was William Steinberg who was appointed next permanent conductor. From 1952, Steinberg established the Pittsburgh Symphony as a sound, if not particularly adventurous, ensemble. André Previn, who succeeded Steinberg in 1976, admitted that the orchestra had become 'a bit sloppy' and embarked on an energetic programme of recordings and tours, expanding the repertoire to include works of the eighteenth and twentieth centuries that had previously been neglected. A festival of English music in 1982 was characteristic of Previn's innovative programming. Since 1971, the orchestra has played in Heinz Hall, a converted cinema. Its season of over 200 concerts included annual visits to New York and Washington, and an ambitious schedule of television appearances.

Philharmonia Hungarica
founded in 1957

Conductors: Zoltán Rozsnyai (1957-60), Miltiades Caradis (1960-67), Alois Springer (1968-75), Reinhard Peters (1975-79), Uri Segal (1979-85), Gilbert Varga (since 1985).

The Philharmonia Hungarica is funded by the state, the province Westphalia and the city of Marl. It was founded with Hungarian musicians that had escaped to the west in 1956. They performed for two years in Vienna, before moving as a group to Marl. The orchestra has made a long series of recordings. These are now also available in the west. The series includes the complete Haydn Symphonies, conducted by Antal Dorati.

Philharmonic Orchestra of Budapest
founded in 1853

Conductors: Ferenc Erkel (1853-71), Hans Richter (1871-75), Sándor Erkel (1875-1900), István Kerner (1900-18), Ernö von Dohnányi (1919-44), Otto Klemperer (1947-50), András Kóridi (since 1968).

The Philharmonic Orchestra of Budapest has also functioned as the accompanying ensemble at the Opera since its opening.

Rotterdam Philharmonic Orchestra
founded in 1918

Conductors: Willem Feltzer (1918-28), Alexander Schmuller (1928-30), Eduard Flipse (1930-62), Franz-Paul Decker (1962-68), Jean Fournet (1968-73), Edo de Waart (1973-79), David Zinman (1979-82), James Conlon (since 1983).

The Rotterdam Philharmonic lost its concert hall, its library and a good deal of its instruments during the German air raids of the Second World War. A new concert hall, the Doelen, now already famous for its acoustic qualities, enabled the orchestra to blossom anew. It now enjoys a first rate reputation at home and abroad.

Eduard Flipse has run the orchestra for more than thirty years. In that time, the Rotterdam Philharmonic have performed a great deal of contemporary music, including many Dutch and even world premières.

The Rotterdam Philharmonic has toured Europe many times since 1949 (including visits to Sandinavia, Belgium, Germany, England, Switzerland, Scotland and Italy). In 1954 at the celebration of the 150th anniversary of the Society for the Promotion of Music, Flipse performed Mahler's *Symphony of Thousands*. The Rotterdam orchestra was supplemented with the Brabants Orchestra, 10 soloists, a choir of 900 and a children's choir of 120. 8500 people attended the concert and Philips recorded the spectacle. At the orchestra's own 40th jubilee in 1958, Flipse was decorated with the Mahler Medal.

Guest conductors throughout the years have included: Eduard van Beinum, Alexander Gibson, Bernard Haitink, Lorin Maazel, Charles Munch, Jean Martinon, Wolfgang Sawallisch and Eugen Jochum.

Royal Philharmonic Orchestra
founded in 1946 by Sir Thomas Beecham

Conductors: Sir Thomas Beecham (1946-61), Rudolf Kempe (1961-75), Antal Dorati (1975-78), Walter Weller (1980-85), André Previn (since 1985).

After the Second World War, Sir Thomas Beecham returned from his concert tours to Australia, Canada and the United States. He was invited to return to his old orchestra, the London Philharmonic, but declined, prefer-

ring to employ an orchestra rather than be employed by one. Consequently, in 1946, he formed the Royal Philharmonic which under his baton became associated with the annual Glyndebourne Festival opera season in Sussex. The orchestra tours frequently, still making regular visits to the United States. The orchestra has made several experiments with the repertoire, often performing pieces associated with the realms of light music, or the jazz or pop genre.

San Francisco Symphony Orchestra
founded in 1911

Conductors: Henry Hadley (1911-15), Alfred Hertz (1915-29), Basil Cameron and Issaïe Dobrowen (1931-34), Pierre Monteux (1935-52), Enrique Jordà (1954-63), Josef Krips (1963-70), Seiji Ozawa (1970-76), Edo de Waart (1976-85), Herbert Blomstedt (since 1985).

Pierre Monteux is the most responsible for making the San Francisco Symphony one of the five top orchestras in the United States. Premières performed in San Francisco: *San Francisco Polyphony*, Legeti (1975); *Improvisation on an Impromptu of Britten*, Walton (1970); *Symphony no. 8*, Harris (1961); *A Flock Descends in the Pentagonal Garden*, Takemitsu (1977); *Musique pour San Francisco*, Milhaud (1972).

Scottish Chamber Orchestra
founded in 1974

Music director: Roderick Byron (1974-83), and Raymond Leppard has been principal guest conductor since 1979.
The orchestra is made up of 37 musicians. It has performed contemporary works from composers including: Hamilton, Harper, Maxwell Davies, Crosse and Benjamin.

Scottish National Orchestra
founded in 1890

Conductors: Sir Georg Henschel (1893-95), William Kes (1895-98), Max Bruch (1898-1900), Sir Frederick Cowen (1900-10), Emil Mlynarski (1910-16). Between 1916 and 1919, the orchestra had no principal conductor. Sir Ronald Landon (1919-20), Václav Talich (1926), Sir John Barbirolli (1933-36), George Szell (1936-39) Aylmer Buesset (1939-40), Warwick Braithwaite (1940-45), Walter Süsskind (1946-52), Karl Rankl

(1952-57), Hans Swarowski (1957-59), Sir Alexander Gibson (1959-84), Neeme Järvi (since 1984).

As its founding, it was named simply the Scottish Orchestra, but received its new title in 1950. The Scottish National Orchestra is also the accompanying ensemble of the Scottish National Opera, founded in 1962. In 1960, Alexander Gibson started the Musica Nova concert series wherein many contemporary works have been performed. Among these have been two English premières, works by Henze, and *Gruppen* by Stockhausen.

Stockholm Philharmonic Orchestra
founded in 1902

Conductors: Tor Aulin (1902-9), Erich Ochs (1914-15), Georg Schneevoigt (1915-24), Wilhelm Sieben (1925-26), Václav Talich (1926-36), Adolf Wiklund (1936-37), Fritz Busch (1937-40), Carl Garaguly (principal guest from 1936 until 1937, principal conductor from 1942 until 1955), Hans Schmidt-Isserstedt (1955-64), Sergiu Comissiona (principal guest 1964-66), Antal Dorati (1966-74), Guennadi Rozhdestvenski (1974-77), Yri Ahronovitch (since 1982).

The Stockholm Philharmonic is subsidised for 40% by the state, 38% by the city and 22% of the costs are covered by ticket sales.
The following works were commissioned by the Stockholm Philharmonic: *Poesis* (1964) and *Kontakinn* (1979) by Lidholm; *Symphony no. 4* (1977) by Börtz; *Requiem for Sweden* (1981) by Welin; Concerto for Organ and Orchestra (1982) by Morthenson and Rosell; *Concerto for Flute and Orchestra* (1981) by Sandström.

The Czech Philharmonic Orchestra
founded in 1894

For the first few years of its life (1894-1901), the Czech Philharmonic was the orchestra of the Prague National Opera. It only became an independent organization when the opera management dismissed its musicians en masse for daring to go on strike. Villém Zemánek was the conductor from 1908 until 1913. He was succeeded by the great Václav Talich, whose combination of inspiration and painstaking discipline made the Philharmonic one of Europe's most esteemed orchestras. Many works by Jánacek, Suk and Nóvak first became known to western audiences through the

tours. Raphael Kubelik, who had frequently appeared with the orchestra during the thirties, was appointed principal conductor. He left his homeland in voluntary exile when the communists became political, and more importantly for him, cultural masters of Czechoslovakia in 1948. Karl Ancerl conducted the Philharmonic from 1950 until 1968, maintaining the internationally high standards of his predecessors while championing predominantly national repertoire. He too left Czechoslovakia in the wake of the political disturbances of 1968, taking up residence in Canada.
Under Václav Neumann, the Czech Philharmonic has continued to enjoy a high reputation. Its frequent international tours and many recordings, make it the most familiar and respected of the Eastern European orchestras.

Toulouse Capitol Orchestra (Orchestre Capitole de Toulouse)
founded in 1974

The Orchestre du Capitole de Toulouse is a regional orchestra and fulfils as such many different obligations. Michel Plasson has been principal conductor since its founding. Together they perform during the symphonic season in the Halle des Grains, and for the opera season, in the Capitole. The orchestra also performs at several festivals, including Aix-en-Provence and Bordeaux. In 1975, this ensemble played the première of Lemeland's *Symphony no. 1*.

USSR State Symphony Orchestra
founded in 1982

The principal conductor of the State Symphony is Guennady Rozhdestvenski. The principal activity is the making of records, usually in large series of complete works. Once in a while, the orchestra performs for the public. They toured outside of the Soviet Union for the first time in 1984.

Washington National Symphony Orchestra
founded in 1931

Conductors: Hans Kindler (founder, 1931-48), Howard Mitchell (1948-69), Antal Dorati (1970-76), Mstislav Rostropovitch (since 1977).

The Washington National Symphony Orchestra has performed premières of compositions including those by: Tansmann (1943), Enesco (1949), Bennett (1976), W. Schuman (1976),

Landowski (1979), Dutilleux (1979), Lutoslawski (1980), Walton (1982), Laderman (1983), Penderecki (1983), and Bernstein.

Vienna Philharmonic
founded in 1842

In the years following the death of Beethoven, it became increasingly apparent that Vienna did not have an orchestra capable of playing his symphonies. This need was filled in 1842 by the establishment of the Vienna Philharmonic, a self-governing body of professional musicians. The conductor was Otto Nicolai, musical director of the Court Opera. His musicians were all familiar faces, members of his opera orchestra who had moved from the pit to the concert platform. In its first years, the Philharmonic performed infrequently, but already by 1845, it had impressed Hector Berlioz with its 'outstanding technical skill' and 'meticulous accuracy of instrumental tuning'. The Revolution of 1848 very nearly put end to the enterprise, but under Karl Eckert and Felix Dessof the orchestra struggled to its feet. The Philharmonic moved to its own concert hall in 1870, the Grosser Musikvereinsaal. In this splendid auditorium, the second and third symphonies of Brahms were heard for the first time. Eight of the modernist Anton Bruckner's symphonies also premièred there. Hans Richter was principal conductor during this golden period. His long reign extended from 1875 through 1898 when Gustav Mahler stepped in for three years. Between 1908 and 1927, Felix Weingartner was principal, maintaining the Philharmonic's remarkable standards throughout the First World War and organizing a triumphant tour to South America in 1922.
After the Weingartner period was a long stretch without a principal conductor. Many glamorous guests performed with the orchestra at that time including: Wilhelm Furtwängler (1927-28), Clemens Krauss (1929-33), Bruno Walter (1933-38), Karl Böhm (1954-56 and 1971-81), Herbert von Karajan (1956-64), Claudio Abbado (since 1971) and Lorin Maazel (1982-1984).
Furtwängler remained to direct during the German occupation, a decision which obliged him to undergo the ignomy of de-Nazification by the Allied Forces after the war. The Philharmonic itself did not meet with such disdain, but stepped out of the rubble of Vienna once again into the forefront of the world's great orchestras. Under recent conductors, including Claudio Abbado and Karl Böhm, the Philharmonic has maintained its reputation and fierce pride. 'We are the successors of artists who learned their craft with Beetho-

ven', boasted Richard Strauss for the orchestra in 1923. Sixty years later, the Vienna Philharmonic still lives up to this grand heritage.

Vienna Symphony Orchestra
founded in 1900

Such is the fame of the Vienna Philharmonic Orchestra, that its hard-working younger sister is little known outside Austria. The Vienna Symphony Orchestra was founded as the Wiener Konzertverein. Ferdinand Löwe, its permanent conductor until 1924, championed the music of his former teacher, Anton Bruckner, whose ninth symphony received its posthumous première with the Vienna Symphony in 1903. Subsequent first performances have included Ravel's *Piano Concerto for the Left Hand*, Boris Blacher's *Requiem*, and, in the opera pit under Karl Böhm, the Viennese premières of Alban Berg's *Lulu* and Richard Strauss's *Daphne*. In 1921, the Konzertverein incorporated another local orchestra. Twelve years later, it changed to its present name.

During the early years, the orchestra attracted the world's most distinguished musicians as guest conductors: Gustav Mahler, Bruno Walter, Richard Strauss, Arnold Schoenberg and Wilhelm Furtwängler. Despite this galaxy of great names, the orchestra had become close to financial ruin when it was adopted as Vienna's principal radio orchestra in 1934. Sponsorship from the City of Vienna and the Austrian Ministry of Education in 1938, further assured its future.

Since the war, the Symphony has been closely associated with a number of eminent conductors, among them, Hans Swarowsky (1946-47), Herbert von Karajan (1948-49), Wolfgang Sawallisch (1960-70), Josef Krips (1970-73), Carlo-Maria Giulini (1973-76) and Guennadi Rozhdestvenski (1981-83).

There have been only a few principal conductors contrasted with the Vienna Symphony Orchestra. Most have received only temporary contracts and haven not been responsible for artistic direction. Only Sawallisch and Giulini were granted more extensive powers. With a season of approximately 120 concerts in the city, frequent broadcasts and annual tours of the provinces, the Vienna Symphony is an essential part of Austria's cultural life while it remains one of the least known (internationally) of the world's outstanding orchestras.

The Vienna Symphony Orchestra has produced a number of smaller ensembles from among its members including: The Haydn Trio, Concentus Musicus, and the Johann Strauss Ensemble.

A recording session in
London under the direction
of Sir Colin Davis.

11

Discographies

Introduction

It remains a very personal decision, the preference for a certain recording. There are many reasons why a performance becomes one's favourite: the interpretation communicates as if to you alone, the performance is interesting in an unorthodox way, the beauty of the sound simply overwhelms, all regardless of the fact that a record was made yesterday or thirty years ago. The opinions expressed here are no unquestioned truths. There are too many personal preferences and too many recordings. Let taste be the ultimate guide.
The following discography sums up the record industries products in terms of more than 500 symphonies of the classical repertoire. LP's as well as CD's have been included and the listings are extensive. Due to advances in 'high technology', many older recordings have been re-released and in the majority of cases, with a much improved sound. Because of this, the discography can serve a historical purpose, making it possible to compare interpretations as these have evolved throughout our century. A note of caution in this respect: a CD of an old analogue recording does not in itself insure improvement. Some remastering does indeed fail.
This discography is definitely not a complete summing up of the recordings available in the local shops. (For that purpose, consult the record company catalogues or the shops themselves.) There is no commercial purpose to the listings presented here. The listings are meant for the record collector (those who indulge in comparisons themselves) and as a helpful guide for the radio listener, concertgoer or music student.
The difference between LP (for example, Philips 6769 054) and CD (for example, Philips **416 417-2**) as well as cassettes (for example, l'Oiseau Lyre *K 168 K 33*) has been so made and where of importance, the date of release has been noted. When a CD has been made of an LP already released, this has also been noted by 'transfer from' or 'remastered'. LP's that are recent releases of much older recordings have been specified for clarity (recorded in, 19..). Concert performances before a live audience have been noted as far as that is known. The practicality of this discography is a result of all these factors; it includes information often sorely lacking on record jackets. The

dates given on jackets are usually only the copyrights. These are the latest release dates but are often confused for the actual recording dates. The commentary that accompanies the listings is not of a competitive nature. A 'best recording' is almost impossible to signify. There are so many excellent choices! The comments here hopefully heighten the differences between these, leaving the ultimate choice up to the reader, listener and music lover.

HUGO ALVÉN (1872-1960)

Symphony nr. 3 in E major, Op. 23
- Stockholm P O / Nils Grevillius
Swedish Soc. SLT 33161
Symphony nr. 4 in c minor (Från Havsbandet), Op. 39
- Söderström, Winbergh, Stockholm P O / Westerberg
  BlueBELL 107 [Turn. TVS 34778/*CT*4778]
- Malmborg, Vikstrom, Stockholm P O / Nils Grevillius
  Swedish Soc. SLT 33186

International music critics say that Alfvén is more comfortable with his symphonic poems (Midsummer watch; Dalecarlian rhapsody) and his musical miniatures, than with his symphonies. His style, reminiscent of Svendsen, Grieg and Strauss, tends to vague in the expanse of the symphony form.
Leif Segerstam recorded Alfvén's First Symphony with the Swedish Radio Orchestra (SLT 333213) and the Second Symphony with the Stockholm Philharmonic. Segerstam's sound is superb, the orchestras are alert. Despite these excellent performances, Alfvén remains unconvincing. The Third Symphony, recorded under Grevillius by the Stockholm Philharmonic, deserves more attention. Perhaps Grevillius lacks the refinement of say, a Stenhammar, but his musical ideas exude a vitality that make this recording a fluid and authoritative interpretation. Alfvén himself conducted the Third with the same orchestra in 1950; the sound is surprisingly clear and clean when heard on the new print (EMI 4E 053-34620). Some devotees, not insistent on a stereo recording, prefer this performance.
The Fourth Symphony appeared in 1919. The subtitle is: From the Farthest Reefs of the Archipelago. Many find that this piece captured the unusual atmosphere of the islands in question, that stretch from Stockholm all the way to the Baltic Sea. This makes it purely romantic programme music. Strauss and Wagner are the obvious inspiration for the orchestration; the score specifies an extended orchestra: four times the usual woodwinds, eight horns, two harps, celesta, piano etc. An impression of nature dominates the music, and no deep emotions are summoned up. The vocalizing is clearly Wagnerian.
The tenor in the Bluebell version is rather loud and unpleasant and Södestrom uses a large vibrato. The performance has colour and atmosphere but isn't very original. The recording, technically, is masterly; the detail of sound is extensive. Apparently it is very

difficult for an orchestra to give a more indulgent performance of this piece. The playing itself is excellent.

In the 1964 recording, Nils Grevillius conducts the singer Gunilla von Malmborg whose vibrato is less gaudy. This recording was made by the Swedish branch of Decca and sounds quite good taking into consideration that it is already twenty years old.

WILLIAM ALWYN (born 1905)

Symphony nr.1
- London P O / Alwyn
  Lyr. SRCS 86
Symphony nr. 2
- London P O / Alwyn
  LYR SRCS 85
Symphony nr. 3
- London P O / Alwyn
  Lyr SRCS 63
Symphony nr. 4
Symphony nr. 5 (Hydriophia)
- London P O / Alwyn
  Lyr SRCS 76

Alwyn's First Symphony appeared in 1950. The Finale of this piece sounds very much like film music, something in which Alwyn is a master. The LPO's version is exemplary. The Second Symphony is from 1953 and like the first, very well orchestrated. This recording is excellent as well. The Third was commissioned by the BBC and had its première with the BBC Symphony and Sir Thomas Beecham. The Fourth is the longest, a good example of the strongly rhetorical, English symphonic tradition. The Fifth (1973) is a short, one movement piece in four sections. The composer's own performances are, of course, reliable, and the Lyrita label guarantees quality.

THOMAS ARNE (1710-78)

Symphonies nrs 1 in C major; 2 in F major; 3 in e minor; 4 in c minor.
- Bournemouth Sinfonietta / Kenneth Montgomery
  HMV Green ESD/TC-ESD 106024-1/-4
  [+WESLEY: Symphony in D major]

According to an anonymous story, Arne, late in his career, having been confronted with the new Mannheimers, determined that he would beat these newcomers at their own game. That he did with these surprising and brilliant symphonies. They are inspired as say, Haydn's middle period symphonic works. Arne has, with apparent ease, here discarded his earlier baroque methods and made the gallant style very much his own.

It is amazing that these symphonies remained totally unknown up until 1973, when they were published as the result of musicological research. It is even probable that the most ambitious work, the Symphony in c minor, never had been published in Arne's lifetime. This recording is especially praiseworthy. The playing by the Bournemouth Sinfonietta, especially in terms of style, is outstanding. It sounds warm and alive. The cassette is also excellent.

MALCOLM ARNOLD (born 1921)

Sinfonietta nr.1, Op. 49
- London S O / Braithwaite
  Lyr SRCS 115
Symphony for Brass, Op. 123
- Philip Jones Brass Ensemble
  Argo ZRG 906

The Sinfonietta by Arnold is a very popular work that gets performed regularly. He wrote the piece in 1955 for two oboes, two horns and strings. The LSO recording is lovely. Symphony for brass takes 26 minutes and is well-crafted for its length. The orchestration betrays Arnold's trumpet-playing past: horn, tuba, four trumpets and four trombones. The Philip Jones ensemble plays with great precision and cohesiveness. The recording quality is excellent.

KURT ATTENBURG (1887-1974)

Symphony nr. 2 in F major, Op. 6
- Swedish Radio S O / Westerberg
  Swedish Soc. SLT 33179

Any fame that Kurt Attenburg enjoys is due to his Sixth Symphony, that won the Schubert Memorial Prize in 1928. His Second Symphony was written in 1912, had two movements originally to which a third was added later. The slow movement builds up to a scherzo in the same manner as Berwald's Symphony Singulière which preceeded Attenburg's piece by seven years. This same movement is quite an evocative work, the opening is really poetic and is more Scandinavian than the movements around it. The work owes much to the German romantic tradition: Schumann, Wagner etc., so much so that one wonders if the idiom is truly Attenburg's own. This performance is convincing. The recording is adequate.

Apparently there is no modern recording of the Sixth Symphony available, but there is a re-release of an old mono version dating from 1929, conducted by Thomas Beecham (EMI 7C-037-35982). Collectors will be surprised at the fresh and lively sound of this recording.

CARL PHILIPP EMANUEL BACH (1714-88)

6 Hamburg Sinfonias, Wq 182/1-6 (complete)
- The English Concert / Trevor Pinnock
  DG Arch CD 4125 300-2 (2533 449)
- Collegium Aureum
  Harmonia Mundi 1 C 065 99691 (nrs 2 - 5)
6 Hamburg Sinfonias, Wq 182/1-6;
Sinfonia in C major, Wq 174
Sinfonia in D major, Wq 176
- Academy of Ancient Music / Christopher Hogwood
  l'Oiseau-Lyre DSLO 557/8
4 Hamburg Sionfonias, Wq 182 : Nrs 1 in G major ; 2 in B flat; 3 in C major; 5 in b minor
- Tel Dig CD ZK8 42843 (AZ6/CX4 42843)
  Liszt Chamber O / Rolla
Sinfonias strings and continuo: in D major, Wq 183/1; in e sharp minor, Wq 183/2; in F major, Wq 183/3; in G

major, Wq 183/4
- Little Orch of London / Leslie Jones
  Nonesuch H 71180
4 Sinfonias, Wq 183/1-4
- English Ch O / Raymond Leppard
  Philips 9502 013
- Münchener Bach Orchester / Karl Richter
  Archiv 2547026

The sharp originality of Carl Philip Emmanuel Bach's genius is nowhere more evident than in the 6 Sinfonias of Wq 132. Bach wrote the sinfonias having left the Prussian Emperor's employ, at last a freer man. The whimsical melodies, the dizzying modulations and the abrupt pauses seem more twentieth century than eighteenth. The capriciousness inherent in this music is most evident in the authentic performance of the Academy of Ancient Music led by Christopher Hogwood. Hogwood continually gives the impression that the music is brand new. The sinfonias with winds sound a bit less original but are nonetheless, brilliantly recorded.

The English Chamber Orchestra's version is less whimsical and more dedicated to the eighteenth century's general style, one of refinement, balance and decoration. This recording is excellent as well. The Collegium Aureum (originally released on BASF) made their début with original instruments performing these sinfonias. Their playing is strongly rhythmical; it has substance. The sound is slightly grainy, but has a masculine freshness to it that is very appealing. The only disappointment is that the Collegium recorded only 4 of the 6 Sinfonias.

The Wq 183 Sinfonias (there are 4 of them) were published in Hamburg in 1780. The music is not only historically important, it has an emotional content that can be devastating. The ECO plays beautifully led by Leppard. The performance is vital and the recording is exemplary in terms of sound as well as balance. It was made in 1969 and re-released in 1981.

Leslie Jones has a broader interpretation. It almost seems as if he is searching for likenesses to Haydn, a composer that he has often performed as well.

The old recording made by Karl Richter and his Bach Orchestra has only historical interest: Emmanuel Bach as played by the German School: very square.

JOHANN CHRISTIAN BACH (1735-82)

6 Sinfonias, Op. 3 (ed. Erik Smith)
- Academy St Martin in the Fields / Marriner
  Philips 9501/7313 001
[a] 6 Sinfonias, Op. 3 (ed. Smith)
[b] 6 Sinfonias , Op. 6
Sinfonias, Op. 8, nrs 2 in G; 3 in D; 4 in F
Sinfonias, Op. 9, nrs 1 in B flat; 2 in E flat, 3 in B flat
6 Sinfonias, Op.18
Sinfonia concertante in F for oboe, cello and orchestra
- [a] Academy SMF / Marriner
  [b] The Netherlands Chamber O / David Zinman
  Philips 6768 336 (5)
Sinfonias Op. 6/6; Op. 18/4 and 6
- Collegium Aureum
  Harmonia Mundi 1C 065/265 99759
Sinfonia in E flat, Op. 9/2

Sinfonia concertante for flute, oboe, violin, cello and orchestra
- English Chamber O / Bonynge
  Decca Ser SA24

Sinfonia concertante in A, for violin, cello and orchestra

Sinfonia in e sharp for double orchestra, Op. 18/1
- Collegium Aureum
  Harmonia Mundi 1C 065 99827

Symphonies (wind-sextet) nr. 1 in E flat; nr. 2 in B flat; nr. 3 in E flat; nr. 4 in B flat; nr. 5 in E flat; nr. 6 in B flat
- Camden Wind Ensemble
  PRT (Precision Records and Tape) GSGC/ZCGC 2033

Sinfonias Op. 6/3; Op. 9/2; Op. 18/2 and 4
- Bournemouth Sinfonietta / Kenneth Montgomery
  HMV ASD/TC - ASD 3544

The Johann Christian Bach Sinfonias appeared with the opus numbers: 3, 6, 8, 9 and 18. Opus 3 was recorded for the first time in 1982 by Neville Marriner and his Academy of St Martin-in-the-fields. The première took place in Carlisle House in Soho Square in 1765. The Sinfonias are written for strings, oboes and horns. The Academy's performance is sheer magic, as is the recording itself. The Collegium Aureum plays the opus 6 elegantly but too seriously, without a smile. The recording doesn't help either; it lacks a certain gloss. More attractive is Kenneth Montgomery's performance with the Bournemouth sinfonietta. The playing is wonderful and the sound, brilliant.

Opus 6 sounds the most polished played by The Netherlands Chamber Orchestra led by David Zinman. Even the recording technicians are musical in this Philips product. In 1982, opus 8, 9 and 18 appeared in a 5 record set, with performances made by Zinman in the late seventies. This set, which is wonderful, does not completely wipe out the memory of Leppard's version made in the sixties. Leppard's sense of style is purer perhaps, and the interpretation is intense. Bonynge's interpretation with the ECO does not measure up to either Zinman or Leppard. This is too bad as Bonynge was the only one to record the Sinfonia concertante of opus 9.

The opus 18 by Collegium Aureum is disappointing. The balance is not good; the soloists sound too hard as a result. In terms of expression, the contrasts are too square. The Sinfonia (opus18/1) is a delicious piece of music that has a Mozart aroma to it. The performance is good, but the overall acoustics prevent the antiphonal character of the piece from working well.

The 6 Sextets were most likely written for Vauxhall and are very appropriate for open air concerts. The Cambden Wind Ensemble, led by the famous bassoonist, Archie Cambden, performs the sextets well. There is a chance that the old, much loved version by the London Wind Ensemble, led by Jack Brymer, will again be included in the LP catalogues.

MILY BALAKIREV (1837-1910)

Symphony nr.1 in C
- Philharmonia O / Karajan
  HMV mono XLP/TC- XLP 60001
- Royal Philharmonic O / Beecham
  HMV SXLP 30171
- City of Birmingham Symphony O / Neeme Järvi

HMV Dig EL 270050-1/4

Symphony nr. 1 in C

Symphony nr. 2 in d minor
- USSR State Academy O / Svetlanov
  HMV ASD 3315

Symphony nr. 2 in d minor
- USSR State Academy O / Svetlanov
  Le Chant du Monde/Harmonia Mundi CD LDC278758, transferred from Eurodisc Melodiya 300 045 Oct. 1984

The Symphony in C major led by Neeme Järvi has great clarity and sonority. The HMV recording is wonderfully direct. There is also much to be said for the Svetlanov version, but the eastern brass will most likely disappoint western listeners. The sound cannot compete with the HMV product. The old recording under Von Karajan was originally released as a 78 record in 1950. It is one of the most inspired of the recordings Von Karajan made with the Philharmonia in their early years of success together. The passion and intensity are appropriate to this often neglected work. The transfer is well done. The equally old stereo version made by Beecham with his own orchestra, has merits of its own. This was one of Sir Thomas' favourite works. The face-lift done by EMI has greatly improved the old recording.

SAMUEL BARBER (1910-81)

Symphony nr.1, Op. 9
- London S O / David Measham
  Uni RHS 342

Samuel Barber's First Symphony was once recorded by the legendary Bruno Walter and the New York Philharmonic on a 78 record. This same piece has been scandalously neglected in the LP age. The work is somewhat dated, to be sure, but Barber never repeated the vitality of this early work. David Measham is a wonderful promoter of this work; his performance is very spiritual and the recording is excellent. It includes Night Flight, a part of the Second Symphony that Barber did not retract.

ARNOLD BAX (1883-1953)

Symphony nr. 2 in e minor, and C major
- London P O / Myer Fredman
  Lyr. SRCS 54

Symphony nr. 3
- Hallé O / Sir John Barbirolli
  HMV Mono EX290107-3

Symphony nr. 4
- Ulster O / Bryden Thomson
  Chan 8312; ABRD/ABTD 1091

Symphony nr. 5 in c sharp minor
- London P O / Raymond Leppard
  Lyr SRCS 58

Symphony nr. 6 in C major
- New Philharmonia O / Norman del Mar
  Lyr SRCS 35

The opinion is that the Second Symphony by Arnold Bax, possesses the strongest imaginative power of all of his seven symphonies; the musical ideas are the richest; the almost wild intensity is astonishing.

Unfortunately, many works by Bax have fallen prey to run-of-the-mill performances or recordings. Myer Fredman, on the other hand, offers us a perfect version. The London Philharmonic sounds like it has known this work throughout its history, and the recording that dates from 1971 is an example of analogue technique at its very best.

The Third Symphony has a power of its own and is generally considered to be Bax's masterpiece. Barbirolli's performance, with its fierce intensity, easily surpasses the more recent recording with Edward Downes. Sir John's way of handling the piece's serenity is inimitable, this serenity that often barely covers the surging tempest beneath. (Louis Foreman in his 1983 biography of Bax, published by Scholar Press, attributes this serenity to Bax's love for Mary Gleaves, one of the few women in his life to make him happy.) There is much to forgive in the quality of sound in the Barbirolli recording. The performance is first rate in spite of this.

The Fourth Symphony was composed in Ireland between 1930 and 1931. The abundant stream of musical thought found in Bax's best symphonies (nrs 2, 3, 5 and 6) is not always especially coherent. In that respect, the Fourth is the least concentrated and most hedonistic of all seven. This distracts nothing from the originality of the piece; rather it emphasizes what one critic wrote of Bax: that a Bax symphony is a drama, full of emotions and led by instinct, rather than a well-built and logical whole. It is unashamedly romantic. Some devotees prefer the Third and Fifth symphonies to the Fourth, but Bryden Thomas' performance is a convincing plea for this piece. He inspires the ultimate from his players when it comes to nuanced dynamics and working on the special atmosphere the piece needs.

The Fifth Symphony in its turn, is considered Bax's best by some. Dedicated to Sibelius, it was performed for the first time in 1934, with Sir Thomas Beecham conducting. Beecham is definitely the most articulate advocate of this Finnish master's work. Raymond Leppard's performance of the Fifth should also help those still in doubt as to Bax's imaginative powers and strong symphonic instincts. The Leppard recording dates from 1972, with the London Philharmonic playing at its very best.

The Sixth Symphony is an ode on the wild beauty of Invernessshire in Scotland where it was composed. The performance, the New Philharmonia conducted by Norman del Mar, is good. It does leave one desiring a more thoughtful and nuanced dynamic, something the piece surely deserves.

LUDWIG VAN BEETHOVEN (1770-1827)

*** Symphonies nrs 1-9 [19 sets, including 8 on CD]
- Soloists, Philharmonia Orchestra and Chorus / Klemperer
  HMV EX 290379-3/9 , also SLS 788 (9 LPs)
- Perry, Baltsa, Cole, Van Dam, Wiener Singverein, Berliner Phil / Karajan
  DG Dig **DDD 415 066-2GH6 (6 discs)**; 415 066-1GH7 (7 LPs); 4GH6
- Tomowa-Sintow, Baltsa, Schreier, Van Dam, Wiener Singverein, Berliner Ph / Karajan
  DG 2740 172/3378 070 (8 LPs)
- Tomova-Sintow, Burmeister, Schreier, Adam, Leipzig and

Berlin Choruses, Leipzig Gewandhaus O / Masur
   Philips **416 274-2PH** [in 1986 dig remastered from 6747
135 - 9/75]; 416 274-1PB6 (1972-74); also Philips Silver
Line **420 701-2PSL** (9/75)
- Van der Sluys, Luger, Van Tulder, Ravelli, Amsterdam
Toonkunst Choir Concertgebouw O/ Mengelberg
   Philips mono **416/200-205-2** [recorded in April, May and
November 1940] transfers Philips 6767 003 (9/77) and
GL5806 (5/65)
- Armstrong, Finnie, Tear, Tomlinson, Philh Chorus,
Philharmonia O / Sanderling
   HMV Dig SLS/*TC-SLS* 5239
- Soloists, Chorus, Chicago S O / Solti
   Decca 11 BB 188/96
- Buchanan, Hodgson, Mitchinson, Howell, Hallé Chorus
and Orch / Loughran
   ASV ALHB 803
- Popp, Obraztsova, Vickers, Talvela; Cleveland O and
Chorus / Maazel
   CBS 79800 (8 LPs)
- Cleveland O / George Szell
   CBS **M5K 42444** (5 compact discs)
- Jones, Schwarz, Kollo, Moll, Choir Vienna Opera, Vienna
Philh / Bernstein
   DG 2740 216/ *3378 090*
- Soloists and Chorus, London P O / Haitink
   Philips 6747 307 (7 LPs) (1975)
- Concertgebouw O / Haitink
   Philips (Dig 04-88) Digital Classics series **416 822-2**
(6 compact discs)
   nr. 1: London S O; nr.2: Concertgebouw O; nr. 3: Vienna
   Philharmonic;
   nr. 4: Israel P O; nr. 5 : Boston Symphony; nr. 7: Vienna
   Philharmonic;
   nr. 8: Cleveland O; nr. 9: Orch des Bayerischen Rund-
   funks / Kubelik
   DGG 2740 155 (8 LPs)
- Te Kanawa, Hamari, Burrows, Holl, Chorus, London S O /
Jochum
   HMV SLS 5178 (8 LPs)
- Sutherland, Horne, King, Talvela, Choir Vienna State
Opera, Vienna P / Schmidt-Isserstedt
   Decca Jub JBA 500/5
- Hargen, Walther, Büchner, Kováts, Berlin Radio Choir,
Dresden Philharmonic / Kegel
   Capriccio / Target **10 451/55** (5 CDs) [transfer
CAPR1001/05, 10 006/7 - 11/84]
- Several orchestras / Furtwängler
   HMV mono dig remastered EX290660-3 (6 LPs):
- Vienna Philharmonic / Furtwängler
   [transfers resp. nr. 1: ALP1324 - 4/56; nr. 2: 1C 149
   5342/9M - 12/80; nr. 3: ALP 1060 - 9/53; nr. 4: ALP 1059 -
   6/53; nr. 5: ALP 1195 - 2/55; nr. 6: ALP 1041 - 12/53; nr.7:
   DB 21106/10 - 9/51]
- Stockholm P O / Furtwängler
   nr. 8: Unicorn WFSS, 9/72;
- Bayreuth Festival Chorus and Orchestra / Schwarzkopf,
Hoengen, Hopf, Edelmann / Furtwängler; 1951 Bayreuth
Festival
   nr. 9: transfer ALP1286/7;
- Berliner Philharmoniker / Furtwängler
   nr. 7 and nr. 8
   DG Mono **415 666-2GH**
- Columbia Symphony O / Walter
   CBS Masterworks dig transfered **MK42009/014, 6 discs**;
transfers nrs 1 and 2: Philips SABL168 - 11/60; nr. 3:
SABL132 - 5/60; nrs 4 and 5: SABL167 - 11/60; nr. 6:
SABL133 - 5/60; nr. 7: SABL166 - 11/60; nr. 8: SABL169/

70 - 11/60; nr. 9 (with Cundari, Rankin, Da Costa,
Wildermann, Westminster Symphonic Choir) from
SABL169/70 - 11/60]

*** Symphony nr.1 in C major, Op. 21
- XVIII Century O / Frans Brüggen
   Philips dig 416329-1PH; *4PH* ; **2PH**

*** Symphony nr. 1 in C major, Op. 21
*** Symphony nr. 2 in D major, Op. 36
- Academy of Ancient Music / Hogwood
   L'Oiseau-Lyre Florilegium, dig 414 338-1OH; *4OH* ; **2OH**
- English Chamber O / Michael Tilson Thomas
   CBS Masterworks dig IM39707; **MK 39707**
- Academy S M F / Marriner
   Philips Seq 6572 074; *7311*
- Columbia S O / Walter
   CBS **MK 42009**
- Berliner Philharmoniker / Karajan
   DG Acc 2542 102 [transfers 1962-cycle 2/63 and 10/79]
and DG 2531 101 [transfers 10/77 and 4/78]; also **DDD 415
505-2GH**
- London S O / Jochum
   EMI Em EMX2015 - 11/79 and 6/83
- Vienna Philharmonic / Bernstein
   DG Sig410 836-1GS from resp 3/80 and 6/84
- New York P O / Bernstein
   CBS **MK 42219**
- Philharmonia / Sanderling
   HMV Dig ASD4151 [originally 11/81]

*** Symphony nr. 1
*** Symphony nr. 3 , in E flat major, Op. 55, 'Eroica'
 - NBC Symphony O / Toscanini
   RCA Red Seal **RD87197** (refurbished ALP1039/40 from
4/53)

*** Symphony nr. 1 in C major, Op. 21
*** Symphony nr. 4 in B flat major, Op. 60
*** Symphony nr. 6 in F major, Op. 68, 'Pastoral'
*** Symphony nr. 7 in A major, Op. 92
- BBC Symphony O / Toscanini
   EMI Treasury Mono EX290930-3 (3 LPs) from resp. 9/38,
12/39, 12/37 and 1935

*** Symphony nr. 1
*** Symphony nr. 3
*** Symphony nr. 4
*** Symphony nr. 5
*** Symphony nr. 6
- Sydney S O / Van Otterloo
   Chan CBR 4001

*** Symphony nr. 1
*** Symphony nr. 4
- Northern Sinfonia / Richard Hickox
   ASV ALH968
- Vienna Philharmonic / Furtwängler
   EMI mono **CDC7 47409**, [transfer HMV EX290660-3 from
6/86]
- Philharmonia O / KLEMPERER
   HMV ED 290270-1; *-4;* [also Ang AE 34423]
- Berliner Philharmoniker / Karajan
   DG Gal 419 048-1; *-4;*
- Vienna Philharmonic / Bernstein
   DG 2531 308; *3301*

*** Symphony nr.1

*** Symphony nr. 5, in c minor, Op. 67
- Philadelphia O / Ricardo Muti
   HMV dig EL270449-1 (10/86); idem *-4* ; **CDC47447-2**
- London P O / Haitink
   Philips 9500 067

*** Symphony nr.1
*** Symphony nr. 7
- Philharmonia O / Klemperer
   EMI **CDC7 47184-2**, [transfers resp. HMV ED290270 and
290328 from 5/85]
- Vienna Philharmonic / Bernstein
   DG **ADD 419 434-2GH**

*** Symphony nr. 1
*** Symphony nr. 8, in F major, Op. 93
- Los Angeles Chamber O and London S O / Gerard
Schwarz
   Delos / John Goldsmith's CD Service **D/CD3013**
- Hallé O / John Barbirolli
   Virtuoso collection/PRT **PVCD8373** [transfer Pye
CSCL70001 from 9/58]
- Orch des Bayerischen Rundfunks / Jochum
   DGG Heliodor 2548 224
- Berliner Philharmoniker / Jochum
- Concertgebouw O / Jochum
   Philips Universo 6580 148
- Vienna Philharmonic / Monteux
   Decca Eclipse ECS 638 [early 60's]

*** Symphony nr. 2
- London S O / Monteux
   Decca SPA 584
- Berliner Philharmoniker / Jochum
   DGG Heliodor 2548 215
- Berliner Philharmoniker / Cluytens
   Classics for Pleasure CFP 193
- Chicago S O / Solti
   Decca SXL 6761
- Leipzig Gewandhaus O / Masur
   Philips Fest 6570 130
- Vienna Philharmonic / Böhm
   DGG 2530 448
- BBC S O / Colin Davis
   Philips 9500 160

*** Symphony nr. 2
*** Symphony nr. 4
- Philharmonia O / Klemperer
   EMI **CDC 747185-2** [transfers resp HMV ED290252-1 and
ED290270-1 from 5/85]
- (nr. 2) Concertgebouw O / Kubelik
   (nr. 4) Israel P O / Kubelik
   DG Priv 2535 441; *3335*
- Vienna Philharmonic / Bernstein
   DG **ADD 423 049-2GH**

*** Symphony nr. 2
*** Symphony nr. 5
- Vienna Philharmonic / Abbado
   DG 423 590-1GH; *4GH;* **2GH**
   [live recording in the 'Grosser Saal', Musikverein in
Vienna]

*** Symphony nr. 2
*** Symphony nr. 7
- NBC Symphony O / Toscanini
   RCA Red Seal mono **RD87198**

[dig refurbished resp from HMV ALP1145 - 7/54 of concerts (Symphony nr. 7) in Carnegie Hall, Nov. 1949 and Oct. 1951, and (Symphony nr. 8) in Carnegie Hall, Nov. 1951]
- Berliner Philharmoniker / Karajan
  DG Galleria **419 050-2GGA** [transfer 2740 172 - 10/77]

*** Symphony nr. 2
*** Symphony nr. 8
London Classical Players / Roger Norrington
EMI dig EL270563-1; *-4;* **CDC7 47698-2**

*** Symphony nr. 3 in E flat major, Op. 55, 'Eroica'
- Orchester des Norddeutschen Rundfunks / Günther Wand
  German Harmonia Mundi / Conifer dig 1C 067 169543-1 (3/86); **CDC169543-2;** also cassette
- Academy S M F / Marriner
  Philips Dig **410 044-2**; 6514 314, and *7337*
- Philharmonia / Klemperer
  ED290271-1 (3/62 and 5/85); **CDC7 47186-2** (10/85); HMV SXLP 30310
  also HMV mono EX 200457-3/5; and SXLP 30310; and ASD 2562
- Columbia Symphony O / Bruno Walter
  RD87197 (9/86), and CBS **MK 42010**
- Concertgebouw O / Monteux
  Philips Fest 6570 204; *7310;* also Philips Legendary Classics **420 853-2**
- London S O / Jochum
  EMI Em EMX 2016; *TC-EMX*
- Hallé O / Loughran
  ASV ALH 901
- Vienna Philharmonic / Bernstein
  DG 2531 310; *3301;* **ADD 413 778-2GH**
- New York P O / Bernstein
  CBS **MK 42220**
- Münchener Philh / Kempe
  CFP 41 4410-1; *-4*
- Los Angeles P O / Giulini
  DG Dig **410 028-2**; 2532 123
- Leipzig Gewandhaus O / Masur
  Philips Fest 6570 165; *7310*
- Philharmonia O / Sanderling
  HMV Dig ASD 4152; *TCC-ASD*
- Vienna Philharmonic / Schmidt-Isserstedt
  Decca Jubilee JB6 (11/66 and 1/78)
- Hallé O / Loughran
  ALH901 (2/77 and 1/82)
- Berliner Philharmoniker / Karajan
  DG dig 415 507-1GH, *-4-GH;* **DDD 415 506-2GH;** also 419 049-1GGA , DG Galleria, and **-2GGA** [from 10/77 and re-release in 4/78 and 1/87]; also DG Acc 2542 103
- Royal Liverpool Ph O / Marek Janowsky
  ASV dig DCA556
- Concertgebouw O / Haitink
  Philips 412 358-1PS (3/71; 3/85)
- Concertgebouw O / Haitink
  Philips (Dig 09-88) **420 538-2**
- Chicago S O / Solti
  Decca SXL6902, and SXL 6829 (9/79, 9/81); also Decca **417 556-2DH** [transfer from 11BB 188-96 9/75]
- Vienna Philharmonic / Erich Kleiber
  Decca mono 414 626-1DM, **2DM;** *-4DM*
  [transfer from Ace of Clubs ACL35 (5/59)]
- Czech P O / Paul Kletski
  Supraphon/Counterpoint **C37-4**
  [transfer from Parliament PLPS129 (10/60)]
- Academy of Ancient Music / Hogwood

L'Oiseau Lyre Florilegium dig 417 235-1OH; **-2OH;** *-4OH*
- Orch of St Lukas / Tilson-Thomas
  CBS **MK 445 16**; and MT 44516; also cassette
- Vienna Philharmonic / Furtwängler
  EMI mono **CDC7-47410-2**, [transfer from HMV EX290660-3 (6/86)]
- Hungary State O / Janos Ferencsik
  Hungaroton/Conifer **HCD12566-2**, [transfer from SLPD12566 (12/84)]
- Vienna Philharmonic / Abbado
  DG dig 419 597-1GH; *4GH;* **2GH**
  [live recording in the 'Grosser Saal', Musikverein in Vienna]
- Vienna Philharmonic / George Szell
  Philips **4210 242**

*** Symphony nr. 4 in B flat major, Op. 60
- Columbia S O / Walter
  CBS **MK 42011**
- Berliner Philharmoniker / Karajan
  DG 2531 104
  alternative recording: DG 2542 104 (also 2535 303)
- London S O / Jochum
  EMI Em EMX 2017
- English CH O / Tilson-Thomas
  CBS Dig 37209
- Leipzig Gewandhaus O / Masur
  Philips Fest 6570 132
- London P O / Haitink
  Philips 9500 258
- Vienna Philharmonic / Hans Schmidt-Isserstedt
  Decca Jubilee JB7
- BBC S O / Colin Davies
  Philips 9500 033
- Bayerisches Staatsorchester / Carlos Kleiber
  Orfeo d'or 100 841B, *MC M100 841B;* **CD C 100 841A**
  [live recording]

*** Symphony nr. 4
*** Symphony nr. 5
- London S O / Wyn Morris
  Pickwick IMP Classics **PCD869**
- Academy of Ancient Music / Hogwood
  L'Oiseau-Lyre Florilegium dig 417 615-1OH; *4OH;* **2OH**
- London S O / Gerard Schwarz
  Delos / John Goldsmith CD Service **D/CD3027**
- New York P O / Bernstein
  CBS **MK 42221**
- Columbia S O / WALTER
  CBS **MK 42011**

*** Symphony nr. 4
*** Symphony nr. 7
- Berliner Philharmoniker / Karajan
  DG **DDD 415 121-2**

*** Symphony nr. 5
- Vienna Philharmonic / Carlos Kleiber
  DG **ADD 415861-2GH** [transfer from 2530 516 (6/75)]
- Berliner Philharmoniker / Furtwängler
  Wilhelm Furtwängler Society / UK Harmonia Mundi / **FURT 100**
  [oririnally the first electric Polydor 78 recording of Furtwängler in 1926]
- Vienna Philharmonic / Furtwängler
  Danacord DACO114
  [live recording Copenhagen 1950; Furtwängler's 10th recorded version]

- Berliner Philharmoniker / Karajan
  DG Galleria **419 051-2GGA** [transfer (dig remastered) of 2740 172 (10/77)];
  also: DG 2531 105; *3301* and Dg Acc 2542 105; *3342*
- Los Angeles P O / Giulini
  DG Dig **DDD 410 028-2GH**; 2532 049; *3302*
- Philharmonia O / Ashkenazy
  Decca Dig **400 060-2**; SXDL 7540; *KSXDC*
- Vienna Philharmonic / Bernstein
  DG 2531 311; *3301*
- Philharmonia O / Sanderling
  HMV Dig ASD 4136; *TCC-ASD*
- London S O / Jochum
  EMI Em EMX 2018; *TC-EMX*
- Concertgebouw O / Jochum
  Philips Universo 6580 145; also **4207 012**
- Orch des Bayerischen Rundfunks / Jochum
  Con CC 7526
- Chicago S O / Solti
  Decca SXL 6762; *KSXC*
- Hallé O / Loughran
  ASV ALH 908

*** Symphony nr. 5
*** Symphony nr. 6
- Concertgebouw O / Erich Kleiber
  Decca mono **417 637-2DH** [dig refurbished of LXT2851 (1/54)]
- Berliner Philharmoniker / Karajan
  DG DIg **DDD 413 932-2GH**

*** Symphony nr. 5
*** Symphony nr. 7
- Concertgebouw O / Haitink
  Philips (Digital Classics serie) **CD 420 540-2;** also: LP and *MC* (9/87)

***Symphony nr. 5 in c minor, Op. 67
***Symphony nr. 8 in F major, Op. 93
- Berliner Philharmoniker / Karajan
  DG Galleria 419 051-1; *-4;* and **-2GGA** [transfer from analogue recording 10/77: 2740 172]
- Philharmonia O / Otto Klemperer
  EMI **CDC7 47187-2**, [transfer from resp ED290252-1 and ED290328-1 (5/85)]
- Vienna Philharmonic / Bernstein
  DG **ADD 419 435-2GH**
  [live recording in 'Grosser Saal', Musikverein in Vienna in resp. 1977 and 1978; transfer from 2740 216 (3/80) and 2531 347 (12/78)]
- Vienna Philharmonic / Schmidt-Isserstedt
  Decca Jubilee JB5
- Münchener Philh / Kempe
  CFP 41 4415-1; *-4*

*** Symphony nr. 5
*** Symphony nr. 9
- Gueden, Wagner, Dermota, Weber, Wiener Singverein, Vienna Philharmonic / Erich Kleiber
  Decca France mono 1592118 (2LPs), [transfer from resp LXT2851 - 1/54 and LXT2725 (10/51)]
- London P O (5th); Harper, Watts, Young, McIntyre; London S Choir and Orch (9th) / Stokowsky
  Decca DPA 599/600

*** Symphony nr. 6, in F major, 'Pastoral'
- Concertgebouw O / Erich Kleiber
  Decca France mono 1592105 [transfer from LXT2851 (1/54)]

- Berliner Philharmoniker / Karajan
  from 1977-cycle, DG Galeria, 415 833-1GGA; also 415
  507-1GH - 6/86 and **-2GH** (6/86)
- New York Chamber O / Gerard Schwarz
  Delos/John Goldsmith CD Service **D/CD3017**
- Vienna Philharmonic / Karl Böhm
  DG Signature 413 977-1GS; [remastering from 1971; also
  413 932-1GS from12/85] and **413 721-2GX2**; -1; -4; from 5/
  86; [also DG 2530 142 (+ nr. 9); see below]
- Academy of St Martin-in-the-Fields / Marriner
  Philips dig 416 385-1PH; **-2PH**; 4PH
- Orch des Nordwest Deutschen Rundfunks / Günther
Wand
  German Harmonia Mundi **CDC7 47526-2**
- London P O / Klaus Tennstedt
  HMV dig EL270476-1; -4; **CDC7 47459-2**
- Philharmonia / Klemperer
  ED290253-1 (10/58 and 5/85); also HMV **CDC 747188-2**;
also ASD 2565
- Cleveland O / Christoph von Dohnányi
  Telarc/Conifer **CD80145**
- Vienna Philharmonic / Bernstein
  DG **ADD 413 779-2GH**
- Vienna Philharmonic / Abbado
  DG 419 779-1GH; 4GH; **2GH**
- Philharmonia O / Ashkenazy
  Decca Dig **410 003-2**; SXDL 7578
- Columbia S O / Walter
  CBS **MK 42012**; also 60107 [early 60's]
- Berliner Philharmoniker / Andre Cluytens
  CfP CFP 40017
- Philadelphia S O / Muti
  HMV ASD 3854
- Hallé O / Loughran
  ASV ALH 902
- London S O / Jochum
  EMI Em EMX 2019
- Concertgebouw O / Jochum
  Philips Seq 6527 045
- Philharmonia O / Sanderling
  HMV ASD 4154
- Leipzig Gewandhaus O / Masur
  Philips Fest 6570 133
- English CH O / Tilson-Thomas
  CBS 76825
- London P O / Haitink
  Philips 9500 256; 7300 544
- Concertgebouw O / Haitink
  Philips (Dig 09-88) **420 541-2**
- Chicago S O / Frits Reiner
  RCA Camden CCV 5053
- Royal P O / Kubelik
  Music for Pleasure Fanfare SIT 60039
- New York P O / Bernstein
  CBS **MK 42222**
- Columbia S O / Walter
  CBS **MK 42012**

*** Symphony nr. 6
*** Symphony nr. 8
- London P O / Klaus Tennstedt
  EMI **CDC7 47459-2** [transfer from EL270476-1 (1/87)]

*** Symphony nr. 6, 'Pastoral'
*** Symphony nr. 9,
- Norman, Fassbaender, Domingo, Berry, Konzertverein
Wiener Staatsopernchor, Vienna Philharmonic / Karl Böhm
  DG **ADD** and **DDD 413 721-2GX2** (2 discs) [transfers fróm

resp 2530 142 (2/72) and 2741 009 (11/81)]

*** Symphony nr.7 in A major, Op. 92
- Vienna Philharmonic / Carlos Kleiber
  DG **ADD 415 862-2GH** [transfer (dig remastered) of 2530
706, 9/76); also Signature 410 932-1GS (4/84)]
- Dresdner Staatskapelle / Jeffrey Tate
  EMI dig EL270544-1; -44; **CDC7 47815-2**
- English Ch O / Michael Tilson-Thomas
  CBS Dig M 39052
- Vienna Philharmonic / Bernstein
  DG 2531 313
- Royal P O / Colin Davis
  HMV SXLP 20038
- London S O / Colin Davis
  Philips 9500 219
- London S O / Jochum
  EMI Em EMX 2020
- Chicago S O / Solti
  Decca SXL 6764
- Vienna Philharmonic / Schmidt-Isserstedt
  Decca Jub JB4
- Orch des Bayerischen Rundfunks / Kubelik
  DG Priv 2535 252
- Staatskapelle Dresden / Kempe
  Orfeo d'or **DMM S 079 8321**
- Marlboro Fest O / Casals
  CBS 60126
- Philharmonia / Ashkenazy
  Decca Dig **411 941-2**; -1DH; -4 (1/84)
- Philharmonia / Klemperer
  EMI ED291341-1; -4; **CDM7 69183-2** [first transfer in
stereo of Columbia SAX2331 - 9/60]

*** Symphony nr. 7
*** Symphony nr. 8
- Vienna Philharmonic / Abbado
  DG 423 364-1GH; 4GH; **2GH**
  [live recordings in the 'Grosser Saal', Musikverein in
Vienna]
- New York Ph O / Bernstein
  CBS **MK 42223**
- Chicago S O / Giulini
  EMI Studio **CDM 7 69031 2**
- Philharmonia O / Klemperer
  HMV ED 290328-1; -4; (1955 stereo recording);
transfer on compact disc: **CDM 7 69183 2**
- Columbia S O / WALTER
  CBS **MK 42013**
- Berliner Philharmoniker / Furtwängler
  DG **ADD 415 660-2GH Mono**

*** Symphony nr. 8
- Berliner Philharmoniker / Karajan
  DG dig 415 507-1GH, idem **2GH**; idem -4GH
- Cleveland O / Dohnányi
  Telarc Dig **CD80090**
- Vienna Philharmonic / Abbado
  Con CC 7503

*** Symphony nr. 9, in d minor, Op. 125
- Murphy, Watkinson, Neill, Howell; Tallis Chamber Choir;
English Ch O / Tilson-Thomas [with nr. 8]
  CBS Masterworks dig 12M 39711 (2 LPs); M2T 39711;
  M2K 39711
- Smickova, Soukupova, Pribyl, Novak, Prague Philhar-
monic Choir, Czech Philharmonic O / Vaclav Neumann
  Denon **C37-7574**, [recorded concert Dec. 76 in Lucerne]

- Donath, Schmidt, König, Estes, Chor und S O des
Bayerischen Rundfunks / Colin Davis
  Philips dig 416 353-1PH; 4PH and 2PH
- Te Kanawa, Hamari, Burrows, Holl; London S Choir and
Orch / Jochum
  EMI EM EMX 2040; and EMI Studio **CDM 7 69030 2**
- Janowitz, Rössl-Majdan, Kmentt, Berry, Wiener
Singverein; Berliner Philharmoniker / Karajan [with nr. 8]
  from 1970 cycle (2740 172), DG Galeria, 415 832-1GGA
and **2GGA**
  also: **ADD 423 204-2GMW** (1988)
- Perry, Baltsa, Cole, Van Dam; Wiener Singverein; Berliner
Philh / Karajan
  DG **DDD 410 987-2GH** (1/85)
- Tomowa-Sintow, Baltsa, Schreier, Van Dam; Wiener
Singverein;
  B P / Karajan [with nr. 8]
- Vaness, Taylor, Jerusalem, Lloyd, Cleveland Chorus and
Orchestra / Christoph von Donahnyi
  Telarc/Conifer DG10120; **DG80120**
- Price, Finnilä, Laubenthal, Rintzler; Concertgebouw Choir
and Concertgebouw O / Haitink
  Philips Classics Dig **410 036-2PH** from 11/84
- Wiens, Hartwig, Lewis, Hermann, Opera Choir Hamburg,
Orch des Nordwest Deutschen Rundfunks / Günther Wand
  German Harmonia Mundi/EMI dig 169595-1; -4; **CDC7
47741-2**
- Chicago Symphony / Solti
  Decca Ovation series LP 417 486-1DB; 4DB (early '70's);
also:
- Norman, Runkel, Schunk, Sotin; Chicago Symphony
Chorus and O / Solti
  Decca dig 417 800-1DH; 4DH; **417 800-2DH**
- Lorengar, Minton, Burrows, Talvela, Chicago S Choir and
Orch / Solti
  Decca 6BB 121/2; KBB2 7041
- Napier, Reynolds, Brilioth, Ridderbusch, Ambrosian
Singers, New Philharmonia / Seiji Ozawa
  Philips **416 884-2PH** (of 6747119 from 1/75)
- Benackova, Lipovsek, Winbergh, Prey; Konzertver-
einigung Wiener Staatsopernchor; Wiener Philharmoniker /
Claudio Abbado
  DG dig 419 598-1GH; 4GH; **2GH**
  [live recording 'Grosser Saal', Musikverein in Vienna, May
1986]
- Kenny, Walker, Power, Salomaa; Schütz Choir, London
Classical Players / Roger Norrington
  EMI Dig EL749221-1; -4; **CDC7 49221-2**
- Schwarzkopf, Höngen, Hopf, Edelmann; Bayreuth Festival
Choir and O / Furtwängler
  HMV mono **CDC7 47081-2** (3/85)
- Curtin, Kopleff, McCollum, Gramm; Chicago Symphony
Choir and Orch / Fritz Reiner
  RCA Papillon mono **GD86532** [transfer from GD86532
(10/62)]
- Jones, Schwarz, Kollo, Moll; Wiener Staatsopernchor;
Vienna Philharmonic / Leonard Bernstein [with nr. 8]
  DG **ADD 410 859-2GH**
  [live recording Wiener Staats Oper (1979); transfer from
2740 216 (3/80)]
- Arroyo, Sarfaty, deVirfilio, Scott; the Juilliard Chorus, New
York P O / Bernstein
  CBS **MK 42224**
- Farrell, Merriman, Peerce, Scott; Robert Shaw Chorale;
NBC S O / Arturo Toscanini
  RCA Red Seal mono **RCCD 1005** and mono **RD85936**
[transfer from EMI ALP1039/40 (4/53)]
- Cundari, Rankin, Da Costa, Wildermann; Westminster

Choir; Columbia S O / Walter

  CBS **MK 42014**; 60506; *-40* ; [transfer MP/MPT39029]
- Norman, Fassbaender, Domingo, Berry; Chorus Wiener Staatsoper; Vienna Philharmonic / Böhm

  DG Dig 2741 009
- Harper, Watts, Young, McIntyre; London S Choir and Orch / Stokowsky

  Decca VIB 1
- Koszut, Fassbaender, Gedda, McIntyre; Münchener Ph Chor und Orch / Kempe

  CfP CFP 41 4418
- Sutherland, Horne, King, Talvela, Choir Wiener Staats Oper, Vienna Philharmonic / Hans Schmidt-Isserstedt
- Armstrong, Reynolds, Tear, Shirley-Quirk; London S Chorus and Orch / Giulini

  HMV SLS 841 (2 LPs)
- Tomowa-Sintow, Burmeister, Schreier, Adam, Dresdner Philh Chor, Berlin RIAS Chor, Leipzig Chor and Gewandhaus O / Masur

  Philips Silver Line **420 701-2PSL** [transfer from 6747 135 (9/75)]

The choice here is not a simple one. There are over 200 recordings, 19 complete sets (with many new releases of separate symphonies and complete cycles), 12 of which were performed by the world's most famous orchestras. More than half the recordings listed are of separate symphonies. A complete comparison would fill a book by itself. Here are just a few remarks concerning this incredible Beethoven harvest.

DRESDNER PHILHARMONIE/HERBERT KEGEL - Seen completely, this is not one of the grandest cycles. Musical vision and vitality are its strongest assets and it is really quite impressive. The orchestra sounds full and well balanced but are no match for, for example, Masur and the Gewandhaus Orchestra.

GEWANDHAUS ORCHESTRA/KURT MASUR - This set (on CD) is to be recommended despite the slight inconsistencies between symphonies. A music critic once said that this performance was reminiscent of Weingartner's pre-war Viennese concerts, a compliment indeed. Both the orchestra and its recorded sound are extremely good. The recordings were made between 1972 and 1974, but were very much improved when they were remastered in 1986.

WILLEM MENGELBERG - This cycle was recorded live in a series of concerts between April and November of 1940. Indeed, it is an historical document which preserves the Beethoven as was once played by one of the century's great conductors. The CDs are clear, the balance good and there are hardly any background noises. Mengelberg is brilliant but can be vulgar when his highly emotional vision goes just a bit too far. The Concertgebouw, Mengelberg and Beethoven are together an unforgettable institution, well-preserved in these recordings.

BERNARD HAITINK - Haitink's first cycle was made in 1975 with the London Philharmonic. The Eighth is the most impressive of that cycle, the Fifth the least successful. Haitink's second was recorded in 1987 with the Concertgebouw shortly before his departure from Amsterdam. This is a sparkling cycle. Both Haitink and his orchestra are in top form. For many, Haitink's second set of Beethoven is clearly a first choice.

WILHELM FURTWÄNGLER - Furtwängler never re-corded the complete Beethoven, unlike his fellow legends, Walter, Klemperer and Toscanini. Furtwängler hated studio recording sessions. Nevertheless HMV made a number of recordings in Vienna (1st, 2nd, 5th and 6th) that later formed the nucleus of a complete set. The 7th was recorded in 1951, the 2nd during a concert in the Albert Hall and the 8th with the Stockholm Philharmonic in Sweden. Furtwängler's greatness is evident throughout. He is the victim, however, of varying degrees of recording incompetence. It is not surprising that critics in the fifties preferred the Toscanini and Von Karajan versions. Furtwängler was especially famous for his Third Symphony, and this recording made in Vienna in 1944 is one of the most beautiful ever recorded.

COLUMBIA S O/BRUNO WALTER - Walter's cycle appeared in 1960 and was unanimously and internationally praised. More than twenty-five years later, collectors are still amazed by this legendary conductor. As was once said by Jeremy Noble, these are 'real interpretations'. His nervous energy is fantastic considering he was past eighty when he was recording. Columbia sounds magnificent, the woodwinds are unique, the brass brilliant, the strings excellent. The digital touch-up done at CBS sounds authentic. The Eroica and the Pastoral are the highlights of this impressive cycle.

LEONARD BERNSTEIN - Bernstein has recorded all nine symphonies with both the New York Philharmonic and the Viennese Philharmonic. The Eroica of the first is that set's best. The second set was made from live performances. Spontaneous and convincing as ever, Bernstein reaches a climax with his Ninth. Everything is powerful and dramatic.

EUGEN JOCHUM - Jochum is the noble representative of the important German conducting tradition. He is an undisputed master at Beethoven. All details are well expressed and the contrasts between the symphonies are never clearer as with Jochum. The Ninth is perhaps the best of the set.

HANS SCHMIDT-ISSERSTEDT - This cycle is consistent throughout and will give a great deal of listening pleasure. All the symphonies are well played and equally well recorded. There are no disappointments. The Ninth is especially well done thanks to superb soloists.

KURT SANDERLING - Sanderling is a lot like Klemperer in the way he handles Beethoven. Both chose strict and disciplined interpretations; there is nothing decorative about them. The First and Second Symphonies are so heavy that one is faintly reminded of 19th century traditions. The disappointing symphony is the Seventh. All in all, the sound is good, the digital recordings are clear, perhaps even a bit too clear. The Philharmonia strings suffer from this flat clarity.

OTTO KLEMPERER - For many, Klemperer's Beethoven is unequalled. He recorded the full cycle twice, the first in 1954 and the second a few years later in stereo. The Third, Fifth and Seventh from the first set were re-released in synthetic stereo. This sparkling set of the odd numbered symphonies is a monument to Klemperer's skills. The stoic Marche Funebre is the most impressive of all versions available. Part of the honour should go to Klemperer's equally legendary producer, Walter Legge. Only the Ninth is disappointing and that is due to the sloppy choir and uninteresting soloists. The Fifth is a masterpiece; its finale is unforgettable.

HERBERT VON KARAJAN - Von Karajan's Beethoven is considered to be in a class by itself by many listeners (and by the conductor himself). As a result of the overwelming publicity campaign that always accompanies his releases and the controversiality of his person, critics are clearly divided into two opposing camps: those who celebrate everything the maestro does, and those who are not impressed with mere prestige but thoughtfully search for deeper musical value. Von Karajan has recorded the whole set of Beethoven's nine symphonies four times.

SIR WILLIAM STERNDALE BENNETT (1816-75)

Symphony in g minor
- Milton Keynes Chamber O / Hilary David Welton

  Milton Keynes Music Series dig MKM861

(only available by postal order: Stables Theatre, Wavendon, Milton Keynes, Bucks)

This Symphony in g minor is the first piece by Bennett to be recorded. The Milton Keynes Chamber Orchestra is not well known. It consists of thirty young musicians, and their enthusiasm is wonderful. The strings are not as ripe as more renowned chamber players, but there is nothing wrong with their technique. The brass is also good. Their performance is neat and stylish. The music itself is perhaps too heavily influenced by Mendelssohn. The musical ideas wear a little thin, but the orchestration in itself is beautiful.

NIELS BENTZON (born 1919)

Symphony nr. 3, Op. 46
Symphony nr. 5 ('Ellipsis'), Op. 61
Symphony nr. 7 ('Three Version's'), Op. 83
- Aarhus City O / Schmidt

  Danish Music Anthology DMAO 56/7

Niels Viggo Bentzon wrote 14 symphonies and 15 piano concerti among the more than 450 works he produced. The quality of his writing is somewhat inconsistent; the symphonies date from his most successful period, however, pieces he wrote in the late forties and early fifties. The idiom reminds one of Nielsen, Hindemith and perhaps Stravinsky, but these symphonies definitely have an identity of their own. The most impressive is the Seventh which is more exciting than the other two. The recording sounds superb.

LUCIANO BERIO (born 1925)

Sinfonia
- Swingle Singers

  New York P O / Berio

  CBS 60259/40

Berio's Sinfonia was commissioned by the New York Philharmonic. The longest movement is a collage of material from Mahler's Second, Beethoven's Pastorale, La Valse by Ravel, Wagner's Reingold and Das

Rosenkavalier by Strauss. The Swingle Singers add their own improvisations. The whole piece is a spontaneous happening. The recording quality is excellent.

HECTOR BERLIOZ (1803-69)

Symphonie fantastique, Op.14
- Concertgebouw O / Sir Colin Davis
  Philips CD 411 425-2
- Philadelphia O / Ricardo Muti
  HMV Dig CDC 747278-2 (EL 270235)
- Berliner Philharmoniker / Karajan
  DG CD 415 352-2 (2530 597/3300 498
- Chicago Symphony O / Claudio Abbado
  DG Dig CD 410 985-2 (414 895-1/4)
- Montreal S O / Charles Dutoit
  Decca Dig CD 4141-203-2 (414 203-1/4)
- Orch Nationale de France / James Conlon
  Erato Dig CD ECD 88028 (NUM/MCE 7510)
- Cleveland O / Lorin Maazel
  Telarc Dig CD 80076 (DG 10076)
- New York P O / Zubin Mehta
  Decca Dig CD 400 046-2 (SXDL/KSXDC 7512)
- London S O / Païta
  Lodia CD LO-CD777
- Czech P O / Kosler
  Supraphon Dig CD C37 7722
- Berliner Philharmoniker / Barenboim
  CBS Dig CD MK39859 (IM / IMT 39859)
- Orchestre de Paris / Charles Münch
  HMV CD CDC747372-2
- Royal P O / Sir Thomas Beecham
  EMI TCC-POR 290115-9

Sir Colin Davis chose the Symphonie fantastique for his first recording with the Concertgebouw Orchestra in 1974. It is an impressive performance. The CD transfer is also an impressive improvement on the LP; there are more details and they are clearer. This CD is stronger than Abbado's made with the Chicago Symphony. Despite the fact that Abbado's cannot compete with all the masterly rivals, his performance is justified and very satisfying. There is a wonderful, dreamy quality to it and the Chicago Symphony is as polished as would be expected. Like Davis, Abbado added the cornet à piston part, imitating Klemperer's first performance.
Davis' earlier version with the London Symphony has less life and colour. The Concertgebouw Orchestra also creates more atmosphere in the slow movement. It is exciting right to the end. Davis is obviously a great interpreter of Berlioz.
Ricardo Muti combines his personal warmth and stubborn fierceness to perform Berlioz very well. Muti has greatly improved Philadelphia's sound. It does not equal what Dutoit achieves with the Montreal Symphony, however. Decca's realism is very difficult to rival. The spectacular and rich sound of the 1987 CD is the most important aspect of Dutoit's version. His interpretation is debatable in itself, especially his slow tempi, but the sound is heavenly. Von Karajan chooses an extremely personal interpretation. His Berlin instrumentalists can fortunately keep up with his Don-Quixote-like campaigns. Von Karajan's tempi are so surprising that they mesmerize. The analogue recording from 1975 is very attractive.

James Conlon is very open-hearted in the first movement. The Waltz sounds gallant if somewhat neurotic. The March creates a strong atmosphere but the Finale is less devilish than most. Maazel has recorded the piece within a space of a few years. The first, produced by CBS, is a disaster. The second, from Telarc, is much better but cannot compete with its rivals.
Zubin Mehta sounds very fresh but is not particularly special. Nevertheless, it is an extraordinary example of Decca's prowess. Poita inspires the London Symphony; the hysterical element, however, takes the upperhand early on and the structure is weakened. The Czechs obviously don't really understand this extremely French music. They play very well but the temperament is all wrong. Barenboims version with the Berlin Philharmonic is disappointing. Charles Munch recorded the Symphonie with the brand new Parisian Orchestra in 1967, but the result was terrible, both the performance and the sound. Pierre Monteux, the great French conductor, surprisingly had problems with his recording in 1952 (Decca). He was inappropriately paired up with the Vienna Philharmonic. In 1951 Van Beinum recorded the Symphonie with the Concertgebouw. No longer available, it was considered first rate for a long time. The only older recording still in the catalogues is Sir Thomas Beecham's performance with the National Orchestra of Radio France (1961). This recording is still considered a classic. This interpretation brings so much new detail to light and the sound is still fresh and exciting. It could even today, very easily win the extensive competition among Berlioz recordings.

LEONARD BERNSTEIN (born 1918)

Symphony nr. 1 (Jeremiah) ('with mezzo soloist')
Symphony nr. 2 ('The Age of Anxiety'), for piano and orchestra
- Israel P O / Bernstein / Lukas Foss pno
  DG CD 415 964-2
Symphony nrs 1 and 2
Symphony nr. 3 (Kaddish)
- Israel P O / composer
  (in nr. 3) boys' choir, Christa Ludwig, Foss, Caballé;
Wager (speaker)
  DG 2709 077

The possibilty to hear Bernstein's music anew, thanks to the CD procedure, will undoubtedly make many sceptical about his music. The Jeremiah Symphony was written when Bernstein was only 20, and despite all, does contain an impressive Lamentation for mezzo-soprano. The Second Symphony is inspired by a poem by W.H. Auden as the title suggests. The Third Symphony is the most impressive. It was written in memory of President Kennedy. The new version makes the underlying discussion between God and man, heaven and earth, much clearer.
The Israel Philharmonic is not as polished as the New York orchestra. The performances are also less powerful than the earlier ones led by Bernstein himself. The composer's warmth is translated well in the old version and the improvement made by the new CD's is immeasurable.

FRANZ BERWALD (1797-1868)

Symphony nr. 1 in g minor (Symphonie)
Symphony nr. 3 in C major (Symphonie)
- Royal P O / Björlin
  HMV Green ESD/TC-ESD 135470
Symphony nr. 1 in g minor
Symphony nr. 2 in D major (Capricieuse)
Symphony nr. 3 in C major
Symphony nr. 4 in E flat
- Gothenburg S O / Neeme Järvi
  DG Dig CD 415 502-2 (415 502-1/4)

Berwald's symphonies were composed in the early 1840's. The Singulière is generally thought to be the most beautiful and it surely is an original piece for its time. Berwald's originality has always been more neglected than it should have been. Björlin leads the Royal Philharmonic in a good performance. It lacks bite, however, and power, but it seems that it was made during a heat wave. The sound, for mid-seventies standards, is good. The transfer to the cassette is not as good.
Neeme Järvi made the CD début of Bergwald's first four symphonies in 1986. These recordings leave all other Berwald recordings far behind. The orchestra plays with energy and spirit. The acoustics of their hall are also perfectly suited to the music. The CD sounds excellent, every detail is extremely clear.

GEORGES BIZET (1838-75)

Symphony in C major
- French National O / Sir Thomas Beecham
  HMV SXLP 30260
- Academy of St Martin-in-the-Fields / Neville Marriner
  Decca Jub 410 167-1/4
- New York P O / Bernstein
  CBS 60112/40
- Orch de la Suisse Romande / Alexander Gibson
  Con. CC/CCT 7562
- London S O / Roberto Benzi
  Philips Seq 6527/7311
- Concertgebouw O / Bernard Haitink
  Philips 9500 443/7300 649
- French National O / Ozawa
  HMV Dig ASD/TCC-ASD 143339-1/4

The recordings listed here are new releases of performances Sir Thomas Beecham made in the sixties. The sound and resonance are both quite good. They are not as polished as that which Neville Marriner achieves with his Academy. The fury of their finale is really wonderful; unfortunately, the Decca technicians used a little too much acoustics. In the Haitink version, the slow movement is especially appealing and the oboe solo is very fine. The acoustic qualities of the Concertgebouw are wide and full. Benzi's interpretation (1966) competes easily with Marriner's and even with Beecham's. The LSO sounds dedicated to its conductor here. The later version with Ozawa conducting the French is also an excellent recording, but there are many who will prefer the lively sound in either the Haitink or Beecham LP. Leonard Bernstein's performance is brilliant; the last two movements are especially exciting.

ARTHUR BLISS (1891-1975)

A Colour Symphony
- Royal P O / Sir Charles Groves
  HMV ASD 3416

The Colour Symphony dates from 1922. This is the first recording made since the composer conducted one himself in the mid-fifties. The story goes that Bliss, inspired by a book that concerned heraldry, composed this series of mood paintings that expounds upon the symbolic meaning of the primary colours. The piece is too episodic to really be considered a symphony. Nevertheless, the music is very effective, having been orchestrated by a great craftsman. The composition is rightly done by this appealing performance.

ERNEST BLOCH (1880-1959)

Israel Symphony (1916)
- Viennese State Opera O / Litschauer
  Vanguard (Nixa) 423
Sinfonia Breve (1953)
- Minneapolis S O / Antal Dorati
  Mercury SRI 75116

Bloch was a Swiss Jew who emigrated to America and wrote most of his works there, explaining why there are so many more recordings available there than in Europe. Many music lovers find Bloch's work difficult to approach. There are also those who find him simply depressing. Nevertheless, Bloch's music impresses with its deep authority. The Viennese recording of the Symphony is particularly good. Both the recording and the performance of the Sinfonia are superb. It remains, however, a very sombre composition.

KARL-BIRGER BLOMDAHL (1916-68)

Symphony nr. 3 (Facetter)
- Stockholm P O / Ehrling
  Cap CAP 1251

Blomdahl was the most influential of men in the Swedish musical world directly following the war. The première of his Third Symphony in 1950, sent shock waves through that world. The 'Aspects' (Facetter) referred to in the title are the tonal possibilities created by the twelve tone system, which are presented in the beginnng of the work. The Ehrling recording is the only one available, and dates from the early sixties.

LUIGI BOCCHERINI (1743-1805)

6 Symphonies, Op. 35: nr. 1 in D major; nr. 2 in E flat major; nr. 3 in A major; nr. 4 in F major; nr. 5 in E flat major; nr. 6 in B flat major
- I Filharmonici di Bologna / Ephrikian
  Telefunken FK 6.35021

Considering that Luigi Boccherini wrote nearly as

much music as Mozart, it would be logical to think him second rate due to the limited number of recordings offered. This is simply untrue. Boccherini's work gives evidence of a great craftsman; his melodies radiate true beauty. His touch was light, but no lighter than Haydn's. Boccherini was able to produce very expressive melancholy, an example being the slow movement of his famous cello concerto. It was none other than Carlo Maria Giulini who conducted the Philharmonia Orchestra in the Symphonies in c minor and E flat major for Columbia in the late fifties. The first of these is a delicious piece; the second is very reminiscent of Haydn. The late recordings (I Filharmonici) miss the highly disciplined approach necessary for these subtle works. The gracious cantilena from the slow movement of the Third Symphony, and the Andante from the Sixth, are especially compelling examples of Boccherini's talent.

ARRIGO BOITO (1842-1918)

Sinfonia in a minor
- Monte Carlo Opera O / Claudia Scimone
  Erato STU 71040

This is an interesting, if not very important novelty. There are no other recordings to compare it with. The performance as well as the recording are faultless.

ALEXANDER BORODIN (1833-87)

Symphony nr. 1, E flat
Symphony nr. 2, b minor
Symphony nr. 3, a minor ('Unfinished')
- USSR Academy S O / Svetlanov
  Chant du Monde LDX 78781/2; K331/2
Symphonies nrs 1 and 3
- USSR Academy S O / Svetlanov
  Chant du Monde CD LDC 278 781
Symphonies nrs 1 and 2 and 3
- Toronto S O / Andrew Davis
  CBS 79214
Symphony nr. 2
- Concertgebouw O / Kondrashin
  Philips 412 070-1/4
- USSR Academy S O / Svetlanov
  Chant du Monde CD LDC 278 272
- Mexico State S O / Bátiz
  ASV (Academy Sound and Vision) Dig ABM/ZCABM 761
- Orchestre de la Suisse Romande / Varviso
  Con CC/CCT 7533

Borodin's work has always been very heavily directed by the likes of Rimsky-Korsakov and Glazunov. Many consider this appropriate. Svetlanov's version is livelier and very characteristic, but western listeners will not find the Russian orchestra in the least bit subtle. Svetlanov's performances are the first to appear on CD. They are technically merely acceptable.
The clear, modern digital sound of the Bátiz recording is preferable. It does make obvious how dependent a conductor is on his technicians, as dependent as he has always been on his musicians. Bátiz's interpretation is inspired. Bátiz takes the first movement quite quickly, reminiscent of the famous recording

led by Jean Martinon with the London Symphony (still available on Decca SPA 281). The slow movement is expressive and the horn solo lovely, but the last scherzo is too much for the Mexican orchestra. Perhaps due to too much repetition, their level is not that of the top European ensembles.
Kondrashin's interpretation is fresh and to the point. Unfortunately, there are noises in the background and a terrible intonation mistake in the slow movement.
Contour has re-released the Second Symphony. It is originally a Decca recording from their golden year 1969, performed by Varviso with the Swiss. The recording is superb, very colourful and it has a brilliant sound. It easily surpasses the recordings Ansermet made with the same orchestra.

WILLIAM BOYCE (1710-79)

Symphonies nrs 1-8
- Bournemouth Sinfonietta / Ronald Thomas
  CRD CD 3413 (CRD 1056/CRDC 4056)
- Academy SMF / Marriner
  Argo ZRG/KZRC 874
Symphonies nrs 4, F major; 5, D major; 8, d minor
- Lucerne Festival O / Baumgartner
  DG Archive Priv 2547/3347 054

Both the Bournemouth recording and the Academy's version are excellent. The symphonies themselves are first class examples of the refined English baroque. Both performances are wonderfully subtle. Thomas especially gives the pieces a shine that his technicians have picked up perfectly. The microphones were probably set up a good distance from the players: the balance is perfect. The tempi are also a little fresher than those Marriner uses. Nevertheless, the Academy's recording is wonderful, using the full acoustics of St John's, Smith Square. The Baumgartner still sounds fresh; it was made in the mid-sixties.

JOHANNES BRAHMS (1833-97)

*** Symphonies nrs 1 to 4
- Columbia S O / Bruno Walter
  CBS M3P/ 3PT 39631 ; (recordings from 1959-60);
  MK 42020 (9/86)
- Wiener Philharmoniker / Böhm
  DGG 2740 154 (4 LPs)
  DG Walkman 413 424-4
- London S O / Boult
  HMV SLS 5009 (4 LPs)
- Philharmonia / Klemperer
  HMV SLS 804 (4 LPs)
  EMI 1C 137 50034/7
- Cleveland O / Szell
  CBS 77 356 (3 LPs)
- Wiener Philharmoniker / Kertesz
  Decca SXLH 6610/13
- Berliner Philharmoniker / Karajan
  DGG 2721 075 (4 LPs)
  1982: DG 2740 193/ 3371 041 (1978 cycle)
  1984: DG 2740 275; 3378 120 (1963-64)
- Gewandhaus O Leipzig / Masur
  Philips 6769/6799 109

- Wiener Philharmoniker / Bernstein
  DG 2741/ *3378* 023; **410 081/4-2**
- Chicago S O / Solti
  Decca D 151 D 4/ *K 151/K 44* (9/79); **421 074-2DM4** [4 discs]
  (12/87)
- Cleveland O / Maazel
  Decca D39 D4
- Philharmonia of New Philharmonia / Giulini
  HMV SLS 5241 (the early 60's)
- Orch des Norddeutschen Rundfunks / Günter Wand
  German Harmonia Mundi/EMI dig DMM EX 155532-3 [2 LPs]
  (11/85)
  EMI **CDC 169530-2** (11/85)

*** Symphony nr. 1 in c minor, Op. 68
- Columbia S O / Walter
  CBS **MK 42020** (9/86)
- Wiener Philharmoniker / Kertesz
  Decca Pickwick CC/ *CT* 7613 (the early 70's)
- Berliner Philharmoniker / Keilberth
  Orfeo **C 070101A**
- Dresdner Staatskapelle / Sanderling
  RCA Gold GL/*GK* 25191
- S O des Norddeutschen Rundfunks / Wand
  EMI and German Harmonia Mundi Dig **1C 567 199974-2**; 1C
  067 99974
- RAI Milano / Celibidache
  Movimento Musica, Anal, **011 003**
- Chicago S O / Solti
  Decca **414 458-2**; SXL/*KSXC* 6924
- Los Angeles P O / Giulini
  DG Dig **410 023-2**; 2532/ *3302* 056
- Wiener Philharmoniker / Bernstein
  DG Dig **410 081-2**; 410 081-1/4
- London P O / Tennstedt
  HMV Dig **CDC 74029-2**; EL 270019-1/*4*
- Wiener Pilharmoniker / Furtwängler
  HMV mono ED 270124-1
- Concertgebouw O / Mengelberg
  Philips mono **416 210-2**
- Concertgebouw O / Haitink
  Philips 6500 519
- Concertgebouw O/ Kondrashin
  Philips 412 064-1/*4*
- NBC S O / Toscanini
  RCA mono **RCCD 1007**
- Phiharmonia / Klemperer
  HMV SXLP 30 217
- Berliner Philharmoniker / Karajan
  DG 2531/*3301* 131; and DG Acc 2542/*3342* 166 (1st
  recording)
  DG dig **423 141-2GH**; 1GH; *4GH* (2nd recording)
- London P O / Jochum
  EMI Em EMX/*TC-EMX* 41 2023-1/*4*
- Hallé O / Loughran
  CfP CFP/*TC-CFP* 4387
- Cleveland O /Dohnanyi
  Teldec ASV dig **8 43479**; 6-; *4-*
- National P O / Païta
  Lodia/John Goldsmith dig **LO-CD 779**; LOD 779
- Hallé O / Stanislaw Skrowaczewski
  Pickwick IMP Classics **PCD 882**
- S O des Bayerischen Rundfunk / Kubelik
  Orfeo dig **C 070101A**

*** Symphony nr. 1
*** Symphony nr. 4, e minor, Op. 98
- resp. Berliner Philharmoniker and Wiener Philharmoniker /

Karl Böhm
  DG Walkman *413 424-4*

*** Symphony nr. 2, D major, Op. 73
- Los Angeles P O / Giulini
  DG Dig **400 066-2** (3/83)
- Concertgebouw O / Kondrashin
  Philips 412 066-1/ *4*
- S O des Norddeutschen Rundfunks / Wand
  German Harmonia Mundi Dig 1C 067 169519-1; **CDC7
  47871-2** (6/87)
  also: EMI EX155532 (2/87)
- Columbia S O / Walter
  CBS **MK 42021** (recorded 1960)
- Wiener Philharmoniker / Bernstein
  DG Dig **410 082-2**; 410 082-1/ *4* (1/84)
- Chicago S O / Solti
  Decca Dig **414 487-2DH** - 8/85; transfer from SXL 6925
- Berliner Philharmoniker / Karajan
  (1) DG Acc 2542/*3342* 167 (11/64) (6/82)
  (2) DG 2531/*3301* 132 (5/59)
  (3) DG dig **423 142-2GH**; 1GH; *4GH* (11/87)
- Philharmonia / Karajan
  1957 recorded: HMV SXLP 30513 (5/81)
  EMI Studio **C 070201**
- London P O / Jochum
  EMI Em EMX/*TC-EMX* 41 2024-1/*4*
- Wiener Philharmoniker / Kertesz
  Decca Jub JB/*KJBC* 83
- Hallé O / Loughran
  CfP CFP/*TC-CFP* 4388
- London P O / Boult
  HMV SXLP/*TC-SXLP* 30529
- S O des Bayerischen Rundfunks / Kubelik
  Orfeo dig **C 070201**
- Royal Liverpool Ph O / Marek Janowski
  ASV dig DCA547

*** Symphony nr. 2
*** Symphony nr. 3
- Wiener Philharmoniker / Böhm
  DG Walkman *415 334-4*

*** Symphony nr. 3, F major, Op. 90
- Wiener Philharmoniker / Bernstein
  DG Dig **410 083-2**; 410 083-1/ *4*
- Chicago S O /Solti
  Decca **414 488-2**; SXL/*KSXC* 6902
- Concertgebouw O/ Haitink
  Philips Seq 412 358-1/ *4*
- Residentie O / Lombard
  Residentie O **CD 56**
- Columbia S O / Walter
  CBS **MK 42022**
- Chicago S O / Reiner
  RCA VICS/*VK* 2043
- Cleveland O / Szell
  BS Anal **MYK 42531**
- Philharmonia / Klemperer
  HMV SXLP/*TC-SXLP* 30255
- Berliner Philharmoniker / Karajan
  DG 2531/ *3301* 133
  DG Acc 2542/*3342* 168
- Wiener Philharmoniker / Karajan
  Decca SET 231 (9/62); Ovation **417 744-2DM** (4/88)
- Dresdner Staatskapelle / Sanderling
  RCA Gold GL/*GK* 25216
- S O des Bayerischen Rundfunks / Kubelik

Orfeo **C 070301** (5/84)
- London P O / Jochum
  EMI Em EMX/*TC-EMX* 41 2025-1/4
- London S O / Boult
  EMI Anal **CDM 769 2032**
- Hallé O / Loughran
  CfP CFP/*TC-CFP* 4389
- Royal Liverpool P O / Janowski
  ASV dig DCA556
- Wiener Philharmoniker / Kertesz
  Decca Jub JB/*KJBC* 84

*** Symphony nr. 4, e minor, Op. 98
- Wiener Philharmoniker / Carlos Kleiber
  DG Dig **400 037-2GH** (9/85), from 2532/ *3302* 003 (4/81)
- Chicago S O / Solti
  Decca **414 563-2**; SXL 6890
- Royal Liverpool P O / Janowski
  ASV Dig DCA/*ZCDCA* 533
- Columbia S O / Walter
  CBS **MK 42023**
- Wiener Philharmoniker / Bernstein
  DG Dig **410 084-2**; 410 084-1/ *4*
- Berliner Philharmoniker / Karajan
  DG 2531/*3301* 134
  DG Acc 2542/*3342* 169
- Philharmonia O / Karajan
  HMV SXLP/*TC-SXLP* 30505 (5/81); **CDM7 69228-2** (4/88)
- Philharmonia O / Klemperer
  HMV SXLP 30214
- Wiener Philharmoniker / Kertesz
  Decca Jub JB/*KJBC* 85
- Concertgebouw O / Haitink
  Philips Seq 6527/*7311* 143
- London P O / Jochum
  EMI Em EMX/*TC-EMX* 2026
- Hallé O / Loughran
  CfP CFP/*TC-CFP* 4390
- Cleveland O / Dohnányi
  Teldec/ASV dig **8 43678**; 6/-; 4/-
- Royal P O / Previn
  Telarc/Conifer **CD 80155**
- S O des Norddeutschen Rundfunks / Wand
  German Harmonia Mundi/Conifer dig **1C567 169530-2**
  and EMI **CDC7475892**
- S O des Bayerischen Rundfunks / Kubelik
  Orfeo dig **C 070401A**

VON KARAJAN CYCLE - When this discography
went to print, the Von Karajan cycle was 25 years old
(1963-1964). The whole set is masterly, and for
many, unrivalled. The second cycle has been successfully transferred to cassette. Comparing the
two, Von Karajan's ideas have stayed the same for
the most part. The Third Symphony is an exception:
it is more powerful the second time around, and less
mannered. The sound in the second set is less
flattering for Berlin than in the first.
KLEMPERER CYCLE - Klemperer's set will always
remain a classic. The remastering has improved it a
great deal. It has almost magical power, especially,
for example, in the Second Symphony. It is hard to
imagine more perfect Brahms.
BOULT CYCLE - When it was first released, this set
was highly praised. It is still one of the best. Boult
gives the music nobility; the performance is pure and
convincing. The Fourth is perhaps a bit too sober.
The First, on the other hand, was for a long time

considered to be the best in the catalogues. The Second has also been often honoured for its extraordinary spontaneity. This cycle is surely worthy of Boult's reputation.

KERTESZ CYCLE - Kertesz leads the Viennese through a wonderful performance. Everything has been considered and well-balanced and all the details are clear. Nothing is exaggerated and the listener is never disappointed. The Decca technicians amaze anew.

SZELL CYCLE - Szell was known for his endless rehearsals. These do pay off in an extremely disciplined orchestra as can be heard in his Brahms. It is all superb, but lacks warmth and spontaneity. The sound is also disappointing when compared with the others here.

BOHM CYCLE - Bohm's set is as whimsical of interpretation as is this conductor's habit. One must take into consideration, however, that Bohm studied the scores with Mandyczewski, a lifelong friend of Brahm's. The slow movements loose their tension because of the extremely slow tempi. The recording sounds flat, especially the strings, something that has been improved, by the way, on the transfer to Walkman.

SOLTI CYCLE - Solti approached Brahms after 25 years of experience in the recording studios. He had expressly neglected the symphonies up until that time. It is clearly to be heard in this performance that Solti studied every aspect of this work before daring to record. Those who think of Solti as a lover of sensation and excitement should listen carefully. His Brahms is sober and well thought out. The orchestra is sublime and the Decca technicians should be very proud of their lively, detailed sound.

MAAZEL CYCLE - The clarity, fullness and shine that the Decca technicians give the Cleveland Orchestra is amazing. Unfortunately, Maazel's interpretaton is unsatisfying. Often the playing is cold and lifeless. Maazel is more successful with Brahms in the concert hall. Still, many consider his performance: 'Von Karajan with an American accent'.

GIULINI CYCLE - These recordings were made in the sixties and released only in the eighties. Giulini presents himself as a great Brahms interpreter. Especially in the First and Second Symphonies, Giulini forces nothing and lets the music create its own drama. The sound in the Fourth is disappointing.

BERNSTEIN CYCLE - As is often the case with records Bernstein makes, these were made in the concert hall before an audience and mixed and matched later in the studio. The spontaneity of such performances is unequalled. Bernstein does play a little too much with the score, however, and one hears more Bernstein than Brahms in some sections. He performs like a Dr Jekyll and Mr Hyde, sometimes brilliant, sometimes cheap. The driving force that is Bernstein is amazing, and his instrumentalists give their all for this controversial conductor.

WALTER CYCLE - Walter recorded this set in the early sixties in the CBS studios just before his death. They have stood the test of time well and the remastered version has cost them nothing. The instruments are well balanced, something often neglected in more recent recordings. Walter is often criticized for his extreme romanticism. He chooses alternative tempi, to be sure, but holds these tempi fast in spite

of the dramatic musical development. His romanticism has a discipline of its own it would seem. Walter is in complete control of the score, especially the first two movements of the First Symphony give us Walter at his best. The Second is also very appealing.

MASUR CYCLE - This is a disappointing set that quickly bores. The orchestra's playing is technically excellent but has no character. A grey performance recorded perhaps on a grey day.

WAND CYCLE - All the ingredients necessary for wonderful Brahms can be found here. This is a marvellous orchestra and a talented conductor. The long lines of the symphonies are beautifully built up; no showy elements are needed. Wand's heritage is the old, German, romantic school that started back with Max Fielder in the Philharmonie in Hamburg (1904). Wand was 74 when he recorded this cycle. His energy is amazing for any age and his interpretations are fiery, electric even. Only Bruno Walter's unforgettable Third Symphony surpasses Wand's performance.

SANDERLING CYCLE -The beautiful Dresden Staats-Kapelle is wonderful in this set. Sanderling leads them well especially in the First and Third Symphonies. The Second is a bit mannered, but Sanderling's Third is perhaps the very best available.

JOCHUM CYCLE - Jochum conducts an English orchestra but sounds every bit the German. His passion for Brahms is evident in the natural expression and complete concentration in his performance. The drama in the First is as natural as the tides. Jochum repeats the exposition in the first movement, something few do. This First Symphony is the highpoint of this cycle. The Fourth is fascinating from the first to the last note. Musically, this cycle threatens Von Karajan's crown. The sound quality is also better than both the Von Karajan and Klemperer sets.

HAITINK CYCLE - Haitink's performance, looking back 18 years, is still excellent. It was recorded by Philips in the early seventies. The Concertgebouw again distinguishes itself in attack, intonation and homogeneity. The Third Symphony, the most difficult of them all, is the best in this cycle. Haitink's command of the score is extraordinary and his obvious affection for the music is evident throughout.

JAMES LOUGHRAN CYCLE - This is a wonderful set and is proof that Loughran is a great Brahms interpreter. The First is fresh from beginning to end and is reminiscent of the great Boult version. The winds are not ideal but the strings have the right feeling for Brahms. The Second has a natural warmth that stays interesting. All repeats are peformed. The Fourth is also wonderfully straightforward. Brahms is allowed to speak for himself. Barbirolli recorded the Brahms with the Hallé Orchestra as well, but long ago. Concerning separate recordings of single symphonies, not part of any set, the following are recommended: Frits Reiner (3rd), Kondrashin (2nd), Mengelberg (1st), Tennstedt (1st), Carlos Kleiber (4th). Some older recordings that can still be recommended: Walter (1st and 3rd), Boult (2nd), Klemperer (1st) and Jochum (4th).

HAVERGAL BRIAN (1876-1972)

Symphony nr. 8 in B flat major
Symphony nr. 9 in a minor
- Royal Liverpool P O / Sir Charles Groves
  HMV ASD 3486
Symphony nr. 10 in c minor
Symphony nr. 21 n E flat major
- Leicestershire Schools S O / Loughran (nr. 10) and Pinkett (nr. 21)
  Uni UNS 265

A group of dedicated admirers set about getting at least part of Brian's compositions recorded about ten years ago. They were convinced that recording companies had shamefully neglected Brian, favouring instead dubious works by the avant-garde. Lyrita had at least recorded both the Sixth and Seventh Symphonies.

Groves gives an able performance of the Ninth, a clearly powerful work with a wonderful atmosphere. The Eighth Symphony is more complicated and really much more puzzling. The performance is also less convincing. Lovers of Mahler will never find the harmonic structure in Brian's work too difficult. His work unfortunately does not enjoy a wide audience, at least not yet. This recording was made in 1978 and released again in 1986. Both the Tenth and the Twenty-First Symphonies have been recorded only once, and those by amateurs. Brian wrote the Tenth as an elderly man, and the Twenty-First when he was over 80. There is no need for caution concerning the unknown orchestra performing here: what they have produced sounds surprisingly successful.

BENJAMIN BRITTEN (1913-76)

Sinfonietta, Op.1
- English Ch O / Del MAr
  Lyrita SRCS 111
Simple Symphony (for strings), Op. 4
- Scottish Baroque Ensemble / Friedman
  Abbey ABY 810
Sinfonia da requiem
Spring Symphony
- London S O / Andre Previn
  HMV SLS/TCC-SLS 5266
Spring Symphony, Op. 44
- Sheila Armstrong / Janet Baker / Robert Tear / St Clement Dane's School Boys' Choir / London S O / André Previn
  HMV ASD/TC-ASD 3650 (4/79)
  ED 29 1047-1 (10/86)
  EMI CD CDC747667-2
Spring Symphony
Simple Symphony for strings
- Jennifer Vyvyan, Norma Procto, Peter Pears, Wandsworth School Boys' Choir / English Ch O / composer
  Decca 410 171-1DJ (3/84)
Sinfonia da requiem (i)
Symphony for cello and orchestra, Op. 68 (ii)
- (ii) Rostropovich / English Ch O / composer
- (ii) Wallfisch / English Ch O / Steuart Bedford
  Chandos Dig CD CHAN8363 (ABRD/ABDT 1126)
- (i) New Philharmonia O / composer (1965)
  Decca SXL 6641

The Simple Symphony is a light work. The Scots play

it with energy, but most rival recordings are better. The best is the one led by the composer himself, collected in a series called 'Britten conducts English music' (Decca SXL 6405) and released later as a separate LP together with the Spring Symphony. Decca has again recorded beautifully (originally for the BBC in 1961), and the English Chamber Orchestra's playing under Britten is sublime.

The Spring Symphony was also recorded by Previn in 1979 and transferred to digital in 1986. It differs slightly from the Britten version in terms of accents. The highpoint is Dame Janet Baker's rendition of Auden's poem in the second movement. Baker sings with a marvellous, dark intensity. Britten's 1961 version for Decca has faster tempi and sharper accents than Previn's. Previn's LP was greatly praised technically when it appeared in 1979, but the transfer to the CD sounds plastic.

Comparing the two versions of the Sinfonia da requiem, Previn's is warmer whereas Britten's is generally accepted as definitive. The Previn version is a good alternative, nevertheless.

Rostropovich plays the cello concerto better than anyone else. It is perhaps a bit dated now, but this is probably the most difficult of Britten's works to appreciate. It takes a good 35 minutes. The recording is fine and the ECO play very well under the composer. The new version of the concerto with Raphael Walfisch, does follow the score more carefully. The score requests the soloist to play 'as first among equals' and not in a prominent, virtuoso manner, distant from the orchestra.

MAX BRUCH (1838-1920)

Symphony nr. 2 in f minor, Op. 36
- Leipzig Gewandhaus O / Kurt Masur
  Philips Digital 411 121-1

The fame of Bruch's Kol Nidrei and his violin concerto overshadow the varied talents of this composer. Bruch also composed two mature symphonies one shortly after the other, in 1868 and 1870. The second is an ambitious work in three movements with its roots clearly grounded in the Leipzig tradition. It is very reminiscent of Schumann. On the one hand, the musical ideas are difficult to recollect, on the other, the orchestration is very well designed. As always with Bruch, there reigns a certain dignity and thoughful determination, but in spite of these, his music cannot carry the weight of a symphony form.

For those who dare to stray from the beaten path, the Gewandhaus Orchestra performance is surely worthy of listening. The recording is warm and naturally in balance; the cassette is of an excellent quality.

ANTON BRUCKNER (1824-96)

*** Symphony nr. 0 (die Nulte), d minor (rev. 1969)
Nr 00, f minor (1863) (Study Symphony)
- USSR State S O / Gennadi Rozhdestvensky
  Le Chant du Monde/Harmonia Mundi LDX78 851/2; **LDC278 851/2**

*** Symphonies nrs 0; 1-9
- Concertgebouw O / Haitink
  Philips 6717 002
- Chicago S O / Barenboim
  DG 2740 253

*** Symphonies nrs 1-9
- Berliner Philharmoniker / Karajan
  DG 2740 264 (dig remastered 6/82) [recording 1975]; **415 985-2GH** (1865 version)
- Dresdner Staatskapelle / Jochum
  HMV SLS 5252 [recording 10 years after SOBR, see below]
- S O des Bayerischen Rundfunks / Jochum
  DG 2740 136

*** Symphony nr. 1, c minor
- Berliner Philharmoniker / Karajan
  DG Dig 2532/*3302* 062
- Concertgebouw O / Haitink
  Philips Seq 6527/*7311* 142
- Bavarian State O / Carlos Kleiber
  Orphelia S145851A (9/86)
- Bavarian State O / Sawallisch
  Orfeo **C14585** (12/86)
- Wiener Philharmoniker / Abbado
  Decca SXL 6494
- Dresdner Staatskapelle / Jochum
  HMV ASD/*TC-ASD* 3825 (Nowak edition 1866 version)
- Wiener Philharmoniker / Knappertsbusch
  Decca LXT 2967 (1954)

*** Symphonies nrs 1 and 5
- Berliner Philharmoniker / Karajan
  DG **415 985-2GH** (2 discs) resp 2740 264 (2/82) and 2702 101 (10/78)
  [the 5th dates from 1975 and is dig remastered]

*** Symphony nr. 2, c minor
- Concertgebouw O / Haitink
  Philips 6527/*7311* 183; also 80 2912 (Haas edition)
- Berliner Philharmoniker / Karajan
  415 988-2GH, transfer from DG Dig 2532/*3302* 063 (12/82) (Haas edition)
- Wiener Philharmoniker / Giulini
  HMV ASD 3146 (Nowak edition)
- Wiener Philharmoniker / Horst Stein
  Decca SXL 6681

*** Symphony nr. 3, d minor
- Berliner Philharmoniker / Karajan
  DG Dig **413 362-2**; 2532/*3302* 007 (7/81) (1888-89 version)
- Wiener Philharmoniker / Böhm
  Decca Jub JB/*KJBC* 126
- S O des Bayerischen Rundfunks / Kubelik
  CBS Dig **MK 39033**; IM/*IMT 39033* (1876-77 version)
- Concertgebouw O / Haitink
  Philips 835217 and SAL 3506 (7/65) (1876-77 version)
- RIAS S O Berlin / Chailly
  Decca 417-1DH (6/86); / -**2DH**; *4DH* (version 1889)
- S O des Hessischen Rundfunks / Inbal
  Teldec/Conifer dig ZK8- / *AZ4*- / **ZK8 - 42922**, transfer from GK 35642 (6/84)
- S O des Bayerischen Rundfunks / Jochum
  DG 2707 116

*** Symphony nr. 3
*** Symphony nr. 4
*** Symphony nr. 8

- S O des Hessischen Rundfunks (Frankfurt) / Inbal
  Tel Dig GK6/*CX4* 35642 [4 records]
  (4th) Tel **ZK8 42921**

*** Symphony nr. 4, e minor ('Romantic')
- Berliner Philharmoniker / Karajan
  DG 2530/*3300* 874 (10/76); **415 277-2**
  also EMI Studio **CDM7 69006-2**, transfer from SLS811 (1/72)
  HMV Master Series EG 290566-1/4 (1/72) and SLS 5086
- Berliner Philharmoniker / Jochum
  DGG Priv 2535 111
- S O des Bayerischen Rundfunks / Jochum
  DGM 19057-8 (12/57)
- Concertgebouw O / Haitink
  Philips 6599 729 (2/68), Philips Seq 6527/*7311* 101, (11/81)
- Wiener Philharmoniker / Haitink
  Philips **412 735-2PH**, / 1PH, / *4PH*
- Berliner Philharmoniker / Muti
  HMV Dig **CDC 747352-2**, transfer from EL 270379 (3/86)
- Chicago S O / Solti
  Decca Dig **410 550-2**; SXDL/ *KSXDC* 7538 (8/81), and EG 290566-1 (1/72) (4/86), also 2530 674 (10/76)
- Wiener Philharmoniker / Böhm
  Decca Jub Anal JB/*KJBC* 120 (1973); **411 581-2DH** (5/85) (revised)
- Berliner Philharmoniker / Tennstedt
  HMV Dig SLS/*TCC-SLS* 5279 (2/83), ook EMI Eminence dig EMX 2102/ *TC-* (12/86) (Haas edition)
- Dresden State O/ Blomstedt
  Denon Dig **C37 7126**
- Philharmonia / Klemperer
  Vox PL 11200 (recording 1963), also HMV SXLP 30167 (5/65) (7/74)
- Columbia S O / Walter
  CBS remastered **MK 42035** [recording 1960]
- Wiener Philharmoniker / Furtwängler
  DG mono **415 664-2GH**
  (recorded Stuttgart Oct 1951, dig refurbished from 2740 201 (1/80)
- S O des Westdeutschen Rundfunks / Wand
  Harmonia Mundi 1C 065 99738
- S O des Hessischen Rundfunks / Inbal
  Teldec Conifer **ZK8 42921** transfer from GK8 35642 (6/84)
- Los Angeles P O / Mehta
  Decca SXL 6695

*** Symphony nr. 5, B flat major
- Berliner Philharmoniker / Karajan
  DG 2707 101/*3370 025* (10/78); **415 985-2GH** (6/87)
- Chicago S O / Solti
  Decca Dig D221 D2/*K 221 K 22*
- S O des Bayerischen Rundfunks / Jochum
  SLPM 13804-5 (recording 1958), and DGS7300
- Concertgebouw O / Haitink
  Philips 6725/*7655* 021
- Czech P O / Lovro von Matacic
  Supraphon **C37-7418** (1/86), transfer from MS 1211/12 (7/73) (1878 version)

*** Symphony nr. 6, A major
- Philharmonia / Klemperer
  HMV SXLP 30448
- Concertgebouw O / Haitink
  Philips 6500 164
- Berliner Philharmoniker / Karajan
  DG 2531/*3301* 295 (11/80); **419 194-2GH** (4/87)
- Chicago S O / Solti
  Decca SXL/*KSXC* 6946 (5/80); **417 389-2DH**

- Berliner Philharmoniker / Joseph Keilberth
Teldec/ASV **8 43194**, dig refurbished from Telefunken
SMA83 (7/64)

*** Symphony nr. 7, E major
- RIAS Orch Berlin / Chailly
Decca Dig **414 290-2**; 414 290-1/*4* (6/85)
- Berliner Philharmoniker / Karajan
DG Anal (1975) 2707 102/*3370 023* ; **419 195-2GH**
DG EG290858-1 (1/72) (7/86)
- Concertgebouw O / Haitink
Philips 6700 038 (2 LPs) (1st recording 12/69), also 6833
253, and Philips Seq 412 359-1/*4* (2/85)
Philips **420 805-2PH**, transfer from 6769 028 (2nd
recording 1979)
- Wiener Philharmoniker / Böhm
DG Signature 413 978-1GS (12/85)
- Berliner Philharmoniker / Jochum
DG Priv 2726 054
- Columbia S O / Walter
CBS Masterworks **M2K 42036**, dig refurbished from
SBRG 72139/40 (12/63)
- Philharmonia / Klemperer
HMV ED 290004-1/*4* (Originalfassung) (11/62) (7/85)
- Dresdner Staatskapelle / Blomstedt
Denon Dig **C37 7286** (8/86)
- Czech P O / Lovro von Matacic
Supraphon **C37-7419**, transfer from SUAST 50809/10
(8/72) (version 1883)
- S O des Südwestdeutschen Rundfunks (Baden-Baden) /
Rosbaud
Vox mono STPL 510752 (12/59) and Turnabout TV
34083S
- S O des Hessischen Rundfunks / Inbal
Teldec/Conifer dig AZ6 43259/*CY4*, **ZK8 43259**
- Concertgebouw O/ Van Beinum
Decca Anal LXT2829-30 [recording 1953], dig refurbished
421 139-2
- Wiener Philharmoniker / Solti
Decca SET 323/4
- Chicago S O / Solti
Decca dig **417 631-2DH**, /-1DH, /*4DH*
- Wiener Philharmoniker / Giulini
DG dig **419 627-2GH**, /-1GH, / -4GH

*** Symphony nr. 8, c minor
- Berliner Philharmoniker / Karajan
(Haas edition) DG 2707 085/*3370 019* [recording 1976];
dig remastered
419 196-2GH2 (6/87)
Columbia 33CX1586-7 and S-3576-B; CfP CFPD/*TC-CFPD* 414434-3/*5* [recording 1958]
- Concertgebouwork / Haitink
(Haas edition) Philips Dig 6769/*7654* 080; **412 465-2PH**
(7/85)
- Wiener Philharmoniker / Giulini
(Nowak edition) DG Dig **415 124-2GH2**; /-1GH (1984)
- London P O / Tennstedt
HMV Dig SLS/*TCC-SLS* 5290
- Chicago S O / Barenboim
DG Dig 2741/*3382* 007
- S O des Westdeutschen Rundfunks / Wand
German Harmonia Mundi HM 1C 153 99853/4
- S O des Hessischen Rundfunks / Inbal
Teldec/Conifer **ZL8 48218**, transfer from GK6 35642
(6/84)
- Philh S O / Païta
Lodia **LO-CD 783/4**

*** Symphony nr. 9, d minor
- Berliner Philharmoniker / Karajan
DG Acc 2542/*3342* 129
419 083-2GH (9/86) from DG 2530/*3300* 828 (6/77)
- Concertgebouworkest / Haitink
Philips Dig **410 039-2PH** (9/83), from: 6514 191/*7337*
- Berliner Philharmoniker / Jochum
HMV EG 290492-1/*4*
- Dresden State O / Jochum
HMV Master Series ASD 4218 (10/82 and 4/86)
- Dresdner Staatskapelle / Blomstedt
Denon dig **C37-7286**
- Wiener Philharmoniker / Mehta
Decca Jub JB/*KJBC* 108
- Columbia S O / Walter
CBS **MK 42037** dig refurbished from Philips SABL179
(6/61) [recording 1959]
- Czech P O / Matacic
Supraphon Dig **C37 7420** transfer from 1110 3179ZA
(version 1894)
- Oslo P O / Yoav Talmi
Chandos dig **CHAN 8458/9** [2 discs]; DBRD2010 [2 LPs]
- Chicago / Solti
Decca **417 295-2DH**; /-1DH, /*4DH* (10/86)
- Chicago Symphony / Giulini
HM V ASD/*JS-ASD* 3382
and SXLP/*TC-SXLP* 30546
- S O des Westdeutschen Rundfunks / Wand
EMI **CDC 7477512**
- S O des Hessischen Rundfunks (Frankfurt) / Inbal
Teldec/ASV dig **8 43303-6** (version 1896)
- Wiener Philharmoniker / Giulini
419 627-2GH; /-1GH (8/87)

This lists includes more than 115 recordings. Together they represent more than fifty years of concertizing in both Europe and America. 31 conductors have led 19 different orchestras. There are 8 distinguished Brucknerians (for example, Von Karajan, Haitink, Walter and Jochum) and some conductors are long deceased (Van Beinum, Keilberth and Rosbaud). Still others have been clearly influenced by their predecessors (Chailly, Barenboim and Muti). The eighties alone have produced 6 complete sets of Bruckner. The most important of these are the Von Karajan, Haitink and Jochum. Of these, many have been separately released as well, often remastered. There are numerous individual recordings as well, for example, Giulini, Inbal and Von Matacic. There are about 12 recordings made by the legendary figures Furtwängler, Klemperer, Walter and Böhm. Four orchestras are responsible for the majority (61) of the recordings: Chicago, Berlin, Dresden and the Bavarian Radio Orchestra, in that order. Jochum performing Bruckner is magic. He is temperamentally close to the reserved Austrian composer and, in spite of his belief in free tempi, 'lives' in his Bruckner. The Dresden players are sometimes less than their colleagues in Berlin or Bavaria, but the EMI technicians have served them well making the Jochum cycle something to be treasured. Haitink has a good grasp of the architecture of these difficult pieces and a fine feeling for their detail. His cycle is a classic. His ability to capture mystery, however, is not as strong as Jochum's. Jochum is more spiritual, something that is quite logical considering the fact that Haitink was only 33 when he recorded his Bruckner and Jochum was a good twenty years

older. Barenboim's Eighth is excellent, his Sixth is admirable and his Ninth, interesting. The digital sound on nrs 1 to 3 is superb. The Third is not complete in some way, the conductor is still searching deeper and cannot measure up to Jochum or Von Karajan in this piece.

SYMPHONY NR. 2 - Haitink uses the longer Haas version and that should please many Bruckner lovers. This intelligent performance is wonderful and fresh. Von Karajan is powerful and polished and is distinguished by his tempi and interpretation. The Nowak version is used but with revisions by the conductor. The Scherzo in this high tempo is feather light, the Finale slow and grand. The digital sound is a bit extreme.

SYMPHONY NR. 3 - Von Karajan's performance is impressive. His command of the score is something unique. (Again he uses the Nowak and Haitink, the Haas version) Despite the numerous rivals, Von Karajan stands alone at a dizzying height. Böhm's performance with the Viennese lacks the imagination found in all the best recordings but the magnificent details and gorgeous orchestra should not go unnoticed.

SYMPHONY NR. 4 - The choice of a Fourth Symphony is the most difficult. Many recordings are wonderful, all for different reasons. Von Karajan has recorded the Fourth twice (HMV and DG). Both are wonderful, lyrical, expressive and technically superb. Jochum is unique in all his Bruckner; his is a nobility that is difficult to challenge. He sails through all the most difficult passages convincingly and subtly. Solti's Fourth is faultless as well, wonderful tempi, amazing concentration in the long passages, crisp and clear architecture. (He uses the Nowak version.) The sound is so clear that it borders on the fake. A more mature sound is the one produced by the Concertgebouw with Haitink (1968, re-released, 1981). Haitink knows the Concertgebouw Hall as no other and plays with the acoustics in this shimmering performance. His recording in Vienna is disappointing as a result. Böhm is clearly at home in the middle of the Austrian musicians with which he recorded his Fourth. Their earthy sonority is inimitable. Decca's recording is the best. It is obvious that Muti had to prove himself with the Berlin Philharmonic in this recording. Tennstedt's performance can survive comparison with Von Karajan's. Furtwängler unfortunately uses a bad score (Eulenburg) in his 1951 performance.

SYMPHONY NR. 5 - Neither polished nor balanced, Von Karajan's recording is still sublime. Jochum's slow movement is better, however. In Solti's version sparks fly. Barenboim's does not measure up to the rest of his performances, and certainly not to Von Karajan's Fifth.

SYMPHONY NR. 6 - Barenboim's Sixth, on the other hand, is very successful. It is one of his best recordings ever. Klemperer also gives a strong performance and never betrays his age at the time of recording. Jochum is a strong competitor, but the sound is not as good as that which DG produced for Barenboim. Solti misses spontaneity especially in the second movement.

SYMPHONY NR. 7 - Von Karajan's HMV recording is grand. The later DG recording is majestic and perhaps more powerful than the first. The rich sound that Haitink inspires from the Concertgebouw rein-

forces their tremendous reputation together. Jochum's performance with Dresden is beautiful but the microphones sound too close. The sound was better when he worked with Berlin. Jochum and Berlin are unbeatable teamed up for the Seventh. Barenboim's vision is deep and admirable but the Chicago Symphony cannot compete with the orchestras in Berlin, Vienna and Amsterdam.
SYMPHONY NR. 8 - Jochum gives a warm performance of this, Bruckner's most exuberant symphony. His is not as intense as say Von Karajan's but is nevertheless convincing right from the mysterious beginning. (Jochum again prefers the Nowak version, Haitink and Von Karajan the Haas.) Von Karajan recorded the Eighth twice, in 1958 and 1976. Both are noble and impressive. Both are also available in excellent cassettes.
SYMPHONY NR.9 - Thanks to the superb playing that makes the Berlin Philharmonic famous, and the excellent recording technique, this Von Karajan Ninth speaks for itself. Mehta's performance has its wonderful moments and the orchestra is also breathtaking at times. Still, this is clearly not the same level as achieved by Von Karajan. Giulini's version is disappointing in respect to his rivals. It is however, as is always the case with Giulini, played with the utmost care. There are unfortunate mistakes in the horn solo in the first movement. Walter's Ninth was recorded when he was 83. The interpretation is of great value, unsentimental, almost athletic. His Scherzo is so fast that it sounds exciting, even threatening rather than hysterical (which is often the case with other conductors) and is as important as the rest of the legendary Walter's work.

GEOFFREY BUSH (born 1920)

Symphony nr. 1
- London S O / Braithwaite
  Lyr SRCS 115

Geoffrey Bush was a student of John Ireland's. The first of his two symphonies appeared in 1954. Bush does not shun the role of composer as mere entertainer, and the first movement and the finale are nice amusements at that, very light and pleasing. The recording sounds fine as is always the case with Lyrita.

ELLIOTT CARTER (born 1908)

Symphony of Three Orchestras
- New York P O / Pierre Boulez
  CBS 76812

Some claim that Elliot Carter is one of the most important post-war American composers.The Symphony is divided between three orchestral groups, each plays four of the twelve sections of the piece. Carter here clearly dedicates himself to atonal polyphony which is very complex. Pierrre Boulez leads the New Yorkers in a fascinating and well-crafted performance of an obviously difficult work.

ERNEST CHAUSSON (1855-99)

Symphony in B major, Op. 20
- Detroit S O / Paul Paray (1959)
  Mercury SRI 75029
- Toulouse Capitole Orch / Plasson (1981)
  EMI/Pathé-Marconi 2C 069 14086
- Basler S O / Armin Jordan (1986)
  Erato/Conifer dig CD ECD88169 (NUM75253)
- Nouvelle Orchestre Symphonique de la RTBF (Bruxelles) / Serebrier (1985)
  Chandos Dig CD CHAN8369 (ABRD1135)
- Czech P O / Kosler
  Supraphon Dig 1110 3404

Chausson's symphony is seldom played in the concert hall, but many famous conductors have recorded it. The symphony has three movements, no scherzo, and is known to be a hommage Chausson wrote for his teacher, César Franck. All four recordings make it clear that there are hidden dangers in the score.
The Paray recording was accepted as definitive for a long time, but the sound quality produced by Mercury is disappointing. Surprising is how French the Detroit orchestra sounds with Paray. Details are clear, the acoustics dry.
Plasson and Jordan both sound quite lyrical, but the structure of the piece is lost. The second movement drifts along without any channelled emotional expression. The Chandos recording is a RTB (Radio-Télévision Belge) production. The sound is natural. It is the only CD available.
The Czech performance competes well with the western versions. Kosler catches the character of the symphony with alert rhythm and a clear feeling for proportion. The woodwinds and brass are fine and the balance is good.

CARLOS CHÁVEZ (1809- 78)

Symphony nr. 1
Symphony nr. 2 (Sinfonia India)
Symphony nr. 3
- London S O / Eduardo Mata
  MMG Dig MCD 10002

Despite the difference in their ages, Eduardo Mata and Carlos Chavez were personal friends. They studied the symphonies together as Chavez had conducted them himself for CBS. The most accessible are the frst three. The Sinfonia India is more of a symphonic poem than its name implies. The performances recorded here are excellently played; technically, they are also superb.

LUIGI CHERUBINI (1760-1842)

Symphony in D·major
- New Philharmonia O / Boettcher
  Philips Seq 412 374-1
- Los Angeles Chamber O / Gerard Schwarz
  Nonesuch D-79023

The classic symphony's roots lie in Italian earth. Mozart's contacts with Italy are well documented. He

surely met Sammartini in Milan. Haydn did his best to compose an Italian opera while Kapellmeister at the Esterházy court. Salieri taught Haydn the Italian manner of singing. Nevertheless, we know little about instrumental music written by the Italians between 1780 and 1830. The Symphony in D major by Cherubini is an example of this neglected repertoire.
Since Toscanini's 'classic' performance, there have been too few new recordings made of this piece. The one made by the New Philharmonia is the best in respect to interpretation and recording technique. The balance is wonderful, the timbre very natural. The cassette is of an excellent quality. Still, this symphony deserves more renown. Cherubini was admired by none other than Beethoven.
The recording made by the Los Angeles Chamber Orchestra in 1981 was done with the JVC Digital Audio System (DAS 90) in the Ambassadeur Auditorium in Pasadena, California. Since its début in 1969, this orchestra has quickly become well known internationally. The director, the American trumpeter Gerard Schwarz gives a very stylish performance of Cherubini.

MUZIO CLEMENTI (1752-1832)

Symphony nr. 1 in C major
Symphony nr. 2 in D major
Symphony nr. 3 in G major (Great National Symphony)
Symphony nr. 4 in D major
- Philharmonia O / Claudio Scimone
  Erato STU 71174

Clementi's fame rests on his piano method (1801) and his Gradus ad Parnassum (1817), loved and hated by all professional pianists, and some amateurs as well. He knew Mozart and challenged him to a piano duel. Clementi also knew Beethoven, was a business man and music publisher. His four symphonies were discovered and partly reconstructed by Pietro Spada. Clementi's fame during his lifetime was as an orchestral, not a keyboard composer. In the Great National Symphony, God Save The King is ingeniously worked into the third movement. (Clementi travelled to England when just fourteen, and spent most of his life there). Scimone leads a sparkling performance and the sound is excellent.

ARNOLD COOKE (born 1906)

Symphony nr. 3
- London P O / Braithwaite
  Lyr SRCS 78

Arnold Cooke, along with his teacher, Hindemith, is doomed to remain an unfashionable composer. His symphony is, however, proof that Cooke can produce a work that deserves more than the occasional radio broadcast. There is no experimental material in the piece, yet it has a freshness that excites more than many avant-garde compositions. Both the performance and recording are satisfactory.

AARON COPLAND (born 1900)

Dance Symphony (i)
Short Symphony nr. 2 (ii)
- (i and ii) London S O / composer
  CBS 61997
- (i) Detroit S O / Antal Dorati
  Decca Dig SXDL/KSXDC 7547
- (ii) St Paul Chamber O / Russell Davies
  Pro Arte Dig CD CCD140 (PAD 140)
- (i) Mexico City P O / Enrique Batiz
  HMV Greensleeve dig ED270375-1
Symphony nr. 3
- Academy SMF / Marriner
  Argo ZRG/KZRC 845
- New York P O / Bernstein (1985)
  DG dig CD 410 170-2GH

Copland is well represented in the record catologues including his three symphonies. He is without doubt an important American composer who also enjoys a certain status internationally.
The Dance Symphony was written in 1929, the Short Symphony, a few years later. Both are short, full of energy and original. The performances led by the composer are excellent. Probably no other conductor could better the LSO's playing of these works. The CBS recording is warmer and more detailed than we are accustomed to with this label. The Dorati version is brilliant and alive. Detroit sounds wonderful, proving again that there are more good American orchestras than just the 'big five'.
In the early days of stereo, Copland recorded the Third Symphony with the LSO for Everest. The newer version is richer and the Philharmonia plays well. Bernstein's version, however, makes the Philharmonia sound pale in comparison. The New Yorkers sound vibrant, and the piece gets a Russian perspective given to it, reminiscent of Prokofiev or Shostakovich. Still, Copland's natural authority is grand and the composer inspires his players completely.

SIR PETER MAXWELL DAVIES (born 1934)

Symphony nr. 3
- BBC P O / Downes
  PRT BBC Dig CD 560 (REGL560)
Sinfonia (1962)
Sinfonia Concertante (1982)
- Scottish Chamber O / Davies
  Unicorn-Kanchana Dig DKP9058 (sponsored by the Scottish Arts Council)

Davies' Third Symphony was written to commemorate the 50th anniversary of the BBC Philharmonic. It was released on the BBC Atrium label. It is a lyrical piece. The First Symphony is reminiscent of Sibelius, the Third, of Mahler. Downes has succeeded in attaining complete dedication from the Manchester orchestra for this recording. According to Davies, his Sinfonia is a hommage on Monteverdi. His Sinfonia Concertante, on the other hand, has classical forms as its inspiration. These forms are subtly woven into Davies work and are only apparent after repeated listening. The performance is wonderful, very

alive, and the solo hornplayer deserves a medal for his playing.

PAUL DUKAS (1865-1935)

Symphony in C major
- Orch Suisse Romande / Amin Jordan
  Erato Dig ECD 88089 (CD); MCE 75175 (cassette)
- London P O / Weller
  Decca SXL 6770

On the one hand, Weller's performance is more cultivated. On the other hand, Jordan's interpretation has more conviction. The Suisse Romande Orchestra plays well here, unfortunately, exceptionally so since the death of Ansermet in 1957. Technically, the Erato recording competes easily with the Decca product.

ANTONIN DVOŘÁK (1841-1904)

*** Symphonies nrs 1- 9
- London S O / Kertesz
  Decca D6D7
- Berliner Philharmoniker / Kubelik
  DG 2740 237

*** Symphony nr. 1 in c minor, Op. 3
- London S O / Kertesz
  Decca Jub JB/KJBC 110
- Prague S O / Neumann
  LPV370 [recorded 1959]
- Czech P O / Neumann
  Supraphon 1110 2877

*** Symphony nr. 2, B flat major, Op. 4
- Prague S O / Neumann
  Supraphon SUA 10025
- London S O / Kertesz
  Decca Jub JB/KJBC 111

*** Symphony nr. 3 in E flat major, Op. 10
- Czech P O / Neumann
  Supraphon Dig C37 7668
- London S O / Kertesz
  Decca Jub JB/KJBC 112
- Prague S O / Smetacek
  Art ALP136 [recorded 1959]
- Scottish National O / Järvi
  Chandos 8575; ABRD/ABTD 1270

*** Symphony nr. 4 in d minor, Op. 13
- Czech P O / Neumann
  Supraphon ALPS137 [1959]; Dig C37 7442 (12/85)
- London S O / Kertesz
  Decca Jub JB/KJBC 113; 417 596-2DH, from SXL6527 (4/67)

*** Symphony nr. 4
*** Symphony nr. 5
*** Symphony nr. 6
- London S O / Kertesz
  Decca 417 596/8 (8/87) [3 discs], transfer from resp SXL65276 (4/67); SXL6273 (3/67) and SXL6253 (11/66)

*** Symphony nr. 5, F major (originally Op. 24, 1975, published

as Op. 76)
- London S O / Kertesz
  Decca Jub JB/KJBC 114; 417 597-2DH (8/87), from SXL6273 (3/67) (7/82)
- Scottisch N O / Järvi
  Chandos dig CHAN8552; ABRD/ABDT 1258

*** Symphony nr. 6 in D major, Op. 60
- Czech P O / Neumann
  Supraphon Dig C37 7242 (12/85)
- London S O / Kertesz
  Decca Jub JB/KJBC 115; 417 598-2DH, transfer from SXL6253 (11/66)
- Philharmonia / Andrew Davis
  CBS Dig 36708
- Scottish National O / Järvi
  Chandos dig CHAN 8530; ABRD/ABTD 1240

*** Symphony nr. 7, d minor, Op. 70
*** Symphony nr. 8, G major, Op. 88
- Berliner Philharmoniker / Kubelik
  DG Walkman 419 088-4

*** Symphony nr. 7
- Philh S O / Païta
  Lodia LO-CD 782 (6/85); LOD 782
- Czech P O / Neumann
  Supraphon C37 7067; 1110 3139 (3/84)
- Concertgebouw O / Colin Davis
  Philips 9500 132/7300 535 (2/77)
- London S O / Kertesz
  Decca Jub JB/KJBC 116 (10/64) (2/82)
- Scottish N O / Neeme Järvi
  Chandos dig CHAN 850; ABRD/ABTD 8501
- Cleveland O / Dohnanyi
  Decca dig 417 564-2DH; 1DH; 4DH
- Wiener Philharmoniker / Maazel
  DG Dig 410 997-2 (8/84); 410 997-1/4
- Chicago S O / Levine
  RCA dig RD85427

*** Symphonies nrs 7, 8 and 9
- Cleveland O / Dohnányi
  Decca 421 082-2DH, transfers from resp. 417 564-1DH (3/87); 414 422-1DH (2/86) and 414 421-1DH (11/86)
- Minnesota S O / Marriner
  Philips Dig 412 542-2PH2 (12/85)

*** Symphony nr. 8
- Columbia S O / Walter
  CBS MK 42038
- Czech P O / Neumann
  Supraphon Dig C37 7073
- Chicago S O / Giulini
  DG Sig 413 980-1/4
- Concertgebouw O / Szell
  Decca ACL46 [recorded 1951]
- Concertgebouw O / Colin Davis
  Philips 9500 317/ 730 611
- Minnesota S O / Marriner
  Philips Dig 6514 050/ 7337 050
- Wiener Philharmoniker / Karajan
  Decca Jub JB/KJBC 71
  Decca Ovation 417 744-2DM, transfer from SXL6169 (4/65) also: DG dig 415 971-1GH; -4GH ; -2GH [2nd recording]
- Berliner Philharmoniker / Kubelik
  DG Priv 2535/3335 397 (7/67) (7/80)
- London S O / Kertesz

Decca Jub JB/*KJBC* 117 (7/63) (9/81)
- Hallé O / Barbirolli
  Pye PRT GSGC/*ZCGC* 2056
- Hallé O / Loughran
  ALH912 (5/82)
- Royal Liverpool P O / Bátiz
  ASV Dig ABM/*ZCABM* 768
- London P O / Handley
  Chandos Dig **CHAN 8323** (1/85); ABRD/*ABTD* 1105 (4/84)
- Cleveland O / Dohnányi
  Decca Dig **414 422-2DH** (2/86); /1DH; /4DH
- Wiener Philharmoniker / Maazel
  DG **415 205-2GH** (5/85), transfer from 2532 034 (5/82)
- Cleveland O / Szell
  FON BC1015 [recorded 1960]

*** Symphony nr. 9, e minor ('die neue Welt')
- Wiener Philharmoniker / Kondrashin
  Decca Dig **400 047-2**; SXDL/*KSXDC* 7510 (3/83) [recorded 1979]
  also: **417 267-1DB** (7/80) (9/86)
- Minnesota S O / Marriner
  Philips Dig 412 224-1/4
- Columbia S O / Walter
  CBS **MK 42039**
- Berliner Philharmoniker / Tennstedt
  HMV Dig **CDC 747071-2** (5/85); EL 270104-1/4
- Concertgebouw O / Colin Davis
  Philips 9500 511/*7300 671* (2/79), and Philips Zigzag 412 921-1/4 ;
  remastered as Philips Silver Line **420 349-2PM**
- Wiener Philharmoniker / Kertesz
  Decca SPA/*KCSP* 87; Ovation **417 724-2DM** , transfer from SXL6291 (11/67)
- London S O / Kertesz
  Decca Jub JB/*KJBC* 118, also SPK/*KCSP* 87
- New Philharmonia / Dorati
  Conifer CC/*CCTC* 7579
- Philharmonia / Giulini
  HMV SXLP/*TC-SXLP* 30163
- Chicago S O / Giulini
  DG 2530/*3300* 881
- Berliner Philharmoniker / Karajan
  (1) HMV ASD/*TC-ASD* 3407
  (2) HMV SXLP/*TC-SXLP* 10049-1/4 ; DG mono **423 525-2GDO 6**; originally: Polydor 67519/24 [series The first recordings 1938-1943]
  (3) DG 138 922/*923 008* ; EMI **CDM7 69005-2**
  (4) Wiener Philharmoniker / Karajan
  DG Dig **415 509-2**; /-1; /-4 (recorded 1985)
- London S O / Rowicki
  Philips Seq 412 003-1/4
- Cleveland O / Szell
  CBS 60150/*40*
- Wiener Philharmoniker / Maazel
  DG Dig **410 032-2** (8/83); 2532/*3302* 079
- London P O / Conlon
  Erato **ECD 88036** (12/84)
- Berliner Philharmoniker / Kubelik
  DG Walkman *413 147-4;* DG Priv 2535/*3335* 473
- London P O / Macal
  CfP CFP/*TC-CFP* 40382 (11/82); **CD-CFP9006**
- New Philharmonia / Stokowski
  RCA VICS/*VK* 2038
- NBC S O / Toscanini
  RCA mono **RCCD 1008**
- Philharmonia / Sawallisch
  Columbia 33CX1677 and SAX2322 [recorded 1960]

- Czech P O / Neumann
  Supraphon **C37 7002**
- Cleveland O / Dohnányi
  Decca **414 421-2DH** (1/87); -1DH (11/86)
- Chicago S O / Solti
  Decca Dig **410 116-2**; /-1; /-4
- Scottish N O / Järvi
  Chandos dig ABRD/*ABTD* 1220; **CHAN 8510** (5/87)
- London P O / Zdenek Macal

*** Symphonies nrs 7; 8; 9
- Cleveland O / Dohnányi
  Decca **421 082-2DH2** [2 discs]

One of Decca's first digital recordings was Kondrashin's version of Dvořák's Ninth Symphony, for many years the absolute best despite many newer alternatives. His classic is threatened, however, by the new CD version recorded by Dohnányi. This spectacular sounding performance is full of exciting moments. Regrettable is the fact that the repeat of the exposition is not played, disturbing the balance between the movements. Dohnányi's performance could easily be the best of the long list of 25 possibilities.

Von Karajan also leaves out the repeat. He has recorded the Ninth four times in his long career. The last time was in 1985 when Von Karajan performed it with the Viennese Philharmonic in a video project. The Viennese however cannot equal Berlin instrumentalists in the earlier Von Karajan versions. Both the brass and the strings sound aggressive. Von Karajan, like Tennstedt, conducts in the best Viennese tradition and doesn't force the piece into an extreme, nationalistic corner. The 1979 Kondrashin recording done with the Viennese is better.

Many conductors have recorded only the last three symphonies. Marriner's Seventh is relaxed but rhythmically weaker than other versions. His Eighth is an idyllic, sunny reading, supported well by the warm Philips sound. In his Ninth, the nostalgic Largo is extremely interesting. All in all, the performances are not as alive as by Neumann, for example. Neumann's performance has more character and his orchestra plays more convincingly. Neumann's Eighth is especially wonderful: the Adagio is beautiful and the winds have a rustic charm in the Scherzo. His Ninth is disappointing, the playing is merely routine.

Many will choose Paita's Seventh as the absolute favourite. The natural passion in the climaxes played here is usually heard only in the concert hall. The dynamic scope of the recording is extraordinary.

Vernon Handley's Eighth is a strong and direct interpretation. Kondrashin's Ninth (Decca) is a wonderful example of the best CD techniques. The Maazel recording has something aggressive about it. Tennstedt's Ninth is disturbing because of the painful fortissimos. Batiz's Eighth demonstrates his unique ability of bringing life into the studio. Kubelik is a high quality alternative; the Liverpool Orchestra's inspired playing make this recording a strong competitior.

Colin Davis' recording of the last three symphonies has been admired for years. The music develops in its own natural way, without eccentric meddling by the conductor. Beautifully played, it is also beautifully recorded.

The amazing remastering techniques in use today make it possible for those who never heard Bruno Walter in the concert hall, to hear this legendary conductor at work (and to hear that the great legend is justified). Walter had no special reputation as a performer of Dvořák. Nevertheless, his performances are as good as the very best. There are a few Walter eccentricities, to be sure: he doesn't hesitate to shorten a rest or even a note that he personally thinks is too long! Still, these recordings are highly recommended.

The Kertesz complete cycle is a monument to Dvořák's art. Most of the recordings are excellent. Kertesz has an authentic interpretation. The London Symphony is very alert. Kertesz quickens the Third a bit too much, perhaps, and the Fourth is the disappointment of the set (if there, in fact, is one). His Ninth has been famous for quite a long while.

EDWARD ELGAR (1857-1934)

Symphony nr. 1, A flat, Op. 55
- Royal P O / Previn
  Philips dig CD 416 612-2
Symphony nr. 1
Symphony nr. 2 E flat major
- London P O / Boult
  HMV CD CDC747204-2 (1986, transfer from ASD/*TC-ASD* 3330 - 4/77, also released as Lyrita SRCS13, originally released in 10/68, as SRCS39; also as: 'Boult conducts Elgar'),
  HMV dig remastered EX2906617-3
- BBC Symphony O / Sir Colin Davis
  RCA Dig RL/*RK* 70748
- Philharmonia O / Barbirolli
  EMI Eminence EMX 41 2084-1/4 (1/86) and: HMV SXLP 30268 (11/78), transfer from HMV ASD540 - 10/63
- London P O / Handley
  Classic for Pleasure CFP/*TC-CFP* 40331 (6/80)
- London P O / Solti
  Decca SXL/*KSXC* 6569 (8/72)
- Philharmonia O / Haitink
  HMV Dig ASD/*TC-ASD* 107794 (1/84)
- Hallé O / Loughran
  ASV ALH/*ZCALH* 907
- Hallé O / Barbirolli
  PRT Precision Records & Tape GSGC/*ZCGC* 2010
- Scottish National O / Alexander Gibson
  RCA VICS 2010
- Royal P O / Previn (1986)
  Philips dig CD 416 612-2PH (416 612-1PH) (6/86)
- London P O / Bryden Thomson
  Chandos Dig CD CHAN8452
Symphony nr. 2, E flat major, Op. 63
- London P O / Bryden Thomas
  Chandos Dig CD CHAN 8452 (ABRD 1162)
- Philharmonia O / Haitink
  HMV CD CDC 747 299-2 (EL 270147-1/4)
- London P O / Handley
  Classics for Pleasure CFP/*TC-CFP* 40350
Symphony nr. 2
- London P O / Solti
  Decca SXL 6723
- Hallé O / Loughran
  ASV ALH/*ZCALH* 906
- Hallé O / Barbirolli
  HMV SXLP/*TC-SXLP* 30287,
  also: EMI Eminence EMX412093, transfer from: HMV ASD610 (12/64)

Elgar has been institutionalized by both concert performances and the recording industry in England. Many conductors outside of England have also dedicated themselves to Elgar, including Toscanini and Pierre Monteux (in spite of the usual French hatred of both Elgar and Brahms). The great Elgar interpreters are most definitely Sir John Barbirolli and Sir Adrian Boult. Their performances are loved still and constantly re-released. The only newcomer to be accepted is André Previn.

Boult met the composer when only 16 and cultivated a friendship with him throughout his lifetime. He was present at the rehearsals when Elgar's First Symphony was being prepared for its première by Richter in London. Boult conducted Elgar all his life; he was almost 70 when he recorded the First in Wlathamstow Assembly Hall in 1967. In that same year, Boult recorded the Second Symphony for the fourth time.

Bryden Thomas' version has not been successful mainly due to the strange tempi. Thomas takes a quarter of an hour longer to finish the Second Symphony than the composer himself, eleven minutes longer in the First. The Chandos technicians, usually very good, go too far in their attempts to create 'ideal' acoustics.

The Previn performance has also been released on CD and is unusually good. Devotees also appreciate Previn's subtle handling of the rhythm. There is nothing forced about his meter. It is worthy to note that neither the great Solti nor Haitink have successfully caught the essence of Elgar's genius.

ZDENEK FIBICH (1850-1900)

Symphony nr. 2 in E flat major, Op. 38
- Brno State P O / Jiri Waldhans
  Sup 410 2165
Symphony nr. 3 in e minor, Op. 53
- Brno State P O / Belohlavek
  Sup 1110 3038

The story goes that Fibich composed his first symphony when only fourteen and his second two years later while studying in Leipzig. Fibich later retracted both works. He composed his known symphonies much later in life; the third was written just two years before his death. It is the second that is performed the most. It is fascinating music if somewhat less inspired melodically than say Dvorák or Smetana. Fibich's musical sentences can be a little square and the development a bit predictable. Nevertheless, the Scherzo from the Second Symphony is colourful and stimulating. The Brno orchestra conducted by Waldhans, gives a rather square performance. The sound is too opaque and the tutti are not clear enough; the overal acoustic quality is satisfactory.
Fibich's Third Symphony could, if better known, win him new friends. The Scherzo, with its striking syncopations, is very charming. The performance Belohlavek gives is very convincing.

CESAR FRANCK (1822-90)

Symphony in d minor
- Chicago S O / Pierre Monteux
  RCA Gold GL/GK 85261

- Concertgebouw O / Mengelberg
  Philips mono CD 416 214-2
- Orch National de France / Bernstein
  DG Dig CD 400 070-2 (3/83); (2532/3302 050) (12/82)
- Orchestre de Paris / Barenboim
  DG Sig 410 833-1/4 and Walkman 413 423-4
- Cleveland O / Maazel
  Decca SXL 6823
- Orch National de la Radiodifusion française / Beecham
  HMV ALP1686 (1958)
- Concertgebouw O / Edo de Waart
  Philips 9500 605/7300 727
- Orchester des Bayerischen Rundfunks / Kondrashin
  Philips Dig 6514/7337
- Philadelphia O / Ricardo Muti
  HMV Dig ASD/TCC-ASD 4175
- Berliner Philharmoniker / Carlo Maria Giulini (4/87)
  DG Digital CD 419 605-2GH (also LP and cassette)
- Wiener Philharmoniker / Furtwängler
  Decca mono CD 417 287-2DH (dig transfer from LXT2905
- 4/54)
- Toulouse Capitol Orch / Plasson
  CD CDC7 47547-2 (3/87)

The Monteux recording (1961) with the Chicago Symphony is just what one would expect from Monteux: every measure is alive, there is a perfect balance between the sections of the orchestra, the interpretation is warm, all the details are handled carefully. The orchestra is wonderful but the recording itself is disappointing.
Mengelberg's version was made in 1940. It is high-powered and truly exciting to listen to. The digital remastering is a wonder; it is as if four decades have been skipped over and the old Concertgebouw plays once more.
That is not the case with the old Von Karajan recording (1969). It is very heavy and the constant tempo changes hold the music back. The historical recording made by the Viennese with Furtwängler will only please Furtwängler fans, and disappoint Franck enthusiasts.
Bernstein devotees have something to celebrate here. The dramatic intensity of this performance never lets up. Despite his slow tempi, Bernstein has the whole piece very much under his control.
Plasson (EMI) needs two minutes less than Bernstein but does not sound hurried. Giulini, on the other hand, uses two minutes more than Bernstein and six more than Plasson. Giulini's rubato is a bit too much and makes the whole interpretation too heavy. Franck specifies poco rall. in the score but Giulini is not satisfied with anything less than molto rall. Giulini feels obviously more at home with opera. Franck enthusiasts that find Bernstein a bit too lively are recommended to choose the Plasson. His tempi are not exaggerated, his rubato is controlled and his music is passionate, not hysterical. Plasson also has Franck's difficult orchestration completely under control.
The old 1958 Beecham recording with the French orchestra has been popular for many years and certainly not without cause. Beecham's genius bestows love and warmth on this symphony and the orchestra is clearly dedicated to this great conductor.

NIELS GADE (1817-90)

Symphony nr. 8 in b minor, Op. 47
- Danish Radio S O / Frandsen
  Danish Music Anthology DMA 046

The Eighth is Gade's last symphony, completed in 1872 when he was in his mid-fifties. It is considered stronger than the rest of his symphonies and stands a good chance of being remembered in history. Gade clearly owes a great deal to Mendelssohn in this work. It is well crafted in spite of the limited thematic material. Both recording and performance are adequate. They lack the clarity found in the better recordings nowadays.

VITTORIO GIANNINI (1903-66)

Symphonie nr. 3
- Eastman Symphonic Wind Ensemble / Roller
  Mercury SRI 75010

In 1958, Giannini's Third Symphony appeared, a very personal and well crafted work. It is definitely neo-classical. The first movement sounds too much like a TV theme tune, but the second movement is lovely. The Eastman Ensemble handles the piece knowledgeably, and the recording is surpringly good.

ALEXANDER GLAZUNOV (1865-1936)

Symphony nr. 1 in E major (Slavyanskaya), Op. 5
Symphony nr. 2 inf sharp minor, Op. 16
Symphony nr. 3 in D major, Op. 33
Symphony nr. 4 in E flat major, Op. 48
Symphony nr. 5 in B flat major, Op. 55
Symphony nr. 6 in c minor, Op. 58
Symphony nr. 7 in F major, Op. 77 (Pastoral'naya)
Symphony nr. 8 in E flat major, Op. 83
- USSR Radio S O / Vladimir Fedoseyev
  Eurodisc/Target 999 000
Symphony (two Russian themes)
- USSR S O / Yevgeny Svetlanov
  Le Chant du Monde/ Harmonia Mundi CD LDC278819
(LDX78819); cassette K478819
Symphonies nrs 2, 4 and 7
- Bamberger Symphoniker / Neeme Järvi
  Orfeo/Harmonia Mundi digital S148852H
Symphonies nrs 1, 5 and 8
- Orchester des Bayerischen Rundfunks / Neeme Järvi
  Orfeo Dig CD 93842H (SO/MO 93842H)

If Glazunov's First Symphony pleases, than the rest will as well. It was the First that brought him fame with the St Petersburg audience. Their surprise at seeing a 16 year old in a school uniform ascend the podium at the work's première, insured a lasting celebrity. According to official Russia, Glazunov is the composer to bridge Borodin and the 20th century. This proves to be true time and again. Stravinsky listened to Glazunov's music often. Rachmaninov's 2nd Piano Concerto is very reminiscent of Glazunov's Second Symphony (compare the second movement in the Rachmaninov with the clarinet melody in the Andante of the Glazunov) and

Sibelius also knew these symphonies well. Fedoseyev leads excellent performances. The Russian brass is brilliant, especially in the climaxes. They handle their parts with true authority. The Svetlanov performance is pleasant if light and is interesting as it is the Shebalin version from 1937. Glazunov's orchestration is beautifully cherished here. The three symphonies recorded by the Germans with Järvi are adequate but the sound is not very good.

REINHOLD GLIÈRE (1875-1956)

Symphony nr. 3 in b minor (Ilya Murometz), Op. 42
- Royal Philharmonic O / Farberman
  Uni Dig PCM; UKC (cassette) 500/1

In Glière's massive programme symphony, fairly thin thematic material is endlessly drawn out. Those who can appreciate Glière's colourful style, will appreciate Farberman's performance, the first one with the score uncut. Farberman's conducting is not especially lively, and the climaxes are performed with a dampened passion. Nonetheless, his endless patience and excellent recording technicians have produced a surprisingly good product.
It is noteworthy that it was Unicorn, and not one of the larger companies (excepting Decca) that was first in the use of digital recording techniques. The balance is very natural and the sound is warm. The transfer to the cassette is adequate, but the LP is far better.

KARL GOLDMARK (1830-1915)

Rustic Wedding Symphony, Op. 26
- Pittsburgh S O / Andre Previn
  Ang SZ/ 4zs (cassette) 37662
- Los Angeles P O / Lopez-Cobos
- Westfalen S O / Reichert
  Turnabout TV 34410S

The Wedding Symphony is one of the three colourful works that appeared in 1875 one after the other. (The other two were the first Violin Concerto and the opera, The Queen of Sheba.) These three guaranteed Goldmark's reputation. Brahms called the large but unpretentious symphony 'clear and faultless'. Previn leads Pittsburgh well. The contrasts are great, the rhythmic drive is strong and the innocent lyric clear. The sound is warm; the cassette is also very rich in atmosphere.
Lopez-Cobos gives a surprising performance. Unfortunately, the tempi are too fast and the work loses some of its charm as a result. Previn's interpretation is the more colourful also due to the wider digital sound, giving the listener a better distance from the orchestra.
The Westphalen performance is clear and attractive, unexpectedly so. But the great magicians Beecham and Bernstein are missed here. Unfortunately, their recordings are no longer available.

EUGENE GOOSSENS (1893-1962)

Symphony nr. 1, Op. 58
- Adelaide S O / David Measham
  Uni KP 8000

Between the two World Wars, Goossens had the reputation of being a considerable composing talent. The First Symphony appeared in 1940. It was appropriately recorded in Australia as Goossens lived there for many years. He conducted the ABC Sydney Symphony Orchestra.
The Symphony is easily approachable. The well constructed score has colour and depth. Measham is surprisingly successful with the orchestra from Adelaide, and the recording was obviously made in good acoustics.

CHARLES GOUNOD (1818-93)

Petite Symphonie, in B Flat (for wind instruments)
- Netherlands Wind Ensemble / Edo de Waart
  Philips Sequ. 412 004-1/4
- Collegium Musicum Pragense
  Supraphon 1411 2844
- (Members of) Hallé O / Barbirolli
  PRT GSGC/ZCGC 2037
- Wind Academy Munich / Brezina
  HM Orfeo Dig CD C051831A (S 051831A)

Taste determines the choice here. The Petite Symphonie is still a wonderful piece of music, fresh, humorous, refined and charmng. The Netherlands Wind Ensemble give a perfect performance. The Collegium Musicum give no less. The Czech flautist uses more vibrato and the clarinet is a bit watery. The Barbirolli recording, dating from the sixties, is still vibrant and indeed acceptable. Barbirolli had an obvious affection for this music.

EDVARD GRIEG (1843-1907)

Symphony, in c minor
- Bergen S O / Anderson
  Decca Dig SXDL/KSXDC 7537
- Göteborg S O / Kamu
  BIS LP 200

The Symphony in c minor was written in Denmark while Grieg was living there, before his 21st year. Grieg forbade performance of this piece having heard Svendsen's First Symphony in 1867. The score was kept in the library in Bergen. The story goes that the score was illegally copied and smuggled to Russia. Ironically enough, the work was performed in 1865 by the Bergen Harmony conducted by none other than... Grieg.
The piece has four movements and takes 37 minutes. The music is only interesting in that it reveals what kind of ideas Grieg was busy with in his young years. The Decca recording is well balanced, detailed and has a good perspective. Okko Kamu's interpretation is as convincing as Andersen's, and his orchestra is more refined than the Bergen Symphony.

JOHANN HALVORSEN (1864-1935)

Symphony nr. 2 (Fatal)
- Oslo Philharmonie / Kartsen Andersen
  NKF 30 301

Johann Halvorsen is somewhat known even outside his native Norway. His countrymen, however, credit Svendsen with greater talent. Halvorsen is so often compared to other composers, that it is difficult to grant him his originality. Nevertheless, his Second Symphony, seen in the light of the post natonalistic idiom, is a work with individual character. It is very interesting music. The performance here is very dedicated to the work. The recording itself is not very good, but there is no other available.

HOWARD HANSON (1896-1981)

Symphony nr. 1, e minor ('Nordic')
Symphony nr. 3
Symphony nr. 2 ('Romantic'), Op. 30
Symphony nr. 4
- Eastman-Rochester O / composer
  Mercury SRI/MRI resp 75112; 75007; 75107

The First Symphony by Howard Hanson is a sober work. This American composer with a Swedish heritage has a musical character all his own. His Second Symphony was commissioned for the Boston Symphony's 50th anniversary. The subtitle, the Romantic, is not exaggerated. The music exudes warmth and is melodious, especially when played with such sensuality as it has been for this recording. Hanson's Fourth Symphony (1943) is an orchestral requiem for his father. The composer leads an authoritative performance, the recording is clear but not ideal.

ROY HARRIS (1898-1979)

Symphony nr. 3 in one movement
- New York P O / Bernstein
  CBS 61 681

The Third Symphony by Harris is considered the greatest American symphony to date. (The only competition is perhaps Walter Piston's Fourth Symphony.) The Bernstein performance is extremely dedicated and successful. He achieves all the daring intrinsic in the piece. It is perhaps less overwhelming than the effect achieved by Koussevitsky when he recorded the piece in 1942. But Bernstein is very close and the recording itself is, of course, very much better. Harris is still only popular with a limited audience.

KARL HARTMANN (1905-63)

Symphony nr. 4 for strings
Symphony nr. 8
- Orchestedes Bayerischen Rundfunks / Rafael Kubelik
  DG 413 650-1

In the fifties, Karl Amadeus Hartmann was all the

rage in Germany but was soon forgotten almost completely. These two symphonies give an impression of what Hartmann was capable of. Kubelik performed the première of the Eighth Symphony in 1962 in Cologne; the recording was made in 1968 but is very good nevertheless. The Fourth appeared right after the war (1946-1947) and is clearly post-impressionistic, as is, as a matter of fact, the Eighth. The structure of both pieces is very tight and, at first, inaccessible. These works are recommended for real lovers of 20th century music only. A complete set of Hartmann's symphonies was made (Wergo 60086) and is perhaps still available in speciality shops.

HAMILTON HARTY (1879-1941)

An Irish Symphony
- Ulster O / Thomson
  Chan Dig CHAN 8314 (CD); ABRD/ABTD (cassette) 1027

The Irish Symphony appeared in 1904 as an entry in a contest for a suite or symphony using Irish melodies. Harty's entry was praised for its superb orchestration, the mark of a true craftsman. The Scherzo is especially exciting, and the Overture is pleasant. The Ulster Orchestra plays very well under Thomson and the recording is wonderful. The cassette is not as good, but acceptable nevertheless.

FRANZ JOSEPH HAYDN (1732-1809)

*** Complete cycle:
Philharmonia Hungarica / Antal Dorati
Decca
nrs 1 - 19: HDNA 1/6
nrs 20 - 35: HDNA B7
nrs 36 - 48: HDNA C13/18
nrs 49 - 56: HDNA D19/22
nrs 65 - 72: HDNA 27/30
nrs 73 - 81: HDNA 31/4
nrs 82 - 87; 88 - 91: HDNA H35/40
nrs 93 - 104: HDNA J41-6

*** Symphonies nrs 6 in D major (Le Matin); 7 in C major (Le Midi); 8 in G major (Le Soir)
- Academy SMF / Marriner
  Philips Dig **411 441-2**; 6514/*7337* 076

*** Symphonies nrs 1 in D major; 2 in C major; 10 in D major; 15 in D major; 18 in G major; 37 in C major
L'Estro Armonico / Solomons
Saga HAYDN 1 (3 LPs)

*** Symphonies nrs 3 in G major; 5 in A major; 11 in E flat major; 27 in G major; 32 in C major; 33 in C major (Morzin Symphonies)
L'Estro Armonico / Solomons
Saga HAYDN 2

*** Symphonies nrs 26 in d minor (Lamentatione); 41 in C major; 43 in E flat major (Merkur); 44 in e minor (Trauersinfonie); 48 in C major (Maria Theresia); 52 in c minor
- L'Estro Armonico / Solomons
  CBS Dig 13M/*13T* 39040 [3 LPs]

*** Symphonies nrs 22 in E flat major (Der Philosoph) and 48

in C major (Maria Theresia)
English Chamber O / Leppard
Philips Seq 6527/*7311* 096

*** Symphonies nrs 22 (Der Philisoph) and 95
Academy SMF / Marriner
Philips 9500 198

*** Symphonies nrs 31 in D major (Hornsignal) and 45 in F sharp (Abschiedsinfonie) and 73 in D major (La Chasse) and 82 in C major (L'Ours) and 83 in g minor (La Poule) and 92 in G major (Oxford) and 101 in D major (The Clock)
Academy of SMF / Marriner
Philips 6768 06 (4LPs)

*** Symphonies nrs 31 and 73
Academy of SMF / Marriner
Philips 9500 518/*7300 674*

*** Symphonies nrs 35 and 38 in C (Echo) and 39 in g minor and 49 in f minor (La Passione) and 58 in F major and 59 in A major (Feuersinfonie)
L'Estro Armonico / Solomons
CBS D3 37861/*40*

*** Symphonies nrs 44 and 49
Academy of SMF /Marriner
Philips 9500 199

*** Symphonies nrs 45 and 101
Academy of SMF / Marriner
Philips 9500 520/*7300 676*

*** Symphony nr. 44 in e minor (Trauersinfonie)
Orch of St John's Smith Square / Lubbock
Pickwick Dig **PCD 820**

*** Symphonies nrs 44, and 47 in B flat major
Orpheus Chamber Orchestra
DG Dig **415 365-2**; /-1; /-4

*** Symphonies nrs 46 and 47
English Chamber O / Barenboim
DG 2531/*3301* 324

*** Symphony nr. 49 in d minor (La Passione)
Orch of St John's Smith Square / Lubbock
Pickwick Dig **PCD 819**

*** Symphonies nrs 22 in E flat major (Der Philosoph); 43 in E flat (Merkur); 44 in e minor (Treuer); 48 in C major (Maria Theresia); 49 in f minor (La Passione); 55 in E flat major (Der Schulmeister); 59 in A major (Feuersinfonie); 85 in B flat major (La Reine); 94 in G major (Paukenschlag); 100 in G major (Military); 103 in E flat major (Drum Roll)
Academy of SMF / Marriner
Philips 6768 003 (6 LPs)

*** Symphonies nrs 60 in C major (Il Distratto) and 63 in C major (LaRoxelane)
Academy of SMF / Marriner
Philips Dig 6514/*7337* 113

*** Symphonies nrs 82 - 87 (Paris Symphonies)
Academy of SMF / Marriner
Philips 6725/*7655* 012 (3 LPs)

*** Symphonies nrs 86 in D major and 98 in B flat major

Concertgebouw O / Colin Davis
Philips 9500 678/*7300 589*

*** Symphonies nrs 93 -104
- Concertgebouw / Colin Davis
  Philips Dig 6725 010/*7655 010*
- Berliner Philharmoniker / Karajan
  DG 2741/*3382* 015 (6 LPs)

*** Symphonies nrs 86 in D major and 87 in A major
Academy of SMF / Marriner
Philips **412 888-2**

*** Symphony nr. 88 in G major
Berliner Philharmoniker / Furtwängler
DG mono **415 661-2**

*** Symphonies nrs 88 and 92 in G major(Oxford)
Wiener Philharmoniker / Bernstein
DG dig **413 777-2**;/-1;/-4

*** Symphonies nrs 88 and 100 in G major (Military)
Columbia S O / Walter
CBS **MK42047**

*** Symphonies nrs 91 in E flat and 92 in G major (Oxford)
Concertgebouw O / Colin Davis
Philips Dig **410 390-2**;/-1;/-4

*** Symphonies nrs 92 in G major (Oxford); 100 in G major (Military) and 101 in D major (The Clock)
Wiener Philharmoniker / Böhm and London P O / Jochum
DG Walkman *415 329-4*

*** Symphonies nrs 93 in D major and 94 (Paukenschlag) and 96 (The Miracle)
- Concertgebouworkest / Colin Davis
  Philips Dig **412 871-2**
- Cleveland O / Szell
  CBS 60148/*40-*

*** Symphonies nrs 93 - 104
Royal P O / Sir Thomas Beecham
HMV SLS 846 (6 LPs)

*** Symphonies nrs 94 and 99
Wiener Philharmoniker / Josef Krips
Decca Ace of Diamonds SDD174

*** Symphonies nrs 96 and 99
Concertgebouw O / Haitink
Philips Universo 6580 151 and Festival 6570

*** Symphonies 94 in G major (Paukenschlag) and 96 in D major (The Miracle)
Academy of Ancient Music / Hogwood
l'Oiseau-Lyre Dig **414 330-2**;/-1;/-4

*** Symphonies nrs 94 in G major (Paukenschlag) and 100 in G major (Military)
London P O / Solti
Decca dig **411 897-2**;/-1;/-4

*** Symphonies nrs 94 and 100
- Berliner Philharmoniker / Karajan
  DG dig **410 869-2**
- London P O / Jochum
  DG 2530 628

- Philharmonia Hungarica / Dorati
  Decca SPA/*KCSP* 494
- New York Philharmonic / Bernstein
  CBS 60267 / *40-*

*** Symphonies nrs 94 in G major (Paukenschlag) and 103 in E flat (Drum Roll) and 104 in D major (London)
London P O / Jochum
DG Walkman *413 424-4*

*** Symphonies nrs 94 and 104
Pittsburgh S O / Previn
CfP CFP4400; *TC /-*

*** Symphonies nrs 95 and 96
Berliner Philharmoniker / Karajan
DG dig 410 867-1;/-4

*** Symphonies nrs 95 in c minor and 97 in C major
Concertgebouw O / Colin Davis
Philips Dig 6514/*7337* 074

*** Symphonies nrs 95 and 101 (The Clock)
Chicago S O / Reiner
RCA VICS/*VK* 2007

*** Symphonies nrs 96 in D major (Miracle) and 100 in G major (Military)
Berliner Philharmoniker / Karajan
DG Dig **410 975-2**

*** Symphonies nrs 97 in C major and 98 in B flat major
Berliner Philharmoniker / Karajan
DG Dig 410 947-1;/-4

*** Symphonies nrs 99 in E flat and 100 in G major (Military)
Berliner Philharmoniker / Karajan
DG Dig 410 958-1;/-4

*** Symphonies nrs 100 in G major (Military) and 103 in E flat (Drum Roll)
Academy of SMF / Marriner
Philips 412 925-1;/-4

*** Symphonies nrs 100 in G major and 104 in D major (London)
- Concertgebouw O / Colin Davis
  Philips **411 449-2** and 9500 510 / *7300 670*
- London P O / Jochum
  DG Privilege 2535-347 / *3355-347*
- Academy of Ancient Music / Hogwood
  l'Oiseau-Lyre **411 833-2**; /-1;/-4
- Philharmonia O / Klemperer
  HMV ED290357-1;/-4

*** Symphonies nrs 101 and 102
- Concertgebouw O / Colin Davis
  Philips 9500 679/*7300 774*
- Berliner Philharmoniker / Karajan
  DG 410 868-1;/-4

*** Symphonies nrs 101 in D major (The Clock) and 103 in E flat (Drum Roll) and 104 in D major (London)
Scottish Chamber O / Leppard
Erato Dig NUM/*MCE* 751412
also: nrs 101 and 104 on CD: **ECD 88079**

*** Symphonies nrs 103 and 104
- Berliner Philharmoniker / Karajan

DG Dig **410 517-2**;/-1;/-4
- Wiener Philharmoniker / Karajan
  Decca VIV55/*KVIC* [recording early 60's)
- Royal P O / Sir Thomas Beecham
  HMV SXLP 30257/*TC-*

It would take an entire book to list, categorize and qualify the conductors and orchestras that have recorded one or more of Haydn's 104 symphonies. Dorati leads the field having recorded the complete set (the only conductor ever to have done so) with the Philharmonia Hungarica. Nrs1-19 and 82-104 have won the most acclaim for him, not to mention the fact that Dorati dared to tackle the immense project in the first place. In terms of quantity, Solomons and l'Estro Armonica are in second place having recorded 29 symphonies (none of the later ones) and Sir Neville Marriner has recorded 26 (including the later numbers 92, 94,100 and 104). Marriner's Academy is brilliant in nrs 44 (Trauersinfonie) and 49 (La Passione). In La Passione especially, the smaller ensembles are the best. Lubbock is wonderful as is the Orpheus Chamber Orchestra from New York whose CD is the most beautifully made.

The Concertgebouw Orchestra under Sir Colin Davis has recorded 16 symphonies (nrs 86, 87, 91-104) and under Sir Bernard Haitink,two (96 and 99). All the Haydn recordings made by the Concertgebouw are true gems. Hogwood, who has caused much excitement with his orchestra in the last few years, has made excellent recordings of 94 (Paukenschlag) and 96 (The Miracle), both for l'Oiseau-Lyre. (It would, by the way, be a pity if in the future, Haydn was only played by authentic ensembles.) Karajan fans will be content to know that he has recorded 11 of the later symphonies (nrs 94-104).

Great conductors of the past have also performed their share of Haydn. A summary follows: Eugen Jochum has performed 10 of the symphonies with the London Philharmonic, the Berlin Philharmonic and the Orchestra of the Bavarian Radio respectively. All of these are true classics. Furtwängler's 88th with the Berliners is one of his most famous records. It can even be recommended to those who do not usually appreciate Furtwängler. It was made in 1951, in the beautiful Jesus Christ Church in Berlin. The recording has been remastered digitally and sounds brand new.

The transfers made of Walter's 88th and100th with the NBC Symphony Orchestra (1961) are disappointing. The whole thing sounds more like a rehearsal than a live concert performance; the slow tempi make it awkward and depressing. Klemperer's version of 100 and 104 are heavy as well, not much to recommend here either. There is something Teutonic about them that is completely inappropriate. Reiner's performances of the 95th and the 101th (The Clock) date from the mid-sixties but still sound quite good. Szell and the Clevelanders are a brilliant combination in the 93rd and 94th. All the details are well taken care of and the rhythm is faultless: truly the work of a perfectionist. Szell gives especially the Menuets a wonderful swing (missing in Bernstein, for example).

Those who prefer a real Viennese version of Haydn will enjoy the Vienna Philharmonic together with the legendary Josef Krips. The playing catches Haydn's

graciousness and joviality in a relaxed and natural way. Nrs 93 -104 have also been recorded by Sir Thomas Beecham and 'his' orchestra: the Royal Philharmonic. These are in a class by themselves. Beecham's greatest talent is in his phrasing: his musicians phrase as naturally as they breathe. Beecham reaches the heart of the music as no other. The balance between the different orchestral sections should serve as a perfect example for all. The span is unfortunately a bit limited in comparison to modern CD technique and Beecham ignores the autographs in nrs. 103 and 104, nevertheless, this is wonderful Haydn.

Last but not least: Karajan. In the early sixties, Von Karajan recorded nrs 103 and 104 with the Vienna Philharmonic for Decca, performances that are still considered fresh. In the newer version with Berlin (hardly a difference between LP and CD!) the 104th has more weight, more value. Karajan rightly repeats the exposition and refrains from eccentricities. The Menuet and Trio are a bit quicker than the Viennese version. The new 103rd has an unmistakeable grandeur.

Michael Haydn (1737-1806)

Symphony P1 in E flat major
Symphony P6 in A major
Symphony P11 in D major
Symphony P12 in C major
- Franz Liszt Chamber O / Janos Rolla
  Teldec/Conifer digital AZ6 431188; ZK8 43188 (CD)
Symphony P16 in G major
Symphony P33 in A major
- Little Orch of London / Leslie Jones
  Pye GSGC 14131
Symphony P16 in G major
- St Paul Chamber O / Russell Davies
  Nonesuch H71323

Perger's catalogue of Michael Haydn's oeuvre includes 50 symphonies, only a handful of which have been recorded. Of the four recorded in Budapest, only the P11 in D major has previously been published and recorded (in 1982 by the RIAS Sinfonietta from Berlin, Gustav Kuhn conducting for EMI Electrola 1 C 15799757/8). The other three are recording premières and are reconstructions from manuscripts in the National Széchényi Library in Budapest. The first, P1 composed in Grosswardein in 1760, has three movements. The others, P6 (Salzburg, 1767) P12 (Salzburg, 1777) and P11, have four movements with the third a Menuet. The best movement of them all is probably the Andante, the second movement of P12. The Trio in P6 is also charming and exciting.

The performances conducted by Janos Rolla are fresh and the orchestra reacts very alertly. One could condemn the heavy vibrato in the horn section, typical for Eastern Europeans' performances, as questionable. The Teldec recording is first rate.

VICTOR HELY-HUTCHINSON
(1901-47)

A Carol Symphony

- Pro Arte O / Rose
  HMV Green ESD/*TC-ESD* 7021

A Carol Symphony by Hely-Hutchinson appeared in the late twenties. The inherent problem of the piece is the carols themselves, precious little gems of old tunes not suited to be treated symphonically. As Constant Lambert once remarked: the only way to play a folktune any new way, is to play it louder. Hely-Hutchinson not only plays the carols 'louder' but, as for example with the Coventry Carol, adds inappropriate Mahlerian harmonies to them. This symphony would never have become known at all if it was not for Sir Thomas Beecham who busily promoted it. The performance is adequate but Guildford Cathedral is not a good place to make such a recording.

HANS WERNER HENZE (born 1926)

Symphonies nrs 1 - 5
- Berliner Philharmoniker / composer
  DG 410 937-1

This recording is a re-release from 1967. Henze is only slightly represented in the record catalogues. The works range from a Stravinsky-like coolness in the First, to an exuberance and expressive brilliance in the Fifth. The recordings, led by the composer, are of course, definitive, but they are very brilliant and lively as well.

ALFRED HILL (1870-1960)

Symphony nr. 4 in c minor (Pursuit of Happiness) (1955)
Symphony nr. 6 in B flat major (Celtic) (1955)
- Melbourne S O / Wilfred Lehmann
  Marco Polo/D sharp 6220345; 8220345 (CD)

The Fourth Symphony by Alfred Hill takes only 19 minutes. Whatever else one might think of Hill, this proves that he was at least extremely efficient in giving his ideas form in this piece. Accepting the romantic idiom, and taking into consideration the times in which Hill worked, this piece can be a pleasure to listen to. If Parry's Fifth Symphony is appreciated, Hill's Fourth deserves the same treatment.
The Celtic Symphony is longer but still less than 24 minutes. The Irish jig is numerously repeated, and for the untrained ear, one jig is frightfully like the next. Nevertheless the music is lively. Technically, it is not as clear a sound as is expected from a CD. Perhaps this is due to the acoustics of the Camberwell Civic Centre in Victoria where the recording was made.

PAUL HINDEMITH (1895-1963)

Mathis der Maler (Symphony)
- Boston S O / William Steinberg
  DG 413 651-1
- Berliner Philharmoniker / Von Karajan
  HMV SXLP/*TC-SXLP* 30536
- London S O / Jascha Horenstein
  Uni RHS/*UKC* 312

Symphonic metamorphoses on themes of Weber
- London S O / Claudio Abbado
  Decca Lon Ent 414 437-1/*4* also: SXL 6398
- Atlanta S O / Robert Shaw
  Telarc Dig DG 10056
- New York P O / Bernstein
  CBS 60288/*40*

Hindemith is well represented in the record catalogues, especially considering the fact that his music is difficult and sells badly. Von Karajan's recording of the Mathis der Maler(1960) still stands as one of the most beautiful ever made. The interpretation is transparent, full of shifting dynamic and wonderful phrasing. The older version Von Karajan made (EMI, with the Philharmonia Orchestra) is thought to be even superior still.
Horenstein's recording was made just before the conductor's death. His interpretation commands attention; it is definitely interesting for Horenstein devotees.
Steinberg leads the Boston Symphony with great control. This recording's advantage lies in the superior balance of the DG sound (1972). In 1957, Steinberg recorded the work for the first time (with the Pittsburgh Symphony). In that same year, the composer conducted the Berlin Philharmonic (12 D-G LPM 18507) but this version has disappeared. Another recording the composer conducted, of the Symphonia Serena (more of a concerto for orchestra than a formal symphony), was also very successful, once again proving Hindemith's directorial talent.
It is always a pleasure to listen to a conductor who puts the music, and especially the score with all its markings, first, and his own, personal ideas, second. Claudio Abbado is such a dignified conductor, and his performance of the Symphonic Metamorphoses, a virtuostic essay for orchestra, is sublime. Robert Shaw, on the other hand, treats the variations in a neo-classical way. The performance is rigid, void of humour and charm.

ALUN HODDINOTT (born 1929)

Symphony nr. 2, Op. 20
- London S O / Norman del Mar
  Oriel ORM 1003

Alan Hoddinott is dedicated to serial music and uses the twelve tone system. This symphony was written in 1962. Too much of the work is slow and pedantic. There is only one recording available.

VAGN HOLMBOE (born 1909)

Symphony nr. 10, Op. 105
- Göteborg S O / Sixten Ehrling
  Cap CAP 1116

This is work that should not be neglected by lovers of Scandanavian symphonic music. The Tenth (of the eleven symphonies) was written for Sixten Ehrling and the Detroit Symphony in 1971. Nielsen devotees will certainly appreciate this piece. There is also a recording of Holmboe's Seventh Symphony, praised as his best by connoisseurs, performed by the Danish Radio Orchestra under John Frandsen (Danish Music Anthology 018).

GUSTAV HOLST (1874- 1934)

Choral Symphony, Op. 41
- London P O / Sir Adrian Boult (with Felicity Palmer)
  HMV ED 290378-1

According to many, this Symphony is wrongfully neglected. It is an ambitious attempt by Holst to set the poems of Keats to music. Boult conducts a straightforward performance and is especially successful in the finale. Boult gives the piece a wholeness. Still, it is not Holst's best work.

ARTHUR HONEGGER (1892-1955)

Symphony no. 1
Symphony no. 2 (for strings and trumpet)
Symphony no. 3 (Liturgique)
Symphony no. 4 (Deliciae basiliensis)
Symphony no. 5 (Di tre re)
- Czech P O / Baudo
  Supraphon 110 1741/3
- Toulouse Capitole Orch / Plasson (2/81)
  EMI 2C 167 16327/9
Symphony nr. 2
- Orch Radio Suisse Romande / Ansermet
  Decca Ace SDD 189
Symphonies nrs. 2 and 3
- Berliner Philharmoniker / Karajan
  DG 2543 805
Symphonies nrs. 1 and 3
- Orchester des Bayerischen Rundfunks / Charles Dutoit
  Erato Dig CD ECD88171; (NUM/*MCE* 75254)
Symphonies nrs 2 and 4
- Orchester des Bayerischen Rundfunks / Charles Dutoit
  Erato/Conifer Dig CD ECD881 78; (NUM75259); also
cassette

Honegger's symphonies are neglected for the most part. They are rarely performed in spite of their obvious worth. The First Symphony was commissioned by Koussevitsky. The Second was written during the war and is a piece wrought with the fear Honegger experienced during the German occupation. The Third was composed towards the end of the war. The Czech recordings were made in the early sixties. The performance is dedicated, to be sure, but the recording is flat and has too much resonance. The Fourth was written for Paul Sacher, using Swiss folk melodies. This is perhaps the most neglected of the symphonies. The Fifth is also powerfully played by the Czechs, even though the sound is again disappointing.
Michel Plasson profited greatly from improved recording techniques in the late seventies. (The Baudo recording was made a decade earlier.) Still, the French orchestra cannot match the Czechs in virtuosity, despite their richer sound.
Ansermet's performance is very powerful, full of spirit. Insiders maintain that Von Karajan's version is the most beautiful Honegger ever played. Perhaps these insiders have never heard the wonderful recording Igor Markevitch made with the Lamoureux

Orchestra in 1957.
Dutoit leads the Bavarians very well and gets given their best efforts. The phrasing Dutoit makes is excellent. Technically, the Erato is far superior to all the other recordings with the exception of perhaps Von Karajan who exists in a class by himself.

ALAN HOVHANESS (born 1911)

Symphony nr. 4, Op. 165
- Eastman Symphonic Wind Ensemble / Roller
  Mercury SRI 75010

This sort of music could rouse a certain curiosity among connoisseurs and enthusiasts. Hovhaness was a student of Martinu's, extremely interested in the East and especially in Armenian music. He was a very fruitful composer (considering the high opus number): he wrote more than fifty symphonies. Hovhaness' Fourth Symphony is rather static; it doesn't contain enough exciting surprises. The Eastman Ensemble plays the piece very intelligently and the recording quality is good.

VINCENT d'INDY (1851-1931)

Symphony nr. 2 in B flat major, Op. 57
- Toulouse Capitole O / Plasson
  EMI 2C 069 73100
Symphonie sur un chant montagnard français (Symphonie cévenole)
- Berner S O / Peter Maag
  Conifer Dig CD CDCF146 (also LP and cassette)

Despite its impressiveness, d'Indy's Second Symphony (1902) is a neglected work. The first recording of this work was made in 1942 by Pierre Monteux and the San Francisco Symphony. Plasson is clearly dedicated to his task here and leads his orchestra well. It cannot be expected, however, that the Toulouse Orchestra is anything more than satisfactory. The Symphonie cévenole is really not a symphony at all. In spite of the difficult piano part, neither is it a concerto. The piece is reminiscent of Fauré's Ballade or Franck's Variations Symphoniques. D'Indy has no other works included in the record catalogues.

CHARLES IVES (1874-1954)

Symphony nr. 2
- Concertgebouw O / Tilson Thomas
  CBS Dig 37300/40
Symphony nr. 3 (The Camp meeting)
- Concertgebouw O / Tilson Thomas
  CBS Dig CD MK37823; (IM/IMT 37823)
- St Paul Chamber O / Russell
  Pro Arte Dig CD CCD140; (PAD/PDC 140)
- Academy SMF / Marriner
  Argo ZRG/KZRC 845
- New York P O / Bernstein
  CBS 60268/40
- Eastman Rochester O / Howard Hanson
  Mercury SRI 75035
Symphony nr. 4
- John Alldis Coir / London P O / Serebrier

Chandos Dig CD CHAN8397, transferred from ABRD/ABDT 1118 (9/85)
- Boston S O / Ozawa
  DG 410-93-1
Symphonies nrs 1 and 2
- Los Angeles P O / Zubin Mehta
  Decca London Enterprise 414 661-1LE

From 1897 until 1902, Charles Ives worked on his Second Symphony. He had to wait another 50 years for Bernstein to conduct the première. The symphony was recorded in 1960, using the composer's handwritten score. Malcolm Goldstein revised that score using material found after Ives' death. Tilson Thomas is the first to record the symphony from this revised score in an excellent recording. The Concertgebouw's playing is wonderful but the CBS technicians are not as successful with this orchestra as their Decca colleagues.
The 1965 recording of the Third Symphony performed by New York is still considered very good. Howard Hanson was the best promoter of contemporary American music for a long time and performs this Ives well. Unfortunately, the microphones sound too close to the players which spoils the recording, something that is often done badly. Russell Davis gives a beautiful performance; there is something intimate about his interpretation.
Ives' Fourth Symphony was written for an immense orchestra. It took 50 years for Stokowski to get round to performing it with the All American Symphony. José Serebrier assisted Stokowski in the preparation of this complex and difficult work. Serebrier does well on his own in the English recording and the Londoners stand by him throughout. Technicians have nightmares about this score. The RCA 1974 recording was received with mixed reviews; after 12 years, the new CD is a good example of the amazing new remastering techniques.
Los Angeles, together with Zubin Mehta, also perform the work well. Their recording is very convincing, but is, unfortunately, one-dimensional in sound.

LEOS JANACEK (1854-1928)

Sinfonietta
- London S O / Claudio Abbado
  Decca SXL 6398
- Pro Arte O / Sir Charles Mackerras
  PRT GSGC/ZCGC (cassette) 2018
- Vienna P O / Mackerras
  Decca Dig. 410 138-2 (CD); SXDL/KSXDC (cassette) 7519 (1983)
- Philharmonia O / Simon Rattle
  HMV Dig ASD/TS-ASD (cassette) 143522-1 (1985)
- Chicago S O / Ozawa
  HMV SXLP 30420
- Czech P O / Ancerl
  Supraphon 50380;PMC/P4C (cassette)
- Czech P O / Vaclav Neumann
  Supraphon / Counterpoint C37 7056 (CD) (1986)
- Vienna P O / Kubelik
  Decca LW5213 (1955)
- Brno Radio P O / Bakala
  Artia ALP122 (1957)

The Sinfonietta is Janacek's most popular orchestral work, probably due to the spectacular opening: nine trumpets, two bass trumpets, two tenor tubas and kettledrums. For a long time, the Bakala performance was considered the best and most authentic. Technically, the recording is not completely satisfactory. Decca brought out an improved version with Kubelik, albeit that this is not the conductor's best performance of the piece. In 1959, the Mackerras recording appeared as a wonderful surprise. It seems that all the trumpeters in London were called upon. Mackerras recorded the Sinfonietta again in 1983, with the Viennese Philharmonic. His is more brilliant than Simon Rattle's version with the V P, but Rattle's is perhaps the favorite among the true romantics. The catalogue was extended when Claudio Abbado made an excellent recording with the London Symphony. Abbado shows us again why he is so famous for his care of detail and his sensitive feeling for the dynamics of a piece.
The recording that differs mostly from the rest is the one made by the Czechs with Neumann. Here are faster tempi and a lighter approach. Everything is more flexible. For example, the tuba ostinato that begins the piece is surprisingly light and supple; it is only the vibrato that gives the Eastern brass players away. All these qualities are enhanced by a good recording. The orchestra plays very near to the microphones. Janacek's heavy orchestration becomes somewhat transparent and less aggressive than on the other recordings.

DANIEL JONES (born 1912)

Symphony nr. 4 (In Memoriam Dylan Thomas)
Symphony nr. 7
- Royal P O / Sir Charles Groves
  Oriel ORM 1002
Symphony nr. 6
- Royal P O / Groves
  Oriel ORM 1004
Symphony nr. 8
Symphony nr. 9
- BBC Elsh S O / Bryden Thomson
  BBC REGL 359

After repeated hearings it becomes evident that Daniel Jones created a very original musical world in his symphonic work. The Fourth and Seventh Symphonies have powerful atmosphere. Sir Charles Groves leads an especially beautiful performance. Jones' Eighth and Ninth Symphonies are also extremely original and pleasing, and Bryden Thomson leads these performances well.

JOSEPH JONGEN (1873-1953)

Symphony Concertant, Op. 18
- San Francisco S O / Michael Murray, organ / Edo de Waart
  Telarc Dig (CD) 80096; DG 10096

There are no harmonic surprises in Joseph Jongen's Symphony. The work dates from 1926 and is obviously the work of a great craftsman. Lovers of Saint-Saëns Third Symphony will appreciate Jongen the most. In particular the Lento misterioso and the spectacular Toccata that closes the piece, are very well written. This performance is very convincing. Murray has the technique to be authoritative with the difficult problems at hand (his Bach recordings are ample proof of that).

WILFRED JOSEPHS (born 1927)

Symphony nr. 5 (Pastoral), Op. 75
- Adelaide S O / Measham
  Uni Dig DKP 9026

Wilfred Josephs is famous for his TV theme tunes and film music. He has obviously no problem in writing very approachable music, even in a more serious genre. His Fifth Symphony is an ambitious work full of glorious sounds. The technical quality of the recording is excellent.

OLAV KIELLAND (born 1901)

Symphony nr. 1
- London P O / composer
  Philips 6529 039

This clearly Norwegian composition (1935) has lots of power. Lovers of Nielsen and Stenhammer will especially appreciate this music. The work is very dramatic and the orchestration is a masterpiece. The composer directs the LPO wonderfully; he was in his eighties at the time. The recording is very natural and very good.

OTTO KLEMPERER (1885-1973)

Symphony nr. 2
- New Philharmonia O / Klemperer
  HMV ED 290332-1

Klemperer's symphony is proof of the creative talents of this great conductor. The paradox lies in the fame Klemperer enjoyed as a musician with the reins firmly in hand; this Mahlerian work presents too many musical ideas of greatly differing quality. Nevertheless, there is enough to please the ear. Both the performance and the recording are good.

OLIVER KNUSSEN (born 1952)

Symphony nr. 3
- Philharmonia O / Michael Tilson Thomas
  Uni Dig RHD 400

At only sixteen, Oliver Knussen directed the première of his First Symphony with the London Symphony when the conductor Istvan Kertesz was suddenly taken ill. He finished his Third Symphony in 1979 which was dedicated to Tilson Thomas. Tilson Thomas performed the première at the Proms that same year. There are hints of Messiaen and Henze in Knussen's work which, nevertheless, remains original and personal. The Third is a one movement piece and takes only 15 minutes. Tilson Thomas has recorded it well; technically, it is adequate.

JOONAS KOKKONEN (born 1921)

Symphony nr. 3
- Finnish Radio O / Berglund
  Finlandia FA 311

Kokkonen is definitely the finest symphonic composer of his generation in Finland. Apart from the Third mentioned here, the radio broadcasts of the Second (Okko Kamu, 1961) and Fourth (Segerstam,1981) are available on the BIS label (BIS LP 189). Kokkonen's Fourth Symphony is generally considered to be his best. This performance of the Third is completely convincing. The Finnish Radio Orchestra plays extremely well and the recording is superb.

LEOPOLD KOZELUCH (1747-1818)

Symphony in F major
Symphony in g minor
- Prague S O / Hlavacek
  Sup 1102078

Kozeluch was a contemporary of both Haydn and Mozart and came from Bohemia. His music is definitely worthy of notice. Both his symphonies, which followed the Parisian symphonies of Haydn, are very well put together and extremely inventive. The rich melodies of his better known colleagues are lacking though. The performance here is lively and the recording is satisfactory.

FRANZ (FRANTISEK) KROMMER (1759-1831)

Symphony in D major, OP. 40
- Prague Chamber O / Frantisek Valjner

The Symphony in D major dates from 1803 and is one of a series of nine. It is a substantial work of considerable power. Beethoven's world comes to mind. According to many, the world of war is also to be heard, with many influences from the French Revolution. The Prague Orchestra is a bit stiff in this performance with Valjnar. A more inspired recording of this interesting music would be very welcome.

EDOUARDO LALO (1823-92)

Symphony in g minor
- French National Radio O / Sir Thomas Beecham
  HMV sxdw 3022
- National Opera Orch of Monte Carlo/ Almeida

This Symphony in g minor should not be confused with the widely played Symphony Espagnole, which itself is actually a violin concerto. Beecham was a champion of this sort of French music (quite irregular for the style of the time), and he is very successful with his French Radio Orchestra. Despite the difference in quality between the two orchestras, the Almeida performance can compete well with the Beecham version. Almeida plays the repeat of the first half. He conducts the piece with great affection.

His is also the much better recording. Beecham's dates from the end of the fifties.

RUED LANGGAARD (1893-1952)

Symphony nr. 6 (Det Himmelrivende)
- Danish Radio S O / Frandsen
  Danish DMA 064

Langaard was somethng of an outsider in the Danish musical world. He has been compared to Ives and Brian. The title of the 1920 Symphony comes from St Paul. Some moments are square and awkward, but the work also has moments of inspiration. The recording was made live at a concert, most probably in 1980. It is acceptable but not noteworthy. The performance is reasonably convincing but suffers from the thin tone of the Danish strings.

ADOLF LINDBLAD (1801-78)

Symphony nr.1 in C major
- Stockholm P O / Okko Kamu
  Cap CAP 1197

Lindblad is credited with fathering the Swedish lieder tradition. Some of his lieder have been recorded by Decca with Elisabeth Söderström. Lindblad did write two symphonies as well. The first appeared in 1832. The Stockholm Orchestra plays with a great deal of charm for Kamu who obviously enjoyed performing the work at hand. The recording is beautiful; it has a very natural balance with enough space around each of the groups of instruments.

FRANZ LISZT (1811-86)

Dante Symphony, G. 109
- Bolshoi Theatre Choir and Orch / Khaikin
  HMV SXLP 30234
- Helmond Concert Choir / Rotterdam P O / James Conlon
  Erato Dig CD ECD 88162 (NUM/MCE 75245)
- Utah Choir and S O / Kojian
  Andante Dig CD ACD72401 (AD72401)
- Chor St Thomas Kirche Leipzig / Leipzig Gewandthaus O / Kurt Masur
  HMV TCC2-POR 54292
- Choeur du Collège Voltaire / Choeur de Genève / Orch Suisse Romande / Lopez-Cobos
  Decca Dig SXDL/KSXDC 7542
- Veronika Kincses / Hungary Broadcast Female Choir/ Budapest S O / György Lehel
  Hungaroton/Conifer CD SLPX11918-2 (also LP and cassette)

Faust Symphony, G.108
- Riegel / Tanglewood Festival Choir / Boston S O / Bernstein
  DG 2707 100
- Royal P O / Beecham
  HMV ALP1737; re-release: SXDW3022 (1960)
- Siegfried Jerusalem / Chicago S O / Georg Solti
  Decca Dig CD 417 399-2DH (also LP and cassette)
- John Aler / Slavic Philharmonic Choir / Rotterdam P O / James Conlon
  Erato Dig CD ECD880682 (NUM/MCE 751582 (2)
- Kozma / Concertgebouw Choir and O / Antal Dorati

Philips Dig 6769/*7654* 089
- Winbergh / Westminster Choir / College Male Choir / Philadelphia O / Ricardo Muti
  HMV Dig SLS/*TC-SLS* 143570-3
- Alexander Young / Beecham Choral Society / Royal P O / Beecham
  HMV SXDW 3022
- Alfonz Bartha / Budapest Choral Society and State Orch / Ferencsik
  DGG Privilege 2535 149
- Werner Krenn / Le Choeur Pro Arte de Lausanne / Orch Suisse Romande / Ansermet
  Decca SET370/1

The recording of the Dante Symphony under Lopez-Cobos is an excellent version. The good balance and refined sound are both remarkable. The Swiss orchestra could have been more brilliant, however, but the winds are mixed well and the choir is luscious, something one would expect from Lopez-Cobos. The opening is especially good.
EMI brought out a series called 'Portrait of the Artist'. Kurt Masur's Dante Symphony was part of this series, a hommage to the conductor for having recorded the complete orchestral works by Liszt. The Masur performance is full and rich. The Inferno section is most likely the best of all versions available. James Conlon, on the other hand, is more brilliant in the Purgatorio section. The Quasi Allegro is noble and reserved. Unfortunately, the sound is perhaps too reserved and does not do justice to Liszt's drama.
György Lehel leads an apocalyptic performance: his Purgatorio is as dramatic as his Inferno. The brass, especially in the opening, is breathtaking. The Andante amoroso is graceful. This Dante Symphony is a special one, easily rivalling the western versions.
The Faust Symphony that James Conlon recorded for Erato is excellent. The choral finales are impressive. Some will probably prefer the Ricardo Muti version. This young Italian has a very special feeling for this symphony.
Bernstein's newer performance with the Boston Symphony is sensitive and brilliant. This is perhaps the first Faust to drive Sir Thomas Beecham, with his record made in the late fifties, from first place. The Bostonians are exciting and the recording is perfectly done. The transfer of the old Beecham recording allows us to treasure this great, early performance.
Ferecsik can not survive a comparison to Beecham, except perhaps, in the choral finale. Ansermet made a deep and beautiful recording for Decca which is still exemplary.
The Concertgebouw's grace and refinement in their 1982 recording for Philips is above criticism. Made during a live concert, the performance lacks drama. Dorati is not at his best here.
The first twelve notes are famous in Faust. Solti attacks these with appetite, and the whole performance is exciting in its virtuosity. The Gretchen section is beautiful and makes clear how ingenius Liszt's orchestration is. As is often the case with Solti, there is a bit too much attention paid to the player's technique, attention that is better dedicated to the music's heart. Those seeking the grand virtuoso should definitely choose Solti.

GEORGE LLOYD (born 1913)

Symphonies nrs 2 (1933) and 9
- BBC P O / Lloyd
  Lyrita/Conifer CD CF139
Symphony nr. 5
- Philharmonia O / Edward Downes
  Lyr SRCS 124
Symphony nr. 7 (1969)
- BBC P O / Lloyd
  Lyrita/Conifer CD CF143
Symphony nr. 8
- Philharmonia O / Downes
  Lyr SRCS 113
Symphony nr. 11 (1985)
- Alban S O / Lloyd
  Conifer Dig CFC144, also CD

George Lloyd's is easy listening music. The Second Symphony is conservative harmonically, surprising as that is considering the time (1933) in which it was composed. The Ninth is a happy piece, often called 'the best answer to the ninth symphony problem'. The Fifth successfully hides the composer's struggle between life and death. The first movement, The Pastoral, gives a false impression of complete happiness. Downes and the Philharmonia give a convincing performance together. The Seventh Symphony is a longer work (50 minutes) and presents us with Lloyd at his best as an orchestrator. There are powerful effects included in the work.
The Albany Symphony was the first to record the Eleventh Symphony. Their hall has remarkable acoustics which helps the orchestra achieve an amazing sound. The long work (55 minutes) seems perhaps, but is not, a Mahler parody. After a long depression in which Lloyd traded in composing for growing mushrooms, it was the Eighth Symphony that was first performed before an audience. The music is very English and should appeal to those attracted to the English renaissance. Lloyd's own performance of his work must be accepted as reliable.

WITOLD LUTOSLAWSKI (born 1913)

Symphonies nrs 1 and 2
- Polish National Radio S O / composer
  EMI 1C 165 03231/6
Symphony nr. 3 (1983)
- Berliner Philharmoniker / composer
  Philips Dig CD 416 387 (also LP and cassette)
- Los Angeles P O / Esa-Pekka Salonen
  CBS Masterworks dig IM 42203

Lutoslawski has never been neglected by the record companies. The recordings listed here of his First and Second Symphonies are available in a boxed set of 6 records, a complete Lutoslawski retrospective. The Second Symphony was finished in 1967. The composer had greatly changed his style in the late fifties. The recordings directed by the composer have a natural authority, of course. These are good examples of Lutoslawski's particular world of sound. The composer himself was very enthusiastic about the Esa-Pekka Salonen performance of his Third Symphony. Philips recordings are better than the CBS. All in all, music for devotees and collectors.

ALBÉRIC MAGNARD (1865-1914)

Symphony nr. 3 in b flat minor, Op. 11
- Orch de la Suisse Romande / Ernest Ansermet
  French Decca 1592 167
Symphony nr. 4 in c sharp minor, Op. 21
- Orch du Capitole de Toulouse / Michel Plasson
  HMV EG 270 150-1/4 [Ang Sera 4XG 60421]

There are plans to record all the Magnard symphonies again. Up to now, only the Ansermet recording (Orchestre de la Suisse Romande) that dates from 1968 is available. This has been transferred, and the new version is faultless. Why Magnard has been neglected for so long is a mystery. It is not his music. The opening of the Third Symphony is wonderful, the Scherzo is very inventive and the Pastoral is musically exciting. The Fourth Symphony was written in 1913. The Toulouse Orchestra plays every note with conviction. The recording has a full sound.

GUSTAV MAHLER (1860-1911)

*** Symphonies nrs 1 and 2
- Cundari, Forrester, Westminster Choir, Columbia S O / Walter
  CBS M3P/*3PT* 39635

*** Symphonies nrs 1 and 4
- Elsie Morison, S O Bayerischen Rundfunk / Kubelik
  DG 415 012-1/4

*** Symphony nr. 1 in D major, ('Titan')
- Chicago S O / Giulini
  HMV (remastered) SXLP/*TC-SXLP* 30548
- Chicago S O / Solti
  Decca Dig **411 731-2**; /-1; /-4
- Chicago S / Abbado
  DG Dig **400 033-2**; 2532/*3320* 020
- London S O / Solti
  Decca SXL 6113 [recording 1969]
- Royal P O / Leinsdorf
  Decca VIV/*KVIC* 57
- Boston S / Leinsdorf
- New York P O / Mehta
  CBS **CD37373**
- S O des Bayerischen Rundfunks / Kubelik
  DG Priv 2535/*3335*
- London S O / Horenstein
  Unicorn RHS/*UKC* 301
- London S O / Levine
  RCA ARL1/*ARK 1*
- London P O / Tennstedt
  HMV EG 290496-1/*4*
- Philadelphia O / Muti
  HMV Dig **CDC 747032-2**; EL 270007-1/4
- S O des Hessischen Rundfunks (Frankfurt) / Inbal
  Denon **C37-7537** (12/85)
- Wiener Philharmoniker / Maazel
  CBS Masterworks dig IM/*IMT* / **MK42141**
- Columbia S O / Walter
  CBS **MK 42031** (9/86)
- Royal P O / Païta
  Lodia **LO-CD 776**; ditto 776
- (original version in 5 parts, with Blumine)
  Boston S O / Osawa
  DG Sig 410 845-1/*4*

- Concertgebouw O / Haitink
  Philips **420 080-2** [2nd recording]
- Hallé Orch / Barbirolli
  Pye/Nixa PRT PVCD8385

*** Symphony nr. 2, ('Resurrection')
- Neblett, Horne, Chicago S Choir and O / Abbado
  DG 2707 094/*3370 015*
- Schwarzkopf, Rössl-Majdan, Philh Ch and O / Klemperer
  HMV SLS 802/*TCC-2POR 54293*
- Concertgebouw O / Klemperer
  D264D2 (9/82) [live recording Concertgebouw 12/7/51]
- Buchanan, Zakai, Chicago S O / Solti
  Decca Dig **410 202-2**; D 229 D 2/*K 229 K 22* [2nd recording]
- Harper, Watts, London S O / Solti
  Decca Jub DJB/*KDJBC* 2001 [1st recording]
- Price, Fassbaender, LSO Chorus, London S O / Stokowsky
  RCA ARL2 0852
- Cundari, Forrester, Westminster Ch, New York P O / Walter
  CBS **M2K 42032**
- Mandac, Finnila, Singing City Choirs, Philadalphia O / Ormandy
  RCA LSB 4003/4
- Mathis, Procter, S O des Bayerischen Rundfunks / Kubelik
  DG 413 524-1/*4* and Walkman *413 149-4* also as DG Priv 2726/*3372* 062
- Mathis, Soffel, London P Choir, London P O / Tennstedt
  HMV Dig **CDS 747041-8**; SLS/*TCC-SLS* 5243
- Armstrong, Baker, Edinburgh Festival Choir and London S O / Bernstein
  CBS M2/*M2T* 32681
- Cotrubas, Ludwig, Wiener Staatsoper Chor, Wiener Philharmoniker / Zubin Mehta
  Decca **414 538-2DH2** [2 discs], transfer from SXL6744/5 (12/75)
- Marton, Norman, Wiener Philharmoniker / Maazel
  M2K 38667, 12M/*12T* 38667
- Philharmonic O / Maazel
  415 959-2GH2 (9/86)
- Auger, Baker, City of Birmingham Chorus and Orchestra / Rattle
  EMI dig EX270598-3 [2 LPs]; **CDS7 47962-8**
- Battle, Forrester, St Louis Orchestra / Slatkin
  Telarc Dig **CD80081-2** (1/85)
- Te Kanawa, Horne, Tanglewood Festival Chorus, Boston S O / Ozawa
  Philips dig **420 824-2PH**; -1PH; *-4PH*
- Donath, Soffel, S O des Hesschischen Rundfunks / Inbal
  Denon Dig **C37 7603/4**

*** Symphony nr. 3 in d minor
- Norman, Wiener Staatopernchor, Wiener Sängerknaben, Wiener Philharmoniker / Abbado
  DG Dig **410 715-2**; 2741/*3382* 010
- Horne, Ellyn Children's Choir, Chicago Chorus and S O / Levine
  RCA **RD 81757**; RL/*RK* 81757
- Watts, Wandsworth School Boys' Choir, Ambrosian Singers, London S O / Solti
  Decca SET 385/6 [1st recording]
- Dernesch, E Ch Choir, Chicago S O /Solti
  Decca Dig **414 268-2**; D281 D2/*K 281 K 22* (4/85) [2nd recording]
- Wenkel, Southend Boys' Choir, London P O Choir, London P O / Tennstedt

HMV Dig **CDS 747405-8**; SLS/*TC-SLS* 5195 (12/86)
- Procter, Wandsworth School Choir, Ambrosian Singers, London S O / Horenstein
  Unicorn RHS 302/3
- Lipton, Schola Cantorum Choir, Boys' Choir, New York P O / Bernstein
  CBS 77206
- Forrester, Los Angeles Philharmonic Ch and Orch / Mehta
  Decca D117 D2, *K117 K22*
- Baltsa, Wiener Staatsoper Chor, Wiener Philharmoniker / Maazel
  CBS Masterworks **M2K 42178**; I2M; *12T*
- Killlebrew, Bonn, Collegium Jesephinum Sängerknaben, Chor des Bayerischen Rundfunks; S O des Westdeutschen Rundfunks (Köln) / Gary Bartini
  German Harmonia Mundi **CDS7 47568-8** [2 discs] transfer from EX169581-3 (12/886)
- Ludwig, Kühn Ch, Prague Philh Ch, Czech P O / Neumann
  Supraphon Dig **C37 7288/9**
- Marjorie Thomas, Tölzer Ch, S O des Bayerischen Rundfunks /Kubelik
  DG 413 5252-1/*4*
- Forrester, Choir NRU, Boys' Choir St Willibrord, Concergebouw O / Haitink

*** Symphony nr. 4 in G major
- Battle, Wiener Philharmoniker / Maazel
  CBS Dig **MK 39072**; IM/*IMT* 39072
- Mathis, Berliner Philharmoniker / Karajan
  DG **415323-2**; 2531/*3301* 205
- Te Kanawa, Chicago S O / Solti
  Decca Dig **410 188-2**; 410 188-1/*4*
- Stahlman / Concertgebouw O / Solti
  Decca SXL2276 [recording 1960]
- Ameling, Concertgebouw O / Haitink
  Philips Silverline **420 350-2PM**, transfer from AXS6000-1/6 (10/68); also: Philips Seq 6527/*7311* 203 [1st recording]
- Alexander/ Concertgebouw O / Haitink
  Philips Dig **412 119-2**; 412 119-1/*4* (4/84) [2nd recording]
- Ritchie, Concertgebouw O / Eduard van Beinum
  Decca mono **421 140-2DH**, transfer from LXT2718 [recording 10/52]
- Concertgebouw O / Mengelberg
  Philips **416 211-2PH** (4/86)
- Popp, London P O / Tennstedt
  HMV Dig **CDC 747024-2**; ASD/*TCC-ASD* 4344
- Harper, Orch RIAS Berlin / Maazel
  Pearl SHE 552
- Blegen, Chicago S O / Levine
  RCA **RDR 80895**
- Della Casa, Chicago S O / Reiner
  RCA Gold GL/*GK* 85256
- New York P O / Walter
  Odys 32160026
- Ameling, Pittsburgh S O / Previn
  HMV ASD/*TC-ASD* 3783
- Hendricks / Israel P O / Mehta
  Decca Dig SXDL/*KSXDC* 7501
- Donath, S O des Hessischen Rundfunks (Frankfurt) / Inbal
  Denon **CO37-7952**
- Raskin, Cleveland O / Szell
  CBS 60124/*40*
- Price, San Francisco S O / De Waart
  Philips Dig 6514/*7337* 201
- Von Stade, Wiener Philharmoniker / Abbado
  DG **413 454-2**; 2530/*3300* 966

*** Symphony nr 5 in c sharp minor
- New Philharmonia O / Barbirolli
  HMV SLS/*TC-SLS* 785
- Berliner Philharmoniker / Karajan
  DG **415 096-2**; 2707 081/*3370 006*
- Philharmonia / Sinopoli
  DG Dig **415 476-2**; -1; -4
- Chicago S O / Solti
  Decca SET 471-2/*KCET2 7001* ; **413 321-2**; /-1; /-4
- Chicago S O / Abbado
  DG 2707 128/*3370 040*
- New York P O / Bernstein
  CBS M2S-698
- Czech P O / Neumann
  Supraphon **2SUP0021**, transfer from 1110 4001/15ZA (12/85)
- S O des Hessischen Rundfunks (Frankfurt) / Inbal
  Denon **CO-1088** (1/87)
- S O des Bayerischen Rundfunks / Kubelik
  DG Walkman *415 335-4*
- Wiener Philharmonker / Maazel
  CBS Masterworks **MK42310**, from I3M 37875 (1/84)
- Los Angeles P O / Mehta
  Decca Ovation **417 730-2DM**, transfer from SXL6806/07 (11/77)

*** Symphony nr. 5
*** Symphony nr. 10
- London P O / Tennstedt
  HMV **CDS 747104-8**; SLS/*TC-SLS* 5169
- Philadelphia O /Levine
  RCA **RD 89205**; RI/*RK* 82905
- Concertgebouw O / Haitink
  Philips 6700 048/*7505 069* (4/72), **416 469-2PH** (1/87)

*** Symphony nr. 6 in a minor
- Berliner Philharmoniker / Karajan
  DG **415 099-2**; 2707 106/*3370 026*
- London P O / Tennstedt
  HMV Dig **CDC 747050-8**; SLS/*TC-SLS* 143574-3/*5*
- Chicago S O / Solti
  Decca **414 674-2**; SET 469/70 (5/86)
- S O des Hessischen Rundfunks (Frankfurt) / Inbal
  Denon **CO-1327/8** [2 discs]
- Chicago S O / Abbado
  DG 2707 117/*3370 031*
- S O des Bayerischen Rundfunks / Kubelik
  DG Priv 2726 065
- (revision Erwin Ratz)
  New York P O / Bernstein
  CBS 77215
- Stockholm P O / Horenstein
  Uni RHS 320/1
- Concertgebouw O / Haitink
  Philips Seq 412 034-1/*4* ; **420 138-2**
- New Philharmonia O / Barbirolli
  CfP CFP/*TC-CFP* 414424-3/*5* [recording 1968]

*** Symphony nr. 7 in e minor
- Chicago S O / Abbado
  DG Dig **413 773-2**; -1; *-4*
- Chicago S O / Solti
  Decca **414 675-2**; SET 518
- Chicago S O / Levine
  RCA **RD 84581**
- S O des Hessischen Rundfunks (Frankfurt) / Inbal
  Denon **CO-1553/4** [2 discs]
- Concertgebouw O / Haitink

Philips Dig **410 398-2**; 410 398-1/*4*
Philips 6700 036
- London P O / Tennstedt
HMV Dig SLS/*TC-SLS* 5238 (12/81), EMI **CDS7 4789-8**
[2 discs]
- S O des Bayerischen Rundfunks / Kubelik
DG Priv 2726 066
- New York P O / Bernstein
419 211-2GH2 (12/86)
- New Philharmonia / Klemperer
CfP CFPD41 4442-3/5

*** Symphony nr. 8 in E flat major, ('Sinfonie der Tausend')
- Harper, Popp, Augèr, Minton, Kollo, Shirley-Quirk, Talvela,
Wiener Sänger Knaben,
Wiener Staatsopernchor and Singverein, Chicago S O /
Solti
Decca **414 493-2**; SET 534-5/*KCET 7006*
- Robinson, Blegen, Sasson, Quivar, Meyers, Riegel,
Luxon, Howell, Tanglewood Festival
Choir, Boston Boys' Choir, Boston S O / Osawa
Philips Dig **410 607-2**; 6769/*7654* 069
- Contrubas, Harper, Van Bork, Finnila, Dieleman, Cochran,
Prey, Sotin, Amsterdam Choir,
Concertgebouw O / Haitink
Philips 6700 049
- Connell, Wiens, Lott, Schmidt, Denize, Versalle,
Hynninen, Sotin; Tiffin Boys' School Choir, London P Choir
and Orchestra / Klaus Tennstedt
EMI dig **CDS7 47625-8**; EX270 474-3; *-5* [2 LPs]
- Arroyo, Spoorenberg, Mathis, Hamari, Procter, Grobe, Fis-
cher-Dieskau, Crass, Regensburger Dom Spatzen,
Münchener Motet Chor, Chor and Orchester des
Bayerischen Rundfunks / Rafael Kubelik
DG **419 433-2GH**, transfer from 2720 033 (10/71)
- Benacková-Capova, Nielsen, Sounová, Soukupová,
Márová, Moser, Schöne, Novák, Prague Philh Choir, Kühn
Choir, Chech Radio Choir, Czech P O / Neumann
Supraphon **C37 7307/8**
- Spoorenberg, Jones, Reynolds, Procter, Mitchinson,
Ruzdjak, McIntyre, Leeds Festival Choir, Orphington Junior
Singers, Highgate Schoolboys' Choir, Finchley Children's
Music Group, London S O / Bernstein
CBS M2S-751

*** Symphony nr. 9 in d minor
- Berliner Philharmoniker / Karajan
DG Dig **410 726-2**
DG 2707 125/ *3370 038* [analogue recording 1980]
- Concertgebouw O / Haitink
Philips **416 466-2**; 6700 021
- London P O / Tennstedt
HMV CDS 747113-8; SLS/*TC-SLS* 5188
- Columbia S O / Walter
CBS 61369/70; remastered: **M2K 42033**
- Chicago S O / Solti
Decca Dig **410 012-2**; D 274 D2/*K 274 K 22*
- London S O / Solti
Decca Jub 410 264-1/*4* [recording 1967]
- Wiener Pilharmoniker / Maazel
CBS Dig **M2K 39721**; 12M/*12T* 39721
- Czech P O / Neumann
Supraphon Dig **C37 7340/1**
- Berliner Philharmoniker / Barbirolli
CfP CFP/*TC-CFP* 414426-3/5 [recording 1964]
- New Philharmonia / Klemperer
HMV SXDW3021 [recording 1967]

*** Symphony nr. 10 in F sharp ('Unfinished'; revision Deryck
Cooke)
- Bournemouth S O / Rattle
HMV Dig **CDS 747301-8**; SLS/*TC-SLS* 5206
- Philadelphia S O / Levine
RCA Dig **RD 84553**; ARC2/*ARK2* 4553

The 1980's brought with them a new peak in Mahler
adoration. Mahler is a must in the programmes of
any and every respected orchestra. Mahler is also a
great challenge for recording technicians and recording companies. As a result, listeners can easily
find more than one hundred different versions of his
works to choose from. Needless to say, none of this
proves that Mahler is either easy to interpret or to
sell. At least twenty-five orchestras have, nevertheless, taken that task upon themselves.
SYMPHONY NR. 1 - There are a half dozen top
recordings of this piece which makes it hard to
choose a number one. Every one of these was made
by top orchestras and conductors and the ultimate
choice will be a difficult and subjective one. Solti
leads the London Symphony in an extraordinary
performance. The magic of the opening is wonderful
and the strings are unusually warm. Leinsdorf's
Decca recording with the Royal Philharmonic is also
an excellent choice. It is a little less poetic than
Kubelik's, however, who is at his very best. Horenstein has fresh ideas and is concentrated in his work.
Levine has the most exciting orchestral sound of
them all. The Giulini recording has been remastered
perfectly; the great performance loses nothing in the
process. Abbado's version is pure and refined, recorded in excellent digital sound. His could be a
possible first choice but is a bit less exciting than the
rest. The 1967 Walter recording is a true classic. The
opening horn section is exquisite. The last movement is less concentrated, unfortunately.
Haitink's second version is an improvement on the
first. His Mahler is, without doubt, first class. This
would be a good alternative for those who think
Leinsdorf a trifle extrovert. Tennstedt's approach is
disciplined and precise. The tempo changes, however, are too abrupt at times. Leinsdorf's performance with Boston rivals his performance with London.
SYMPHONY NR. 2 - Abbado's Second was the first
Mahler that he recorded. It is very convincing. The
Chicago Symphony's dedication is exemplary. Other
versions (Klemperer, Solti etc. are more emotionally
demanding). Klemperer's performance is perhaps
his most interesting on record. The raw emotion in
his work is surprising. His tempi are amazingly slow
in the last movement. The choir and soloists are
thrilling. This is definitely one of EMI's best recordings. Solti's first recording with the London Symphony (an analogue recording made by Decca) is
one of his greatest achievements. Despite the brilliant playing in his second version with Chicago,
Solti's first has been and will remain a strong favourite. Bernstein made a film for television at the same
time as recording his very personal version of the
Second. Both soloists are sublime. Tennstedt's is a
dedicated performance, but the neurotic tensions of
the work are somehow weakened. Kubelik's approach is very refined but the recording itself misses
grandeur. Mehta and Klemperer stock the finale with
overflowing emotion. Mehta's performance with the

Viennese is especially appealing. Stokowsky recorded Mahler for the first time when he was over 90.
His performance is youthful(!) and direct. Ormandy
was the first to ever record this symphony (in the
early 30's with the Minneapolis Symphony). His
performance of it is still fresh, a touch too emotional
perhaps but loyal to the score and its power.
SYMPHONY NR. 3 - Levine's performance is rhythmic and strong; he uses wonderful tempi and sounds
warmer than either Horenstein or Haitink. Horenstein refrains from romantic exaggeration here and
makes one shiver with excitement. Haitink is as
dedicated and honest as ever. The simplicity of his
second movement is touching. Solti's version with
the London Symphony is disappointing. In his second try, this time with Chicago, he revenges himself
completely. This second Solti has been remastered
for CD and the resonance and background noise are
both much improved. Neumann is heavy and boring
which is unfortunate. The Czech Philharmonic is capable of much better playing. Christa Ludwig is also
let down by this conductor. Tennstedt's recording
for HMV is very impressive. Bernstein's (his first of
the Mahler symphonies) is strong and passionate
and not overly exaggerated (a Bernstein tendency to
be sure). This brilliant conductor is so much more
impressive when he can control himself and respect
the style at hand.
SYMPHONY NR. 4 - In December, 1958, Reiner
recorded this symphony with the Chicago Symphony. That performance has now been remastered
for CD. Reiner's interpretation is very personal.
Everything he does sounds spontaneous. The Viennese influence on this American recording is unmistakeable. Lisa della Casa has a magical voice. Van
Beinum's 1951 recording is also available on CD.
This is one of the classic versions of the 4th. The
beauty is breathtaking. Van Beinum's performance
rivals Walter's with the New York Philharmonic.
Mengelberg's 1939 version (before the war!) has
also been remastered. For many, this is the best 4th
this side of heaven's gates. The magnificent Jo
Vincent is the soloist. Haitink's two versions were
made 16 years apart, the first with Elly Ameling (12/
67) and the second with Roberta Alexander (4/83).
The second recording is especially wonderful thanks
to the Concertgebouw Orchestra's extraordinary
playing. The Adagio is no longer a sober meditation
but an ecstatic aria. After having been successful
with the earlier symphonies, Abbado's 4th is disappointing, especially in the slow movement. The 1967
Szell performance with Cleveland has been an inside
favourite for many years. What at first may seem cool
and distant, this interpretation allows the score to
speak for itself. The wonderful orchestral playing is
unrivalled. 20 years have dated this record a bit
perhaps, but many will still appreciate this performance as a highpoint in Szell's career. Three later
recordings are also to be recommended: Von Karajan with Berlin, Tennstedt with the London Philharmonic and Levine with the Chicago Symphony.
SYMPHONY NR. 5 - Tennstedt's 5th is mature and
thoughtful. This is a first class recording. Levine's
interpretation is also very convincing. The Philadelphians are at their best here. Solti, working with
Chicago, is also quite good. This 1971 recording has
been remastered. Solti takes the death march a bit
quicker than almost anyone else. It is melancholic

rather than tragic. The absolute classic among the recordings of Mahler's 5th is undoubtedly Barbirolli's. The exuberance of his interpretation is totally convincing as are his tempi. This entire performance is a credit to Barbirolli's knowledge of the score and the concentration with which he leads the work.
SYMPHONY NR. 6 - The 1970 recording directed by Haitink has been re-released in the Philips Seq. series. The interpretation is refined and thoughtful, a performance well done. The remastering is not completely successful, however; the upper registers are thin, proof that remastering is not necessarily an improvement. Von Karajan's 6th is magnificent due to the superior playing that is the hallmark of the Berlin Philharmonic. The Andante Moderato is simple and lyrical, a style Karajan does not often use. Mahler's 6th was the first recording that Solti made having been named principal conductor in Chicago. As he has said himself, it was love at first sight (or sound!) between orchestra and conductor. Solti has a unique, extrovert manner in dealing with Mahler. Maazel lacks the depth needed in this work. Kubelik's version of the 6th is probably the best of his Mahler cycle. The 1969 sound quality is still competitive with more recent recordings. Bernstein's live performance is in a class by itself. The excitement of the hall comes alive. Horenstein's version also deserves attention. His interpretation, distinctive due to the slower tempi, is sober and noble.
SYMPHONY NR. 7 - Abbado's understanding of Mahler is clearest in this wonderful performance of perhaps the most difficult of the symphonies. The precision and polish of the Chicago Symphony are laudable. This is also the most successful recording the DG technicians have ever made with Chicago. Klemperer's 7th is not one of his best. Levine's 7th is as good as the rest of his Mahler and Haitink's second version with the Concertgebouw is just what would be expected: beauty and perfection. The excitement that Haitink usually produces with Mahler is a bit tempered in this symphony. The more one listens to this interpretation, the more appropriate it seems. Solti's 7th is as wonderful as his 6th. Tennstedt leads a London Philharmonic playing in top form. This digital recording is clear down to the smallest detail.
SYMPHONY NR. 8 - The classic among the 8th Symphonies available is without doubt Solti's performance with the Chicago Symphony and some European choirs. All soloists and instrumentalists involved are inspired by Solti's direction of the unique piece. Another breathtaking Symphony of Thousands is Bernstein's live performance in Walthanstow Town Hall. Unfortunately, this supreme performance is compromised by microphones standing too close to the players. The atmosphere is lost. Philips' digital recording of Ozawa leading the Boston Symphony is quite good. The playing and the singing is all wonderful but some intensity is missing. Solti and Bernstein are too powerful rivals for Ozawa. Neumann's version is a poor competitor. Even for this massive work, Kubelik chooses for refinement and his technicians are amazingly good at adapting to this unusual interpretation. Many will find this refinement out of place for such an exciting 'happening' as Mahler's 8th. Anyone lucky enough to find an old (1954) Philips recording (ABL3024-5, or EP SC-6012) of a live

performance by the Rotterdam Philharmonic led by Flipse (with the soloists Annie Bijster, Annie Hermes, Annie Woud, Hilde Zadek, Frans Vroons, Herman Schey, Gottlob Frick and David Hollestelle) will also possess a true classic.
SYMPHONY NR. 9 - There are really only three rivals here: Haitink, von Karajan and Solti. Many will favour Haitink. His great performance has been recorded very well. The first movement is tentative, the second, perfectly timed and the third, extrovert and brilliant, a wonderful culmination. Von Karajan's 1980 analogue recording is extremely intense. Karajan recorded the 9th again after only two years and during live performances in Berlin. The difference in these performances is the distinct optimism that shines through the second of the two, doing away with all of Mahler's fatalistic doom. Solti's version with Chicago is perhaps a bit too cerebral. The outer movements are mystical, the middle movement lacks charm. Solti's earlier recording with the London Philharmonic is warmer and more spontaneous. The Viennese play magnificently for Maazel in the 9th Symphony. Nothing is mannered or superficial as sometimes is the case. The sound is excellent. It is the most successful of Maazel's whole cycle.

FRANK MARTIN (1890-1974)

Petite Symphonie concertante
- Sydney S O / Willem van Otterloo
  Chan ABR/ABT (cassette) 1060
- Czech P O / Kodadova; Ruzickova / dir. Vajnar

Frank Martin's Petite Symphony concertante is widely recognized as his masterpiece. The balance between the double strings and the three solo instruments presents a problem for recording. The mono recording under Ansermet (Decca LXT 2631) is well balanced in this respect. In this Chandos recording, the soloists are perhaps too prominently placed. Nevertheless, the recording has atmosphere and many of the subtle contrasts are recorded just right. The Sydney string players miss a certain flair; the performance is, however, the best available: very dedicated and successful. In the Supraphon recording, the soloists are too close to the microphone so their role is out of proportion. Vajnar uses slow tempi that give the piece lots of room, but often the tempi are under those specified in the score. His takes four minutes longer than Van Otterloo, also longer than the Paul Sacher recording (the piece is dedicated to Sacher) made in the seventies on the Swiss Composers label. The Symphonie pour orchestre burlesque ('Geneva' - 1915) and the Symphonie (1937) are both, unfortunately, no longer available.

BOHUSLAV MARTINU (1890-1959)

Sinfonietta La Jolla
- Prague Chamber O / Hnat
  Supraphon 110 1619
Symphony nr. 1
- Czech P O / Vaclav Neumann
  Supraphon SUP2166
Symphony nr. 2
Symphony nr. 6 (Fantaisies symphoniques)

- Czech P O / Neumann
  Supraphon SUP 2096
Symphony nr. 3
Symphony nr. 4
Symphony nr. 5
- Czech P O / Neumann
  Supraphon SUP 2771/2
Sinfonietta La Jolla
Symphony nr. 4
- Royal Liverpool P O / Weller
  HMV ASD/TC-ASD 3888
Symphony nr. 4
- Czech P O / Turnovsky
  Supraphon SUAST 50669
Symphony nr. 5
- Louisville O / Whitney
  RCA Gold Seal GL 25058
Symphony nr. 6
- Boston Symphony O / Charles Munch
  RCA RB-16030
- New Philharmonia O / Bialoguski
  Unicorn RHS 309

The First Symphony appeared in 1942, the year Martinu arrived in the United States. The Neumann recording is excellent; the sound is acceptable. The Czechs play very well, but the acoustics of the House of Artists in Prague are too resonant.
The Second, the most relaxed of the 6 symphonies, dates from 1943. The Third is the most powerful of the symphonies from the war years. The Fourth is perhaps the most attractive of them all and the Fifth is also a wonderful symphony; it has more colour than the bleak war-time pieces. Charles Munch and the Boston Symphony recorded the Sixth, a later work. Martinu wrote the work for them.
Some will probably remember the greatly loved versions led by Turnovsky or Karl Ancerl. Early lovers of Martinu were enchanted with these performances.
Walter Weller is at his best in the Scherzo of the Fourth Symphony. He drives the orchestra along; the sound is wonderful. The Liverpool strings lack shine, however, and the winds cannot compete with the Czechs. Perhaps the orchestra wasn't given enough time to learn the piece thoroughly. The same can be said for Sinfonietta La Jolla. Hnat's direction is excellent, however, as is the recording.

VINCENC MASEK (1755-1831)

Symphony in D sharp major
- Prague Chamber O / Vajnar
  Sup 111-2809

Masek was born just a year before Mozart. He was famous as a keyboard player, making tours throughout Germany, Holland and Denmark. He became director of the St Nicholas Choir in the Mala Strana in Prague. Even though this symphony is not extraordinary, it is very good music (the D sharp was used at the time to signify a piece that is actually in E flat) and the performance here has a contagious enthusiasm. The recording quality is good.

WILLIAM MATHIAS (born 1934)

Symphony nr.1, Op. 31
and DANIEL JONES
Symphony nr. 6
- Royal P O / Charles Groves
  Oriel ORM 1004

Mathias and Jones differ in generation but are both examples of contemporary Welsh music. Mathias' First Symphony was commissioned for the Llandaff Festival of 1966. It is a tonal work that is held together by its rhythmic power (in that respect, reminiscent of Stravinsky, especially in the Scherzo) and it tends to be aggressive. Jones' music is more memorable despite its being much more conservative. The recording of both is well done.

FELIX MENDELSSOHN (1809-47)

*** Symphonies nrs 1 - 5
- London S O / Abbado
  DG Dig 415 353-2; /-1; /-4 [2nd recording]
- Berliner Philharmoniker (with soloists and choir in nr 2) / Karajan
  DG 2740 128/3371 020 [recording 1975]

*** Symphony nr. 1 in c minor, Op.11
*** Symphony nr. 2 in B flat major, Op. 52
- New Philharmonia / Sawallisch
  Philips 6768 030

*** Symphony nr. 1
*** Symphony nr. 4 in A major, Op. 90
- London P O / Haitink
  Philips 9500 708/7300 803

*** Symphony nr. 1
*** Symphony nr. 5 ('Reformation')
- Wiener Philharmoniker / Dohnáhnyi
  Decca SXL 6818

*** Symphony nr. 2
- Ghazarin, Gruberova, Krenn, Wiener Staats Opernchor, Wiener Singverein, Wiener Philharmoniker / Dohnányi
  Decca D133 D2

*** Symphony nr. 2
*** Symphony nr. 3 ('Scottish')
- (nr. 2) Price, Burton, Jerusalem, London P O and Choir / Chailly
- (nr. 3) London S O / Chailly
  Philips 6769 042/7699 128

*** Symphonies nrs 3 ('Scottish'), 4 ('Italian') and 5 ('Reformation')
- Israel P O / Bernstein
  DG 415 018-1/4 [live recordings]

*** Symphony nr. 3 in a minor, Op. 56
- Hungary State O / Ivan Fischer
  Hungaroton Dig HCD 12660-2
- London S O / Abbado
  DG Dig 415 973-2; /-1; /-4
- London S O / Peter Maag
  Decca SPA/KCSP 503
- Scottish National O / Alexander Gibson

CfP CFP/TC-CFP 40270
- New Philharmonia / Muti
  HMV ASD 3184
- S O des Bayerischen Rundfunks / Colin Davis
  Orfeo Dig C 089841A; S-/
- Wiener Philharmoniker / Dohnányi
  Decca SXL 6954, dig remastered as Decca Ovation 417 458-1DB
- London P O / Haitink
  Philips 9500 535/7300 678 (1979)
  dig remastered: Philips Zigzag 420 011-1PM/4PM
- S O des Bayerischen Rundfunk / Andrew Davis
  CBS Dig 37282/40
- Berliner Philharmoniker / Karajan
  DG 2530 126/3300 181
- Israel P O / Bernstein
  DG 2531/3301 256

*** Symphony nr. 3
*** Symphony nr. 4 in A major, Op. 90
- Acadamy SMF / Marriner
  Argo 411 931-2ZH (11/84); ZRG/KZRC 926 (6/81)
- London S O /Abbado
  Decca Jub JB/KJBC 103 and SXL6363 (9/68) [1st recording]
- Orch of St John Smith's Square / Lubbock
  ASV Quicksilva QS6004; transfer from WEA Enigma K 53588; also ABM 774 ACM
- London P O / Bychkov
  Philips dig 420 211-2PH; -/4PH
- Chicago S O / Solti
  414 665-2DH; /-1DH (4/86)
- Philharmonia / Klemperer
  HMV ED 290579-1/4
- Wiener Philharmoniker / Dohnányi
  Decca Ovation 417 731-2DM, transfers of SXL6954 (7/80) and SXDL7500 (7/79)

*** Symphony nr. 3
*** Symphony nr. 5 in d minor, Op. 107
- New Philharmonia / Sawallisch
  Philips 6768 031

*** Symphony nr. 4
*** Symphony nr. 5
- New Philharmonia / Sawallisch
  Philips SAL 3727 and Philips Seq 412 008-1/4

*** Symphony nr. 3
*** Symphony nr. 10
- Gewandhaus Orchester Leipzig / Masur
  RCA Gold GL/GK 25330

*** Symphony nr. 4 ('Italian')
- Philharmonia O / Sinopoli
  DG Dig 410 974-2; 415 974-1/4
  also DG Dig 410 862; 410 862-1/4
- Boston S O / Colin Davis
  Philips Zigzag 412 928-1/-4 (10/85)
  Philips Silver Line 420 653-2PM, transfer from 9500 068 (11/76)
- London S O / Abbado
  Decca VIV/KVIC 33
- Berliner Philharmoniker / Tennstedt
  HMV Dig ASD/TCC-ASD 3963
- Wiener Philharmoniker / Dohnányi
  Decca Dig SXDL/ KSXDC 7500; Ovation 417 731-2DM
- London S O / Previn
  [1st recording] RCA SB6847 and RCA Gold GL/GK 12703

[2nd recording] HMV ASD/TC-ASD 3763
- Cleveland O / Szell
  CBS 60147/40 and CBS Classics 61019
- Philharmonia / Cantelli
  World Mono SH/TC-SH 290
- New Philharmonia / Muti
  HMV ASD3365
- Philharmonia / Klemperer
  HMV SXLP30178
- Israel P O / Solti
  Decca Ace of Diamonds SDD121
- l'Orch de la Suisse Romande / Ansermet
  Decca SXL 6166
- Concertgebouw O / Haitink
  Philips Universo 6580 027
- Gewandhaus Orchester Leipzig / Masur
  RCA Gold GL/GK 25307
- Philharmonia / Wallberg
  HMV TC-IDL 502
- Berliner Philharmoniker / Karajan
  DG Galleria 415 848-2GGA, dig remastered from (anal.) 2720 068 [recording 1971]

*** Symphony nr. 4
*** Symphony nr. 5, Op.107
- London S O / Abbado
  DG Dig 415 974-2; 415 974-1/4
- NBC S O / Toscanini
  RCA mono RCCD 1007
- English Ch O / Leppard
  Erato EPR/MCE 15533
- Israel P O / Bernstein
  DG 2531/3301 097
- Berliner Philharmoniker / Karajan
  DG Sig 2543/3343 511 (9/74) (12/75) (11/83)
- Hungary State O / Ivan Fischer
  Hungaroton Dig HCD12414-2

*** Symphony nr. 5
- Philharmonia / Muti
  HMV ASD/TC-ASD 3781
- Berliner Philharmoniker / Karajan
  DG Galleria 419 870-2GGA; /1GGA; / -4GGA, transfer from 2720 046 - 9/72

*** Symphonies for strings, nrs 6 in E flat major; 7 in d minor; 10 in b minor
- Ensemble 13 Baden Baden / Reichert
- nrs 9 in c minor; 10 in b minor; 12 in g minor
  London Festival O / Ross Pope
  Hyperion dig A66196/KA66196

*** Symphonies for strings, nrs 2 in D major; 3 in e minor; 5 in B flat minor; 6 in E flat minor
- Poland Chamber O / Maksymiuk
  HMV Green ESD 7123

Four conductors have recorded the entire symphonic cycle: Abbado, Dohnányi, Karajan and Sawallisch. Even considering only the five most important symphonies, there are more than sixty in the catalogues to choose from, half of which are recordings of the Italian Symphony! Many are older, especially of the Fourth Symphony. These older recordings should definitely be considered competitive with the all too idealistically presented CDs. It would be a shame to dismiss impressive performances because of their so-called out-dated technology.

The Peter Maag version (with the Swiss orchestra) for example, is a sublime recording of Mendelssohn. The Allegro Vivace in the first movement is more relaxed than in any other version giving it a wonderful rhythmic swing. The piece is too often aggressively played: virtuosity for its own sake (Solti is the best, or worse in this respect). The Cantelli performance deserves notice as well. This conductor is a master of balances: the details and sense of ensemble in his orchestra are perfect. Nothing to idolize here, as with a Furtwängler or a Toscanini: this conductor serves the music and not himself. Now more than a quarter of a century old, Cantelli's recording is still first class.

The Von Karajan cycle is of renowned Berlin quality, of course. Sawallisch is a reserved yet highly talented Mendelssohn performer. Abbado is stylish and very beautifully recorded, and Dohnányi is a safe choice. Nevertheless, connoisseurs are recommended to look beyond the complete sets. John Lubbock's recording of the Third and Fourth Symphonies with a small string ensemble (better here than St Martin-in-the-Fields) and beautifully clear brass (no mistakes by the technicians), is marvellous. Or perhaps Klemperer's version of the Fourth with the Philharmonia: to be sure, the slow tempi are vintage Klemperer, but the playing is inspired, has humour and is less square than one would expect from this legendary conductor. All in all, this recording should not be too easily dismissed. Among more modern conductors, Previn has recorded the Fourth twice. Both are exuberant performances. The two outer movements are not played in breathless tempi as is so often the tendency among younger conductors.

OLIVIER MESSIAEN (born 1908)

Turangalîla symphony
- Béroff (pno) / Loriod (ondes martenot) / London S O / Previn
  HMV SLS/*TC-SLS* 5117

Messiaen wrote his Turangalîla symphony when the symphonic form was suffering an all time low. Nevertheless, this work is a true masterpiece. Messiaen's conception is epic: all mankind is included. The title is Sanskrit: Turanga, time; Lîla, love. The music is inspired by the legend of Tristan and Isolde.
Turangalila belongs in the concert hall more than in the studio. Still, André Previn has successfully recorded a lively, direct interpretation that summons up Messiaen's atmosphere. The recording technicians have made it all possible, of course, but Previn's work should be lauded. He is at his best in the jazzy fifth movement. The mystery of the opening is highly evocative.

NICOLAI MIASKOVSKY (1881-1950)

Symphony nr. 21, Op. 51
- New Philharmonia O / David Measham
  Uni RHS346

Miaskovsky's 21st symphony is easily his most beautiful. It is also the one most frequently recorded.

David Measham knows how to balance Miaskovsky's melancholy and nostalgia, and from the contemplative opening passages right through to the poetic last bars, Measham does the score justice. The symphony is perhaps conservative for its time, but it has easily withstood the test of time, better perhaps than more inventive works from the forties. The instruments all sound reliable and the recording is, for the most part, acceptable. The highest ranges do miss some clarity and space.

DARIUS MILHAUD (1892-1974)

Symphonies pour petit orchestre nrs 1-5
Symphony nr. 6 (with soloists)
- Luxembourg Radio S O / Milhaud
  Vox STGBY626
Symphony nr. 6
- Louisville O / Mester
  RCA Gold Seal GL25020

It is so surprising that the rich oeuvre of Darius Milhaud so seldom appears in the modern recording catalogues.The best of his six symphonies is the third (subtitled Serenade). Some collectors undoubtedly remember the 78 record with Walter Goehr. None of the symphonies is longer than four minutes, and it is all wonderful music. The performance conducted by the composer must be accepted as the best, despite the disappointing recording technique. The recording is too direct; the pianissimos cannot be registered.
The Sixth Symphony dates from 1955 and was commissioned for the 75th anniversary of the Boston Symphony Orchestra. The Louisville Orchestra can not compete internationally, but it is competent in this performance and very dedicated as well.

ANTHONY MILNER (born 1925)

Symphony nr. 1, Op. 28
- BBC S O / Lionel Friend
  Hyp A 66158

This recording of Milner's First Symphony will be important to insiders. The piece was commissioned by the BBC. Amazingly enough for contemporary music, having heard the piece once, there is an immediate desire to hear it again. Milner belongs to the same musical world as Tippett, Piston and Holmboe. The recording is clear and well balanced.

ERNEST J. MOERAN (1894-1950)

Symphony in g minor
- New Philharmonia O / Sir Adrian Boult
  Lyr SRCS70
- English Sinfonia / Dikes

Moeran wrote his wonderful symphony between 1934 and 1937. Sir Adrian Boult gives a brilliant performance, ordered and with a grand sound. As is always the case with Boult, he never forces the musical progressions; he does have the ebb and flow of the work strictly under control. He lets the sym-

phony express itself.
The more robust performance with Dikes complements Boult's version in many ways. Dikes punctuates the movements more, aggressively perhaps. But the subtle rubatos of the master conductor are lost. Dikes' chamber orchestra has a pleasant compactness and directness, but the more atmospheric of the two is definitely the Lyrita recording.

WOLFGANG AMADEUS MOZART (1756-91)

*** Symphonies nrs 1, 4-6, 7, 7a, K45a/Anh221 ('Alte Lambacher'); 8-20, 42-48, 50, K161/ K141a; 51, K196/121/ K207a; 52 in C, K208/102/ K213c; 55, K208/ 102/ K45b; in G ('Neue Lambacher')
- Academy SMF / Marriner
  Philips 416 619-2PH6 [6 discs] (8/86); 6747 099[8 LPs] (10/74) also nrs 13 - 16: Argo ZRG594

*** Symphonies nrs 1 in E flat major, K16; in a minor ('Odense'), K16a; 4 in D, K19; in F, K19a
- Odense S O / Vetö
  Unicorn Dig DKP/*DKPC* 9039

*** Symphonies nrs 1 in E flat major, K16; 4 in D, K19; in F , K19a; 5 in B flat major, K22; in D, K32; 11 in D, K84/ K73q; 13 in F , K112; 44 in D , K73e; 45 in D , K73n; 46 in C , K96/ K111b; (48) in D, K111/ 120/ K111a; 47 in D, K97/K73m
- Academy of Ancient Music / Schröder / Hogwood
  l'Oiseau Lyre/Florilegium D167 D 3/*K 167 K 33* (6/82); **417 140-2OH2** (2/87)

*** Symphonies nrs 6 in F , K43; 7 in D, K45; 8 in D, K48; 40 in g minor, K550 (2nd version); in F , K42a; in B flat major, K45b; in D, K46a (K51); in G (New Lambacher); in B flat major, K74g (K216); in G, K425a (K444)
- Academy of Ancient Music / Schröder / Hogwood
  (volume 1) l'Oiseau Lyre D 173 D 3/*K 173 K 33*

*** Symphonies nrs 9 in C , K73; 14 in A , K114; 15 in G, K124; 16 in C , K128; 17 in G, K129; in D , K325; in D, K62a/K100; (42) in F, K75; in G, K75b/K110
- Academy of Ancient Music / Schröder / Hogwood
  (volume 2) l'Oiseau Lyre 168 D 3/*K 168 K 33*

*** Symphonies nrs 18 in F, K130; '50' in D, K141a/ 161-3; 19 in E flat major, K132; 20 in D, K133; 21 in A, K134; in D, K135; 26 in E flat major, K184/ 161a; 27 in G, K199/ 161b; 22 in C, K162; 23 in D, K181/ 162b; 24 in B flat major, K182/ 173dA
- Academy of Ancient Music / Schröder / Hogwood
  (volume 3, the Salzburg Symphonies) l'Oiseau Lyre/ Florilegium **417 592-2OH3** ; D 169 D3 /*K 169 K 33*

*** Symphonies nr. 25 in g minor, K173dB (K183); nr. 29 in A major, K186a (K201); nr. 30 in D major, K 186b (K202); D major, K189b (K203); nr. 28 in C major, K189k (K200); D major, K207a (K121); D major, K213a (K204)
- Academy of Ancient Music / Schröder / Hogwood
  (volume 4) l'Oiseau Lyre Florilegium **417 841-2OH3** [3 discs], transfer from D170D3 (9/80)

*** Symphonies nrs 1-41 (complete)
- Berliner Philharmoniker / Böhm
  DG 2740 109 and 110 [15 LPs]

*** Symphonies nrs 21-41 (complete)
- Academy SMF / Marriner
Philips **415 954-2** [6 discs]; 6769 032 [8 LPs] (10/71) and
6769 043 (9/80)

*** Symphonies nrs 25 in g minor, K183; 26 in E flat major,
K184; 27 in G, K199
- Academy of Ancient Music / Schröder / Hogwood
l'Oiseau Lyre 414 472-1/4 ; also: D 170 D 3/ *K 170 K 33*

*** Symphonies nrs 25 in g minor, K183; 29 in A, K201
- English Ch O / Benjamin Britten
Decca SXL 6879
- Academy SMF / Marriner
Decca Ser 411 717-1

*** Symphonies nrs 25; 31 ('Paris'); 33; 34; 35 ('Haffner'); 36
('Linz'); 38 ('Prague'); 39; 40; 41 ('Jupiter')
- Philharmonia O and New Philharmonia O / Klemperer
HMV EX 290482-3/*9* [6 LPs and 9 cassettes] and
SLS5048

*** Symphonies nrs 25, K183; 40, K550
- Concertgebouw O / Harnoncourt
Tel Dig **ZK8**; AZ6/*CX4* 42935

*** Symphonies nrs 25 and 40
- Wiener Philharmoniker / Kertesz
Decca SXL6617
- Scottish Chamber O / Conlon
Erato/ Conifer **ECD88078**, transfer from NUM75119 (4/85)

*** Symphonies nrs 26 in E flat major, K184; 31 in D
('Paris'), K297; 38 in D ('Prague'), K504
- Berliner Philharmoniker / Böhm
DG Acc 2542/*3342* 127

*** Symphonies nrs 28 in C and 33 in B flat major
- Wiener Philharmoniker / Levine
DG dig **419 606-2GH**; -1GH; *-4GH*

*** Symphonies nrs 28 in C, K200; 41 in C ('Jupiter'), K551
- Dresden State O / Colin Davis
Philips Dig 6514/*7337* 206

*** Symphonies nrs 29; 39 in E flat major, K543
- Dresden State O / Colin Davis
Philips 6514/*7337* 205

*** Symphonies nrs 33 and 36
- English Ch O / Colin Davis
l'Oiseau Lyre SOL266

*** Symphonies nrs 39 and 41
- Dresden State O / Colin Davis
Philips Dig **410 046-2**

*** Symphonies nrs 29 and 33
- English Baroque Soloists / Gardiner
Philips Dig **412 736-2**, /-1; /-4
- Berliner Philharmoniker / Karajan
DGG Privilege 2535 155

*** Symphonies nrs 29, 30 and 34
- English Ch O / Barenboim
HMV ASD2806

*** Symphonies nrs 29 in A, K201; 35 in D ('Haffner'), K385

- Wiener Philharmoniker / Kertesz
Decca SXL6616
- Wiener Philharmoniker / Böhm
DG **413 734-2GH**, transfer from 2531 335 (9/81)

*** Symphonies nrs 40 and 41
- Wiener Philharmoniker / Böhm
DG **413 547-2**; 2580 780

*** Symphonies nrs 29 in A, 35 in D, 40 in g minor
- Academy SMF / Marriner
Philips Silver Line **420 486 043** (9/80)

*** Symphonies nrs 29 in A, K201; 39 in E flat major, K543
- Concertgebouw O / Harnoncourt
Tel Dig **ZK8 43017**; AZ6/*CY4* 43017

*** Symphonies nrs 31 in D ('Paris'), K297; 33 in B flat
major, K319
- Concertgebouw O / Harnoncourt
Tel Dig **ZK8 42817**; AZ6/*CX4* 42817

*** Symphonies nrs 31 in D, 35 in D
- XVIIIth Century O / Brüggen
Philips **416 490-2PH** (12/86); -1PH

*** Symphonies nrs 31 in D ('Paris'), K297; 34 in C, K338; 39
in E flat major, K543; 40 in g minor, K550
- English Chamber O / Barenboim
HMV *TCC2-POR 154598-9*

*** Symphonies nrs 31 in D ('Paris'); 35 in D ('Haffner'); 40 in
g minor, K550; 41 in C ('Jupiter'),
- Berliner Philharmoniker / Böhm
DG Walkman *413 151-4*

*** Symphonies nrs 31 in D ('Paris'), K297; 40 in g minor,
K550
- Academy of Ancient Music / Schröder / Hogwood
l'Oiseau Lyre **410 197-2**; DSDL/*KDSLC* 716

*** Symphonies nrs 31 in D ('Paris'), K297; 41 in C
('Jupiter'), K551
- Stuttgarter K O / Conlon
Erato Dig **ECD 88029**; NUM/*MCE* 75107

*** Symphonies nrs 32, K318; 35 ('Haffner'); 36 ('Linz'); 41
('Jupiter')
- English Ch O / Barenboim
HMV *TCC2-POR 54298*

*** Symphonies 35, 38 and 39
- English Ch O / Barenboim
EMI Eminence EMX2097; *TC/-*, from ASD2327 (9/67) and
ASD2424 (8/68)

*** Symphonies nrs 32 in G, K318; 35 in D ('Haffner'), K385;
39 in E flat major, K543
- English Ch O / Tate
HMV Dig **CDC 747 327-2**; EL 270253-1/*4*
- English Ch O / Mackerras
ASV Dig DCA/*ZCDCA* 543

*** Symphonies nrs 32, K318; 35 in D ('Haffner'), K385; 36 in
C ('Linz'), K425; 38 in D ('Prague'), K504; 39 in E flat major,
K543; 40 in g minor, K550; 41 in C ('Jupiter'), K551
- Berliner Philharmoniker / Karajan
DG 2740 189/*3371 038*

*** Symphony nr. 33
- Concertgebouw O / Harnoncourt
Philips 642817 (1/83); **842817** (3/85)

*** Symphonies nrs 34 in C, K338; 35 in D ('Haffner'), K385
- Concertgebouw O / Harnoncourt
Tel Dig **ZK8 42703**; AZ6/*CX4* 42703

*** Symphonies nrs 34 in C, K338; 41 in C ('Jupiter'), K551
- Academy of Ancient Music / Schröder / Hogwood
l'Oiseau Lyre **411 658-2**; -1; *-4*

*** Symphonies nrs 35 ('Haffner'); 36 in C ('Linz')
- Academy of Ancient Music / Schröder / Hogwood
l'Oiseau Lyre DSLO/*KDSLC* 602

*** Symphonies nrs 35 ('Haffner'); 36 ('Linz'); 38-40; 41
('Jupiter')
- Columbia S O / Walter
CBS M3P/*3PT* 39627 [3 LPs]

*** Symphony nr. 36 in C ('Linz'); 'The birth of a perform-
ance' (rehearsal)
- Columbia S O / Walter
CBS DC/*DCT* 40182

*** Symphonies nrs 35 and 39
- Columbia S O / Walter
CBS **MK42026**

***Symphonies nrs 35 ('Haffner'); 40 in g minor, K550
- Academy SMF / Marriner
Philips Seq 412 367-1/*4*

*** Symphonies nrs 35 in D ('Haffner'), K385; 41 in C
('Jupiter'), K551
- Wiener Philharmoniker / Bernstein
DG Dig **415 305-2**; -1; *-4*

*** Symphonies nrs 36 in C ('Linz'), K425; 38 in D ('Prague'),
K504
- English Ch O / Tate
HMV Dig **CDC 747442-2**; EL 270306-1/*4*
- Columbia S O / Walter
CBS **MK 42027**
- English Ch O / Colin Davis
Pickwick Con CC/*CCTC* 7581
- Berliner Philharmoniker / Karajan
DG Sig 410 840-1/*4*
- Wiener Philharmoniker Bernstein
DG dig **415 962-2GH**, /-1GH; /-4GH
[recording Grosser Saal Musikverein Vienna, Oct. 84,
Oct. 85]
- Prague Ch O / Mackerras
Telarc/Conifer **CD80148**

*** Symphony nr. 38
- English Ch O / Britten
Decca SXL6539

*** Symphonies nrs 38 in D ('Prague'), K504; 39 E flat major,
K543
- Stuttgart Ch O / Conlon
Erato Dig **ECD 88093**; NUM/*MCE* 75180
- Academy of Ancient Music / Schröder / Hogwood
l'Oiseau Lyre Dig **410 233-2**; 410 233-1/4
- Chamber Orch of Europe / Alexander Schneider
ASV dig **CDCO E806**; COE 806

*** Symphonies nrs 38 in D ('Prague'), K504; 41 in C ('Jupiter'), K551
- Concertgebouw O / Harnoncourt
  Tel Dig **ZL8 48219**; DX6 48219

*** Symphonies nrs 38 in D; nr. 39 in E flat major
- Wiener Philharmoniker / Böhm
  DG **413 735-2GH** (5/85)

*** Symphonies nrs 38 ('Prague'); 39 in E flat, K543; 40 in g minor, K550; 41 in C ('Jupiter'), K551
- Berliner Philharmoniker / Böhm
  DG Acc 2725/*3374* 104

*** Symphonies nrs 38 ('Prague'); 39 in E flat
- Academy of Ancient Music / Schröder / Hogwood
  l'Oiseau Lyre **410 233-2**; -1; -4
- Berliner Philharmoniker / Karajan
  DG 2531/*3301* 137
- Academy SMF / Marriner
  EL 270308-1 (9/86); **CDC7 47334-2** (12/86)

*** Symphonies nrs 39 in E flat, K543; 40 in g minor, K550
- Wiener Philharmoniker / Bernstein
  DG Dig **413 776-2**; -1; -4
- Berliner Philharmoniker / Karajan
  HMV SXLP/*TC-SXLP* 30527
- London S O / Colin Davis
  Philips Universo 6580
- Concertgebouw O / Josef Krips
  Philips 6500 430
- Bamberger Symphoniker / Jochum
  Orfeo/HM **CO45901A**, transfer from SO45832H (12/83)

*** Symphony nr 40 in g minor, K550
- XVIIIth Century O / Brüggen
  Philips Dig **416 329-2**; -1; -4 [live recording Nijmegen, The Netherlands 1986]
- Orch of St John's Square / Lubbock
  Pickwick Dig **PCD 820**
- English Ch O / Benjamin Britten
  Decca Jub JB*KJBC* 107
- Furtwängler
  HMV DB 6997/9 (2/50)

*** Symphonies nrs 40 in g minor, K550; 41 in C ('Jupiter'), K551
- English Ch O / Tate
  HMV Dig **CDC 747147-2** (7/85); EL 270154-1/4 (2/85)
- English Ch O / Barenboim
  EMI EMX 41 2074-1/4
- London S O / Abbado
  DG Galleria **415 841-2GGA**, transfer from 2531 273 (11/80)
- Columbia S O / Walter
  CBS **MK 42028**
- Chamber Orch of Europe / Solti
  Decca **414 334-2;** /-1; /-4
  [recorded in the Alte Oper, Frankfurt]
- London P O / Mackerras
  CfP CFP/*TC-CFP* 40253 (11/76)
- Praags Ch O / Mackerras
  Telarc/Conifer **CD 80 139** (5/87)
- Berliner Philharmoniker / Karajan
  DG 2531/*3301* 138
- Wiener Philharmoniker / Karajan
  Decca VIVB/*KVIC* 6
- Chicago S O / Levine
  RCA Dig **RCD 14413**
- Academy of Ancient Music / Schröder / Hogwood

l'Oiseau Lyre Florilegium **417 557-2OH** (4/87), transfer from D172D4 (5/83)
  also **410 197-2OH** (6/84) and **411 658 2OH** (11/84)

*** Symphonies nrs 35, 36, 38, 39, 40, 41
- Wiener Philharmoniker / Bernstein
  DG dig **419 427-2GH3** [3 discs]; 2GH3 [3 LPs]; *4GH3*
  [live recorded in the Grosser Saal Musikverein, Vienna, 1981-85]
  transfers of resp 413 776-1GH; 415 305-1GH; 415 962-1GH

*** Symphony nr. 41
- Boston S O / Jochum
  DGG 2530 357
- Boston S O / Leinsdorf
  RCA Victoria VL89576
- Royal P O / Beecham
  HMV SXLP/*TC-SXLP* 30443
- XVIIIth Century O / Brüggen
  Philips **420 241-2PH** [live recording]

THE EARLY SYMPHONIES - Jaap Schröder and Christopher Hogwood have recorded the numbered symphonies (Mozart wrote more than the 41 that he numbered) and give with this work a monumental view of the results obtained by contemporary, 'authentic' performance practices. Especially evident in the early symphonies, authentic instruments (when played well as is the case with Hogwood's Academy of Ancient Music) make the score more transparent. The different sections of the orchestra are better profiled. The symphonies sound exciting and brand new.

Neville Marriner accepts the early scores without question (as compared to Böhm who does not, always considering the later symphonies when approaching the early works). Marriner's performance is wonderfully light. There is an obvious, uncomplicated delight in the Mozart. The rhythm is articulated and exact and the balance is excellent. Nothing postured or fake. Philips has achieved an almost perfect sound and all the details are clear (on the wonderful CD as well).

THE LATER SYMPHONIES - The LP's and especiallly CD's available of Mozart's later symphonies are so numerous and so varied (the 'Amadeus' effect of the Eighties) that the choice is difficult at best. Only a true lover of Mozart and one with infinite patience can find his way through the jungle of recordings available.

Those listeners who are satisfied with only the 'authentic' interpretations should compare the recordings made by Gardiner and Schröder/Hogwood. Number 29 is very different as played by these two groups and therefore makes good material for comparison. The balance, tempo, phrasing and rhetoric are quite distinguishable. Gardiner begins quietly but is very authoritative in the tutti. The AAM sounds less dedicated: the contrasts are a bit vague and the musical ideas are not as polished. This is but one comparison and the differences although evident and worthy of consideration, are still minimal. Bruggen's polished performance should appeal to just about everyone. His interpretation is warm; he has an obvious affection for the music. The sound is subtler than in other performances with authentic instruments. As compared to Hogwood, the Orchestra of the XVIIIth Century clearly expresses its

conductor's identity. Bruggen's tempi are most likely slower than in Mozart's time (Hummel suggests min=96 for the first movement, Bruggen plays at min=66). The interpretation is almost romantic despite the minimal vibrato used. Bruggen makes it clear that authenticity is only relative, even in these self conscious 'authentic' times. It is probably better to consider his work in terms of the standard performances, Colin Davis or Jeffrey Tate, for example, and judge him when compared to the best available on modern instruments.

Bruggen's performance of the 40th Symphony is the most convincing since the Furtwängler version of 1950 (HMV DB6997/9). There are still those who will not consider an authentic performance of any kind, even with a conductor of international importance. Bruggen's orchestra of 40 musicians is better than all the other authentic groups. He is also a greater conductor than the other authentics: nothing but praise here. The orchestra is technically brilliant and Bruggen is an exciting conductor. Rarely are his movements ineffective or vague in performance. His Mozart is much more interesting than that played by a dozen so-called maestros now entrusted with these great works on the international concert scene. Hopefully, the general audience will accept Bruggen's authentic instruments and thus be able to enjoy truly inspiring Mozart.

NRS 25, 28, 29, 30 ETC.: AAM/HOGWOOD. **417 841-20H3** - These symphonies are included in volume 4 of the complete project. A comparison with more traditional interpretations gives us faster slow movements and probably a better idea of what Mozart heard seated behind the harpsichord when performing his own works. Hogwood's players sound a bit stoic and distant, especially in the slow movements. Nevertheless, these performances are quite different and much better than the ones now expected and accepted as conventional.

NRS 29, 35, 40: ASMF/ MARRINER; PHILIPS SILVER LINE **420 486-2PM** -
This version of the 40th was recorded in 1970. It is difficult not to sucumb to Marriner's appealing work. The tempi are extraordinary and the orchestra creates a marvellous atmosphere. The sound is rather dated though. The acoustics are a bit much, especially in the basses in the Haffner Symphony. Nevertheless, these recordings are highly recommended.

NRS 32, 35, 39: MACKERRAS/TATE - In the early Seventies, Mackerras recorded these symphonies for CfP. After ten years he recorded them again, this time with the English Chamber Orchestra. Tate recorded them with the ECO as well. The differences could not be greater. Mackerras plays with much faster tempi than Tate. Those who choose for elegance should choose Tate. The faster tempi give a persistence and excitement to Mackerras' version but threaten the accuracy. Never one to bet on charm, Mackerras' Haffner is so fast that clarity and articulation are both sorely lacking.

THE COMPLETE SET: ASMF/MARRINER - This set of the later symphonies is excellent. The most amazing aspect of this monumental project is that there is not a trace of routine to be heard in any of the symphonies, except perhaps in the Jupiter (where the playing is a trifle less exciting than in the rest). The ASMF rivals the ECO under Tate; its sound is fuller than the ECO, the strings are more polished. Even the tempi

have more wit and humour than with Tate.
NRS 38, 39: CHAMBER ORCHESTRA OF EUROPE/
ALEXANDER SCHNEIDER; HMV/ASV dig **COE806** -
The talented members of the European Chamber
Orchestra are perhaps young, nevertheless they
perform in many ways much better than their older
colleagues even when led by conductors the likes of
Tate or Bernstein. Schneider, their permanent conductor, leads them in a wonderful version, old fash-
ioned in some respects perhaps, but always refreshing and animated. Schneider's tempi are conservative (rather like Bohm who refuses to be hurried); his
Andantes are even slower than Bohm's. The 16th
notes in the Finale of nr. 39 however, are played
better, more articulated and clearer, than done by
even the Viennese under Bernstein! These performances are rhythmic and strong in spite of the tempi,
and the stylish phrasing, especially by the soloists, is
more successful than that which the Viennese or
even Marriner's musicians have produced.
NRS 39 AND 40: SOLTI/TATE - The European Chamber Orchestra is alert   der Solti and the details are
all clear. Solti's inte. :tation, however, is rather
excessive an   the w   leaves a rather messy
impression. The version v :h Tate is preferable. It is
more sparklii i and spontaneous. Tate also plays all
the repeats, Solti none of them.
NRS 39 AND 40: JOCHUM/BAMBERGER; on Orfeo -
This excellent performance is consistent throughout and much preferable to Bernstein's version on
DG. The sound quality is also better with Jochum,
fuller and more detailed. Tate, however, will still be
favourite with many Mozart lovers. Conlon's performance of 39 and 40 is a safe choice, wonderful
sound, good balance. Conlon lacks an identity in
many ways though: the Giovanni aspect of the Prague Symphony is lost as a result.
NRS 31 AND 35: BRUGGEN, NR. 35: HOGWOOD - Of
all the authentic performances now available (Hogwood and AAM, English Baroque Soloists/Gardiner,
Harnoncourt with CO), Bruggen's excellence pre-
vails. Between Hogwood's and Bruggen's recordings are six years of ever-changing views concerning
authentic performance practices. The differences
could not be greater. Bruggen's strings are subtle
and articulated but have a beautifully vague and full
tone; the woodwinds (which include of course the
wooden flutes) are clear and well-balanced and the
trumpets in the tutti, together with the kettle drums,
bite their way through and take their rightful share of
attention. Not Mozart that everyone will love, but for
those willing to be swept off their feet by something
completely new, perfection indeed.
NRS 30, 31, 32: VPHO/ LEVINE, CONCERTGEBOUW
O/HARNONCOURT - James Levine and the Viennese
take a healthy stand with Mozart's 30th and leave him
be. The humour and teasing is wonderful. Their
precision in performance is just what the score
demands. The Paris Symphony gets a straight-faced
interpretation as well. It is a pleasing and ironic
performance. Harnoncourt rivals Levine with the
Concertgebouw's version of the Parisian. The conti-
nuity is missing, however, as Harnoncourt switches
styles throughout. The orchestra sounds surprisingly awkward, almost Walteresque, and the whole
is not very convincing.
NRS 35, 36 ('LINZ'), 38 ('PRAGUE') - The ECO under
Tate is pleasing in every way perhaps due in part to

the size of the orchestra. Barenboim directs exceedingly lively performances, rhythmic and well-crafted
and well-balanced despite the few moments when
the brass get the better part of the strings. The
Marriner version is first class. His Academy, in many
ways better than the ECO, sound more like a symphony than a chamber orchestra. Tate and Jochum
are rather similar in terms of interpretation.
Jochum's Nr. 41 is the far better of the two however,
recorded with the Boston Symphony for DG.
NRS 32 AND 36: CONCERTGEBOUW O/HARNON-
COURT - The whole series is questionable. This
orchestra doesn't for some reason fit this conductor
with this music. The result is too heavy and slightly
depressing Mozart.
NRS 36 AND 38: VPHO/ BERNSTEIN - Bernstein
followed his instincts here and appropriately left the
Mozart to the Viennese. The strings are velvety and
the brass sweet. Many things are exaggerated, but
the orchestra saves the performance with their gorgeous phrasing and general alertness.
NRS 25 AND 40: SCOTTISH CH O/CONLON -
Conlon's tempi are refreshing especially in comparison to Harnoncourt's. He gives the Scots enough
time to develop the musical lines while ensuring that
the larger phrases remain in tact. The Scottish
Chamber Orchestra, not very well known, has a
warmer sound than even the Concertgebouw which
should surprise many. More the pity that their work
gets such little attention.
NRS 29 AND 39: VPHO/ BOHM; CO/HARNON-
COURT; DRESDEN STATE O/COLIN DAVIS - Bohm's
performance with the Viennese is much warmer than
his own with the Berliners. Nevertheless, the best
here is unquestionably Sir Colin Davis and the
Dresdner State Kapelle. Pure Mozart, pure musicality, not a hint of exaggeration of any type or school,
this is a marvellous recording. The sound is magnificent. Harnoncourt's tempi (too fast) and the overly
realistic sound (too loud) just can not compete.
NRS 29 AND 35: BOHM - These transfers of the 1977
and 1981 recordings that Bohm made with the
Viennese have been carefully constructed by the
technicians at DG. The analogue sound and balance
are pleasing, the background noise is almost nonex-
istent. The orchestra plays beautifully, detailed and
relaxed. Bohm is at his best here, despite the rather
slow tempi (the first movement of the 29th!). The
41st is one of the very best.
NRS 35, 36, 38, 39, 40, 41 COLUMBIA SO/WALTER;
M3P39627 (36 and 38 on CD) CBS mono **CD40182**
with the famous rehearsal of the 'Linz' (6/85) - This
set is an exceptional one and not only because of its
historical value. The famous rehearsal of the 'Linz'
that Walter leads with his Los Angeles musicians
makes evident his relationship with this orchestra.
Always the gentleman, Walter works out details to
the utmost. Walter is of course a product of the late
19th century German Romantic School. His Mozart
is nevertheless vital and lively and worthy of one's attention. Compared with the impersonal and light
Mozart performances of late, it is refreshing to hear
the richness of the melodies as performed by the
Columbia Symphony. The excellent solo oboist and
bassonist deserve mention. No lovers of these great
symphonies should ignore performances by such a
'great' orchestra.
NRS 29, 39: BERLIN PO/KARAJAN DG**423 374-**

2GH./-1GH/-4GH. (cf CO/Harnoncourt **8 43107**) -
The Harnoncourt version has a scratchy sound, the
tempi are eccentric and the balance is wrong. The
fortes sound more angry than full (Andante in nr.
29). The Menuet in nr. 39 is absurd and has no
relationship to the trio, and the strings are buried by
the brass in the Finale. How does Karajan fare in
comparison? The DG sound is definitely friendlier,
almost mild. The dynamic contrasts, however are
barely audible and the nuances practically non-
existent. The interpretation in general has an unpleasant stiffness. The balance is good.
NRS 40 AND 41: NEW PHILHARMONIA/GIULINI;
Decca Ovation **417 727-2DM** (4/88 transfer from a
1965 recording) - These recordings are still pleasant. The orchestral playing is excellent. Giulini has
been criticized for his interpretation, nevertheless
the direct and dedicated performance should appeal
to many. The balance that Giulini maintains between
warmth on the one hand, and classical refinement
and style on the other,is truly musical.
NRS 35, 40, 41: RADIO SO TURIN /KARAJAN; DG
mono **423 525-2GD04** - These recordings were
made in 1942 when 'Das Wunder Karajan' was 34.
The interpretation borders on the bizarre. Where is
the need for these recordings when there are so
many good versions of these pieces? (the Karajan
cult at its worst). His own reaction to these records
at a later date was 'I must have been drunk at the
time'!
NRS 38 AND 39 V PHILHARMONIKER/LEVINE; DG
423 086-2GH/-1GH; -4GH. - Nr. 38 was performed
for the first time in Prague in 1786 with 25 strings.
Despite a much larger string section, Levine successfully gives a light and transparent performance.
The soft touch and flowing tempi are excellent. In nr.
39, he tends to be pompous. This is not Beethoven,
please.
NRS 40 and 41: PHILHARMONIA/KLEMPERER; EMI
CDC7 47852-2 (reconstructed from Columbia SAX
2486 from 11/63) - The general opinion about Klemperer should revise itself after experiencing these
wonderful performances. The stiffness and rough-
ness that this genius gets criticized for so often are
completely gone. The slow tempi are there, of
course. There are few repeats and not much real
Mozart charm. Nevertheless the performance is
essentially refined and decorative. Nr. 40 is especially fascinating. These recordings, dating from the
Sixties, still sound fresh and alive.
NRS 36 AND 38, 40 AND 41: PRAGUE CHAMBER O/
MACKERRAS; Telarc/Conifer respectively **CD80148**
and **CD80139** (10 and5/87) - The number of recordings of these late symphonies, many of which of
such good quality, and the fact that Mozart lovers
have such strong personal views, makes recom-
mending one performance a perilous task. Mackerras has obviously been influenced by the 'authentic'
school, yet doesn't let himself go far enough in that
style. The harpsichord is there, the repeats as well,
and the strings play lightly and with a lot of articulation. Even the kettledrums have the same intensity as
with an authentic authority like Roger Norrington
and his London Classical Players.The acoustics are
altogether wrong though, which is unfortunate.
Mackerras has long been an established recording
talent. These performances are stronger than his
1976 work with the London PO. In nr. 40, Mackerras

is the first since Benjamin Britten to give such a personal and characteristic performance. The clarity of these recordings along with the structural transparency and brilliant tempi are what make these performances so attractive.

NRS 40 AND 41 LONDON SO/ABBADO; DFG Galleria **415 841-2GGA** - These transfers to CD, in light of the numerous recordings available, are rather redundant. They serve to prove, however, that not every esteemed conductor is automatically a Mozart conductor as well.

CARL NIELSEN (1865-1931)

Symphony nr. 1 in g minor, Op. 7 (1894)
- Danish Radio S O / Thomas Jensen
  Decca LXT2748 (1952)
Symphony nr. 1
Symphony nr. 3 (Sinfonia espansiva), Op. 27 (1912)
- Gomez / Rayner Cook / London S O / Ole Schmidt (1/75) (1/80)
  Uni KPM 7001/*UKC 7130*
Symphony nr. 2 ('The Four Tempers'), Op. 16
- London S O / Schmidt
  Uni KPM 7002/*UKC 7250*
- Göteborg S O / Myung-Whun Chung
  BIS CD 247 (LP/*MC 247*)
Symphony nr. 3
- Hassing / Sjoberg / Danish Radio S O / Erik Tuxen
  Decca LXT2697 (1952)
- Rehling / Hansen / Danish Radio S O / Ahronovich
  Uni Kanchana KP/*UKC 8006* (11/82)
Symphony nr. 4
- Danish Radio O / Grondahl
  EMX290444-3 (5/52) (7/85)
- Berliner Philharmoniker / Karajan
  DG Dig CD 413 313-2 (2532/*3302* 029) (3/82)
- London S O / Schmidt
  Uni KPM7004 (1/75) (2/81)
- Swedish Radio S O / Esa-Pekka Salonen
  CBS Dig CD MK42093 (also LP and cassette)
- City of Birmingham S O / Simon Rattle
  HMV Dig CD C7 47503-2, transfer from EL270260-1/4 (11/85)
- London Ph O / Markevich
  Turnabout TV34050
Symphony nr. 4 and nr. 5
- Danish Radio S O / Blomstedt
  HMV *TCC2-POR 54593-9*
Symphony nr. 5, Op. 50 (1922)
- Danish Radio S O / Jensen
  Decca LXT2980 (1954)
- Bournemouth S O / Berglund
  EMI Em EMX/*TC-EMX* 2033
- Danish Radio S O / Kubelik
  HMV Dig EL 270352-1/4
- Concertgebouw O / Kondrashin
  Philips 412 069-1/4
Symphony nr. 6 (Sinfonia semplice) (1925)
Symphony nr. 4
- London S O / Schmidt
  Uni KPM 7006/*UKC 7460*
- Danish Radio S O / Jensen
  Decca LW5132 (1954)
- Hallé Orchestra / Barbirolli
  PRT GSGC/*ZCGC* 2031

Nielsen was an unknown outside of Sweden until after the Second World War. His impressive performances and recordings with the Danish Radio Orchestra made him famous in Europe. The catalogues are now full of Nielsen and the old recordings are still available.

Thomas Jensen and Erik Tuxen led the recordings made in the fifties, then considered very successful. Their successor, Ole Schmidt, was not as popular with the Scandanavian public. Nevertheless, Schmidt's version of the Second with the London Symphony is still the best one since Jensen. A close second is Myung-Whun Chung's performance with the Gothenburg Orchestra. Chung has a natural affinity for Nielsen, but the Gothenburg players cannot match London's standard. Schmidt has also recorded the Third but that performance is not one of the best. The Espansiva was also recorded during a concert in 1981 led by Ahronovich. The strength of the recording lies in the strings who play with lyrical intensity. This music is in the Danish musician's blood and Ahronovich leads them well, better than Blomstedt.

The best version (for those who insist on a modern recording) of the Fourth Symphony is probably Von Karajan's with the Berlin Philharmonic. The orchestra's playing is perfect and Von Karajan's interpretation, majestic. As is often the case with Von Karajan, the brass is perhaps a bit too reserved, especially when compared to pioneer recordings made by Launy Grondahl (again with the Danish Radio Orchestra) in the early fifties. Simon Rattle has released the Fourth on CD. Rattle's grasp of the score is better than both Von Karajan and Salonen who tend to break up Nielsen's long lines. The EMI technicians gave Rattle a beautiful balance. Salonen's recording for CBS is egocentric if not eccentric. He breaks up the music with all sorts of unmarked rests and allargandos.

Berglund's Fifth is a bit better than Schmidt's. Kubelik recorded the Fifth during a concert. His is a very personal vision. The orchestra is relaxed under Kubelik. The pianissimo at the opening is breathtaking.

The Sixth has been recorded by Ole Schmidt and is an unqualified success. He leaves all rivals behind with his natural and captivating interpretation.

GOESTA NYSTROEM (1890-1966)

Sinfonia breve
- Gothenburg S O / Ehrling
  Cap CAP 1116
Sinfonia concertante for cello and O
- Stockholm P O / Lavotha, Göran Nilsson
  Cap Dig CAP 1272

Nystroem lived for many years in Paris, trying to build up a career as both a painter and a musician. On the one hand, he belongs in a group with Dardel and Grünewald, on the other hand, he was greatly influenced by Honegger, Suaguet and even Bloch. The Sinfonia breve was written between 1929 and 1931 and is performed well. It must be taken into consideration, however, that a half a century after its composition, this work has lost its appeal. The concertante symphony was written in the war years and has many pleasant passages. This symphony is much worthier than the Sinfonia del mar. The soloist, Elemér Lavotha, is superb, as are the players of the Stockholm Philharmonic.

HUBERT PARRY (1848-1918)

Symphony nr. 5 in b minor
- London P O / Sir Adrian Boult
  HMV ASD 3725

Sir Adrian Boult recorded this piece just before retirement. His conducting career was much longer than expected and longer than any of his colleagues. Parry's Fifth was the composer's last symphony. The style is reminiscent of Brahms. The slow movement is especially impressive. Performance and recording are both exemplary: a worthy finale for Boult's career.

WILHELM PETERSON-BERGER (1867-1942)

Symphony nr. 2 in E flat major (Sunnanfärd)
- Swedish Radio S O / Westerberg
  EMI 7C 061 35455

Peterson-Berger is best known in his native Sweden for his short instrumental works inspired by the folk tradition. He composed five symphonies; the Second is subtitled, Journey To The Sun. It was written in the first ten years of this century. The first movement's opening is very promising. The second movement enchants with its dreamy quality. As a whole, however, the symphony lacks coherence. It is well to note, that Petersen-Berger's piece is more popular than works by Alfvén or Rangström. The performance and recording are both faultless.

WALTER PISTON (1894-1976)

Symphony nr. 3
- Eastman-Rochester O / Hanson
  Mercury SRI 75107

Walter Piston wrote his Third Symphony in 1947; it had been commissioned by the Koussevitsky Music Foundation. There are no programme implications known, nevertheless, the piece is strongly subjective and often very sombre. The Scherzo is a fierce and biting movement, but the Finale is more optimistic. This particular symphony is praised as an excellent example of the American symphonic repertoire. The sound on this recording is not ideal; it does have substance though, and the details can be clearly heard.

SERGE PROKOFIEV (1891-1953)

Symphony nr. 1 in D ('Classic'), Op. 25
- Berliner Philharmoniker / Herbert von Karajan
  DG Dig CD 400 034-2 (2532/*3302* 031)
- Los Angeles Ch O / Schwarz
  Delos Dig CD D/CD 3021 (also LP and cassette)

- London S O / Claudio Abbado
  Pickwick Con CC/*CCTC* 7576
  also: (including Symphony nr. 3) Decca SXL 6469) (10/70)
- Academy SMF / Marriner
  Decca Jub 410 167-1/*4* (12/73) (8/84)
- Chicago S O / Giulini
  Dig Sig 410 838-1/*4* ; (2530/*3302* 783)
- New York P O / Bernstein
  CBS 60112/*40*
Symphony nr. 1
Symphony nr. 4 in C, Op. 112 (revised version 1947)
- Scottish National O / Neeme Järvi
  Chandos Dig CD CHAN 8400; (ABRD/*ABDT* 1137)
Symphony nr. 1
Symphony nr. 7 in c sharp minor, Op. 131
- London S O / Previn
  HMV EG 290298-1/*4* (11/78) (8/85)
- Philharmonia / Nicolai Malko
  HMV SXLP/*TC-SXLP* 30437 (6/55) (5/80)
Symphony nr. 2 in d minor, Op. 40
- Scottish National O / Järvi
  Chandos Dig CD CHAN 8368; (ABRD/*ABDT* 1134)
- London P O / Weller
  Decca SXL 6945
Symphony nr. 3 in c minor, Op. 44
- Concertgebouw O / Kondrashin
  Philips 412 070-1/*4*
- Junge Deutsche Philharmonia / Ricardo Chailly
  DG Dig 410 998-1/*4* (8/84)
- Scottish National O / Järvi (original version 1930)
  Chandos Dig CD CHAN 8401; (ABRD/*ABDT* 1138)
Symphony nr. 5 in B flat, Op. 100
- Berliner Philharmoniker / Karajan
  DG Sig 410 992-1/*4*
- Israel P O / Bernstein
  CBS Dig CD 35877 (also LP and cassette)
- St Louis S O / Felix Slatkin
  RCA Dig CD RD85035; (*RK* 85035) and CD RCDI 5035;
  (ARCI/*ARKI* 5035)
Symphony nr. 6 in E flat, Op. 111
- Scottish National O / Järvi
  Chandos Dig CD CHAN8359; (ABRD/*ABDT* 1122)
Symphony nr. 7 in C sharp, Op. 131
Sinfonietta in A, Op. 5/48
- Scottish National O / Järvi
  Chandos Dig CD CHAN 8442; (ABRD/*ABDT* 1154)
- (only Sinfonietta) Moscow Radio O / Dzhemal Dalgat
  HMV/Melodiya ASD 2765 (4/72)
- (only Sionfonietta) Philharmonia O / Muti
  HMV SLS5110 (4/78)

Perhaps due to the immense popularity of both Peter and the Wolf and the Classic Symphony, Prokofiev has always been a favourite with the record companies. There are 20 recordings listed here, just the tip of the iceberg. More important 20th century composers are neglected in favour of Prokofiev. His popularity did take some time, however, to develop. The Classic Symphony is a parody of 18th century symphonic music. There is more 20th century music in the piece than the title suggests. This First Symphony has been interpreted quite a number of different ways. The three recordings that are the best older ones are the one conducted by Ferenc Fricasay with the Berlin Radio Orchestra (RIAS), Ansermet with the orchestra of the Conservatoire in Paris (1954) and especially, Efraim Kurz's performance with the Philharmonia (1958). Of the newer recordings,

Schwarz with the Los Angeles Chamber Orchestra is very good. The lyric is relaxed and appealing. The balance is good. Neeme Järvi's version with the Scots is a bit flat, but the slow movement is a real 'douceur', wonderfully reminiscent of the pioneer recording led by Koussevitsky in 1931. The old Nicolai Malko record is still loved. This was the first stereo recording EMI ever made (1955). The transfer has preserved the original sound well. Bernstein's performance is precise. Abbado's is fresh and well played, but misses the shimmering quality of the old Kurtz recording. Previn's version exudes warmth and vitality. Von Karajan's performance is, as is to be expected, brilliant and polished. The middle movements could do with a bit more charm (as in the Marriner record) and the balance is not natural.

The Second Symphony is the heaviest and most dissonant of the series. Walter Weller gives an impressive performance of this difficult score. The other two to be recommended are Järvi and Chandos.

Järvi's Third is successful in the Andante. Chailly's DG recording with the German Youth Orchestra is an achievement. It cannot compete, however, with Abbado's for Decca. Kondrashin's live performance is ruined by the concert hall noises.

The Fourth Symphony (1930, revised 1946) is not really a finished work. It is actually a ballet for Diaghlev, The Prodigal Son. Late in his life, the composer drastically revised the work and extended it from 23 to 37 minutes. He also added a piano part. The Fourth has not been recorded often. The older versions are Georges Sebastien for Urania and Martinon for Turnabout (TV370525). Järvi directed the 1947 version and his is a more successful performance than either Rozhdestvensky's with the USSR Symphony (1958) or Weller's with the London Philharmonic on Decca.

The Fifth Symphony is the obvious favourite of the record companies. The glittering orchestration shows off the CD technique as it did both the hi-fi and stereo systems. Von Karajan's 1971 recording is still the best, according to many. Jarvi built up a great reputation with his Prokofiev and his recording is also grand. Chandos improved his reputation with this piece as well. The Bernstein version is a mixture of several concert performances. Bernstein is the best in building up a heavily romantic climax. Slatkin leads the St Louis Orchestra in an excellent performance, fresh and lyrically innocent, but it cannot compete with Bernstein's power.

Perhaps the grandest of the cycle, the Sixth has been recorded well by several conductors. The Scots play it well under Järvi. That goes for the Seventh Symphony as well which has also been released on CD. The 1955 Nicolai Malko recording with the Philharmonia was rereleased in 1980. The Previn recording with the London Symphony (1978) also returned to the catalogues, in 1985.

Prokofiev's Sinfonietta was written in 1909 and revised twice, in 1914 and 1929. It is a wonderful piece but has never come close to being as popular as the Classic Symphony. Järvi has performed it with the Scottish National and Dalgat recorded it in Moscow. The newest is Muti's recording with the Philharmonia, made in 1978.

SERGEI RACHMANINOV (1873-1943)

Symphony nr. 1 in d minor, Op. 13
Symphony nr. 2 in e minor, Op. 27
Symphony nr. 3 in a minor, Op. 44
- Concertgebouw O / Wladimir Ashkenazy
  Decca Dig CD 411 657-2; (SXDL/*KSXDC* 7603)
  resp 400 081-2; (SXDL/*KSXDC* 7653)
  and 410 231-2; (SXDL/*KSXDC* 7531
- Berliner Philharmoniker / Maazel
  DG Dig 413 784-1/*4*
  resp 2532/*3302* 102 and 2532/*3302* 065
- Orch de la Suisse Romande and London P O / Weller
  Decca Jub JB/*KJBC* 91, resp 92 and 93
- Rotterdam P O / Edo de Waart
  Philips 6768 148
- London S O / Previn
  HMV ASD/*TCC-ASD* 3137 and 3369 and 2889
  [Symphony nr. 2 also EMI CD CDC747159-2, transfer from
  ASD2889 (4/73)]
Symphony nr. 2
- Royal P O / Previn
  Telarc Dig CD 80113; transfer DG10113 (10/85)
- Royal P O / Yuri Temirkanov
  Classics for Pleasure CFP414508 (also cassette), transfer
  HMV ASD3606 (11/78)
- Los Angeles P O / Simon Rattle
  HMV Dig CD CDC747062-2; (EL270052-1/*4*)
- Philharmonia / Ling Tung
  ASV ACM 2016
Symphony nr. 3
- Nat P O / Stokowski
  Desmar DSM 1007

Rachmaninov's three symphonies have had a strange history in terms of the recording industry. For a long while, they were neglected by all but the Russians. Now there are at least 5 complete sets available. The Second is considered to be the masterpiece of the three, but on whose recommendation is not clear. The Third is the most neglected, especially in the concert hall, perhaps due to its length. This symphony was played often in England, though; Sir Malcom Sargent had it in his repertoire. The older versions of the symphonies were made by Kurt Sanderling (Leningrad Orchestra at the end of the fifties), William Steinberg (with Pittsburgh in 1955), Eugene Ormandy (Philharmonia in that same year), Adrian Boult (1958) and Paul Paray (in Detroit in 1959).

Of the newer versions, both the De Waart and Previn recordings are popular. The Previn is the better; the Rotterdam Orchestra misses a bit of the melancholy inherent in Rachmaninov. Ashkenazy's set performed with the Concertgebouw is very different due to the extreme tempi Ashkenazy chooses. The First is the best; throughout the set, it is clear how much the Concertgebouw enjoys working with this pianist/conductor. Weller's First with the Suisse Romande lacks some of the richness needed in the second movement. His Second, with the London Philharmonic, is better, but this same orchestra (the strings in particular) sound warmer with Previn. Ling Tung's performance is not up to standard. Rattle's recording in Los Angeles is also disappointing but the acoustic quality of the Chandler Pavilion, the home of the LA O, is to blame. An excellent digital recording is the one made in the Henry Wood Hall in Glasgow with the Scottish National and Alexander Gibson. The performance is spontaneous and the sound is natural.

After having performed it on tour in America, the London Symphony recorded the Third Symphony successfully with Previn. The LSO has never sounded so virtuostic on record. Stokowski, who performed the première in 1936, recorded the piece forty years later with a select group of musicians. The result is terribly exciting. The interpretation is whimsical and some of the tempi are almost fatal (as in the Finale). Nevertheless, the energy and inspirational talents of the elderly Stokowski are amazing.

JOACHIM RAFF (1822- 82)

Symphony nr. 5 (Leonore)
- London P O / Hermann

Raff's eleven symphonies are, for the most part, long forgotten. Thanks to Bernard Hermann and a generous Unicorn, it is still possible to enjoy the best of Raff's symphonic works. This colourful programme music is very reminiscent of Mendelssohn. It is well played and the recording is very clear.

TURE RANGSTRÖM (1884-1947)

Symphony nr.1 in c sharp minor (In memoriam August Strindberg)
- Swedish Radio S O / Segerstam
  EMI 7C 061 35712
Symphony nr. 3 in D flat major (Song Under The Stars)
- Halsinborg S O / Frandsen
  EMI 7C 061 35774
Symphony nr. 2
- ORF (East German Radio O) / Leif Segerstam
  EMI Conifer 7C-061 35291

Ture Rangström was a contemporary of Bax and Bloch but could not measure up to their craftsmanship and orchestral experience. Rangström's talent lies in his lieder; these are considered among the best of the twentieth century.
The Swedish Radio Orchestra and Leif Segerstam do their best to make
the First Symphony convincing but they cannot reduce the banality of some of the thematic material. The recording is really first rate and improves the chances for Rangström's symphonic offerings.
The Third Symphony (1929) is gaudy at best. The performers are uninterested and the recording uninteresting. A 1984 recording (by the Symphony Orchestra of the Austrian Radio) of the Second Symphony is perhaps even gaudier. It is probably the poorest symphony ever recorded.

ALAN RAWSTHORNE (1905-71)

Symphony nr. 1
Symphonic Studies
- London P O / John Pritchard
  Lyr SRCS 90

This is the first stereo version of Rawsthorne's

Symphonic Studies. The Studies were written before the war and are considered to be his most original work and probably, his masterpiece. Rawsthorne's followers are convinced that his First Symphony is unduly neglected. It is a well crafted and original piece to be sure. Pritchard leads the LPO in a musically satisfying performance; the recording sounds full and detailed.

NICOLAI RIMSKY-KORSAKOV (1844-1908)

Antar (Symphony nr. 2), Op. 9
- Rotterdam P O / David Zinman
  Philips Dig 9500/7300 971
Symphony nr. 1 in d minor, Op. 1 (2nd version)
Symphony nr. 2 (Antar)
Symphony nr. 3 in C, Op. 32
- USSR State O / Svetlanov
  Chant du Monde CD 278771/3; (LXD/K4 78771/3)
Symphony nr. 2
- Orch de la Suisse Romande / Ansermet
  Decca LW5326 (1954)
Symphony nr. 3 in C, Op. 32
- London S O / Yondani Butt
  ASV Dig DCA/ZCDCA 538
Sheherazade (symphonic suite), Op. 35
- Concertgebouw O / Kondrashin
  Philips CD 400 021-2; (9500 681/7300)
- London P O / Haitink
  Philips 416 861-1/4
- Philadelphia O / Ricardo Muti
  HMV Dig CD CDC747023-2; (ASD/TCC-ASD 4188)
- Wiener Philharmoniker / Previn
  Philips Dig CD 411 479-2; (6514/7337 231)
- London S O / Tjeknavorian
  Andante CD CDACD 85701
- Moscow Radio S O / Fewdoseyev
  JVC/Target VCD 519
- Boston S O / Osawa
  DG Walkman 413 155-4
- Orch de la Suisse Romande / Ansermet
  Decca CD 414 124-2
- Berliner Philharmoniker / Maazel
  DG Dig CD 415 512-2 (also LP and cassette)
- London S O / Markevich
  Philips On Tour 416 221-4
- Montreal S O / Dutoit
  Decca Dig CD 410 253-2 (also LP and cassette)

As a young officer in the Russian Navy, Rimsky-Korsakov travelled around the world and wrote his First Symphony on the trip (1865). This was the first symphony ever written by a Russian. Svetlanov has made an impressive Russian recording of the piece (originally on Melodiya).
Antar was written in 1869. David Zinman's performance is warm and colourful and the melodies are well contoured. The older version recorded by Ansermet, for a long time an important Rimsky-Korsakov promoter, is exciting; this wonderfully orchestrated pseudo-oriental piece is pure luxury.
The Third Symphony is not Rimsky-Korsakov's strongest work but Svetlanov makes it appealing. The brass screams a bit but that is to Russian tastes. Butt's performance with the London Symphony is much flatter but has a certain refinement that is convincing.

Kondrashin's Scheherazade is fortunate to have a perfect sound and equally perfect resonance. The former concert master, Herman Krebbers, grandly leads the Concertgebouw through this performance. Haitink's 1974 recording with the London Philharmonic was one of the most beautiful for more than a decade but now tends to show its age. Rodney Friend, the concertmaster in London, dominates the performance as Krebbers does.
Muti's interpretation is a bit hysterical. His bravura is reminiscent of Stokowski who also made a big show of this piece. Previn, performing with the Viennese, chooses an unsentimental approach to the story. Maazel's interpretation lacks involvement and the acoustics of the Philharmonia are not good on CD. Dutoit, with slower tempi and lots of warmth, follows a lyrical path, an act of self-discipline for this conductor to be sure. The Moscow Radio Orchestra's performance is impressive and the cymbals at the end are amazing. The whole thing is exciting but never elegant. The recording is technically excellent.

CYRIL ROOTHAM (1875-1938)

Symphony nr. 1 in c minor
- London P O / Handley
  Lyr SRCS 103

Rootham wrote the first of his two symphonies in 1932. It was immediately evident that he was a born symphonic craftsman. The orchestration of the work is remarkable. The recording technicians have achieved a natural sound that is also remarkable. There will probably only be few who find this work original or powerful; neverthless both the work and recording are to be admired.

GIOACCHINO ROSSINI (1782-1868)

Sinfonia al conventello
- Los Angeles P O / Schwarz
  None Dig D/D4 79023 (cassette)

Actually, Rossini's Sinfonia is not symphonic at all, but rather an overture. It is an early work and Rossini used the thematic material again in Il Signor Bruschino. The later opera overtures are more brilliant than this one. The recording includes Cherubini's Symphony in D major (see above).

ALBERT ROUSSEL (1869-1937)

Symphony nr. 3 in g minor, Op. 42
- New York P O / Pierre Boulez
  CBS 76519
Symphony nr. 3
Symphony nr. 4 in A major, Op. 53
- Orch de la Suisse Romande / Ansermet
  Decca Eclipse ECS673
Symphony nr. 2 in B flat major, Op. 23
Symphony nr. 4
- French National O / Charles Dutoit
  Erato/Conifer Dig NUM75284; CD: ECD88226
Symphony nr.1 in d minor, Op. 7
Symphony nr. 3

- French National O / Dutoit
  Erato/Conifer NUM75283; CD: ECD8825
Symphony nr. 4
- Philharmonia / Karajan
  HMV mono XLP/*TC-XLP* 60003
Symphony nr. 3
Symphony nr. 4
- Lamoreux Orch, Paris / Charles Münch
  Erato EPR/*MCE*
Symphony nr. 2
- Concerts Colonne / Pierre Dervaux
  EMI Pathé-Marconi/Conifer C2 26 069 73096

Ansermet's recording of Roussel's Fourth is not one of his best. The later recording (1965) under Munch has the unmistakeble advantage of being performed by obviously dedicated players. Both can compete in technical terms with modern records. They cannot overshadow, however, Bernstein's interpretation of the Third or Von Karajan's excellent recording of the Fourth. Karajan's Fourth has dominated the market since 1949! In particular it is the brass that makes this performance so memorable. Boulez's performance of the Third doesn't have much to recommend it. The first movement is played too slowly, the acoustic qualities are just too much and the violins are quite shrill. Roussel's Second Symphony is neglected both in the concert hall and the recording studio. Jean Martinon performed the Second on tour with the BBC Symphony in the fifties, but this pioneer's work is lost to us. The Pierre Dervaux performance has been a white elephant for a long time. The new recordings on CD with Dutoit conducting the French National are excellent; the recording technicians from Erato have obviously profited from all the newest developments.

EDMUND RUBBRA (1901-86)

Symphony nr. 5 in B flay major, Op. 63
- Melbourne S O / Schönzeler
Symphony nr. 6, Op. 80
Symphony nr. 8 (Hommage à Teilhard de Chardin), Op. 132
- Philharmonia O / del Mar
  Lyr SRCS 127
Symphony nr. 7, Op. 88
- London S O / Vernon Handley
  Lyr SRCS119
- London P O / Adrian Boult
  Lyrita SRCS 41
Symphony nr. 2
- New Philharmonia / Handley
  Lyr SRCS 96
Symphony nr.10 (Sinfonia da camera)
- Bournemouth Sinfonietta / Schönzeler
  RCA RL 25027

Repeated listening to Rubbra's pieces is essential in trying to comprehend this difficult oeuvre. The Fifth Symphony is a noble work in the tradition of Elgar and Sibelius. Despite the fact that the Melbourne Orchestra is not one of the world's best, it plays Rubbra for all its worth and the strings especially, have an extra charm. The sound is fuller and more complete than the old recording made by Barbirolli with the Hallé Orchestra in the fifties. Of all his symphonic works, the Sixth is favoured by Rubbra

enthusiasts. The Eight is a hommage on Teilhard de Chardin and possesses a certain mysterious quality. Both performance (by Del Mar) and recording are excellent. The Seventh (1956) is also well recorded, this time the honours go to Boult. The Tenth (1975) was written for a chamber orchestra. The scrupulous performance led by Schönzeler has very nuanced dynamics and the balance is perfect.

CAMILLE SAINT-SAËNS (1835-1921)

Symphony nr. 3 in c minor, Op. 78
- Philippe Lefèbre / Orchestre National de Paris / Seiji Ozawa (1987)
  EMI Dig CD CDC747477-2; (EL2700499-1/*4*)
- Hurford / Montreal S O / Dutoit (3/83)
  Decca Dig CD 410 201-2; (SXDL/*KSXDC* 7590)
- Philadelphia O / Ormandy
  Telarc Dig CD 8005; (DG 10051)
- Rawsthorne / London P O / Batiz
  ASV Dig CD CDDCA524; (DCA/*ZCDCA* 524 (9/84)
- Jean Guillou / San Francisco S O / de Waart
  Philips Dig CD 412 619-2 (also LP and cassette)
- Cochereau / Berliner Philharmoniker / Karajan
  DG Dig CD 00 063-2; (2532/*3302* 045)
- Litaize / Chicago S O / Barenboim
  DG Walkman *413 424-4* (7/86)
  DG Gal 415 847-1/4 (4/76) and DG2530/*3300* 619
- Orch National de la Radiodiffusion française / Jean Martinon
  HMV Gren ESD/*TC-ESD* 173191-1/*4*
- City of Birmingham S O / Frémaux
  HMV Green ESD 7038
- Rawsthorne / Royal Liverpool P O / Tjeknavorian
  Chalfont Dig SDG 312
- Dupré / Detroit S O / Paray
  Mercury SRI 75003
- Boston S O / Munch
  RCA Gold GL/*GK* 14039
- Los Angeles P O / Mehta
  Decca SXL 6482
- Orch Suisse Romande / Ansermet
  Decca VIV/*KVIC* 51
- Parker Smith / London P O / Baudo
  EMI Em EMX/*TC-EMX* 41
- New York P O / Bernstein
  CBS 60137/*40*

Many musicians consider the organ symphony a difficult piece to record. Nevertheless, there are several successful performances available. In the seventies, Daniel Barenboim's performance with the Chicago Symphony was considered the best. Then came the digital eighties when the ASV recording with the London Philharmonic and Batiz took over first place. (This recording is better in the LP version than in the CD which was mastered in Japan.) The new CD version by Montreal and led by Dutoit, however, conquers all. The recording is brilliant and Dutoit has a natural feeling for the score. Barenboim's is still a superlative performance and exudes a special warmth from the first to the last note. Martinon also leads a noble performance which is very well recorded. Ormandy's balance is wrong. The organ is brought forward as if it were a concerto, and the piano is barely audible. The San Francisco Symphony is also disappointing. Berlin, as usual, plays superbly under Von Karajan but the

recording has a forced balance that is disturbing. A new French version on CD is superb, performed by the National Orchestra of Paris under Ozawa. Ozawa is obviously enchanted with the music. He lets the structure shine through and all the details are clear. The strings are wonderful. Perhaps Ozawa is free to swing through a piece that he only takes seriously in part. The finale is delicious and technically, the recording is perfection. The organ played stands in the Cathedral in Chartres (the same one used in the Barenboim recording).

AULIS SALLINEN (born 1935)

Symphony nr. 1
Symphony nr. 3
- Finnish Radio S O / Kamu/Berglund
  BIS LP41

Sallinen's two symphonies are more appealing for collectors than music lovers in general who prefer recordings of his operas. The First Symphony (1970) is, however, an attractive piece in one movement, diatonically composed and full of rather ghostly sounds. The Third (1975) is a very imaginative piece. One sometimes is reminded of Sibelius or Britten. Both performance and recording are first rate.

FRANZ SCHMIDT (1874-1939)

Symphony nr. 3 in A major
- Slavich P O / Pesek
  Sup Dig 11103394
Symphony nr. 4 in C major
- Viennese P / Mehta
  Decca SXL 6544

Schmidt composed his Third Symphony in 1928. The first recording made of the piece was in 1977, and in 1980 Decca released a second. This Decca recording is unfortunately of a disappointing quality technically. This century of Schoenberg has neglected the likes of Schmidt. His Fourth Symphony is very popular with the Viennese public, however, and the performance the Viennese Philharmonie gives attests to this fact.

ARNOLD SCHOENBERG (1874-1951)

Chamber Symphony nr.1, Op. 9
- Berlin P O / Sinopoli
  DG Dig 2532 02
- Los Angeles P O / Zubin Mehta
  Decca London Ent 414 440-1

Little known, Schoenberg did write one symphony which is performed well by Sinopoli and his Berlin instrumentalists. His interpretation places the music, in a positive way, back in the idiom of the late romantics (Richard Strauss). The orchestral sound is glorious on this recording. Other interpretations have more detail perhaps, but miss the warm-blooded sound Sinopoli makes.
Schoenberg would be pleased to know what a splen-

did orchestra the Los Angeles Philharmonic has become, one of America's best. Schoenberg spent his last years in Los Angeles and would be happy to hear them play his Chamber Symphony so well. The very high tempi are perhaps questionable, but Zubin Mehta successfully calls forth all the deep emotions inherent in this late piece of romanticism.

FRANZ SCHUBERT (1797-1828)

*** Symphonies nrs 1-3; 4 ('Tragic'); 5-7; 8 ('Unfinished'); 9 ('Great'); 10 in D, D.936a
- Academy SMF / Marriner
  Philips Dig **412 176-2** [6 discs]; -1 [7 LPs]; -4 [5 cassettes]

*** Symphonies nrs 1-9
- Berliner Philharmoniker / Böhm
  DG 2740 127/*3378 082*
- Berliner Philharmoniker / Karajan
  HMV SLS/*TC-SLS* 5127
- Dresdner Staatskapelle / Sawallisch
  Philips 6747 491
- Bamberger Symphoniker / Horst Stein
  Eurodisc/RCA dig 302 358 [5 LPs]; **610 599** [4 discs]
- Rundfunk Orch Köln / Günther Wand
  German Harmonia Mundi / EMI EX155527-3 [5 LPs]

*** Symphonies nrs 1 in D. D.823; 4 in c minor ('Tragic'), D.147
- Academy SMF / Marriner
  Philips Dig 6514/*7337* 261

*** Symphonies nrs 2 in B flat major, D.125; 6 in C, D.589
- Academy SMF / Marriner
  Philips Dig 6514/*7337* 208

*** Symphonies nrs 3 in D, D.200; 5 in B flat major, D.485
- Royal P O / Thomas Beecham
  HMV SXLP/TC-SXLP 30204
- Academy SMF / Marriner
  Philips 6514/*7337* 149
- Berliner Philharmoniker / Barenboim
  CBS Masterworks **MK 39671**; IM; *IMT*

*** Symphonies nrs 3 in D, D.200; 8 in b minor ('Unfinished'), D.759
- Wiener Philharmoniker / Carlos Kleiber
  DG **415 601-2**; 2531/*3301* 124
- Royal P O / Beecham
  HMV SXLP 30204 (6/60) (2/76)
- City of London Sinfonia / Richard Hickox
- Pickwick IMP Red Label **PCD 848**

*** Symphonies nrs 4 in c minor ('Tragic'), D.417; 5 in B flat major, D.485
- Academy SMF / Marriner
  Philips Dig **410 045-2**
- Wiener Philharmoniker / Kertesz
  Decca Jub/*KJBC* 75

*** Symphonies nrs 5 in B flat major, D.485; 8 in b minor ('Unfinished'), D.759
- Wiener Philharmoniker / Solti
  Decca Dig **414 371-2**; -1; -4 (9/85)
- Columbia S O of New York P O / Walter
  CBS **MK 42048**
- Berliner Philharmoniker / Karajan
  HMV EG 290572-1/*4*

- Philharmonia O / Klemperer
  HMV 290460-1/*4*

*** Symphony nr. 6 in b minor ('Unfinished')
- Royal P O / Thomas Beecham
  HMV SXLP/*TC-sxlp* 30443; and EMI mono ENC108 (9/61)

*** Symphony nr. 8 in b minor ('Unfinished'), D.759
- Philharmonia O / Sinopoli
  DG Dig **410 862-2**; -1; -4
- Berliner Philharmoniker / Karajan
  DG Sig 413 982-1/*4*
  also: DG Galleria **415 848-2GGA**, transfer from SLPM 139001 (4/66)
- Philharmonia O / Karajan
  HMV SXLP 30513
- Academy SMF / Marriner
  Philips **412 472-2**
  (Newbould edition) Philips 411 439-1/*4*
- Boston S O / Colin Davis
  Philips Dig **410 393-2**; -1; -4
- Berliner Philharmoniker / Böhm
  DG Walkman *413 157-4* ; and DG Sig 2543/*3343* 506
- Wiener Philharmoniker / Kertesz
  Decca Jub JB/*KJBC* 76
- Wiener Philharmoniker / Josef Krips
  Con CC/*CCT* 7503
- New York P O / Bernstein
  CBS 60106/*40*
- Boston S O / Colin Davis
  Philips Dig **410 393-2**; -1; -4

*** Symphonies nrs 8; 9 in C ('Great')
- Berliner Philharmoniker / Böhm
  DG Acc 2725/*3374* 103

*** Symphony nr. 9 in C ('Great'), D.944
- Wiener Philharmoniker / Solti
  Decca Dig **400 082-2** (3/83);
  and: SXDL/*KSXDC* 7557 (10/82)
- Concertgebouw O / Haitink
  Philips 416 245-1/*4*; and Philips 9500 097/*7300 510*
- Columbia S O / Walter
  CBS **MK 42049**
- Philharmonia O / Klemperer
  HMV ED 290426-1/*4* (9/61)
- Chicago S O / Levine
  DG Dig **413 437-2**; -1; -4 (9/84)
- Berliner Philharmoniker / Tennstedt
  HMV ASD/*TC-ASD* 143662-1/*4*
- Dresdner Staatskapelle / Böhm
  [live recording Kulturpalast in Dresden, 1 Dec. 1979]
  DG 2531/*3301* 352; Galleria **419 484-2GGA**; *4GGA*
- Dresdner Staatskapelle / Tate
  EMI dig **CDC7 47482-2**; EL 270 500-1; -4
- London S O / Krips
  Decca SPA 467
- Hallé Orch / Barbirolli
  EMI Em EMX/*TC-EMX* 2010
- London P O / Boult
  HMV SXLP/*TC-SXLP* 30558
- S O des Bayerischen Rundfunks / Jochum
  Con CC/*CCT* 7512
- Wiener Philharmoniker / Kertesz
  Decca Jub JB77
- Boston S O / Steinberg
  RCA VICS/*VK* 2036
- Berliner Philharmoniker / Barenboim

CBS Masterworks dig **MK 42316**; IM-
- London P O / Boult
  SXLP 30558 (12/72) (3/83)

NRS 5 AND 8, NR. 9: BPH/KARAJAN; EMI/HMV MASTER SERIES resp. EG290572-1 and EG 290612-1 - Von Karajan is without doubt closely associated with the German-Austrian repertoire, nevertheless his Schubert recordings are not all equally good. The 8th is sombre and grand, cool in its power. The 9th is a bit too quick and sounds stubborn and stiff. The accents are so forced. It is neither poetic nor powerful enough.
NRS 3 AND 8: VIENNESE PHO/KLEIBER; DG **4415 601-2GH** from 2531 124 (11/79) [cf Nr. 8 V PHO/ Solti, **414 371-2DH** (9/85)] - Carlos Kleiber is not as at home with Schubert as he is with Beethoven. Perhaps he's just too restless. The Unfinished is satisfactory if one can live with the tempi. The lyrical aspect is underdone. Solti is much to be preferred.
NR. 9 CLEVELAND/DOHNANYI; TELARC/CONIFER **CD80110** (from DG10110) [cf VPHO/Solti, Decca **400 082-2DH** (3/83) and SXDL7557 (10/82) and Chicago/Levine **413 437-2GH**: -1Gh (10/84)] - Dohnányi has too high a tempo and sounds hurried throughout. The orchestral playing is anything but terrific. Schubert's exacting score is not taken literally enough; not all the repeats are played. The technical quality of the CD is not up to standard. Levine's style of conducting suits this symphony. He is light and fast without compromising the quality of playing. The sound is excellent. Even so, Solti's performance will probably appeal to more listeners.
NR. 8: VPHO/HARNONCOURT TELEC/CONIFER dig **ZK8-43187**; *AZ/-*,*CY4/-* [cf BostonSO/Davis 410 393-1PH (4/84) - Harnoncourt does not quite measure up to the others in the Schubert competition. He cannot make enough of a difference between the drama of the first movement and the serenity of the second. Solti's subtle interpretation is a clear winner. Every possible gradation of dynamic and every conceivable nuance is clear and polished.
NRS 5 AND 8: COLUMBIA SO/WALTER; CBS MASTERWORKS, **MK42048**, transfer from Philips SABL209 (2/62). NR. 9 IDEM CBS MK42049, from Philips SBRG720202 (7/62) - Those used to and charmed by more modern conductors and their idea of an exciting Schubert will be disappointed in Walter. His performance is never boring, just less dynamic and grander perhaps than his younger, more self- conscious colleagues. Walter's Schubert is warm and musical; the melodies really sing (Scherzo in the 9th) and the beauties are carried along on a waltz-like tempo. He plays no repeats, excusing them as a long gone habit of former times (some modern versions include every repeat ad absurdum, an example being Solti's repeat of the Finale). Walter does have the irritating habit of 'correcting' the score, something one must learn to live with in order to appreciate him. The performance is wonderful nevertheless; it includes audibly different pp and ppp.
NR. 5: ST JOHN'S SMITH SQUARE/LUBBOCK PICK-WICK/MP; RED LABEL **PCD819** - This is a pleasant, fresh and unpretentious version of Schubert's most remarkable symphony. The playing mirrors the conductor's musicality but misses the finesse possible under his more prestigious colleagues.

NRS 4 (TRAGIC), 8 AND 9: CHICAGO SO/GIULINI; DG419 108-1GX2 (recorded in 1977-78) - These are refined and characteristic performances.The Unfinished has strong dramatic as well as very intimate moments. In the 9th, the difficult tempo changes are handled very well. Chicago is sublime in all three symphonies. The dynamic scale of the recordings is surprising, seemingly unlimited.

NR. 8: BOSTON SO/COLIN DAVIS; VPHO/HARNONCOURT - The Unfinished survives Harnoncourt's sometimes strange romantic intentions. There is definitely drama in his performance. More will feel at home in the domestic atmosphere Davis creates. His tempi are slower and the general impression is more placid.

NR. 9: BERLIN PO/BARENBOIM; CBS MASTERWORKS dig MK42316; IM/-;IMT/- [cf London PHO/ Boult SXLP 30558 (12/72) (3/83); VPHO/Solti- see above; Chicago SO-see above; Dresden SK/Tate CDC7 47482-2; EL270500-1] - Many insiders are of the opinion that Sir Adrian Boult's recording is absolute perfection. The one that comes closest is Solti's for Decca. Barenboim is way behind these two, not able to let the music speak for itself. The 9th cannot endure too much personal opinion. The naturalness of the best recordings hide the great craftsmen behind them. Levine joins Barenboim way behind Boult and Solti (although his version is wonderfully light and airy). Tate is disappointing; his version is nevertheless warmer than Klemperer's with whom he is often compared. Tate's tempi are too slow and the orchestra sounds sluggish.

CYCLES NRS 1-9: COLOGNE R SO/GUNTER WAND, GERMAN HARMONIA MUNDI/EMI DIG EX15527-3 (5 LP's); NRS 1+2: CDC7 47874-2 AND 1C 065 199772-1 (4/81); NRS 3+6: CDC7 47875-2 AND 1C 067 1999988-1 (3/85); NRS 4+8: CDC7 47976-2 1C 067 169518-1 (1/85) - Günther Wand, the publicity-shy conductor who is barely known outside his native Germany, proves himself to be a truly great conductor with his Schubert series. His whole performance is laden with inspired, almost prophetic moments (the Coda of the first movement of the Unfinished with woodwinds and brass has a ghost-like quality that portrays Schubert's personal desperation perfectly); the niveau is unattainably high. His performance of the Great Symphony is no less amazing, one of the most beautiful performances every recorded of anything. The two horns that open the piece announce in themselves that something extraordinary is about to happen. The LP's are completely without noise and are easily mistakable for CD's.

Wand's act, as they say, is a hard one to follow. Marriner is most successful in the early symphonies where the playing is extremely pure and gracious. Those who have ever heard Beecham's recording of the 6th (EMI mono ENC108-9/61) will remember it fondly.

NR. 9: VPHO/MUTI EMI DIG CDC7 47697-2; EL270562-1/-4 [cf CO/Haitink416 245-1PM (2/77) (5/86)] - Muti's performance is very personal and extremely Italian. He has a rather absurd respect for the score and plays all the repeats. The orchestra sounds as Viennese as it is but Muti succeeds in combining that with his own southernness. The melodies are Verdi-like, Rossini is heard in the oboe solo. The amount of energy throughout the performance is amazing; there is no other version that has the drive that Muti has in this recording. Boult (EMI) and Haitink (Philips) have what Muti lacks, however, a feeling for the typically Schubertian ambivalence: fear, mystery and horror on the one hand and the will to survive and prevail on the other. Muti is better than Levine (DG) and Solti (Decca), his is the more involving performance. Nevertheless, Haitink especially has a clearer understanding of Schubert and his idiom.

NRS 1-9: BERLIN PHO/BÖHM; 419 318-2GHH; NRS 1+2: 2530 216 (4/72); NRS 3+4+6: 2720 062 (5/73); NRS 5+8: 1139 162 (5/67); NR. 9: 138 877 (1/64) - Böhm has often been praised for his version of the 9th. Each to his own taste. Böhm's relaxed and grand approach does have its moments but misses the drive that is inherent in the score. The lapses in tempo are also something peculiar to Böhm. Most of the same applies to the Unfinished. The phrasing is impeccable but Marriner, for instance, has clearer long lines which make the whole more exciting. Böhm has more warmth than Marriner in any case. Wand's performance is still the favourite by comparison.

NRS. 8 AND 9: BERLIN PHO/KARAJAN; DG 423 219-2GMW, from 139001 (4/66) and 139043 (2/71); Nrs 5 and 8: idem; EMI CDM7 69016-2 from SLS5127 (2/79) - For some reason or other, Karajan has never won in his struggle with Schubert's symphonies. Of the two recordings of the 8th, the one for DG is the better. The 9th cannot be included among Karajan's successes, to say the least. One waits for human contact to no avail. The 5th misses Böhm's charm, Wand's suppleness and Beecham's nobility.

NRS 3 AND 5: BPH/BARENBOIM; CBS MASTERWORKS DIG MK39671-1;IM/-;/- [cf Royal PHO/ Beecham SXLP30204 (2/76) (6/80)] - This should be a safe combination: an orchestra that knows the work through and through and an internationally distinguished conductor. And to be sure, to an extent, this is a very successful performance. No dynamic marking goes unplayed throughout but the spontaneity is sorely lacking. It is precisely the spontaneity that makes Beecham's version so irresistable. Barenboim's seriousness is a bit tiresome.

NRS 3 AND 8: CITY OF LONDON SINFONIA/HICKOX, PICKWICK; IMP RED LABEL PCD848 [cf VPHO/ Kleiber 415 601-2GH (12/85)] - Hickox and his ensemble give a good performance together. There is nothing surprising about it and so it should be a safe choice for many.

NRS 1-6, 8 AND 9: BAMBERGER SYMPHONIKER/ STEIN; EURODISC/RCA DIG 610 599; 302358 [cf Masur 412 176-2PH6; Wand EX155527] - Horst Stein is little known outside of Switzerland (he is Sawallisch's successor at the l'Orchestre de la Suisse Romande since 1980 and principal at the excellent Bamberger Symphoniker). The recordings have a very natural sound with light acoustics. The solo instruments are highlighted too much (the horns in the opening of the 9th, for example, with their unfortunate mistakes, should have been corrected). Stein's interpretation of the 1st is exemplary, better than even Wand's wonderful performance. The 3rd and the 5th are also very good under Stein. Furtwängler, Boult, Walter and Barbirolli are all better in the 8th and 9th, but Stein is excellent not only in the 1st as mentioned, but also in the 5th and 6th.

NR. 9: BERLIN PHO/FURTWANGLER; DG MONO 415 660-2GH (recorded in the Jesus Christ Church in Dec.,1951) dig refurbished from DGM18015-6 (3/55) - Furtwängler's performance will endure. His 9th is especially important, placing the work as it does in the context of the 19th century German musical tradition where it belongs. The Berliners play so beautifully in the Finale that they must be heard to be believed.

NRS 8 AND 9: CO/MENGELBERG; PHILIPS DIG REFURBISHED MONO 416 212 2-PH [from GL5689 recorded before a live audience in November,1939 and December 1940 (2/65)] - These recordings make it very clear why Mengelberg was so popular and influential with his audience in the years between the two world wars. Notwithstanding personal preferences concerning the interpretation, the Concertgebouw's playing under Mengelberg is of the highest order, legendary and unique. Remastering has made it possible for this recording to survive forty years beautifully intact.

NR. 9: NBC SO/TOSCANINI; RCA MONO GL85246 (third recording released in 1959) - Toscanini's first recording of this piece was made in 1941 with the Philadelphians. It was subtler and had more nuanced phrasing than this recording. His second version was also better than this one. The playing had an unforgettable vitality also missing in this his last version.

NR. 9: DRESDNER S K/BOHM; DG GALLERIA 419 484-2GGA [live performance recorded at the Palace of Culture, Dec.,1979 from 2531 352 (1/82)] - Böhm first recorded the 9th in 1964 in Berlin, a record that was extremely popular up until the early Seventies. This later version was made when Böhm was 85. His energy at the time and the vitality of the performance is amazing. As one critic put it: The typically Austrian energy is laden with typically Austrian lyric. There are faults to be sure, nevertheless the rapport Böhm has with the Dresden musicians is excellent. The second movement is perhaps a bit more businesslike than the earlier recording. The ultimate choice is between this recording by Böhm, Solti's for Decca (400 082-2DH) and Walter's for CBS (MK42049).

ROBERT SCHUMANN (1810-56)

*** Symphonies nrs 1-4
- Concertgebouw O / Haitink
  Philips Dig 412 126-2; from 412 852-1PH3 (1/86) and 411 104-1PH (4/84)
    nr. 1 in B flat major, Op. 38 [recording 2/83]
    nr. 2 in C major, Op. 61 [recording 1/84]
    nr. 3 in E flat major, Op. 97 [recording 1981]
    nr. 4 in de minor, Op. 120 [recording 12/84]
- Dresdner Staatskapelle / Sawallisch
  EMI 1C 149 02418/20
- Berliner Philharmoniker / Karajan
  DG 2740 129

*** Symphony nr. 1 in B flat major ('Frühling')
- Berliner Philharmoniker / Kubelik
  DG Walkman 413 157-4
- Rundfunk S O Stuttgart / Marriner
  Capriccio CD 10 063; C27/CC27 078

*** Symphonies nrs 1 in B flat major, Op. 38 ('Frühling'); 3 in E flat major ('Rheinische'), Op. 97
- Chicago S O / Barenboim
  DG Sig 2543/*3343* 504
- Dresdner Staatskapelle / Otmar Suitner
  Denon **CO-1516**
- Royal Liverpool P O / Marek Janowski
  Chandos ASV dig DCA 587/*ZC*-

*** Symphonies nrs 1 ('Frühling'); 4 in d minor, Op. 120
- Berliner Philharmoniker / Karajan
  DG Gal 419 065-1/*4*
- Wiener Philharmoniker / Bernstein
  DG Dig **415 274-2**; -1; -*4*
- Dresdner Staatskapelle / Sawallisch
  HMV SXLP/*TC-SXLP* 30526
- Berliner Philharmoniker / Kubelik
  Con CC/*CCT* 7532

*** Symphony nr. 2
- Wiener Philharmoniker / Sinopoli
  DG Dig **410 863-2**; -1; -*4*

*** Symphonies nrs 2; 3 and 4
- Rundfunk Orch Stuttgart / Marriner
  Capriccio/Target dig C27 106/7; *CC27*- ; **10 093/4** [2 discs]

*** Symphony nr. 3 in E flat major('Rheinische')
- Los Angeles P O / Giulini
  DG Dig **400 062-2**; 2532/*3302* 040
- Concertgebouw O / Haitink
  Philips Dig **411 104-2**; -1; -*4*
- Berliner Philharmoniker / Kubelik
  Con CC/*CCT* 7538
- London P O / Tennstedt
  EMI Master Series EG 291069-1 (12/79)

*** Symphony nr. 4 ind minor, Op.120
- Berliner Philharmoniker / Karajan
  DG Sig 413 982-1/*4* (1/87)
- Berliner Philharmoniker / Furtwängler
  DG mono **415 661-2**
- Berliner Philharmoniker / Tennstedt
  HMV Dig ASD/*TCC-ASD* 3963

There are quite a number of good recordings available of the individual symphonies. A short summary follows:
NR. 2: VPHO/BERNSTEIN; DG **419 190-2GH**; /-*4GH* (recorded in the Grosser Saal, Vienna, Nov., 1985) [cf Berliner P/Kubelik; Contour Classics CC 7537 (4/65) (9/75)] - Bernstein's Schumann cycle is exaggerated and pretentious. He wants so much expression that he goes too far. Schumann was not, of course, some sort of early Mahler. The Karajan performance, on the other hand, is a classic. Sawallisch is also to be recommended (re-released by EMI/Electrola in 1984). Both Kubelik and Haitink are successful with Schumann. Kubelik's appealing recordings are also available separately. Haitink is clearly dedicated to achieving good musical balance and he is especially great in the imaginative Second Symphony. Despite being recorded over a period of three years, the Haitink cycle is consistent. It is not a high point of the orchestra's (or conductor's) career, however. Clarity, details and rhetoric are lacking. Many are still of the opinion that Schumann was not the symphonic power that he should have

been, especially in terms of his obvious genius for the piano. Nevertheless, many have done their best to perform the complete cycle. Many critics still concern themselves with both the works and their interpreters.
NR. 1: V PHO/FURTWANGLER; DECCA MONO **417 287-2DH** (refinished from LXT 2905 dated 4/54) - Accepting the rather poor sound for what it is, this recording is still probably the most important of the First Symphony. The technical quality is bad, the background noise (it is a live performance with public) too loud, the tempi are rather slow, nevertheless, the dramatic energy is marvellous. Furtwängler takes advantage of many possible freedoms and enhances the piece with a magic reminiscent of Berlioz.
NR. 4: BERLIN PO/FURTWANGLER; DG MONO **415 661-2GH** [recorded in Titania Palace, Berlin, Dec. 18,1949, refinished from 2535 805 (7/78)] - For insiders, this is the most beautiful recording ever made of the Fourth Symphony. It is an inspiration how the interpretation matches the musical material with such perfection.
NRS 2 AND 4: ROYAL LIVERPOOL PHO/MAREK JANOWSKY; (HMV) ASV DIG DCA562; [cf for nr.4 B PHO/Karajan 419 065-1GGA (11/72) (11/74) and WPHO/Bernstein, see above] - This recording with the RLPHO was not generally accepted when it first appeared. Janowski made it after being contracted to train the orchestra for three years. Despite the criticisms, the ensemble playing is faultless and has the enthusiasm of a live performance. Janowski's interpretation is no more eccentric than Bernstein's. It seems that all conductors after Furtwängler have their own ideas about Schumann's tempi. The Second Symphony is the more successful of the two.
NR. 4: BERLIN PHO/TENNSTEDT (recording 1980) dig EG290568-1 - It is difficult to even recognize the Berliners in this grainy and noisy recording. Tennstedt's vision has absolutely no romance or refinement.
NR.1 (Früling): STUTTGARTER RADIO O/MARRINER; CAPRICCIO/TARGET DIG **CD10-063**, CD-028 - This orchestra is excellent: the strings are full and warm and the woodwinds clear and smooth. The balance is also excellent and the digital recording quality faultless. Marriner's approach is very direct and has a spring-like freshness. The rhythm is marvellous.
For those who are interested in Schumann's very first version of his First Symphony (published by Breitkopf and Härtel, autograph in the Library of Congress), there is a recording made by the Berlin State Kapell under Otmar Suitner. Suitner's relaxed interpretation together with the wonderful balance and acoustics of the Jesus Christ Church in Berlin, make this unique performance a true treasure.
NR.3: TENNSTEDT/EMI MASTER SERIES EG291069-1 - This is a strong performance despite the tendency to feel that Tennstedt is in over his head with this music.
NRS1 AND 4: BERLIN PHO/KARAJAN; DG419 069-1GGA - A convincing performance that needs only a bit of help from Von Karajan perhaps.
NR. 3: BERLIN PHO/KARAJAN; DG GALLERIA **419 870-2GGA** [from 2720 046 (9/72)] - Karajan's complete cycle is in a class by itself. The Third Symphony is especially extraordinary. The orches-

tral playing is superbly led and the dichotomy between freshness and gravity inherent in the score is realized as never before.

ALEXANDER SCRIABIN (1872-1915)

Symphony nr. 1 in E, Op. 26
- Toczyska / Myers / Westminster Choir / Philadelphia O / Ricardo Muti
  HMV Dig CD CDC747349-2; (EL 270270-1/*4*)
Symphony nr. 1
Symphony nr. 2 in c minor, Op. 29
Symphony nr. 3 in c minor ('Le divin poème'), Op. 43
- Soffel / Tenzi / Frankfurter Kantorei / Saschowa pno / Radio S O Frankfurt / Inbal
  Philips 6769 041
Symphony nr. 2
- Scottish National O / Neeme Järvi
  Chandos Dig CD CHAN8462; (ABRD1176 LP and cassette)
Symphony nr. 3
- BBC S O / Pritchard
  BBC Dig CD 520; (REGL/*ZCF* 520)
- Concertgebouw O / Kondrashin
  Etcetera / Harmonia Mundi CD KTC1027 ; (ETC/*ETX* 1027((2/76)

The First Symphony is a long, six movement piece written in 1900. The score is rhapsodic, reminiscent of the Art Nouveau trend. The piece has been recorded by Svetlanov, Inbal and Muti. Muti's is the best: the orchestral playing is superior and the technical quality is the best of the three. Muti's direction is refined. He highlights many beautiful passages missed in the other interpretations.
The Third is a mammoth symphony with quadrupled woodwinds, eight horns and five trumpets (1903). Many commentators have done their best to prove the value of the work but it is less than original. The BBC has recorded Pritchard's interpretation well; the complex score is easier to unravel, and therefore perhaps to appreciate, on CD.
Kondrashin's recording for Etcetera has more to say. It was made during a live performance in 1976; the sound quality is not up to standard (the Philips recording under Inbal is much better as is the digital BBC recording). The BBC is the best sound; Kondrashin is the best interpreter.
The First, Second and Third Symphonies have been recorded with the Radio Orchestra of Frankfurt under Inbal. These recordings have a silkier sound than Svetlanov's performance with the Russians. The Russians are intoxicating nevertheless.

HUMPHRY SEARLE (born 1915)

Symphony nr. 1, Op. 23
- London P O / Boult
Symphony nr. 2, Op. 33
- London P O / Josef Krips

Josef Krips spent one of his last recording sessions performing an extremely expressive Second Symphony by Searle. As is true of the First Symphony, the Second is based on the twelve tone serial system but is also traditionally English in form. The Boult recording dates from the early sixties but still sounds excellent.

DMITRI SHOSTAKOVICH (1906-75)

*** Symphonies nrs 1-15 (complete)
- Moscow S O / Kondrashin
  HMV Dig EX 290387-3 [12 LPs]

*** Symphony nr. 1 in F major
- BBC Welsh S O /Mariss Jansons
  BBC Records dig REN637X; **CD637X**
- Philadelphia O / Ormandy
  CBS 72081 (9/60)
- Scottish N O / Järvi
  Chandos ABRD1148 (4/86)

*** Symphonies nrs 1 in F, Op. 10; 6 in b minor, Op. 54
- Scottish National O / Järvi
  Chandos

*** Symphonies nrs 1 in f minor, Op. 10; 9 in E flat major, Op. 70
- London P O / Haitink
  Decca Dig **414 677-2**; SXDL/*KSXDC* 7515 (5/81)

*** Symphonies nrs 2 ('October Revolution'), Op. 14; 3 ('The First of May'), Op. 20
- London P O en Choir / Haitink
  Decca Dig SXDL/*KSXDC* 7535

***Symphony nr. 4 in c minor, Op. 43
- London P O / Haitink
  Decca Dig SXL/*KSXC* 6927

*** Symphony nr. 5 in d minor, Op. 47
- Concertgebouw O / Haitink
  Decca Dig **410 017-2** (9/82); SXDL/*KSXDC* 7551
- Berliner Philharmoniker / Bychkov
  Philips Digital Classics **420 069-2**; -1; -*4*
- Cleveland O / Maazel
  Telarc Dig **CD 80067**; DG 10067
- New York P O / Bernstein
  CBS **CD 35854**; 35854/*40*
  also: 60117 (12/60)
- London S O / Previn
  RCA Gold GL/*GK* 42690
- Bournemouth S O / Berglund
  EMI Em EMX/*TC-EMX* 2034

*** Symphony nr. 6 in b minor, Op. 54
- London S O / Previn
  HMV ASD 3029
- New York P O / Bernstein
  CBS 72730 (10/69)
- Mavrinsky
  EMI ASD2805 (7/72)

*** Symphonies nrs 6 in b minor, Op. 54; 9 in E flat minor, Op. 70
- Concertgebouw O / Kondrashin
  Philips 412 073-1/*4*
- Wiener Philharmoniker / Bernstein
  DG dig **419 771-2GH**; -1GH
  [live recording, Grosser Saal Musikverein, Vienna, 1985 and 1986]

***Symphonies nrs 6 in b minor, Op. 54; 11 in g minor (1905), Op.103
- Bournemouth S O / Berglund
  HMV SLS 5177; *TCC2-POR 54286*

- Concertgebouw O / Haitink
  Decca Dig **411 939-2**; -1; -*4*

*** Symphony nr. 7 ('Leningrad')
- London P O / Haitink
  Decca Dig D 213 D 2/*K 213 K 22*
- Concertgebouw O / Haitink
  Decca Dig **412 392-2**
- Bournemouth S O / Berglund
  HMV SLS 897 (10/74); EMI Master Series, dig remastered, EG291135-1 (6/87);
  CDC7 47651-2

*** Symphony nr. 8 in c minor, Op. 64
- Concertgebouw O / Haitink
  Decca Dig **411 616-2**; SXDL/*KSXDC* 7621
- Bournemouth S O / Barshai
  HMV Dig EL 270290-1/*4*
- London S O / Previn
  HMV ASD 2917

*** Symphony nr. 9 in E flat major
- London P O / Haitink
  SXDL7515 (5/81); **414 677-2DH** (6/86)

*** Symphony nr. 10 in e minor, Op. 93
- Berliner Philharmoniker / Karajan
  DG Dig **413 361-2**; 2532/*3302* 030
- London P O / Andrew Davis
  CfP CFP 41 4472-1/*4*
- London P O / Haitink
  Decca SXL/*KSXC* 6838
- New York P O / Mitropoulos
  CBS mono 61457
- London S O / Previn
  HMV ASD/*TCC-ASD* 4405

*** Symphony nr. 12 in d minor ('1917'), Op. 112
- Concertgebouw O / Haitink
  Decca Dig SXDL/*KSXDC* 7577

*** Symphony nr. 13 in b sharp minor ('Babi Yar'), Op. 113
- Concertgebouw O, Rintzler and Choir/ Haitink
  Decca Dig **417 261-2** ; also Dig 414 410-1/*4*
- Petkov, London S O Choir, London S O / Previn
  HMV ASD/*TC-ASD* 3911
- Shirley-Quirk, S O and Chor des Bayerischen Rundfunks / Kondrashin
- Storojev, City of Birmingham Chorus, CB Choir, Warwick University Chorus, City of Birmingham S O / Okko Kamu
  Chandos dig **CHAN8540**; ABRD/*ABTD* 1248

*** Symphony nr. 14, Op. 135
- Varady, Wenkel, Fisher-Dieskau, Concertgebouw O / Haitink
  Decca Dig SXDL/*KSXDC* 7532 (1/82); **417 514-2DH** (3/87)
- Dubiak, Bushkin, New York P O / Bernstein
  CBS Dig 74084/*40*

*** Symphony nr. 15 in A, Op. 141
- London P O / Haitink
  Decca SXL/*KSXC* 6906

The first complete set of Shostakovich symphonies was recorded by HMV in 1975, performed by a group of Russian conductors. Ten years later, a cycle was released with Kondrashin conducting everything himself (recorded between 1962 and May,1975).

This is the only set available in the West conducted by a single man (who happens to be one of the best Russians).The questions remain: is this the standard one should measure other recordings to and are there single symphonies better recorded since the appearance of Kondrashin's set? The answer is yes to both. Kondrashin has succeeded in producing a true standard (despite the fact that recording standards in general have changed since 1975). There are, however, superior performances now available that have been made in the last ten years. Kondrashin's Fourth is historic. It was recorded shortly after the première in a difficult political situation. Actually all of the first four of the symphonies are excellent.The Sixth is strong, serious yet subtle, almost Mahlerian in its violence: very impressive. Both the Eighth and the Ninth are good despite hurried tempi. The Tenth is stoic. The Eleventh and Twelfth sparkle in a metallic way. By the time we reach the 13th, 14th and 15th symphonies, all doubts as to the brilliance of this set have dissipated. Kondrashin was inspired and passionate when performing music that was so important to him personally. He directed many of the premières before recording.

Haitink has been lauded for his version of the Seventh (Leningrad). The deep, tragic centre lies in the Adagio, one of Shostakovich's most beautiful slow movements. The passionate lament has a nobility that is destroyed in the violent finale. The sonata form is very clear in Haitink's performance; he makes more of the exposition than just a quarter of an hour's loud noise. Haitink's 12th is no less successful, very sonorous. It is as if the conductor asks how anyone could ever doubt the work's being a true masterpiece.

Mitropoulos, Karajan, Mravinsky, Previn and Rattle have all recorded the Tenth. The Rattle version has much to be said for it. The tempi are a bit slow though. Rattle's general interpretation is uncertain. Previn and Karajan are more sure of themselves with this piece.

Jarvi recorded the First Symphony very dramatically (especially clear on the CD). The rests, important in Jarvi's interpretation, are truly silent. Those looking for a fuller orchestral sound should choose Haitink. His Ninth is one of the most beautiful of his series. The p and pp sound more like mf, nevertheless what for a long time seemed like a loose string of sounds becomes a true symphony with Haitink. The much less difficult First Symphony is less successful and one would do better to choose Jarvi.

The Twelfth ('1917') is the most popular with the Russians, a brilliant and very symbolic piece like a big black, white and red poster, painted to be understood immediately. Gennadi Rozhdestvensky plays the piece for all its worth. His Finale is the ultimate in screaming drama. The agitation and propaganda in the work are big as life.

JEAN SIBELIUS (1865-1957)

*** Symphonies nrs 1-7
- Boston S O / Colin Davis
  Philips 6709 011 [5 LPs]
- Philharmonia / Ashkenazy
  Decca dig 417 378-1DM5 [5 LPs]; -*4DM4* ; **416 600-2PH4**
  [4 discs]

*** Symphony nr. 1 in e minor, Op. 39
- Philharmonia O / Ashkenazy
  Decca Dig **414 534-2**; -1; *-4* (9/86)
- City of Birmingham S O / Rattle
  HMV Dig EL 270309-1/*4* (11/85); EMI **CDC7 47515-2**
- Berliner Philharmoniker / Karajan
  HMV Dig ASD*TCC-ASD* 4097
- Wiener Pilharmoniker / Maazel
  Decca Jub JB/*KJBC* 42

*** Symphonies nrs 1 in e minor, Op. 39; 7 in C, Op. 105
- Bournemouth S O / Berglund
  HMV Green ESD/*TC-ESD* 7095
- Scottish National O / Gibson
  Chan Dig **CHAN 8344**; ABRD/*ABTD* 1086

*** Symphony nr. 2 in D, Op. 43
- Philharmonia O / Ashkenazy
  Decca Dig **410 206-2**; SXDL/*KSXDL* 7513
- Boston S O / Colin Davis
  Philips Silver Line **420 490-2PM**, transfer from 9500 141 (4/77)
- Scottish National O / Gibson
  Chan Dig **CHAN 8303**; ABRD/*ABTD* 1062
- City of Birmingham S O / Rattle
  HMV Dig EL 270160-1/*4*
- Göteborg S O / Järvi
  BIS Dig **CD 252**; LP 252
- Berliner Philharmoniker / Karajan
  HMV Dig ASD/*TC-ASD* 4060
- Wiener Philharmoniker / Bernstein
  DG dig **419 172-2GH**; -1GH; *-4GH*
  live recording Grosser Saal Musikverein, Vienna, 10/86
- Wiener Philharmoniker / Maazel
  Decca Jub JB 43
- NBC S O / Leopold Stokowski
  Dell'Arte mono DA 9004
- London S O / Pierre Monteux
  Con CC/*CCT* 7563
- Concertgebouw O/ Eduard van Beinum
  Philips Seq 6527/*7311* 111 (from 6570/*7310* 0540)
- Hallé Orch / Barbirolli
  EMI Em EMX/*TC-EMX* 2006

*** Symphony nr. 3 in C, Op. 52
- Göteborg S O / Järvi
  BIS Dig **CD 228**; LP 228
- Philharmonia O / Ashkenazy
  Decca Dig **414 267-2**; -1; *-4*
- Bournemouth S O / Berglund
  HMV Green ESD*TC-ESD* 7094
- Scottish N O / Gibson
  Chandos ABRD1097 (8/84)

*** Symphonies nrs 3, 4, 5, and 6
- Scottish N O / Gibson
  Chandos **CHAN 83889/9** [2 discs]; transfer from ABRD1097 (8/84) and 1074 (7/83)

*** Symphonies nrs 3 in C, Op. 52; 6 in d minor, Op. 104
- Boston S O / Colin Davis
  Philips 9500 142

*** Symphonies nrs 3 en 7
- City of Birmingham S O / Rattle
  EM dig EL 270 496-1; **CDC7 47450**

*** Symphony nr. 4 in a minor, Op. 63

- Göteborg S O / Järvi
  BIS Dig **CD 263**; LP 263
- Philharmonia / Ashkenazy
  Decca Dig **400 056-2**; SXDL/*KSXDC* 7517 (3/83)
- Wiener Philharmoniker / Maazel
  Decca Jub JB/*KJBC* 45
- Berliner Philharmoniker / Karajan
  415 107-2GH (6/85)

*** Symphonies nrs 4 in a minor, Op. 63; 5 in E flat major, Op. 82
- Berliner Philharmoniker / Karajan
  HMV EG 290613-1/*4*

*** Symphonies nrs 4 in a minor, Op. 63; 6 in d minor, Op. 104
- Berliner Philharmoniker / Karajan
  DG **415 107-2**

*** Symphonies nrs 4 in a minor, Op. 63; 7 in C, Op. 105
- Helsinki P O / Berglund
  EMI Dig **CDC 747443-2**; transfer from HMV EL 270099-1/*4* (9/84)

*** Symphony nr. 5 in E flat major, Op. 82
- Philharmonia O / Rattle
  HMV Dig **CDC 747006-2**; ASD/*TC-ASD* 4168
- Philharmonia O / Ashkenazy
  Decca Dig **410 016-2**; SXDL/*KSXDC* 7541
- Berliner Philharmoniker / Karajan
  HMV ASD/*TC-ASD* 3409
- Philharmonia O / Ashkenazy
  Decca Dig **400 016-2**; SXDL/*KSXDC* 7541
- Philharmonia O / Esa-Pekka Salonen
  CBS Masterworks dig **MK 42366**; M-; *MT-*

*** Symphony nrs 5 in E flat major, Op. 82; 7 in C, Op. 105
- Berliner Philharmoniker / Karajan
  DG **415 108-2**

*** Symphony nr. 6 ind minor, Op. 104
- Göteborg S O / Järvi
  BIS Dig **CD 237**; LP 237

*** Symphonies nrs 6 in d minor, Op. 104; 7 in C, Op. 105
- Berliner Philharmoniker / Karajan
  DG Acc 2542/*3342* 137

*** Symphony nr. 7
- Philharmonia O / Ashkenazy
  Decca **411 935-2**; SXDL/*KSXDC* 7580
- Göteborg S O / Neeme Järvi
  BIS/Conifer **CD311**
- Berliner Philharmoniker / Karajan
  415 108-2GH (6/85)

The complete cycle performed by Ashkenazy of Sibelius' symphonies is a large project led by a great musical thinker. His grasp of the scores is unquestionable despite possible reserves as to his ability to communicate something personal and unique. The niveau is consistent throughout and more extraordinary, he is obviously deeply aware of the development the composer himself underwent while working on the symphonies. These performances are influential yet never very touching. The CD technique gives the sound an openness that is refreshing. The listener is in intimate contact with the players as it were. A demanding listener would ask more emotion

from Ashkenazy perhaps, in the woodwind solos of the 4th, or in the strings in the second movement of the 7th. Nevertheless, the cycle demands listening. Ashkenazy has a great deal to say about Sibelius. The only rival among living conductors is Sir Colin Davis. His tempi are ideal. The recordings are beautiful and yet there is something lacking in the cycle as a whole. The same is true of both the Maazel and Von Karajan cycles.

After refinishing, Davis' performance of the Second Symphony with the Boston Symphony (Philips Silver Line **420 490-2PM**) has been greatly improved. At its appearance, it was written that Davis had achieved the right balance 'between the nationalistic-romantic heritage on the one hand, and the classical strength of Sibelius' thought on the other' Audiences will not be holding their breath throughout this performance however; nevertheless, it is a strong interpretation of great vision. Davis has three rivals for his complete cycle on CD: the SNO under Gibson, Neeme Jarvi on BIS and Ashkenazy.

All three are well recorded. For the Second, Jarvi is perhaps the best choice, and for the Fifth, Von Karajan.

Simon Rattle is very successful with the First Symphony (HMV). The older recordings: Karajans' from 1930 (World Records), Stokowsky on dell'Arte, Szell on Philips and the unforgettable Beecham recording of 1937 (World Records) and the equally unforgettable Von Karajan from 1966 (DG), are all of another class entirely, a class that seems impossible to achieve these days. (Did conductors have more time for rest and study then? Were there more reheasals? Were there more concert performances before a recording? These questions in themselves are their own answers.) Rattle comes close, however, despite the fact that certain mannerisms mar his interpretation.

There are at least 5 CD's of the First Symphony, all quite different. Ashkenazy's and Rattle's have already been mentioned, neither of which really compete with older versions on LP.

If the listener is set on Bernstein, perhaps the Second Symphony is the best choice. The recording is from 1968 (New York Philharmonic) and has intensity and great drama.

Rattle's Third, as well as his Seventh, are marvellous. One critic wrote:'Few have driven as deep into this symphonic landscape since the days of Kajanus'. A great compliment indeed. The recording quality is excellent.

There are at least 7 versions of the Fourth Symphony on CD. Beecham was the first to record the piece in 1937. Forty years later, a second Englishman followed: Sir Colin Davis (with the Boston Symphony, now transferred to CD). In the early Fifties, Karajan recorded it, followed a year later by Ormandy. Maazel joined them in the Sixties. Of all these non-Scandanavians, Davis is probably the most successful in delving into the work's dark character. Fifty years after Beecham, Rattle now joins the select few. Karajan has recorded the Fourth no fewer than three times (the Fifth four times!). The Fourth dating from 1978 (ASD3485, later **CDM7 69244-2**) is beautiful. It is both epic and intimate at the same time. The Fifth from 1985 is the one to be most recommended. There are a half dozen versions of the Fifth on CD and a lot more on LP. The Philharmonia has performed the piece numerous times throughout the years: twice with Karajan, with Pretre (RCA), Ashkenazy (Decca) and Rattle (EMI). Era Pekka-Salonen's is a well prepared version with great nuances. This talented young Fin creates exceedingly beautiful moments, at the cost of the overall structure perhaps, nevertheless, worthy of mention. Eris Tuxen on Decca, Kajanus and Koussevitsky as well as the first mono recording under Karajan (1953 for Columbia): these were the great Sibelius performances.

There are at least 6 CD's of the Sixth Symphony. All have something to be said for them but Karajan's version is in a class by itself. Von Karajan conducted the piece for the first time in Stockholm in 1930. His best performance was in 1955 with the Philharmonia. (Many believe Karajan's years with the Philharmonia were his best) Berglund and Jarvi represent the Scandanavians with wonderful performances. Rattle's has more authority however,which is the least one would expect with such strong regional competition.

BEDRICH SMETANA (1824-84)

Festival Symphony in E major
- Czech P O / Sejna
  Sup 50875

In Smetana's Festival Symphony there are passages taken from the national anthem of Austria (melody composed by Haydn). As is often the case, pieces written with such occasions in mind are only mediocre. The Scherzo is the exception here: it is quite charming. Sejna does his best to save the piece, but the recording itself is not up to what Supraphon usually produces.

LUDWIG SPOHR (1784-1859)

Symphony nr. 6 in G major ('Historical'), Op. 116
Symphony nr. 9 in b minor ('The Seasons'), Op. 143
- Bavarian Radio O / Karl Rickenbacher
  Orfeo C 094841 CD (S094841 A)

The Sixth Symphony (1839) inspired the hateful comment in the press: 'Spohr, mixed with Bach and Beethoven'. The Bavarian orchestra gives a very dedicated performance. The character is one-dimensional, however; succeeding movements are all the same. The Scherzo is unsuccessful Beethoven and the last movements are second-rate Schumann. Perhaps if Rickenbacher had had a more disciplined approach, something could have been saved from these two symphonies.

KARL STAMITZ (1745-1801)

Sinfonia concertante in D major
(violin, viola and orchestra)
- English Chamber O / Stern, Zukerman / Daniel Barenboim
  CBS DC 40167

This light weight piece of the symphonic repertoire was recorded to fill up an LP with Mozart's Sinfonia

Concertante (see Mozart discography). It is a wonderful opportunity for Stern and Zukerman to play with the rival parts; the sparks fly as these two perform together. The balance is unnaturally direct and that is a shame. The same LP also contains the Sinfonia Concertante by Pleyel.

CHARLES STANFORD (1852-1924)

Symphony nr. 3 in f minor
- Bournemouth Sinfonietta / Norman del Mar
  HMV ASD/TCD-ASD (cassette) 4221
- Bournemouth Sinfonietta / del Mar
  EMI Greensleave EM291154-3
  sponsored by Harveys of Bristol

Stanford was a fruitful composer, originally from Ireland. He wrote 11 theatre works, 30 church pieces, 100 short choral works, 7 symphonies and numerous concerti. He taught composition at the Royal College of Music and was professor at Cambridge University. These qualifications do not make him a great composer in themselves. There, opinions greatly differ. Standford's Third and most wonderful symphony is a rich and attractive work and owes a great deal to Brahms. Unfortunately, Stanford's Irish Symphony (1887) appeared just one year after Brahm's Fourth. The melodic similarities are painful to say the least. Del Mar conducts a warm and mature performance. The recording is very good. The cassette is excellent, very clear and with a lively sound.

WILHELM STENHAMMER
(1871-1927)

Symphony nr.1 in F major
- Göteborg S O / Neeme Järvi
  BIS LP/MC 219 (1983), also CD (1987)
Symphony nr. 2 in g minor, Op. 34
- Stockholm P O / Stig Westerberg
  Cap CAP/TC-CAPI 1151
- Göteborg S O / Järvi
  NIS CD 251 (LP251)

Stenhammer wrote his First Symphony in 1902 and 1903. After the première, he retracted the score to revise it thoroughly. When Hans Richter wanted to perform the piece, the composer again insisted on a revision. This revision did not come in time for the Göteborg Symphony's recording, and so this version is not the composer's intention. The BIS recording is excellent.
The Second Symphony, contemporary with Nielsen's Fourth and Sibelius' Fifth, is unlike both of these. The Stockholm Philharmonic and Stig Westerberg make a very good case for the piece with their performance. The strings are warm and the brass is good. The sound is lively, even compared to the digitals of today.
The Göteborg S O was Stenhammer's own orchestra. He led the first performance in 1915. Neeme Järvi chooses a more compact interpretation than Westerberg's version on Caprice. The first is 42'37", the second, 46'55". The sound on the CD is very impressive.

ROBERT STILL (1910-70)

Symphony nr. 3 (1960)
- London S O / Sir Eugene Goossens
Symphony nr. 4
- Royal P O / Myer Fredman
  Lyrita SRCS 46

Robert Still's Third Symphony is generally thought to be an attractive piece with an extended orchestration. It is, however, not something to be listened to too often. Goossen's performance dates from 1962. The Fourth Symphony reveals the composer's interest in psychology. It is inspired by a complicated case involving a paranoid young man. The Fredman recording is very recent.

RICHARD STRAUSS (1864-1949)

Eine Alpensinfonie (1913)
- Berlin P O / Karajan
  DG Dig 400 039-2 CD (2532/3302)
- Concertgebouw O / Haitink
  Philips Dig 416 156-2 CD (416 156-1/4)
- Bavarian Radio O / Solti
  Decca 414 676-2 CD (SXL 6059)
- Dresden State O / Rudolf Kempe
  HMV TCC-2 POR 54279 (ASD 3173)
- Philadelphia P O / Andre Previn
  HMV Dig ASD/TC-ASD 143577-1/4
- Los Angeles P O / Mehta
  Decca Jub JB/KJBC 139
- Royal P O / Kempe
  RCA GOld GI/GK 42697
- London P O / Andrew Davis
  CBS Dig 37292
Symphonia Domestica, Op. 53
- Vienna P / Lorin Maazel
  DG Dig 413 654-2 CD

The Alpen Symphony is obviously popular with orchestras (or recording companies?) considering the number of LP's available. Kempe was a great Strauss conductor; that is clear in this recording too. The Dresden orchestra has a cultivated and vital tone and Kempe adds a new warmth to the score. The EMI recording is a good example of analogue technique. The Von Karajan version is digital, but the details are not as clear as in the Solti version, for example. Nevertheless, the Von Karajan performance is also first rate.
Previn leads a superb Philadelphia Orchestra and the technique of his record is also excellent, better perhaps than the Von Karajan. Still, many devotees will prefer the Kempe recording.
The Solti performance was recorded in the Herkulessaal in Munich. The brass section is unforgettable. The Davis recording has a certain freshness to it, but sounds a little pre-packaged. The Haitink version (Philips) has a more natural sound than the Von Karajan digital; it is also rounder and less frantic than the Solti recording. Haitink gives his interpretation a great deal of character.
The Symphonica Domestica is far less popular. It has been neglected for the past ten years. (Romain Rolland found the erotic scene especially distasteful). Those who remember the old mono LP recorded

by Clemens Krauss are convinced that the score holds treasures missed by most conductors up until now. Von Karajan has called the piece one of Strauss' greatest, and in the 1974 recording, the players sounds very appreciative of the score. Maazel worked against heavy prejudices when he recorded the piece. He succeeds in giving a good performance and the recording is exemplary. But again, the great Strauss interpreter, Kempe, must be favoured.

IGOR STRAVINSKY (1882-1971)

Symphony in C major
Symphony in three movements
- Orch de la Suisse Romande / Dutoit
  Decca Dig 414 272-2 (CD); SXDL/KSXDC (cassette) 7543
- London P O / Sir Colin Davis
  PH Seq 6527/7311 (cassette) 127
- Israel P O / Bernstein
  DG Dig 415 128-2 (CD); 415 128-1/4 (cassette)
Symphony in C major
Symphony of Psalms
- Columbia S O / Stravinsky (1964)
Symphony of Psalms
- Berlin S O / Ricardo Chailly
  Decca Dig 414 078-1DH;2DH (CD) (1985)
- Atlanta S O / Lane
  Telarc (CD) 80105 (1985)
- London S O / Bernstein
  LP 76670 (1978)

The Orchestre de la Suisse Romande played better for these recordings under Dutoit, than for the earlier ones in the sixties with Ansermet (re-released on Decca: Lon Ent 414 062-1). This is quite an accomplishment for Dutoit, a fast rising directoral star. He understands the virile spirit of Stravinsky's score perfectly. The recorded sound is superb. It was recorded in Victoria Hall in Geneva and the sound is rich and full. The CD is even better, registering even the lowest tones clearly and without aggression. It will be very diificult to better this production.
Davis' interpretation of the Symphony in C major is wonderfully alert. The London Symphony is inspired. The Symphony in Three Movements is too fast and too tense if we compare it to Stravinsky's own interpretation. The sound is good; the cassette is only partly successful: the low level of transfer ruins the highest registers.
The excellence of the 78 recording that Stravinsky made before the war of the Symphony of Psalms (with the Walter Straram Chorus and Orchestra) has not, up until now, been equalled. The technical mistakes of the old record are, of course, not repeated in the new. The composer himself, even in the newer, less successful production, performs the work on a much higher level than conductors such as Ansermet and Ancerl.
Bernstein (1978, London) and Chailly (1985, Berlin) have also recorded the Symphony of Psalms. Chailly's production is far from ideal. He is rather abrupt with the score, and the Jesus Christ Church in Berlin does not lend itself to recording this piece. Chailly races through the work. He needs only 20 minutes and 17 seconds to play it, compared to Bernstein's 24 minutes and 15 seconds. Bernstein's choir is more inspired and the entire production is

better formulated. The end of the third movement (Laudate Eum in timpano et choro) is a good moment to compare the two interpretations more closely. Bernstein's tempo and phrasing are completely contagious and convincing; Chailly's version is flat and square.
Despite the fact that it is only two dimensional, the CBS recording is excellent. In the Berlin recording, the CD has an extra dimension, but that extra dimension also emphasizes the less than perfect acoustics. The Atlanta recording of this same piece is run-of-the-mill, both in interpretation and recording quality.

KAROL SZYMANOVSKI (1882-1937)

Symphony nr. 2 in B flat major, Op. 19
Symphony nr. 3 ('Night song'), Op.27
Symphony nr. 4 (Sinfonia concertante for piano and orchestra)
- Polish National Radio S O / Kasprzyk (nr. 2)
- Polish N R S O / Semkov, and Ochman, Radio Choir from Krakow (nr. 3)
- Polish N R S O / Piotr Paleczyny pno / Semkow
  HMV SLS 5242
- Detroit S O / Dorati; Karczykowski; Jewell Chorale (nrs. 2 and 3)
  Decca Dig SXDL/KSXDC (cassette) 7524
- Polish N R S O / Felicia Blumenthal pno / Kord (nr. 4)
  Uni RHS 347

The first set of symphonies appeared in 1982 for the anniversary of Szymanovski's birth (the First Symphony was never finished). Conducted by Kasprzyk, this performance has wonderful atmosphere. Paleczyny is a great pianist even though little known in the west. His playing is very subtle and he changes moods easily as the score demands.The Third Symphony is also performed well: lots of detail and ample proof of Kasprzyk's thorough knowledge of the piece.
The Dorati recording is the first western, commercial performance of Szymanovski's work. Dorati has caught the pieces well and the recording is wonderfully proportioned. Rowicki's version appeared in 1962; it is more sensual and earthy. The Dorati recording will appeal to more listeners.
The Second Symphony dates from 1909 to 1911. It is more difficult than the Third and unusually formal. There are only two movements, the second of which is a set of variations ending with a fugue. Strauss and Scriabin influences are clearly heard. The cassette is very good quality.
Felicia Blumenthal plays the solo part with determination in the performance conducted by Kord, however, more determined than inspired.

PIOTR ILYICH TCHAIKOVSKY (1840-93)

*** Symphonies 1-6
- Berliner Philharmoniker / Karajan
  DG 2740 219 [6 LPs]/3378 084 [5 cassettes]
- [incl Manfred Symphony]
  Concertgebouw O / Haitink
  Philips 6768 267 [7 LPs]
- [incl Manfred Symphony]
  Philharmonia of New Philharmonia O / Muti

HMV SLS 154530-3 [7 LPs]

*** Manfred Symphony, Op. 58
- Oslo P O / Mariss Jansons
  Chandos ABRD/ABTD 1245; CHAN8535 (5/88)
- Philharmonia O / Muti
  HMV Dig CDC 747412-2; ASD/TCC-ASD 4169 (7/82)
- New Philharmonia O /Ashkenazy
  Decca SXL/KSXC 6853
- London P O / Rostropovich
  EMI Eminence EMX/TC-EMX 41 2060-1/4
- Concertgebouw O / Haitink
  Philips 9500 778/7300 853

*** Symphonies nrs 1 in g minor, Op. 13 ('Winter Dreams'); 2 in c minor, Op. 17 ('Little Russian'); 3 in D gr, Op. 29 ('The Polish Symphony')
- Berliner Philharmoniker / Karajan
  DG 415 024-1/4

*** Symphony nr. 1 in g minor ('Winter Dreams'), Op. 13
- Oslo P O / Jansons
  Can Dig CHAN 8402; from ABRD/ABTD 1139 (11/85)
- Berliner Philharmoniker / Karajan
  DG 2531/3301 284
- London P O / Rostropovitch
  EMI Em EMX/TC-EMX 41 2061-1/4 (10/77)
- Concertgebouw O / Haitink
  Philips 9500 777/7300 851

*** Symphony nr 2 in c minor ('Little Russian')
- London S O / Simon
  Chan Dig CHAN 8304; ABRD/ABTD 1071
- Berliner Philharmoniker / Karajan
  DG 2531/3301 285
- Philharmonia O / Muti
  HMV ASD/TC-ASD 3488
- Oslo P O / Mariss Jansons
  Chandos dig CHAN 8460 (11/87); ABRD/ ABTD 1173
- Pittsburgh S O / Maazel
  Telarc/Conifer CD80131 (recorded in 1987)
- Wiener Philharmoniker / Maazel
  Decca JB21 (12/77) (recorded in 1964)
- Chicago S O / Abbado
  CBS IM39359 (7/85)

**Symphony nr. 3 in D major ('The Polish Symphony')
- Berliner Philharmoniker / Karajan
  DG 2531/3301 286
  DG 415 024-1GX (10/85)
- London P O / Rostropovitch
  EMI Eminence EMX/TC-EMX 41 2063-1/4 (11/77) (10/84)
- Concertgebouw O / Haitink
  Philips 9500 776/7300 850
- Oslo P O / Jansons
  Chandos Dig CHAN 8463; ABRD/ABTD 1179

*** Symphonies nrs 4-6
- Leningrad P O / Mravinsky
  DG 413 541-1/4 ; 419 745-2GH2
  from: (nr. 4) SLPM 138657 (6/61)
  (nr. 5) SLPM 138658 (10/61)
  (nr. 6) SLPM 138659 (11/61)
- Philharmonia / Ashkenazy
  Decca D 249 D 4/K 249 K 44

*** Symphony nr. 4 in f minor, Op. 36
- Oslo P O / Jansons

Can Dig **CHAN 8361**; ABRD/*ABTD* 1124 (9/85)
- Wiener Philharmoniker / Karajan
  DG Dig (Telemondial Video Project) **415 348-2GH**; -1GH; -*4GH*
- Berliner Philharmoniker / Karajan
  DG 2530/*3300* 883 (6/78)
- London S O / Rozhdestvensky
  IMP Classics **PCD867**
- Leipzig Gewandhaus Orch / Masur
  Teldec/ASV **8 43339**; 6/-; *4 /-* (288)
- Cleveland O / Maazel
  Telarc Dig **CD 80047**; DG 10047 (12/83)
- Chicago S O / Solti
  Decca **414 192-2DH** (5/84); /-1DH (12/84)
- Pittsburgh S O / Previn
  400 090-2PH (5/83)
- Wiener Philharmoniker / Abbado
  DG Sig 2543/*3343* 522
- Concertgebouw O / Haitink
  Philips Seq 6527/*7311* 191
- Philharmonia O / Ashkenazy
  Decca SXL/*KSXC* 6919
- Philharmonia / Muti
  HMV ASD 3816
- London S O / Markevitch
  Con CC/*CCT* 7595/*7310*

*** Symphony nr 5 in e minor, Op. 64
- Oslo P O / Jansons
  Chan Dig **CHAN 835**; ABRD/*ABTD* 1111 (3/85)
- London S O / Gennadi Rozhdestvensky
  Pickwick IMP Classics **PCD 875**
- Royal P O / Previn
  Telarc Dig **CD 80107**; DG 10107
- Berliner Philharmoniker / Kempe
  CfP CFP 41 4478-1/*4*
- Chicago S O / Abbado
  CBS Dig IM/*IMT* 42094
- London S O / Abbado
  DG Sig 410 831-1/*4*
- Philharmonia / Ashkenazy
  Decca SXL/*KSXC* 6884
- Philharmonia O / Muti
  HMV ASD/*TC-ASD* 3717
- Berliner Philharmoniker / Karajan
  DG 2530/*3300* 699
- Cleveland O / Szell
  CBS 60154/*40*
- Concertgebouw O / Paul van Kempen
  Philips Legendary Classics mono **420 858-2PLC**; from ABL 3000 (1/55)

*** Symphonies nrs 5-6
- Philadelphia O / Muti
  HMV *TCC2-POR 54284*
- London S O and Wiener Philharmoniker / Abbado
  DG Walkman *413 429-4*

*** Symphony nr. 6 in b minor ('Pathétique'), Op. 74
- Philharmonia O / Ashkenazy
  Decca **411 615-2** (5/84); (Anal) SXL/*KSXC* 6941 (8/81) (4/87)
  and **417 463-4DB**
- Concertgebouw O / Haitink
  Philips 412 937-1/*4* ; also: 9500/*7300* 739
- Philadelphia O / Muti
  HMV EG 290499-1/*4*
- Philharmonia O / Muti

HMV ASD/*TC-ASD* 3901
- Philharmonia O / Kletzki
  CfP CFP/*TC-CFP* 41 2066-1/*4*
- Cleveland O / Dohnányi
  Telarc/Conifer **CD80130**
- Nat P O / Païta
  Lodia Dig **LO-CD 778**
- Wiener Philharmoniker / Karajan
  DG **415 095-2**; -1; *-4*
- Berliner Philharmoniker / Karajan
  DG Acc 2542/*3342* 154
  DG 2530/*3300* 774
  DG Galleria 415 468-1GH (6/77) (9/87)
- Philharmonia / Karajan
  HMV SXLP/*TC-SXLP* 30534
- Philadelphia O / Ormandy
  CBS 60155/*40*
- London P O / Rostropovitch
  EMI Em EMX/*TC-EMX* 41 2066-1/*4*
- London P O / Enrique Bátiz
  ASV dig DCA566; *ZCDCA566*
- Oslo P O / Jansons
  Chandos dig **CHAN8446** (5/87); from ABRD1158 (1/87)
- New York P O / Bernstein
  DG dig **419 604-2GH**; -1GH; *-4GH*
  [live recording, Avery Fisher Hall New York, 8/86]
- Chicago S O / Solti
  Decca Ovation **417 708-2DM** transfer from SXL6874 (9/77)
- Leipzig Gewandhaus / Kurt Masur
  Teldec ASV dig 6 43340; 4-/ ; **08 43340**
- Boston S O / Ozawa
  Erato/Conifer dig **ECD88242**; NUM75305; *MCE/-*
- Chicago S O / Abbado
  CBS Masterworks dig **MK42368**; M/-; *MT/-* (4/88)
- Czech P O / Lovro von Matacic
  Supraphon/Counterpoint Gems **2SUP0008**, from 110 485 (12/71)
- London S O / Rozhdestvensky
  Pickwick IMP Classics **PCD878**
- Concertgebouw O / Bychkov
  Philips dig **420 925-2PH**; /-1PH; /- *4PH*

In 1985 Tchaikovsky's First, Fourth and Fifth Symphonies were released on the relatively unknown label, Chandos. These performances by the Philharmonie of Oslo led by Mariss Jansons dumbfounded the musical world. How could an unknown label with a relatively unknown orchestra (certainly not one of the world's top five) produce such brilliant Tchaikovsky? The music critics were and still are unanimous in their praise. The cycle was completed in 1987 and still leads all others in the extensive discography of this popular Russian. Mariss Jansons' direction is refreshing, well thought out and in many ways reveals aspects of these works as yet undiscovered. His direct approach has wonderful vitality which he combines with refinement. The interpretation is extremely Russian, exciting and contagious.

FIRST SYMPHONY - Jansons connects the many threads of this work like a spider in her web, all clear yet interdependent. The usual renditions of the First are messy, unable to sort out Tchaikovsky's complex themes. The Chandos technicians have produced a marvellous sound, transparent yet warm. The strings sound clear and melodious.

Those who want a more suggestive version should choose Rostropovitsj. His is more vivid Tchaikovsky

but less controlled as well. Karajan's majestic performance is a strong rival. He makes the symphony greater and more magnificent than it really is. There are moments that are truly breathtaking. Jansons is on a much smaller scale by comparison but sounds more appropriate to the piece.

SECOND SYMPHONY - Jansons recorded the Second Symphony last. Maazel (with Pittsburgh where he is artistic director) began with the Second. Both are strong contenders and both on CD (Maazel did record the Second with the Vienna Philharmonic 25 years ago), Jansons' is the more emotional of the two. He does avoid romantic excesses however and his tempi are better balanced. In the 'expressivo' passages, Jansons adds just the right touch of freedom and has better phrasing than Maazel. The lively Scherzo and the pure happiness that exudes from the Norwegian's Finale are unrivalled (Abbado goes just a bit too far in enjoying the Finale). There are beautiful moments in the Pittsburgh performance as well. The woodwinds are exceedingly refined. Nevertheless, the general approach taken by Maazel is too controlled. Abbado (CBS) is plagued by uneven tempi.

THIRD SYMPHONY - Jansons seems to have resolved all possible problems in his performance of this difficult score. His is also the only version on CD (the Third is neglected by the record companies). Rostropovitsj's Third with the London Symphony (1977) was successful for the time but cannot now compare with Jansons. Neither does Rostropovitsj survive comparison with the brilliant Karajan. The pianissimos from Berlin are magic (an effect created by close microphones and good mixing techniques). Jansons' Third is his most successful of all the symphonies and even the legendary Karajan with his wonderful Berliners cannot supersede him.

SIXTH SYMPHONY - There are at least 25 recordings of the Sixth Symphony available. More amazing is that Jansons again leads the field. The London Philharmonic under Batiz is extrovert and beautiful. The quality of the ASV recording is very good. The brass are sublime. The whole performance is a touch prosaic though and never really convincing as a concert. Ashkenazy is also extrovert and fresh. His Decca recording is analogue however and many will prefer Jansons' digital CD.

Bernstein takes 15 minutes more to play the Pathétique (59 minutes) than Jansons (whose performance is not at all hurried!). Bernstein uses the time to display his unique ability to hypnotize. His vision is different from all others, yet, this time at least, there is nothing hysterical about it. The New Yorkers play as never before. The intensity and power of their performance is fascinating.

The London Symphony has recorded the Fifth and Sixth Symphonies with Rozhdestvensky on CD. The ensemble could use more polish but Rozhdestvensky is determined to capture the spontaneity of a live performance and succeeds in this. There was probably minimal editing done on the tape which has a special effect all its own. The Concertgebouw's version of the Pathétique has the simple advantage of a better orchestra. Bychhov's interpretation is disappointing however, as is the unusually low standard of sound produced by Philips.

Tennstedt's performance of the Fourth Symphony is as refined as would be expected with the Leipzig

Gewandhaus Orchestra. Despite the relationship the East Germans are bound to have with the Russians, Tennstedt's interpretation is extremely German and in that respect comparable to Bohm and Klemperer (both of whom recorded the piece at the end of their careers).

Abbado's second version of the Pathétique (1988, with the Chicago Symphony, the first was made in 1973 with the Viennese Philharmonic) is disappointing. There is no tension and the level of playing is surprisingly low for one of America's best orchestras. Mravinsky's 1961 recordings of the 4th, 5th and 6th symphonies with the Leningrad Philharmonic are classics. They have now been successfully transferred to CD and are still wonderful examples of high quality recording techniques as well as of musical interpretation. All of Mravinsky's decisions in terms of the interpretation are based on his thorough study of the score. The detail is extensive and the orchestra is obviously dedicated and inventive. Ironically enough, Mravinsky's work is very different from Jansons. (Jansons was for many years Mravinsky's assistant in Leningrad.)

Dohnányi leads Cleveland in a very controlled performance of the Pathétique, a recording well-suited to 'easy listening'. Ozawa's version for Erato is excellent. The playing is impeccable and the interpretation loving. One would, however, expect more personality from Ozawa. Paul Kletzki's Pathétique (1960) with the Philharmonia was for many years the absolute favourite. The recording has been remastered for CfP and the sound is remarkably good: lively and well-balanced.

Karajan made his first stereo recording of the 6th with the Philharmonia (in Kingsway Hall) for EMI in 1959. The sound is surprisingly rich considering the fact that it was recorded almost thirty years ago. Solti's 6th is disappointing and lacks maturity and warmth. Haitink has recorded the 6th twice. The second is the better of the two in technical terms. Some will appreciate Haitink's sober and noble interpretation but for many, it will be less exciting than Karajan's or any of the Russians', not to mention the ever favourite Jansons.

SIR MICHAEL TIPPETT (born 1905)

Symphony nr. 2
- London S O / Davis
  Argo ZRG 535
Symphonies nrs. 1 and 2
- London S O / Davis
  Decca 414 091-1/-4
Symphony nr. 4
- Chicago S O / Solti
  Decca 414 091-1/-4

The English are very fond of Tippett's rich and masterly Second Symphony. Colin Davis leads a favoured performance. The recording is excellent. All four symphonies appeared separately on three labels: Argo, Philips and Decca. The international merger that produced Polygram made it possible to offer the four as a set which was released to celebrate the composer's eightieth birthday.

EDUARD TUBIN (1905-82)

Symphony nr. 2 ('The Legendary')
Symphony nr. 6
- Swedish Radio S O / Jarvi
  BIS CD 304 (LP304)
Symphony nr. 4
- Bergen S O / Järvi
  BIS LP227
Symphony nr. 9 (Sinfonia semplice)
- Gothenburg S O / Järvi
  BIS LP 264

Eduard Tubin fled his native Estland to settle in Sweden in 1944. Despite the fact that the Swedes basically ignored him, all ten of his symphonies have been recorded. At the première of the First in 1934, Tubin caused quite a sensation. The Second and Sixth form a good introduction to Tubin's musical world. The Second was composed in the summer of 1937 and despite its title, has no specific thematic material. The Fourth dates from 1944; Tubin revised this work at the end of his life. The Bergen Orchestra plays enthusiastically. The recording was made at a live concert: the sound is very natural and the pressing is excellent. In the Sixth (1954), one hears Prokofiev throughout (even including the orchestration). Järvi and his dedicated Radio musicians will convert many into enthusiasts of this music.

RALPH VAUGHAN WILLIAMS
(1872-1958)

*** Cyclus: Symphonies nrs 1-9
- Soloists, London S Choir, London S O / André Previn
  RCA RL43371 (7 LPs)
- Soloists, London P Choir, London P O and New Philharmonia / Sir Adrian Boult
  HMV SLS154708-3; TC-SLS 154708

*** A Sea Symphony (nr. 1)
- Harper, Shirley-Quirk, London Symphony Choir, London S O / Previn
  RCA Gold Seal GL/GK 89689, transfer from SER5585 (4/70)
- Armstrong, Carol Case, London P Choir, London P O / Adrian Boult
  HMV Green ESD/TS-ESD / 7104; also dig remastered as EX290617 from ASD 3330 (4/77)

*** A London Symphony (nr. 2)
- London P O / Boult
  EMI CDC7 47213-2, transfer from HMV ASD2740 (10/71) [recorded in 1970]
- London S O / Previn
  RCA Gold Seal Gl/GK89690 transfer from SB6960 (8/72) also: RD 89826 (11/86)
- Hallé Orchestra / Sir John Barbirolli
  (1st recording) PVCD8375 (12/86) transfer from Pye GSGC14012 (3/65)
  (2nd recording) EMI Eminence EMX412087-1/-4 ; from ASD 2360 (4/68) [recorded in 1963]
- London P O / Haitink
  EMI CDC7 49394-1; from EL74934-1/-4 (12/87)
- Royal P O / Previn
  Telarc / Conifer CD80138

*** A Pastoral Symphony (nr. 3)

- London S O / Previn
  RCA Gold Seal Gl/GK89691, from SB6861 (9/72); also RD89827

*** A Pastoral Symphony (nr. 5)
- New Philharmonia and London P O / Boult
  EMI CDC7 47214-2, from HMV ED2900408-1 (5/85) and ED290418 (8/85)

*** A Pastoral Symphony (nr. 6)
- Price / New Philharmonia / Boult
  HMV ED290480-1;/-4

*** Symphony nr. 4
- London S O / Previn
  RCVA Gold Seal Gl/GK89692, from SB6801 (9/69)
- New Philharmonia / Boult
  HMV Greensleve ED290417-1;/-4, from ASD2375 (6/68)

*** Symphony nr. 4 and nr. 5
- BBC S O / Ralph Vaughan Williams
  Hallé / Barbirolli Orchestra
  EMI Treasure mono EH7449396-1; /-4 from resp HMV DB3367/70 (1/38) and HMV C3388/92 (5/44)

*** Symphony nr. 4 and nr. 6
- New Philharmonia / Boult
  EMI CDC7 47215-2, from resp ASD2375 and ASD2329 (10/67)
- Royal P O / Berglund
  Bournemouth S O / Berglund
  EMI EMX 41 2072-1;/-4
- New York Philharmonic / Mitropoulos and Stokowski
  CBS 61432

*** Symphony nr. 6
- London S O / Boult
  HMV ED290258-1;/-4

*** Symphony nr. 5 in D major
- Royal Liverpool P O / Vernon Handley
  EMI Eminence dig CD-EMX 9512, from EMX2112 (8/87)
- London S O / Bryden Thomas
  CHAN 8554 and ABRD/ABTD 1260
- London S O / Previn
  RCA Gold Seal GL/GK89693, from SB6856 (3/72); also RD89882
- London P O / Boult
  ED290 418-1 (4/70) (8/85)
- Royal P O / Gibson
  HMV Dig ASD/TCC-ASD /143441-1;/-4
- Philharmonia / Barbirolli
  HMV TCC2-POR54280

*** Sinfonia Antarctica (nr. 7)
- Richardson, Harper, Ambrosian Singers, London S O / Previn
  RCA Gold Seal GL/GK89695, from SB6736 (3/69); also RD89883 (12/86)
- Burrowes, London Philharmonic Choir, London S O / Boult
  EMI Greensleve ED291204-1;/-4
  CDC7 47216-2; dig refurbished from ASD2631 (11/70)
- Armstrong, London P Choir and London S O / Haitink
  CDC7 47516-2, from HMV dig EL270318-1;/-4
- Ritchie, Choir, Hallé Orchestra / Barbirolli
  SJB100 (2/54) (2/78)

*** Symphony nr. 6 in e minor and nr. 8 in d minor

- London S O / Previn
  RCA Gold Seal GL/GK89694, from SB6769 (10/68)
  (nr 8) also: **RD89884** (12/86)

*** Symphony nr. 6 and nr. 9
- London S O / Previn
  RD89827 (1/87)

*** Symphony nr. 8
- Hallé Orchestra / Barbirolli
  PRT **PVCD8380**, from Pye Golden Guinea GSGC14061
  (5/66)

*** Symphony nr. 8 and nr. 9
- London P O / Boult
  EMI **CDC7 47217-2**, from resp ASD2469 (9/69) and 2581
  (9/70)

*** Symphony nr. 9
- London S O / Previn
  RCA Golden Seal GL/GK89696, from SB6842 (6/71)

André Previn recorded the complete cycle between 1968 and 1972. In the Second, Third and Fifth Symphonies especially, his is a very deep interpretation. The Fourth is unexpectedly disappointing. The whole cycle, nevertheless, is refreshing.
The Boult cycle dates from the late Sixties. Insiders will probably prefer this one. Boult's long study of the scores is in evidence and his work is consistent and convincing throughout. The recordings have been remastered but were excellent anyway. The Fourth is especially excellent. This was Sir Adrian's first stereo recording. Some might expect a bit more fire and excitement.
Barbirolli was also an enthusiastic Vaughan Williams conductor. His version of the Fifth with the Philharmonia Orchestra is memorable for many. His second version of the Second Symphony (with the Hallé Orchestra) is more relaxed and has more authority than his first performance for Pye.
Many will still fondly remember the performances led by the composer himself. Previn is very good but cannot match Boult's superior vision.

JAN VORISEK (1791-1825)

Symphony in D major
- English Chamber O / Charles Mackerras
  Philips Seq 6527/7311 129

Vorisek is the closest that the Czechs came to having

their own Beethoven. The finale of his Symphony in D has some of the characteristics of Beethoven's Fourth. There is nothing that suggests plagiarism, however; Vorisek was talented with the idiom we associate with Beethoven. There was once a beautiful performance by the Prague Chamber Orchestra of this piece on Supraphon; it is no longer available. In comparison, the Mackerras version is disappointing. The Philips sound is good.

RICHARD WAGNER (1813-83)

Symphony in C major
- Berlin P / Gerdes
  DG 2543 817
- San Francisco S O / De Waart
  Philips Dig 6514/7337 380

Wagner wrote his symphony while still a teenager. There is little that is Wagnerian about it. It is highly reminiscent of Mendelssohn and Weber. The Gerdes interpretation is clear and the recording good.
The De Waart performance is a splendid reading of this youthful score. The melodies are given a Schubertesque shine and the sound is very full. The recording is excellent.

WILLIAM WALTON (1902-83)

Symphony nr. 1 in b minor
- Scottish National O / Alexander Gibson
  Chan Dig CD CHAN 8313 (ABRD/*ABDT* 1095)
- London S O / Sir Hamilton Harty
  Decca mono 414 659-1/4
- London S O / Previn
  RCA GL/*GK* 42707
- Royal Liverpool P O / Vernon Handley
  ASV ACM/*ZCACM* 2006
- Philharmonia O / Haitink
  HMV Dig ASD/*TCC-ASD* 4091
Symphony nr. 2
- London S O / Previn
  HMV ASD 2990

The Gibson version of Walton's First Symphony is convincing in a certain way, but the orchestra is not exact enough in performing this dark, intense music. The recording is excellent even if the kettle drums are a bit aggressive. The CD sounds weak. The historical recording under Sir Hamilton Harty, recorded in December,1935 (recorded within a month of the

piece's appearance and transferred to 78), is certainly more emotional than any other version. Harty makes the work warm, and the playing is surprisingly good considering the level of orchestras at the time. There is noise in the recording, however, that takes some getting used to.
Previn's performance of the First is wonderful. His tempi seem a little fast at the beginning, but he builds up the tension in the finale in a great way. Previn's interpretation is a good representation of the tense thirties and, at the same time, Walton's then youthful spirits. The Scherzo is marked 'Presto con malizia' and maliciousness is exactly what Previn achieves. In the Haitink version, the malicious devil is muzzled and the dynamics of the piece lose some power. Still, Haitink plays a shimmering slow movement. Vernon Handles's interpretation resembles Haitink's: the vision has scope but misses the rough edges.
Georg Solti and the Cleveland Orchestra have also made a brilliant recording, but it only competes with Previn and does not surpass him. Previn's is livelier in the outer movements and more romantic in the middle, slow movement. Technically, Previn's recording is also very good.

KURT WEILL (1900-50)

Symphony nr. 1 (1921)
Symphony nr. 2 (1934)
- Leipzig Gewandhaus O / De Waart
  Philips Seq 6527/7311 25
- BBC S O / Bertini
  Decca Lon Ent 414 660-1/4

Despite a warm sound and excellent soloists, the De Waart interpretation misses some of the bite and intensity of this music. Given more disciplined musicians, the Bertini interpretation is more preferable. The First Symphony Weill wrote while still a student with Busoni in Berlin in 1921. The influences clearly come from Mahler and Schoenberg, and Busoni was not satisfied with his student. The Second is obviously a more mature work that is reminiscent of the symphonies of Shostakovich and Kabelevsky.

Index

Abbado, Claudio 153
Abel, Carl Friedrich 29
Academy of Ancient Music 166, 183
Academy of St Martin-in-the-Fields 171, 183
Accademia Santa Cecilia Orchestra, Rome 141, 171, 177
Alvén, Hugo 196
Alwyn, William 197
Andriessen, Hendrik 146
Ansermet, Ernest 153
Arnold, Malcolm 197
Attenburg, Kurt 197
Auden, W.H. 136, 146
Auer, Max 101
Baaren, Kees van 147
Bach, Carl Philipp Emanuel 21, 197
Bach, Johann Christian 16, 21, 29, 197
Bach, Johann Sebastian 15, 21, 75, 88, 94
Badings, Henk 146
Balakirev, Mily 110, 124, 198
Bamberger Symphoniker 183
Barber, Samuel 133, 198
Barbirolli, John 154
Barenboim, Daniel 154
Barraud, Henri 144
Bartók, Béla 147
Baudrier, Yves 147
Bavarian Radio Orchestra 8, 163, 169
Bax, Arnold 148, 198
BBC Symphony Orchestra 163, 176, 184
Beecham, Sir Thomas 155
Beethoven, Ludwig Von 15, 17, 24, 45-62, 74, 89, 198
Beinum, Eduard van 155
Benjamin, Arthur 136
Bennett, William Sterndale 202
Bentzon, Niels 202
Benzi, Roberto 156
Berg, Alban 131, 135, 136, 146
Berio, Luciano 162, 202
Berlin Philharmonic Orchestra 163, 167, 183
Berlioz, Hector 51, 74, 83, 88, 104, 145, 203
Bernstein, Leonard 146, 156, 203

Berwald, Franz Adolf 91, 203
Bizet, Georges 88, 93, 203
Bliss, Arthur 150, 204
Bloch, Ernest 136, 204
Blomdahl, Karl-Birger 204
Boccherini, Luigi 22, 204
Böhm, Karl 161
Boito, Arrigo 204
Borodin, Alexander 110, 116, 204
Boston Symphony Orchestra 133, 136, 141, 163, 168, 169, 219
Boulez, Pierre 161
Boult, Sir Adrian 161
Bournemouth Sinfonietta 184
Boyce, William 20, 204
Brahms, Johannes 88-94, 95, 112, 115, 204
Bree, Johannes Bernardus van 81
Brian, Havergal 149, 206
Britten, Benjamin 136, 149, 156, 206
Bruch, Max 113, 116, 147, 207
Bruckner, Anton 94-105, 207
Brüggen, Frans 162
Bülow, Hans Von 101, 105, 114, 116
Bush, Geoffry 209
Carter, Elliott 145, 209
Chailly, Riccardo 162
Chausson, Ernest 96, 102, 209
Chavez, Carlos 209
Cherubini, Luigi 24, 50, 209
Chicago Symphony Orchestra 177, 185
City of Birmingham Symphony Orchestra 162
Clementi, Muzio 55, 209
Cleveland Orchestra 170, 179, 185
Cocteau, Jean 135, 145, 151
Collegium Aureum 185
Concertgebouw Orchestra (Amsterdam) 150, 155, 162, 165, 166, 168, 172, 185
Cooke, Arnold 209
Copland, Aaron 145, 146, 210
Corneille 108
Cosima 101
Covent Garden, Royal Opera House 155, 165, 177

Cui, César 106, 109, 110
Czech Philharmonic Orchestra 169, 173, 193
Da Ponte, Lorenzo 29
Dalcroze, Jean 136
David, Johann Nepumuk 143, 144, 146
Davidov, Vladimir 'Bob' 114
Davies, Peter Maxwell 148, 210
Davis, Andrew 162
Davis, Colin 162
Debussy, Claude 108, 134, 135, 136, 154
Detroit Symphony Orchestra 186
Deutsch, Otto Erich 64
Diabelli, Anton 61
Diaghilev, Sergei 135, 153, 171
Dittersdorf, Karl Ditters von 23
Dorati, Antal 163
Dresden Staatskapelle 176, 186
Dukas, Paul 108, 145, 147, 210
Duparc, Henri 102
Dupré, Marcel 147
Dutilleux, Henri 144
Dutoit, Charles 163
Dvorák, Antonin 112, 114-123, 210
Elgar, Sir Edward 129, 148, 211
English Chamber Orchestra 155, 169, 186
English Concert 186
Esterházy, Prince Nicolaus 19, 20, 22
Evans, Edwin 91
Ferenc Liszt Chamber Orchestra 186
Fibich, Zdenek 109, 212
Franck, César 88, 96, 102, 128, 212
Furtwängler, Wilhelm 163
Gade, Niels 75, 83, 115, 132, 212
Galuppi, Baldassare 19
Gewandhaus Orchestra 163, 171, 173
Giannini, Vittorio 212
Gibson, Alexander 164
Giulini, Carl Maria 164
Glazunov, Alexander 116, 125, 146, 212
Glière, Reinhold 112, 133, 213

Glinka, Mikhail 106
Gluck, Christoph Willibald 23
Glyndebourne Festival Opera 162, 165
Goethe, Wolfgang Von 67, 108
Goldmark, Karl 213
Goossens, Eugene 164, 213
Gossec, François Joseph 23
Gounod, Charles 88, 102, 112, 213
Grieg, Edvard 112, 113, 115, 213
Grillparzer, Franz 48
Group des Six 145, 150, 151
Groves, Charles 164
Haas, Robert 101
Haitink, Bernard 165
Hallé Orchestra 154, 186
Halvorsen, Johann 213
Handel, George Frideric 15
Hanson, Howard 213
Harnoncourt, Nicolaus 162, 165
Harris, Roy 213
Hartmann, Karl Amadeus 143, 146, 213
Harty, Sir Hamilton 214
Haydn, Franz Joseph 19-27, 29, 74, 214
Haydn, Michael 19, 215
Hely-Hutchinson, Victor 215
Henze, Hans Werner 148, 150, 216
Hill, Alfred 216
Hindemith, Paul 143, 144, 216
Hoddinott, Alun 216
Hoffmann, E.T.A. 69
Hofmannsthal, Hugo Von 105
Hogwood, Christopher 166
Holmboe, Vagn 216
Holst, Gustav 149, 150, 216
Honegger, Arthur 129, 143, 144, 151, 216
Houston Symphony Orchestra 164
Hovhaness, Alan 217
Huberman, Bronislav 178
Indy, Vincent d' 102, 128, 145, 151, 217
Israel Philharmonic Orchestra 171, 172, 178, 186
Ives, Charles 141, 142, 145, 156, 217
Janácek, Leos 125, 217

Järvi, Neeme 166
Joachim, Joseph 93
Jochum, Eugen 166
Jolivet, André 147
Jones, Daniel 217
Jongen, Joseph 217
Jordan, Armin 166
Josephs, Wilfred 218
Kalback, Max 93
Kalliwoda, Wilhelm 86
Karajan, Herbert Von 166
Keuris, Tristan 148
Kielland, Olav 218
Kleiber, Erich 167
Klemperer, Otto 167, 218
Knussen, Oliver 218
Kokkonen, Jonas 218
Kondrashin, Kirill 168
Koussevitsky, Sergei Alexandrovich 112, 133, 135, 136, 142, 151, 168
Kozeluch, Leopold 218
Krips, Josef 169
Krommer, Franz 218
Kubelik, Rafael 169
Lalo, Edouard 218
Langgaard, Rued 218
Leipzig Gewandhaus Orchestra 187
Leningrad Philharmonic Orchestra 187
Leonhardt, Gustav 162, 165, 166
Leppard, Raymond 169
Leroux 145
Lesur, Daniel 147
Lindblad, Adolf 218
Liszt, Franz 24, 70, 88, 101, 116, 124, 218
Lloyd, George 219
London Philharmonic Orchestra 155, 162, 165, 167, 168, 179, 187
London Symphony Orchestra 163, 166, 176, 188
Los Angeles Chamber Orchestra 171
Los Angeles Philharmonic Orchestra 172, 188
Los Angeles Symphony Orchestra 164, 181
Löwe, Ferdinand 95, 101
Lutoslavski, Witold 150, 219

Luzern Festival Orchestra 188
Maazel, Lorin 170
Maeterlinck, Maurice 108
Mackerras, Sir Charles 170
Maelzel, Johann Nepomuk 52, 53, 56
Magnard, Albéric 219
Mahler, Alma 127, 132
Mahler, Gustav 83, 126-133, 136, 142, 168, 172, 219
Malko, Nicolai 170
Maria Theresa, Empress 23
Marie Antoinette, Queen 22
Markevich, Igor 170
Marriner, Neville 171
Martin, Frank 131, 154, 222
Martinon, Jean 171
Martinu, Bohislav 125, 151, 222
Marx, Adolf 76
Masek, Vincenc 222
Massenet, Jules 96, 112
Masur, Kurt 171
Mathias, William 223
Meck, Nadezhda Von 107, 111, 114
Mehta, Zubin 172
Mendelssohn Bartholdy, Felix 51, 70, 75, 83-87, 109, 111, 115, 223
Mengelberg, Willem 155, 172
Messiaen, Olivier 144, 145, 147, 148, 224
Meyerbeer 145
Miaskovsky, Nicolai 224
Milhaud, Darius 129, 135, 144, 145, 151, 224
Millner, Anthony 224
Milyukova, Antonina 107, 111
Minnesota Orchestra 171
Moeran, Ernest 224
Monteux, Pierre 150
Montreal Symphony Orchestra (Orchestre Symphonique de Monréal) 172, 188
Morzin, Count 19, 20
Moscow Philharmonic 168
Mozart, Leopold 19, 20, 29-43, 74
Mozart, Nannerl 29
Mozart, Wolfgang Amadeus 21, 29, 224
Mravinsky, Yevgeni 166, 172
Muck, Karl 141

Münch, Charles 173
Mussorgsky, Modest 106, 110, 125
Muti, Ricardo 173
Napoleon 51
National Orchestra of France 170
NBC Symphony Orchestra 181, 189
Neuhauss, Gustav 143
Neumann, Václav 173
New York Philharmonic Orchestra 172, 178, 181, 189
Nielsen, Carl 132, 228
Nikisch, Arthur 96, 121
Norrington, Roger 174
Nystroem, Gösta 228
Orchestra of the Bayerische Rundfunk 163, 169
Orchestra of the XVIIIth Century 162, 189
Orchestre de la Suisse Romande 154, 166, 176, 191
Orchestre de Paris 155, 190
Orchestre des Concerts Colonne 128, 190
Orchestre des Concerts Lamoureux 128, 171, 190
Orchestre National de France 190
Orchestre Philharmonique de Paris 173
Orchestre Philharmonique de Radio France (Orchestre de ORTF) 190
Orel, Alfred 101
Ormandy, Eugene 133, 174
Ozawa, Seiji 174
Parry, Hubert 228
Pears, Peter 136
Peterson-Berger, Wilhelm 228
Philadelphia Orchestra 173, 174, 178, 181, 191
Philharmonia Hungarica 163, 192
Philharmonia Leningrad 176
Philharmonia Orchestra 177, 191
Philharmonic Orchestra of Budapest 192
Philharmonic Orchestra of Oslo 191
Pijper, Willem 146, 147, 148

Piston, Walter 228
Pittsburgh Symphony Orchestra 170, 175, 178, 191
Prague Philharmonia 179
Previn, André 175
Pritchard, John 175
Prokofiev, Sergei 133, 141, 228
Rachmaninov, Sergei 121, 125, 172, 229
Raff, Joachim 230
Rangström, Ture 143, 230
Rameau 23
Ravel, Maurice 143, 147, 150
Rawsthorne, Alan 230
Redlich, Hans 103
Residential Orchestra of The Hague 171, 180
Richter, Hans 96, 129
Ries, Ferdinand 52
Rimsky-Korsakov, Nicolai 106, 110, 124, 133, 135, 143, 230
Rootham, Cyril 230
Rossini, Gioacchino 67, 70, 141, 230
Rostropovich, Mstislav 175
Rotterdam Philharmonic Orchestra 181, 192
Rousseau, Jean-Jacques 69
Roussel, Albert 129, 130, 144, 230
Royal Philharmonic Orchestra 165, 192
Rozhdestvensky, Gennadi 176
Rubbra, Edmund 149, 231
Rubinstein, Anton 107, 108, 109, 110, 133
Rubinstein, Arthur 143
Rubinstein, Nicolas 107, 108, 109, 111

Saint-Saëns, Camille 88, 96, 102, 113, 231
Salieri, Antonio 24, 45
Sallinen, Aulis 231
Sammartini, Giovanni Battista 19, 22
Sanderling, Kurt 176
San Francisco Symphony Orchestra 192
Satie, Eric 145, 151
Sawallisch, Wolfgang 176
Scarlatti, Domenico 16, 22
Schalk, Franz 101
Schat, Peter 147
Schiller, Friedrich 45, 62
Schmidt, Franz 231
Schoenberg, Arnold 130, 131, 135, 231
Schubert, Franz 24, 64-73, 232
Schumann, Clara 73, 85, 86, 89, 115
Schumann, Robert 46, 62, 74-83, 84, 89, 115, 233
Scottish National Orchestra 164, 166, 192
Scriabin, Alexander 125, 142, 234
Searle, Humphry 234
Shostakovich, Dmitri 125, 141, 142, 143, 146, 172, 235
Sibelius, Jean 106, 107, 123-125, 235
Simpson, Robert 101
Sinopoli, Giuseppe 176
Smetana, Bedrich 70, 106, 124, 237
Solti, Sir Georg 177
Spohr, Ludwig 75, 76, 237
Stamitz, Anton 25

Stamitz, Johann 19, 25, 237
Stamitz, Karl 25
Stanford, Charles 237
Steinberg, William 146, 173, 178
Stenhammer, Wilhelm 132, 237
Still, Robert 237
Stockholm Philharmonic Orchestra 176, 193
Stockholm Symphony Orchestra 171
Stokowski, Leopold 178
Straus, Richard 70, 88, 105, 127, 172, 237
Stravinsky, Igor 124, 134, 136, 145, 148, 150, 153, 238
Svetlanov, Yevgeny 178
Swedish Radio Orchestra 179
Sydney Symphony Orchestra 164
Symphony Orchestra of Göteborg 163, 166
Symphony Orchestra of Montreal 163
Symphony Orchestra of Radio Berlin 170
Symphony Orchestra of the Süddeutschen Rundfunk 171
Szell, George 178
Szymanovski, Karol 143, 238
Tchaikovsky, Piotr Ilyich 106-114, 238
Tennstedt, Klaus 179
Thalberg, Sigismond 86
Tilson Thomas, Michael 179
Tippett, Michael 149, 240
Toronto Symphony Orchestra 162
Toscanini, Arturo 179

Toulouse Capital Orchestra 193
Tubin, Eduard 240
USSR State Symphony Orchestra 178, 193
Vaughan Williams, Ralph 147, 148, 149, 150, 162, 240
Vaurabourg, Andrée 151
Verhulst, Johannes 75, 87
Vermeulen, Matthijs 143, 146, 147
Vidal, Paul 108
Vienna Philharmonic Orchestra 102, 163, 193
Vorisek, Jan 241
Waart, Edo de 180
Wagemans, Jan 148
Wagenseil, Georg 19, 20, 29
Wagner, Richard 53, 67, 88, 101, 103, 126, 241
Walter, Bruno 127, 128, 155, 181
Walton, William 150, 241
Washington National Symphony Orchestra 193
Weber, Constanze 29, 70
Webern, Anton Von 131, 135, 136
Weill, Kurt 241
Wieck, Clara 84
Wiener Symphoniker 164, 167, 194
Williamson, Malcolm 150
Wittgenstein, V. 145
Wood, Sir Henry 123
Zweers, Bernard 106, 122,156